Lecture Notes in Computer Science 8012

Commenced Publication in 1973
Founding and Former Series Editors:
Gerhard Goos, Juris Hartmanis, and Jan van Leeuwen

Aaron Marcus (Ed.)

Design, User Experience, and Usability

Design Philosophy, Methods, and Tools

Second International Conference, DUXU 2013
Held as Part of HCI International 2013
Las Vegas, NV, USA, July 21-26, 2013
Proceedings, Part I

 Springer

Volume Editor

Aaron Marcus
Aaron Marcus and Associates, Inc.
1196 Euclid Avenue, Suite 1F
Berkeley, CA 94708, USA
E-mail: aaron.marcus@amanda.com

ISSN 0302-9743   e-ISSN 1611-3349
ISBN 978-3-642-39228-3   e-ISBN 978-3-642-39229-0
DOI 10.1007/978-3-642-39229-0
Springer Heidelberg Dordrecht London New York

Library of Congress Control Number: 2013941914

CR Subject Classification (1998): H.5, H.4, H.3, K.4

LNCS Sublibrary: SL 3 – Information Systems and Application, incl. Internet/Web and HCI

Typesetting: Camera-ready by author, data conversion by Scientific Publishing Services, Chennai, India

Printed on acid-free paper

Springer is part of Springer Science+Business Media (www.springer.com)

Foreword

The 15th International Conference on Human–Computer Interaction, HCI International 2013, was held in Las Vegas, Nevada, USA, 21–26 July 2013, incorporating 12 conferences / thematic areas:

Thematic areas:

- Human–Computer Interaction
- Human Interface and the Management of Information

Affiliated conferences:

- 10th International Conference on Engineering Psychology and Cognitive Ergonomics
- 7th International Conference on Universal Access in Human–Computer Interaction
- 5th International Conference on Virtual, Augmented and Mixed Reality
- 5th International Conference on Cross-Cultural Design
- 5th International Conference on Online Communities and Social Computing
- 7th International Conference on Augmented Cognition
- 4th International Conference on Digital Human Modeling and Applications in Health, Safety, Ergonomics and Risk Management
- 2nd International Conference on Design, User Experience and Usability
- 1st International Conference on Distributed, Ambient and Pervasive Interactions
- 1st International Conference on Human Aspects of Information Security, Privacy and Trust

A total of 5210 individuals from academia, research institutes, industry and governmental agencies from 70 countries submitted contributions, and 1666 papers and 303 posters were included in the program. These papers address the latest research and development efforts and highlight the human aspects of design and use of computing systems. The papers accepted for presentation thoroughly cover the entire field of Human–Computer Interaction, addressing major advances in knowledge and effective use of computers in a variety of application areas.

This volume, edited by Aaron Marcus, contains papers focusing on the thematic area of Design, User Experience and Usability, and addressing the following major topics:

- Design Philosophy
- Usability Methods and Tools
- Design Processes, Methods and Tools

The remaining volumes of the HCI International 2013 proceedings are:

- Volume 1, LNCS 8004, Human–Computer Interaction: Human-Centred Design Approaches, Methods, Tools and Environments (Part I), edited by Masaaki Kurosu
- Volume 2, LNCS 8005, Human–Computer Interaction: Applications and Services (Part II), edited by Masaaki Kurosu
- Volume 3, LNCS 8006, Human–Computer Interaction: Users and Contexts of Use (Part III), edited by Masaaki Kurosu
- Volume 4, LNCS 8007, Human–Computer Interaction: Interaction Modalities and Techniques (Part IV), edited by Masaaki Kurosu
- Volume 5, LNCS 8008, Human–Computer Interaction: Towards Intelligent and Implicit Interaction (Part V), edited by Masaaki Kurosu
- Volume 6, LNCS 8009, Universal Access in Human–Computer Interaction: Design Methods, Tools and Interaction Techniques for eInclusion (Part I), edited by Constantine Stephanidis and Margherita Antona
- Volume 7, LNCS 8010, Universal Access in Human–Computer Interaction: User and Context Diversity (Part II), edited by Constantine Stephanidis and Margherita Antona
- Volume 8, LNCS 8011, Universal Access in Human–Computer Interaction: Applications and Services for Quality of Life (Part III), edited by Constantine Stephanidis and Margherita Antona
- Volume 10, LNCS 8013, Design, User Experience, and Usability: Health, Learning, Playing, Cultural, and Cross-Cultural User Experience (Part II), edited by Aaron Marcus
- Volume 11, LNCS 8014, Design, User Experience, and Usability: User Experience in Novel Technological Environments (Part III), edited by Aaron Marcus
- Volume 12, LNCS 8015, Design, User Experience, and Usability: Web, Mobile and Product Design (Part IV), edited by Aaron Marcus
- Volume 13, LNCS 8016, Human Interface and the Management of Information: Information and Interaction Design (Part I), edited by Sakae Yamamoto
- Volume 14, LNCS 8017, Human Interface and the Management of Information: Information and Interaction for Health, Safety, Mobility and Complex Environments (Part II), edited by Sakae Yamamoto
- Volume 15, LNCS 8018, Human Interface and the Management of Information: Information and Interaction for Learning, Culture, Collaboration and Business (Part III), edited by Sakae Yamamoto
- Volume 16, LNAI 8019, Engineering Psychology and Cognitive Ergonomics: Understanding Human Cognition (Part I), edited by Don Harris
- Volume 17, LNAI 8020, Engineering Psychology and Cognitive Ergonomics: Applications and Services (Part II), edited by Don Harris
- Volume 18, LNCS 8021, Virtual, Augmented and Mixed Reality: Designing and Developing Augmented and Virtual Environments (Part I), edited by Randall Shumaker
- Volume 19, LNCS 8022, Virtual, Augmented and Mixed Reality: Systems and Applications (Part II), edited by Randall Shumaker

- Volume 20, LNCS 8023, Cross-Cultural Design: Methods, Practice and Case Studies (Part I), edited by P.L. Patrick Rau
- Volume 21, LNCS 8024, Cross-Cultural Design: Cultural Differences in Everyday Life (Part II), edited by P.L. Patrick Rau
- Volume 22, LNCS 8025, Digital Human Modeling and Applications in Health, Safety, Ergonomics and Risk Management: Healthcare and Safety of the Environment and Transport (Part I), edited by Vincent G. Duffy
- Volume 23, LNCS 8026, Digital Human Modeling and Applications in Health, Safety, Ergonomics and Risk Management: Human Body Modeling and Ergonomics (Part II), edited by Vincent G. Duffy
- Volume 24, LNAI 8027, Foundations of Augmented Cognition, edited by Dylan D. Schmorrow and Cali M. Fidopiastis
- Volume 25, LNCS 8028, Distributed, Ambient and Pervasive Interactions, edited by Norbert Streitz and Constantine Stephanidis
- Volume 26, LNCS 8029, Online Communities and Social Computing, edited by A. Ant Ozok and Panayiotis Zaphiris
- Volume 27, LNCS 8030, Human Aspects of Information Security, Privacy and Trust, edited by Louis Marinos and Ioannis Askoxylakis
- Volume 28, CCIS 373, HCI International 2013 Posters Proceedings (Part I), edited by Constantine Stephanidis
- Volume 29, CCIS 374, HCI International 2013 Posters Proceedings (Part II), edited by Constantine Stephanidis

I would like to thank the Program Chairs and the members of the Program Boards of all affiliated conferences and thematic areas, listed below, for their contribution to the highest scientific quality and the overall success of the HCI International 2013 conference.

This conference could not have been possible without the continuous support and advice of the Founding Chair and Conference Scientific Advisor, Prof. Gavriel Salvendy, as well as the dedicated work and outstanding efforts of the Communications Chair and Editor of HCI International News, Abbas Moallem.

I would also like to thank for their contribution towards the smooth organization of the HCI International 2013 Conference the members of the Human–Computer Interaction Laboratory of ICS-FORTH, and in particular George Paparoulis, Maria Pitsoulaki, Stavroula Ntoa, Maria Bouhli and George Kapnas.

May 2013
Constantine Stephanidis
General Chair, HCI International 2013

Organization

Human–Computer Interaction

Program Chair: Masaaki Kurosu, Japan

Jose Abdelnour-Nocera, UK
Sebastiano Bagnara, Italy
Simone Barbosa, Brazil
Tomas Berns, Sweden
Nigel Bevan, UK
Simone Borsci, UK
Apala Lahiri Chavan, India
Sherry Chen, Taiwan
Kevin Clark, USA
Torkil Clemmensen, Denmark
Xiaowen Fang, USA
Shin'ichi Fukuzumi, Japan
Vicki Hanson, UK
Ayako Hashizume, Japan
Anzai Hiroyuki, Italy
Sheue-Ling Hwang, Taiwan
Wonil Hwang, South Korea
Minna Isomursu, Finland
Yong Gu Ji, South Korea
Esther Jun, USA
Mitsuhiko Karashima, Japan

Kyungdoh Kim, South Korea
Heidi Krömker, Germany
Chen Ling, USA
Yan Liu, USA
Zhengjie Liu, P.R. China
Loïc Martínez Normand, Spain
Chang S. Nam, USA
Naoko Okuizumi, Japan
Noriko Osaka, Japan
Philippe Palanque, France
Hans Persson, Sweden
Ling Rothrock, USA
Naoki Sakakibara, Japan
Dominique Scapin, France
Guangfeng Song, USA
Sanjay Tripathi, India
Chui Yin Wong, Malaysia
Toshiki Yamaoka, Japan
Kazuhiko Yamazaki, Japan
Ryoji Yoshitake, Japan
Silvia Zimmermann, Switzerland

Human Interface and the Management of Information

Program Chair: Sakae Yamamoto, Japan

Hans-Jorg Bullinger, Germany
Alan Chan, Hong Kong
Gilsoo Cho, South Korea
Jon R. Gunderson, USA
Shin'ichi Fukuzumi, Japan
Michitaka Hirose, Japan
Jhilmil Jain, USA
Yasufumi Kume, Japan

Mark Lehto, USA
Hiroyuki Miki, Japan
Hirohiko Mori, Japan
Fiona Fui-Hoon Nah, USA
Shogo Nishida, Japan
Robert Proctor, USA
Youngho Rhee, South Korea
Katsunori Shimohara, Japan

Michale Smith, USA
Tsutomu Tabe, Japan
Hiroshi Tsuji, Japan

Kim-Phuong Vu, USA
Tomio Watanabe, Japan
Hidekazu Yoshikawa, Japan

Engineering Psychology and Cognitive Ergonomics

Program Chair: Don Harris, UK

Guy Andre Boy, USA
Joakim Dahlman, Sweden
Trevor Dobbins, UK
Mike Feary, USA
Shan Fu, P.R. China
Michaela Heese, Austria
Hung-Sying Jing, Taiwan
Wen-Chin Li, Taiwan
Mark A. Neerincx, The Netherlands
Jan M. Noyes, UK
Taezoon Park, Singapore

Paul Salmon, Australia
Axel Schulte, Germany
Siraj Shaikh, UK
Sarah C. Sharples, UK
Anthony Smoker, UK
Neville A. Stanton, UK
Alex Stedmon, UK
Xianghong Sun, P.R. China
Andrew Thatcher, South Africa
Matthew J.W. Thomas, Australia
Rolf Zon, The Netherlands

Universal Access in Human–Computer Interaction

Program Chairs: Constantine Stephanidis, Greece, and Margherita Antona, Greece

Julio Abascal, Spain
Ray Adams, UK
Gisela Susanne Bahr, USA
Margit Betke, USA
Christian Bühler, Germany
Stefan Carmien, Spain
Jerzy Charytonowicz, Poland
Carlos Duarte, Portugal
Pier Luigi Emiliani, Italy
Qin Gao, P.R. China
Andrina Granić, Croatia
Andreas Holzinger, Austria
Josette Jones, USA
Simeon Keates, UK

Georgios Kouroupetroglou, Greece
Patrick Langdon, UK
Seongil Lee, Korea
Ana Isabel B.B. Paraguay, Brazil
Helen Petrie, UK
Michael Pieper, Germany
Enrico Pontelli, USA
Jaime Sanchez, Chile
Anthony Savidis, Greece
Christian Stary, Austria
Hirotada Ueda, Japan
Gerhard Weber, Germany
Harald Weber, Germany

Virtual, Augmented and Mixed Reality

Program Chair: Randall Shumaker, USA

Waymon Armstrong, USA
Juan Cendan, USA
Rudy Darken, USA
Cali M. Fidopiastis, USA
Charles Hughes, USA
David Kaber, USA
Hirokazu Kato, Japan
Denis Laurendeau, Canada
Fotis Liarokapis, UK

Mark Livingston, USA
Michael Macedonia, USA
Gordon Mair, UK
Jose San Martin, Spain
Jacquelyn Morie, USA
Albert "Skip" Rizzo, USA
Kay Stanney, USA
Christopher Stapleton, USA
Gregory Welch, USA

Cross-Cultural Design

Program Chair: P.L. Patrick Rau, P.R. China

Pilsung Choe, P.R. China
Henry Been-Lirn Duh, Singapore
Vanessa Evers, The Netherlands
Paul Fu, USA
Zhiyong Fu, P.R. China
Fu Guo, P.R. China
Sung H. Han, Korea
Toshikazu Kato, Japan
Dyi-Yih Michael Lin, Taiwan
Rungtai Lin, Taiwan

Sheau-Farn Max Liang, Taiwan
Liang Ma, P.R. China
Alexander Mädche, Germany
Katsuhiko Ogawa, Japan
Tom Plocher, USA
Kerstin Röse, Germany
Supriya Singh, Australia
Hsiu-Ping Yueh, Taiwan
Liang (Leon) Zeng, USA
Chen Zhao, USA

Online Communities and Social Computing

Program Chairs: A. Ant Ozok, USA, and Panayiotis Zaphiris, Cyprus

Areej Al-Wabil, Saudi Arabia
Leonelo Almeida, Brazil
Bjørn Andersen, Norway
Chee Siang Ang, UK
Aneesha Bakharia, Australia
Ania Bobrowicz, UK
Paul Cairns, UK
Farzin Deravi, UK
Andri Ioannou, Cyprus
Slava Kisilevich, Germany

Niki Lambropoulos, Greece
Effie Law, Switzerland
Soo Ling Lim, UK
Fernando Loizides, Cyprus
Gabriele Meiselwitz, USA
Anthony Norcio, USA
Elaine Raybourn, USA
Panote Siriaraya, UK
David Stuart, UK
June Wei, USA

Augmented Cognition

Program Chairs: Dylan D. Schmorrow, USA, and Cali M. Fidopiastis, USA

Robert Arrabito, Canada
Richard Backs, USA
Chris Berka, USA
Joseph Cohn, USA
Martha E. Crosby, USA
Julie Drexler, USA
Ivy Estabrooke, USA
Chris Forsythe, USA
Wai Tat Fu, USA
Rodolphe Gentili, USA
Marc Grootjen, The Netherlands
Jefferson Grubb, USA
Ming Hou, Canada

Santosh Mathan, USA
Rob Matthews, Australia
Dennis McBride, USA
Jeff Morrison, USA
Mark A. Neerincx, The Netherlands
Denise Nicholson, USA
Banu Onaral, USA
Lee Sciarini, USA
Kay Stanney, USA
Roy Stripling, USA
Rob Taylor, UK
Karl van Orden, USA

Digital Human Modeling and Applications in Health, Safety, Ergonomics and Risk Management

Program Chair: Vincent G. Duffy, USA and Russia

Karim Abdel-Malek, USA
Giuseppe Andreoni, Italy
Daniel Carruth, USA
Eliza Yingzi Du, USA
Enda Fallon, Ireland
Afzal Godil, USA
Ravindra Goonetilleke, Hong Kong
Bo Hoege, Germany
Waldemar Karwowski, USA
Zhizhong Li, P.R. China

Kang Li, USA
Tim Marler, USA
Michelle Robertson, USA
Matthias Rötting, Germany
Peter Vink, The Netherlands
Mao-Jiun Wang, Taiwan
Xuguang Wang, France
Jingzhou (James) Yang, USA
Xiugan Yuan, P.R. China
Gülcin Yücel Hoge, Germany

Design, User Experience, and Usability

Program Chair: Aaron Marcus, USA

Sisira Adikari, Australia
Ronald Baecker, Canada
Arne Berger, Germany
Jamie Blustein, Canada

Ana Boa-Ventura, USA
Jan Brejcha, Czech Republic
Lorenzo Cantoni, Switzerland
Maximilian Eibl, Germany

Anthony Faiola, USA
Emilie Gould, USA
Zelda Harrison, USA
Rüdiger Heimgärtner, Germany
Brigitte Herrmann, Germany
Steffen Hess, Germany
Kaleem Khan, Canada

Jennifer McGinn, USA
Francisco Rebelo, Portugal
Michael Renner, Switzerland
Kerem Rızvanoğlu, Turkey
Marcelo Soares, Brazil
Christian Sturm, Germany
Michele Visciola, Italy

Distributed, Ambient and Pervasive Interactions

Program Chairs: Norbert Streitz, Germany, and Constantine Stephanidis, Greece

Emile Aarts, The Netherlands
Adnan Abu-Dayya, Qatar
Juan Carlos Augusto, UK
Boris de Ruyter, The Netherlands
Anind Dey, USA
Dimitris Grammenos, Greece
Nuno M. Guimaraes, Portugal
Shin'ichi Konomi, Japan
Carsten Magerkurth, Switzerland

Christian Müller-Tomfelde, Australia
Fabio Paternó, Italy
Gilles Privat, France
Harald Reiterer, Germany
Carsten Röcker, Germany
Reiner Wichert, Germany
Woontack Woo, South Korea
Xenophon Zabulis, Greece

Human Aspects of Information Security, Privacy and Trust

Program Chairs: Louis Marinos, ENISA EU, and Ioannis Askoxylakis, Greece

Claudio Agostino Ardagna, Italy
Zinaida Benenson, Germany
Daniele Catteddu, Italy
Raoul Chiesa, Italy
Bryan Cline, USA
Sadie Creese, UK
Jorge Cuellar, Germany
Marc Dacier, USA
Dieter Gollmann, Germany
Kirstie Hawkey, Canada
Jaap-Henk Hoepman, The Netherlands
Cagatay Karabat, Turkey
Angelos Keromytis, USA
Ayako Komatsu, Japan

Ronald Leenes, The Netherlands
Javier Lopez, Spain
Steve Marsh, Canada
Gregorio Martinez, Spain
Emilio Mordini, Italy
Yuko Murayama, Japan
Masakatsu Nishigaki, Japan
Aljosa Pasic, Spain
Milan Petković, The Netherlands
Joachim Posegga, Germany
Jean-Jacques Quisquater, Belgium
Damien Sauveron, France
George Spanoudakis, UK
Kerry-Lynn Thomson, South Africa

Julien Touzeau, France
Theo Tryfonas, UK
João Vilela, Portugal

Claire Vishik, UK
Melanie Volkamer, Germany

External Reviewers

Maysoon Abulkhair, Saudi Arabia
Ilia Adami, Greece
Vishal Barot, UK
Stephan Böhm, Germany
Vassilis Charissis, UK
Francisco Cipolla-Ficarra, Spain
Maria De Marsico, Italy
Marc Fabri, UK
David Fonseca, Spain
Linda Harley, USA
Yasushi Ikei, Japan
Wei Ji, USA
Nouf Khashman, Canada
John Killilea, USA
Iosif Klironomos, Greece
Ute Klotz, Switzerland
Maria Korozi, Greece
Kentaro Kotani, Japan

Vassilis Kouroumalis, Greece
Stephanie Lackey, USA
Janelle LaMarche, USA
Asterios Leonidis, Greece
Nickolas Macchiarella, USA
George Margetis, Greece
Matthew Marraffino, USA
Joseph Mercado, USA
Claudia Mont'Alvão, Brazil
Yoichi Motomura, Japan
Karsten Nebe, Germany
Stavroula Ntoa, Greece
Martin Osen, Austria
Stephen Prior, UK
Farid Shirazi, Canada
Jan Stelovsky, USA
Sarah Swierenga, USA

HCI International 2014

The 16th International Conference on Human–Computer Interaction, HCI International 2014, will be held jointly with the affiliated conferences in the summer of 2014. It will cover a broad spectrum of themes related to Human–Computer Interaction, including theoretical issues, methods, tools, processes and case studies in HCI design, as well as novel interaction techniques, interfaces and applications. The proceedings will be published by Springer. More information about the topics, as well as the venue and dates of the conference, will be announced through the HCI International Conference series website: http://www.hci-international.org/

General Chair
Professor Constantine Stephanidis
University of Crete and ICS-FORTH
Heraklion, Crete, Greece
Email: cs@ics.forth.gr

Table of Contents – Part I

Design Philosophy

Reframed Contexts: Design Thinking for Agile User Experience
Design.. 3
   Sisira Adikari, Craig McDonald, and John Campbell

An Individual Differences Approach to Design Fixation: Comparing
Laboratory and Field Research 13
   Brooke G. Bellows, Jordan F. Higgins, and Robert J. Youmans

Techno-imagination and Implicit Knowledge......................... 22
   Jiří Bystřický

Context as a System, Product as a Component, and the Relationship
as Experience 29
   WonJoon Chung and Sara Fortier

On the Poetry of Design 38
   Arash Faroughi and Roozbeh Faroughi

Future Fashion – At the Interface 48
   Patricia J. Flanagan and Katia Fabiola Canepa Vega

Haptic Interface Aesthetics – 'Feedback Loops, Live Coding and How to
Harness the Potential of Embodied Estrangement in Artistic Practices
and Aesthetic Theories within Interface Culture' 58
   Patricia J. Flanagan

Is Reality Real? Thoughts and Conjectures about Culture, Self,
Intersubjectivity and Parallel Worlds in Digital Technologies 68
   *Ana Carol Pontes de França, Marcelo Márcio Soares, and
   Luciano Rogério de Lemos Meira*

The Lack of Subjective Experience in Hybrid Intelligent Agents in
Interactive Storytelling 74
   Olivier Guy and Ronan Champagnat

Towards Determinants of User-Intuitive Web Interface Signs........... 84
   Muhammad Nazrul Islam

Sci-Fi Movies and the Pessimistic View for the Future Controlled
Society of Totalitarianism 94
   Masaaki Kurosu

Interactive Design and the Human Experience: What Can Industrial
Design Teach Us   100
  Neil Matthiessen

Location, Location, Location: About Home Networking Devices
Location and Features   107
  Abbas Moallem

Metacommunication and Semiotic Engineering: Insights from a Study
with Mediated HCI   115
  *Ingrid Teixeira Monteiro, Clarisse Sieckenius de Souza, and
  Carla Faria Leitão*

Hypertext in Mutation: The Mapping of a Mythos   125
  Tara Ogaick and WonJoon Chung

Social Movement Information Design and a Curriculum of Proper
Knowledge Consumption   134
  Gabriel Y. Schaffzin

Shifting the Focus: An Objective Look at Design Fixation   144
  *Melissa A.B. Smith, Robert J. Youmans, Brooke G. Bellows, and
  Matthew S. Peterson*

Semiotics of Void and Information Representation   152
  Kumiko Tanaka-Ishii

Of Hoverboards and Hypertext   162
  Daniel Yule and Jamie Blustein

User-Mobile Phone Interactions: A Postphenomenology Analysis   171
  Bin Zhang and Hua Dong

Usability Methods and Tools

Assessing Designs of Interactive Voice Response Systems for Better
Usability   183
  Siddhartha Asthana, Pushpendra Singh, and Amarjeet Singh

User Interaction Forensics: Detecting and Interpreting the User's
Footprints during Touch Interaction   193
  Kai Breiner

The Conjunction Fallacy and Its Impacts in the User's Data Acquisition
Process   203
  *Fábio Campos, Dino Lincoln, Maria Neves, Walter Correia, and
  Marcelo Soares*

Remote Usability Evaluation Using Eye Tracking Enhanced with
Intelligent Data Analysis... 212
  Piotr Chynał, Janusz Sobecki, and Jerzy M. Szymański

Beyond Satisfaction Questionnaires: "Hacking" the Online Survey 222
  Andrea L. Evans

A Component-Based Evaluation Protocol for Clinical Decision Support
Interfaces 232
  *Alessandro Febretti, Karen Dunn Lopez, Janet Stifter,
  Andrew E. Johnson, Gail M. Keenan, and Diana J. Wilkie*

Human in the Loop: A Model to Integrate Interaction Issues in
Complex Simulations 242
  *Stefano Filippi, Daniela Barattin, Francesco Ferrise,
  Monica Bordegoni, and Umberto Cugini*

Towards a Holistic Tool for the Selection and Validation of Usability
Method Sets Supporting Human-Centered Design 252
  Holger Fischer, Benjamin Strenge, and Karsten Nebe

VMUXE: An Approach to User Experience Evaluation for Virtual
Museums 262
  *Bianca Gockel, Holger Graf, Alfonsina Pagano, Sofia Pescarin, and
  Joakim Eriksson*

Customer Recruitment: Ethical, Legal and Practical Issues 273
  Kristyn Greenwood and Angela Johnston

Novel Method of Evaluating GUI Design from the Viewpoint of Worker
Experience: Central Control Systems for Social Infrastructure 283
  *Daiki Hama, Mai Kurioka, Mariko Kato, Ken Imamura, and
  Miwa Nakanishi*

Understand System's Relative Effectiveness Using Adapted Confusion
Matrix 294
  Nan Jiang and Haibin Liu

Development of a General Internet Attitude Scale 303
  Mary Joyce and Jurek Kirakowski

The Usability Perception Scale (UPscale): A Measure for Evaluating
Feedback Displays 312
  Beth Karlin and Rebecca Ford

System for Evaluating Usability and User Experience by Analyzing
Repeated Patterns 322
  Young Bin Kim, Shin Jin Kang, and Chang Hun Kim

\

A Color Model in the Usability of Computer Interface Applied to Users
with Low Vision 330
   Cínthia Costa Kulpa, Fábio Gonçalves Teixeira, and
   Régio Pierre Da Silva

Usability of Virtual Worlds 340
   Haind Lu, Tobias Brockmann, and Stefan Stieglitz

Assessing Perceived Experience with Magnitude Estimation 349
   Mick McGee, Misha Vaughan, and Joseph Dumas

SINGRAR Usability Study 359
   Isabel L. Nunes and Mário Simões-Marques

Development and Validation of an Instrument to Measure the Usability
of Educational Artifacts Created with Web 2.0 Applications 369
   Tihomir Orehovački and Nikolina Žajdela Hrustek

Ergonomic Evaluation of Usability with Users – Application of the
Technique of Cooperative Evaluation 379
   Marcelo Penha, Walter Correia, Marcelo Soares,
   Fábio Campos, and Marina Barros

Using Eye-Tracking to Test and Improve Website Design 389
   Anna Prisacari and Thomas Holme

The Dimensions of Positive and Negative User Experiences with
Interactive Products 399
   Gabrielle Provost and Jean-Marc Robert

Participatory Design and Usability: A Behavioral Approach of Workers'
Attitudes in the Work Environment 409
   Dierci Marcio Cunha da Silveira

Merging Methodologies: Combining Individual and Group
Card Sorting 417
   Robert L. Thomas and Ian Johnson

Engaging Citizens with UX Design 427
   Kate Walser

Design Processes, Methods and Tools

Eliciting User Requirements and Acceptance for Customizing Mobile
Device System Architecture 439
   Katrin Arning, Bianka Trevisan, Martina Ziefle, and
   Eva-Maria Jakobs

User Experience Starts at the Keystroke Level: The Model of User
Experience (MUX) 449
    Stefan Brandenburg, Marlene Vogel, and Uwe Drewitz

Designing iDTV Applications from Participatory Use of Patterns 459
    Samuel B. Buchdid, Roberto Pereira, and
    Maria Cecília C. Baranauskas

Design Process and Knowledge Searching Model Based on User
Creativity 469
    Chia-Ling Chang and Ding-Bang Luh

Activity-Based Context-Aware Model 479
    Yuanyuan Chen, Zhengjie Liu, and Juhani Vainio

Satisfying Consumers' Needs through Systematic Empathic Design
Model 488
    Ming-Hsuan Hsieh, Ding-Bang Luh, Cheng-Yong Huang, and
    Chia-Hsiang Ma

How to Observe, Share and Apply in Design Process? Focusing on
International Design Workshops as a Case Study 498
    Namgyu Kang and Hidetsugu Suto

Modelling User Behaviour and Experience – The R2D2 Networks
Approach 506
    Amela Karahasanović and Asbjørn Følstad

Community Participation Support Using an ICF-Based
Community Map 516
    Satoru Kitamura, Koji Kitamura, Yoshifumi Nishida,
    Ken-Ichiro Sakae, Junko Yasuda, and Hiroshi Mizoguchi

Pragmatic Approach to Cost Benefit Analysis of User Centered
Design 525
    Izumi Kohno, Hiroko Yasu, Satoshi Sugawara, and
    Masahiro Nishikawa

Innovative Behavioral Intention and Creativity Achievement in Design:
Test of an Integrated Model 535
    Chia-Chen Lu and Ding-Bang Luh

A Design Process for New Concept Development 545
    Ding-Bang Luh, Frank (Ming-Hung) Chen, and Vincent (I-Hsun) Ku

How to Create a User Experience Story 554
    Ioanna Michailidou, Constantin von Saucken, and Udo Lindemann

Prototyping with Experience Workshop 564
    Jussi Mikkonen and Yi-Ta Hsieh

Keeping User Centred Design (UCD) Alive and Well in Your
Organisation: Taking an Agile Approach 573
  Colette Raison and Snezna Schmidt

Design Thinking Methodology for the Design of Interactive Real-Time
Applications... 583
  Diego Sandino, Luis M. Matey, and Gorka Vélez

User Involvement in Idea Brainstorming of Design Process: Finding the
Effective Strategy in Social Network Service 593
  Shu-Chuan Chiu and Kiyoshi Tomimatsu

Understanding the UX Designer's Role within Agile Teams 599
  *Tiago Silva da Silva, Milene Selbach Silveira,
  Claudia de O. Melo, and Luiz Claudio Parzianello*

Designing for Resonance by Evocative Objects: An Experiential
Interaction Design Method 610
  Chih-Sheng Su and Rung-Huei Liang

Usagame – A New Methodology to Support User Centered Design of
Touchscreen Applications 620
  Pedro Vinagre and Isabel L. Nunes

A Method for Teaching Affordance for User Experience Design in
Interactive Media Design Education 630
  Asım Evren Yantaç

Author Index 639

Table of Contents – Part II

Cross-Cultural and Intercultural User Experience

A Novel Reading Technique Application: Exploring Arabic Children
Experience... 3
   Maram S. Alhafzy, Ebtesam A. Alomari, Hind H. Mahdy, and
   Maysoon F. Abulkhair

Observation Analysis Method for Culture Centered Design – Proposal
of KH Method... 11
   Kaho Asano and Kazuhiko Yamazaki

Lessons Learned from Projects in Japan and Korea Relevant for
Intercultural HCI Development 20
   Martin Blankl, Peter Biersack, and Rüdiger Heimgärtner

Usability Evaluation of Two Chinese Segmentation Methods in
Subtitles to Scaffold Chinese Novice 28
   Chih-Kai Chang

Young Egyptians Use of Social Networks and the January 2011
Revolution 38
   Ghada R. El Said

Designing for a Thumb: An Ideal Mobile Touchscreen Interface for
Chinese Users 44
   Qian Fei

Examining Interdisciplinary Prototyping in the Context of Cultural
Communication... 54
   Michael Heidt

Intercultural User Interface Design – Culture-Centered HCI Design
– Cross-Cultural User Interface Design: Different Terminology or
Different Approaches? 62
   Rüdiger Heimgärtner

User-Experience and Science-Fiction in Chinese, Indian, and Japanese
Films... 72
   Aaron Marcus

Two Solitudes Revisited: A Cross-Cultural Exploration of Online Image
Searcher's Behaviors... 79
   Elaine Ménard, Nouf Khashman, and Jonathan Dorey

Usability Assessment in the Multicultural Approach 89
Maria Lúcia L.R. Okimoto, Cristina Olaverri Monreal, and Klaus-Josef Bengler

Lessons from Intercultural Project Management for the Intercultural
HCI Design Process 95
Yvonne Schoper and Rüdiger Heimgärtner

Localization beyond National Characteristics: The Impact of Language
on Users' Performance with Different Menu Structures............... 105
Christian Sturm, Gerhard Strube, and Sara Gouda

Tracing Technology Diffusion of Social Media with Culturally Localized
User Experience Approach 115
Huatong Sun

The Interactive Media between Human and the Sacred: An Example
for Taiwanese Spiritual Practice 121
Pi-Fen Wang

Banner Evaluation Predicted by Eye Tracking Performance and the
Median Thinking Style 129
Man-Ying Wang, Da-Lung Tang, Chih-Tung Kao, and Vincent C. Sun

Intercultural Design for Use – Extending Usage-Centered Design by
Cultural Aspects... 139
Helmut Windl and Rüdiger Heimgärtner

A Usability Testing of Chinese Character Writing System for Foreign
Learners 149
Manlai You and Yu-Jie Xu

Designing for the Learning and Culture Experience

A Cross-Cultural Evaluation of HCI Student Performance - Reflections
for the Curriculum 161
José Abdelnour-Nocera, Ann Austin, Mario Michaelides, and Sunila Modi

Desirability of a Teaching and Learning Tool for Thai Dance Body
Motion 171
Worawat Choensawat, Kingkarn Sookhanaphibarn, Chommanad Kijkhun, and Kozaburo Hachimura

Improving User Experience in e-Learning, the Case of the Open
University of Catalonia 180
Eva de Lera, Magí Almirall, Llorenç Valverde, and Mercè Gisbert

Math Fluency through Game Design 189
    Wanda Eugene, Tiffany Barnes, and Jennifer Wilson

Musical Experience Development Model Based on Service Design
Thinking.. 199
    Sunyoung Kim and Eui-Chul Jung

Investigation of Interaction Modalities Designed for Immersive
Visualizations Using Commodity Devices in the Classroom 209
    Kira Lawrence, Alisa Maas, Neera Pradhan, Treschiel Ford,
    Jacqueline Shinker, and Amy Ulinski Banic

Legibility in Children's Reading: The Methodological Development of
an Experiment for Reading Printed and Digital Texts 219
    Daniel Lourenço and Solange Coutinho

PALMA: Usability Testing of an Application for Adult Literacy
in Brazil 229
    Francimar Rodrigues Maciel

Setting Conditions for Learning: Mediated Play and Socio-material
Dialogue 238
    Emanuela Marchetti and Eva Petersson Brooks

The Learning Machine: Mobile UX Design That Combines Information
Design with Persuasion Design...................................... 247
    Aaron Marcus, Yuan Peng, and Nicola Lecca

Information Accessibility in Museums with a Focus on Technology and
Cognitive Process 257
    Laura B. Martins and Felipe Gabriele

Luz, Câmera, Libras!: How a Mobile Game Can Improve the Learning
of Sign Languages.. 266
    Guilherme Moura, Luis Arthur Vasconcelos, Aline Cavalcanti,
    Felipe Breyer, Daliton da Silva, João Marcelo Teixeira,
    Crystian Leão, and Judith Kelner

Toward Social Media Based Writing 276
    John Sadauskas, Daragh Byrne, and Robert K. Atkinson

Participatory Design for Mobile Application for Academic Management
in a Brazilian University 286
    José Guilherme Santa Rosa, Andrei Gurgel, and
    Marcel de Oliveira Passos

YUSR: Speech Recognition Software for Dyslexics.................... 296
    Mounira Taileb, Reem Al-Saggaf, Amal Al-Ghamdi,
    Maha Al-Zebaidi, and Sultana Al-Sahafi

Measuring Usability of the Mobile Mathematics Curriculum-Based
Measurement Application with Children 304
   Mengping Tsuei, Hsin-Yin Chou, and Bo-Sheng Chen

Teachers and Children Playing with Factorization: Putting Prime
Slaughter to the Test 311
   Andrea Valente and Emanuela Marchetti

Towards a Common Implementation Framework for Online Virtual
Museums 321
   Katarzyna Wilkosinska, Andreas Aderhold, Holger Graf, and
   Yvonne Jung

Designing for the Health and Quality of Life Experience

Towards an Arabic Language Augmentative and Alternative
Communication Application for Autism 333
   Bayan Al-Arifi, Arwa Al-Rubaian, Ghadah Al-Ofisan,
   Norah Al-Romi, and Areej Al-Wabil

Improving Autistic Children's Social Skills Using Virtual Reality 342
   Omaima Bamasak, Roa'a Braik, Hadeel Al-Tayari, Shatha Al-Harbi,
   Ghadeer Al-Semairi, and Malak Abu-Hnaidi

Lazy Eye Shooter: Making a Game Therapy for Visual Recovery in
Adult Amblyopia Usable 352
   Jessica D. Bayliss, Indu Vedamurthy, Mor Nahum,
   Dennis Levi, and Daphne Bavelier

Designing Supportive Mobile Technology for Stable Diabetes 361
   Katherine S. Blondon and Predrag Klasnja

Application of Rhetorical Appeals in Interactive Design for Health 371
   Sauman Chu and G. Mauricio Mejia

Addressing Human Computer Interaction Issues of Electronic Health
Record in Clinical Encounters 381
   Martina A. Clarke, Linsey M. Steege, Joi L. Moore,
   Jeffery L. Belden, Richelle J. Koopman, and
   Min Soon Kim

Designing Co-located Tabletop Interaction for Rehabilitation of Brain
Injury   391
   Jonathan Duckworth, Patrick R. Thomas, David Shum, and
   Peter H. Wilson

Paindroid: A Mobile Tool for Pain Visualization and Management   401
   Tor-Morten Grønli, Gheorghita Ghinea, Fotios Spyridonis, and
   Jarle Hansen

Usability Testing Medical Devices: A Practical Guide to Minimizing
Risk and Maximizing Success   407
   Chris Hass and Dan Berlin

Exploring the Need for, and Feasibility of, a Web-Based
Self-management Resource for Teenage and Young Adult Cancer
Survivors in the UK   417
   Louise Moody, Andy Turner, Jane Osmond,
   Joanna Kosmala-Anderson, Louise Hooker, and Lynn Batehup

Avatar Interfaces for Biobehavioral Feedback   424
   Tylar Murray, Delquawn Hardy, Donna Spruijt-Metz,
   Eric Hekler, and Andrew Raij

Participatory Interaction Design for the Healthcare Service Field   435
   Takuichi Nishimura, M. Kobayakawa, M. Nakajima,
   K.C. Yamada, T. Fukuhara, M. Hamasaki, H. Miwa,
   Kentaro Watanabe, Y. Sakamoto, T. Sunaga, and Yoichi Motomura

Virtual Environment to Treat Social Anxiety   442
   Ana Paula Cláudio, Maria Beatriz Carmo, Tânia Pinheiro,
   Francisco Esteves, and Eder Lopes

Development and Evaluation of a Knowledge-Based Method for the
Treatment of Use-Oriented and Technical Risks Using the Example of
Medical Devices   452
   Simon Plogmann, Armin Janß, Arne Jansen-Troy, and
   Klaus Radermacher

Interactive System for Solving Children Communication Disorder   462
   Wafaa M. Shalash, Malak Bas-sam, and Ghada Shawly

Game-Based Interactive Media in Behavioral Medicine: Creating
Serious Affective-Cognitive-Environmental-Social Integration
Experiences   470
   Alasdair G. Thin and Marientina Gotsis

A Mobile Prototype for Clinical Emergency Calls   480
   Cornelius Wille, Thomas Marx, and Adam Maciak

Games and Gamification

The Design in the Development of Exergames: A New Game for the
Contribute to Control Childhood Obesity 491
    Marina Barros, André Neves, Walter Correia,
    Marcelo Marcio Soares, and Fábio Campos

Case Study: Identifying Gamification Opportunities in Sales
Applications.. 501
    Joëlle Carignan and Sally Lawler Kennedy

Interactive Doodles: A Comparative Analysis of the Usability and
Playability of Google Trademark Games between 2010 and 2012 508
    Breno José Andrade de Carvalho, Marcelo Marcio Soares,
    Andre Menezes Marques das Neves, and Rodrigo Pessoa Medeiros

Exploring Adjustable Interactive Rings in Game Playing: Preliminary
Results 518
    Leonardo Cunha de Miranda, Heiko Hornung, Roberto Pereira, and
    Maria Cecília C. Baranauskas

Gamification at Work: Designing Engaging Business Software.......... 528
    Janaki Kumar

Stand Up, Heroes!: Gamification for Standing People on Crowded
Public Transportation 538
    Itaru Kuramoto, Takuya Ishibashi, Keiko Yamamoto, and
    Yoshihiro Tsujino

Applying Gamification in Customer Service Application to Improve
Agents' Efficiency and Satisfaction 548
    Prerna Makanawala, Jaideep Godara, Eliad Goldwasser, and
    Hang Le

Perception of Gamification: Between Graphical Design and Persuasive
Design... 558
    Cathie Marache-Francisco and Eric Brangier

Interactive Rock Climbing Playground Equipment: Modeling through
Service 568
    Mikiko Oono, Koji Kitamura, Yoshifumi Nishida, and
    Yoichi Motomura

Work and Gameplay in the Transparent 'Magic Circle' of Gamification:
Insights from a Gameful Collaborative Review Exercise 577
    Răzvan Rughiniş

Augmenting Yu-Gi-Oh! Trading Card Game as Persuasive Transmedia
Storytelling 587
    Mizuki Sakamoto and Tatsuo Nakajima

How Gamification and Behavioral Science Can Drive Social Change
One Employee at a Time... 597
    Susan Hunt Stevens

Bridging the Gap between Consumer and Enterprise Applications
through Gamification.. 602
    Tim Thianthai and Bingjun Zhou

Gamification: When It works, When It Doesn't 608
    Erika Noll Webb

Author Index... 615

Table of Contents – Part III

Designing for Safe and Secure Environments

Rap Backs: Continuous Workforce Monitoring to Improve Patient
Safety in Long-Term Care 3
    *Fuad Abujarad, Sarah J. Swierenga, Toni A. Dennis, and
Lori A. Post*

Join the Ride! User Requirements and Interface Design Guidelines
for a Commuter Carpooling Platform 10
    Katrin Arning, Martina Ziefle, and Heike Muehlhans

SustainDesign – A Project with Young Creative People 20
    Roby Attisano

Using Virtual Reality to Examine Hazard Perception in Package
Design 30
    *Hande Ayanoğlu, Francisco Rebelo, Emília Duarte,
Paulo Noriega, and Luís Teixeira*

Multi-touch Based Standard UI Design of Car Navigation System
for Providing Information of Surrounding Areas 40
    Jung-Min Choi

Designing Technology for Older People – The Role of Technical
Self-confidence in Usability of an Inclusive Heating Control 49
    Nicola Combe, David Harrison, and Hua Dong

Effects of In-Car Navigation Systems on User Perception of the Spatial
Environment 57
    Mehmet Göktürk and Ali Pakkan

Analysis and Evaluation of Wireless Ad Hoc Network Performance
for a Disaster Communication Model and Scenarios 65
    Koichi Gyoda

Improving Management of Medical Equipment 75
    Yu Hao, Yida Gong, and Young Mi (Christina) Choi

Safety of Natural Disasters 85
    *Lamiaa F. Ibrahim, Reem Albatati, Samah Batawil, Rudainah Shilli,
Mai Bakeer, and Tsneem Abo Al Laban*

Interaction Design Using a Child Behavior-Geometry Database 95
    Hiroyuki Kakara, Yoshifumi Nishida, and Hiroshi Mizoguchi

Classifying Energy-Related Events Using Electromagnetic Field
Signatures 105
    Anand S. Kulkarni and Karla Conn Welch

Department of Homeland Security Websites Uncoupled: An Evaluation
of Online Counterterrorism and Security Information across Agencies ... 112
    Anna L. Langhorne

Development of an Unconventional Unmanned Coaxial Rotorcraft:
GremLion 120
    Feng Lin, Kevin Z.Y. Ang, Fei Wang, Ben M. Chen,
    Tong Heng Lee, Beiqing Yang, Miaobo Dong, Xiangxu Dong,
    Jinqiang Cui, Swee King Phang, Biao Wang, Delin Luo,
    Shiyu Zhao, Mingfeng Yin, Kun Li, Kemao Peng, and Guowei Cai

Heuristic Evaluation of iCalamityGuide Application 130
    Aaron Marcus, Scott Abromowitz, and Maysoon F. Abulkhair

The Driving Machine: Mobile UX Design That Combines Information
Design with Persuasion Design.................................... 140
    Aaron Marcus and Scott Abromowitz

Human Error in Aviation: The Behavior of Pilots Facing the Modern
Technology 150
    Isnard Thomas Martins, Edgard Thomas Martins,
    Marcelo Marcio Soares, and Lia Giraldo da Silva Augusto

Breaking Technological Paradigms – Sustainable Design in Air
Transport Multi-mission 160
    Edgard Thomas Martins, Isnard Thomas Martins, and
    Marcelo Marcio Soares

Ergonomics Aspects in Operators of the Electric Power Control and
Operation Centers 169
    Miguel Melo, Luiz Bueno Silva, Ana Almeida, and Francisco Rebelo

HALO the Winning Entry to the DARPA UAVForge Challenge 2012 ... 179
    Stephen D. Prior, Siu-Tsen Shen, Mehmet Ali Erbil,
    Mantas Brazinskas, and Witold Mielniczek

Main Usability Issues in Using Virtual Environments for Older
Population Warning Studies 189
    Lara Reis, Emília Duarte, and Francisco Rebelo

Merging Two Worlds Together 199
    Alex Schieder

Are Emergency Egress Signs Strong Enough to Overlap the Influence
of the Environmental Variables? 205
  Elisângela Vilar, Francisco Rebelo, Paulo Noriega, Luís Teixeira,
  Emília Duarte, and Ernesto Filgueiras

Calculation of Areas of Permanence in Public Spaces, According
to Solar Radiation Simulated Conditions 215
  Julie A. Waldron and Jorge H. Salazar

Designing for Smart and Ambient Devices

Design Methodology for Body Tracking Based Applications - A Kinect
Case Study... 227
  Felipe Breyer, Bernardo Reis, Luis Arthur Vasconcelos,
  Aline Cavalcanti, João Marcelo Teixeira, and Judith Kelner

Empowering Electronic Divas through Beauty Technology 237
  Katia Fabiola Canepa Vega and Hugo Fuks

An Empirical Study of the Characteristics of Interactive Projection
Systems in Multi-media Exhibits 246
  Ting-Han Chen and Shiau-Yuan Du

Evaluation of Effects of Textures Attached to Mobile Devices
on Pointing Accuracy.. 255
  Yoshitomo Fukatsu, Tatsuhito Oe, Yuki Kuno,
  Buntarou Shizuki, and Jiro Tanaka

A Proposal for Optimization Method of Vibration Pattern of Mobile
Device with Interactive Genetic Algorithm 264
  Makoto Fukumoto and Takafumi Ienaga

NUI-Based Floor Navigation — A Case Study 270
  Ulrich Furbach and Markus Maron

Capturing Nursing Interactions from Mobile Sensor Data and In-Room
Sensors 280
  Sozo Inoue, Kousuke Hayashida, Masato Nakamura,
  Yasunobu Nohara, and Naoki Nakashima

Creating Instantly Disappearing Prints Using Thermochromic
Paint and Thermal Printer in an Interactive Art Installation 290
  Miu-Ling Lam

Fashioning Embodied Interfaces: Open Wearables Crafting 296
  Valérie Lamontagne

InTouch: Crossing Social Interaction with Perception 306
  Rung-Huei Liang, Wei-Ming Chung, Hsin-Liu Kao, and
  Tsen-Ying Lin

A Pilot Study of the Intuitiveness of Smartphone Camera Interface
for Elderly Users 316
  Hyunju Shin, DaeSung Ahn, and Junghyun Han

Designing for Virtual and Augmented Environments

Sharing Kinetic Interactions for Mobile Devices 327
  Bashar Altakrouri, Darren Carlson, and Andreas Schrader

Virtual Reality Immersion: An Important Tool for Diagnostic
Analysis and Rehabilitation of People with Disabilities 337
  Helda O. Barros, Marcelo Marcio Soares, Epitácio L. Rolim Filho,
  Walter Correia, and Fábio Campos

Virtual Reality Applied to the Study of the Interaction
between the User and the Built Space: A Literature Review 345
  Alexana Vilar Soares Calado, Marcelo Marcio Soares,
  Fabio Campos, and Walter Correia

Gestural, Emergent and Expressive: Three Research Themes for Haptic
Interaction 352
  Jared Donovan, Gavin Sade, and Jennifer Seevinck

Sense of Presence in a VR-Based Study on Behavioral Compliance
with Warnings 362
  Emília Duarte, Francisco Rebelo, Luís Teixeira, Elisângela Vilar,
  Júlia Teles, and Paulo Noriega

Interactive Shopping Experience through Immersive Store
Environments 372
  Kunal Mankodiya, Rolando Martins, Jonathan Francis,
  Elmer Garduno, Rajeev Gandhi, and Priya Narasimhan

Minimal Yet Integral – Designing a Gestural Interface 383
  Martin Osen

Efficient Information Representation Method for Driver-Centered
AR-HUD System 393
  Hyesun Park and Kyong-ho Kim

Towards Medical Cyber-Physical Systems: Multimodal Augmented
Reality for Doctors and Knowledge Discovery about Patients 401
  Daniel Sonntag, Sonja Zillner, Christian Schulz,
  Markus Weber, and Takumi Toyama

Border Crosser: A Robot as Mediator between the Virtual and Real
World   411
    Anke Tallig, Wolfram Hardt, and Maximilian Eibl

Strategy for the Development of a Walk-In-Place Interface for Virtual
Reality   419
    Luís Teixeira, Elisângela Vilar, Emília Duarte, Paulo Noriega,
    Francisco Rebelo, and Fernando Moreira da Silva

Emotional and Persuasion Design

Exhibiting Emotion: Capturing Visitors' Emotional Responses
to Museum Artefacts   429
    Genevieve Alelis, Ania Bobrowicz, and Chee Siang Ang

Blinklifier: A Case Study for Prototyping Wearable Computers
in Technology and Visual Arts   439
    Katia Fabiola Canepa Vega, Patricia J. Flanagan, and Hugo Fuks

Emotional Experience and Interactive Design in the Workplace   446
    Kuo-Pin Chen and Wen-Huei Chou

A Study on Time Differences between Actual Advertisement
Viewing and Retrospective Perception   455
    Miao-Hsien Chuang and Chiwu Huang

Semiotic Analysis for Gestural and Emotional Human – Computer
Interaction   465
    Roman Danylak

Evaluating Emotional Responses to the Interior Design of a Hospital
Room: A Study Using Virtual Reality   475
    Susana Dinis, Emília Duarte, Paulo Noriega, Luís Teixeira,
    Elisângela Vilar, and Francisco Rebelo

Changing Eating Behaviors through a Cooking-Based Website
for the Whole Family   484
    Marc Fabri, Andrew Wall, and Pip Trevorrow

Design for Relaxation during Milk Expression Using Biofeedback   494
    Loe Feijs, Jeanine Kierkels, Nicolle H. van Schijndel, and
    Marjolein van Lieshout

Designing Ludic Engagement in an Interactive Virtual Dressing Room
System – A Comparative Study   504
    Yi Gao and Eva Petersson Brooks

Humor Illustration Design, a Summary of Illustrations, Designs, and
Projects 513
    Jochen Gasser

Increasing Trust in Personal Informatics Tools 520
    Luis G. Jaimes, Tylar Murray, and Andrew Raij

Feed-In Tariff Personal Carbon Allowance: A Case Study
of Psychological Change 530
    Takayoshi Kitamura, Asao Takamatsu, Hirotake Ishii, and
    Hiroshi Shimoda

Positive Design: New Challenges, Opportunities, and Responsibilities
for Design.. 540
    Anna Elisabeth Pohlmeyer

Tassophonics: Nanotechnology as the Magical Unknown............... 548
    Audrey Samson and Kristina Andersen

Engineering Awareness^{TM}: An e-Service Design Approach
for Behavioral Change in Healthcare and Well-Being 558
    Alberto Sanna, Sauro Vicini, Sara Bellini, Ilaria Baroni, and
    Alice Rosi

Designing a Product Satisfaction Model Using Customer
Segmentation and Information Consolidation 568
    Meng-Dar Shieh

Design Matters: Mid-Term Results from a Multi-Design Fuel Economy
Feedback Experiment.. 578
    Tai Stillwater and Kenneth S. Kurani

Running to Behavior Change 585
    Pip Trevorrow and Marc Fabri

Well-Being on the Go: An IoT Vending Machine Service
for the Promotion of Healthy Behaviors and Lifestyles 594
    Sauro Vicini, Sara Bellini, Alice Rosi, and Alberto Sanna

Author Index... 605

Table of Contents – Part IV

DUXU in Business and the Enterprise

User-Centered Soft Innovation in Established Business Fields   3
  Henning Breuer, Zeno Wolze, and Elisabeth Umbach

The Adoption of Mobile Internet: Industry and Users Experiences   13
  *Manuel José Damásio, Inês Teixeira-Botelho, Sara Henriques, and
  Patrícia Dias*

Branding "for All": Toward the Definition of Inclusive Toolkits of
Analysis and Visual Communication for Brand Identities   23
  Giuseppe Di Bucchianico, Stefania Camplone, and Stefano Picciani

Studies on the Design Marketing Strategies in the Experiential
Economy through the Case Study of 'the Starbucks Company'   30
  Yung Joo Jang and Eui-Chul Jung

A Dependency-Sharing Tool for Global Software Engineering   37
  Douglas Lee, Allen E. Milewski, and Daniela Rosca

Management of Individual and Organizational Design Knowledge   47
  Tz-Ying Lin and Ding-Bang Luh

Ultrabooks™ and Windows 8: A *touchy* UX Story   57
  Daria Loi

The Innovation Machine: Mobile UX Design Combining Information
and Persuasion Design to Change Behavior   67
  Aaron Marcus, Megan Chiou, Chirag Narula, and Allan Yu

Web-Portal Solution for Supporting In-Country Reviews   77
  Michael Oettli and Tasos Panagis

User Experience Transformation in Telco Companies: Turkcell Case   84
  Seda Alpkaya and Cem Sakarya

Human-Centered Communication Planning: A Conceptual Approach . . .   94
  Tim Schneidermeier, Florian Maier, and Johannes Schricker

Online Advertising as a New Story: Effects of User-Driven Photo
Advertisement in Social Media   103
  Min Shin and Da Young Ju

An Applied Ergonomics Study on IT User Interaction in a Large
Hydroelectric Company in the Northeast of Brazil 113
  Marcelo Márcio Soares, Fabio Campos, Walter Correia,
  André Neves, Joao Corte, and Saul Mendonca

Design and Usability: A Case Study on Selecting Exhibitors for the
National Fair of Craftwork – FENEARTE - Recife, PE, Brazil 121
  Tibério Tabosa, Virginia Cavalcanti, Ana Andrade,
  Erimar Cordeiro, and Germannya D´Garcia

How to Design Experiences: Macro UX versus Micro UX Approach 130
  Constantin von Saucken, Ioanna Michailidou, and Udo Lindemann

A User Centred Approach to Determining the Impact of Faster
Broadband on Small and Medium Sized Enterprises 140
  Doug Williams, Andy Gower, Joshan Meenowa, and Jon Wakeling

A User Centred Approach to Evaluating the Future Demand for
Bandwidth from Consumers 150
  Doug Williams, Andy Gower, Joshan Meenowa, and Jon Wakeling

Designing for the Web Experience

Examining User Experience of Cruise Online Search Funnel 163
  Asta Adukaite, Alessandro Inversini, and Lorenzo Cantoni

A User Experience Study of Airline Websites 173
  Mahmut Ekşioğlu, Esin Kırış, Tuğba Çakır, Merve Güvendik,
  Efsane D. Koyutürk, and Merve Yılmaz

Exploring Offline Browsing Patterns to Enhance the Online
Environment 183
  Xiaopeng Guo, Jie Gao, Yujing Zeng, and Zhenghua Zhang

Usability of County Election Websites 193
  Cyd Harrell, Andrea Fineman, Ethan Newby, Dana Chisnell, and
  Whitney Quesenbery

Analysis of Query Entries of a Job Search Engine 203
  Yeolib Kim

The Effect of Feedback within Social Media in Tourism Experiences 212
  Jeongmi (Jamie) Kim, Daniel R. Fesenmaier, and Steven L. Johnson

Fulfilled and Missed Requirements for Online Reservation Systems:
An Empirical Investigation of Austrian and Swiss Hotels 221
  Gerhard F. Knolmayer, Viola Sini, and Polina Chelnokova

Geospatial Web Interfaces, Why Are They So "Complicated"? 231
  Erick López-Ornelas, Rocío Abascal-Mena, and
  J. Sergio Zepeda-Hernández

Behind Livia's Villa: A Case Study for the Devolution of Large Scale
Interactive "in-site" to "on-line" Application 238
  Guido Lucci Baldassari, Emanuel Demetrescu, Sofia Pescarin,
  Joakim Eriksson, and Holger Graf

Evaluating a Web-Based Tool for Crowdsourced Navigation Stress
Tests 248
  Florian Meier, Alexander Bazo, Manuel Burghardt, and
  Christian Wolff

Ergonomic Evaluation of Websites Focusing on the Human-Computer
Interface so as to Improve Access to the Web Especially by People with
Visual Disabilities 257
  André R. Melo, Marcelo Márcio Soares, Fabio Campos, and
  Walter Correia

Evaluating Interaction with Websites: Case Study of a Government
Website of the Brazilian Ministry of Labor and Employment 265
  Fabiane R. Fernandes, Luis Carlos Paschoarelli, and
  José Carlos P. da Silva

From the Ground-Up: Role of Usability and Aesthetics Evaluation
in Creating a Knowledge-Based Website for the U.S. Army Corps of
Engineers 274
  Dennis B. Propst, Sarah J. Swierenga, Graham L. Pierce,
  Eunseong Jeong, and Constantinos K. Coursaris

Selection and Implementation of Navigation and Information Search
Strategies in Bank Web Sites: Turkish Case 284
  Özgürol Öztürk and Kerem Rızvanoğlu

Content as Conversation in Government Websites 294
  Janice (Ginny) Redish

Re-thinking Bookmark Management – Less Choice Is More Efficient 304
  Siu-Tsen Shen and Stephen D. Prior

User-Centered Evaluation of a Discovery Layer System with Google
Scholar 313
  Tao Zhang

Product Design

Modeling Consumer Sensitivity for Product Design and Perceived
Usability... 325
   Tareq Ahram, Waldemar Karwowski, and Nabin Sapkota

Developing ISO 9241-151 Product Certification Process: Challenges 334
   Kürşat Çağıltay, Ozge Alacam, Nihan Ocak, and Feride Erdal

Application of Virtual Reality Technologies in Consumer Product
Usability... 342
   Christianne Soares Falcão and Marcelo Márcio Soares

User Experience on Product Display Page: At Tmall.com 352
   Jie Gao, Yujing Zeng, Xiaopeng Guo, and Zhenghua Zhang

Evaluation of a New Cockpit Color Concept under Mesopic Lighting
for Urban Driving.. 359
   *Martin Götze, Antonia S. Conti, Andreas Keinath, Tarek Said, and
   Klaus Bengler*

Proactive Home Furnishings: Inspiring from Interactive Art for
Designing Functional Aesthetics in a Space........................ 367
   Scottie Chih-Chieh Huang

Design and Evaluation of a Predictive Model for Smartphone
Selection... 376
   Yerika Jimenez and Patricia Morreale

TRIGGER: Maximizing Functional Effect of Using Products 385
   Kyung-Bo Min and Eui-Chul Jung

An Experimental Study for Applying Generative Design to Electronic
Consumer Products 392
   Ming-Huang Lin and Lin-Chien Lee

dJOE: Design Jigsaw On sitE: A Computational Interface of Displacing
Ideas in the Design Productive Process 402
   Chia-Hui Nico Lo, Ih-Cheng Lai, and Teng-Wen Chang

A Proposal of Design Method of Obtaining the Construction Items of
Mental Models in Product Design 408
   Naoya Okazawa and Toshiki Yamaoka

Design of Experience: Measuring the Co-production with the Consumer
Engagement during the Product Development Process 414
   *Sabrina Oliveira, Virgínia Kistmann, Adriano Heemann, and
   Maria Lúcia L.R. Okimoto*

Open Design: Non-professional User-Designers Creating Products for
Citizen Science: A Case Study of Beekeepers 424
  Robert Phillips, Yelena Ford, Karl Sadler, Sarah Silve, and
  Sharon Baurley

Design Guidelines for Coffee Vending Machines 432
  Tim Schneidermeier, Manuel Burghardt, and Christian Wolff

Beyond Comprehension: A Usability Study on User Instruction Manual
for Stove with Steam Function 441
  Carla Galvão Spinillo and Kelli C.A.S. Smythe

The Relationship between Preference and Stare Duration on Bicycle.... 450
  Jin-Han Tseng, Ding-Bang Luh, and Zhi-Hong Liang

Exploring Prior Experience and the Effects of Age on Product
Interaction and Learning 457
  Christopher R. Wilkinson, Patrick Langdon, and P. John Clarkson

Information and Knowledge Design and Visualisation

Visualizing Information Associated with Architectural Design
Variations and Simulations 469
  David Aurelio

Texture and Relative Movement in Moving Image 478
  Yen-Ting Cho

Graphical Displays in Eco-Feedback: A Cognitive Approach 486
  Rebecca Ford and Beth Karlin

Dot, Line, Network: Helping Individuals Make Sense of "New Data" 496
  Emilie W. Gould

Developing a Concept Interface Design of ATM Systems Based on
Human-Centred Design Processes 506
  Satoru Inoue, Hajime Hirako, Toshiya Sasaki, Hisae Aoyama,
  Yutaka Fukuda, and Kazuhiko Yamazaki

A Study of the Satisfaction Level of User Experience in Digital Media
Space Accordance with Differences in Flow Characteristic 515
  Youngtae Kim and Eui-Chul Jung

Trial of Diagnostic to Find Preferable Job Using the Visual Image
Information Interaction: Prototype Development and Evaluation in
Global Human Resources Matching Site 525
  Akira Kondo and Naoko Kondo

Scaffolding Computer Supported Argumentation Processes through
Mini Map Based Interaction Techniques 533
   Nguyen-Thinh Le, Sabine Niebuhr, David Drexler, and
   Niels Pinkwart

Designing Discovery Experience for Big Data Interaction: A Case
of Web-Based Knowledge Mining and Interactive Visualization
Platform.. 543
   Qing Liu, Mihaela Vorvoreanu, Krishna P.C. Madhavan, and
   Ann F. McKenna

Interactive Visualization of Evolving Force-Directed Graphs 553
   Walter M. Rafelsberger

CHARM Pad: Ontology-Based Tool for Learning Systematic Knowledge
about Nursing 560
   Munehiko Sasajima, Satoshi Nishimura, Yoshinobu Kitamura,
   Akemi Hirao, Kanetoshi Hattori, Akemi Nakamura,
   Hiroe Takahashi, Yoshiyuki Takaoka, and Riichiro Mizoguchi

SysML-Based Approach for Automation Software Development –
Explorative Usability Evaluation of the Provided Notation 568
   Daniel Schütz, Martin Obermeier, and Birgit Vogel-Heuser

Usability Design and Testing of an Interface for Search and Retrieval of
Social Web Data 575
   Dimitris Spiliotopoulos, Ruben Bouwmeester,
   Georgios Kouroupetroglou, Pepi Stavropoulou, and
   Dimitrios Tsonos

Looking beyond the Single Pane of Glass: Visualization and Perspective
in Enterprise Network 581
   Maria C. Velez-Rojas, Serge Mankovskii, Michael Roberts,
   Steven Greenspan, and Esin Kırış

Investigating the Effect of Visualization on User Performance of
Information Systems 591
   Xiaojun Yuan

Effects of Domain Knowledge on User Performance and Perception in a
Knowledge Domain Visualization System 601
   Xiaojun Yuan, Chaomei Chen, Xiangmin Zhang, Josh Avery, and
   Tao Xu

Exploring Information-Triage: Speculative Interface Tools to Help
College Students Conduct Online Research 611
   Liese Zahabi

Mobile Applications and Services

M-Commerce Usability: An Explorative Study on Turkish Private
Shopping Apps and Mobile Sites 623
   Özgürol Öztürk and Kerem Rızvanoğlu

Smart Metering with Smartphones: User-Centered Design of a Mobile
Application in the Context of Energy Efficiency 631
   Stephan Böhm and Lee Szwec

End-User Development of Mobile Mashups 641
   Cinzia Cappiello, Maristella Matera, and Matteo Picozzi

A New Framework for Increasing User Engagement in Mobile
Applications Using Machine Learning Techniques 651
   Merve Gençer, Gökhan Bilgin, Özgür Zan, and Tansel Voyvodaoğlu

User-Originated Innovation of Mobile Financial Services 660
   Päivi Heikkilä, Heli Järventie-Ahonen, and Sirpa Riihiaho

A Service Design on Driving Like Living 666
   Hung-Pin Hsu

Feature Evaluation for Mobile Applications: A Design Science Approach
Based on Evolutionary Software Prototypes 673
   Bodo Igler

ARS Module of Contents Management System Using Cell Phones 682
   Toshikazu Iitaka

9/11 Memorial App: A Case Study of Serious Smart Phone UX
Design.. 691
   Tobias Komischke

The Travel Machine: Mobile UX Design That Combines Information
Design with Persuasion Design.................................... 696
   Aaron Marcus, Theresa Karolina Schieder, and Lorenzo Cantoni

Sharing Life Experiences with Friends Based on Individual's Locality ... 706
   Mohsin Ali Memon and Jiro Tanaka

Usability Testing of Mobile Applications Store: Purchase, Search and
Reviews 714
   Wilson Prata, Claudia Renata Mont'Alvão, and Manuela Quaresma

Addressing Animated Transitions already in Mobile App Storyboards.... 723
   Marcus Trapp and René Yasmin

Meta-design Approach for Mobile Platforms Supporting Creative
Tourism Experiences 733
   Iis P. Tussyadiah

Determining the Effect of Menu Element Size on Usability of Mobile
Applications.. 740
  Shelly Welch and Si-Jung Kim

Author Index.. 751

Part I
Design Philosophy

Reframed Contexts: Design Thinking for Agile User Experience Design

Sisira Adikari, Craig McDonald, and John Campbell

School of Information Systems and Accounting
University of Canberra ACT 2601 Australia
{Sisira.Adikari,Craig.McDonald,John.Campbell}@canberra.edu.au

Abstract. The effectiveness of user experience design is dependent on many factors including complete and accurate contextual information, design approaches, and methods followed. The recent HCI literature clearly shows that there is a growing research interest on integration of User Experience (UX) design and agile software development. A framework based on design thinking is proposed that enhances the current user experience design by integration of three design approaches - design thinking, designing for user experience and agile software development. These three different design approaches of the framework complement each other to benefit effective derivation of contextual requirements that include functionality of the system as well as aspects of total user experience based on the shared understanding gained from stakeholders in the context. Implications of each design approach on stakeholders and the context are discussed in detail to show the significance and value of the proposed framework on the whole design and design process. It is expected that the proposed framework is capable of enhancing the design quality and user experience of products, systems, and services created through agile software development approaches.

Keywords: user experience, agile software development, human-centered design, human-computer interaction, design thinking.

1   Introduction

The recent literature in the field of Human-Computer Interaction (HCI) and Software Engineering clearly shows that there is a growing research interest on integration of User Experience (UX) design and agile software development. UX is a concept central to interaction design and concerns how a user feels about an artifact when using it in the real world [1]. Although the UX evolved from classical usability, the main focus of UX is distinctive in creating positive user experience mainly by means of pleasure, joy, excitement, fun, attitudes, emotions and added values when the user interacts with an artifact. Traditional usability is the practice of making things (products, systems and services) easy to use and it is often equated with user experience [2]. UX has emerged to cover the components of users' interactions with, and reactions to, products that go beyond effectiveness, efficiency, and conventional

A. Marcus (Ed.): DUXU/HCII 2013, Part I, LNCS 8012, pp. 3–12, 2013.

interpretations of satisfaction. Similar to User-Centered Design (UCD), the prime focus of UX studies is on the user and the associated context of use. Such studies often take the user into account in the iterative design and evaluation of the product, system or service. Accordingly, a deep understanding of the user and the context of use is important in designing artifacts for optimum UX. Often these studies begin with time-consuming up-front activities such as contextual enquiries, interviews, definition of UX and usability goals, creation of personas and usage scenarios etc., resulting in extensive documentation.

On the other hand, Agile Software Development is light-weight, customer-oriented and a highly collaborative approach that follows a continual exploration of the business need as the basis to gather and refine software requirements to develop quality software. A key objective of the agile software development is to deliver quality software products in a cost and time effective manner through a series of short iterative and incremental development cycles. Each iteration of the agile software development produces a version of working software that emphasizes a business value to the customer ensuring that all agreed requirements have been met.

The integration of UX design into agile software development has been widely discussed in the literature highlighting that UX aspects are not well addressed in agile software development [3]. A recent publication on two case studies of UX design and agile development highlighted the narrow focus of UX aspects in agile development iteration despite the presence of a dedicated UX team in the project [4]. A key challenge faced by UX design for agile software development is the building an in-depth understanding of the user and the context of use in a manner that adds business value for agile software development process and activities. Building of such understanding has to be light-weight, time-optimized and effective with the quick turnaround of simple artifacts that contain easy to understand and 'just right' information. The customer- orientation nature of the agile software development emphasizes the customer as the main source of information for software requirements. Accordingly, software developers interact closely with the customer to elicit all types of software requirements including user requirements. The distinction between the user and the customer in agile software development has been identified by many authors. For example, Bayer et al. [5] considers a user is the individual who interacts with the system being designed directly whereas the customer is a larger term that bears one role or many roles such as a user, or an indirect user of a system. The customer can also be a dependent user on the output of the system, or a user who prepares input for a system, decides on the need for a system and approves the purchase of a system etc. Moreover the authors emphasize that understanding the users is key to getting the design right and understanding the other customers of the system may be key to getting the system accepted. In another example, having analyzed few research studies, Kautz [6] points out that although customer representatives act with decision power, they only a possess a limited understanding of the users' needs because they are not the actual users of the software to be developed, who in turn may have the necessary knowledge, but not the authority to decide on system features.

This paper proposes a rapid, solution-oriented framework to simulate the contextual environment in which key stakeholders and users can develop a shared understanding of the whole experience which then can be used as the main source of information for agile software development. The framework is based on three design approaches: design thinking, user experience design and agile software design.

The paper is organized in the following order. Following the introduction, Section 2 presents a brief overview of Design Thinking, concept of design, design thinking process models, empathy in design thinking, and reframed contexts in design thinking. Section 3 details the design of the integrated framework of design thinking, user experience design and agile software development and how the proposed framework will add business value by means of rapid contextual analysis and solution design.

2   Design Thinking

In the last two decades, 'design thinking' has matured immensely to gain a wider popularity in many fields even outside the design profession and considered as an exciting new paradigm for dealing with problems in many disciplines [7]. Design thinking has been recognized as a widespread approach to solve socially ambiguous design problems [8]. An early definition of design thinking by Cross et al. [9] outlines design thinking as a study of the cognitive processes that are manifested in design action, as well as something inherent within human cognition [10]. According to Dunne and Martin [11], design thinking is the way designers think and apply their mental processes to design objects, services or systems, as distinct from the end result of elegant and useful products. A widely cited definition by Brown [12] describes design thinking as an approach of human-centered innovation that uses the designer's sensibility and methods to match people's needs with what is technologically feasible and what a viable business strategy can convert into customer value and market opportunity. The emphasis of the Brown's definition highlights two important points. Firstly, design thinking is an approach to creating a new or enhanced feasible solution situation meeting customer needs with added value. Second, design thinking is an approach for designing; hence design is an integral part of design thinking. Accordingly, the main idea behind design thinking is how designers progress the design process with a creative mind towards design solutions discovering new opportunities.

For a deeper understanding of design thinking, it is important to gain a clear view of what is meant by design, the concept of design and how design and the concept of design relate to design thinking. There are many definitions of design given by many authors in different disciplines because design is multifaceted and not limited or belongs to a particular field or discipline. Design is a broad concept which has developed a very substantial literature over time across a variety of disciplines and fields [13]. Accordingly, design has been conceptualized differently, such as a process (action), a creation (artifact, product, system or service), as planning, as intention etc. In the literature, the design has been widely and mostly defined as a process as well as a creation. For example, an early definition of design specified by IEEE standard IEEE 610.12-90 [14] outlines that design is both the process of defining the architecture, components, interfaces, and other characteristics of a system or component and the result of that process. Another example [15] states design refers to the creative process of specifying something new and to the representations that are produced during the process. These definitions clearly point out that design is both a process and a creation.

Based on a research study towards a clear, unambiguous and a formal definition of the design concept, Ralph and Wand [16] concluded that although there are many varying definitions given for design by many authors, there is no clear, precise and generally accepted definition available for the concept of the design. According to their analysis, they see the design activity as a process aimed at generating a specification of a design object. These include the environment in which the object will exist, the goals ascribed to the object, the desired structural and behavioral properties of the object (requirements), a given set of component types (primitives), and constraints that limit the acceptable solutions. The design object is the design outcomes such as an artifact, product, system or service. This design view on the concept of design from an artifact point of view is shown in Figure 1 where the artifact is situated in the application domain which is essentially a part of the external environment. We consider the application domain as an activity system and the artifact as an artifact of the activity system.

Figure 1 shows a view of concept of design that can be interpreted as a representation of creating an artifact that meets the design requirements of the application domain in order to accomplish design goals ascribed by the external environment. There are many other systems in the external environment which may or may not be interacting with the application domain (activity system). These systems in the external environment collectively ascribe the goals of the activity system. Hence, a holistic system view of design is essential for the design and for the implementation of system artifacts of any activity system. This systems view of design is shown in Figure 2.

Systems and associated components such as users and stakeholders are different in nature and behavior. Accordingly, design thinking requires specific focus to gain a deeper understanding and an extended view of the whole systems landscape holistically in capturing contextual information as much as possible to identify system issues, constraints, system goals and requirements. Explained as a design thinking capability framework [12], these focus areas are:

- Empathy - view contexts holistically from multiple human perspectives
- Integrative thinking - see all of the aspects of a situation for creative solutions
- Optimism - optimize one potential solution over other alternatives
- Experimentalism - explore the situations in creative ways to-wards new directions
- Collaboration - collaborate with interdisciplinary actors for innovative solutions.

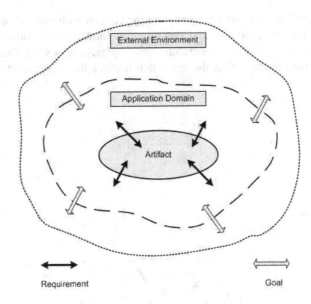

Fig. 1. The Concept of design – artifact, separate domains, goals and requirements [16]

2.1   Design Thinking Process Models

In this section, we analyze three designs thinking models reported in the literature to highlight the similarities between these models and how they relate to problem solving leading to creativity and innovation.

Eris [17] presented a model named Divergent-Convergent Inquiry based Design Thinking Model (DCIDT) that describes design thinking as divergent and convergent inquiry associated with two fundamental modalities: divergent and convergent questioning. The DCIDT model is shown in Figure 3.

In this model, design requirements are transformed through Generative Design Questions (GDQ) into a series of design concepts. GDQs are used to create, synthesize and expand concepts, which subsequently transformed into design decisions or specifications through Deep Reasoning Questions (DRQ). The purpose of the DRQs is to analyze, evaluate, and validate design concepts (Cs) towards viable design decisions specifications. The model presented by Dunn and Martin [11] consists of four activities namely: Abduction, Deduction, Test, and Induction (see Figure 4). In this model, the Abduction activity focuses on generating ideas and during the Deduction activity, those ideas will be analyzed to predict likely consequences. All predictions will then be tested and valid outcome will be generalized during the Induction stage.

The design thinking model presented by Brown [21][26] details how design thinking happens by means of three overlapping spaces namely: Inspiration, Ideation and Implementation. There are a number of sub activities in each space, which are described as a system of spaces rather than a pre-defined series of orderly steps. These activities and how they overlap between spaces are shown in Figure 5.

The 'inspiration' space motivates to explore the context with empathy and human-centeredness to identify problems and opportunities through direct observation and understanding; 'ideation' is for generating, developing, and testing ideas towards solutions, and 'implementation' is the space that realizes the viable solutions for the context.

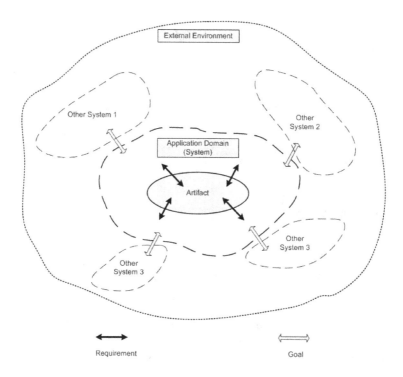

Fig. 2. Systems view of design - artifact, separate domains, goals and requirements

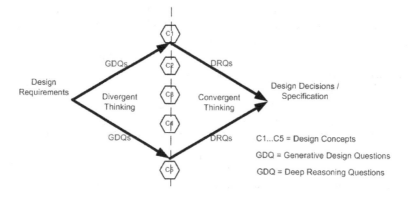

Fig. 3. Divergent-Convergent Inquiry based Design Thinking Model [17]

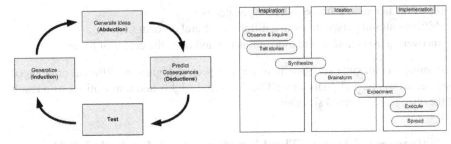

Fig. 4. Design thinking process model proposed by Dunn and Martin [11]

Fig. 5. Design thinking process model proposed by Brown [26]

All these three models share common characteristics such as holistic contextual exploration, integrative thinking based idea generation, creation and evaluation of viable solutions and realization of solutions in the context. The nature of the design thinking process poses the natural potential to reframe new solutions or enhance solutions with better ideas, hence the innovation-centered design solutions for contextual problems.

2.2 Empathy – An Important Challenge in Design Thinking

Much of the design thinking is impacted by many mental aspects such as cognition, affection and conation. Moreover the emotional concerns of all system users have been acknowledged as important in design [18], which leads to empathy as the focus of design. This informs and inspires designers to create designs matching user needs and wants [19]. Importantly, design thinking is considered to be a complex design behavior within a complex context and the actual behavior is determined by combined cognitive, motivational and emotional processes in the context [20].

As highlighted in [21], a successful design program should focus on three mutually reinforcing elements: insight, observation, and empathy with the aim of translating observations into insights and insights into design solutions thus leading to products and services. Accordingly, we consider that empathy as the most important challenge in design thinking that reflects emotional aspects and experience of all users in context.

2.3 Reframed Contexts in Design Thinking

Framing and reframing of problem situations have been stressed as a process of reflection that is presented through appreciation, action, and re-appreciation [22]. Whilst framing is the cognitive process that explores a contextual situation in capturing, analyzing and creating knowledge, the reframing is the process of exploration of the same contextual situation from multiple perspectives to create new knowledge. Reframing allows visualizing how the users in a different or changed or less contextual situation might complete their tasks in achieving user goals. A recent publication [23] detailed reframing as a method of synthesis through highlighting the following strengths to see a different reality:

- recasting an existing frame in a new perspective
- shifting cultural perspectives to a different cultural domain
- uncovering associations and hidden links to and from the center of focus

Reframing a contextual situation in a new perspective highlights different or changed user needs, wants, and goals as well as different insights and implications as a result of the changed contextual situation.

3   Integrated Design Thinking Framework for Agile UX Design

Adikari et al. proposed a UX design framework titled 'Design Science Research Framework for Designing and Assessing UX [24]' as well as another framework for integrating usability into agile requirements engineering [25]. In this section we propose an enhanced framework that integrates the concept of design thinking and reframed contexts with designing for UX framework (designated as Framework 1) and usability in agile software development framework (designated as Framework 2). The proposed enhanced framework based on design thinking is shown in Figure 6.

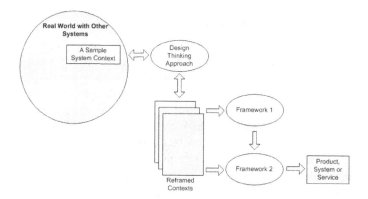

Fig. 6. Integrated framework for agile UX design

Figure 6 shows a sample system context being explored with other relevant systems in the real world using design thinking approach to create reframed contexts. The important emphasis is that the design thinking approach is not only limited to the sample system context, but also considers a holistic view of all relevant and interacting systems in the real world (systems view) for the contextual exploration and to create reframed contexts. The new knowledge of the reframed contexts are subsequently used by Framework 1 (designing for user experience) and Framework 2 (usability in agile software development) to create enhanced products, systems or services. Emphasis of a systems view extends the focus on the broader areas of the problem situation within the context of the sample system context.

4   Conclusions

In this paper, we have presented an enhanced framework based on design thinking and reframed contexts for agile user experience design. The concept of design thinking, design in general, the design process and three design thinking process models discussed are to emphasize the importance and the significance of design thinking towards solutions for contextual problems. Existing frameworks proposed by Adikari et al. on designing for UX and usability in agile software development is also used as part of the enhanced framework.

The main contribution of the paper is to highlight a new approach of contextual exploration using design thinking and holistic systems view to create reframed contexts and generate new knowledge. Reframing contexts for different situations highlights a broader focus of the problem to reveal hidden issues, hidden links and unclear systems interactions etc. It is expected that the proposed framework is capable of enhancing the design quality and user experience of products, systems, and services created through agile software development approaches.

References

1. Rogers, Y., Sharp, H., Preece, J.: Interaction design: beyond human-computer interaction. John Wiley & Sons (2011)
2. Kuniavsky, M.: Smart Things: Ubiquitous Computing User Experience Design. Morgan Kaufmann (2010)
3. Chamberlain, S., Sharp, H., Maiden, N.A.M.: Towards a framework for integrating Agile development and usercentred design. In: Abrahamsson, P., Marchesi, M., Succi, G. (eds.) XP 2006. LNCS, vol. 4044, pp. 143–153. Springer, Heidelberg (2006)
4. Najafi, M., Toyoshiba, L.: Two Case Studies of User Experience Design and Agile Development. In: AGILE 2008 Conference (2008)
5. Beyer, H., Holtzblatt, K., Baker, L.: An Agile Customer-Centered Method: Rapid Contextual Design. In: Zannier, C., Erdogmus, H., Lindstrom, L. (eds.) XP/Agile Universe 2004. LNCS, vol. 3134, pp. 50–59. Springer, Heidelberg (2004)
6. Kautz, K.: Customer and User Involvement in Agile Software Development. In: Abrahamsson, P., Marchesi, M., Maurer, F. (eds.) XP 2009. LNBIP, vol. 31, pp. 168–173. Springer, Heidelberg (2009)
7. Dorst, D., Stewart, S., Staudinger, I., Paton, B., Dong, D.: Introduction. In: DTRS8 Proceedings of the 8th Design Thinking Research Symposium (2010)
8. Lindberg, T., Gumienny, R., Jobst, B., Meinel, C.: Is There a Need for a Design Thinking Process? In: DTRS8 Proceedings of the 8th Design Thinking Research Symposium (2010)
9. Cross, N., Dorst, K., Roozenburg, N.: Preface to Research in Design Thinking. In: Research in Design Thinking (1992)
10. Cross, N.: Design Thinking: Understanding How Designers Think and Work. Berg Publishers, Oxford (2011)
11. Dunne, D., Martin, R.: Design thinking and how it will change management education: An interview and discussion. Academy of Management Learning & Education 5, 512–523 (2006)
12. Brown, T.: Design Thinking. In: Harvard Business Review, pp. 85–92 (June 2008)

13. McKay, J., Marshall, P., Heath, G.: An exploration of the concept of design in information systems. In: Hart, D., Gregor, S. (eds.) Information Systems Foundation: The Role of Design Science, D, ANU ePress (2010)
14. IEEE610.12-1990: IEEE Standard Glossary of Software Engineering Terminology. IEEE (1990)
15. Benyon, D.: Designing Interactive Systems. Pearson (2010)
16. Ralph, P., Wand, Y.: A proposal for a formal definition of the design concept. In: Lyytinen, K., Loucopoulos, P., Mylopoulos, J., Robinson, B. (eds.) Design Requirements Workshop. LNBIP, vol. 14, pp. 103–136. Springer, Heidelberg (2009)
17. Eris, O.: Insisting on Truth at the Expense of Conceptualization: Can Engineering Portfolios Help? International Journal of Engineering Education 22, 551–559 (2006)
18. McDonagh, D., Denton, H.: Design and Emotion. Journal of Engineering Design 20, 433–435 (2009)
19. Merlijn, K., Froukje, S.V.: A framework for empathy in design: stepping into and out of the user's life. Journal of Engineering Design 20, 437–448 (2009)
20. Badke Schaub, P.G., Roozenburg, N.F.M., Cardoso, C.: Design thinking: a paradigm on its way from dilution to meaninglessness? In: Proceedings of the 8th Design Thinking Research Symposium, DTRS8 (2010)
21. Brown, T.: Change by Design: How Design Thinking Transform Organizations and Inspires Innovation. HarperCollins, New York (2009)
22. Schon, D.A.: The reflective practitioner: How professionals think in action. Basic Books, New York (1995)
23. Kolko, J.: Abductive Thinking and Sensemaking: The Drivers of Design Synthesis. Design Issues 26, 15–28 (2010)
24. Adikari, S., McDonald, C., Campbell, J.: A Design Science Framework for Designing and Assessing User Experience. In: Jacko, J.A. (ed.) Human-Computer Interaction, Part I, HCII 2011. LNCS, vol. 6761, pp. 25–34. Springer, Heidelberg (2011)
25. Adikari, S., McDonald, C., Campbell, J.: Little Design Up-Front: A Design Science Approach to Integrating Usability into Agile Requirements Engineering. In: Jacko, J.A. (ed.) HCI International 2009, Part I. LNCS, vol. 5610, pp. 549–558. Springer, Heidelberg (2009)
26. Brown, T.: Innovation through Design Thinking, Boston, Massachuttes, USA. MIT World: Dean's Innovative Leader Series, http://mitworld.mit.edu/video/357/ (accessed March 10, 2013)

An Individual Differences Approach to Design Fixation: Comparing Laboratory and Field Research

Brooke G. Bellows, Jordan F. Higgins, and Robert J. Youmans

George Mason University, Human Factors & Applied Cognition, MSN 3F5,
4000 University Drive, Fairfax VA 22030, USA
bbellows@gmu.edu

Abstract. The current study investigates the effects of environmental disruptions and individual differences in working memory capacity on design performance in controlled laboratory and field settings. In the laboratory, we measured participants' working memory capacity, asked them to view a poster design, then asked them to design their own poster in either a silent or distracting environment. The results of the study revealed a main effect of working memory capacity on design behavior, but no effect of environment. In the field, we asked practicing designers to take an online working memory capacity test, then to describe their distractibility and ideal work environment while designing. The results suggest that working memory capacity may influence perceived distractibility.

Keywords: Design fixation, creativity, design, working memory capacity, interruptions.

1 Introduction

Among the many factors that likely contribute to strong design, one is the ability to abandon past design solutions to produce innovative, new ideas. Unfortunately, past research has shown that design fixation, a form of conceptual rigidity during the design process, can severely impair designers' creativity and innovative output [1]. Design fixation is often described as an adherence to previously established ideas or concepts and is especially problematic when negative design features from previously established work are retained through the creative ideation process. Design fixation has been shown to have such robust effects that it affects both novice and expert designers similarly in a vast number of creative domains (e.g., mechanical engineering, industrial design, architecture). In order to develop methods to increase innovation by reducing design fixation, it is critical that the factors influencing design fixation behavior are identified.

Environmental factors, such as interruptions, may have a strong influence on design fixation behavior. Interruptions are a regular occurrence in most work environments but there are opposing views as to whether interruptions help or hurt primary task performance in contexts such as problem solving [2], VCR programming [3], and

A. Marcus (Ed.): DUXU/HCII 2013, Part I, LNCS 8012, pp. 13–21, 2013.

computer productivity [4]. Interruptions have been identified as a potential environmental factor eliciting differences in ability to maintain memory for previously viewed concepts [5] which is assumed to be a main component of design fixation behavior. Previous research has shown that high working memory capacity (WMC) can provide some resistance to environmental interference [6], but this finding may be task and context specific.

WMC is a fundamental cognitive process that is sometimes thought of as a mental work space. It is an active memory store that is implicated in goal maintenance and attentional control. Previous research has argued that individual differences in working memory capacity may affect designers' propensity to fixate [7,8] because the design conceptualization process requires designers to access and manipulate many ideas at a time while working towards a design goal. Some differences that have been found to exist between individuals with low WMC and individuals with high WMC include the abilities to inhibit non-goal relevant information and to suppress intrusion from previously viewed concepts [9]. This means that designers with low working memory capacity may not be able to inhibit information that is unimportant for their current project. They may be more likely than high WMC designers to encode negative aspects of examples that could lead to a degradation of their work.

1.1 Research Goals

This study sought to explore the relationship between environment, working memory capacity, and design performance in two settings: a controlled laboratory and in the field. In the laboratory, we made use of the controlled conditions to explore designers' ability to resist design fixation and produce an original design. One hypothesis is that WMC might predict designers' likelihood of fixating on previous concepts. Specifically, people with low WMC would fixate more than people with higher WMC. The second hypothesis is that there will be an interaction between WMC and design environment. We expect that people with High WMC will be resistant to the interference of interruptions and their design performance will remain largely unchanged, but individuals with Low WMC will be unable to remember elements from the original design and become de-fixated in the distracting environment.

Similarly, we believe that individual differences in working memory will have an effect on professional designers in field settings. It is predicted that designers with low working memory capacity will be more likely seek out a work environment that features less distractions, such as a home office or cubicle setting, and more likely to report negative consequences of distractions in the work environment. Designers with high working memory capacity were predicted to experience less of a negative impact from distractions in the work environment and would not have a strong preference for work environment.

2 Method

2.1 Participants – Laboratory

A total of 71 undergraduate and graduate students (53 females, 18 males) aged between 17-52 years (M=21 years) participated for course credit. Forty-two percent of the students were enrolled as psychology majors and 58% of the students were enrolled in a range of other majors offered at the university.

2.2   Materials and Procedure – Laboratory

Participants in our study performed two tasks in a counterbalanced order. The first task was the Automated Operation Span (AOSPAN), an automated version of an operation span task which was designed to measure WMC [10]. AOSPAN requires that participants try to hold a series of letters in their memory system, and then recall them at some later point in time (see Fig. 1).

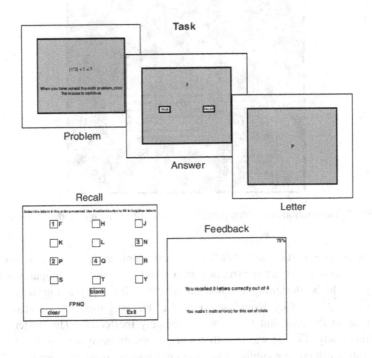

Fig. 1. Illustration of the automated operation span task procedure

The task is demanding because after the presentation of each letter, participants are required to answer a true or false arithmetic question that prevents most participants from using mnemonics or other rehearsal strategies, and therefore AOSPAN is said to measure how well participants can maintain target information (the letters) while also avoiding memory interference caused by distraction (the math problems). The program ran on a standard desktop computer equipped with E-Prime 2.0 software. Although AOSPAN produces several dependent variables related to WMC, in this paper, the Overall AOSPAN Scores of each participant were used in all analyses. An 85% math accuracy criterion was enforced to confirm participants were accurately solving the math equations in addition to retaining the letters.

Fig. 2. The fixation poster that participants saw prior to their own design efforts

After measuring participants' WMC, the participants were assigned to one of two experimental conditions, an interruption or a silent condition. Participants were told that they would be designing a poster to advertise for a psychology organization. They were told that they would see a poster that was used to advertise for this organization in the past, but that it was extremely ineffective. The poster that was used in this study (Fig. 2) was one that had previously been demonstrated to create strong fixation effects in a similar population of undergraduate students [7]. The poster was designed to contain 23 predefined, quantifiable fixation features that could be counted post hoc by the researchers as evidence of fixation. Participants were instructed that they would be given two minutes to view the example poster so that they could attempt to design a more effective and original poster for the organization. After viewing the fixation poster for two minutes, participants were then given ten minutes to mentally prepare their own design. In the silent condition, participants spent this time planning quietly while in the interruption condition participants were shown pre-solved math problems on a computer display every 20s. We asked participants to quickly respond aloud whether they believed the problem had a correct or incorrect solution displayed. Finally, all participants were given blank sheets of paper, a ruler, and colored pencils, and were asked to spend another ten minutes developing a sketch of their original poster design.

2.3 Participants – Field

Participants were 63 designers recruited through professional networks and online forums (23 females, 40 males), 19 participants were removed for incomplete survey responses. The remaining 44 designers (16 females, 28 males) were aged between 18-69 years (M = 30 years). Approximately 45% of designers described their current professional status as student, with the remaining 55% representing a broad range of professional titles in the field of design (e.g. Senior Designer, Art Director). Participants reported years of formal design training: 9% reported no training, 2% reported less than 1 year, 77% reported 1-4 years, and 11% reported 5 or more years.

2.4 Method and Procedure – Field

A survey exploring distractions in the workplace, adapted from a previously used instrument [11], was disseminated online to facilitate data collection from participants in remote work environments. Upon clicking a hyperlink, the participant was taken to a web-based tool (http://fluidsurveys.com/) that was used to administer a survey that collected three types of information: demographic information about the designer, information about their design experience and work environment, and self-reported scores from an online test of working memory.

After reviewing an informed consent form, participants were asked to respond to the demographic survey with questions about his or her experience as a designer and the conditions of their work environment. Questions were formed as Likert-scales with responses ranging from 1-5. Next, participants were asked to perform a web-based N-back task (http://cognitivefun.net/test/4) that assessed their individual working memory capacity. After a brief set of instructions, participants were presented with a series of images, and asked to click on the screen when recognizing an image that had been presented two images before the current image. The percent of images correctly identified were recorded and participants entered their scores from the N-back task into the survey. Finally, participants were taken to an online debriefing letter after submitting their survey responses. Submissions that failed to enter the proper format for working memory scores were removed from consideration for analysis.

3 Results

3.1 Results - Laboratory

Each poster was judged for the presence or absence of the predefined fixation features. Seven participants were excluded from the analysis for failing to meet the 85% math accuracy criterion during the AOSPAN.

Fig. 3. Examples of less fixated (left) and more fixated (right) poster designs

A quasi-experimental Analysis of Variance (ANOVA) was conducted to test a 2 (WMC: high, low) x 2 (Environment: Silent, Interruption). The results revealed a significant main effect of WMC $F(1,60) = 4.74$, $p < 0.05$. On average, participants with Low working memory copied a larger number of the previously viewed features into their designs (M = 3.71) than those with High WMC (M = 2.77). The main effect of environment on fixation features copied was not significant $F(1,60) = 0.49$, ns. No significant interaction was found between interruption condition and WMC on

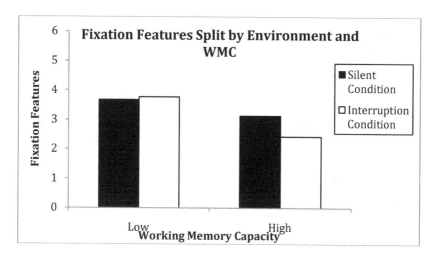

Fig. 4. The mean number of fixation features split by working memory capacity and design environment

fixation features copied $F(1,60) = 0.36$, ns. Although there was a disproportionate quantity of males and females, a Pearson Correlation showed that there was no significant difference in fixation by gender ($r = -.13$, ns). There was also no reliable relationship found between fixation and major ($r = .15$, ns).

3.2   Results – Field

Three ANOVAs were conducted to test the hypothesis that differences would exist between responses to three survey questions regarding impact of environment on productivity split by WMC (High, Low). A mean-split was conducted on WMC scores.

Survey Questions	Low WMC	High WMC
Q1. Do you ever feel as though distractions in the workplace impact your productivity?	4.17*	3.52*
Q2. Would you extend, or have you extended your working hours by coming in early or staying late to avoid distractions?	4.10	3.64
Q3. Which of the following statements best describes your ideal work environment?	2.58	3.08

Fig. 5. Response averages split by WMC. For Q1 and Q2, a score of 1 indicated a response of 'never' and a 5 indicated 'frequently'. For Q3, a score of 1 indicated 'I enjoy multi-tasking, and I work better in an environment with significant activity' and a 5 indicated 'I prefer to have privacy while working, and am easily distracted by other people or things not pertaining to work'. (* = $p<.05$)

The results revealed that on average Low WMC designers reliably rated that distractions more frequently impact their work than High WMC designers; $F(1,41)=4.43$, $p<.05$. Participants in the Low WMC group also responded that they were more likely than High WMC designers to want to extend their work hours in order to avoid distractions, but this result was only marginally significant; $F(1,42)=1.98$, $p=.16$. As for preference on work environment, Low WMC and High WMC designers did not differ significantly; $F(1,42)=1.29$, ns.

4   Discussion

The goal of this study was to begin to explore two factors that could potentially influence design behavior. Our results suggest that working memory capacity predicts susceptibility to design fixation and distraction, but it is unclear how environment impacts design performance.

The results from this study revealed that working memory capacity has an effect on design in both controlled and applied settings. The laboratory research provides support that individual differences in WMC can predict a designer's propensity to fixate on previous designs. Designing may be a resource dependent activity where Low WMC designers lack the cognitive capacity to develop new ideas while holding on to past ideas, and high WMC designers may be able develop new ideas while also holding onto past ideas in memory. Another possible explanation for this finding is that Low WMC participants failed to maintain the goal of developing a completely original poster, while High WMC participants were better able to preserve their objective and consequently suppress the non-goal relevant fixation poster. This result, although perhaps counter-intuitive, is in keeping with research [e.g., 12] that has shown that across a variety of contexts people with High WMC are better able to maintain more goal relevant information while suppressing non-goal relevant information than those with Low WMC.

The data from the field setting, although only preliminary, lends support to the hypothesis that individual differences in working memory capacity also affect professional designers in real world contexts. Interestingly, although Low WMC designers reported that they were easily distracted by workplace interruptions they did not respond reliably differently than High WMC designers in regard to environmental preference. These results indicate, regardless of WMC, that most designers prefer a relatively neutral environment with an intermediate amount of distraction. Some research even suggests that there can be creative benefits that can be brought about by taking time off task [2], but this was not substantiated by our laboratory results. Often the effect of the interruption on primary task performance is largely dependent on the type, frequency, and importance of the interruption [4], so one possible explanation for the absence of an effect in our laboratory task is that the interruption was not demanding enough to produce a quantifiable change in participants' design behavior.

With the event of modern day technology, interruptions are ubiquitous and come in a wide variety of forms (e.g., IMs, emails, text messages, phone calls). Correspondingly, a majority of the design professionals who completed our survey reported technology as the primary source of distraction when they design. The implication of this is that in order for further progress to be made toward finding the paramount environment for innovation, the impact of these types of interruptions during the design process needs to be better understood.

References

1. Jansson, D.G., Smith, S.M.: Design fixation. Design Studies 12, 3–11 (1991)
2. Beeftink, F., van Eerde, W., Rutte, C.G.: The effect of interruptions and breaks on insight and impasses: Do you need a break right now? Creativity Research Journal 20(4), 358–364 (2008)
3. Monk, C.A., Trafton, J.G., Boehm-Davis, D.A.: The effect of interruption duration and demand on resuming suspended goals. Journal of Experimental Psychology: Applied 14(4), 299 (2008)

4. Cutrell, E., Czerwinski, M., Horvitz, E.: Notification, disruption, and memory: Effects of messaging interruptions on memory and performance (2001)
5. Delaney, P.F., Sahakyan, L.: Unexpected costs of high working memory capacity following directed forgetting and contextual change manipulations. Memory & cognition 35(5), 1074–1082 (2007)
6. Kane, M.J., Engle, R.W.: Working-memory capacity, proactive interference, and divided attention: Limits on long-term memory retrieval. Journal of Experimental Psychology: Learning, Memory, & Cognition 26, 336–358 (2000)
7. Bellows, B.G., Higgins, J.F., Smith, M.A., Youmans, R.J.: The Effects of Individual Differences in Working Memory Capacity and Design Environment on Design Fixation. In: Proceedings of the Human Factors and Ergonomics Society Annual Meeting, vol. 56(1), pp. 1977–1981. SAGE Publications (2012)
8. Youmans, R.J.: Design Fixation in the Wild: Design Environments and Their Influence on Fixation. The Journal of Creative Behavior 45(2), 101–107 (2011)
9. Redick, T.S., Broadway, J.M., Meier, M.E., Kuriakose, P.S., Unsworth, N., Kane, M.J., Engle, R.W.: Measuring working memory capacity with automated complex span tasks. European Journal of Psychological Assessment 28(3), 164 (2012)
10. Unsworth, N., Heitz, R.P., Schrock, J.C., Engle, R.W.: An automated version of the operation span task. Behavior Research Methods 37, 498–505 (2005)
11. Public Policy Polling, Survey of 606 American Workers. Unpublished instrument. (August 2010), http://www.workplaceoptions.com/ (retrieved)
12. Conway, A.R., Cowan, N., Bunting, M.F.: The cocktail party phenomenon revisited: The importance of working memory capacity. Psychonomic Bulletin & Review 8(2), 331–335 (2001)

Techno-imagination and Implicit Knowledge

Jiří Bystřický

Academy of Fine Arts, Prague, Czech Republic
`jiribystricky@seznam.cz`

Abstract. Techno-imagination is the ability to encode and decode images created by devices. This technological shift has caused a departure from images towards an alphanumeric codification of knowledge. This has led to the disconnection between thinking and speaking, caused by new computer codes. The paper discusses the effects of this paradigm shift on the mental processing of vision data and on the relation between concepts and images. We conclude our exploration with a strategy to define a concept of media to allow for both of its features: mediality and transparency.

Keywords: image, mediality, transparency, art, imaging, instrumentality.

1 Introduction

"Post Modern fantasy operates in the coordinate system whose axes are orbital, synchronistic, and combinatorial." (Sloterdijk, 2001: 48-49)

If we accept Flusser's concept of techno-imagination, we can accordingly describe a film, its production and consumption from the phenomenological perspective. Thus, we can interpret techno-imagination as the ability to encode and decode images ("techno-images") created by devices (or "apparatuses" in Flusser's terms). The hypothesis is that the techno-imagination is radically different from traditional imagination. The difference can be explained using the following description: the actual "reading" and "writing" of techno-images (e.g., photos, movies, television programs) have a set of completely different requirements for the reception and interpretation of these phenomena than is the case for "reading" and "writing" of classical paintings (e.g., mosaics, cave drawings, sketches on glass plates). This turnover has redefined writing as a term for departing from the images towards the alphanumeric codification of knowledge: "Writing is the withdrawing from images, as it allows images to spread into concepts." (Flusser, 1999: 35)

This turnover also meant a change in the perspectives of knowledge and the creation of forms of opinion. A part of the modern requirements for the devices from their users determines the possibility of their use and application. This requires a cognitive adaptation to the changed nature of the object of knowledge. Flusser talks about relational learning of objects, things or reality, about the establishment of the so-called ideographic formats of things. "... (F)or our consideration, what is crucial is the observation that the new computer codes are "ideographic", i.e., that they suspend the link between thinking and speaking. Elite thinking has been emancipated from the

A. Marcus (Ed.): DUXU/HCII 2013, Part I, LNCS 8012, pp. 22–28, 2013.

discursive structure of our language and now it experiences and judges the world and itself not as processes anymore, but as computations, such as the movements of relational fields." (Flusser, 1999: 51)

We can say that the ideography of codes is also a kind of division between the pre-technological period and our own contemporary knowledge-society. Our present time is a period introducing combinatorics and computation in the system of thought which interrupted a relatively close relationship between thought and its articulation in speech. After turning from painting to writing, the difference is established between thinking and its articulation in speech.

This is the stage that is characterized by a distinction between idea and representation in an unusual, yet sharper, difference. In the case of ideas, for example, a film does not mediate reality, only a fiction pointing to the reality. The idea, therefore, presents symbols representing reality. The representation itself does not mean anything because it only displays something that lies in front of us. In contrast, the idea means something, although it refers to something that is not here, but what it represents and that it replaces the displayed thing. The representation is actually displaying symbols, valid under the agreement, that the displayed represents the reality which we do not have before us.

Aware of this more powerful difference, we can further say that in today's complex world, which surrounds us with networks, technologies, satellites, mobile phones, etc., techno-images are transmitted through a system of a codified universe where most of the "messages" consist of techno-images, rather than traditional texts, as it was in the early last century. Techno-imagination informs the perception field according to the construction of the devices.

Nevertheless, the game still remains twofold: first, the significantly new and informative nature of the creation and production of technical images as innovative representation, which resemble a plan (or a "map" in Flusser's terms) not only for orientation, but primarily for our decision making. Second, a completely instrumental, quantitative view of the mere reproduction of images to influence the audience. In the latter case, we are talking about structural constraints of knowledge objectivity. The belief in a vision, or representation, brings some unwelcome consequences. Apparently, under the influence of our culture, the traditions and transmitted forms of knowing that we are willing to trust is in almost everything we see. This is a kind of conditionality which is difficult to overcome and which prevents us more or less from critical exploration. The effect of the contribution of the new means of communication in the system of knowledge, such as visualization, can thus not only be altered at the level of the forms of judgment, and the need to search for an interface for an available "form of reality", but also on the level of impact that can have long-term neutralization effects. This means that the novel forms of opinions, imaging innovation, and forms of thinking miss their intent: techno-imagination in this regard is rather suppressed.

This unintended effect, however, illustrates well the understanding of the difference which arose from the new forms of pictures and the necessary revision of opinions in a system of knowledge: that nature that speaks to the camera is different than the one that speaks to our eye. (Benjamin, 1979: 35)

2   Neutralization and Transparency

The aesthetics of display gives us a critical tool against the superficial illusion that what images make visible, can be also possible. For, as Plato reminds us: the real world is invisible.

In fact, the procedure of seeking an instrumental combination of the abstract and the real for movements which are concealed by the self-motion of images that limit and sometimes prevent vision is somehow a countermovement against the dominance of surface, covering what allows for something to be seen. Beyond this movement of the vision, we must learn to see the way how neutralizations make that vision possible.

In a certain metaphor: for the seen, so far, there was almost anything other to be seen. We ask for neutralization processes of motion, procesualities that enable for the creation of static units that make objects degrade before us, balanced and yet separate things, differences from what we actually see.

We do not see the object as an object, which is just a backward reconstruction from our senses. We see only through a certain restraint, a stopping of the process, an interruption of lines, etc..: we register therefore states not as facts, i.e. the states of matter according to Wittgenstein (as a breaking free from a logical procedure), but we see just what lets us to be 'seen'. What remains in the visual field by itself distinguishable from the procedure of vision: we see the effects of transparency. The instrumentalization of association is therefore a framework for rendering which calls for a reconstruction of the seen: not so to stop us to see an image, but rather so that, if possible, to offer also what was currently hidden by the process of becoming visible.

The structure and composition of the abstract and the real world is therefore a reference to the unseen in a vision, hidden too much by the contemporary, streamlined and technologically mediated visibility and, therefore, a reference moving towards another order of connecting the universal and the individual. To be able to connect the variable and the constant, which does not peak in a fatality of an image seen once and forever, but for such a connection that still offers the movement of beauty towards what equals beauty. That is, to harmonize the differences which allows beauty. And to express the surface through depth which does not offers itself cheaply by being just visible.

For quite a long time, we have already known that "the concept of time, the only reality of which according to Bachelard was the reality of a moment, could be built only on our ignorance of our speed in the world, which is entirely devoted to the law of motion, and hence the creator of illusion of immobility." (Virilio 2010: 107)

The aesthetics of display is thus a strategy that pauses on the first thing that offers itself to display, by looking behind the picture for what the image does not depict.

It is so mainly due to the purity of imaging, which allows for the initiative of a phenomenon to bring the initiative of mediation that still leaves in the game everything the images leave behind. In short, what we cannot yet see, wants to speak in the language of images. Paul Klee assessed the situation by saying that art allow us to see. We can add to the second part of his sentence by saying: "no matter in what reality it is actually happening." "The aesthetically formed spirit lets before the thing it deals with just defile what equals the spirit, and what it understands or hopes to make equal to itself." (Adorno 1997: 74)

The aesthetics of display leads to the restoration of forms that are silenced by a certain type of imaging. The form in the world of images is only thanks to the speech of display, which is never content with what is given. The form still seeks a place to express all that did not make it still through the established units. For even this speech does not want to be silenced once and for all only because it has not found an adequate expression.

The form seeks, on the contrary, ways of duplication, supplementation (Derrida), to replace the missing part of a whole, for which there is no available way of expression, a term (Lyotard). Thinking, however, gets doubled by the interaction of transparency with mediality, thus unlearns to just copy the so-called reality, which is unavailable in principle, so reality can be only more or less successfully replaced. Transparency is not just a certain way of seeing thoroughly, but also an instruction on how to see, through what to see, therefore, how to get through the gap of dividing things and phenomena.

3   Medium Image and Concept

"Image technique always refers to the metaphysics of imagination: as if there were two ways of understanding the transition from one image to another." (Deleuze 2006: 72)

Let us say that the display is effective, when displaying by the image also shows a change in the potential state of affairs at different levels of explication. If we can follow the movement of a concept definition through an image, including a change of position expressing the current level of state of affairs, then just showing the concept shows the change itself. In this situation, we can say that the "practice" of a concept as a medium is the reconstruction of the thinking "format" in order to be able to build up the "state of things" again from other levels and into new structures; basically, it is to finish a chosen formalization of abstraction. On the other hand, the aim of an image as a medium is a formalization of vision. Philosophy of the media is then the examination and seeking of positions, where the two media encounter and may overlap each other, so it is the necessary "comparability" between different forms of mediation, often described as a "modulation", and used by the aforementioned Deleuze to describe analogue synthesizers as necessary "... introduction of immediate connections between the different elements". (Deleuze 2003: 95) We are therefore talking about mediality as the original operator of mediation.

We understand mediality basically as an instant background, say, as an "operator of mediation": i.e. a multilevel background with a hidden hierarchy for communication with different orders, i.e. between complexity and the reality, or between the universe and multiverse. Thanks to mediality, we are able to work with the objects from the objectivation world without knowing to what extent they are related to the foundations of the subject. We can nevertheless say that, thanks to the hidden systematics of the real world which we perceive as a background, the heterogenic objects are in a certain unity which makes this world depictable. Mediality philosophy then follows its own, so-called zero state of media thinking: "The philosophy of mediality looks into the thinking in the zero medium, i.e. in what the thinking mediates the thinking itself." (Bystřický 2007: 32)

When applying the direct connections, it can be said that the concept uses one part of the spectrum of mediation, while the image uses the other part. This allows a processing at two levels: abstraction and imagination.

The conceptual order is, in its majority, "codified" by the mediation of abstract determining. That is to say that the order is constituted as a theory of a certain type of use of the forms of transparency, i.e. - showing at displaying - that is available to the level of mediation.

The term thus leads to the definition through determination, scaling the difference between inner and outer space levels of localization, between what the term is opening up and then proceeds to another level: the term leaves thus in the game the movement of the transfer of the thinking levels in which the change in the starting position of the concept is happening. Both the medias are differentiated between "identification" with the help of distinguishing the unchanging positions and definiteness, and, with the help of restrictions which in turn may change the position. The concepts are thus shown as locally arranged distinctions; that is to say as a place of a unique overlap between the real and the virtual that can be used just because they can be thought of as a form of mediation without altering the position from which they are based. This then brings us to another aspect, the concepts and images that the mediation procedures allow: namely, that in addition to its unique and indisputable transitive function, these procedures allow mediation as a system of transparency. The medium of a concept thus generates abstract forms; the media the image then generates the regimes of imagination.

The media of the image as a part of the system of transparency allows establishing the topic of vision. The image media can thus represent the vision itself as visibility and therefore as a taxonomy of transparency: it represents seeing through visibility. The actual images are indeed a secondary operation, but their contribution is not in the order of access to the primary data, but how by displaying and pointing out they bring attention to a specific functionality, efficiency, utility, and "application" of certain forms of transparency, such as, e.g. painting, photography, film images. They do so in the broad sense of the word mediation, because it is about what you can actually see when it can be displayed.

While the practice of concepts refers to the possibility of using a specific access point for mediation between complexity and reality, the whole is framed by images of the whole's current application: i.e. a situation where we can ask how much the mediation acts as an operator of thinking, what type of mediation it is. Namely, the transparency and display which makes something as "noticeable" in the same regime in which "something" is given to be perceived.

In principle, this allows the sharing of data as data, content as a separate and stand-alone content, etc. Consequently, we are talking about the establishment of certain facts as certain versions of some limit values, because "if every fact is assembled from option, then the fact is a "limit value". (Flusser 1996: 249)

The obvious difference is already at the level of the approach to mediation: the concepts work in a primary regime of mediation, reconstruct the accesses to what is giving to us as a giving givenness; images highlight those systems of transparency, in which we can show the giving givenness: i.e. to show it in vision. The images allow us to see through more accurately, through what the given is given: an understanding of the regimes that certain structures and data released into the game of vision and have become so our world visible through technologies. "While the pre-image designers had to fight against the objective world, we are already confronted with a "materialized spirit"." (Flusser 1981: 19)

4   Conclusion

To conclude, we may ask how to actually define the term "media" to fulfill its two main characteristics: mediality and transparency.

To connect the two defining features of the media we need two things. First, perhaps a new platform for the unification and diversification as a new approach to the concept of media which points to an essential hierarchization of the unification while it refers to the different levels of rationalization. "... (W)hat a structure carries and serves as its internal borders, is the tightest circuit between the current image and the virtual image." (Deleuze 2006: 85)

Second, we need an establishment of forms of knowledge that also introduces a corresponding difference of order which subsequently allows those forms. It is not, therefore, a static concept of the known equation of concept, subject and knowledge, but rather a concept of the formation and transparency, as the establishment of the subject in the regime of control of an environment, in which thinking operates as his or her own mediator. We speak therefore about a specific association between the virtual and the real image. "More greater circles will be able to develop, corresponding to increasingly deeper layers of reality and increasingly higher levels of memory and thinking." (Deleuze 2006: 85)

This is also to say that what is constituted through the performance of subjectivity as an object is something dual because what moves from the background of the subject to the forefront of transparency of the same subject is a kind of "making visible" just by setting the direction of constitution of the subject, which simultaneously moves in the direction of the concept, practiced thereof on a higher level, to make the named at the same time as something divided from what it names. Transparency must lead to the emancipation of thought from the concept and knowledge must lead to show the control methods that originated in the individual knowledge.

Kupka's view of the matter is similar: "... an artist can never present a completely and totally authentic idea he or she chose; he artist decides (...) on the lines and modulated positions, profiles and the relationships between volumes. (...) A large part of the work lies in the combination and the understanding and awareness of it." (Kupka 1999: 187) We could, with some exaggeration, call it a temptation for birth.

References

1. Adorno, T.W.: Estetická teorie. Panglos, Praha (1997)
2. Benjamin, W.: Work and its source. Odeon, Prague (1979)
3. Bystřícký, J.: Elektronická kultura a medialita. VaN 999, Praha (2007) ISBN 978-80-86391-28-1
4. Sloterdijk, P.: Tau von den Bermudas. Uber Einige Regime der Einbildungskraft. Frankfurt a/M. Suhrkamp (2001)
5. Deleuze, G.: Film 2. Obraz-čas. NFA, Praha (2006) ISBN 80-7004-127-7
6. Deleuze, G., Bacon, F.: The Logic of Sensation. Univerzity of Minnesota Press, Minnesota (2003) ISBN 978-0-8166-4341-7
7. Flusser, V.: Medienkultur, Fischer, Frankfurt (1999)
8. Flusser, V.: Moc obrazu. Výtvarné umění, 3–4, s. 117–121 (1996); ISSN 0862-9927
9. Flusser, V.: Fotografieren als Bildermachen. In: Standpunkte, European Photography, Göttingen (1981)
10. Kupka, F.: Tvoření v umění výtvarném. Brody, Praha (1999) ISBN 80-86112-16-0
11. Virilio, P.: Estetika mizení. Pavel Mervart, Červený Kostelec (2010) ISBN: 978-80-87378-21-2.

Context as a System, Product as a Component, and the Relationship as Experience

WonJoon Chung and Sara Fortier

School of Industrial Design, Carleton University, Ottawa, ON, Canada
wonjoon_chung@carleton.ca, sarafortier@gmail.com

Abstract. Currently, User Experience Design (UXD) is spotlighted as one of the most topical areas in design. It is an umbrella term that explains all aspects of a user's experience with a given context, including the interface, graphic design, industrial design, and interaction (Merholz P. , 2007). Particularly, the notion of UXD is rooted in human factors and ergonomics that focus on physical, cognitive and emotional interaction between human users, machines and a contextual environment. In the industrial design field, the idea of UXD is not a new but an ancient concept that has been discussed in different terms such as ergonomics, anthropometrics, and affordance, etc., and whose main focus is a positive and rich experience. The current development of SNS (Social Networking Services) and smartphone technology, however, has created possibilities for new types of user experience design. Sander (Sanders, 2002) mentions this possibility as new design space where "designers will transform from being designers of "stuff" (e.g., products, communication pieces, etc.) to being the builders of scaffolds for experiencing.", and where industrial designers will now confront different challenges to discover and develop new types of products with different interface designs for novel user experience. For example, tablet computers like the Apple iPad already have changed the activity of computing from a static environment to almost everywhere. Based on the theoretical framework that "a context as a system, a product as a component, and the relationship between them as an experience", we propose three main research questions. These questions are 1) how a current professional UX designer in practice has redefined UX design themselves, 2) what specific actions are performed and 3) what supports they provide for their client. Through careful in-depth interviews with seven professional UX designers in experience-centric design firms, including IDEO and Adaptive Path etc., in US and Canada, we propose several critical notions and foundational references for UX designers.

Keywords: User Experience Design (UXD), total experience, empathy, systemic thinking.

1   Background

Human experience is innately a personal activity and thereby evokes different meanings for different people (Sanders, 2001). It is usually caused by our physical, cognitive and emotional interaction with the world surrounding us. John Dewy

A. Marcus (Ed.): DUXU/HCII 2013, Part I, LNCS 8012, pp. 29–37, 2013.

(Dewey, 1934) insisted that our experience is governed by a series of historical events during our life. He states that "our interpretation of the present world is influenced by our past experience while our future goals will be shaped by the interpretation of our current experience" (Dewey, 1934). This statement shows that one's desirable experience in the future could be forecasted by understanding his or her past experience as well as current behaviors.

Some have identified the principles of experience from business and technological perspectives (Joseph and Gilmore, 1998; Zomerdijk and Voss., 2010; Stuart, 2006) and others in design fields have looked healthier and richer applications for this topic. In industrial design fields in particular, some factors or components that contribute to a positive experience for end users have been studied. For example, the fields of anthropometrics and ergonomics have focused on positive physical experiences such as comfort (Vink, 2005) while cognitive human factors and Kansai engineering have stressed cognitive and emotional experiences such as pleasure (Jordan, 2000).

Basically, the aforementioned studies have focused on our physical experience locked in an analog world. The basic unit in the analog world is the atoms. It is a fundamental component needed to create material value. The material value, then, affects the ownership of something which is of crucial importance in an analog world. On the other hand, secondary space that we have is the digital world. Instead of atoms, the digital world consists of "bits" which have only two numeric values, either 0 or 1. Moreover, bits allow for easy transforming, replicating and dispersing information which augment the experiential value rather than that of ownership. In other words, sharing experience in the digital world is much easier and simpler than that in the analog world. Furthermore, the experiential value leads to the notion, "sharing". Instead of owning something, shared experience with others is a crucial matter in digital world and this is also related to the notion of "service".

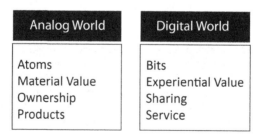

Fig. 1. The foundational difference between a digital world and an analog world

2   Examples of New User Experience Design (UXD)

Based on an understanding of the theoretical framework of these two different worlds, some key concerns for the future UX designers are discussed in this section. Firstly, the value of experience will be more emphasized than that of ownership. One example of this notion would be the newly made title, "rentrepreneur" (Baedeker, 2011). This is a person who rent his or her personal belongings that he or she does not often use. They rent out items such as cars, couches, costumes, and even their dog! Some elderly people who want companionship with a pet but who cannot handle the responsibility of caring for their own pet may wish to rent someone's dog when they want companionship.

In a similar vein, Airbnb, an online community based company, is doing their business to connect travelers who are looking for difference experience and economic accommodation service rather than staying in a hotel room to an owner of room or house who want to share a room in their place or entire house while he or she goes away. Currently, this company founded in 2008 has more than 250,000 lists of places from a private room to an igloo in 30,000 cities and 192 countries (Hempel, 2011). The basic principles of the two cases, the "rentrepreneur" and "Airbnb", are all about sharing experience.

Fig. 2. The image of the rentrepreneur (http://www.thedailybeast.com/newsweek/2011/11/20/how-to-make-money-when-economy-is-failing.html) and the airbnb's company logo (www.airbnb.com)

Rather than emphasizing product design, the secondary aspect that is explored is that of service design. In this situation, a good service refers to the benefits of a product and its channel through which users could engage with the service. For example, Starbucks is a place that provides better service and aims to improve the entire customer experience of enjoying a cup of coffee. The numbers of touchpoints1 in the place have been carefully designed to increase customer's total experience. For example, the wooden tables and the leather couches provide comfort and a relaxed experience. In addition, other touchpoints such as the incandescent lightings, Wi-Fi internet service, relaxed background music, and coffee aroma will accelerates a customer's positive experience in being there.

In terms of the concept of a total experience, another good example is the airport lounge service that Porter airlines provides. Porter is a regional airline company in Canada. By providing a better airport lounge service, Porter has increased a customer's entire flight experience. In general, an airport lounge service is only for business or first class passengers. However, Porter provides a similar lounge service for everyone who booked their flight. Similar to other airport lounges for business or

---

[1] Touchpoints occur whenever a customer or user come into contact with a part of an organization, whether it be a product, interface, customer service call, in-store interaction, or point of purchase display. They occur across several channels and at multiple points in time (Fortier, 2012).

Fig. 3. Images of Porter airline lounge in Ottawa international airport, ON, Canada

first class ticket holders, Porter provides an Internet café service, coffees, beverages, newspapers and snacks for free to all their passengers. Furthermore, they put home-like-furniture and undisruptive table lamps to increase a cozy and relaxed experience for their customers.

Lastly, new types of collaboration at work will be introduced. For example, Local Motors, a U.S based the first car company that co-create vehicles with its virtual multidisciplinary community of diverse groups of experts such as car designers, fabricators, engineers, enthusiasts and customers from around the world (Anderson, 2010). Moreover, this company provides an 'engaging experience' for their customers so that they learn about cars and customize the car they would like to have.   Through these new types of collaboration, this 40-employee company has received around 44,000 car designs a year, shared knowledge and insights. In fact, with 3,600 innovators, the company developed a car five times faster than the traditional way to make a car, and used 100 times less capital (Anderson, 2010).

Fig. 4. 2009 Rally Fighter, designed by Sangho Kim, with the Local Motors Community (http://www.cartype.com/pages/4078/local_motors_rally_fighter_2009)

Based on the understanding of the new trend described above and the flux of current technological developments in SNS (social networking service), powerful broadband, cloud sourcing, hi-speed Internet and smartphone, etc., more diverse services and experience will be introduced and available through new products or applications in near future. Moreover, the new product or application will reduce the distance between the digital and the analog world due to the demand of flexible accessibility from the analog to the digital world or vice versa.

For the purpose of meeting the requirements for the new trend, some have proposed ways to achieve it by evoking the user's dreams through indirect investigation, games (Shedroff, 2009) and the use of emphatic research to understand complexities of the user's life (Merholz et al., 2008). In a similar vein, Sanders (2001) suggests participatory design is a way to engage users in the design process so that designers could discover a user's feeling, memories, experience, and dreams for their future offerings.   Beyond the academic perspective to see the phenomenon, the next chapter attempts to investigate current approach for UXD in practice.

3   Method

As the popularity of UXD grows and evolves, the population of UX designers in the field has been rapidly escalating. For this reason, this study has employed an in-depth interview as an empirical investigation to understand how industry leaders on this topic illuminate this new field of inquiry. Through careful in-depth interviews with seven experience-centric design and consulting firms, this study attempt to discover areas such as; 1) how current professional UX designers in practice defines UX design by themselves, 2) what specific approach they do, and 3) what supports they provide for their client.

For the purpose of analysis, the narrative data from the interviews were transcribed and analyzed based on Auerbach and Silverstein's (Auerbach, Carl F., and Louise B. Silverstein., 2003) methodology, where relevant text is highlighted and grouped into repeating ideas. Then, the repeating ideas are categorized into patterns that are related to the research questions.   In addition, a careful screening procedure to choose appropriate interviewees has been made by reviewing whether their core business offering is user experience design or not.

In order to understand the most comprehensive components of experience design, the selected interviewee had a minimum of five years of professional experience in this field. Also, the list of companies was primarily identified based on public reputation and expert opinions in order to assure that they were appropriate design firms. Furthermore, companies who had a global presence, were active in social media and contributed regularly to reputable publications were pursued (Fortier, 2012).

3.1   Interviews

Setting. The in-depth interviews were conducted remotely via telephone as well as on-site, in-depth interviews. The three on-site interviews took place in casual environments at the IDEO office in Palo Alto, California, including the lunchroom and a public meeting room. As the telephone interviews were conducted remotely, some interviews were conducted during regular working hours, where participants were reached on their office phones, while others preferred to be contacted at home or on a mobile phone. Participants were located in either Canada or the United States, depending on their company headquarters (Fortier, 2012).

Measurement Instruments. The interviews were conducted using an interview protocol. Interview questions moved from the general to the specific in order to build rapport with the participant and avoid establishing a set, where the participant would be inclined to provide predisposed answers (Sommer, 1997). A list of ten to fifteen questions was asked based on the duration and direction of the interview. Consequently, at times some questions were omitted, while others were added ad-hoc during the course of the interview to delve deeper into a particular topic of interest when relevant. Furthermore, questions were asked in an open-ended format and focused mainly on the meaning of experience design, the research and design methods used, and perspectives of the respective firms. Probes were also used to further explain an abstract concept or obtain supplementary information on a certain question (Fortier, 2012).

Data Collection. Interviews began by providing participants with a general overview of the study, helping to set the context for obtaining information relevant to the research problem. The interviewer also requested each participant's oral consent in identifying the design firm's company name in the reported findings. At which point, participants were informed that their responses would not be attributed to them in any way and they would remain anonymous in the findings and thesis. In order to ensure accuracy of data collection, participants were also asked for permission to audio record the interview session. As the phone interviews were held with participants who live outside of Canada (e.g. United States), oral consent versus written consent was more appropriate. Each interview lasted between 30 and 45 minutes.

Data Analysis. Due to the semi-structured and open-ended question format, data analysis involved a coding process to categorize and label the data into meaningful chunks. The goal was to draw out major themes or relationships in the hopes of developing a set of design patterns. Firstly, from the raw transcript, relevant text was selected and transferred to a separate document. Relevant text is text that relates in anyway to the research questions and theoretical framework (Auerbach and Silverstein., 2003). Subsequently, the relevant text was scanned for repeating ideas which are similar ideas expressed by two or more research participants. Repeating ideas were first identified in the separate transcripts and then combined with the repeating ideas from all other transcripts. After all, a master list of repeating ideas was created, where all repeating ideas assimilated from the individual interview transcripts were combined. At this stage, ideas were either amalgamated, re-grouped, or discarded as orphan text. Then, the repeating ideas grouped into themes. The process was designed to be transparent and systematic in order to ensure the validity of the results (Auerbach and Silverstein., 2003). In sum, five patterns emerged and are discussed in detail in the following chapter (Fortier, 2012).

4   Result

The seven interviews on experience-centric design firms provided a wealth of knowledge of UXD in practice in response to the three research questions; 1) how do current UX designers in practice defines UX design by themselves?, 2) what are specific actions they perform?, and 3) what types of supports they provide for their client?.

4.1   Holistic and Systemic Perspectives

In regards to the definition of UXD for the first question, most participants had similar opinions. When asked to describe the meaning of experience design almost all participants responded that it involves a consideration, beyond one interaction, to how all the interactions fit together within a broader experience. In describing this concept one participant stated,

"The experience of opening the packaging also contributes to the experience that you have with the object itself. So it's really a case of not just concentrating on one particular instance of interaction but going beyond that and seeing how these interactions get together and form a whole experience."

Many have emphasized the holistic perspective as the most important factor for experience design. It involves every single interaction we have with the whole chain of events that lead us to experience the offerings. So, a holistic perspective is about going beyond one particular instance of interaction with a product and seeing how multiple interactions form a whole experience. For example, Starbucks pays great attention to the holistic perspective from designing the café from the moment a consumer walks in and leaves the place. People like going there not only to drink a coffee but to have an entire experience. People tend to consider Starbucks café as a warm, cozy, and safe place that evoke the sort of legendary coffee shop of Europe. In order to have a holistic perspective, it is necessary for UX designers to have a systematical viewpoint to see the given design context. Like a system consists of multiple components and their relationship to make the system running, the holistic perspectives allow designers to see products as a components, the given design context as a system, and the interactions among the components, the system and end users as experience.   For example, if a hiking trail is a given design context, a bench is one of products in the context. From the systemic perspective, the hiking trail is a system and the bench is one of components in the system. In this sense, the design of a bench does not have to be traditional bench shape but it can be anything (e.g. a log or a stone) as long as it supports the system. Also, participants in the interview stressed that a holistic perspective is something to be carried through all phases and approaches of designing for experience. This also requires a holistic picture of everyone involved, not only the end user. As such it must take into account the whole person; appreciating the user as a complex, multi-faceted human being.

4.2   Design Research and Design Synthesis

It was clearly shown that UX designers focused heavily on both design research and synthesis. In the research, first, they try to learn about their clients as well as end users in terms of their culture and business. Immersive in-depth research techniques, such as ethnography and observation are utilized to understand user's perspective and emotional latent needs such as pains, needs, and desires. By employing qualitative and quantitative research methods, they tried to make an emotional connection with the users as well as clients. Once they have made an emotional connection, then, almost of all project members including clients wanted to develop empathy for users through team involvement in all design phases and soliciting user feedback through high and low fidelity concept testing and iterative prototyping throughout. Often designers represent the empathy through a narrative story explaining how an offering fits into one's life and a particular context in which they will be using in. Through the series of those activities, designers try to find opportunity and change viewpoint from usability or functionality to desirability.

4.3   Harmonious Relationship

As we mentioned briefly above, user experience originates from every single touchpoints in the given context and their harmonious relationship. Almost all companies we interviewed advocated that their capabilities are to deliver consistent touchpoints to increase the impact of experience centric product, service and system design in their organization. Explicitly, when asked the reasoning behind their success one firm responded,

"If you are looking for experience design you should come to us, because we are looking at what's happening, what technologies you have, what the brand is, taking the pulse of the people that are out there. Looking at the pulse of the people who are buying watches, looking at materials, looking at finishes, looking at the packaging, looking at the brand promise that would show up in advertising. Looking at the point of sales display. Integrating across all those touchpoints, that's where we get our strength."

In order to make better harmonious relationship among the touchpoints, integrating the experience consistently across all touchpoints and resenting a coherent brand story tied seamlessly across all touchpoints will be crucial factor. Specifically, the notion of consistency in this case was extended to a company's brand identity, philosophy or a concept of particular project. Designers try to make sure that they are consistently showcasing similar concepts and images of what they offer. For example, companies like Apple and Alessi have done a very good job at consistently communicating their design concept.

5   Discussion

This study has attempted to reveal some important concerns to conduct better user experience design. It insists that designers must shift their perspective from the isolated product or service towards a holistic perspective to interconnect products, context and users throughout the design approach. Due to the current rapid technical development allowing the gap between an analog world and a digital world to be reduced, the area of experience design would be a new market and a competitive battleground. This phenomenon could aid in redirecting organizational focus and help companies to recognize that every touchpoint impacts the greater experience. In addition, the shift in the existing client-designer paradigm towards collaborative co-creating design ascertains that designers will play a greater role as facilitator, communicator and enabler for their clients.

References

1. Anderson, C.: WIRED Magazine. In: The Next Industrial Revolution, Atoms Are the New Bits, New York, NY, USA (2010),
   http://en.wikipedia.org/wiki/Local_Motors (retrieved)
2. Auerbach, C.F.: Qualitative data: An introduction to coding and analysis. New York University Press, New York (2003)
3. Auerbach, C.F., Silverstein, L.B.: Qualitative data: An introduction to coding and analysis. New York University Press, New York (2003)
4. Baedeker, R.: How to Make Money When Economy Is Failing. Newsweek (November 21, 2011)
5. Dewey, J.: Art as Experience. The Berkley Publishing Group, New York (1934)
6. Fortier, S.: A Systems Approach to Rich User Experience Design. Mater of Design (MDes) Thesis. Carleton University Press, Ottwa (2012)
7. Hempel, J.: With Neighborhoods, Airbnb expands its horizons. CNN Money (November 13, 2011)
8. Jordan, P.W.: Designing Pleasurable Products. Taylor & Francis, London (2000)
9. Merholz, P.: Peter in Conversation with Don Norman about UX & Innovation (2007),
   http://www.adaptivepath.com/ideas/e000862 (retrieved)
10. Merholz, P.B.: Subject to change: Creating great products and services for an uncertain world. O'Reilly Media, Sebastopol (2008)
11. Pine, J.B., Gilmore, J.H.: Welcome to the experience economy. Harvard Business Revew 76, 97–105 (1998)
12. Sanders, E.B.-N.: Virtuosos of the experience domain. Paper presented at the 2001 IDSA Education Conference IDSA (2001)
13. Sanders, E.B.-N.: Scaffolds for Experiencing in the New Design Space. In: Information Design Institute for Information Design Japan (Editors), IID.J, Graphic-Sha Publishing Co., Ltd. (2002)
14. Shedroff, N.: Experience design 1.1. Experience Design Books, San Francisco (2009)
15. Sommer, B.: A practical guide to behavioral research: Tools and techniques, 4th edn. Oxford University Press, New York (1997)
16. Stuart, I.F.: Designing and executing memorable service experiences: Lights, camera, experiment, integrate, action! Business Horizons 49, 149–159 (2006)
17. Vink, P.: Comfort and design: principles and good practice. CRC Press, Danvers (2005)
18. Zomerdijk, L.G., Voss, C.A.: Service design for experience-centric services. Journal of Service Research 13(1), 67–82 (2010)

On the Poetry of Design

Arash Faroughi and Roozbeh Faroughi

Cologne University of Applied Sciences, Germany
University of Burgos, Spain
{arash.faroughi,roozbeh.faroughi}@fh-koeln.de

Abstract. This paper seeks to answer the questions why the original design concept was invented and what disciplines were responsible for its development. Therefore, significant works from the Classical Antiquity and Renaissance are selected for analyzing the invention of the original design. The paper comes to the conclusion that design was created from the disciplines poetry, music, philosophy, rhetoric, painting, sculpture and architecture. Especially, poetry was of particular importance for design. Finally, the paper describes how the poetry of design is related to interaction design.

Keywords: Disegno, Design theory, Renaissance, Poetry.

1 Introduction

The designer of today is faced with enormous tasks of accomplishing a wide range of skills. These skills often seem contradictory. John Kolko describes the education of a designer as follows: "We must train generalists. We must train specialists" [19]. Hence, according to Robert Bauer, a 'Renaissance Man' who can unify the technical, economic, cultural and artistic creativity is currently sought [5]. Interestingly, design as a standalone concept was already developed in the Renaissance for the first time with the Italian term 'Disegno'. Giorgio Vasari placed Disegno over the three arts: architecture, sculpture and painting [31]. It was the primary concept of supporting innovations by bringing ideas to life and creating "never-before-seen" things [8]. For Leonardo da Vinci, Disegno was not only a science but also a deity which can produce infinitely far more things than nature [10]. Hence, the Renaissance period could be labeled as the Golden Age of Design.

This paper aims to bring a new perspective to design theory. It seeks to answer the questions why the original design concept was invented. The departure point of this analysis is the philosophy of Aristotle, who argued that we can only know each thing if we recognize its original causes [4]. In achieving this, the paper first describes the selected books which were significant for this analysis. Then, it points out, which disciplines were responsible for the invention of the original design. Finally, it introduces the poetical philosophy of design and how it is connected to interaction design.

A. Marcus (Ed.): DUXU/HCII 2013, Part I, LNCS 8012, pp. 38–47, 2013.
© Springer-Verlag Berlin Heidelberg 2013

2   Selected Works

In recent related works, we have studied the original design concept with its method and techniques [14][15][16]. As mentioned before, this analysis aims to find out why design was invented. Hence, the paper analyzes the origin of the design concept. Therefore, significant works are selected and divided into two parts: The first part consists of six main authors of the classical antiquity - three Greek (Plato, Aristotle and Plotinus) and three Roman authors (Cicero, Horace and Quintilian) - which significantly influenced the first design concept and the Renaissance thinking. The second part includes writings of six important Italian Renaissance humanists beginning with Francesco Petrarch who is known as the father of Humanism and ending with Giovanni Pico della Mirandola who authored the book 'De hominis dignitate' (Oration on the Dignity of Man) which was called the 'Manifesto of the Renaissance'. In addition, to understand how these writings influenced the development of design and the Renaissance thinking, it is necessary to consider other important works from authors such as Alberti [1][2], Da Vinci[11], Ghiberti [17],Vasari [31] and Vitruvius [32]. Figure 1 and Table 1 present the selected authors and their writings.

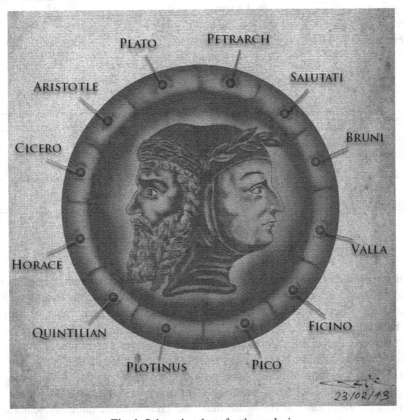

Fig. 1. Selected authors for the analysis

Table 1. Selected books for the analysis

Author	Book	Year
Plato	*'Ion'*	~ 399 BCE
	'Symposium'	~ 385–380 BCE
	'Phaedo'	~ 385–378 BCE
	'Timaeus'	~ 360 BCE
Aristotle	*'Poetics'*	~ 335 BCE
	'Nicomachean Ethics'	~ 350 BCE
	'Metaphysics'	~ 350 BCE
	'Rhetoric'	~ 367-347 BCE
Cicero (Marcus Tullius Cicero)	*'De Oratore'*	55 BCE
Horace (Quintus Horatius Flaccus)	*'Epistula Ad Pisones'* (*'Ars Poetica'*)	~ 18 BCE
Quintilian (Marcus Fabius Quintilianus)	*'Institutio Oratoria'*	~ 95
Plotinus	*'Enneads'*	~ 270
Petrarch (Francesco Petrarca)	*'On the Solitary Life'* *'De sui ipsius et multorum aliorum ignorantia'*	~ 1346 – 1356 ~ 1368
Coluccio Salutati	*'De laboribus Herculis'*	1406
Leonardo Bruni	*'De studiis et litteris'*	~ 1426
Lorenzo Valla	*'De voluptate'*	1431
Marsilio Ficino	*'Theologia Platonica'* *'De amore'*	1482 1484
Pico (Giovanni Pico della Mirandola)	*'De hominis dignitate'*	1486

3   Disciplines of the Original Design

One of the peculiarities of that time was that the Renaissance humanists tried to free themselves from the scholastic restraints of the Middle Age and to initiate a 'New Golden Age'. They found a way by studying the classic antiquity and by learning from the ideal past.

Furthermore, they tried to form a new order of sciences and thinking. Hence, the Renaissance period can be labeled as an age of increasing, decreasing, comparing and especially harmonizing different disciplines. The goal of the Renaissance to harmonize different disciplines was surely influenced by the book of Cicero 'De Oratore' ('On the Orator'). He wrote that "the great men of antiquity, embracing something of superior magnificence in their ideas, appear to me to have seen further into the nature of things than visual faculties of our minds can penetrate" [9, p.197]. Moreover, he argued that all things "formed one system and were linked together in strict union" and cannot be separated from each other. The same effect could be seen in the disciplines, which were "linked together in one bond of union", and it was possible to discover a wonderful correspondence and harmony of all sciences. Therefore, design can be called a product of such a harmonization process.

Of particular importance for the invention of design was poetry. During the Renaissance period, it grew up to the art of all arts [30] and can thus also be called the mother of design. The term poetry is etymologically derived from the Ancient Greek word 'poiesis' which means 'to make' or 'to create things'. Interestingly, classical authors like Aristotle, Cicero or Diogenes Laertius divided sciences in three categories: the theoretical, the practical and the poetical [4][9][20]. The poetical sciences concern the activities for the creation of a work or work piece. Apart of poetry, as depicted in Figure 2, design was especially invented from the disciplines music, philosophy, rhetoric, painting, sculpture and architecture. In the following, the correspondence of the different disciplines to poetry is described and the question why they were necessary for the invention of design is answered.

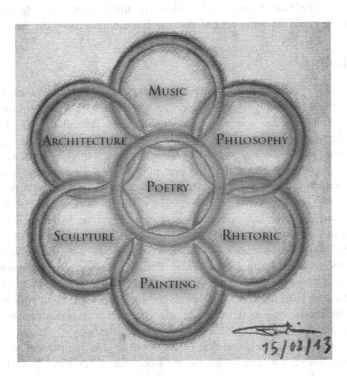

Fig. 2. Disciplines of the original design

3.1   Music

In the Renaissance, music was called the 'unknown method' [12] and the 'true magic' [13]. It had the magical power to combine contrasted things. Music was the science of reconciliation of opposites and love in relation to harmony and rhythm [27]. Hence, music was strongly connected to the theory of harmony, which was also important for the creation of things. Alberti defined harmony with the following words: "harmony as that consonance of sounds which is pleasant to the ears". For him, the same effect could also be achieved with the eyes. Beauty was the "harmony of all parts in relation to one another" [2].

In the Classical Antiquity, there was a great correspondence of poetry and music. Music and harmony were parts of poetry [3] and the poets of that time were also musicians who sang their own verses. Both arts had the capacity to inspire oneself and others and Plato's theory of 'Poetic Inspiration' was of particular importance for the invention of design. Plato argued in his early dialogue 'Ion' that poetry was not a 'techne' (art or skill) but rather a product of divine inspiration [25]. The Renaissance linked the artist with the poet1 and thus the artist's inspiration was also divine. Zuccari claimed that 'Disegno' has an etymological meaning: 'Segno di Dio' (sign of God in Man) [33]. As an inspired creator and as a lover, the artist had the divine ability to see the true beauty, only with his mind. According to his genius imagination, he could invent never-before-seen things and envision the future.

3.2   Philosophy

Pico criticized the lack of appreciation for Ancient philosophy with the following words: "For the whole study of philosophy (such is the unhappy plight of our time) is occasion for contempt and contumely, rather than honor and glory. The deadly and monstrous persuasion has invaded practically all minds, that philosophy ought not to be studied at all or by very few people; as though it were a thing of little worth" [12]. Moreover, he pointed out that the true philosopher was not someone who sought money or profit but wisdom. For the Renaissance, true richness should be sciences. For Castiglione, sciences were the noblest gift of the humanity [7]. Furthermore, a philosopher was a universally educated person who strived to know not only the divine but also the human things [9]. The true or ideal poet was also a philosopher [24] who dealt thus with human subjects. Hence, the focus of the Renaissance turned more towards the human rather than God and was the reason why the scientists and thinkers started to study non-Christian sources. The Renaissance can be labeled as the rebirth of philosophical thinking. For design, the focus on human and philosophy was necessary for its invention. The theory of 'Disegno' was mainly based on the neoplatonic, pythagorean, aristotelian and epicurean philosophy.

Another interesting correspondence between poetry and philosophy was the fact that Plato was not only a philosopher for the Renaissance but also a poet. Especially Ficino believed that Plato used poetry for hiding the truth behind allegories and the

---

[1] Cennini was the first who establish the connection between artist and poet [8].

mask of figurative language [13]. Even Pythagoras, Socrates and Orpheus wrapped the secrets and the mysteries of their philosophy in "veils of poetry" [12] [13].

3.3   Rhetoric

For Quintilian, the negative definition of rhetoric as 'the power of persuading' had its origin from Isocrates, who characterized rhetoric with the words: 'worker of persuasion'[29, p.303]. Rhetoric was the "power of a bad man" [29, p.301] to speak in a persuasive manner for transforming the inferior position to a superior one and to succeed without regard to morality. It had the ability to control and steer the hearts of the hearers to any direction that is desired by the orator. Furthermore, Quintilian argued that Plato didn't criticize the 'true rhetoric'. He argued: "Plato does not regard rhetoric as an evil, but holds that true rhetoric is impossible for any save a just and good man" [29, p.313]. Hence, the true or ideal orator should be a good man and should use the power of rhetoric to lead others to the good. For Quintilian, rhetoric was the 'science of speaking well' [29, p. 317]. This definition "includes all the virtues of oratory and the character of the orator as well, since no man can speak well who is not good himself." [29, p. 317]. For design, this thinking was relevant: Only a good person can create good things.

The rhetorical system was of great importance for the invention of design. The Renaissance used it to extent the theory of poetry and also painting. Especially the rhetorical parts 'inventio' (invention), 'dispositio' (arrangement) and 'elocutio' (style) were adapted to the mentioned theories. Moreover, Salutati ordered poetry as a part of rhetoric and defined that the poetic style is a necessity for creating a graceful and dignified speech [30]. In poetry, it was not only important 'what' but also 'how' it is said or written. For Bruni, it was a barren attainment to say only the truth without using the "art of expression" [6, p. 124].These two sides should not be separated but build a perfect familiarity. For him, poetry had "a stronger attraction for us than any other form of expression" [6, p.131]. For design, this high status of form and beauty was essential for its invention. In addition, the similar goal of poetry and rhetoric was also relevant for design. As Horace pointed out, poetry should be delightful and useful [18]. Rhetoric had also the goal to delight and inform the hearer [29]. For this reason, design should unify utility ('utilitas') with beauty ('venustas') [31].

3.4   Painting

As Castiglione described, nature was like an elegant and great painting and aimed to create the most perfect [7]. Alberti characterized it as the extraordinary master of all things [1]. For him, painting is like an "open window" through which the outside world could be observed [1, p. 39]. Da Vinci used the metaphor of a mirror to describe the goal of a painter: "His mind will (...) be like a mirror, reflecting truly every object placed before it, and become, as it were, a second Nature [11, p. 206]. The mirror metaphor and the philosophy behind painting were derived from Plato, who defined painting as the imitation ('mimesis') of things [28]. The Renaissance had increased the value of Plato's definition: The painter must clearly understand the things in nature in order to imitate it. Hence, he must observe and analyze things in nature to create the most beautiful and perfect thing. This thinking played a significant part in design.

'*Ut picture poesis*' (As is painting so is poetry) was a statement of Horace [18], *who described the correspondence between painting and poetry.* Even Da Vinci analyzed the similarities between both arts and defined painting as 'silent poetry' and poetry as 'blind painting' [11]. For Cennini, the painter was like a poet free in mind and had the fantasy to create things, which were never seen in nature [8]. According to him, design ('disegno') was the bridge between mind and hand. Hence, the artist was able to design things solely in the mind and then, ultimately, to hold them in his hands.

3.5 Sculpture

For the Italian Renaissance, the ancient Greek sculptors embodied the excellence of the art. Therefore, they tried to imitate beauty and perfection. For design, sculpture played an important role for the invention of modeling ('modello') or prototyping. As Vasari pointed out, "sculptors, when they wish to work a figure in marble, are accustomed to make what is called a model for it in clay or plaster" [31, p. 148]. This technique was also used in architecture and was responsible for evaluating the design concept. Accordingly, the artist could represent his idea in a three dimensional model in order to define how it could look like in reality. Hence, it was possible to evaluate the effect of the work on the viewer and to verify their "quality" ('qualitas') [2]. Furthermore, it made it easier for the laymen to understand the artist's intention and to calculate the costs. Mostly important for the invention of Design was also the work of Ghiberti. He described that two theories were necessary for sculpture: the theory of drawing ('teorica disegno') and the theory of perspective ('prospettiva'). "In going around from view to view", the sculptor must analyze his work from different perspectives in order to understand his concept completely.

Vasari defined sculpture as "an art which by removing all that is superfluous from the material under treatment reduces it to that form designed in the artist's mind" [31, p. 143]. This definition was strongly derived from Plotinus' theory of Beauty and was used by Pico as a poetical allegory for describing the dignity of man. Like a "sculptor of himself" ('plastes et fictor sui ipsius'), man had the freedom to form his nature according to his desires and judgement [12]. This freedom was according to Pico God's greatest gift to Humanity. Man was allowed to be whatever he chose to be [12]. Hence, he was a sculptor or designer of his own identity.

3.6 Architecture

With his treatise '*De Architectura libri decem*' Vitruvius wrote the oldest book on architecture by being the only one which survived from the Classical Antiquity. For him, architecture was divided in three parts: "*the art of buildings, the making of timepieces, and the construction of machinery*" [32, p.22]. The goal of architecture was not only to develop buildings, but also to create complex things. Of particular importance for design was his arguing that all created things *"must be built with due reference to 'firmitas' (stability), 'utilitas' (utility) and 'venustas' (beauty)"* [32].

Etymologically, the term 'architecture' is composed of the Greek words 'arché' (supreme, principle, first) and 'techné' (art, craft, work), which thus means 'first art' or 'supreme work'. This meaning was also relevant for the invention of design and can be described by Aristotle's theory of poetical sciences. For him, all created things were produced by nature or art. Moreover, things were unions of form and matter. However, all artistic or artificial things could only be created, when the form of it was already in the mind of the creator [4]. The form was the cause and the principle ('arché') for the creation of the thing. This thinking was related on Plato's 'Theory of Forms'. Due to Vasari, design ('Disegno') was "like a form or idea of all objects in nature" [31, p. 205]. Moreover, he described that "design is not other than a visible expression and declaration of our inner conception and of that others have imagined and given form to in their idea" [31, p. 205]. Hence, design was the principle and the supreme work of all artificial and artistic things.

Moreover, based on Plato's dialogue 'Timaeus' [26], the Renaissance humanists like Ficino characterized God as an architect who artfully created the universe [13]. Therefore, Cellini and Vasari described God as a designer, who was responsible for the design of all things ('primo disegno') [23]. For this reason, the artist had the poetical power to understand the 'primo disegno' with his mind and thus the essence of all things.

4   Relation to Interaction Design

From the point of view of interaction design, Aristotle created an interesting philosophy of poetics. For him, poetry was not the imitation of things, but of action. Poetry should describe *"how certain sorts of persons would act in certain sorts of situations"* [3, p. 8]. Hence, it was necessary to characterize the persons and to analyze what *"sort of thing they seek or avoid"* [3, p. 8]. Furthermore, he wrote *"that the poet's function is to describe, not the thing that has happened, but a kind of thing that might happen"* [3, p. 12]. For this reason, the aim of poetry was to define, what *"such a kind of man will probably or necessarily say or do"* [3, p. 12]. Therefore, poetry was *"something more philosophic and of graver import than history"*[3, p.12]. It had dealt not with the past, but referred to the creation of a possible future. Also relevant for interaction design is that Manetti defined the creation of things as the meaning of life. According to him, the purpose of mankind was to reinvent, beautify and complete the world [21]. Hence, the poetry of design is to invent a better world and thus to help persons to interact better in the future.

5   Conclusion

In summary, the aim of the paper was to find out which disciplines were responsible for the invention of the original design. Therefore, we first analyzed significant works from the Classical Antiquity and Renaissance. Based on our analysis, we defined poetry, music, philosophy, rhetoric, painting, sculpture and architecture as the main disciplines. Then, we described the correspondence of the different disciplines to poetry and answered the question to why they were necessary for the original design. Finally, we described how the poetry of design is related to interaction design.

References

1. Alberti, L.B.: De Pictura, 1435, translated by Spencer, J. R., On Painting, Revised Edition. Yale University Press, New Haven (1967)
2. Alberti, L.B.: De re aedificatoria, 1452, translated by Rykwert, J., On the Art of Building in Teh Books. MIT Press, Cambridge (1988)
3. Aristotle. Aristotle on the Art of Poetry, 335 BCE, Translated by Bywater, I. Dodo Press, USA (2006)
4. Aristotle.: The Metaphysics of Aristotle, 350 BCE, Translated by M'Mahon, J. H. Henry G. Bohn, Covent Garden (1857)
5. Bauer, R.: Design Thinking: Strategische Innovation ist mehr als technischer Fortschritt. APA - Austria Press Agentur, Austria (2008)
6. de Bruni Arezzo, L.: De Studiis et Litteris, 1426. Cambridge University Press, Cambridge (1912)
7. Castiglione, B.: The Book of the Courtier from the Italian of Count Baldassare Castiglione, 1528, Translated by Sir Hobby, D.N (1900)
8. Cennini, C.: Il libro dell"arte, 1400, translated by Thompson, D.V., The Craftsman"s Handbook. Dover Publications, New York (1965)
9. Cicero, M.T.: On Oratory and Orators, 55 BCE, Translated or Edited by Watson, J.S. Southern Illinois University Press, Carbondale (1970)
10. Da Vinci, L., von der Malerei, T.: 1570. Translated by: Ludwig, H., 1925, Reprint. Eugen Diedrichs, Tillmann Roeder, Jena, München (1989)
11. Da Vinci, L.: Treatise on Painting, 1570, Translated by Rigaud, J. F. High Holborn, Architectural Library, London (1892)
12. Della Mirandola, G.P.: Oration on the Dignity of Man, 1486, translated by Caponigri, A. R. Gateway Editions. Washington, D.C (1996)
13. Ficino, M.: Evermore Shall Be So, Ficino on Plato's Parmenides, 1484, translated by Farndell. Shepheard – Walwyn (Publishers) Ltd., London (2008)
14. Faroughi, A., Faroughi, R.: Design Re-Thinking: From Italian Renaissance to Strategic Design Architecture. In: Marjanovic, D., Storga, M., Pavkovic, N., Bojcetic, N. (eds.) The 12th International Design Conference on DS 70: Proceedings of DESIGN 2012, Dubrovnik, pp. 1967–1976 (2012)
15. Faroughi, A., Faroughi, R.: Über die Synthese der MCI basierend auf dem Ursprung des Designs. In: Reiterer, H., Deussen, O. (eds.) Mensch & Computer 2012: Interaktiv Informiert – Allgegenwärtig und Allumfassend!?, pp. 213–222. Oldenbourg, München (2012)
16. Faroughi, R., Faroughi, A.: Design-Denken in der Renaissance. In: Reiterer, H., Deussen, O. (eds.) Mensch & Computer 2012 – Workshopband: Interaktiv Informiert – Allgegenwärtig und Allumfassend!?, pp. 203–211. Oldenbourg, München (2012)
17. Ghiberti, L., Bartoli, L. I., 1447. Universtiy of Michigan, Giunti, Napoli (1998)
18. Horace: Epistles Book II and Epistle to the Pisones 'Ars Poetica'. In: 18 BCE, Edited by: Rudd, N., Cambridge University Press, New York (1989)
19. Kolko, J.: The Conflicting Rhetoric of Design Education. Interactions magazine (2011)

20. Laertius, D.: Vitae philosophorum, 300, translated by: Apelt, O. Leben und Meinungen berühmter Philosophen. Erster und Zweiter Band. Felix Meiner, Leibzig (1921)
21. Manetti, G.: De dignitate et excellentia hominis libri IV. Two Views of Man: Pope Innocent III-On the Misery of Man; Giannozzo Manetti- On the Dignity of Man 1452, translated by Murchland B. Ungar, New York (1966)
22. Murray, C.: Key Writers on Art: From Antiquity to the Nineteenth Century. Routledge, London (2003)
23. Nova, A.: Benvenuto Cellini. In: Schreurs, A. (ed.) Kunst und Kunsttheorie im 16. Jahrhundert. Böhlau, Köln (2003)
24. Petrarch, F.: De vita solitaria. The Life of Solitude, translated by: Zeitlin, J., pp. 1346–1356. Univsersity of Illinois Press, Illinois (1924)
25. Ion, P.: 399 BCE, Platons Werke. Verlag von Wilhelm Engelmann, Leipzig (1850)
26. Plato's Timaeus, P.: 360 BCE, translated by Jowett, B. Serenity Publishers, USA (2009)
27. Plato.: Symposium, 385 – 380 BCE, Translated by Jowett, B. In The Dialogues of Plato. Charles Scriber's Sons, New York (1911)
28. Plato.: The Republic, 380 BCE, Translated by Allen, R.E. Yale University Press, New Haven (2006)
29. Quintillian.: Institutio Oratoria, 95 , translated by Butler, H.E. Loeb Classical Library edition, London (1920).
30. Salutati, C.: De laboribus Herculis, 1406. In: Ullman, B.L. (ed.) Aedibus Thesauri Mundi, vol. 1 (1951)
31. Vasari, G.: Le vite dei più eccellenti architetti, pittori et scultori italiani, 1568, translated by Brown, B.B. et al, Vasari on Technique. Dover Publications, New York (1960)
32. Vitruvius, P.: De Architectura libri decem, 22 BC, Vitruvius: The Ten Books on Architecture. Echo Lib, UK (2008)
33. Zuccari, F.: L'Idea de Pittori Scultori Ed Architetti, 1607, Lightning Source, UK (2011)

Future Fashion – At the Interface

Patricia J. Flanagan[1] and Katia Fabiola Canepa Vega[2]

[1] Hong Kong Baptist University, Academy of Visual Arts,
5 Hereford Rd, Kowloon Tong, Hong Kong SAR, The People's Republic of China
tricia@triciaflanagan.com
[2] PUC-rio Departamento de Informática, Pontifícia Universidade Católica do Rio De Janeiro,
Rua Marquês de Sâo Vicente, 225
Gávea Rio de Janeiro RJ 22451 9000, Brasil
katia.canepa@gmail.com

Abstract. Imagining the future, we create sci-fi predictions visualized through telematic imagery, involving stage sets and costumes. Looking back at sci-fi's imagination we find it depicts the ideologies of the period in history when it was created far more accurately than it manages to predict future materials or functions. This article focuses on the body, but goes beyond the traditional perspectives of fashion, to consider *wearables* as an interface between the body and the world. Two key concepts will be presented in order to interpret future fashion, they are: 'fungibility' and 'empathy', which will be discussed through examples of clothing as a means for expressing data. User interfaces of the future will acknowledge the relationship between people, places and things as emergent spaces that generate meaning through everyday activity and therefore ones in which users themselves act as co-designers.

Keywords: Wearables, Fungibility, Empathy, Blinklifier, Snoothood Surreal, Snoothood Chinoiserie, Blinklifier, Reverse Predictive Practices, Sleep Disorders, Snoring, Humanistic Computing, Technogenesis, Interface Aesthetics, Interface Culture.

1   Introduction

Futuristic fashion depicts the ideologies of the period in history when they were created far more accurately than they manage to predict future materials or functions. For example, the birth control belts in Aldous Huxley's 1930 dystopian vision 'Brave New World' are shown in the 1980 film version as clear plastic Malthusian belts worn around the hips supporting white computoseption dials (resembling the dials of analogue desk telephones of the 1980's). The belts are worn over Spandex unitards. The materials used are the latest technologies available at the time of the film's creation, and so even though the film is set in 2540 it presents a clearly 1980's vision of 2540. As in most utopian films, as well as being dated by the materials used, the function of the depicted technology grapples with debates of the time as much as it anticipates the future condition. In this case with social issues surrounding the contraception debate.

A. Marcus (Ed.): DUXU/HCII 2013, Part I, LNCS 8012, pp. 48–57, 2013.
© Springer-Verlag Berlin Heidelberg 2013

Beyond the traditional perspectives of fashion, *wearables* can be considered as an interface between the body and the world living in the fuzzy border between private, intimate, personal space and the public realm. Fashion beyond aesthetic design, engages with flows of information and integrates seamlessly with the physical world – blurring the boundaries between body, clothing, and the physical environment, between the real and the artificial. In 'Everyware: The Dawning Age of Ubiquitous Computing', 2006, Adam Greenfield proposed that software is evolving into every environmental object. One realm of this colonization is the infusion of technology into the fabrics of our clothing that might be referred to as 'everywear'. [3] An example of 'everywear' is Hussein Chayalan's use of memory wire to elevate the skirt of a dress that disappears under a tailored jacket. Future applications of this technology could be in reaction to environmental changes in temperature or the wearers desire to change style from day to evening wear. Simultaneously, the line is blurring between the real and the artificial body. From cosmetic surgery and implanted technologies such as pacemakers, to tapping into the blood stream to charge body batteries and conductive tattoos, biotechnology is mashing-up the chemistry and biology of the body with new intelligent materials.

For example in Western Australia, Oron Catts Biowear experiments successfully produced test-tube-grown tissue. This technique might solve ethical issues in the fashion industry, for example, culturing skins that he calls 'victimless leather'. Increased mobility and cultural cross-fertilization mean artists and designers are becoming interdisciplinary practitioners who work across multiple fields. Artists and designers are collaborating with computer scientists, psychologists, biologists, sociologists, anthropologists, and industrial designers.

Fungibility. Two key concepts to understand the future are fungibility (i.e., exchangeability) and empathy. An example of something fungible is money: in that it is able to replace or be replaced by another identical item. With money everything can be classified in terms of its exchange value and traded without regard to its physical form. A more recent, fungible form that appeared in the 1950s is binary computer code. Digital code is mutually interchangeable and so it seems that all phenomena can lose their 'bodily form' and live as numerical codes that can be materialized in different ways. The data used to produce an image can be exchanged to present sounds, for example.

Neil Harbisson has achromatopsy, meaning he cannot see colors; he has been wearing a small computer to enable him to hear color since 2004. Harbisson reported that adaption time was required to memorize sounds associated with colors, but quickly the association felt natural, then he expanded the spectrum to include colors invisible to the human eye, such as infrared and ultraviolet. The color combinations of clothing may be chosen by selecting musical scores, Harbisson now dresses to sound good rather than look good – he wore 'C major' to present a lecture for TED in 2012. By inverting the role of sensors and actuators a future dress may change color in response to sounds in the environment. Clothing becomes a means for expressing data. This is just one potential future in which fashion, beyond aesthetic design, will engage with flow of information and integrate seamlessly with the physical world – blurring the boundaries between body, clothing, and the physical environment.

This is my fashion forecast for 2029: the date when some predict, following Moore's Law, computing capacity will equal that of the human mind. Ray Kurzweil, applying Moore's Law to neuroscience, predicts we shall understand the complexity of the mind at the same time as we reach its processing capacity. This future moment is known as Singularity. [7] The precedents of Singularity began with early experiments in electrode-stimulus mind control by José Delgado, who implanted electrodes into a bull's head to control its behavior. For his death-defying experiment Delgado armed with a radio-control device, was able to calm a charging bull. Mapping the human mind's electronic signals produces bio-data that can be used to send signals directly to intelligent clothing, which can respond. The details of fashion's future are currently fuzzy; what is clear is that keyboard/screen-mediated human-computer interaction will be a thing of the past. Communication through brainwaves or other somatic sources will be able to create changes, movements, colors, and sounds in our fully-fashioned future.

Think of Mathew Barney's crystal prosthetic legs in his art-house film 'Cremaster Cycle' or Alexander McQueen's intricately hand-carved ash-wood prosthetic legs for paralympian Amiee Mullins, and add technology. The user experience of computer-mediated objects can now be directed by thought alone, not action. Miguel Nicolelis' experiments first showed this potential by recording monkey brain waves. By replaying them, he found he could control a robotic arm. Surprisingly, after the monkey mastered controlling the robotic arm through its movements, it eventually learned it could control the arm by the thought of the movement alone. [10] Wearables such as neuroprosthetic limbs for assisting the disabled, and extending the potential of the able bodied are becoming a reality.

Humanistic Computing. Humanistic Intelligence is a term promulgated by Steve Mann who pioneered wearable computers. [8] He describes a framework in which wearable computers become integral to a harmonious interaction between our human body/mind. With 'critical design' in mind we created 'Blinklifier' (see Figure 1), a wearable computer that amplifies voluntary and involuntary eyelid movement into a visible light array. Blinklifier uses bio-data to directly interact with the computer. Although the light array can be consciously controlled, it is designed to avoid conscious interaction and instead directly amplify the body's expression. The experiments have implications for user interfaces. Blinklifier doesn't look like a computer; its electronic components are nearly invisible. The technology is a mash up with beauty products and fashion styling, into a consumable fashion image of the future. An Arduino microcontroller translates the metalized eyelashes' blinking movements into signals transmitted through conductive eyeliner (bare conductive ink) to light up LEDs embedded in the headdress. Facial expressions such as winking and blinking are gestures that are amplified in the headdress. Close your eye and you turn on the lights above that eye. Beyond such defined signals, the eyelids are constantly blinking which activates patterning arrays. Facial expressions are complex but easily recognized and naturally understood. The predominant model within HCI is to reduce expression into easily recognized signals, icons that directly represent functions. Alternately Blinklifier 'transfers the site of this interface from computer-embodied functions to open-ended, positive feedback loops 'connecting digital information with the entire affective register operative in the embodied viewer-participant... [] ...by bypassing investment in more effective technical 'solutions', it invests in the body's capacity to supplement technology – the potential it holds for 'collaborating' with the information presented by the interface in order to create images' in this case visual light patterns. [4] By their amplification through bodily worn devices, something usually overlooked in everyday life can become a rich source of knowledge, or open the potential for new ways of communicating our emotions and of understanding others. Coming back to the cinematic, Godfrey Reggio's 'Koyaanisqatsi' was a film that questioned human intervention into nature; that was in 1982 - today critical design is posing questions about the intervention of technology into the nature of humanity itself.

There are two types of design; 'affirmative' design which focuses on problem solving and market viability and 'critical' design which challenges pre-conceived notions of the way we live in the world, presenting alternatives models and thought provoking experiences. Reggio's work, like Blinklifier, does not try to affirm current trends, rather it challenges us to consider the human - technology relationship. Are we becoming reliant on electronic representations of the body's emotions to the extent that we are losing our innate capacity to register the complexity of natural emotional signals, or, is humanistic computing our natural technogenesis?

Empathy. As we approach Singularity, empathy becomes a primary distinguishing factor between comprehending the world through a data stream vs. a physical, tactile experience. Empathy seems to be a purely emotional response but research indicates human beings are ethical by nature. Empathy is less ephemeral than we previously thought; it can now be understood as a chemical phenomenon. We are homo-empathic as a biological trait to ensure our survival. In 1990, a group of neuroscientists discovered mirror neurons in the premotor cortex through which the motor activity of the brain can mirror the action of others. [5] This means that when we witness something happening to another our bodies mirror the emotion. These brain circuits can keep us from estranging ourselves from others. Indeed we do physically feel another's pain.

Computer based technology tools give us access to a broader range of information but at the same time act as a buffer zone between physical contact with the natural world. In this way they amplify some senses while at the same time nullifying others. Our ability to empathize with one another is desensitized when we live large portions of our lives in telematic fantasy world, removed from reality and framed by the screen. How does this change when technology leaves the screen and augments reality, when the separation between human and computer becomes seamlessly integrated? Three-dimensional body scanners enable fashion designers to work on their collections virtually and customers to visualize their wardrobe selections on their body before the garments are physically manufactured. These technologies are profoundly changing the fashion industry. Blurring the line between the physical and digital body, Hussein Chalayan in collaboration with Nick Knight presented his 2008 fashion collection to an admiring public audience in virtual catwalk shows. The models were projections walking down the runway.

These mediated fashions are indicative of what Guy Debord called 'the society of the spectacle', where authentic experience is replaced with its representation. [1] Debord was a member of the French 'Situationists' whose ideas about art and design attempted to engage with the moment. Like the Italian 'Futurists' they embraced motion, movement and dynamism and identified fashion as a prophetic social phenomenon, promulgating their vision of future society. The Futurists were from different art and design disciplines, but they shared a vision. Vincenzo Fani, known as Volt, produced fashion with fantastic titles in homage to mechanical modernity and speed, titles such as machine-gun woman or the antenna-radio-telegraph creature. Contemporary artists are likewise exploring our culture – the digital era.

2   Case Study - Prototype

Extending the Blinklifier experiment discussed above, and further exploring humanistic computing and feedback loops we designed Snoothood. A wearable pillow that surrounds the head and alerts the wearer through haptic vibration if he/she begins to snore, thus enabling his/her bedmate to continue to sleep undisturbed. Based on a skivvy design that holds sensors in place around the neck, embedded inside a padded sculpted hood is an Arduino single-board microcontroller and vibrator.

Aesthetically there are two design versions of Snoothood. The first is Snoothood Surreal that is shaped like an egg on its side, the large end of which acts as a pillow for side sleepers. Where the scale corresponds to the width of the shoulder to support the neck comfortably. If you prefer sleeping on your back there is also enough padding behind the head. The ears and eyes are totally enclosed blocking out light and sound. There is an opening around the nose, mouth and chin; imagine Edvard Munch's iconic painting 'The Scream' (1895) and you have an image of this opening. The fully felted headpiece has the appearance of a surrealist sculpture – an egg sitting atop a human figure. The Snoothood is created from handmade white felt. This white fluffy material and its sculptural form, evoke a metaphoric image of a cloud around the head, an apt reference for dreaming and sleep. The second version Snoothood Chinoiserie references the shape of ancient Chinese pillows. These were traditionally ceramic or wooden as well as textile and were blockish, bow or dog-bone shaped, cradling the neck. This style of neck pillow was used widely across Asia and as far south in the Asia Pacific region as Papua New Guinea where young men grew their hair to be used in felted head dresses worn by the tribal chief. Snoodhood Chinoiserie, like Surreal, is sculpted from white felt. The pillow form is connected to a balaclava style hood fully enclosing the head and neck. It has circular pads quilted over the ears and an elliptical opening around the mouth, nose and chin. To remove the headpiece the neck and yoke sections have been overlapped and the diagonal opening is modeled on the traditional cheongsam or changshan in mandarin known as qipao (chipao).

Fig. 1. Blinklifier 2012

Fig. 2. Prototype of Snoothood Surreal with hand made felt samples in foreground

Background. Sleep is a fundamental human need, and the lack of it can have deleterious consequences. Till Roenneberg from the Ludwig-Maximilians University uses the term 'social jetlag' to refer to a modern phenomenon. [12] Our body rhythms are set by three different clocks; the diurnal motion of the sun, the body's biological clock and the social clock. The biological clock is set by the daily exposure to sun light, but the social clock does not often correspond to the natural environmental one, in fact as we spend most of our modern lives indoors and in front of electronic light sources our body clocks tend to be set to stay awake increasingly later, while our social clocks (articulated by the alarm clock) are set earlier to deal with busy work schedules. Ultimately this results in a lack of sleep during the working week and overcompensating by sleeping in on weekends, this pattern is what Roenneberg calls social jetlag. Research has linked sleep to memory, learning, metabolism and the immune system. Sleep deprivation leads to health consequences such as obesity, hypertension, diabetes and cancer, and is linked to diseases such as chronic heart failure, chronic obstructive pulmonary disease and alzheimer's disease. [13] The holy grail of sleep analysis is the 'polysomnography', which involves overnight recording of sleep, respiration, cardiovascular function and movement through data from bio-signals such as EEC, EOG, EMG, airflow, respiration rates, oxygen saturation, snoring, ECG and body position. [11] This testing involves patients spending the night in well equipped sleep labs.

Examples of Similar Devices. There are many researchers working on sleep analysis. Mahsan Rofouei's wearable neck-cuff system, is a portable home use system for real-time monitoring and visualization of sleep data useful for detection of obstructive sleep apnea and other sleep disorders. The neck-cuff collects data that is sent by Bluetooth to a smart phone or nearby computer where specialists analyze it for diagnosis. The system components are an oximetry sensor, microphone, accelerometer and antenna. The advancement is in the portability of the unit, so that data collection can take place at home, which is less expensive and less of a disruption in the life of the patient than an overnight stay in a sleep lab. [9] IPhone released Lark, a wristband that performs actigraphy - a method of tracking motion during sleep. [14] The data is sent via Bluetooth to a smart phone and it can be viewed later. Like Snoothood, this system contains a vibrator as a silent alarm, but in their case it vibrates on the wrist rather than over the ear and at the time you set, rather than through bio-data signals as in our device. Similarly to Snoothood the output signal is silent vibration and the bedmates comfort is a consideration within the design concept.

The Somnus Sleep Shirt from Nyx Devices is a t-shirt that measures the movement in the abdominal cavity through stretch sensors on the back and front of a tight t-shirt. The movement of the abdomen is associated with breathing when in deep sleep. [15] Another smart t-shirt design by S. Puzzuoli has embedded textile sensors that survey ECG, breath and body movement. The data is preprocessed before transmission and then sent via Bluetooth to a recording device. [13] The examples above are all designed for home use, the Lark and Somnus provide a limited range of data that may not be reliable for medical diagnosis but have applications for home treatment and self-analysis.

Potential Applications. The objectives of the Snoothood project are not to diagnose medical conditions, but to see sleep deprivation as a societal problem. By presenting the Snoothood as the locus of discussion and prompting debate surrounding social jetlag and other sleep related conditions. Experiments are currently being conducted with volunteers who are invited to sleep with the Snoothood to test its effectiveness in alerting them to snoring and not disturbing their bedmate. They are interviewed before and after the experience to discuss their sleeping issues and gauge the hoods performance. A photographic portrait of the sleeper in bed wearing the hood provides visual documentation. An exhibition of a series of these photographs, printed at human scale, will provide a forum for a wider discussion on issues such as social jet lag. A short text statement hung beside each image will provide information about sleep issues drawn from individual responses.

Further Development – Relaxation and Creativity. There is a common saying when faced with a problem that you don't know how to solve which is to 'sleep on it'- meaning not to make your decision about a plan or idea immediately, but wait until the next day in order to have more time to think about it. A moment of insight often occurs just before we wake. It is common practice to keep a diary by the bed in order to record these 'aha' moments. Recent research posits that people are more likely to solve problems with insight if they are in a positive mood and that watching comedy videos for example could enhance this. Hypothetically this state of lightheartedness could also be induced by involvement in a humorous and playful art project such as ours. In order to test this hypothesis, we aim to track brain activity in search of the *aha* moment. Kounios and Beeman's research found 'distinct patterns of brain activity preceding problems solved with insight versus those solved analytically.

Before the presentation of problems to be solved with insight, EEG revealed greater neural activity over the temporal lobes of both cerebral hemispheres (i.e., around the ears) and over mid frontal cortex.' [6]

The next stage of the Snoothoods project is to enable analysis of individual sleeping habits. The data recorded during sleep is used to create bespoke personalized textiles as a visual record of an individual's sleep patterns. The data from the Snoothood sensors is used as live code to actuate motion in a series of rollers that draw thread through a dye bath. In addition to the sensors in the original prototype, three EEG sensors are added in the hood's lining, located above the cerebral hemispheres and over the mid frontal cortex. The weft-dying machine, is a purpose built contraption that lays alongside the bed with half the rollers parallel to the head of the bed and half parallel to the foot of the bed. They are connected in pairs by weft threads that are reeled slowly through dye baths. The brain and sound wave data is communicated live via Xbee through an Arduino processor that controls the speed of the rollers. Hence, the speed of motion is reflected in depth of the dye color, faster speed equals paler color as there is less time in the dye; the deeper the sleep the slower the rollers, the darker the color. Spikes in activity, such as waking, snoring or lighter sleep are visible as lighter sections of thread because the rollers are moving faster during these activities. Each night the thread is dyed and each day it is woven into a unique textile that becomes a visual and tactile record of the night before.

An extension of the interview process that took place in the earlier version of Snoothood is the addition of a dream diary kept by the bed for ease of recording ideas as they come to mind, or reflections upon waking. Results of this experiment are entirely speculative but it is imagined that through the transmogrification of fungible bio-data into other physical forms and visual patterns, new insights may be possible. This is a technique coined by Lewis Lancaster called *reverse predictive practice.*

The placement of this performance installation in an art gallery with window to street frontage, frames the work for the audience. Online documentation is telematic imagery that reaches out to virtual audiences; the production has involved stage sets and costumes, a Sci-Fi imagination that questions the ideologies and conditions of the period in history in which we live.

Examples of Similar Artworks. Janine Antoni's 'Slumber' is a performance-based installation in which the artist slept in the art gallery overnight attached to an EKG machine. Each morning she printed a graph of the data collected and then by day wove cloth from raw cotton fabric incorporating the pattern from the graph by weaving in strips of fabric torn from her nightdress. She has performed this work in a number of galleries: her dream blanket is now over 200 feet long.

Mischer' traxler's 'The Idea of a Tree' is a solar powered machine that translates the suns energy into colored thread using a similar system to ours. In this piece the work takes place in a trailer-like construction outdoors. The thread, a dye bath and a glue bath are mounted on a slowly elevating platform that moves at a continuous speed throughout the day. The dyed and sticky thread is pulled through the baths by a revolving plastic-form; the speed that it turns is dependent on the suns strength.

The result is a colored wrapped form that maps the sunlight of the day in its thickness and depth of color. When the form has dried it is removed from the plastic form and used in the production of a series of household products, such as stools and lampshades.

Snoothoods have similar aesthetic elements to the works above in regard to Antoni's theme of mapping sleep and weaving and Micher' traxler's method of dying using data feeds. Micher' traxler's work is similarly concerned with linking natural rhythms with mechanical /technological ones. The Snoothoods project is unique in its focus on the interface as an experiment in humanistic computing with a direct and unconscious connection between body and machine.

3   Conclusions

The challenge of fashion is that it celebrates the new through perpetual change. Originality is proof of progress; to be fashionable is to be desirable, yet at the same time fashion seeks consensus or legitimization to be accepted. It is this paradox that keeps fashion in motion. *Future- ism* is about looking forward, be it Volt, Madeleine Vionnet, Issey Miyake or Rei Kawakubo, creative designers are not only creating objects and clothing but conceiving new modes of living in the world.

Art and fashion can create an image of the future, just as the space-age-inspired futurism of Pierre Cardin's 1960's catwalk shows did in the past. These dreams pave the way for technologies and societies of the future.

But for user interfaces to become genuinely intelligent interactive systems, we must enable the development of interactive systems that can recognize unpredictable state changes, such as emotion, intention, desire, empathy, etc.

User interfaces of the future will acknowledge the relationship between people, places and things as emergent spaces that generate meaning through everyday activity and therefore ones in which users themselves act as co-designers. As we develop more intelligent technologies what is revealed is how little we understand of the complexity that makes up our own human form. By adopting an approach in which objects mediate human beings and human beings mediate objects we can acknowledge an alternative to the predominant separation of humans and things. The challenge is to fashion a future that is not based on predicting utopian visions but one that is responsive to changing conditions and acknowledges both mind and body.

Acknowledgments. The author notes that this paper is related to and was prepared simultaneously with "Fashion Futurism" by the author, which appeared in User Experience, Vol. 13, No. 2, 2013, pp. (in press). Blinklifier photo credit: Dicky Ma, Snoothoods photo credit: Patricia Flangan. We would like to acknowledge the support of the Wearables Lab, Academy of Visual Arts, Hong Kong Baptist University and sponsors Seeed Studios Shenzehn The Peoples Republic of China and The Woolmark Company Australia. Snoothoods was designed at Haptic InterFace 2012 in collaboration with Prof. Hugo Fuks from the PUKrio Departamento de Informática, Pontifícia Universidade Católica do Rio De Janeiro, Brasil.

References

1. Debord, G.: The Society of the Spectacle, translation by F., Perlman, and J., Supak. Black & Red (1970); rev. ed. (1977)
2. Gibson, W.: We Can't Know What the Future Will Bring, http://online.wsj.com/article/ SB10001424052970204425904578072641200585334.html
3. Greenfield, A.: Everyware: The dawning age of ubiquitous computing. New Riders, Berkeley (2006)
4. Hansen, M.B.N.: Affect as medium, or the 'digital-facial-image', pp. 151–165. D.A.P./Distributed Art Publishers [distributor], Rotterdam (2003), in art, doi:10.1177/14704129030022004
5. Keysers, C.: Mirror neurons – are we ethical by nature. In: Brockman, M. (ed.) What's next?: Dispatches on the Future of Science: Original Essays from a New Generation of Scientists. Vintage Books, New York (2009)
6. Kounios, J., Beeman, M.: The aha! moment: The cognitive neuroscience of insight. Current Directions in Psychological Science 18(4), 210 (2009), doi:10.1111/j.1467-8721.2009.01638.x
7. Kurzweil, R.: Singularity: Ubiquity interviews ray kurzweil, p. 1 (January 2006), doi:10.1145/1119621.1117663
8. Mann, S.: Wearable computing: Toward humanistic intelligence. IEEE Intelligent Systems 16(3), 10–15 (2001), doi:10.1109/5254.940020
9. Rofouei, M., Sinclair, M., Bittner, R., Blank, T., Saw, N., DeJean, G., Heffron, J.: A Non-invasive Wearable Neck-Cuff System for Real-Time Sleep Monitoring. In: Proc. BSN, pp. 156–161 (2011)
10. Nicolelis, M.: Beyond boundaries: The new neuroscience of connecting brains with machines–and how it will change our lives. Times Books, New York (2011)
11. Rajagopal, M.K., Villegas, R.: E., Towards Wearable Sleep Diagnostic Systems for Point-of-Care Applications. In: 2013 IEEE Point-of-Care Healthcare Technologies (PHT), Bangalore, India, January 16-18 (2013)
12. Roenneberg, T., Allebrandt, K., Merrow, M., Vetter, C.: Social jetlag and obesity. Current Biology 22(10), 939–943 (2012), doi:10.1016/j.cub.2012.03.038
13. Puzzuoli, S., Marcheschi, P., Bianchi, A.M., Mendez Garcia, M.O., De Rossi, D., Landini, L.: Remote Transmission and Analysis of Signals from Wearable Devices in Sleep Disorders Evaluation
14. Saenz, A.: iPhone Wristband Tracks Your Sleep, Vibrates You Awake, and Lets Your Mate Sleep In' Singularity Hub, http://singularityhub.com/2011/10/03/ iphone-wristband-tracks-your-sleep-vibrates-you-awake-and-lets-your-mate-sleep-in/
15. Ijem, W.: How well are you sleeping? Ask your pajamas, http://singularityhub.com/2011/06/27/ how-well-are-you-sleeping-ask-your-pajamas

Haptic Interface Aesthetics – 'Feedback Loops, Live Coding and How to Harness the Potential of Embodied Estrangement in Artistic Practices and Aesthetic Theories within Interface Culture'

Patricia J. Flanagan

Hong Kong Baptist University, Academy of Visual Arts, 5 Hereford Rd, Kowloon Tong,
Hong Kong SAR, P.R. China
tricia@triciaflanagan.com

Abstract. This article describes interface aesthetics from a trans-disciplinary perspective and reports on the findings of research into haptic interfaces through discussion of a series of prototypes and their potential as 'critical' design as opposed to 'affirmative design'. The article begins with analysis of the body - machine relationship positing human technogenesis as the framework for further discussion into humanistic computing; the use of feedback loops and live coding as artistic medium; and discusses outcome potentials such as reverse predictive practices and the notion of estrangement to stimulate thought and debate.

Keywords: Haptic Interface, Feedback Loops, Live Coding, Estrangement, Wearables Lab, Interface Aesthetics, Interface Culture, Wearables, Reverse Predictive Practices, Embodied Estrangement, User Interface, Human Computer Interaction, Human Technogenesis, Trans-disciplinary Research, Critical Design, Bamboo Whisper, Blinklifier, Snoothoods, Pulse Swarm.

1 Introduction

The Webster's Ninth Collegiate Dictionary defines an interface as 'a surface forming a common boundary of two bodies, spaces, phases.'

Scanning the plethora of citations across a range of dictionaries the term is used in many contexts including chemical, biological and sociological.

This article, 'Haptic Interface aesthetics: feedback loops, live coding and how to harness the potential of embodied estrangement in artistic practices and aesthetic theories within interface culture' is informed by research as principle investigator of the Haptic InterFace (HIF) project and current work as Assistant Professor and director of The Wearables Lab, a new trans-disciplinary lab for innovation, at the Academy of Visual Arts at Hong Kong Baptist University in the Special Administrative Region of the Peoples Republic of China.

A. Marcus (Ed.): DUXU/HCII 2013, Part I, LNCS 8012, pp. 58–67, 2013.
© Springer-Verlag Berlin Heidelberg 2013

2   The Expanded Field of Interface Aesthetics

Human-computer interaction studies have largely focused on the screen interface and concern themselves with how humans interface with information and computer technology (ICT) systems, focusing on issues such as how we approach bandwidth, processor speed and storage capacity, and gauging their success on user satisfaction statistics.

A contemporary approach to human-computer interaction could be viewed as an inversion of this; as design ICT systems are increasingly considering how computers approach humans. With the radical miniaturization of electronics, sensors and actuators combined with bio- and nano-technologies and global digital networks, information is now more than ever before directly embedded into everything imaginable. The bonds between human and computer are merging in ways that were previously only the dreams of science fiction. It is within this 'human-computer-confluence' that this paper considers an expanded field of interface aesthetics, one in which haptic interfaces have become the most interesting resource for the scope of design explorations.

Using the term 'haptic interface' is problematic and so as not to mislead the reader, it would be helpful to define my use of it here.

Since the beginning of 'interface aesthetics' in experimental digital art in the 1960's, the term haptic was adopted by game design engineers to refer to a very specific set of parameters such as rumble packs, mouse, keyboard, i.e. tools to communicate with the screen based information of the game.

Media studies have historically promulgated 'interface' synonymously to refer to 'human-to-software interfaces'. Brenda Laurel's 'The Art of Human-Computer Interface Design' (1990) [9] and Lev Manovich's 'The Interface as a new Aesthetic Category' (2000) [11] both contain many examples of this phenomenon. Manovich's work is to be applauded for its analysis of context ie: the relationship between subject, object and medium, but as Florian Cramer points out, his use of the term 'interface' could be replaced with 'media', and 'aesthetics' for 'phenomenology', or in other words the interface as machine and aesthetics as human. Reinforcing this Cartesian dichotomy is the common categorization of a programming interface (API) as opposed to a user interface (UI). [5] This inherent duality is unproductive to the scope of this article, which rather considers a future condition in which end users are extended programmers and programmers are users.

If we step outside disciplines we can further broaden our understanding. For example within Humanities 'interface' is a term used generally to refer to a common boundary. Whether that boundary is physical, visible, tactile or tangible, the profusion of interfaces in daily life means there is clearly a social dimension active within human-computer interfaces that effects cultural practices in ways that go well beyond the traditional user seated before a computer screen.

The 'human-computer-confluence' can be reimagined through the relative fluidity of notions such as 'live coding' and 'feedback loops', in which the programming interface is itself a user interface, and in terms of their potentiality in which case the artists work involves sculpting the interface/interaction – playing in the fluid transmogrification of space between programmer and user, designer and consumer. '…interface does not stop at the computer's surface but goes beyond the buttons and reaches 'back' into history, and 'through' to the human senses and perception, 'behind' the concept of the interface, 'down' into the machine, 'out' into society and culture.'[1]

It is the aesthetics of this boundary that I consider the *haptic interface*.

3   Trans-Disciplinary Research Methodology

Across all disciplines the potential of interface aesthetics is increasingly expanding through collaboration and exploration at the conjuncture of aesthetic theories and working methodologies. This combined with the mash-up of new and old technologies from both analogue and digital realms and experiments in haptic and tactile interfaces creates new and unexpected experiences. [1].

The artistic methods proposed in this research stem from trans-disciplinary praxis, and consider the aesthetic and emotional experience of the wearer as primary to pragmatic and functional enhancements.

The research took place in the Wearables lab and references a broad range of methodologies that are intrinsically intertwined in the creation of prototypes (e.g. Design practice, computer science, systems theories, media arts, performance, sculpture, engineering and the humanities). The methods generically embrace 'process as research' and support collaborative practice in the generation of ideas in an interdisciplinary knowledge domain.

The HIF project brought a group of twenty professionals and creative thinkers from many backgrounds and cultures together for an intensive ten-day workshop to explore haptic interfaces. The resulting prototypes were presented as a pop up exhibition within the larger context of a curated exhibition of selected wearable works titled 'Haptic InterFace' at the Koo Ming Kown Exhibition Gallery, Kowloon Tong, Hong Kong.

Following are descriptions of some of the prototypes developed, collaborators names are in brackets, for more information about HIF visit http://hapticinterface.hkbu.edu.hk.

4   Prototypes and Directions for Future Work

Imagine wearing shoes that enable you to physically sense an awareness of another person walking. Sensors on the bottom of your shoes communicate via microcontrollers through smartphones to actuators located on top of another wearer's shoes. When that person sits to rest, you will feel the weight lift. When they run, you feel increased pressure and faster rhythm of the activity and visa versa, they can feel you too. People wearing the prototype shoes, and strangely sensing each other's activity, are currently walking around Trier in Germany, and Brisbane in Australia.

---

[1] (Andersen & Pold, 2010) p.9.

An odd sense of awareness of the body rhythms of another person emerges in the mind of the partners. In this application the locations highlight the global diurnal disjuncture, for example dancing at a nightclub overlaps an early morning walk. (J. Donavan, D. Gilgen,)

Imagine a second skin interface that tangibly communicates through touch. When a New Zealand weaver, Hong Kong fashion designer and Portuguese media engineer put their heads together the result was a touch-sensitive kinetic dress that reacts, releasing a swarm of 'butterflies' to flutter around the wearer's neck. 'Nitinol' shape memory wire opens the collar and enables featherweight PVC butterflies to emerge, when the memory wire cools it relaxes, causing the collar to close again enveloping the butterflies. Life and theatre are poetically intertwined in this expressive garment. (M. Chueng, S. Coelho, K. Henson).

By wearing specially designed white leather gauntlets, with ostrich feather plumage highlighted by a diffused pulsating red light, two people can sense each other's presence even when they are out of visible range. The prototype gauntlets read the pulse of one person and send it as vibration to the other as haptic feedback. The proximity of the communication is, near field in contrast to the smart shoes mentioned above.

In informal trials, a couple wearing the gauntlets in a domestic environment reported that there was an enhanced sense of connection between them supported by a subtle awareness that the other was within proximity, before they approached the boundaries of being seen they were felt.

This experience sounds like a physical manifestation of the film editor's trick of overlaying 'fade in/out' to join spliced footage without the viewer experiencing any visual jolt. This is often done aurally by overlaying the audio from an image so that it can be heard just before the corresponding vision, cushioning the transition. In this prototype the experience is through haptic means. It would be difficult to surprise somebody if you could sense their pulse just before they appeared.

Further investigation could test the effect on the body's biorhythms with prolonged use in cohabitation. Perhaps with greater implications, the production of many cuffs and their trial with larger groups will enable exploration of 'swarm behavior.' [5] (G. Sade, P. Bracks, D. Brough) For more information on this project visit http://kuuki.com.au/.

5   Analysis

The Haptic Interface workshop provided a space, both physically and mentally for participants to step outside their daily professions and spend focused time reflecting on one theme and exploring it through hands on experimentation and praxis. Creativity was enhanced by participant initiated 'circle workshops' in quick response to a problem when it arose. This structure was embedded into the program and designed to maximize skill and knowledge sharing. Another contributing factor was the careful selection of a dynamic mix of participants with differing skills sets, cultures and experience and an induction into the trans-disciplinary and multi-cultural work environment. In this, everyone works with different languages, methodologies and has different ideas and expectations about outcomes. As the introduction alluded, even the terminology provides fodder for contentious debate. An open-minded attitude enables progress, and in fact, it is at the point where differing perspectives collide that sparks of creative ideas emerge. The misunderstanding and misinterpretations provide richness to the workshop forum that is both challenging and fruitful.

Projects such as these are reimagining our perception of time and space and our presence within it. Chris Salter suggests 'human and technical beings and processes are so intimately bound up in a conglomeration of relations that it makes it difficult, if not impossible to tease out separate essences for each.'[2]

Bernard Stiegler [14], Mark Hansen [7] and N. Katherine Hayles [8] would agree, they claim the relationship of human and machine to be fundamental to our natural evolution as a species, and propose human 'technogenesis'[3] as a framework with which to deconstruct and rethink the body-technology binary.

The tools we work with mediate our relationship with the physical materials that the real world is made of. When you work with your hands on a medium you gain an inherent understanding of the properties of that material that are difficult to explain or learn by means other than doing it.

Hand tools act as extensions of the body, their use often involves gestures that the body learns to work with, without conscious thought an idea can flow from the mind through the hands into a work of sculpture for example.

Mechanical tools usually declare their function by their physical structure. There is a mechanical logic at work when you see the operation of a typewriter or a bicycle that you can imagine by looking at the design.

With digital tools this mechanical logic has become invisible. There is no correlation between the material presence of the machine and its potential, which now depends on a network of divergent activities, differing relations between the machine and software packages, 'an ontology of techniques – that assumes the original relatedness between the material and the immaterial as its condition of possibility.'[4]

The fungibility of code enables fluid transformation between media. The representation of information in slightly altered states, or new forms, underlie the artistic tactics employed in the projects described in the case studies.

6   Case Studies

The author collaborated on four projects, which shall be briefly introduced and then the focus will turn to one project for a more in detailed case study. 'Blinklifier' is a wearable computer that amplifies eyelid movements into a visible light array. It uses bio-data directly to interact with the computer, although it can be consciously

---

[2] (Salter, 2010) p.xxxiv.
[3] The belief that humans and technics are coevolving.
[4] (Benjamin, 2005)p.229.

controlled, it is designed to avoid conscious interaction and instead directly amplify the body's expression. Facial expressions are complex but easily recognized and naturally understood. By their amplification through bodily worn devices, something usually overlooked in everyday life can become a rich source of knowledge, or open potential for new ways of communicating our emotions and of understanding others. [6] Details of this project are published in the article.

Extending this research we designed the 'Snoothoods', which are wearable pillows that surround the head and alert the wearer if he/she begins to snore. Based on a skivvy design around the neck that holds sensors in place, an Arduino single-board microcontroller and vibrator are embedded inside a padded sculpted hood.

Two versions were designed, a Western and an Asian; the first is shaped like an egg laid on its side. This fully felted headpiece has the appearance of a surrealist sculpture, made from white felt, metaphorically evoking a cloud as an apt reference for dreaming and sleep. The second draws on the form of a traditional Chinese pillow, cushioning the back of the neck. This bow shaped form is permanently affixed to the neck and hood. (Flanagan, P. Vega, K., Fuks, H.) The aims and objectives of this project are expounded in the article 'Future Fashion – at the interface' also found in this volume so it will not be further discussed here.

'Peripatetic people' is an installation that explores virtual reality through the construction of a series of analogue machines that present 3D visual representations of people. Simple electronic input devices such as motion sensors and output speakers with mp3 players create an immersive environment for audiences to interact with virtual people in a room that on first glance is filled with mechanical apparatus and lights. Upon closer inspection it is possible to look in macro detail at a persons body, the wrinkles of their skin, the weathered leather of their shoes, the rings on their fingers, the proximity to which breaks with conventional rules of privacy. The visitor becomes voyeur, but at the same time it is their presence that sets the work in motion, as the virtual people discuss their ideas of boundaries and borders the visitor is forced to consider their own.

Common to both of these projects is' what Steven Mann terms 'humanistic computing'. The concept of direct communication between human and computer without involving conscious thought, exploring the notion of connection directly between bio data and techno data. [10] To further explore humanistic computing, bio data and experiment with feedback loops we created 'bamboo whisper'. A set of wicker wearable microcontrollers that communicate through the reconfiguration of data: from spoken words into visual movement and percussive sound. The hats are reminiscent of elongated Victorian bonnets: they measure the volume from the voice of one wearer and amplify it into kinetic energy in the other's bonnet. One person experiences the voice of the other visually, through the movement of the brim above her eyes, and aurally through the chattering noise that the movement creates in the bamboo reeds from which the hat is constructed.

The hat vibrates causing the brim sticks to chatter; in this way the voice is translated into a kind of whisper. Each hat responds to the other, engaging the wearers in an immersive, interactive, haptic, audio-visual experience. Both devices incorporate an electronic system powered by an Arduino Lilypad. Via integrated microphones and XBee radio the voice of one wearer is transmitted into movement and sound of the brim sticks and vibration felt on the other wearers neck.

In this work as in 'blinklifier' above the computer components and circuits are not hidden but barely visible. The circuitry has been inlaid into the structure of the felt at manufacture and onto the surface of the bamboo. The result is a product that seamlessly integrates traditional craftsmanship with what could be described as embodied magical capabilities.

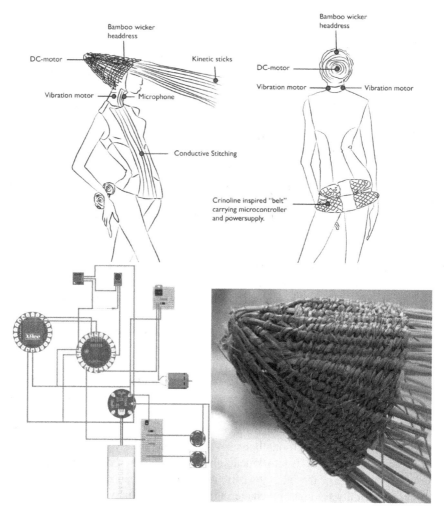

Fig. 1. Bamboo Whisper components and their locations, plus detail of weaving structure. (Illustration: Flanagan, Frankjaer).

7   Reverse Predictive Practices

In response to increased computing power and speed, artists are drawing on live data as a medium in their work to create responsive, ever-changing, experience environments. As we store ever-increasing amounts of digital data and our retrieval systems are capable of finding thousands of examples in response to any keyword there is a need to seek the most efficient method of communicating the presence and meaning of a wide range of analytic patterns.

Speaking at the NODEM conference in Hong Kong Prof. Lewis Lancaster gave a lecture called 'Europeana and the Future of the Archive' in which he boldly declared that he had to give up writing in order to see it. His research into reverse predictive practices and imaging data is inspirational. A very effective way to analyze large amounts of data is through its visualization. His experiments with reverse predictive practices grew out of a mass of data that was correlated through scanning of textual corpora such as canonical texts, archival documents and digital records of artifacts.

By changing natural language into abstract images, for example text characters into blue dots, the data can display word occurrence and patterning by tonal and density changes. In this way anomalous patterning found in past data sources can express new meanings and unprecedented readings. In Lancaster's work one such anomaly in patterning revealed that men travelled more widely that women during the period in Asian history that the text was written. The focus becomes one of asking the right questions in response to data evidence that is visually apparent. Rather than a codex system as in previously established methods of dissemination, the revelations that become apparent are specifically tied to the digital.

In Bamboo Whisper verbal language becomes a rhythmic and visual pattern. It will be interesting to examine how this new media can be interpreted and provide insight in a reverse predictive sense into the original language, speaker, content and context. I am encouraged by a previous project in which I recorded audio from speakers discussing their relationship to the ocean or rivers. Interviews took around the world place in Italian, German and English, which became part of an interactive installation called Preserved Fish that has visited audiences in Europe and Australia and will travel to Hong Kong Maritime Museum in 2014. To maintain a sense of cultural integrity in the work it was decided to play the soundscapes using the original voice. A short excerpt is translated and available, but the experience overwhelmingly is a musical one. A sense of richness emerges in the appreciation of individual culture through the rhythms and the intonation of its language in a way that would be impossible if one was to focus on the translation of individual words.

Reverse predictive practice is just one example of the potential of the expanded field of interface aesthetics through the fungibility of digital data.

8   Conclusion and Future Work

The objectives of our design products are open to conjecture. Rather than the traditional aim of design to solve set problems, affirm consumer behavior, and prove validity of product for market, our aim is to produce 'critical' design that poses carefully crafted questions that break away from the media representation of reality and challenge the way we experience the world by estranging perception and presenting reality askew. Critical design will never be popular in mainstream culture and therefore will often remain as bespoke individual works that challenge audiences to think. Affirmative design on the other hand is fundamentally unsustainable.

The participant's prototypes from the Haptic InterFace workshop will be further developed and the final results exhibited 12 months after the initial workshop. At that time further analysis of the results will be conducted.

All interfaces involve the translation of signs and signals and as such, interfaces are as key to the inner-workings of the computer as they are to our sense perception of the techno-savvy contemporary world.

In the knowledge that the way we perceive our contemporary environment is through these interfaces, our objectives are that of stimulating discussion, posing questions and generating dialogue. 'The designer becomes the coauthor of the experience[5] and the artists role is no longer that of the object maker but has become one of social agent. The focus on 'sign and object' has evolved to 'signal and software'. The objectives are in terms of 'social sculpture' [3] and the interface is in terms of 'relational aesthetics' [4].

Acknowledgments. I would like to thank all the workshop participants and acknowledge the support of Hong Kong Baptist University Academy of Visual Arts and the Wearables Lab workshop sponsors Seeed Studios Shenzhen and The Woolmark Company Australia. Bamboo Whisper was developed in collaboration with Raune Frankjaer of Department of Design at the University of Applied Sciences in Trier/Germany. Blinklifier was developed in collaboration with Katia Vega of Department of Informatics, PUC-Rio, Brazil, Snoothoods were developed in collaboration with Katia Vega and Prof. Hugo Fuks of Department of Informatics, PUC-Rio, Brazil.

References

1. Andersen, C.U., Pold, S.: Interface criticism: Aesthetics beyond the buttons. Aarhus University Press, Aarhus [Denmark] (2010)
2. Benjamin, A.E.: Plurality of actions: Notes on an ontology of techniques. In: Benjamin, A.E., Brouwer, J. (eds.) ARt & D: Research and development in art, pp. 224–229. D.A.P./Distributed Art Publishers, Rotterdam (2005)
3. Beuys, J.: Speech made during live satellite telecast of opening of documenta 6, (June 16, 1977)
4. Bourriaud, N.: Relational aesthetics. Les Presses du Réel, France (2002)
5. Cramer, F.: What is interface aesthetics, or what could it be (not)? In: Andersen, C.U., Pold, S. (eds.) Interface Criticism: Aesthetics Beyond Buttons, pp. 117–117. Aarhus University Press, Aarhus (2010)

---

[5] Raby, F. (2003). Design noir: The secret life of electronic objects. In G. Stocker, C. Schöpf & A. (. Ars Electronica Linz (Eds.), (). Ostfildern-Ruit, Germany: Hatje Cantz.

6. Flanagan, P., Vega, K.: Blinklifier: The power of feedback loops for amplifying expressions through bodily worn objects. In: 10th Asia Pacific Conference on Computer Human Interaction (APCHI 2012), Matsue, Japan (August 2012)
7. Hansen, M.: Embodiment: The machinic and the human. In: Benjamin, A.E., Brouwer, J. (eds.) ARt & D: Research and development in art, pp. 151–165. D.A.P./Distributed Art Publishers [distributor], Rotterdam (2005)
8. Hayles, N.K.: How we think: Digital media and contemporary technogenesis. The University of Chicago Press, Chicago (2012)
9. Laurel, B., Mountford, S.J.: The art of human-computer interface design. Addison-Wesley Pub. Co., Reading (1990)
10. Mann, S.: Wearable computing: Toward humanistic intelligence. IEEE Intelligent Systems 16(3), 10–15 (2001), doi:10.1109/5254.940020
11. Manovich, L.: The Interface as a New Aesthetic Category, http://www.voyd.com/ttlg/textual/manovichtext.htm (accessed March 1, 2013)
12. Raby, F.: Design noir: The secret life of electronic objects. In: Stocker, G., Schöpf, C., Linz, A.A.E. (eds.) Hatje Cantz, Ostfildern-Ruit (2003)
13. Salter, C.: Entangled: Technology and the transformation of performance. MIT Press, Cambridge (1967)
14. Stiegler, B.: Technics and time. Stanford University Press, Stanford (1998)

Is Reality Real? Thoughts and Conjectures about Culture, Self, Intersubjectivity and Parallel Worlds in Digital Technologies

Ana Carol Pontes de França[1], Marcelo Márcio Soares[1],
and Luciano Rogério de Lemos Meira[2]

[1] Post graduate Program in Design, Federal University of Pernambuco, Brazil
[2] Post graduate Program in Cognitive Psychology,
Federal University of Pernambuco, Brazil
acpsicologa@gmail.com, marcelo2@nlink.com,
luciano@meira.com

Abstract. This article makes a brief foray into state-of-the-art in Virtual Reality technologies and into semiotic studies in the field of Human-Computer Interaction in order to invite the reader to think about human´s current situation. From this perspective, we shall seek to raise new questions about the forms of communication and interaction mediated by digital technologies. These forms deal with the fact of fiction and non-fiction going hand-in-hand, taking shape in images which, and in virtual beings who, co-inhabit both our imagination and the scenarios which comprise the parallel worlds of virtual environments. This thinking is indispensable for us to understand, for example, the implications of these changes on children and young people development and how we conceive education in today´s world. Therefore, this article is based on: 1) studies that led to the dissertation entitled *Digital Self: exploring the "I" construction on the Internet*, submitted to the Post graduate Program in Cognitive Psychology at the Federal University of Pernambuco, 2) discussions kindled at the Laboratory of Interactional Analysis and Videography, which is linked to the Post graduate Program in Cognitive Psychology, and 3) discussions and projects developed in partnership between the Center for Informatics, Department of Design and Human Factors Researchers at Federal University of Pernambuco.

Keywords: Virtual Reality (VR), Human-Computer Interaction, Semiotics, Sense of Self.

1 Introduction

With the emergence of Virtual Reality and the increasingly frequent presence of digital technologies in everyday life, some considerations and ways to question the world we live in have become imperative and ever more frequent.

Questions like: does reality exist? Are we who think we are? Could we be living in a Matrix? In the contemporary world what cannot be taken for a simulation? Could it be that our lives are governed by us, or are we at the mercy of a computer program

A. Marcus (Ed.): DUXU/HCII 2013, Part I, LNCS 8012, pp. 68–73, 2013.

that controls our minds? Are we of flesh and blood or could our likenesses be a mental projection of our digital "I"? Could it be that we are "awake", aware of what is happening to us? Or could it be that we have fallen asleep, having given ourselves over to our wishes, while machines dominate the world and feed themselves on our energies, and our being?

The idea of parallel virtual worlds counterpointing the idea of reality as something that is out there, independent of us, marks an evolutionary moment in the history of the human race in which we have become ever more dependent on digital technologies, this being a special feature that has arisen from the changes observed, given the increasingly frequent and extensive presence of Virtual Reality and digital technologies in our lives.

In general, we are immersed more and more in digital culture so that we might experiment with and experience the Internet and cyberspace as real phenomena that affect our lives and our subjectivities, our ways of being and of living in society.

In this perspective, we have started to be influenced by technological devices and digital environments from the moment we get up until bedtime in ways to have more often fiction and imagination in our everyday life.

In order to better illustrate the above statement, let us take as an example a typical day in the everyday routine of screens, displays and icons with which we live: a day filled of updating online profiles on social networks and virtual communities of practice focused on education, work or even entertainment. Situations in which any commercial designation may well no longer to make sense, since the supposed "subscribers", "clients" or "users", are involved in weaving a plot that intertwines their on-line and off-line lives and destinies in order to give meaning to life and actions in the world doing reference to the forms of life that they are very familiar in face-to-face world [1, 2, 3].

In this sense, the convergence and the technological advances of the resources of audio, video, computing, and imaging make it possible for users to immerse themselves in three-dimensional virtual environments, which have texture, mass and dynamic interactions, in order not only to dive in an illusion, but to contextually undergo the experience that lead to the sensation of physical involvement.

2   But finally, What Is Virtual Reality (VR)?

In general, Virtual Reality (VR) is a term that is applied to computer-simulated environments. As the definition itself suggests, these environments simulate physical presence in both the physical and virtual environments.

Also known for describing a wide variety of applications frequently associated with 3-D, immersive and visual environments, experiences in Virtual Reality arise from sense-perceptual experiences that cover visual, auditory, tactile and kinesthetic experiences by means of multimodal and stereoscopic devices or three-dimensional images that enable users to step into and interact in parallel worlds.

Originally conceived to serve both military purposes as for educational, work, leisure and entertainment situations, Virtual Reality can create situations and provide experiences similar to those existing in the physical world, and yet it may differ from "reality" by creating simulations of fictitious and even unlikely situations.

3   Culture and Subjectivity in Virtual Environments

In order to better understand how interactions, communications and the human processes of subjectification occur in virtual environments, we make a link to an integrative perspective that considers the real and virtual as continuous.

According to de França [2], "in this context, paradoxically, digital culture allows us to experience our own identity as being fluid, multiple and complex by supporting our practices with resources that allow us to compensate the lack of a physical body".

To do so, we resort to a theoretical-conceptual approach that focuses on a conception of a dialogic subject [4, 5, 6, 7, 8, 9, 10, 11] and of an interactional subject [12, 13, 14, 15] which is rescued form the polysemic flow - or from a range of possible meanings and senses – by the narrative form of how people talk about themselves [16, 17].

In these terms, we stress the importance of language in the representation of oneself in virtual environments, which confers on a computational artifact the property of operating as an extension of the individual's cognition beyond the body.

4   Self, Intersubjectivity and Semiotic Mediation

With paradigms changes, modern conceptions grant space to the socio-cultural-historical perspective that emphasizes language and narrative constructions, giving a new contour to the notions of self and reality.

This reality, permeated by what is symbolic, is no longer independent of the cognoscent subject, since historical and situational reflection is adopted as the kernel of psychological activity [5, 6, 13, 11, 8, 9].

In this framework, semiotic mediation gains a place of prominence. Based on intersubjective actions, semiotic mediation confers a primary and central aspect to signs, which allows us to assign a personal meaning to the objects with which we relate ourselves, bearing in mind that, by itself, the object does not have an intrinsic character that acts on the individual [12].

Founded on this perspective, we emphasize the pragmatic aspect of communication to the detriment of a watertight, crystallized structure, which means we consider the notion of genesis involved in an uninterrupted dialogic process.

In this process, intersubjectivity is related to our awareness of others as well as to an orientation to the other that allows communication be established from the beginning of life [7].

Taking these considerations as a starting point, we join this to a perspective that characterizes the self as a discursive, social and narratively structured construction that emerges and develops in the course of the dialogic sequences of action, established by interlocutors located in time and space.

In this construction, new versions of self are possible thanks to semiotic mediation, the influences of social norms that regulate our actions and the specific situations in which they occur.

These new contours of the self are marked in the moments of interaction between the participants, from the way that people describe themselves and are described while they dialogue with each other's, which makes it vital for us to consider the message frameworks by the human action of making sense.

Thus, in the continuous flow of communicative action, the person, the user of the discourse [18], reveals himself/herself to be a unique being, with differentiated characteristics and powers and with a history that is distinct from those whom he/she considers as his/her peers; a being who acts together with many others in different face-to-face and virtual scenarios, wherever he/she transits while simultaneously he/she shows himself/herself to respond and to be responsible vis-à-vis to the others.

In this case, we consider the Self as an embodied reason, simultaneously one and multiple, a discursive construction that confers presence on all those that are significant at the time, even in cases where these others are metaphorically incorporated into the context [19, 20].

Thinking about Self in these terms lead us to consider that the emergence and development of a sense of continuity do not correspond to an exclusively individual movement, but to a situational and dynamic dialogical phenomenon that involves the other parties that make up the system.

5   User-Centred Design and the Conception of Environments Based on Virtual Reality (VR)

To produce a useful and easy to use system is always a challenge, especially if we want to create environments based on Virtual Reality (VR), as such environments are created for people, flesh and blood users, with goals, wishes and expectations, so much so that during the development process of a product, the focus must not be restricted to the technology itself, but may shall also consider the active participation of the user [21].

In other words, as the term itself suggests, in User-Centered Design, the focus of the development process is on the user who collaborates in trying to ensure that the product could be more widely accepted and received by other users.

Nevertheless, why the focus on the user? Because according to Preece, Rogers and Sharp [21], "a well designed system should extract human skills and judgments to the maximum extent and be directly relevant to the job in question. It should support users, and not limit their actions. All this implies much less technique and more philosophy."

In this perspective, the ethnographic method is often used, although the interpretation and presentation of data remains a challenge for the design.

6   Conclusion

The increasing spread of digital technologies based on Virtual Reality throws up socio-cultural implications never seen before in human history.

Face the current situation, Ergonomics and usability researchers, dedicated to analyzing systems with focus on users, need to take into consideration that people leave their marks and style while interacting in virtual environments.

Accordingly, to study users' needs requires thinking about every possible requirement, considering even the desires and experiences of users. Therefore, it is important to talk to users about their experiences to propose Virtual Reality systems that resemble the expectations of society.

Finally we caution that the mere presence of technology does not guarantee an active and effective collaboration, marked by interactional and dialogical potential in order to develop social participation, self-knowledge, the development of individual and group identity as well as the production of content and critical attitude to face the problems and challenges of the contemporary world.

References

1. de França, A.C.P.: Self Digital: explorações acerca da construção do "eu" na internet. In: Dissertação de Mestrado, UFPE, Recife (2008)
2. de França, A.C.P.: Cultura digital, intersubjetividade e colaboração. In: VII Congresso Internacional de Tecnologia na Educação. Recife/PE. VII Congresso Internacional de Tecnologia na Educação: Educação, Trabalho e Humanismo, pp. 114–117 (2009a)
3. de França, A.C.P.: Subjetividade, protagonismo e autoria na internet. Cultura Garança 6, 115–120 (2009b)
4. Mead, J.: Mind, self and society from the standpoint of a social behaviorist. University of Chicago, Chicago (1934),
   http://spartan.ac.brocku.ca/~lward/Mead/pubs2/mindself
   (accessed in Febraury 2007)
5. Bakhtin, M.: Marxismo e filosofia da linguagem. Annablume/Hucitec, São Paulo (2002a)
6. Bakhtin, M.: Problemas da póetica de Dostoievski. Forense Universitária, Rio de Janeiro (2002b)
7. Lyra, M.C.D.P.: O modelo EEA para a investigação da emergência e desenvolvimento da comunicação e do self: bases conceituais e fundamentos teóricometodológicos. Estudos de Psicologia 11(1), 25–33 (2006)
8. Valsiner, J.: Temporal integration of structures within the Dialogical Self. In: Keynote Lecture at the 3rd International Conference on Dialogical Self. Warsaw (August 28, 2004)
9. Valsiner, J.: Scaffolding within the structure of Dialogical Self: Hierarquical dynamics of semiotic mediation. New Ideas in Psychology 23, 197–206 (2005)
10. Hermans, H.J.M., Hermans-Jansen, E.: Self narratives:the construction of meaning in psychotherapy. The Guilford Press, New York (1995)
11. Hermans, H.: The dialogical self: Toward a theory of personal and cultural positioning. Culture & Psychology 7(3), 243–281 (2001)

12. Bezerra, H., Meira, L.: Zona de Desenvolvimento Proximal: Interfaces com os processos de intersubjetivação. In: Meira, L., Spinillo, A.G. (eds.) Psicologia Cognitiva: Cultura, Desenvolvimento e Aprendizagem, Universitária da UFPE, Recife (2006)
13. Peres, F.: Diálogo e autoria:do desenvolvimento ao uso de sistemas de informação. In: Tese de Doutorado, UFPE, Psicologia Cognitiva, Recife (2007)
14. Melo, P.H.F.: Uma perspectiva semiótico-interacional da emergência e manutenção de redes sociais na Internet. Dissertação de Mestrado. Programa de Pós-Graduação em Psicologia Cognitiva UFPE (2007)
15. Oliveira, R.: Uso de marcas verbais para os aspectos não-verbais da conversação em salas de bate-papo na internet.Dissertação de mestrado. Programa de Pós-Graduação em Psicologia Cognitiva UFPE (2007)
16. Chandler, M.: Surviving in time:the persistence of identity in this culture and that. Culture & Psychology 6(2), 209–231 (2000)
17. Chandler, M., et al.: Personal persistence, Identity Development, and Suicide: A Study of Native and Non-native North American Adolescents. Monographs of the Society for Research in Child Development (April 2003)
18. Guanaes, C., Japur, M.: Construcionismo social e metapsicologia:um diálogo sobre o conceito de Self. Psicologia: Teoria e Pesquisa 19(2), 135–143 (2003)
19. Lakoff, G., Johnson, M.: Metaphors we live by. University of Chicago, Chicago (1980)
20. Lakoff, G., Johnson, M.: Who are we? In: Philosophy in the flesh: the embodied mind and its challenge to western thought. Basic Books, New York (1999)
21. Preece, J., Rogers, Y., Sharp, H.: Design de interação – Além da interação homem-computador. Bookman, Porto Alegre (2005)

The Lack of Subjective Experience in Hybrid Intelligent Agents in Interactive Storytelling

Olivier Guy and Ronan Champagnat

Université La Rochelle/L3i
Pôle Science et Technologie
17042 La Rochelle, France
olsat@yahoo.com, ronan.champagnat@univ-lr.fr

Abstract. We need a model for non-player characters (NPCs) in interactive storytelling, and recent advances in neurocognitive science have not brought to a close the controversies of the subjective and objective experience being both verses of the same coin. The NPCs are still made desperately from a 'third party' point f view, the exact opposite of the subjective experience, while we want to show that this method only produces weaker user experience. This is a hard problem, described by David Chalmers in the philosophy of the mind: we know what it is to be ourselves, we know what the outside world looks like from our point of view, but we have no idea what it is to be something, or even more difficult, someone else. Our goal as in Crawford is to reach the meaningful interaction with the NPC and we want to prove that this may not be attained through third party cognitive models. As a prospective we invite the developers to work on psychodynamic psychology. Moreover, French psychodynamics are a valuable intercultural tool spread in the entire Latin world and can be powerful to describe, heal, and treat human features, while Fodor's followers have exclusive theoretical access to our game models. It is a good way to introduce diversity in our community.

1 Introduction

This work takes place among the dialectics of subjective experience, by opposition to the objective experience reflected mostly in the field of the philosophy of the mind. There is a major gap in the description of the mind with on the one hand the experience of the subject and the other hand what is described by a third party — the objective experience. These problems have been brought to light by papers such as `What is it like to be a bat?' by Thomas Nagel, [Nagel 1974] which explains no matter how deep we might know how the brain and perceptual system of bat works, we have no idea what it is to be one — hence the title. We may have many different models — and we will speak in-depth of a few of them later- for the human agent, we lack the subjective side of the problem.

The notion of pre-reflective self-consciousness is related to the idea that experiences have a subjective 'feel' to them, a certain -phenomenal- quality of 'what it is like' or what it 'feels' like to have them. As it is usually expressed outside of

A. Marcus (Ed.): DUXU/HCII 2013, Part I, LNCS 8012, pp. 74–83, 2013.

phenomenological texts, to undergo a conscious experience necessarily means that there is something it is like for the subject to have that experience [Searle 1992].

Our goal is to show that our current working models are all inspired with objective psychology: cognitive, neuroscience, or behaviorism. We would like to prove that we need more subjective experience-side psychology in our models. The reason for such a problem is that subjective experience as described by Chalmers is very complicated. Moreover, it has been best described by Lacan in France, who has the reputation for being impossible to be translated in English. In the end our models, and we will show examples, are disappointing. As a prospective we would like to incite IT specialists to reflect on this major problem of objective/subjective dichotomy in the design of the characters.

In this paper we will follow the topology of Espen Aarseth in that we are willing to build a theoretical model that is capable of making a mimetic world, by opposition to arbitrary, which does not seem to be a concern in Katherine Isbisker. It may seem superfluous to specify this point, but in psychology, the closer we will want to be to the truth of the human psyche and the more it will make a difference. In the case of a deterministic game, our study will target the simulation of the relationship between the storyteller and the user, while, in the case of a non-deterministic application we would be in the context of providing a model for a verbose agent that would tell a story in natural language [Aarseth, et al., 2003]. Our niche is between the logic of cognitive science which believes in some objectivity of thought as matter of research, and social psychology, the scientific study of how people's thoughts, feelings, and behaviors are influenced by the actual, imagined, or implied presence of others, studied empirically, but by a third party.

The works of Stephane Donikian (Donikian, 2004) exposed the even growing antagonism of the approaches in the field of cognitive science and the substantial lack of federative models to propose an architecture allowing to connect together the various functions used in the human behavior even for the simplest ones. Reproducing the human behavior takes the developing of formalisms to model. We also need systems to simulate autonomous anthropomorphic characters. We do not have any theory for determining either the necessary or sufficient structures needed to support their particular capabilities. It is a basic tenet of cognitive sciences in the so called identification problem that choosing the one out of several candidate models that best describes a given set of results, is unsolvable in principle (Fum, Missier, & Stocco, 2007) (Anderson, 1976)

In this context we try to point out a matter that is on the border of three different subjects, philosophy of the mind, mind models, and neurocognitive science. Our premise is that subjective experience is absent of the current models for interactive storytelling. We would like to go further and tell how interactive media could be profitable to the models of subjective experience, mostly psychoanalysis.

We will try to prove that everything that we try to simulate in a storytelling, can boil down to a table-top RPG[1], [Delmas, Champagnat , Augeraud 2009] hence can boil down to a psychodynamic perspective, i.e. a story being told from a game master,

---

[1] Role playing game.

who has all the NPCs[2] in its power, [Velsen, Josh , Gustav 2009] to a user who receives the story.

- We will try to tell the difference between subjective experience and objective experience.
- We have then tried to show possible gaps within the state of the art.

2   Distinctions between Objective Point of View and Subjective Experience

The distinction with subjective experience is the one that is made by Chalmers, the famous philosopher of the mind (Chalmers, 1996), when he speaks of a `whir of information processing'- e.g. a whir of information processing happens when it comes to solve the problem of subjective experience, while there are, according to him, easy problems. It is obviously not as simple as the one as put by Donikian in the objective point of view. Chalmers says that reacting to environmental stimuli is an `easy problem', although no expert would qualify such a problem of easy, the model can be easily put into words. By comparison with the `hard problem of subjective experience', we could probably be calling it easy. Telling a story is a subjective experience matter because it requires psychodynamic interaction, should it be synchronous or asynchronous — a story can be received in the meantime it is told or not.

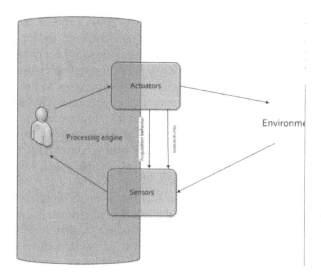

Fig. 1. The representation of the anthropoid agent in Donikian as in Von Uexküll (Uexküll, 1956)

---

[2] Non-player character.

When we speak of storytelling, we imply that `Style is the man' (Lacan J., 1966) as used to say Jacques Lacan. The enunciation of the story and its style contain more than just the behavior of the man with its environment. It contains a part of its psyche. The social decryptions by Roland Barthes of a number of habits such as the way of dressing connote the intimate of the subject. Thus there is a semiology of the appearances, which bears value of the vision of the world that the individual has of herself and of her environment. Then telling a story boils down to a psychodynamic interaction between two people more accurately than just between her and her environment.

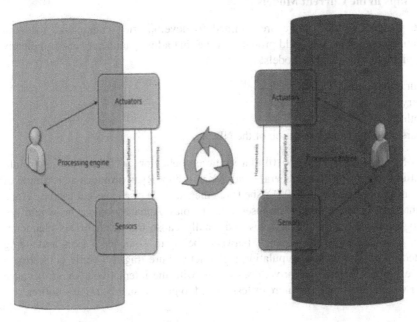

Fig. 2. In our views, the mind of the storyteller — should it be an emergent agent or not, through his NPCs; meets the psyche of the user

Still according to Donikian the goal of our work as designers of characters is to make them look credible or `natural-looking' so to say. To that purpose we would have a multiple layer of a cognitive architecture that would fit a classic cognitive doctrine that would be in accordance with Fodor or Pylyshyn. Mind that the natural isomorphism of the cognitivism is not agreed obviously, and that Edelman, Reeke, and the psychoanalysts showed different aspects of the problem, this is what we will try to show here.

Then an idea could be of considering the matter of storytelling as a relationship between two individuals with transference, mechanisms of defense, fantasies, and desires. A storytelling tells as much on a literal level of understanding, than it tells about the storyteller, according to Paul Ricoeur of whose works are based on the relationships between the two times of the narrative, the one of the life, and the one of the affective action.

More than anything: the relationship of the human being to another is a `narrative identity'. It means that we build our identity out of the story that we tell of ourselves — or through the stories that we tell to other by ourselves. Hence our question: why try to make a character,   world,   story, look natural out of scratch by the machine, while storytelling results of an interaction - the story being told from a human to another?.

3   A Short Comparative Analysis of the Iago Character

3.1   Gaps in the Current Models

On the prospective side if we are inclined to develop `rich characters', meaning `qualitative characters', we could probably argue that a few parameters are completely off the picture in the current models:

- Natural language;
- Poetry;
- Depth;
- Diversity in the characterization of the NPCs...

Nicolas Szilas states (Szilas, 2010) that irrational behaviors so far are not taken into account in the industry. At a general level, Marie-Laure Ryan provides an example of a linear negative case (Ryan, 2001) She takes the example of a classical tragedy Anna Karenina, and observes that if the user were to play Anna Karenina, he would not want to behave the way she behaves and finally cause the death of his character. There's a considerable discrepancy between being in someone's skin and being separated by an interface, manipulating a character. Pure tragedy, while consisting a perfect example of linear narrative, does not fit with the interactive context, because the user would not want to be more or less forced to go into such a tragic solution.'

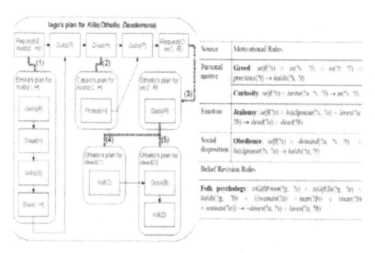

Fig. 3. A behavioral model for Iago's plan for Othello to kill Desdemona in Othello (Chang & Soo, 2008)

We may infer two reasons: the first is that no NPC is designed to be a tragic character. As tragic as the game scenario may be, and after thinking our characters as logical and rational machines for decades, the gamer could not think the same meaningfulness in his characters as the designers if the latter figured tragic ones. This would be a brand new way of playing, for a new line of games, and a new generation of players: tragedy is not fun; games so far are to be fun. In the end we know that a behavior that could be closer to poetry than to rationality poses a lot of problems in terms of simulations. Psychoanalysis takes into account those behaviors.

As a matter of fact the character is much more subtle as the following lines reveals:

'Now, I do love her too;
Not out of absolute lust, though, peradventure,
I stand accountant for as great a sin,
But partly led to diet my revenge,
For that I do suspect the lusty Moor
Hath leap'd into my seat: the thought whereof
Doth, like a poisonous mineral, gnaw my inwards;
And nothing can or shall content my soul
Till I am even'd with him, wife for wife;
Or, failing so, yet that I put the Moor
At least into a jealousy so strong
That judgment cannot cure. He also says: I'll have our Michael Cassio on the hip,
Abuse him to the Moor in the rank garb... '
(Shakespeare, 2012)

`Iago is the acid which comes from our failed narcissistic relationships; it slowly eats into our object articulations, even the most honestly loving. This corrosive and underhand action of the deathwish drive seems even more vowed to be efficient that Othello, deep in himself does not have a character built only on idealized and toned down tenderness, without any other constituent: his Moorish blood reminds the heredity of the id that froths beneath the surface of his `noble' apparent behavior.` (Bergeret, 2003).

What Jean Bergeret tries to show through this analysis is what can be universal in Iago. The reader may appreciate the poetics of the prose in which he describes the char acter, even though it is only a translation from the French. We can see that from the rough work of BDI to the non-interactive piece of Shakespeare there is a huge discrepancy. The first question is: what if he was to act in an interactive environment, how would he behave? The second question could be: do we have enough analysis, poetics or depth, to simulate him, to have a convincing Iago in the sense of our state of the art with either (Bergeret, 2003) or (Chang & Soo, 2008)?.

As we may see, this excerpt is pure subjective experience from the character of Iago, though it is harder to see where the diagram is going, probably because it tries to rationalize `a whirl of information', into a very terse formula. Indeed, psychoanalysis is more verbose, but we cannot be ambitious in our narratives while trying to avoid the use of natural language. It seems on the one hand that some psychologist/philosophers believe that they can bridge the gap between the subjective experience and the logic of machinery.

'Subjective psychological phenomena are the legitimate concern of psychologists, but these must not be confused with thoughts and their laws which, given their objectivity and concern with truth, are the proper subject matter for logicians. Logic is set apart because it alone is charged with 'the task of discovering the laws of truth, not the laws of taking things to be true or of thinking'. [Hutto 2003] Thoughts are therefore implicitly within the grasp of logic, thus within the grasp of computers. While Lacan says that the truth of the thoughts is not even within the grasp of the subject who produces them... This is one of the rules of poetry. Those schools of thought are very significant of the intellectual severance between the Latin world and the – dominant- English speaking world.

4   Lacanian Concepts Which Could Be of Use to Design a NPC

We offer quadrangular characters to the acumen of the designer instead of the classic Fodorism. They are prompted by, as subjects, desire, mesmerized by The Thing — Das Ding in German, which Lacan derived from Kant- trying to get a kick — for lack of a better expression- until they are put on the path of self-destruction, and organized by the symbolic law. These concepts are part of the human experience, we are persuaded of it, thus they lack in our models so far.

4.1   The Thing

We could say of the Thing that it magnetizes the desire. Every object of desire is under some aspect a delusion. We only imagine that we desire such or such object. In reality, the desire, through the objects it seems to expect, only looks for one thing: the Thing, of which it will never have any representation, which is not a goal since it cannot be reached, but around which the desire never ceases to revolve. So far we have been able to make characters that want to stuff themselves on experience points or gold coins, but this concept helps us understand something no so logical with hu man psyche: what's the point of being rich and powerful up to a certain point? And more than this, why are we trying to reach a point beyond the one we thought we originally wanted to go?.

- The young woman who enters medical school thinking that she will help old people while unconsciously she wants to please her dad;
- The man who becomes a priest and paints because he has unsolved desires with his mom;
- The man who turns to angry politics because he had absent parents and wants to fill a gap...

This brings us to the second concept, enjoyment: the use and abuse of pleasures until there are put on the path of self-destruction.

4.2   Enjoyment

The principle of pleasure explained by Freud is the principle of limitation of pleas ure, since it imposes to get a kick out of life as little as possible. But at the same time as he seeks pleasure while limiting it, the subject strives, constantly, to overcome the limits of the pleasure principle. Getting a kick is that uncomfortable position that hurts and is pleasant at the same time... For lack of a better translation for *jouissance* we chose to use this way of saying it: having a pleasure that hurts a little at the same time, such as having sex, or watching people fight.

It does not mean that the attempt for the maximization of the pleasure results in the coming of more pleasure. There's a degree of pleasure that the subject cannot tolerate that Lacan calls *jouissance* in the seminaire VII and that we could call an abuse of pleasure. The deathwish is the constant desire to overcome the principle of pleasure and to reunite with The Thing and to get more kick out it. In this sense, getting a kick is a path to death — seminaire XVII.

Why did Iago act like that then? Yes, he did break it all, but what a kick must it have been to watch everything fall apart.

We could find examples in rich and good looking people who waste their lives before 30 with sex, drugs, and parties...

4.3   The Law and the Other

The desire takes us towards The Thing is the reverse of the law. The Other — with a big O- designates what the subject depends upon, the place of its determinations, and also what is required to put order in the human world in the subject, i.e. the place of the law. It is an organizing instance, not a repressive one.

We want to leave to the imagination of the developer the leeway of using these concepts which are among the most powerful to describe the human psyche in La can's theory. There are obviously many others, but the first step is to take into consideration the existence of the unconscious, which is completely left behind by the other models. In our model we have, at least more depth than just:' NPC wants money because money is useful, NPC locates money, and NPC takes money'.

5   Conclusion

Psychoanalytical models can be as efficient as neurocognitive ones, but not of the same sort. Psychoanalysis is much more on the side of history, of the humanities, than on the life sciences. No one has ever asked an historian, a sociologist, an economist, a controlled experimental check of his results. Why then when we assume that story telling is closer to psychoanalysis than cognitive science should we have the judgment filter? This is not the same order of things, as Blaise Pascal might have said. There are different kinds of science in which the criteria of observation and verification are not identical. Psychoanalysis and neuroscience seem to involve logically each other, in a parallel way lately.

Every one of which could claim to be true, while the other may or may not be true or false. Each side of the coin can coexist with the other, joined and separated at the same time, and the other could be intact or erased. Obviously, today, subjective experience and objective experience are both sides of the same coin. The storytellers and characters as automatons is a mistake that we should avoid in order not to repeat the same imbalance that exists within the design of computer apps in general — humanities are underrepresented in computer development.

The dichotomy made by Chalmers in the easy and hard problems of the mind is useful in the sense that so far our models are practical but tries to solve what he calls easy problems such as perception, navigation in complex environments, path planning, memory but they tend to be very far in a qualitative way from anything that we need to solve the complicated problems posed by the poetics of IS.

References

1. Aarseth, E., Smedstad, S.M., Sunnanâ, L.: A MULTI-DIMENSIONAL TYPOLOGY OF GAMES. Utrecht, s.n (2003)
2. Bergeret, J.: Lapersonnalite normale etpathologique. D unod, Paris (2003)
3. Cavazza, M., Pizzi, D.: International conference on entertainment. In: TID SE (2006)
4. Cavazza, M., Pizzi, D.: University of Teeside (2012), http://wwwscm.tees.ac.uk/f.charles/bovary.php (retrieved May 21, 2012)
5. Cavazza, M., Pizzi, D.: Merchant of Venice. University of Teeside: http://www-scm.tees.ac.uk/f.charles/merchant-of-venice.php (retrieved May 21, 2012)
6. Chalmers, D.: The Conscious Mind. In: Search of a Fundamental Theory, Oxford University Press, Oxford (1996)
7. Chang, H.M., Soo, V.W.: International Conference on Intelligent Technologies for Interactive Entertainment (2008)
8. Crawford, C.: Artists and engineers as cats and dogs: implications for interactive storytelling. Computer graphics (2002)
9. Delmas, G., Champagnat, R., Augeraud, M.: From tabletop RPG to interactive storytelling: Definition of a story manager for videogames. In: Iurgel, I.A., Zagalo, N., Petta, P. (eds.) ICIDS 2009. LNCS, vol. 5915, pp. 121–126. Springer, Heidelberg (2009)
10. Donikian, S.: Modélisation, contrôle et animation d'agents virtuels autonomes évoluant dans des environnements informés et structurés. HDR IFSIC, Rennes (2004)
11. Fodor, J.: The modularity ofthe mind. Cambridge University Press, Cambridge (1983)
12. Hutto, D.: Wittgenstein and the end of philosophy. Palgrave Macmillan, New York (2003)
13. Lacan, J.: Le séminaire sur l'Identification IX. le seuil, Paris (1962)
14. Lacan, J.: Le seminaire VII. Le seuil, Paris (1986)
15. Lacan, J.: Seminaire VII. Seuil, Paris (2006)
16. Lacan, J.: Seminaire XI Quatre concepts fondamentaux de la psychanalyse. Le seuil, Paris (1973)
17. Lacan, J.: Seminaire XVII. Seuil, Paris (2006)
18. Lacan, J.: Les complexes familiaux dans la formation de l'individu, Paris (1966)
19. Lacan, J.: Les complexes familiaux dans la formation de l'individu. Navarrin, Paris (1966)
20. Nagel, T.: What is it like to be a bat? In: The Philosophical Review (1974)

21. Peinado, F., Cavazza, M., Pizzi, D.: Revisiting character-based affective storytelling under a narrative BDI framework. In: Spierling, U., Szilas, N. (eds.) ICIDS 2008. LNCS, vol. 5334, pp. 83–88. Springer, Heidelberg (2008)
22. Racamier. L'inceste et l'incestuel. College de Psychanalyse, Paris (1995)
23. Ryan, M.-L.: Beyond Myth and Metaphor - The Case of Narrative in Digital Media. The International Journal of Computer Game Research (2001)
24. Searle, J.R.: The Rediscovery of the Mind. MIT press, Cambridge (1992)
25. Staller, Sloman, & Ben-Zeev, Perspective effects in nondeontic versions of the Wason selection task. Memory & Cognition (2001)
26. Szilas (2010) Requirements for Computational Models of Interactive Narrative. In: AAAI (2010)
27. van Velsen, M., Williams, J., Verhulsdonck, G.: Table-Top Gaming Narratology for Digital Interactive Storytelling. In: Iurgel, I.A., Zagalo, N., Petta, P. (eds.) ICIDS 2009. LNCS, vol. 5915, pp. 109–120. Springer, Heidelberg (2009)

Towards Determinants of User-Intuitive
Web Interface Signs

Muhammad Nazrul Islam

Turku Centre for Computer Science (TUCS)
Department of Information Technologies
Åbo Akademi University, 20520 Turku, Finland
nazrulturku@gmail.com

Abstract. User interfaces of web applications encompass a number of objects like navigation links, buttons, icons, labels, thumbnails, symbols, etc. which are defined in this paper as interface signs. Designing interface signs to be intuitive to the users is widely accepted to have a significant effect on enhancing web usability. Interface signs design principles are semiotics by nature, as semiotics is the doctrine of signs. Thus, the fundamental objective of this study is to reveal the determinants of user-intuitive interface signs for enhancing web usability from a semiotics perspective. To attain this research objective, an extensive user study was conducted with twenty six participants following a semi-structured interview approach. The preliminary results provide a number of determinants and their attributes to interpret properly the meaning of interface signs.

Keywords: Semiotics, interface sign, web usability, user interface design, web sign ontology.

1 Introduction

The smallest elements of web user interfaces such as navigational links, small images, thumbnails, short text, command buttons and the like are called interface signs in this research. Interface signs act as communication artifacts in the UI to convey web content and system functionalities. Designing intuitive interface signs is essential in order to achieve user satisfaction, proper task performance, user communication, system learnability, effective and efficient use, etc... i.e., according to usability standards [1],[2],[3],[4]. These interface signs' design principles are semiotics by nature as semiotics is considered as the science of signs [5].

Semiotics can be defined as "the study of signs, signification, and signifying systems" [6]. A semiotic model proposed by Peirce [5] consists of a triadic relationship containing the *representamen* (the sign itself that stands for something to somebody in some respect or capacity), the *object* (actual thing the sign stands for) and the *interpretant* (created in the mind of the interpreter an equivalent or more developed sign). A sign requires the existence of these three constituents concurrently. According to semiotics theories an interface sign (*representamen*) needs

A. Marcus (Ed.): DUXU/HCII 2013, Part I, LNCS 8012, pp. 84–93, 2013.

to be designed intuitively so that it creates a sense in the perceiver's (*interpretant*) mind to understand the actual meaning (*object*) of this sign. Therefore, semiotics research on web interface in particular focuses mainly on the language of the web interface and its usability.

The interface signs are designed as encoded form in the UI. End users decode these signs in order to obtain the desired information or to perform specific tasks. End users can perform the desired task or obtain the information accurately only when end users' interpretant matches the referential object of the interface signs with the designer's interpretant. There is no one-to-one link between the sign and its referential object [7]. Moreover, different interpreters may interpret a sign in a number of ways. As a result, some signs might be very easy to interpret for some users while some others may not. Therefore, the fundamental objective of this study is to reveal the determinants of user-intuitive interface signs for boosting web usability from semiotics point of view. A fundamental research question for this research is formulated as "What are the determinants of user-intuitive user interface signs from a semiotics perspective in order to improve web usability?".

This paper is organized as follows. Previous works related to this study are discussed briefly in section 2. In section 3, the study method is presented. The study results are discussed in section 4. The conclusion and ideas for future work are presented in the final section.

2   Related Research

Some research related to semiotics perception in user interfaces has been conducted in the HCI research area in the last decade [8]. This section provides a brief overview of a few selected research related to this study.

Bolchini et al. [9] included 'interface signs' as one of the design and evaluation dimensions of web user interface. They proposed a set of heuristics to be used as an additional toolkit to evaluate web interface signs. Andersen [10] provides a methodological framework to analyse HCI rooted in the semiotics. In his work, Andersen showed how computer based signs mediated peoples' interaction with the computer systems.

De Souza [1] introduced semiotic engineering in HCI, where she treated HCI as a new triangle consisting of the user, the designer, and the system. De Souza et al. [11] proposed a semiotic engineering evaluation method in HCI named Semiotic Inspection Method (SIM), encompassing five core steps [12]: (i) inspection of the metalinguistic signs, (ii) inspection of the static signs, (iii) inspection of the dynamic signs, (iv) comparison of the designers' meta-communication message produced in the prior three steps, and (v) summary evaluation of the quality of entire meta-communication of designer to user.

A user study conducted by Islam [13] showed that users' inaccurate interpretations of interface signs were significantly aligned with usability problems and, as a consequence, with their effects on overall web usability. In another study, he investigated issues related to web interface signs' re-design and their meaning's intuitiveness [14], [15]. These study results provide a set of semiotics considerations to design and evaluate web interface signs.

An empirical study conducted by Islam & Tétard [16], showed that integrating semiotic perception in usability testing produced a set of benefits that contributed to the usability evaluation such as providing an overall idea of interface signs' intuitiveness, helping to find usability problems, recommending possible solutions, and conveying the understandability of interface signs.

3   Research Method

A user study following a semi structured user interview research method was conducted to attain the research objective. The following steps were followed to perform the user study effectively as well as efficiently.

1. *Define the study objective* – the objective of this study was to reveal the factors of users' interpretations of interface signs. In other words, to observe the determinants why some interface signs are more intuitive to the end users while some others are not.

2. *Develop study instrument* -
   - *Selecting the web interface signs* – interface signs were retrieved from the user interfaces of two web application domains (online calendar and email application) and two web domains (university and museum websites that belong to educational and cultural heritage web domains respectively). A total of 18 interface signs were selected from each domain thus a total of 72 interface signs were selected for this test. In this stage, webpage snapshots for each of the 72 signs were taken and stored. A few heuristics were employed to select the interface signs. These were: (*h1*) signs used to provide most common information or functionalities in a particular application; (*h2*) signs provide same information or functionalities but only differ by its representamen; (*h3*) signs which did not fit with heuristics h1 & h2 but seemed important for this study. A list of selected example signs is shown in Table 1.
   - *Prepare pre-test questionnaires* – a set of questions were prepared to obtain the data related to the participants' demographic profile, their experience and familiarity with selected web applications, and the like.
   - *Develop interview question* – the questions were developed based on the main objective of this study. Three types of questions: open ended, probing, and closed questions were developed following the interview guidelines suggested by Stanton & Young [17]. In this stage, a data collection sheet is also prepared to make it easy to transcribe and store the transcribed data. An example set of questions is presented in Table 2.

3. *Piloting the test* – a pilot test was conducted with two test subjects. Pilot test's outcomes were considered to finalize the order of the questions, make clear and concise questions, order the display of interface signs, and the like.

4. *Recruit appropriate test-subjects* – a total of 26 students were recruited as test subjects for this research project since (i) users who have internet access facility as well as are familiar with web browsing could be considered as the potential users of the selected web applications, (ii) the study was planned to be conducted on web user interface, (iii) it was easy to access students as test subjects.

Table 1. A list of selected example interface signs

Interface sign	Application/Website	Domain	Heuristic
Library	University of Oulu	educational	*h1*
EXHIBITIONS	Design Museum	cultural heritage	*h1*
Add Event	Yahoo! calendar	online calendar	*h2*
New	Hotmail calendar		
CREATE	Google calendar		
	Yahoo! mail	e-mail	*h3*

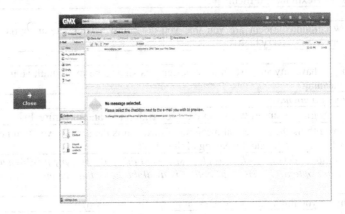

Fig. 1. A sign presented without context (left side) and with context marked by rectangle (right side), snapshot taken from www.gmx.com dated on September, 2012

5. *Conduct test* – the actual test was conducted with 26 participants at the usability laboratory at Åbo Akademi University during late 2012. Each test was conducted one by one. The following activities were followed in each test session with each participant. Firstly test subjects filled up pre-test questionnaires; secondly a short lecture was given to inform the test subjects about the test in general like test procedure, test participants' roles, etc.; and finally test subjects seated in front of a computer and gave answers to a set of questions (see Table 2) for each interface sign presented to them. Selected interface signs were presented to test subjects in two arrangements through the presentation software Microsoft® PowerPoint: (i) *sign without context,* where only the sign was presented without the source webpage and only retaining the original size and color, and (ii) *sign with context,* where the source webpage snapshot was presented and the interface sign was marked by a red-color rectangle. Test subjects were not allowed to click on the signs, they were only supposed to respond to a number of questions for each interface sign. Each test session was audio and video recorded. An example of a user's response for a sign is presented in Table 2.

Table 2. An example of a test-subject's responses

Sign presented without context (see left side one in figure 1)	
Q1:	What could be the referential meaning of this sign?
A:	*"It seems difficult to me. 'Right arrow' icon is conflicting with the word 'close'. Why close used in email. Generally it uses in computer to close a folder, but i do not know whether in email there is any necessity to close the window. However, since this sign is taken from email application, it may used to close an open email."*
Q2:	Why do you think this as the referential meaning of this sign?
	"Familiarytiy with computer uses, where I used this sign close an open window."
Q3:	How much complicacy / difficulty do you feel to interpret this sign? [score: 1(very easy) - 7(extremely difficult)]
	"4"
Q4:	How certain/confident are you that you are right in your interpretation? [score: 1(very low) - 7(very high)]
	"5"
Q5:	Do you have any suggestion to re-design this sign to be more intuitive to interpret its meaning?
	"No, I do not have."
Sign presented with context (see right side one in figure 1)	
Q1:	Do you think the referential meaning of this sign is the same as you told before? If not, what is the referential meaning of this sign?
A:	*"I do not understand why this close sign is at this position. why it is? Where is the sign out option? No sign out option is availabe here, that means it may be sign-out."*
Q2:	Why do you think this as the referential meaning of this sign?
	"There is no sign out option in this page and the position of this sign."
Q3:	How much complicacy / difficulty do you feel to interpret this sign? [score: 1(very easy) - 7(extremely difficult)]
	"6"
Q4:	How certain/confident are you that you are right in your interpretation? [score: 1(very low) - 7(very high)]
	"6"
Q5:	Do you have any alternate suggestions for redesigning this sign that might be comparatively more intuitive to interpret its meaning properly?
	"It is better to use a sign 'Sign-out'."
Q1:	Why do you think that this (proposed alternative sign) sign is more intuitive than the said one?
A:	*"The word 'close' is mostly used for closing window not for signing out. Moreover, icon of 'right arrow' is not clear to me. If a cross or back arrow icon is used here, then it still will not make the sense properly. Better not to use any icon. Use only the text 'Sign-out'."*

6. *Transcribe and gather interview data* – the test videos were then replayed and transcribed fully into text. Transcribed data were gathered in a Microsoft® Excel spreadsheet. Data was organized in columns (asked questions) and rows (participants' responses) for each participant. Both qualitative and quantitative data were collected through this test. Interface signs were presented in two arrangements (*with context* and *without context*), minimum number of questions answered was 4 for each presented sign thus a large volume of data [26

(participants) x 72 (interface signs) x 2 (sign presented with and without context) x 4 (minimum no. of questions responded)] was collected from this test.

7. *Analysis of the study data* – Marshall [18] suggests that a careful reading and summarization of descriptive text can be sufficient for a general evaluation of qualitative data. Therefore, firstly a careful reading and summarization of descriptive text was performed. The study data were then preliminary analyzed following a basic process of qualitative data analysis model named *noticing, collecting & thinking* model suggested by Seidel [19].

4   Study Results

The preliminary results help us identify a number of determinants and their attributes to interpret the meaning of interface signs from a semiotics perspective. These determinants and attributes could be used as semiotics considerations for the design and evaluation of user-intuitive interface signs. The determinants and their attributes observed so far are briefly presented in this section.

User's presupposed knowledge: The user's presupposed knowledge refers to the user's pre-familiarity with interface signs and their referential meaning. A user can interpret a sign because of his/her familiarity with that sign. For instance, a user can easily understand and interpret the meaning of the sign 'Inbox' because of his/her familiarity with this sign in some email applications. In such case, the basis for interpreting the sign's meaning accurately is the presupposed knowledge of the web application domain. This study found a set of user presupposed knowledge to interpret interface signs such as: (i) user's presupposed knowledge of internet or web use; (ii) web application domain; (iii) website's / application's real world environment; (iv) web application domain's real world environment; (v) computer use; (vi) mobile phone uses, etc... An instance of user response for a sign 'Logout' is presented in Table 3. A user response to this sign showed that the bases of the user's accurate interpretation with high confidence and no complexity were (i) all kinds of web application have this sign, i.e., pre-familiar with this sign in other web applications, (ii) underlining of the sign which refers to its interactivity. This example of user response showed how a user's presupposed knowledge of internet/web use helped to interpret the 'Logout' sign.

Interface signs' interactivity: This study found that web interface signs could be used for different purposes such as (i) decorative or aesthetic (sign used only for aesthetic purpose); (ii) indicative (one cannot interact with this sign and the sign is used only to provide suggestions or hints in the UI, e.g., a webpage title could be treated as an indicative sign); (iii) interactive (one can interact with this sign only for getting some indication or hints, not for performing a task , e.g., there might be some interface signs in UI that may provide some messages or hints only if a cursor put or move on these signs); (iv) functional (e.g., interactive sign to perform a task such as to submit an online form); and (v) navigational (e.g., interact with sign to go through to further details information, e.g., navigate to other pages to access related information). The interactive, functional and navigational interface signs could have

Table 3. Examples of user responses for six interface signs (presented without context)

Sign and Domains	Meaning	Basis	Conf	Comp
Logout (email applcation)	"It means log out from email application. It's a hyperlink as it has underline."	"All kind of web application has this sign. Underline refers to hyperlink since the 19s internet."	7	1
Library (university web)	"It is navigational. Its for the library of university where you can get many services like read books, rent books."	"I have seen this before. For the icon it helps me more. Otherwise I may thought it as a programming library."	7	1
(university web)	"It means twitter. what i linked it with the twitter, a social media."	"It is colored. So I am more confident it is twitter. Only the confusion is whether it is for sharing or visiting the university social network page. "	5	2
f (university web)	"Button for function. "	"I guess it. This letter f is used in mathematics for function. "	1	6
SHOP (museum web)	"For the shopping site. Not the online shop but it is a tourist shop at the museum. It is a navigational label. I will not surprised more if it is web shop but in that case probably I will give it names as webshop."	"Interpret based on the word meaning."	5	2
WEBSHOP (museum web)	"it refers to online museum shop. It is navigational."	"The word and my familair with web uses."	7	1

two states: active (one can click on it) and inactive (one cannot click on it). An instance of user response for the sign 'Logout' presented in Table 3 showed how the underline helped the user to interpret and understand its interactive purpose.

Ontological classification: From a designer's perspective, a set of knowledge presupposed and pointed by an interface sign (i.e. a semiotic unit) is defined as 'Ontology' [2]. Speroni also listed a set of web sign ontologies in [2] such as interlocutor ontology, website ontology, commonsense ontology, web domain ontology, internet ontology, topic ontology, and context ontology. Based on Speroni's definition and concept of ontology, interface signs were classified into different ontological signs in this study. The study observed that the interpretation accuracy, confidence and complexity of users' interpretations of interface signs varied depending on different ontological signs. Thus interface sign ontology is treated as a determinant to interpret sign meaning. For instance, the '' sign (see Figure 1) belongs to website ontology [2], as this sign is not commonly used in email or any other online applications and is very specific to GMX email application. The 'Logout' (see Table 3) sign belongs to internet ontology [2], as this sign is commonly used in many online applications. These both signs actually stand for signing out from an online system. But this study showed that, while presented without context, these two signs were interpreted differently by two test subjects (see Table 2 and 3). Their interpretations showed that the sign belonging to internet ontology was interpreted accurately with high confidence and no complexity whereas the sign belonging to website ontology was interpreted inaccurately (confused) with comparatively less confidence and high complexity. A more detailed about this determinant is discussed in [20]).

Amplification Features of Interfaces Signs: This study observed that a few features of interface signs assisted users in interpreting interface signs accurately with comparatively less complexity and high confidence. These are listed here as amplification features. These features are individually not enough to express the meaning properly and generally append with other signs. The attributes of amplification features are (i) appended small image, (ii) appended thumbnail, (iii) appended icon with textual sign, (iv) appended short text, (v) appended indicative text with iconic sign, (vi) appended abbreviated letter (e.g., e, m, i, etc.) with textual sign, etc... For instance (see Table 3), the sign 'Shop' in museum website will not make complete sense as it may be confusing to the user whether the sign refers to the information of a physical museum shop or whether it will bring the user to the online museum shop. Again a sign 'Webshop' refers to the same thing and the user grasp its meaning without any confusion only because of the word 'web'. The word 'web' separately does not make any sense but when appended with another word 'shop', it strengthens the user's interpretation of a sign.

Interface Sign Position: The position of a sign in the user interface assists in making sense when interpreting a sign's meaning. This study observed a few attributes of this feature such as user habit, neighbor signs, etc. Users are used to see some interface signs in some particular positions in web pages for instance interface signs that provide accessibility features for disabled people (e.g., sign for resizing text) are mostly placed in the upper left side of a webpage. Neighbor signs make sense when interpreting a sign, even if the user may not be familiar with this sign. For instance, the sign 'Agendum' is not familiar to a user and therefore a user may be unable to interpret the sign's meaning without context whereas in context user may be able to interpret the meaning properly only because of the understanding of the neighbor signs - 'Day', 'Week', 'Month', etc. These neighbor signs help the user making sense about the meaning of 'Agendum' sign in Hotmail application. Again the sign '' (see Figure 1 and Table 2) was accurately interpreted by a user when presented with context. The position of this sign on the web page was one of the bases to interpret this sign accurately, since the user was used to interface signs located at this specific position for signing out in some other online applications.

Sign Color: Sign colors positively affect user interpretations of interface signs. Color, light, and contrast are also often used to express the interactivity of interface signs. In other words, interface signs color helps users understanding whether a sign is active or inactive, currently visited or already visited. This study observed a few attributes of this feature such as color contrast, user attention, brand color, interactivity suggestions, sign importance, etc. For instance, the Facebook sign (see Table 3) was interpreted as a mathematical function since in mathematics 'Function' is represented by the symbol f and the sign is presented as black grey color. The same user interpreted the Twitter sign (see Table 3) accurately. The user was familiar with Facebook use and had an idea about social media in general but failed to interpret the sign only because of its lack of brand color (blue). The Twitter sign held its brand color and was therefore interpreted accurately.

Matching Features of Interface Sign: An accurate interpretation of interface signs depends on the matching of interpretant and object. The interface sign's object and the user's interpretant need to match to interpret the meaning of interface sign properly. There are a few attributes of this matching feature such as (i) conventions, (ii) underline reality, (iii) clearness of designer's motivation, (iv) correspondence with the real world object, (v) functional similarities, etc. The concepts of paradigm and syntagm could be used here. For instance, a user accurately interpreted the interface sign ' Library ' (see Table 3). According to him, the sign might have been interpreted it as a programming library if the sign only used the word 'Library', since the word 'Library' refers to both concepts (university library service and programming library) in the educational web domain. The small images of books motivated him to interpret the sign accurately (i.e., to access the university library services). Thus the matching attributes like clearness of designer's motivation (by the appended small images) and correspondence with the real world object (as how the images look like) assisted him in making sense when interpreting the sign meaning.

5   Conclusion and Future Work

This empirical user study provided a set of determinants and their attributes for interpreting web interface signs and grasping their referential meaning. The observed determinants and attributes could be used as semiotics consideration for designing and evaluating user-intuitive interface signs to enhance web usability. For instance, the attribute 'brand color' of the 'interface sign color' determinant provided a semiotic consideration in the form of a design guideline: 'maintain the interface sign's brand color, if it exists'. However, these are not claimed to be a complete set of determinants and attributes. Therefore, the author intends (i) to perform a rigorous analysis on the study data and (ii) to consider the outcomes of other studies conducted through user observation and expert inspection to produce a complete set of determinants for designing user-intuitive interface signs. The findings of these (comparative study, user tests) studies will be converged to propose a semiotic mode for user interface sign design and evaluation. In the final phase, an empirical user study will be conducted to validate and refine the semiotic model.

References

1. de Souze, C.S.: The Semiotic Engineering of Human-Computer Interaction. The MIT Press, Cambridge (2005)
2. Speroni, M.: Mastering the Semiotics of Information-Intensive Web Interfaces. Unpublished doctoral dissertation, Faculty of Communication Sciences, University of Lugano, Swizerland (2006)
3. Islam, M.N., Ali, M., Al-Mamun, A., Islam, M.: Semiotics Explorations on Designing the Information Intensive Web Interfaces. International Arab Journal of Information Technology 7(1), 45–54 (2010)
4. Islam, M.N.: Semiotics of the Web Interface: Analysis and Guidelines. Journal of Computer Science and Technology (JCS&T) 8(3), 166–167 (2008)
5. Peirce, C.S.: Collected Writings (8 Vols.) Ed. C. Hartshorne, P. Weiss & A. Burks, vol. 1-8. Harvard University Press (1931-1952)
6. Robert, S., Robert, B., Sandy, F.L.: New Vocabularies in Film Semiotics: Structuralism, Post-Structuralism and Beyond. Taylor & Francis, London (1992)
7. Frege, G.: Begriffsschrift, English Translation. Journal van Heijenoort, 1–82 (1879)
8. Islam, M.N.: A Systematic Literature Review of Semiotics Perception in User Interfaces. Journal of Systems and Information Technology (JSIT) 15(1), 45–77 (2013)
9. Bolchini, D., Chatterji, R., Speroni, M.: Developing heuristics for the semiotics inspection of websites. In: 27th ACM International Conference on Design of Communication (SIGDOC 2009), pp. 67–71. ACM Press, USA (2009)
10. Andersen, P.B.: A Theory of Computer Semiotics. Cambridge Uni. Press, UK (1997)
11. de Souza, C.S., Leitão, C.F., Prates, R.O., da Silva, E.J.: The Semiotic Inspection Method. In: VII Brazilian Symposium on Human Factors in Computing Systems (IHC 2006), pp. 148–157. ACM Press (2006)
12. Salgado, L.C.D.-C., de Souza, C.S., Leitão, C.F.: A semiotic inspection of ICDL. In: de Lucena, C.J.P. (ed.) Monografias em Ciência da Computação, No. 31/09, Brazil (2009)
13. Islam, M.N.: A Semiotics Perspective to Web Usability: An Empirical case Study. IADIS Interfaces and Human Computer Interaction 2011, 19–28 (2011)
14. Islam, M.N.: Towards Designing Users' Intuitive Web Interface. In: 6th International Conference on Complex, Intelligent, and Software Intensive Systems (CISIS 2012), pp. 513–518. IEEE Computer Society (2012)
15. Islam, M.N.: Semiotics Perception towards Designing Users' Intuitive Web User Interface: A Study on Interface Signs. In: Rahman, H., Mesquita, A., Ramos, I., Pernici, B. (eds.) MCIS 2012. LNBIP, vol. 129, pp. 139–155. Springer, Heidelberg (2012)
16. Islam, M.N., Tetard, F.: Integrating Semiotics Perception in Usability Testing to Improve Usability Evaluation. In: Garcia-Ruiz, M.A. (ed.) Cases on Usability Engineering: Design and Development of Digital Products, pp. 145–169. IGI Global, USA (2013)
17. Stanton, N.S., Young, M.S.: A guide to methodology in Ergonomics. Taylor & Francis, UK (1999)
18. Marshall, J.G.: Using evaluation research methods to improve quality. Health Libraries Review 12, 159–172 (1995)
19. Seidel, J.: Qualitative Data Analyisis. The Ethnograph v5 Manual, Appendix E (1998), http://www.qualisresearch.com/
20. Islam, M.N.: Towards Exploring Web Interface Sign Ontology: A User Study. In: 15th HCI International 2013. Springer (2013)

Sci-Fi Movies and the Pessimistic View for the Future Controlled Society of Totalitarianism

Masaaki Kurosu

The Open University of Japan
2-11 Wakaba, Mihama-ku
Chiba-shi 261-8586, Japan
masaakikurosu@spa.nifty.com

Abstract. The author proposes a view that most science-fiction movies that described not just the future technological development but the life in the future social organization are pessimistic and depict dystopian, rather than utopian societies. They can provide useful guidance to increase our awareness of what technology might bring to the user experience and of how we should take care for not falling into such a social organization.

Keywords: Sci-Fi movie, future society, dystopia, utopia, totalitarianism.

1   Introduction

Since the optimistic earliest work of science-fiction (sci-fi) movies such as "A Trip to the Moon" (1902) by Georges Méliérs, movies categorized as such have been describing the state of possible future development of technology such as "Ralph 124C 41+ (one to foresee for many)" (1911) by Hugo Gernsback (though not a movie) as well as monsters and aliens as the subjects of entertainment. On the other hands, there are some serious movies that described the life in the future society. I point out that future societies described in such movies tend to be mostly dystopian ones, rather than utopian, although some of their stories have positive endings in order to satisfy the audience.

Fig. 1. A scene from "A Trip to the Moon" (1902)

A. Marcus (Ed.): DUXU/HCII 2013, Part I, LNCS 8012, pp. 94–99, 2013.
© Springer-Verlag Berlin Heidelberg 2013

2   Utopia and Dystopia

The criterion that differentiates dystopia from the utopia may vary, depending on the movie analyst's viewpoint. Some could claim that even a free and wealthy country can be categorized as a dystopia, if people living there cannot have a positive attitude and mindset, which will lead to a negative result, the opposite of a happy life. What is such a life? The PERMA Model describes it.

The PERMA Model was developed by a positive psychologist, Martin Seligman, and was published in his influential 2011 book "Flourish". PERMA, an acronym for a model of well-being, proposes five building blocks of well-being and happiness:

— Positive emotions: feeling good
— Engagement: being completely absorbed in activities
— Relationships: being authentically connected to others
— Meaning: purposeful existence
— Achievement: a sense of accomplishment and success

However, in this discussion, I believe many sci-fi movies describing the life in the future society take an opposite view, and I shall focus on their self-evident dystopia and, in particular, totalitarianism.

Table 1. A tentative classification of dystopian sci-fi movies

Happy Ending	Unhappy Ending
"Metropolis" (1927) by Fritz Lang	"1984" (1956) by Michael Anderson
"Fahrenheit 451" (1966) by Francois Truffaut	"THX-1138" (1970) by George Lucas
"Logan's Run" (1976) by Michael Anderson	"ZPG" (1971) by Michael Campus
	"Soylent Green" (1973) by Richard Fleischer
	"1984" (1984) by Michael Radford

In Table 1, I tentatively listed sci-fi movies that deal with a future society under the control of totalitarianism. This table excludes sci-fi movies that are not focused on the totalitarian organization of a future society even though the situation is set in the dystopian future.

This is the reason why such movies as "Shame" (1968) by Ingmar Bergman, "A Clockwork Orange" (1971) by Stanley Kubrick, "Futureworld" (1976) by Richard T. Heffron, "Time of the Wolf" (2003) by Michael Haneke, etc., were not included in the table. The table is not yet complete; upon further analysis, additional movies could be added.

3   Dystopia in the Real World

I am a movie lover and watch one to two movies per day! I have found it rather difficult to find sci-fi movies that describe a utopia. One reason for the imbalanced proportion between utopian and dystopian movies might be the historical facts of human civilization, in which there have been many totalitarian and autocratic societies. We can remind ourselves of such cases as Germany under the regime of Hitler, the Soviet Union under Stalin, China under Mao Zedong, Cambodia under Pol Pot, and more and more if we limit the list just to World War 2 and afterwards.

Most movies are made to entertain audiences. Sometimes, however, serious themes, such as the nature of dystopia, will be adopted for raising the consciousness of people about their own futures, so they will be able to avoid the circumstances that will lead them again into dystopia.

4   How Can Dystopia Become Possible?

Some dystopian movies include an explanation of the process by which the society has come to accept such a regime. For example, "1984" refers to a nuclear war, "Soylent Green" mentions a population explosion and the consequent shortage of food, and "ZPG" and "Logan's Run" also refers to a population explosion. "Metropolis" and "THX-1138" do not have such causes; hence the audience is placed into an unexpected situation from the beginning without any explanatory narrative.

So, how were the totalitarian and autocratic societies possible in the real world? Examples that I have cited in the previous section were cases in which an older regime was destroyed, and people believed in propaganda that a better society will come about. This belief delivered controlling power to a totalitarian leader. Today, many of the countries mentioned above are more democratic, which seems to suggest that a totalitarian society is a transitional state before the eventual emergence of a democracy.

This leads to a next question: Is democratic society the final form that will last forever? If we think about the future not far from present time, with the likely circumstances of an energy crisis, the shortage of underground resources, the shortage of food, the population explosion, and the cost of upgrading developing countries, it seems reasonable to think the entire world will be thrown into turmoil.

Table 2. Negative aspects in dystopian sci-fi movies

	Domination	Propaganda	Behavior Monitoring	Mind Control
"Metropolis" (1927) by Fritz Lang	Rich			
"1984" (1954) by Rudolph Cartier "1984" (1956) by Michael Anderson "1984" (1984) By Michael Radford	Party	"Hate."	AV system, spy	Special Device
"Fahrenheit 451" (1966) by Francois Truffaut	Firefighters	"Waste books!"	People	
"2001 A Space Odyssey" (1968) by Stanley Kubrick	HAL		Robot	
"THX-1138" (1970) by George Lucas	Government	"What's wrong?"	People	Red capsule
"ZPG" (1971) by Michael Campus	Government	"No babies!"	Flying object	
"Solaris" (1972) by Andrei Arsenyevich Tarkovsky "Solaris" (2002) by Steven Soderbergh	Solaris		Through mind	Solaris reads the mind
"Soylent Green" (1973) by Richard Fleischer	Government	"Eat Soylent Green!"		
"Logan's Run" (1976) by Michael Anderson	Government	"Life must end at 30!"		

5   Dystopia and Future Technology

From the viewpoint of user experience, it would be good to focus on the development of devices and systems to achieve positive objectives, like those described in the PERMA Model. However, we should also consider how the future devices and information/communication technology (ICT) can be used to control society, which would lead us into a negative life experience.

Table 2 shows how domination, propaganda, behavior monitoring, and mind control are described in several dystopian sci-fi movies. Domination concerns social organization and is less related to ICT. Future technology may be related to propaganda and mind control, but here I shall focus on behavior monitoring. Regarding this aspect, the ubiquitous technology will be one of the plausible means to achieve the controlled totalitarian society.

The following technologies are available now and will be reinforced in the near future. They all have the potential to deliver information to those in control of governments, systems, communication networks, and devices:

Mobile Device. Devices such as laptops, tablet PCs, and smart phones equipped with global positioning system (GPS) can send the location of the device user.

Internet-Related System. Internet-related system gives personal information such as preferences, political attitudes, social groupings, and other personal information to those in control by analyzing the contents of SNS, blog, email and the log data of illegal access to the prohibited sites. Such technologies for the Big Data as data mining, massively parallel machine, grid computing, distributed file system and others have already been realized.

Small Chips. Small chips such as RFID and IC-tags, implemented in many varieties of personal and professional objects, will send the location and handling information of the object (or the person) to people in control.

Video Cameras. Video cameras are now set up at various places in and out of homes, business and government buildings, travel-system stations and routes, and commercial shops of all kinds and are already used to trace the move of suspects.

Surveillance by Satellite or Airplane. This kind of system will provide the detailed pictures and specific locations of particular objects and people. Although it is influenced by the weather condition and the vegetation and is unable to make the reconnaissance of people in underground, video camera will give some supplemental information.

Biometrics. Biometric system including physiological, psychological, and behavioral measures will give information about and provide accurate identification of the person.

Scene Analysis and Pattern Recognition. This kind of technology analyzes the pictures taken by organizations, government, and individuals that will give sufficient information to identify people, places, and objects in almost any environment or location.

When such technologies are in the hands of those who have a strong will to control people, the world drifts quickly and inexorably to a state far worse than those described in dystopian sci-fi movies. To wake us up and to help us prepare for the future, we can thank and learn much from sci-fi movies, even the most dystopian, about the possible future state of the world. Then we, as the audience, can and should utilize that information to stimulate our good-natured imagination to navigate better alternatives.

Reference

1. Seligman, M.E.: Flourish. Random House Australia, North Sydney (2011)

Interactive Design and the Human Experience: What Can Industrial Design Teach Us

Neil Matthiessen

University of South Florida St. Petersburg, Program in Graphic Design
St. Petersburg, FL, USA
matthiessen@usfsp.edu

Abstract. With more than a third of PC users, 37 percent are now turning to Smartphones and Tablets to surf the Internet and access entertainment. With this dynamic shift, the use of the wide-open Web has migrated to a semi-closed platform, or Apps, that uses the Internet for data transportation, something once performed by a browser. Users are accessing data all at the same time these devices are becoming intergraded into every aspect of modern life. User interfaces and experiences are changing and designers and developers have to become aware of addressing these changes.

Keywords: User Experience, Industrial Design, Design, Mobile Computing.

1 Introduction

Mobile Computing, Smartphones and Tablets, continue to become such an integral part of contemporary society. These devices have created a large shift in terms of connectivity. With more than a third of PC users, 37 percent are now turning to Smartphones and Tablets to surf the Internet and access entertainment [1]. With this dynamic shift, the use of the wide-open Web has migrated to a semi-closed platform, or Apps, that uses the Internet for data transportation, something once performed by a browser. This shift is not always by choice or rejection of the Web, but out of convenience. These Apps provide the user with ease and a direct link to the user task, as well as simplifying the user life [2].

Mobile devices are no longer just a connection to information, but are starting to become incorporated into everyday living. Car manufacturers, like Ford, are increasing Bluetooth integration to allow mobile devices to stream music through the cars' audio systems, while the company Visteon is planning on mobile devices to become fully integrated into the car. Their aim is to go beyond replacing the car stereo and will do so with the developed Device to Vehicle HMI (human/machine interface). The HMI concept looks at operating the vehicle entertainment system, climate control and other systems with personal mobile devices. What is unique about this system is that there is an integrated dock to provide power, but the system is entirely wireless which allows anyone in the car with the appropriate device to have control over certain aspects. Though tight coupling between consumer electronics and

A. Marcus (Ed.): DUXU/HCII 2013, Part I, LNCS 8012, pp. 100–106, 2013.

the automotive industry can be very problematic: a cell phone has a typical lifespan of 18 months and an automobile an estimated lifecycle of 8 to 10 years."[3] The consumer lifespan of a tablet has not been established yet, but it is safe to say that a car will typically last beyond consumer electronics.

The car is not the only product that is starting to couple mobile devices. Other examples include home electronics such as TVs, sound systems, heating/cooling systems, coffee makers and electrical outlets for homeowners to be in control of their energy. The majority of these products, however, will outlive the mobile devices. This is an issue with all consumer electronics that are starting to integrate mobile devices into their products. But Companies like Qualcomm have developed and continue to better chipsets, on a open-source networking, so that communication between the product and multiple devices from various manufacturers improves.

With the shift from accessing content, games and entertainment from the PC to mobile devices, users are being accustomed to do more with these devices. They are now being trained and accepting to use their devices to do things beyond the web and control various items and tasks on location. As the shift continues to grow, designers are going to be confronted by new challenges, and the focus will keep growing and developing content driven sites, application interfaces, and ultimately to virtual control panels. The user experience is not tied to the physical, but is manifested itself into the entire experience, virtual and physical.

2   The User Experience

As the shift keeps moving into these semi-closed connections and integrated products with mobile devices, the user has to go beyond the novelty and even usability. The developments of these Apps have to provide a connection and a desire for the users. Apple App store alone has 425,000 apps and developers have created an incredible array of over 100,000 native iPad apps [4]. The competition is abundant so to keep the user interested, a connection needs to go beyond usability. Technology and user interface design should start to be seen as not just about usability or functionality, but also in the same light as any physical object. The virtual world and the physical world are becoming integrated and as designers the approach should be looked at not separate but integrated. "Dreyfuss stated, "Industrial design is a means of making sure the machine created attractive commodities that work better because they are designed better. It is coincidental, but equally important" [5].

Since the development of the computer, there has been a separation between the hardware and software. The hardware, especially the devices that we handle have fallen to the industrial designers. But the software has not always been thought of the same way in its design and development. There are unique attributes to the virtual, where one cannot see the physical, so a perceptual language grows to help a user navigate in this new environment. Technological advances in the modern era has philosophically created a disconnect, "It is a product of a modern world view that seeks to separate and purify the categories of the human and the technical, ignoring and downplaying the degree to which humans and objects have always mutually shaped each other" [6]. The use of tools is infused in humanity. There cannot be a separation to human and nonhuman devices because we are interconnected. But anytime changes take place, people must be able to perceive the value and understand it [7].

This separation can be seen in how usability was originally defined as the degree of efficiency and effectiveness of use within a specified range of users, tasks, tools, and environment [8]. This is the very basic concept of usability. But to be able to quantitatively discern usability, Shackel [9] who suggested four dimensions of usability: effectiveness, learn ability, flexibility, and attitude. Usability in this sense only looked at the mechanical aspect; did this do what it was intended to do and could the user complete the task? This way of looking at usability ignored the emotional side of humans. This is especially true when this comes to consumer products. For example, when a consumer decides to purchase a car they do think about usability or function of a car. If that was all consumers wanted then all cars could look exactly the same. Instead, consumers think about the place of a car in their life — how it fits their budget, their desire for comfort, their need for peace of mind, the aesthetics [10]. Functionality and usability are expected, but the user experience goes beyond functionality. Users are also looking for pleasure in products use [11], and emotional, experiential aspects related to appeal, aesthetics, or product image [12]. This can be seen in how mobility devices are not just devices; they have been marketed to consumers on a emotional level. The connections to these devices are more then just utilitarian to the user; they are becoming a central device for modern day living.

The user experience is not being tied to just the ease and use of a product or a software, but the over all experience. Accessing content via the Internet that once was a stationary event in front of a computer, is now nomadic. All users can now access information, content, and entertainment almost anywhere and at anytime. The experiences for each user changes and because of their environment, how they access content has changed. The way that consumers are accessing products is changing, so now they are starting to have choices of how to interact with products. The new definition of usability of a consumer electronic product is "satisfying the users in terms of both the performance and the image and impression felt by them."[13] This is not just related to consumer electronic devices, but to all things that a person interacts with. Developing Apps, Web Sites, Software, have all become the extension of the product or the company. The best products talk to their potential customers on an emotional level, as well as satisfying functional needs [14].

The physical experience is being replicated into the virtual environment. There are many factors that have to be considered in the design process, the experience that the user will have will be based on there perceived experience with the interaction they have, but this will be coupled with other experiences they have had in the past with similar products. Users bring their past experiences with them.

> "Design choices about visual similarity to existing products may affect customer perceptions of value by affect designed to and the extent to which the product stimulates analogical reasoning, which facilitates the

cognitive change necessary for resolving incongruity; and the design choices about the product's visual appeal influence the extent to which the product stimulates positive affect infusion, which also facilitates cognitive change. As the incongruity triggered by the innovation's novelty is (not) resolved, the cognitive and emotional responses to it change, making the perception of its value a dynamic constructive enable transfer of knowledge from available trigger cognitions and emotions with a positive effect on perceived value." [15]

Though if the functionality or what the user perceives to not be, achieves the same level or a better experience from the user's experience, this can have a negative effect. Especially in mobile devices, the Apps are an extension of the physical device and perceptions of the device is placed into the App. Also if the App is an extension of a company, the perceptions of that company can be transferred to either the physical or virtual aspects; meaning that if a user has a favorable view of the company prior to the use of the companies' virtual presence, that view is carried over. Though the virtual presence of a company can have an affect on the overall company favorability.

3   Design Choices

Usability has gone beyond the pure functionality, once a user learns to use and navigate; the emotional and cultural needs rise. To the user, functionality does not end with usability, but is the self being satisfied. This is ambiguous. How do these emotional needs get met? One method is "understanding of people's sensorial perceptions and cultural values, where products have added value, meeting user's true needs and making their experience more meaningful." [16] The user experience is not just tied to the interface or the product, but the user projects their understanding through a set of values and understanding that they have learned through their culture and social upbringing. The user does not just bring past experiences of knowledge that can be directly related to interface or product, but they bring a large set of knowledge that has virtually no connection.

As technology tries to create a compatibility that works for all, through standardizations, "there is a danger of a loss of cultural identity and tradition." [17] It makes sense to try to create standardizations in technology, but the human factor is easily lost. The Industrial Designers Society of America defines one aspect of the responsibility of an Industrial Designer "The industrial designer's unique contribution places emphasis on those aspects of the product or system that relate most directly to human characteristics, needs and interests. This contribution requires specialized understanding of visual, tactile, safety and convenience criteria, with concern for the user." [18] Most of the development of software has been centralized in or by USA developers. The concerns of the users have been thought of, but only on one level, western culture. To be able to truly develop a connection to the user beyond functionality, cultural factors need to be addressed.

Another aspect that developers have to start to pay attention to is how the user will interact with the Apps. Mobile devices allow the user to access content from virtually anywhere, but design decisions and usability are still made on the idea that a person will access the content in a consistent manner. As users access data nomadically, development has to take into consideration the potential way that users will access the data. The physical world plays a major role in the satisfaction of experience. Users usually do not associate these two things to the emotional connection, but if a user is attempting to access data and they are in a situation that is adding stress, they will develop a negative attitude to that App or site.

4　Safety

Developers need to start to address the potential safety issues that a user may have. Though an argument can be made that it is the user's responsibility to access data in a safe manner, but functionality does play a role when and where a user may access the data.

> (…) well-designed device that reduces distraction at the operational level may actually undermine driving safety if it encourages drivers to use the device more frequently while driving. This usability paradox occurs when increased ease of use reduces the distraction of any particular interaction but increases overall risk by encouraging drivers to use the device more frequently. This tendency for drivers to adapt to improvements and thereby undermine the expected safety benefits is a common phenomenon. For example, when roadway improvements are made (lanes widened, shoulders added, lighting improved), speeds increase. Drivers may view hands-free cell phones as safe to use while driving and so make more calls than they would with a handheld cell phone. [19]

Most of these Apps take into account usability, but may have overlooked the issue of time of use. Most App development is based on a specific task, and the development sets out to accomplish that task. When devices are mobile, an approach has to be developed by the development team to identify how a user will use the App. Though an App is virtual, the fact remains that a user is able to be nomadic with their mobile device and the Apps.

5　Conclusion

The way people access information, entertainment, and social networks are changing rapidly. Even the way that productive software is changing. Usability will always be at the core but people are looking beyond the function; they are looking at the experience. The line between software and product continues to blur. Content has become truly mobile and mobile devices are becoming multifunction devices. Devices now have the ability to allow people to communicate, find information and control various products, all on one device. These devices are chameleons; a development of an App is not for whichever device but the App becomes the device and the App becomes the product. As content is accessed on the move and content is becoming accessed in a semi-closed avenue, usability has to extend out beyond just function. Designer and developers of software have to start to think more like industrial designers, to think that they are creating product.

References

1. Connected Intelligence, http://www.connected-intelligence.com/about-us/press-releases/37-pc-users-migrate-activities-mobile-devices-according-npd-group-0
2. Wired, http://www.wired.com/magazine/2010/08/ff_webrip/all/
3. Gil-Castiñeira, F., Chaves-Diéguez, D., González-Castaño, F.J.: Integration of Nomadic Devices with Automotive User Interfaces
4. Apple, http://www.apple.com/pr/library/2011/07/07Apples-App-Store-Downloads-Top-15-Billion.html
5. Dreyfuss, H.: Designing for People New York, Simon and Schuster (1955)
6. Latour, B.: We Have Never Been Modern, Harvard University Press (1993)
7. Rindova, V.P., Petkova, A.P.: When Is a New Thing a Good Thing? Technological Change, Product Form Design, and Perceptions of Value for Product Innovations. Organization Science 18(2), 217–232 (2007)
8. Bennet, J.: Managing to Meet Usability Requirements: Establishing and Meeting Software Development Goals. In: Bennet, J., Case, D., Sandelin, J., Smith, M. (eds.) Visual Display Terminals, Englewood Cliffs, NJ, pp. 161–184. Prentice-Hall (1984)
9. Shackel, B.: Ergonomics in Design for Usability. In: Harrison, M.D., Monk, A.F. (eds.) People and Computers: Designing for Usability, Proceedings of the 2nd Conference of Human-Computer Interaction Specialist Group British Computer Society, Cambridge University Press, Cambridge (1986)
10. Companies spent the 20th century managing efficiencies. They must spend the 21st century managing experiences.
11. Jordan, P.W.: Human Factors for Pleasure in Product Use. Applied Ergonomics 29(1), 25–33 (1998)
12. Suri, J.F., Marsh, M.: Scenario Building As An Ergonomics Method In Consumer Product Design. Applied Ergonomics 31(1), 151–157 (2000)
13. Han, S.H., Yun, M.H., Kwahk, J., Hong, S.W.: Usability of Consumer Electronic Products. International Journal of Industrial Ergonomics 28(3-4), 143–151 (2001)
14. Good Design Can Cash In On The Gray, http://profeng.com/columns/good-design-can-cash-in-on-the-grey-pound
15. Rindova, V.P., Petkova, A.P.: Technological Change, Product Form Design, and Perceptions of Value for Produce Innovations 18(2), 217–232 (2007)

16. Li, H., Sun, X., Zhang, K.: Culture-Centered Design: Cultural Factors in Interface Usability and Usability Test. In: Eighth ACIS International Conference on Software Engineering, Artificial Intelligence, Networking, and Parallel/Distributed Computing, vol. 3, pp. 1084–1088. IEEE Conference Publication (2007)
17. Li, H., Sun, X., Zhang, K.: Culture-Centered Design: Cultural Factors in Interface Usability and Usability Test. In: Eighth ACIS International Conference on Software Engineering, Artificial Intelligence, Networking, and Parallel/Distributed Computing, vol. 3, pp. 1084–1088. IEEE Conference Publication (2007)
18. What is Industrial Design, http://www.idsa.org/what-is-industrial-design
19. Lee, J.D., Strayer, D.L.: Preface to the Special Section on Driver Distraction, Human Factors. The Journal of the Human Factors and Ergonomics Society Winter 46, 583–586 (2004)

Location, Location, Location: About Home Networking Devices Location and Features

Abbas Moallem[*]

College of Engineering, San José State University, USA
abbas.moallem@sjsu.edu

Abstract. A home. It is where people spend most of their family time. It is a place to gather friends. It is somewhere to escape the world in the comfort of someplace that is our own. And it is a location that is filled with a variety of big and small appliances and devices. The number of appliances, their size, shape, and their features change over and over again, and based on the advancement in technology, there are changes in the needs of consumers alongside a certain expectation of comfort and productivity. One of the properties of a device in a home is the location in which people place it. Where to place the device depends, among other things, on its use and the features that the device offers as well as its aesthetics. This study investigates the location of home networking devices, also known as routers, in modern houses. It also looks at how router features accommodate users based on the location where people keep the devices and how their needs have evolved.

For this study, 95 participants were surveyed about the location of their home networking devices (routers) location then, 43 locations were evaluated from houses located in Silicon Valley, California. The results provide the data on the rooms where people keep their routers, their physical location, and certain idiosyncrasies of their usage. In light of this study we have extracted some results and hypothesized some guidelines for future designs of routers in the consumer market.

Keywords: Home Networking, Network Device Location, Device Location versus Features, Router Location.

1 Introduction

Whether or not you live in a small apartment or a luxurious house, the device and appliances that you choose for your home, their size, features, location, aesthetics, and cost are all important factors in your decision. A rapid review of some home appliances over time illustrates how much they have evolved as technology has advanced and expectations of comfort have risen. Take, for example, a telephone device at home. Early phones were a luxury item that gradually turned into a home necessity in western countries. Soon the telephone became an important device often found in the kitchen, living room or family room.

---

[*] Dr. Abbas Moallem is an adjunct professor at San Jose State University, and California State University, East Bay where he teaches HCI and human factors. He has been working as a user experience architect and usability expert for the past twenty years in Silicon Valley California.

A. Marcus (Ed.): DUXU/HCII 2013, Part I, LNCS 8012, pp. 107–114, 2013.

Telephone usage has changed drastically from that lonesome, lavish device in a single room. And yet despite this, a telephone's main feature, allowing two parties to communicate by voice, has not changed but instead been expanded on. So many features have been added to it, while at the same time its location at home, size and aesthetics have evolved a lot. The most traditional location for a phone in a US household is in the kitchen, mounted on a wall. [1]

Another item that technology has radically affected in households is the clock. Clocks range from large grandfather clocks in the living room to smaller and fancier ones. Eventually the time display traditionally associated with clocks became incorporated into most devices. Just think about how many time-displays you might have in your house. I could count up to six, and that was excluding cell-phones and computers.

With the speedy expansion of the Internet and Internet-based technologies in homes, an Internet connection has become a basic utility like electricity, gas, or water. Consequently, a wireless home is becoming almost a standard item in a house independent to the size of each individual home [2]. From a dial up modem in the computer to a smart appliance that needs to communicate with networking devices, home networking devices are continuously changing [3]. This study tries to understand how these devices are used from the location they are placed in, aesthetics, size, and positioning. The study should provide us with some input as to how to improve these devices based on their actual usage. To the best of our knowledge, no other study has been yet been conducted from this perspective [4].

2   Method

In this investigation to learn where and how people use their home networking devices (i.e. routers), two studies were conducted in parallel:

Group 1 (Online Questionnaire): 95 participants completed the online survey (self-reported).

Group 2 (Location Investigated): Information about 43 houses and the location of the networking devices was collected in a paper survey including pictures of the device location.

To better understand the pattern of usage, a follow-up study on seven locations selected among the second group is in progress. These seven houses are all located in Silicon Valley, California in the United States. The process of visiting each location and evaluating the location and configuration of the networking device was investigated along with a semi-structured interview with one of the homeowners—the person who most often managed the home networking devices.

3   Results

3.1   Survey 1 Results

In the first survey, 95 participants reported the size of their home, the room where the device was located, and the device brand. 38% of the homes are 1-2 bedroom apartments/houses, 17% are 3 bedroom houses or town houses, 40% are 4 bedroom houses, and 5% are other type of facilities.

The networking device (router) is said to be placed in the living room in 45% of the cases, while 28% stayed in the bedroom, 13% in the office, 3% the garage, 2% a spare room, and 8% in other locations. Almost all of the brands are represented in the participant sample group: Berkin 4%, Dlinks 11%, Linksys 20%, AT&T 22 %, NETGEAR 24%, and other brands 19% (Fig 1).

This result shows that overall users are most likely to keep their networking device in their living room or bedroom. There does not seem to be a much of a correlation between this preference and the size of the apartment/house (Fig 2, 3 and 4). However, in bigger four bedroom homes with Silicon Valley standards, the likelihood of an office being the area of placement for the router increases. While manufacturers often claim a wide area of coverage for wireless connections, it seems that this is not always the case as certain obstructions are not taken into account. This is one reason that users keep their devices close to entertainment devices such as televisions, sound systems, or laptops depending on usage. The proximity to the entertainment unit would thus allow for a wired connection as well.

In addition, since wireless devices do not cope well in transmitting with the presence of physical obstructions such as cabinets or drawers, mirrors, glasses, metallic objects, thick walls and ceilings, users are limited when it comes to the choice of room for their router. To get the better signal, the user is almost stuck choosing their living room or bedroom.

The other issue that users are confronted with is interference with neighboring wireless networks, microwave ovens, 2.4 GHz cordless telephones, Bluetooth devices, wireless baby monitors or other similar devices. Since solving the interference often requires the difficulty of management or a change of channel and the SSID on users' router, most users instead turn to changing the physical closeness of their router rather than managing their home networking for a better efficiency.

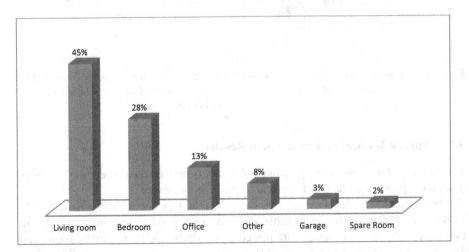

Fig. 1. Room where networking device (router) is located. (95 Locations in Silicon Valley, California, USA)

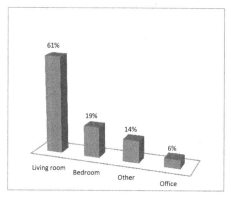

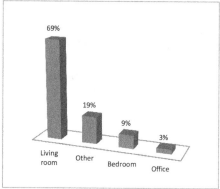

Fig. 2. Room where networking device (router) is located in 1-2 bedroom apt. or houses

Fig. 3. Room where networking device (router) is located in 3 bedrooms houses

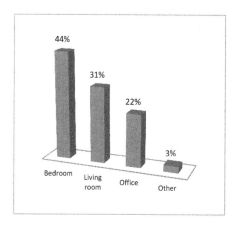

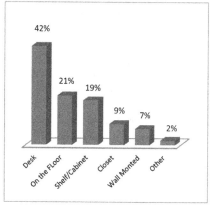

Fig. 4. Room where networking device (router) is located in 4 bedroom houses

Fig. 5. Area where networking device (router) is located in a 1-3 bedroom home (43 Locations)

3.2   Survey 2- Location Investigation Results

The result of the second survey includes the data from the room where the device is placed and pictures of the exact physical location of the device.

The physical location of the devices indicates that 42% are placed on a desk, 21% on the floor, 19% on a shelves or cabinet, 9% in a closet and 7% mounted on walls. In this same study, 23% of devices are placed in a bedroom, 49% in a living room, and 5% in each of the following locations: garage, spare room or other location. This survey thus provides support on the previous one in terms as to the commonality of where the device is located (Fig. 2 & 5).

The physical location of the device in each room seems to be in accordance with the room placement. On a shelf or desk close to a computer seems to be a natural choice, but still 21% of people keep their router on the floor. A closer look at the provided pictures indicated that in most of the cases the wireless device was also very close to a cable plug and Internet cable in the electrical cabinet. While some devices offer the wall mounting feature for the device, only 7% were placed so.

The data taken from the pictures provided were classified and revealed that:

- Routers were mostly placed next to an appliance like a telephone or computer (Figure 6).
- Multiple wires around the router create a very unpleasant and cluttered situation (Figure 7).
- Positioning of the device is horizontal or vertical according to the design of the device (Figures 8 and 9).
- Most of the devices were placed in the open and were not hidden (Figure 9).

Fig. 6. Router on desk close to telephone   **Fig. 7.** Multiple wires around the router

Fig. 8. Router in open air with vertical positioning   **Fig. 9.** Router on desk with horizontal positioning

4   Data Analysis and Design Concepts

The results from this empirical study tend to suggest a pattern of behavior in most networking device usage at home, including the following:

- Most people place their router in the living room
- Routers are almost always placed close to other electronic devices such as a computer
- The mixture of wires from other devices creates a very common chaotic situation around the router
- Most users seem to be unaware of certain positions of the router that would offer optimal performances in accordance to range
- Only a very small number of the users observed mounted the router on the wall or placed the router in a discrete location such as in a closet or the garage
- Although most of the routers observed offered multiple USB ports for connecting an external storage drive, no one observed in this sample was shown to use them
- Although most of the router models evaluated in this study offered up to four wired connections and one to two USB ports, in addition to an ADC adapter wire and a main network connection, it has been observed that it is rare for any of these additions to be used
- When the offered ports are used, it seems that the multiplicity of the wired device makes the routers, which are designed for vertical positioning, somehow unstable

The results from my observed study tend to suggest a common pattern of behavior in most networking device usage at home. In addition, it helps us to extrapolate a number of issues that seem to not yet have been considered in current designs.

In light of this study, in this section we are going to look at some current identified issues, define some possible technological or environmental changes for home networking, and then try to hypothesize some guidelines for future designs of routers in the consumer market.

Some observations of current router design:

- Current router design does not offer wireless coverage in a large enough diameter to offer strong signals throughout a house independent of where the user chooses to place the router in the house.
- The router offers some features that only a small percentage of users utilize, but ultimately the cost of these features is paid by all users. This includes the number of USB ports or card reading ports, and to some degree the number of Ethernet ports.
- Routers seem to have been designed with the wrong assumption about the positioning of the devices. For example, it is assumed that people might use the wall mounting fixture but in reality a very small percentile choose to employ that facet. Again this assumption creates an ignored feature that a majority of customers still have to bear the cost of.
- Average users often have difficulty understanding the documentation, labeling, and information on the package. These provide an explanation of the features but not

what it is they do. For example, text on a router package indicates "Dual Band avoid interference," or "DLNA Media Server," but it does not indicate what DLNA does for the user. More scenario-based information or help could read: "Suitable for a 2-bedroom home with cable; share media (video, pictures, and music from a central location)". Without this, it becomes common for customers to purchase products that do not fit their true needs.

- Most networking devices seem to have been designed in imitation of a competitor's product rather than based on what users really need. A good example of this is the USB ports on routers, which are rarely used but continuously offered.
- Whenever users need to use multiple ports such as connecting the USB ports or adding Ethernet cables, the small device becomes very hard to position and creates a messy environment that is not necessary or pleasant to have in a living room, and in some cases may even be dangerous.
- Users have a hard time understanding that they can change the device's configuration by logging into the user interface of the device to make further changes. Even when they are shown how to do so, they are discouraged by its complexity as well as worried about changing something incorrectly and having it affect their network.
- The device designs do not seem to take into consideration the reality of new homes and systems. The router offers the USB port while most of the devices now connect wirelessly to the network.

Now let's take a look at some possible technological or environmental changes in home networking and hypothesize some guidelines for future designs of routers in the consumer market.

- There are going to be more and more smart devices that require wireless access for full operation, such as refrigerators, heating systems with temperature controls, surveillances systems, washing machines, and so on. These devices are going to be positioned all around in the household and will thus require the home networking device to provide sufficient signal to reach all appliances around the house.
- The device should offer an incorporated capability (internal drive) to back up the system configuration of all connected devices.
- The user should be able to communicate with the device directly though a touch screen, rather than through a computer interface.
- The device should have a test feature to detect and problem solve any issues, periodically scan the network, and show the status of the system.
- The device should include a security features that works well and is easy to manage.
- The device should be built in a way that can be incorporated as a display into a specific location.
- Interaction with the device should be extremely easy for average homeowners/users. The users will not be able to handle the complexity of a featured home networking system if it is not easy to understand and operate.
- Device should be very robust and offer one-click functionality to users in case of any issues so that the device will diagnose and problem-solve the issues.

5   Conclusion

Although this study offers some indication about how the networking devices are used, the number of houses, their type, size and locations are among other factors that need to be taken in consideration in future studies. On top of that, the houses studied in this sample are located in one of the most developed areas on the planet: Silicon Valley, California in the United States, and so do not reflect other geographical locations or residences, especially those in a more urban city setting. Further studies are needed to evaluate the usage of routers in different types of homes and apartments located in big and rural cities.

Acknowledgments. The author would like to acknowledge his students at the ISE 217 HCI class at San Jose State University and Nassim Moallem, for data gathering and assistance in this study.

References

1. Mueller, M.: Universal service in telephone history: A reconstruction. Elsevier (1993)
2. Moallem, A.: Why should home networking be complicated? In: Cheng, J., Kunz, T. (eds.) Advances in Usability Evaluation: part II. CRC Press (2013)
3. Russell, D.M., Gossweiler, R.: On the Design of Personal & Communal Large Information Scale Appliances. In: Abowd, G.D., Brumitt, B., Shafer, S. (eds.) UbiComp 2001. LNCS, vol. 2201, pp. 354–361. Springer, Heidelberg (2001)
4. Sharpe, W.P., Stenton, S.P.: Information Appliances. In: Jacko, J.A., Sears, A. (eds.) The Human-Computer Interaction Handbook: Fundamentals, Evolving Technologies and Emerging Applications. Laurence Erlbaum Associate Publisher (2003)
5. Geuss, M.: Router Tips to Make Your Wireless Faster. In: PCWorld (October 18, 2011)
6. http://www.pcworld.com/article/242112/router_tips_to_make_your_wireless_faster.html

Metacommunication and Semiotic Engineering: Insights from a Study with Mediated HCI

Ingrid Teixeira Monteiro, Clarisse Sieckenius de Souza, and Carla Faria Leitão

SERG / Departamento de Informática, PUC-Rio
Rua Marquês de São Vicente 225
22451-900 Rio de Janeiro, RJ – Brazil
{imonteiro,clarisse,cfaria}@inf.puc-rio.br

Abstract. Semiotic perspectives on HCI take human-computer interaction as a special case of computer-mediated human communication. Through the interface, systems designers communicate to users their design vision as well as how the system can or should be used for a variety of purposes. To date, there hasn't been enough empirical research in HCI exploring this complex phenomenon. This paper reports an empirical research about metacommunication in HCI and discusses how and why semiotically-inspired research can contribute to advance knowledge in this field. The aim of the discussion is to motivate and justify more research projects in this interdisciplinary territory and to present semiotic engineering concepts and tools that can be used to carry them out.

Keywords: Semiotic engineering, computer-mediated human communication, end-user development, mediated web navigation.

1 Introduction

Human-Computer Interaction is an interdisciplinary field *par excellence*. Semiotics, however, in spite of its indisputable contribution to all investigations involving representations, interpretation and communication, is hardly listed among the disciplines that have influenced HCI to this date [1]. Although the straightforward explanation for this is that semiotic theories look plainly esoteric to most non-semioticians, a justification to perpetuate HCI's impermeability to semiotic influence cannot be easily sustained. To be sure, the effectiveness of this discipline's contribution depends on the semioticians' willingness to revisit and revise the foundations of their discipline in order to produce *usable* concepts, models and methods for the benefit of non-semiotician [2]. However, successful cross-disciplinary initiatives in this context also depend on compelling *cases*, which demonstrate the distinctive contribution of a semiotic perspective while responding to relevant HCI challenges and opportunities. This paper takes the latter course and discusses one such case against the backdrop of new kinds of social participation brought about by the Web 2.0.

De Souza [3] argues that semiotics can provide solid conceptual foundations for the design of technology that *mediates* one's participation in contemporary society and shapes the signs that can be used to express one's intent, beliefs, values, capacities, social engagement, etc. This, in and of itself, is a strong reason to stimulate more

A. Marcus (Ed.): DUXU/HCII 2013, Part I, LNCS 8012, pp. 115–124, 2013.

research projects at the intersection between semiotics and HCI. What must not be forgotten is that interested researchers must have concrete examples of what they should be looking at and looking for.

In response to this need, our paper concisely presents how semiotics has been used in a qualitative empirical study that explored new kinds of technology-enabled social interaction. The study is described in detail in Monteiro's dissertation [4] and a subsequent technical report [5]. Here we only describe how it was conducted and highlight its main findings with selected pieces of evidence collected in various experiments with users. Our goal is to discuss how this kind of research can be conducted and how it opens the door to promising investigations about *metacommunication* and *mediated HCI*. We strongly believe that such investigations are particularly relevant to improve the design of technologies that support end-user development and wider social participation in the Web 2.0.

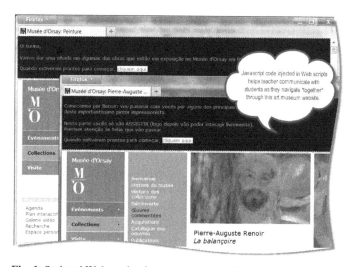

Fig. 1. Scripted Web navigation creates new kinds of social experience

For a quick illustration of applications that can benefit from semiotically-informed research, let us think of software that enables users to customize their experience with Web applications. In Fig. 1 above we show how a Portuguese-speaking art teacher might combine two Firefox Add-ons, Greasemonkey [6] and iMacros [7], to create new learning experiences for her students. Greasemonkey injects JavaScript code into existing Web pages as they are loaded in the browser while iMacros records sequences of interaction steps. With both, the teacher produces a scripted tour across the Musée d'Orsay's website. By sharing her scripts with students, who cannot speak French, the teacher achieves among other things two important effects. She creates new software upon existing software and thus communicates new things about what the original software communicates to her. And she mediates her students' learning experience by means of a digital representation of herself, which virtually encounters and guides each student in a technologically amplified educational environment.

Using a semiotic theory of human-computer interaction to analyze and design for experiences like the one above has at least one major advantage. The hallmark of semiotic perspectives on HCI is to expand the scope of the phenomenon under study and say that, in fact, we should not be speaking strictly of user-system interaction (or its recent reconceptualization referred to as *user experience*). Rather, what goes on as people interact with computer technologies is that they (knowingly or not) engage in a very specific kind of computer-mediated human communication. Through the interface, software designers and developers communicate with software users. They tell them things like how the software product could or should be used, when, where, why and what for. It is only when users, through interaction itself, *get the message* (*i. e.* achieve a satisfying interpretation of what the software product *means*) that technology begins to be used successfully.

Once we accept that software producers and software consumers communicate through systems interfaces, we not only include 'more humans' (*i. e.* users *and* designers) in our scope of investigation, but also gain a unified theoretical framework that can account for semiotic processes taking place on the designers' side, on the users' side and also in their the digital mediator's side, the system's. In short, semiotic theories and methods can support the investigation of a very large and relevant span of computer-mediated communication, unlike any other breed of theory currently used in HCI.

In the following sections we will show how this can be done. Section 2 briefly characterizes semiotic engineering [8], the specific HCI theory that we work with, and presents the Web Navigation Helper (WNH), a user agent that supports mediated interaction with Web applications. Section 3 concisely reports how we collected metacommunication evidence in a lengthy case study carried out by Monteiro [4, 5]. Section 4 highlights the main findings of the reported study and discusses the relevance of this sort of investigation, making the case for more semiotically-inspired research in HCI. Finally, section 5 concludes the paper with suggested items for future research.

2   Semiotic Engineering and End-User Metacommunication with the Web Navigation Helper

Semiotic engineering is a comprehensive theory of HCI dedicated to the study of how designers (one person or a team) and users communicate through systems interfaces. A system's interface acts as the designer's deputy, telling the user what the designer knows about users, what the designed system does, how and why, the designer's vision of how his product benefits the users, how it attends to their needs and meets their expectations [8]. The communication of the designers' vision is received by the user as he or she interacts with the system and discovers the meanings designed into it. This is called metacommunication (communication about communication) and constitutes the prime object of investigation for semiotic engineering. The most striking distinction proposed by this theory compared to other theories in HCI is, as already mentioned, to postulate that designers of interactive software are active participants in the process of interaction.

In order to be of any scientific value, semiotic engineering must provide appropriate tools for researchers to investigate metacomunication and draw valid conclusions that can be subsequently evaluated and used in theory and practice. In response to this requirement we have developed specialized methods to analyze how the designers' communication is emitted through the interface and how it is received by users [9]. Additionally, in recent years, we have started to use technology to help us collect empirical data of metacommunication, namely the Web Navigation Helper (WNH).

WNH is a script-based user agent originally developed to help users with special needs navigate the Web [10, 4]. It is built on top of CoScripter [11] and implemented as an extension of Firefox. While CoScripter is a macro recorder for the Web, WNH is a tool to create and deploy user-defined dialogs that shown on screen as the recorded macro executes. Such dialogs explicitly address the targeted user and, by means of typical interface elements like dropdown lists, text boxes and buttons, among others, they keep parallel interaction *about* the web page in reference. This is done in such a way that all information required to interact with this web page is collected in the parallel conversation between WNH and its user before it is passed on as a macro parameter to the web page. Consequently, WNH *mediates* interaction between users and web applications.

Fig. 2. WNH dialogs help foreign visitors use a local website

For illustration, take the snapshot shown in Fig. 2. The sidebar on the left of the browser window shows a WNH dialog in English. It has been specifically designed to help English-speaking users interested in checking flight information in a Brazilian website (Infraero's) whose interface is only available in Portuguese. The dialog creator included not only the necessary instructions for the addressed user (instructions in 1 and 2 at the top of the sidebar) and a dropdown list at the bottom to collect the user's input and execute the macro, but also useful tips about the official names of some major airports that differ from the name by which they are known to the locals.

The style and content of the dialog on the sidebar signify important things to researchers interested in metacommunication. For example, they provide powerful evidence of how the dialog creator *interprets* and *receives* metacommunication originally encoded in the web page to which the dialog refers (see part of the original web page on the main area of the browser window in Fig. 2). The comment about famous airports' local names, for example, indicates that the dialog creator finds that this is important information missing in the original web page design (where it is not included). Likewise, WNH dialogs reveal their creators' ability to *rephrase* (and in some cases to *repurpose*) metacommunication by means of *interactive computer vocabulary*.

To create mediation, dialog authors can use the WNH dialog editor. It works in combination with CoScripter and allows them: to record scripts for specific tasks; to create mediation dialogs that can be inserted before or after selected script steps; to create mediation dialogs to introduce, capture and explain information that must be passed on to the running script; and to create "online help" pages associated with mediation dialogs, which can include all the range of elements that HTML can handle (text, images, video, audio, etc.). An important feature of the WNH dialog editor is that authors can choose to import into their own dialogs the same interactive elements as are used in the original web page design (see this in Fig. 2, where a dropdown list with exactly the same elements as are shown on Infraero's web page appears at the bottom of the mediation dialog in the sidebar). Alternatively, authors can choose different widgets and even constrain parameters or change properties to improve the quality of mediation (*e. g.* use option buttons rather than a dropdown list, with only the sub-set of choices that make sense to a particular user audience that the dialog author is about to address).

Given this general characterization, the next sections show how semiotic engineering research can be carried out with WNH and the kinds of results it can achieve.

3   Collecting Evidence of End-User Semiotic Engineering

Starting in 2008, we have carried out a number of empirical studies with WNH. Initially, we were mainly interested in building the user agent [10] and exploring its potential as an accessibility tool [12, 13]. Later, however, research carried out by Monteiro [4, 5] showed that accessibility was in fact only one of many possible purposes for which WNH could be used. Insights about the use of WNH as a semiotic engineering research instrument emerged from lengthy empirical investigation with different groups of participants, focusing on different aspects of the users' experience.

When a complete working WNH prototype was finally implemented, an in-depth research could at last be conducted. The overall rationale of the research was: (1) to select a website with *interesting* metacommunication features to be explored; (2) to identify a group of potential users who had barriers to interact with the website by themselves; (3) to identify another group of users who did not have such barriers and who expressed their disposition to *help* the challenged users by creating mediation dialogs for them to achieve a specific task in the selected website; (4) to contrast the communication created by *helpers* with the website's communication achieved through the original interface; and (5) to observe how the group of *helpees* reacted and used the proposed mediation dialogs while achieving a specific scripted task. This research covers a wide spectrum of metacommunication, allowing researchers to have valuable insights on this sort of computer-mediated communication and the technologies that can be designed and developed to explore and enhance it in the context of the Web 2.0.

The first step in our empirical study was to select a website where metacommunication was likely to challenge at least part of the designers' intended audience. Communicability issues were important for two reasons: if there weren't communicability problems, then mediation dialogs would not be needed; additionally, the complete experiment would allow us to appreciate how communicability issues might affect dialog creators and subsequently the dialog end-users. Thus we chose an online mortgage calculator, which was part of a major Brazilian bank's website. As a cultural clarification, we should add that mortgage prices are a big concern in Brazilian society, cross-cutting age ranges (from young adults to elderly citizens) and economic classes (from lower income to higher income). Even citizens who do not have to pay mortgage themselves are usually concerned with mortgage paid by family members or other people with whom they are closely related.

We analyzed the website and identified communicability issues in it. The next step was to think of a group of users that were very likely to have problems *interacting* with the application (but no problems understanding what a mortgage is and the kinds of information required to calculate loan installments if they – or someone in their family – wanted to buy an apartment). Our choice was to work with a group of six elderly users (63-82), who were taking an introductory course on how to use the Internet. These were middle class citizens, interested in gaining digital literacy to benefit from opportunities brought about by the Internet. All of them knew how to use a Web browser and do basic navigation across web pages. In the remainder of this paper we will refer to this group as WNH *helpees*.

Dialog creators, which we will refer to as WNH *helpers* from now on, were two individual selected from a group of four volunteers who designed and implemented mediation dialogs for targeted elderly users to interact with the web application in this study. They were savvy Internet users, with enough technical knowledge to record a mortgage calculation script and define mediation dialogs to address the *helpees* and collect input data from them to complete the calculation script. They were also adequately familiar with the needs of elderly users. We selected dialogs from two individuals from the *helpers* group: one (*helper 1*) was a graduate student doing research in Web accessibility; the other (*helper 2*) was an instructor of an introductory Internet course for the elderly. They were chosen because we wanted to have some contrast in mediation styles.

The *helpers'* dialogs were used in a subsequent test with the group of *helpees*. After they watched a demonstration of WNH and played with it for a while, participants were asked to use it and calculate how much they should pay if they were to buy a property whose value was R\$ 100.000,00. We provided them with fictional financial information about the loaner's family income, the period of the loan, etc. None of the participants had any difficulty to understand that. So, we split them in two groups:

three of the *helpees* interacted with dialogs created by *helper 1*; the other used dialogs created by *helper 2*. Their activity was recorded with audio and screen-capture software. After it was over, each participant was interviewed about his experience with computers, his thoughts and impressions about the activity they did in the test, and about WNH. For lack of space in this paper, we will not go into the details of rich evidence we were able to collect. The interested reader should look at [5] for these. In the following we only summarize the main findings and discuss their contributions.

4   Investigating Metacommunication with WNH

One of the richest evidence we got came from the *helpers'* dialogs themselves. In **Table 1** we contrast a portion of the original website's communication (column 1) with the corresponding communication presented by *helper 1* (column 2) and *helper 2* (column 3) for the end users of WNH mediation dialogs. Notice not only the difference in style, when addressing the *helpees*, but also important discrepancies in interpretation. For example, *helper 2* asks the *helpee* to say where he or she *lives* (row 2), whereas the requested information is actually about where the property is located (possibly somewhere else). The same sort of discrepancy appears in row 5, where *helper 2* asks for the *helpee*'s date of birth instead of that of the oldest person who is going to contribute to paying the mortgage. Another greatly interesting piece of evidence in Table 1 is the contrasting style of *helper 1* and *helper 2*. Notice how *helper 2* is fixated on talking about *the mouse*, the *indicator* (the clickable arrow with which to open a dropdown list), the *white space*, while *helper 1* is not worried with it at all.

Table 1. How helpers received the original metacommunication

Original website	Helper 1	Helper 2
In which city is the property located?	Select the city where the property is located.	Click with the mouse on the indicator below and choose the city where you live.
What is the approximate value of the property?	Inform the value of the property you want to buy. Please, inform the value correctly. It is very important for the calculation.	Write, in the white space below, the value of the property you want the loan for.
What is the gross family income?	Inform the total value of your household income.	Inform in the white space below your monthly income.
What is the birth date of the oldest person contributing to pay the mortgage?	Inform the birth date of the older person contributing to the household income.	Write in the white space below your birth date.

Both groups of *helpees* were able to achieve the task, even if the actual calculation (in view of interpretation discrepancies verified among *helpers*) might not be correct in a real case situation. The accuracy of the calculation was irrelevant for our study, which concentrated solely on mediated metacommunication. So, in the following we discuss further findings and their significance.

One of the most tangible benefits of WNH as perceived by all *helpees* was to break interaction into small steps. This was not only observed during their task activities, but also in their verbal manifestation later, in the post-test interview. For example, one participant said: "There is no way to be complicated. [...] You cannot be lost, because it is sequential. [...] There is nothing there to complicate [things] and you cannot make mistakes." All *helpees* reached the end of the task, although some of them experienced problems along the way.

One of the recurring problems was that mediation dialogs had no error-recovery resources in place. If a participant entered the wrong input, for example, he or she had to start the script over again. More than that, a close look at Table 1 shows that both *helpers* created dialogs that explicitly concentrated on trying to prevent errors (with detailed information and occasional help pages, not shown in Table 1). One of them (*helper 1*) also used in-line formatting as means to verify input and prevent error for such things as typing "3oo" (with literals instead of digits) when the intended input was "300". This strategy was not used by *helper 2*. So, the group of *helpees* using her dialogs failed to anticipate which was the correct format for currency and dates, for instance, and this led to script errors. A remarkable characteristic of both styles of mediation dialogs – and of the original website interface as well – is the little (if any) attention paid to communicating what to do in case of errors. In Table 1 there is an interesting illustration of how oblivious we can be of our metacommunication interlocutor's real needs. In row 3, *helper 1* warns the *helpee* against errors by saying: "Please, inform the value correctly. It is very important for the calculation." Notice that there is no explicit information about *which format* is right; only a communication about the consequences of using the wrong one.

Valuable evidence for researchers interested in semiotic engineering was the fact that both *helpers* were familiar with the needs of elderly users. Be it because of research activity (*helper 1*) or professional practice (*helper 2*), they knew that this group of users is prone to much hesitation and therefore needs constant coaching and reassurance, especially – as was the case – if they are novice users. Although mediation dialogs tended to take care of the coaching reasonably well, it was evident that *helpers* did not pay as much attention to reassuring the *helpees* along the way. Throughout the test, participants would constantly turn to the researcher in search of approval and confirmation that what they had done was right. The only evidence of dialogs for this purpose was a single *"Congratulations! You've successfully achieved task."* closure dialog designed by *helper 1*. *Helper 2*, curiously, didn't even include a closure communication in his mediation dialog. As a result, dialogs were much more impersonal than they had to be, giving evidence that even in very simple metacommunication dialogs as were necessary in this experiment, savvy end users haven't explored the opportunities to come closer to their interlocutors and thus communicate with them more effectively.

This study gave us privileged access to conditions and effects of actual end-user semiotic engineering. *Helpers* were engaged in the same *kind* of activity as professional HCI designers are when they build interfaces for full-fledged Web applications, for example. Deciding how to address the users, how to tell them what to do and what not to do, providing them with the necessary information and appropriate technical or domain knowledge for productive interaction – all of this was part of the *helpers'* task in our experiment. The study also raised many more questions than it gave us answers, proving its worth in long-term research about topics that the HCI community hasn't been investigating systematically. Could it be doing it? Should it be doing it?

5   Opportunity for New Kinds of HCI Research

With the advent of Web 2.0, crowd sourcing, end-user development and content sharing initiatives have become possible and popular. Data mashups and website deployment are within reach for a rapidly increasing number of non-technical users, eager to participate in novel large-scale social processes enabled by web technologies. Our introductory illustration of what can be done with Greasemonkey [6] and iMacros [7] suggests how technology has been changing our lives in depth and breadth.

Although there has been more communication-centered investigations presented in major HCI conferences in recent years, they tend to rely on social psychology and other social sciences (see for example [14, 15, 16, 17]) but not in semiotics. This paper has shown, however, that semiotic engineering offers an opportunity for new kinds of research in HCI. Let us begin with the possibly disturbing fact that, in our case study with WNH, *helpers* may have led their *helpees* astray by introducing misinterpreted communication in their mediation dialogs. This piece of evidence shows once again the power of WNH as an empirical research tool. It also shows the importance of investigating how end users who build mashups and other kinds of content or applications using previously existing software interpret third party's meanings and express their own with new software. Clearly, the effects of misunderstandings resulting from HCI design blunders are propagated and potentially magnified in important ways. Hence the relevance of this kind of research.

Another line of investigation that we take as equally important is how to promote *good* metacommunication among professional HCI designers in the first place. This kind of research is vital to raise the overall quality of end user software engineering that so critically depends on what development tools communicate to end users who are about to build software of their own. WNH is no exception: one of our immediate concerns is to improve both its interfaces, for *helpers* and *helpees*. Additionally, we are working to support end user semiotic engineering more effectively, which would encourage savvier users to represent their intent, beliefs, values, knowledge and capacities more expressively through software interfaces. In this way, they would be readier to enjoy the new kinds of social participation brought about by the Web 2.0.

Acknowledgement. Authors thank FAPERJ and CNPq for supporting this research.

References

1. Rogers, Y.: HCI Theory: Classical, Modern, and Contemporary. Synthesis Lectures on Human-Centered Informatics. Calif. Morgan & Claypool, San Francisco (2012)
2. Nadin, M.: Reassessing the foundations of semiotics: Preliminaries. International Journal of Signs and Semiotic Systems 2(1) (January-June 2012)
3. de Souza, C.S.: Semiotics and Human-Computer Interaction. In: Soegaard, M., Dam, R.F. (eds.) Encyclopedia of Human-Computer Interaction, vol. 25, Interaction-Design.Org, Aarhus (2012),
   `http://www.interaction-design.org/encyclopedia/semiotics_and_human-computer_interaction.html`
4. Monteiro, I.T.: Acessibilidade por diálogos de mediação: Desenvolvimento e avaliação de um assistente de navegação para a Web. Rio de Janeiro: Pontifícia Universidade Católica do Rio de Janeiro, 198 p. MSc Dissertation (2011)
5. Monteiro, I.T., Leitão, C.F., de Souza, C.S.: Interacting with the Web Navigation Helper: First Lessons about Mediated Metacommunication for Increased Accessibility. In: Lucena, C.J.P. (ed.) Monografias em Ciência da Computação MCC (January 2013),
   `http://bib-di.inf.puc-rio.br/techreports/`
6. Greasemonkey, `http://wiki.greasespot.net/Greasemonkey`
7. iMacros, `http://wiki.imacros.net/Main_Page`
8. de Souza, C.S.: The semiotic engineering of human-computer interaction. The MIT Press, Cambridge (2005)
9. de Souza, C.S., Leitão, C.F.: Semiotic Engineering Methods for Scientific Research in HCI. Calif. Morgan & Claypool, San Francisco (2009)
10. Intrator, C., de Souza, C.S.: Using web scripts to improve accessibility. In: IHC 2008. Proceedings of the VIII Brazilian Symposium on Human Factors in Computing Systems, pp. 292–295. Sociedade Brasileira de Computação, Porto Alegre (2008)
11. Leshed, G., Haber, H.B., Matthews, T., Lau, T.: CoScripter: automating & sharing how-to knowledge in the enterprise. In: Proceedings of the SIGCHI Conference on Human Factors in Computing Systems (CHI 2008), pp. 1719–1728. ACM, New York (2008)
12. Intrator, C.: Using Scripts to Improve Web Accessibility. Rio de Janeiro: Pontifícia Universidade Católica do Rio de Janeiro, p. 105. MSc Dissertation (2009)
13. Teixeira Monteiro, I., Sieckenius de Souza, C.: Embedded cultural features in the design of an accessibility agent for the web. In: Stephanidis, C. (ed.) Universal Access in HCI, Part I, HCII 2011. LNCS, vol. 6765, pp. 295–304. Springer, Heidelberg (2011)
14. Sundar, S.S., Oh, J., Bellur, S., Jia, H., Kim, H.-S.: Interactivity as self-expression: a field experiment with customization and blogging. In: Proceedings of the SIGCHI Conference on Human Factors in Computing Systems (CHI 2012), pp. 395–404. ACM, New York (2012)
15. Dabbish, L., Kraut, R., Patton, P.: Communication and commitment in an online game team. In: Proceedings of the SIGCHI Conference on Human Factors in Computing Systems (CHI 2012), pp. 879–888. ACM, New York (2012)
16. Otsuka, K.: Multimodal conversation scene analysis for understanding people's communicative behaviors in face-to-face meetings. In: Salvendy, G., Smith, M.J. (eds.) HCII 2011, Part II. LNCS, vol. 6772, pp. 171–179. Springer, Heidelberg (2011)
17. Weiss, A., Mirnig, N., Buchner, R., Förster, F., Tscheligi, M.: Transferring Human-Human Interaction Studies to HRI Scenarios in Public Space. In: Campos, P., Graham, N., Jorge, J., Nunes, N., Palanque, P., Winckler, M. (eds.) INTERACT 2011, Part II. LNCS, vol. 6947, pp. 230–247. Springer, Heidelberg (2011)

Hypertext in Mutation: The Mapping of a Mythos

Tara Ogaick and WonJoon Chung

Carleton University, School of Industrial Design, Ottawa, Canada
{tara_ogaick,wonjoon_chung}@carleton.ca

Abstract. Currently, hypertext exists in its earlier state as webpage, connected to various other nodes of relevant information or advertising online, in interactive narratives such as Geoff Ryman's *253*, as hyperlinks housed within static documents like PDF's or Word files, or hyperlinks shelved between layers of blogging data and Facebook walls (to name a few social media outlets). Hypertext is understood as operating between poles – as a means of electronic or digital freedom granted to the reader, or as the opposite, the illusion of freedom granted by a controlled system set up by the author. This paper explores the third space for hypertext by making use of the process of using hypertext; the space wherein a user or participant is directly interacting with hypertext and thus influences the reader-author relationship by creating a subjective reading (and therefore a subjective document) of a series of nodes and proposes that appropriate interface can create design synthesis.

Keywords: hypertext, design synthesis, interaction styles, interface.

1 An Introduction to Hypertext

1.1 The Conception of Hypertext

Vannevar Bush presented the concept of a machine that could house different documents and media styles which would be available to anyone and allow people to gain and share knowledge [4]. However, this concept was hindered by the need for a physical artifact, and in particular, one that could withstand a subset of machines to perform various tasks (projector, etc.) By 1987, Jeff Conklin was introducing hypertext-proper. Jeff Conklin and Ted Nelson, pioneers of the hypertext interaction style, expose how digital media overcome the barriers of the physical machine that Vannevar Bush presented in 1945 [6][9]. Interestingly, the language that Conklin uses to describe hypertext presents a seemingly utopic and radical system. He writes,

> *Mechanisms are being devised which allow direct machine-supported references from one textual chunk to another; new interfaces provide the user with the ability to interact directly with these chunks and to establish new relationships between them. These extensions of the traditional text fall under the general category of hypertext (also known as nonlinear text). [6]*[1]

---

[1] p. 17

A. Marcus (Ed.): DUXU/HCII 2013, Part I, LNCS 8012, pp. 125–133, 2013.
© Springer-Verlag Berlin Heidelberg 2013

Conklin's statements regarding the tasks available to hypertext are appropriate – it does indeed allow for referencing between documents beyond the scope of the page the participant may be using, but the term "interact" is a misnomer. In 2001, Marie-Laure Ryan describes the difference between interaction and narrativity as play versus meaning.[2] The ability to "click" to open another node of information should perhaps be considered the first sign that hypertext was fantasized as having the power to produce nonlinear means of knowledge building and sharing and interacting with the original source file, but that this is under scrutiny. This is echoed by other researchers interested in the notion that hypertext is nonlinear.[3]

One of Conklin's statements regarding the potential that hypertext espouses is that it should not be properly representable on a printed sheet of paper [6].[4] Yet, much like the desktop metaphor famously praised by the Xerox Company that produced the Star User Interface and presented an interface style that bridged the gap between the technology of the computer and the physical counterpoint of the office desktop, hypertext is still most often referenced as a "page" – especially in relation to databasing and knowledge sharing [5].[5]

1.2   Metaphor and Its Influence on Developing Interfaces

The metaphor of the desktop provided users the affordances necessary to intuit functions of the interface and appreciate the GUI (graphical user interface) developed by Xerox in the 80s [5]. This included the presentation of text documents as icons, and by using the pointer as metaphorical "hand-tool" to perform actions such as move

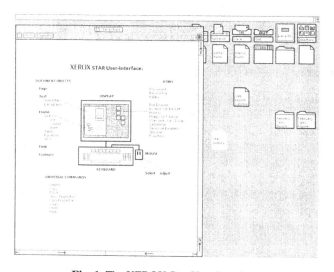

Fig. 1. The XEROX Star User-Interface

---

[2] p. 45

[3] A few of these authors are, Smith and Wilson, 1993; Kendrick, 2001; Ryan, 2009; Pope, 2010.

[4] p. 17

[5] p. 517

and copy, users were presented with a style of interaction that invited a performance between physical reality (outside the computer), and digital reality (inside the computer) [5].[6] This was a revolutionary development because it combined human needs psychologically by providing a reference point grounded in reality (that of a physical desktop), with the digital landscape of the desktop.

1.3   Examples of Interfaces that Use Metaphor

The use of metaphor for the development of new interfaces has expanded beyond the desktop. Some examples of this expansion include TapGlance (using a magnifier tool for inter- and intra- application navigation for mobile phones) [11].[7] The MagicBook (for augmented reality devices, this metaphor is espoused in a physical book) [2], and Toolglass and Magic Lenses (for use in digital media as a window pane metaphor that allows for multiple layers of data to appear or be hidden) [1].[8] These are three examples, but there are others that are less focused on a type of computer device or screen such as haptic animals that still rely on metaphor (the haptic noses, haptic fur, and so forth). This paper, however, is focused on hypertext as a new style of interaction with idea creation and relation capacity that haptic devices are not as focused on. However, tangible interaction will be touched on as smart phones and devices are already integrating this style into hypertext. For example, reading software on the iPad that includes the ability to touch on any word and be given a dictionary definition.

Fig. 2. The MagicBook Interface

---

[6] p. 520
[7] p. 386
[8] p. 73

These tools may be interpreted as metaphors for the original hypertext. They are tools developed and designed to enhance learning and the manipulation of data, to envision layers and wander through these layers while remaining connected to an original context, and as methods to enhance interaction rather than simply deriving meaning from collected data. While one might see fragments of these tools in some software, they do not appear in popular media items like laptops or smartphones.

1.4   Metaphor in Hypertext

A paper by Ece Merdivan and Nesrin Ozdener in 2011 examined the effects of different metaphor in relation to hypertext in specific. Their study was relevant to the need for tools promoting knowledge and learning and are thus applicable to developing a discussion on metaphor both in interface design and in hypertext. According to the results of the study, metaphor is just as important as the way it is used [9].[9] Moreover, the use of metaphor offers conflicting results for the ability to create nonlinear texts and student comprehension and absorption of knowledge [9]. In this instance, one is able to see where meaning is both attained via metaphor and proper nonlinear creation and the discrepancy where meaning is lost in the interpretation and knowledge acquisition of data at the end of the hypertext [9].

In fact, the authors conclude that "Future studies can develop strategies to enable students to read the whole content text before hypertext construction" [9]. This statement furthers the conflict buried in research on hypertext and the desire for it to synonymously promote creativity and challenge linearity. Here, Merdivan and Ozdener state explicitly that one must see the entirety of the hypertext (its map; its linear structure) before one is able to access the potential for the nonlinear.

2   Mutations in Form

2.1   Storytelling and Gaming

Marie-Laure Ryan, one of the most renowned critics of interactive fiction as well as one of its greatest champions, posits that there is a particularly interesting design problem that affects interactive fiction. What she does not predict is how relevant this problem becomes for interaction designers and user experience designers. In her seminal text, *From Narrative Games to Playable Stories: Toward a Poetics of Interactive Narratives*, she writes that this design problem is how to integrate "...the user's activity into a framework that fulfills the basic condition of narrativity: a

---

[9] p. 280

sequence of events involving thinking individuals, linked by causal relations, motivated by a conflict, and aiming at its resolution" [12].[10] One may even propose that the balance between user experience and the product itself are what is most at stake in the design process.

Interactive fiction, as presented by Ryan, invites its users into a lifelike scenario where one has access to input whatever one wishes (similar to the Holodeck in Star Trek, according to Ryan) [12].[11] Contrary to this, hypertext fiction is a controlled environment that limits the amount of input a user can contribute and thereby becomes a challenge for the participant to figure out how to speak to/with the hypertext [12]. The author supplements the definition of hypertext developed by Conklin and other preliminary authors of the time with that of a need for interaction. Ryan notes that

> *What hypertext gains in actual feasibility over the Holodeck, thanks to the simplicity of its algorithm, it loses in ability to create narrative meaning and immersion in a fictional world: narrative is a linear, causal sequence of events whose significance depends on their position on a temporal axis, while hypertext is a network of textual fragments that can be read in many different orders. Unless the user's choices are severely restricted, it is highly unlikely that they will produce a sequence that respects narrative logic.* [12].[12]

Therefore, what Ryan points out is that hypertext in its desirable and fantasized format of the explicitly nonlinear would render the meaningful meaningless by enforcing a lack of connection between nodes of information.

It is therefore necessary to maintain some sort of link between materials in order to maintain meaning. This is also reminiscent of metaphor; the necessity for metaphor to maintain a connection with something in reality, which has been ingrained into current models of language and semiotics, is what makes metaphor or its uses successful. Probably the most interesting example of this mutation is the interactive fiction, *Façade*. In *Façade*, the user is allowed to input whatever text they desire, so that they have the freedom to use language in its fantasized state. It is almost perfect use of natural language. The characters react to the input of text and the story revolves around how the user interacts and chooses to use this power. The number of endings one can achieve are seemingly endless. However, these interactions and the ability for meaning to remain active in the fiction is built on metaphor and although one can insert random language and text into the space of Grace and Trip's home, the punishment that the user faces is the ending of the narrative and their dismissal from the space.

---

[10] p. 43

[11] p. 44

[12] p. 44

Fig. 3. A screenshot of Andrew Stern and Michael Mateas' *Façade*, interactive theatre where a user inputs text to communicate with the two characters depicted here, Grace and Trip

2.2   The Rules of Engagement

Furthermore, Ryan makes a distinction between a narrative game and a playable story. According to the author's definition, "...in a narrative game, gameplay is meant to enhance gameplay, while in a playable story, gameplay is meant to produce a story" [12].[13] Likewise, there are differentiations in what these types of interaction can render regarding pleasure. On the one hand, interacting where one does not try to "win" or where there is no predictable outcome produces pleasure in free play and imagination. Conversely, interacting where there are set rules and guidelines allows users the pleasure of "winning" or overcoming challenges and feeling satisfied in the completion of a task [12].[14] One may imagine that Conklin's imagined hypertext should have produced the feeling of pleasure described as the pleasure in free play and exploration rather than of winning or completion. However, one might venture that in current exploration of hypertext and their imagined metaphorical developments such as Toolglass etc, free play is hindered by both the set regulations and direct metaphor of the page, or else hindered by the learning curve or inaccessible nature of the development of these other tools.

Similar to the early stages of interaction style development and assessment, one may venture that successful interface design should include a variety of styles. Gosling and Crawford further the debate on narrative games versus storytelling by considering the difference between passive observation and the active participation

---

[13] p. 45
[14] p. 46

and creation that happens when one plays games [7].[15] It is becoming equally important to blend these two styles; users of both interactive fiction and interactive media want to be able to manipulate and develop their devices while still being able to participate passively in an experience. One sees this most obviously in Apple users versus Android users. Android users claim one of the perks of the Android user experience is the freedom to adapt and change their experience, whereas Apple users claim the user experience comes in the completed package of the iOS.

3   Interface for Design Synthesis

The paper up until this point has been a review of the hypertext interface style as well as interactive tools for interfaces such as the Toolglass application, and finally an overview of interactive narrative as a means of understanding the presence of necessity for metaphor in the design of new styles. Interactivity in text has been expanded to alternate mediums. Instead of needing a computer, mouse, and keyboard, the development of smart phones, tablets, and locative media (amongst other more practical products) have enabled hypertext to reach new users and be implemented across different products [3].[16] It is through this development that one is able to recognize problems with hypertext and design. Bizzocchi and Woodbury enumerate these problems:

> *This problematic relationship can be seen as a conflict between two design domains: the design of narrative and story and the design of interactive experience. For many storytellers working in the traditional media, the design of narrative seeks a particular kind of outcome—a state of immersive surrender to the work. The reader engages in a suspension of disbelief, ignores the objective reality of the conditions of reception, and surrenders to the world of the story [3].[17]*

One must establish a context, or a relationship, between types of narrative immersion and interactivity to ensure that hypertext remain meaningful. Moreover, this problematic relationship calls into question whether or not hypertext has evolved beyond its primary functions from the time of Vannevar Bush and Jeff Conklin.

We propose that there is flexibility and further evolution of the hypertext interface to fulfill the power behind the process of moving between links and nodes, and that satisfies and propels story and narrative to its most appropriate quality of establishing a meaningful story. Through an appropriate interface, users have the ability to co-create a story in a non-linear fashion (thereby distancing themselves from the potential bias of one sole storyteller), without physical proximity to one-another (which may cause inconsistencies in participation or feelings of collaboration), apart from environmental constraints, and with access to the larger database and networking potential that digital interfaces allow.

---

[15] p. 139
[16] p. 550
[17] p. 551

3.1   Brief Proposal of Methodology

In order to explore the potential for hypertext and non-linear design, we will first determine the set of characteristics that define hypertext and attempt to connect these characteristics to the analog world. This will help us test whether or not hypertext influences an aspect of design – its storytelling potential, for example – without developing and designing a finished digital product. Indeed, one of the most crucial aspects for testing will be to create a hypertext-like process developed for storytelling in user scenarios that focuses on the backstory rather than its finished product.

3.2   Workshops for Comparative Studies

Furthermore, workshops will be conducted to test this process and develop a firm set of criteria for future work in hypertext-influenced design. These workshops will compare the current meaningfulness of user scenarios in the design process against our hypertext-influenced user scenario creation. This design process has been chosen for its 1) use of metaphor for storytelling, 2) its capacity to use empathy and sympathy in order to produce meaningfulness for an artifact, 3) its capacity to create a more holistic understanding of the product, and 4) for the notion that storytelling moves design from its requirements to a space between fantasy and reality. Hypertext-influenced design does not need to remain relegated to the process part of design. We propose that this work will influence interface design as well as work in augmented reality which is still criticized for its remarkable capacity to affect the metaphor for what is human.

In order to fully actualize the potential for this cyborg interface that consciously acknowledges the limitations of interactive narratives, we will appropriate Aaron Koblin's expressions of visualization; of metaphor and the propensity for all users to contribute within the boundaries of their own abilities, interactive narrative components such as the ability to link between nodes when the reader chooses, human-computer interaction styles such as direct manipulation and natural language, and an awareness of design knowledge and processes for co-design and collaboration articulated by authors such as Nigel Cross and Elizabeth Sanders.

References

1. Bier, E.A., Stone, M.C., Pier, K., Buxton, W., DeRose, T.D.: Toolglass and Magic Lenses: The See-Through Interface. In: Proceedings of SIGGRAPH 1993, pp. 73–80 (1993)
2. Billinghurst, M., Kato, H., Poupyrev, I.: The MagicBook: A Transitional AR Interface, pp. 1–14. CiteSeer (2001)
3. Bizzocchi, J., Woodbury, R.F.: A case study in the design of interactive narrative: The subversion of the interface. Simulation & Gaming 34(4), 550–568 (2003)
4. Bush, V.: As We May Think. The Atlantic Monthly (July 1945); Reprinted in ACM Interactions 3(2) (March 1996)
5. Smith, D.C., Irby, C., Kimball, R., Harslem, E.: The Star User Interface: An Overview. Submitted to the AFIPS 1982 National Computer Conference

6. Conklin, J.: Hypertext: an introduction and survey. Computer 20(9), 17–41 (1987)
7. Gosling, V.K., Crawford, G.: Game Scenes: Theorizing Digital Game Audiences. Games and Culture 6(2), 131–154 (2011)
8. Hornecker, E., Buur, J.: Getting a Grip on Tangible Interaction: A Framework on Physical Space and Social Interaction. In: CHI 2006 Proceeding of the Designing for Tangible Interactions, pp. 437–446 (2006)
9. Merdivan, E., Ozdener, N.: Effects of different metaphor usage on hypertext learning. Behaviour and Information Technology 30(20), 273–285 (2011)
10. Nelson, T.: Dream Machines: New Freedoms Through Computer Screens— A Minority Report. In: Computer Lib: You Can and Must Understand Computers Now (1974) (Self-published)
11. Robbins, D.C., Lee, B., Fernandez, R.: TapGlance: Designing a Unified Smartphone Interface. In: ACM, pp. 386–394 (2008)
12. Ryan, M.L.: From Narrative Games to Playable Stories: Toward a Poetics of Interactive Narratives. StoryWorlds, A Journal of Narrative Studies (1), 43–59 (2009)

Social Movement Information Design and a Curriculum of Proper Knowledge Consumption

Gabriel Y. Schaffzin

Massachusetts College of Art & Design, Dynamic Media Institute
gyschaffzin@massart.edu

Abstract. Narrowing in on two contemporary social movements as a case study, this analysis will use a mainstay of information design, Edward Tufte, as well as a lesser-known pioneer in the field, Otto Neurath, to consider the ways in which the infographics associated with those movements can be looked at critically. Using Tufte's popularity and commercial success as an indication of his strong influence on this field, questions about the appreciation of efficiency or validity of message at the expense of craft, nuance, and meaning making will be raised, eventually concluding that a new approach to the consumption of information design is necessary.

1 Graphic and Information Design and Social Movements

A review of the relationship between social activism and graphic design over the past century [16] illustrates the ways in which graphic designers have integrated themselves into or extracted themselves from the active participation in social movement design. From radical movement publications on the Left at the turn of the century, through to the emergence and dominance of the commercial design field, ties between design and activism were strengthened as the former became a commercially driven discipline, providing the talent and distribution channels necessary for mainstream attention.

The modern "information design" discipline under the umbrella of the graphic design field has, perhaps, a misleadingly broad name. Arguably, information designers are those who focus on using maps, charts, illustrations, graphs, and other graphic-heavy visual elements to convey their message—with a strong emphasis on the simplification of that message [6]. With a brief nod to DaVinci's *Vitruvian Man*, William Playfair's *Commercial and Political Atlas*, and Dr. John Snow's work mapping the cholera outbreak in London in the 1850s, we observe information designers' use of visualized data to convey messages in a universal form—imagery [29].

Considering this universality, especially combined with information design's ability to handle quickly large amounts of data, it is logical that commercial designers are looking to the field as a way to improve corporate communication [6]. But while documentation of Snow's maps or Playfair's atlas is relatively commonplace, there is little written about the use of information design in contemporary social movements. In order to gain a critical understanding of social movement information design, therefore, it would follow as worthwhile to apply contemporary information design principles to those graphics being produced for social movements today.

A. Marcus (Ed.): DUXU/HCII 2013, Part I, LNCS 8012, pp. 134–143, 2013.

2   A Tuftean Framework

To begin, it would be helpful to review the work of perhaps the most prominent information designer of our time, Dr. Edward Tufte [2]. His *The Visual Display of Quantitative Information*, originally published in 1983, presents a thorough overview of the history of information design, as well as a set of principles to be used in effective graphics which maintain the integrity of their respective data. Since the publication of *Visual Display*, he has built up an empire of self-published work and self-orchestrated seminars. The *New York Times* noted in 1998 that, "his skills seem uniquely suited to the moment: he knows how to turn seas of information into navigable—even scenic—waterways" [24]. His "Sparklines" and other mechanisms have made him a mainstay in the information design field, providing him the opportunity to have significant influence over the way corporations and government organizations present data [2].

In his fourth and most recent volume, *Beautiful Evidence* [28], Tufte presents a list of six principles: Comparisons; Causality, Mechanism, Structure, Explanation; Multivariate Analysis; Integration of Evidence; Documentation; and Content Counts Most of All. A critique using these principles can be useful in helping to dissect a visual language from an analytical perspective—how well an argument is presented via the design of the data associated with that argument, or, as Tufte notes, "to appraise their quality, relevance, and integrity." The fact that social movement design's subject matter may differ from traditional corporate or scientific presentations is moot according to Tufte's assertion that "the fundamental principles of analytical design apply broadly, and are indifferent to language or culture or century or the technology of information display." He goes on: "Human activities, after all, take place in intensely comparative and multivariate contexts filled with causal ideas: intervention, purpose, responsibility, consequence, explanation, intention, action, prevention, diagnosis, strategy, decision, influence, planning."

For Tufte, applying his modernist approach to any social movement information design would provide a fruitful understanding of those designs' "quality, relevance, and integrity." But what does this application look like using real-world examples? This analysis takes two movements featuring widespread use of infographics and data visualization—the Occupy Wall Street and the anti-SOPA/anti-PIPA movements—and attempts such an application.

3   Comparing the Social Movements

3.1   Occupy Wall Street

Generally speaking,[1] the Occupy movement (sometimes called "Occupy Wall Street" or "OWS") refers to a global protest against the economic and social injustices caused

---

[1] Note that, due to the disparate nature of the Occupy movement, there is no official manifesto or handbook to reference.

by what its members believe to be capitalism's power over government and the individual—a power which the movement posits has led to a severely skewed distribution of wealth throughout the developed world. Of particular note is the movement's emphasis on "horizontal" organization, governed by consensus processes: decisions are made at "general assembly" meetings[2] via predetermined methods that are designed to ensure broad agreement across the group. In September of 2011, occupations—or camps of protestors in public locations—began appearing in hundreds of cities around the world. After the majority of camps were evicted by local authorities, the movement continued as a network of smaller groups, planning direct action protests and awareness campaigns. Each camp and associated social action share a general theme (representing the "99%" of the population who are affected by the aforementioned unfair distribution of wealth) but there is no official body which governs each one as a collective [1].

3.2   Anti-SOPA/Anti-PIPA

In October 2011, the Electronic Frontier Foundation[3] began encouraging constituents to contact their Congressional representatives to voice concern over legislation being debated on the floors of the U.S. House of Representatives and U.S. Senate, the Stop Online Privacy Act (SOPA, formerly Combating Online Infringement and Counterfeits Act, or COICA) and Protect Intellectual Property Act (PIPA) [3], [22], [27]. The organization expressed fears over what they felt were over-reaching measures to protect intellectual property—measures that would, according to them, invade users' privacy and censor free speech online. The following month, Congressional mark-up hearings were held, featuring five representatives from the media industry and one representative from technology giant Google. Taking note of the lack of representation, more technology companies—Facebook, eBay, and others—joined together in opposition of the legislation [10]. Google itself hired "at least 15 lobbying firms" to counter the bills [31].

On November 16, the efforts of the technology lobby crossed over into mainstream attention when the online micro-blogging site, Tumblr, began "censoring" user dashboards by blocking out text on the site with black squares. Soon after, other online giants made similar gestures—all to protest SOPA and PIPA [7]. As coverage of SOPA and PIPA moved into the mainstream, more content regarding the legislation and the movement against it was being produced and distributed, especially online.

---

[2] General assembly refers to "a time and place for Occupy Boston announcements and proposals." It is open to anyone and is governed by consensus process—proposals are made and passed via broad agreement, hand signals are used to indicate various points of process, and a team of at least 11 facilitators ensure the process is executed as previously agreed upon. For more, see: http://bit.ly/tsBIoE

[3] A non-profit advocacy group, described as committed to "confront[ing] cutting-edge issues defending free speech, privacy, innovation, and consumer rights" [26].

3.3   The Comparison

Looking at these two contemporary social movements and their respective use of information design is an exercise that could prove useful to both social and political actors, as well as designers. The comparison between these two movements in particular, however, can also prove a bit complicated.

On the one hand, there are concrete variations between the two movements: Occupy presents itself as a horizontal movement, while anti-SOPA/anti-PIPA began as a technology lobby initiative, eventually gaining broader support via specific for- and not-for-profit organizations (i.e. Tumblr, Wikipedia, et al.). Additionally, the former resists assigning itself one singular message or goal, whereas the latter rallied constituents around defeating two very specific pieces of legislation [23], [7].

The two movements are not, however, mutually exclusive. In fact, one of the tenets of the Occupy movement is to support freedom of speech and resist censorship. As such, various groups within the movement expressed support for the SOPA/PIPA opposition, going so far as to encourage activists to "Occupy SOPA" by contacting local representatives [20]. Even though members of the movement had previously expressed resistance engaging with the political system, the threat posed by these bills was enough to inspire action [13].

Beyond the complications in comparing the two movements, a thorough investigation of every infographic associated with each movement is, arguably, impossible; neither movement has an "official" producer or repository for promotional or informational content, let alone the specifically visual. One collection of Occupy related graphics (including a number of anti-SOPA/anti-PIPA focused designs) resides at OccupyDesign.org, whose administrators describe the site's goal as "building a visual language for the 99 percent" [19]. Produced and maintained by a group of volunteers, the site presents itself as a toolkit for both those who do and do not self-identify as designers. It provides visual elements that can be reproduced and distributed on signs, banners, or online. Initially, the focus of the group was on producing infographics and iconography for the movement—sometimes using data-sets received from constituents. Eventually, the site expanded into posters and other designed pieces related to the movement. When asked how "infographics" are classified as such by site administrators, team member Max Slavkin [25] noted, "I guess it's been more of a 'know it when we see it' approach."

This relatively liberal approach is noted beyond OccupyDesign, as well, when observing each movement's respective design subject-matter (one can find graphics describing the purpose of a movement, descriptions of its members and makeup, its goals and effects, and so on) and content (both movement's causes are represented in a quantitative or qualitative manner). An attempt to contextualize each movement's visuals by aesthetic is similarly evasive: one observes a range of aesthetics from large blocks of text to pictograms, graphs, and even Rodchenko-esque "voice ripples".[4]

---

[4] Copyright and space considerations precluded the inclusion of the actual graphics referenced here. Please see http://occupydesign.org/gallery/all?field_type_tid=3 and https://google.com/takeaction/past-actions/end-piracy-not-liberty/

4   Application of the Tuftean Framework

The highly varied nature of the information graphics produced for and by the Occupy and anti-SOPA/anti-PIPA movements is rather revealing in itself. Even the pure volume of designs from which to pull a sample to analyze is an indication of the popularity of the infographic form among these particular movements. But does the value placed on the form distract from the motives or meaning behind the design?

According to Tufte, "Evidence is evidence" [29]. Encouraging a "comparative and multivariate" approach certainly makes sense for economic or scientific considerations—fields in which empirical data drives much of what is taught. But what this approach ignores are considerations such as—among others—the intangibility of movement objectives, the multichannel nature of graphic presentation (in movement literature, on posters, during collective action), and the importance of anonymity for some movement actors (especially those supporting contentious causes).

For instance, an application of the Tuftean principles suggests that OccupyDesign's information graphics are relatively weak: they normally only contain few pieces of data, they are presented with very simple visual cues (in black and white, without more than a few different icons, etc.), and they are much stronger (in a Tuftean manner) when a number of them are viewed together at the same time. These designs, however, were prepared for use in collective physical action—occupations and protests. The pioneers of information design were not able to take the channels and media we have available today into consideration: Playfair and Snow were sending their designs to be printed in books or journals. But as the use of information design moves beyond the medical and economic—and into commercial advertising, social advocacy, etc.—the ways in which we evaluate this design must adapt accordingly.

Concurrently, a reevaluation of the field's approach to "integrity" is also in order. Tufte promotes documentation as a requirement for strong analytical design—an assertion that is hard to refute when considering the importance of delineating between fact and fiction. But at what point does an emphasis on documentation overshadow an expression of belief? Does improper citation of sources regarding a movement's reach, distract from the designer's intent to portray a large scale action? On the other hand, an emphasis on expression through design—rather than on solely conveying scientifically accurate information about or for a movement—leaves perhaps too much in what Milton Glaser calls "the category of consciousness-raising." He goes on to argue that "How can you penetrate people's immunity is always the fundamental question of a designer's work" [8]. Does penetration without an emphasis on fact—turning to shock value—further polarize an already dichotomous discourse?

5   Challenges to Information Design's Inherent Objectivity

To be sure, Tufte's strong emphasis on science and empirical information in the design field has drawn indirect criticism from a number of designers. Two in particular, Jessica Helfand and William Drenttel, write in 2002 [4] of the dangers of applying principles of what Tufte might call "well-designed graphics" to the scientific. "The appeal of information designis that it offers instant credibility." They continue, "But it's a false authority, particularly because we buy into the form so unquestioningly."

Robin Greeley has also presented a similar warning, though she approaches the dangers from the perspective of the designer, rather than the observer. In her 1998 review of designer Richard Duardo's "Aztlan Poster" [9], she offers an interrogation of cultural hegemony in graphic design. She argues that "Design in our present decade cannot be thought of solely in terms of an object or product; rather, it must be considered as a process carried out with a nexus of particular social relations (cultural, economic, symbolic)." Further, she encourages current designers to consider the field's "metapraxis," a place where meaning becomes attached to objects, images, and words: "The ability to engage in this metapraxis is part of what sets designers off from nondesigners, especially in this age of personal computers and cottage industry design, when professional status alone no longer defines a field."

In raising the various considerations which must be acknowledged while designing information, and in focusing on the specific value of the professional designer, Greeley calls into question the very nature of Tufte's mission, one which the *New York Times* describes as "proselytizing, winning converts and turning a profit in the process." Tufte, in the same article, notes that he is "expanding [his] teaching to reach people directly" [24]. This willingness to open the task of information design to the masses—a willingness upon which his entire business model is predicated—stands in direct contrast to the work of a philosopher whose influence on the information design field dates back to nearly 60 years before the publishing of *The Visual Display of Quantitative Information.*

6   Otto Neurath, Isotype, and the Transformer

As a founding member of the Vienna Circle's logical positivist movement, Otto Neurath believed that the expression of fact was of utmost importance, especially in a Europe having recently been ravaged by World War I. During his tenure as director of various local museums in Leipzig and Vienna, Neurath designed exhibits for citizens that explained statistics and policies about local communities and their various economic and social concerns [15]. Confounded by the complexities of expressing statistical knowledge through verbal language and the rules which accompany it, Neurath turned to a system of pictograms, designed and arranged (sometimes alongside written language) with a logic he felt unattainable through words alone. These pictograms addressed, too, his struggle to convey relevant information in a clear manner, to be consumed and understood by an international audience—a "de-babelzation" of sorts. Neurath eventually titled this mode of information transfer the *International System Of TYpographic Picture Education,* or *Isotype* [15], [18].

To be sure, Isotype presented a way for Neurath to balance his struggle with the form of language—the rules and considerations associated with the written and spoken word—and his belief, as a logical positivist, that language could still convey universal fact. In his introductory text to Isotype, Neurath notes that "To make a picture is more responsible than to make a statement, because pictures make a greater effect and have a longer existence" [18]. Considering the devastating effects of World War I on the world around him, it is no surprise that "responsibility" is a priority of Neurath's. Developing a language based on the universality of imagery was of utmost importance to him, as he believed it could usher in, according to designer and educator Ellen Lupton, a more "egalitarian culture," one in which "pictorial information would dissolve cultural differences" [15]. As Marie Neurath (née Reidemeister), Otto Neurath's wife and colleague, writes, Neurath wanted to develop "charts meaning something for everyone," he wanted to make sure "that they excluded nobody, that they allowed several levels of understanding…as a means of education that is neutral, provides objective facts and leaves judgement and evaluation to the viewer" [17].

This seemingly utopian vision required overcoming many obstacles. Neurath set out to take on the practicalities of building Isotype into a truly international language (all the while dodging the oppressive regimes of the pre-World War II nations of Europe) by building a team of designers–most notably of whom, Gerd Arntz, had significant influence on the eventual look and feel of Isotype's famous wood cut aesthetic [15]. Nearly 80 years after Neurath's introduction of Isotype, the language's staying power is, arguably, evident only in this aesthetic's influence on current information design and data visualization pictography and, perhaps, in the addition of the term "isotype" to design's lexicon. In 1972, 27 years after Neurath's death, Marie retired, depositing the full cache of the project's documents and publications into an archive at the University of Reading, outside London [15].

But Isotype may have more to teach us, particularly on a philosophical or theoretical level. Neurath's system was built around the premise that language exists as an object tied to nature, though still formed by the observer of this nature [15]. This belief can be explicitly seen in Isotype's strong emphasis on the role of what Neurath called the "transformer." As Robin Kinross writes in his book [12] *The Transformer*, "Neurath developed the notion of transformer (it was 'Transformator' in German) to describe the process of analysing, selecting, ordering, and then *making visual* [emphasis his] some information, data, ideas, implications."

This process was a detailed one, with the transformer working with stakeholders and subject matter experts, gaining a strong understanding of an issue before building the Isotype pictograms to represent it. This included considering the audience of the language and what symbols would better resonate with them [17]. When a disciple of Neurath's, Rudolph Modley, took his knowledge of Isotype to the United States in the 1930s and 1940s, he opted not to include the role of transformer. Instead, his goal was to reach as broad an audience as possible by bringing, for example, the pictograms to school children as "symbol sheets." In doing so, he alienated Neurath. As Eric Kindle, curator of The Otto and Marie Neurath Isotype Collection at the University of Reading, noted, "it led to [a reduction in] the richness of presentation of information" [11]. By removing the transformer and attempting to bring the principles of Isotype to the masses, much was lost in the development of and the resulting meaning of the language. As such, Neurath and his team sought to control every element of the design and production of Isotype.

7   Moving away from a Focus on the Design Side

It can be said, perhaps, that this focus on control of production led to Isotype's eventual downfall. This is not to detract from the system's influence on the generations of designers who came after its inception amidst a war torn Europe. Neurath's approach is contextualized when viewed alongside more contemporary theorists such as Robin Greeley; attempts at controlling or changing the way design or media is made is nothing new. This phenomenon is what Neil Postman refers to in his work, *Technopoly: The Surrender of Culture to Technology*, when he notes that "no one can reasonably object to the rational use of techniques to achieve human purposes." He goes on to call out the precise subject matter of Neurath's efforts: "...Language itself is a kind of technique—an invisible technology—and through it we achieve more than clarity and efficiency. We achieve humanity—or inhumanity. The question with language, as with any other technique or machine, is and always has been, Who is to be the master? Will we control it, or will it control us? The argument, in short, is not with technique. The argument is with the triumph of technique, with techniques that become sanctified and rule out the possibilities of other ones" [21].

Information design, certainly, is a technique—one that stands to offer significant aide to those working to understand a complex situation. After all, as media philosopher Villem Flusser asserts "Images are mediations between the world and human beings...the world is not immediately accessible to them and therefore images are needed to make it comprehensible" [5]. But the trust we place in these images becomes dangerous as our critical eyes become lackadaisical and the techniques to produce them become sanctified. "They are supposed to be maps but they turn into screens," Flusser continues, "Human beings forget they created the images in order to orientate themselves in the world" [5].

To attempt a methodical or scientific evaluation of the information graphics produced by Occupy, anti-SOPA/anti-PIPA, or any social movements is a futile exercise—they are infinite, produced by countless designers, distributed, cited, even modified throughout countless channels on a plethora of platforms. As graphics associated with movements, this is both expected and acceptable: the way the pieces are designed, viewed, and spread are all products of the nuance and meaning-making infused into them. The way they are understood is a product of the meaning their audiences seek. They need not be held accountable to the tenets of "truth." We need not scold our designers for not producing them in accordance with Tuftean (or any other) principles. Rather, we must remember what Otto Neurath already knew when developing Isotype: there is a translation that takes place between the feelings, the words, and the images that make up an information design. Then, perhaps, we can teach design consumers to do so with a critical eye and a willingness to look past technique.

Nearly 15 years after Greeley's "Aztlan" essay, designers are still faced with the fact that their field is inherently commercially driven. But in the era of Apple, Inc.'s dominance in the consumer market, in a time when "design thinking" is part of the business lexicon, and the "Technology, Entertainment, and Design" conference is perhaps one of the most widespread,[5] surely the observers (the victims, even) of all of this technique-celebrated design are ready for a re-education regarding consumption: a framework, not to produce beautiful, "well-designed information," but one to consume it responsibly.

This framework would require the development of a curriculum of "proper" knowledge consumption, one that challenges viewers of design to answer Postman's rhetorical query with an emphatic, "*we* will control *it*, and not vice versa." Certainly, countless design degrees have been predicated on a similar goal. But, taking into consideration the channels available to our next generation of digital natives (even if these channels may be co-opted by purely commercial interests), perhaps there are new ways to reach our design consumers, making sure that they understand what Otto Neurath once did: one must always consider the forces at work on the knowledge around us.

References

1. About UslOccupyWallSt.org (2011), http://occupywallst.org/about/ (accessed December 9, 2011)
2. Aston, A.: Tufte's Invisible Yet Ubiquitous Influence (June 10, 2009), http://businessweek.com/stories/2009-06-10/tuftes-invisible-yet-ubiquitous-influencebusinessweek-business-news-stock-market-and-financial-advice (accessed April 17, 2012)
3. Combating Online Infringement and Counterfeits Act (2010; 111th Congress; S. 3804) - GovTrack.us (September 20, 2010), http://govtrack.us/congress/bills/111/s3804 (accessed April 28, 2012)
4. Drenttel, W., Helfand, J.: Wonders Revealed: Design and Faux Science (October 14, 2002), http://chapters.aiga.org/resources/content/1/9/1/3/documents/AIGA_Clear_Wonders_Revealed.pdf (accessed April 16, 2012)
5. Flusser, V.: Towards a Philosophy of Photography, pp. 9–10. Reaktion, London (1983)
6. Gadney, M., et al.: You are here (2012), http://eyemagazine.com/feature/article/you-are-here (accessed April 8, 2012)
7. Galvez, M., et al.: RB 196: The Rally Cry of SOPA (April 2, 2012), http://wilkins.law.harvard.edu/podcasts/mediaberkman/radioberkman/2012-03-30_SOPA.mp3 (accessed April 26, 2012)
8. Glaser, M., Mayer, P.: Introduction. In: Glaser, M. (ed.) Graphic Design, pp. 229–230. The Overlook Press, Inc., Woodstock (1973)
9. Greeley, R.A.: Richard Duardo's 'Aztlán' poster: Interrogating cultural hegemony in graphic design. Design Issues 14(1), 21–34 (1998)
10. Higginbotham, S.: SOPA Media Coverage Dissected. Panel at SXSW Interactive 2012. Also ft. Bialer, Jake, Hart, Kim, and Stelter, Brian. Austin, TX (March 10, 2012)
11. Kindel, E.: Personal interview (August 9, 2012)
12. Kinross, R.: The Transformer, p. 6. Hyphen Press, London (2009)

---

[5] As of Jun 2011, the videos on the TED website reached over 500 views [14].

13. Klein, E.: You're creating a vision of the sort of society you want to have in miniature (October 3, 2011), http://www.washingtonpost.com/blogs/ezra-klein/post/youre-creating-a-vision-of-the-sort-of-society-you-want-to-have-in-miniature/2011/08/25/gIQAXVg7HL_blog.html
14. Lawler, R.: 500M Views in 5 Years: How TEDTalks Did It | Online Video News (June 27, 2011), http://gigaom.com/video/tedtalks-5-years/ (accessed October 8, 2012)
15. Lupton, E.: Reading Isotype. Design Issues 3(2), 47–58 (1986)
16. Margolin, V.: Rebellion, Reform, and Revolution: American Graphic Design for Social Change. Design Issues 5(1) (Autumn 1988)
17. Neurath, M., Kinross, R.: The Transformer: Principles of Making Isotype Charts, pp. 26, 75. Hyphen, London (2009)
18. Neurath, O.: International Picture Language; the First Rules of Isotype, pp. 12–15. K. Paul, Trench, Trubner & Co. Ltd., London (1936)
19. Occupy Design, http://occupydesign.org (accessed April 8, 2012)
20. Occupy SOPA-The movement to rid the world of the SOPA bill, http://occupysopa.org/ (accessed April 29, 2012)
21. Postman, N.: Technopoly: The Surrender of Culture to Technology, p. 142. Vintage Books, New York (1993)
22. Preventing Real Online Threats to Economic Creativity and Theft of Intellectual Property Act of 2011 (S. 968) - GovTrack.us (May 11, 2012), http://govtrack.us/congress/bills/112/s968 (accessed April 28, 2012)
23. Schwartz, M.: Pre-Occupied. The origins and future of Occupy Wall Street (November 28, 2011), http://www.newyorker.com/reporting/2011/11/28/111128fa_fact_schwartz (accessed December 9, 2011)
24. Shapley, D.: The da Vinci of Data (March 30, 1998), http://nytimes.com/1998/03/30/business/the-da-vinci-of-data.html (accessed April 26, 2012)
25. Slavkin, M.: Phone Interview (April 12, 2012)
26. SOPA/PIPA: Internet Blacklist Legislation | Electronic Frontier Foundation, http://eff.org/issues/coica-internet-censorship-and-copyright-bill (accessed April 26, 2012)
27. Stop Online Piracy Act (H.R. 3261) - GovTrack.us (October 26, 2011), http://govtrack.us/congress/bills/112/hr3261 (accessed April 28, 2012)
28. Tufte, E.: Beautiful Evidence, pp. 9, 122–139. Graphics Press, Cheshire (2006)
29. Tufte, E.: The Visual Display of Quantitative Information, 2nd edn. Graphics Press, Cheshire (2001)
30. Wyatt, E.: Lines Drawn on Antipiracy Bills (December 14, 2011), http://nytimes.com/2011/12/15/technology/lines-are-drawn-on-legislation-against-internet-piracy.html (accessed April 28, 2012)

Shifting the Focus: An Objective Look at Design Fixation

Melissa A.B. Smith, Robert J. Youmans, Brooke G. Bellows,
and Matthew S. Peterson

George Mason University, Human Factors & Applied Cognition, MSN 3F5,
4000 University Drive, Fairfax VA 22030, USA
msmith32@gmu.edu

Abstract. Design fixation is a robust phenomenon that has been shown to affect amateurs, experts, and groups of designers across a variety of design domains. An area of confusion concerning the concept of design fixation is whether it is a conscious decision made by a designer or an unconscious action that occurs without awareness. The current research addresses this issue by utilizing eye tracking as an objective measure, in conjunction with subjective feedback, and design performance data to gain insight into the underlying processes of design fixation. It was found that there are major discrepancies in what people remember looking at, what people actually looked at, and what features designers fixated on. These findings inspire a fount of new research questions, as well as a possible rethinking of current design processes.

Keywords: Design fixation, eye tracking, creativity, design.

1   Introduction

A growing body of empirical research has shown that developing ideas that are different from past examples is sometimes more difficult than people assume, even when past designs are suboptimal. Strangely, research has demonstrated that designers often suffer from design fixation, a limitation in a designer's creative output due to an overreliance on features of preexisting designs, or a specific body of knowledge directly associated with a problem [1].

The first studies to examine fixation effects in designers were conducted by Jansson & Smith [1]. In these studies, designers were shown an example of a failed product or system (e.g., a spill-proof coffee cup that would still spill coffee), and then they were given some time in which to come up with an improved product. Some designers were able to think of new ideas, but many designers seemed somehow anchored to the examples that had been shown to them (even though they were explicitly told to create original designs). The research was a compelling example of how design fixation could limit a designer's creative thinking at the very beginning of new product's development.

Recent work on design fixation has tended to focus on what can be done to prevent it. For example, Youmans [2] manipulated whether or not engineers interacted with physical prototyping materials during the design process, and found that engineers

A. Marcus (Ed.): DUXU/HCII 2013, Part I, LNCS 8012, pp. 144–151, 2013.

who did not use physical prototypes were more likely to fixate on the previous design. The conclusion of this experiment was that, somehow, the physical prototypes alleviated the fixation effects.

Other research in this same domain has shown that taking breaks [3], incorporating recognized good design heuristics [4], and utilizing various computer applications [5] all reduce fixation, but they have done little to explain what mental mechanisms are responsible for fixation effects. Most researchers agree that design fixation likely occurs during the very early conceptual design process, and some have argued that working memory capacity (WMC) could have an effect on design fixation (e.g., [6],[7]), but, plainly stated, one of the main problems in preventing the reduction of design fixation is that nobody is really sure exactly why design fixation occurs, or to whom it is more or less likely to affect [8].

The current study was designed to investigate design fixation using techniques Human Factors Engineers call *task analyses*. Task analyses are a collection of methods that systematically measuring how humans perform a task in order to better understand why it is difficult, and optimize it with respect to human capabilities [9], [10]. In this case, the task analysis techniques were used to measure participants' eye movements during a design task. Past research has demonstrated that eye movements are a real-time link to the cognitive processes of a person because people rarely look at what they perceive to be task-irrelevant information [11]. Further, the locus of attention during scene viewing is a strong predictor of which objects in a scene are being encoded in memory [12]. Because eye gaze predicts both active processing of information and memory formation, in our study we hypothesized that the elements of a design that participants look at first or most frequently might be an indication of which design elements they would be most likely to be fixate on in future designs.

The objective of the present research was to investigate why design fixation occurs. Eye movements were hypothesized to be especially important in understanding designer behavior, because they have long been linked to cognitive processes, and because prior research suggests that locus of attention during scene viewing is a strong predictor of which objects in a scene are encoded in memory [12].

1.1   Goals of the Research

The first goal of our research was to test whether participants can accurately recall how they spend time critiquing a previous design. The second and third goals were to confirm whether or not participants' memories or participants' eye movements predicted subsequent design fixations. One of the ongoing questions in regard to design fixation is whether it occurs consciously, with the designer actively deciding to include a previous design element, or subconsciously, with the design element being included without the designer being aware of what they are doing [8]. Thus, the method of combining subjective report and eye tracking data provides a technique of testing whether participants were intentionally fixating to features of a prior design, unconsciously fixating, or both.

2   Method

2.1   Participants

Twenty-one (21) students (mean age = 21.72 years, 4 males) from George Mason University were included in this study. Participants were undergraduate students who received partial course credit for their participation.

2.2   Materials

An SR Research Eye Link II head-mounted eye tracker was used in conjunction with a program created in Experiment Builder. Eye movement data was analyzed in SR Research Data Viewer. The program was run on a Macintosh desktop computer, and participants used a chinrest while viewing the poster to maintain a consistent head position for the eye tracking.

2.3   Procedure

Upon entering the laboratory, participants were fitted with the SR Research Eye Link II head-mounted eye tracker that recorded their eye movements. Once the eye tracker had been calibrated, participants were instructed to view a poster that was displayed on a computer screen in front of them (see Figure 1). They were told that the poster had been used to advertise a student organization last year, but had been ineffective in helping to gain new members.

Fig. 1. The fixation poster that participants saw prior to their own design efforts

Participants were then told that we wanted them to spend time critiquing the old poster for two minutes so that they could attempt to design an original, more effective new poster afterward. After viewing the fixation poster for two minutes, both the fixation poster and the eye-tracking equipment were removed. Participants were then given ten minutes to mentally prepare their own design, a feature of the experiment designed to mimic the conceptual design phase that is often identified in studio design work. Following this ten-minute period, the participants were given blank sheets of paper, a ruler, and a set of 16 colored pencils, and they were asked to spend another ten minutes developing a rough sketch of their poster design.

The Fixation Poster. The example poster used in this study to create design fixation effects (Figure 2) was one that had been demonstrated to create strong fixation effects in a similar population of undergraduate students (see [7]). The poster has been carefully designed by the experimenters to contain a total of 25 'fixation' features, specific design elements of the poster that had been identified in advance as those that might be potentially copied by participants. By identifying these features in advance, we could then quantify the level of design fixation that was appearing in new posters that our participants designed by counting the number of fixation features they contained.

Survey. A survey was given at the end of the experiment to gather basic demographic information, in addition to qualitative data about the strategies that were adopted by the participants during the design task. Questions asked other than the written text, what was the first visual element you looked at, what single visual element of the poster did you find yourself looking at most frequently, and what single visual element did you find yourself looking at for the longest length of time?

3   Results

Posters created by the participants were graded for fixations based on the 25 established 'fixation' features from the original example poster. In the subsequent results, a fixation is an element from the fixation poster that was included in a designed poster. There was an average of 2.84 fixations in each created poster; two of these posters are shown in Figure 2. Two study-blind judges graded the posters and had an inter-rater reliability of $r = .96$. We analyzed our data in order to address the main goals of the project. First, we compared whether participants' memories of how they spent their own time critiquing a previous design was consistent with the data we had gathered about their eye movements. Next, we analyzed whether participants' memories about their design critiques, or their eye movement data, predicted subsequent design fixations. Finally, we looked at the survey data that we had collected for any additional insights about what might be predisposing participants to fixation effects.

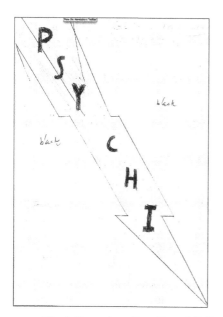

Fig. 2. Examples of less fixated (left) and more fixated (right) poster designs

3.1   Subjective Recall of Eye Movements

One of the research goals was to find out if participants were able to subjectively remember what they actually looked at on the fixation poster first, most frequently, and longest, based on their recorded eye movements. Zero percent (0%) of participants had a match between their subjective recall and objective eye movements of where they looked first; 10% of participants had a match for where they looked most frequently; 5% had a match on where they looked longest.

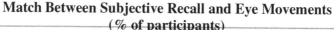

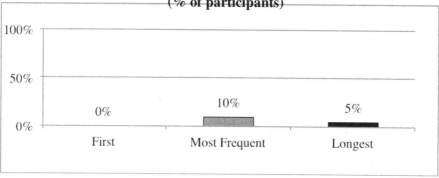

Fig. 3. The percentage of participants where a match was found between a participant's subjective recall and their objective eye movements of where they fixated first, most frequently, and longest

3.2   Subjective Recall and Fixation Effects

In Section 3.1, it was noted that participants were not often successful in matching their subjective recall of what they looked at first, most frequently, and longest. What a participant subjectively remembered looking at first, most frequently, and longest could theoretically lend insight into which elements they may have likely consciously fixated upon when designing their own posters. Participants were most likely to have fixated on what they remembered looking at first – but, even then, only 29% of participants fixated upon what they subjectively stated looking at first. Nineteen percent (19%) of participants fixated on what they subjectively looked at most frequently and 14% of participants fixated on what they subjectively looked at the longest; see Figure 4.

Did Subjective Recall and Eye Movements Predict Fixation?

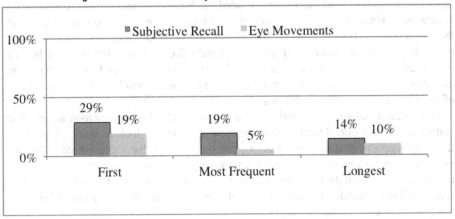

Fig. 4. The percentage of participants that fixated on a feature that was subjectively recalled as looked at first, most frequently, or for the longest duration, and the objective eye movements of each

3.3   Eye Movements and Fixation Effects

High percentages of matches between fixations and first, most frequent, or long lasting eye movements might be taken as evidence that how people spend time looking at an example design could indicate where fixation is likely to subsequently occur. To test whether participants eye movements predicted subsequent design fixation effects, we analyzed which features of the design participants looked at first, most frequently, and for the longest duration, then confirmed whether or not each of these matched with *any* fixation feature in that participant's final poster design. As shown in Figure 4, neither what participants looked at first, most frequently, or for the longest duration was a very good predictor of what they would fixate on.

4   Discussion

We analyzed our data in order to address how accurate people were with remembering where they looked on a poster, if where they looked would be an indicator for fixation, and if what they remembered looking at would be an indicator for fixation. We chose not focus on the effectiveness of their designed posters, but instead on which elements from the original poster they had included, which we termed 'fixations.

There appears to be distinct mismatches between what people remembered looking at on a poster and what they were actually looking at based on their eye movements, correctly matching an average of only 5% of the time across the three questions (see Figure 3). There is also a disconnect between both the subjective recall and objective eye movements and what participants fixated on. Subjective recall was, overall, fairly inaccurate when matched with the objective eye movements, but we wanted to see if the subjective recall would predict fixations included on the designed poster. However, subjective recall predicted an average of only 20.7% across the three trials. We then tried to see if eye movements, an objective measure, would predict fixations included in the designed posters, but that only predicted a fixation on average 11.3% of the time across the three questions.

Our research suggests that designers have poor recall of what they look at, and that neither subjective nor objective data about what designers look at correctly predicts fixation effects very accurately. Given that past research has demonstrated that eye movements are a real-time link to the cognitive processes of a person [11], and that the locus of attention during scene viewing is a strong predictor of which objects in a scene are being encoded in memory [12], it is puzzling that neither measure here was more predictive of fixation behavior.

Further research is clearly needed to determine what is causing design fixation, but one interesting theory of what is happening could be that, because participants were told this was a bad example of a poster, participants spent much of their time thinking and looking at elements of the example poster that they did not like. Later, when they were asked to design their own poster, they did not include those things they had disliked in their designed posters, but they may have been unconsciously primed to think about some of the elements that had not drawn their attention [8]. To use a coffee filter as a metaphor, the elements a participant considered "bad" in the previous design were eliminated, but the rest of the features that had not received attention then made an appearance in the final product. Continuing research will hopefully provide more insight into the underlying processes of design fixation.

References

1. Jansson, D.G., Smith, S.M.: Design fixation. Design Studies 12, 3–11 (1991)
2. Youmans, R.J.: The effects of physical prototyping and group work on the reduction of design fixation. Design Studies 32, 115–138 (2010)
3. Smith, S.M., Linsey, J.: A three-pronged approach for overcoming design fixation. The Journal of Creative Behavior 45, 83–91 (2011)

4. Yilmaz, S., Seifert, C.M., Gonzalez, R.: Cognitive heuristics in design: Instructional strategies to increase creativity in idea generation. Artificial Intelligence for Engineering Design, Analysis and Manufacturing 24, 335–355 (2010)
5. Dong, A., Sarkar, S.: Unfixing design fixation: From cause to computer simulation. The Journal of Creative Behavior 45, 147–159 (2011)
6. Youmans, R.J.: Design fixation in the wild: Design environments and their influence on fixation. The Journal of Creative Behavior 45, 101–107 (2011)
7. Bellows, B.G., Higgins, J.F., Smith, M.A., Youmans, R.J.: The Effects of Individual Differences in Working Memory Capacity and Design Environment on Design Fixation. In: Proceedings of the Human Factors and Ergonomics Society 56th Annual Meeting 2012, vol. 56, pp. 1977–1981 (2012), doi:10.1177/1071181312561293.
8. Youmans, R.J., Arciszewski, T.: Design fixation: A cloak of many colors. In: Proceedings of the 2012 Design, Computing, and Cognition Conference, College Station, Texas (2012)
9. Wickens, C.D., Lee, J.D., Liu, Y., Gordon Becker, S.E.: An Introduction to Human Factors in Engineering, 2nd edn. Pearson Prentice Hall, Upper Saddle River (2004)
10. Kirwan, B., Ainsworth, L.K. (eds.): A guide to task analysis: the task analysis working group. CRC (1992)
11. Hayhoe, M.M., Ballard, D.H.: Mechanisms of gaze control in natural vision. Oxford Handbook of Eye Movements, pp. 607–617. Oxford Library of Psychology (2011)
12. Peterson, M.S., Beck, M.R.: Eye Movements and Memory. Oxford Handbook of Eye Movements, pp. 579–592. Oxford Library of Psychology (2011)
13. Ericsson, K.A., Krampe, R.T., Tesch-Romer, C.: The role of deliberate practice in the acquisition of expert performance. Psychological Review 100, 363–406 (1993)

Semiotics of Void and Information Representation

Kumiko Tanaka-Ishii

Kyushu University
kumiko@ait.kyushu-u.ac.jp

Abstract. The objective of this article is to present a semiotic analysis of void—which in this article is the spacio-temporal empty space existing in any representation—in order to consider the representation of quality and to show how this is essential in human representation yet difficult to process computationally. First, a summary of reference to void is presented through a comparison between Western and Eastern cultural approaches to void. A semiotic model of void is then developed by applying both Saussurian and Peircian frameworks and explaining how the two frameworks become equivalent when applied to void, as well as how void is essentially a structural entity. After analysis of various semiotic kinds of void, the article examines the difficulty of computational handling of void and suggests possible paths towards a more human-oriented form of information representation.

Keywords: semiotics, information representation, void, structure, index, icon, design.

1   Void in Information Representation

Void in this article signifies the spacio-temporal empty space existing in a representation. Spatially, void indicates the empty spaces among content. For example, every character space in this article, the space framing the text, and the space between lines are all part of the void. Temporally, void consists of the non-event periods between consecutive temporal events.

From this definition, void exists everywhere, in any kind of spacio-temporal representation. The design of void partly defines how well the representation as a whole communicates. It requires consideration of the size, frequency, and density of void among non-void occurrences. Such representations naturally include any computational representation, inclusively of all automatic syntheses. For example, the reason why people find most automatic syntheses *mechanical* partly lies in the lack of naturalness in the design of void.

Void at first seems no more than something *left out* after articulating content or an event, and thus unworthy for analysis. Signification by void, such as the naturalness noted above, however, suggests that void itself speaks. Consideration of a representation that communicates well cannot leave void literally as emptiness without any concrete content. In other words, void in a representation has meaning or at least adds meaning to non-void content and events.

A. Marcus (Ed.): DUXU/HCII 2013, Part I, LNCS 8012, pp. 152–161, 2013.

Fig. 1. Uemura Shōen, *Feathered Snow*, Color on Silk, Shōwa Period, 1944 Yamatane Museum of Art, Tokyo, Japan. Original in color.

The first objective of this article is to consider void semiotically. Semiotics is adopted here as the theoretical basis for analysis of any media with meaning. Such semiotic analysis of void would provide insights on the essential differences between human and computational semiotic systems. This understanding would naturally push us to seek better information representation and design. This leads to the question, however, of *better* in which way? Hence, this article examines this question with respect to HCI and UX after brief reference to the previous conjecture on void and semiotic modeling of void.

2 West vs. East: A Brief Summary of Previous References to Void

The historical focus on the notion of void contrasts between the West and East. The West, with the theoretical traditions of ancient Greek philosophy and Christianity, valued rational minds which typically required classifying an analysis target into a few components. Since clarity was valued, void, which tends to remain ambiguous, was avoided. This led to the tendency of void not to develop as a subject itself, with the result that either nothing is left blank or blankness is considered something leftover and unworthy for analysis. For example, Western paintings before the modern era have the strong tendency to fill the whole canvas, as established through the study of perspective, which is the effect obtained by a representation exterior to the subject estate.

In contrast, in the East the notion of void has been considered central in different kinds of representation. This is supported by the philosophical background of Buddhism, in which void is considered the source of holism from which everything is generated. Ambiguity has not been considered something to be avoided. In Eastern representation, the question of how to organize blankness often became a subject itself.

In Japan, void is described through the term '間' (read *ma*, literally meaning *something in between*), and the notion has been considered important through every kind of representation. Figure 1 shows one example of painting making use of void. Minami in [6] indicates how the notion of *ma* governs every Japanese cultural representation, including language, painting, poetry, theater, film, ritual, music, dance, architecture, and martial arts. Moreover, the notion of *ma* appears in various Japanese words. For example, the term *mistake* in Japanese is *ma-chigai* whose literal translation is *ma* taken incorrectly. In China, as well, the mention of void has a long history with respect to Lao-zi's philosophy of Taoism [2]. The notion developed mainly through the term '无' (read *wú*, meaning *none*), although there are other related terms such as '空' (read *kong*, meaning *empty*), as raised by [2].

The two contrastive cultural approaches of East and West towards void, however, have become closer under the influence of globalization. From the Western side, one typical example can be seen in a modern trend in cognitive science, through the distinction of *figure* and *ground*. Originally, the ground remained the less interesting estate, but Gestalt psychology then indicated how the figure and ground can get reversed [4]. In parallel to such increased focus on targets which had acquired less focus in the West, the East has also acquired a great influence of Western rationalism, resulting in less emphasis on traditional Eastern cultural notions. Within this current, the mention of void seems to have decreased, resulting in rare consideration within frameworks of an international, academic, theoretical basis, including semiotics. Even when void is mentioned, the argument entails analysis of a specific Eastern artistic genre, as seen for Chinese painting [2], garden rock placement [1], or art related to Buddhism [3].

Before going on to semiotic consideration of void, note that there is a question of whether voids with different cultural backgrounds can be considered as one. For example, voids in China and Japan are not identical, as seen from how they are primarily articulated. Briefly, Chinese void has a more absolute notion, considered as the source of the yin-yang contrast in Chinese philosophical thought, whereas Japanese void is more relative to other, non-void existences. Even with such different cultural backgrounds, both types of voids influenced each other throughout history. Precisely speaking, every void has a cultural color, and analysis of the different notions would be interesting. In this article, however, in addition to the limitation of space, since the context lies in information representation, which currently concerns every culture, I consider the universality of void in an abstract manner.

3   Semiotic Modeling of Void

Modeling void by the theory of semiotics in fact is challenging, since the focus of semiotics is on what is articulated in the form of a sign. Void at first only seems something left out, the remaining resource after some articulation is made. Thus, considering void as a sign could even sound contradictory. Partly because of such contradiction, void has rarely been considered to form a semiotic target,

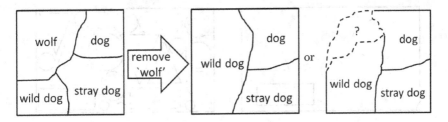

Fig. 2. Saussurian traditional semiotic field formed from relations among signs, filling the semantic field taken from [5] (left, center) and an alternative (right)

even though a substantial variety of representation targets have been considered within semiotics [7]. Some exceptions exist, as found in [2], which suggests considering void (*le vide* in Cheng, i.e., emptiness) by means of semiology, but even here the application of fundamental semiotic theories to the notion of void has been limited, made only through analysis of Chinese paintings.

3.1   Model of Void

First of all, we must consider the plausibility of considering void as a kind of sign. Above all, Saussure emphasized how the meanings of signs are defined relatively within the holistic system of value such that each sign cannot exist absolutely. Saussure raises an example of wolf and dog to explain this in [9]. Maruyama illustrates this idea as shown in Figure 2 (left), in which every area surrounded by a contour is considered as an articulated sign [5][page 96]. If one of the signs (e.g., wolf) did not exist or was removed, the signs placed next to the original would take its place (center), by changing the contour of the semantics of the other signs, such as dog and wild dog.

This image well illustrates the relativity of the values of signs. When one sign is removed, however, should the whole semantic field be completely filled? If the notion of "wolf" did not exist or disappeared, wouldn't there be the possibility of having a semantic portion in which wolves are considered as unknown animals, different from both wild dogs and dogs? Moreover, how could this relative change in the notion be explained in relation to the social convention having the effect of stabilizing the semantic meaning of a sign? I consider that the Saussurian notion of relativity does not necessarily mean that the semantic field should be completely filled. Rather, it could leave space for something unknown or undefined. This can be represented by changing both the contours of every sign and the contour of the whole semantic field, with some semantic borders left obscure, as denoted by the dashed lines in the rightmost figure.

Upon allowing such "left out" or unknown spaces in the semantic field, we find out that these spaces do possess meaning by themselves, as illustrated in Figure 3. Here, objects with various shapes represent non-void signs, and the left-out spaces represent undefined spaces existing within the field. The left-out spaces could have obscure borders (denoted by dashed lines), as seen previously.

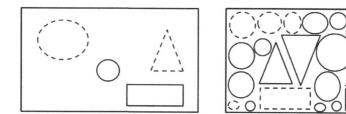

Fig. 3. Semiotic fields with voids

Comparing the two figures in Figure 3, anyone would feel that in the right figure, the objects (i.e., the non-void signs) are more densely placed, suggesting a further connotation that the semiotic space is more tightly packed than that on the left. This could suggest further, for example, how the semantic domain either has much left to be studied (left) or is well established (right), depending on the target field. Even from this simple example, we see that void generates meaning. The void in Figure 1 also provokes imagination of the cold, dim, cloudy winter sky, which effectively highlights the ladies' clothing colors.

Void thus can be considered to form a sign and become a target of semiotics. Indeed, in the East, the notion of void has been considered through a sign, or 无. Even without verification, [2] naturally considered *le vide* within the context of semiotics. In the Saussurian sign model, the signifier is deemed the representation of void, and the meaning raised through the existence of void constitutes the signified. For example, in the case of Figure 1, the signifier is deemed the blank space, whereas the meaning raised through imagination (the dim sky, the effect of highlighting the clothing, etc.) forms the signified.

Comparing void and non-void signs, void as a sign has two characteristics. First, it influences the context, or the *system*, directly. In the same example of Figure 1, the void part is defined by the placement of other non-void signs (namely, the ladies). The final setting of void constitutes the relation or the context of the other non-void signs. Such directness in relation to the sign system as a whole characterizes void. Saussure emphasized how the meaning of a sign should be considered within the holistic system of the sign. Void, if admitted to consideration as a sign, is then a typical sign that directly concerns the whole semiotic field, the holistic semiotic system itself.

Second, void is defined through its use. Void is the space that remains after placing other non-void signs within void itself. This explanation itself shows how void is defined self-referentially. In the same example of Figure 1, the placement of other non-void signs is the *use* of blank area, which defines what and how void exists here. The painter must have searched for the optimal composition in terms of use of void, and the final choice defines the content of the void. The reason why void directly influences the system lies in its way of being defined through its use. In other words, void is a self-referential sign, which acquires its content through the use of itself.

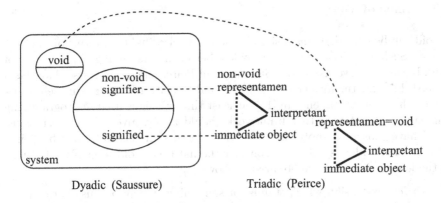

Fig. 4. Void as a sign

So far, we have considered Saussure's framework. Alternatively, Peirce's semiotic framework can model such reflexivity in semiotics. In [11], I argued how the Peircian and Saussurian frameworks might correspond differently from what had been believed, through analysis of different computer programming paradigms. According to this conclusion, by considering Peirce's dynamical object to correspond to Saussure's thing, two relata of the Peircian triadic sign, the representamen and immediate object, correspond to the relata of the Saussurian dyadic sign, the signifier and signified. The third of Peirce's relata, the interpretant, is found in the Saussurian framework in the form of difference.

This new correspondence applies naturally to a semiotic discussion of void as a sign, as shown in Figure 4. The left side of the figure shows the Saussurian model, in which there are two signs, void and non-void. In a usual semiotic representation, there could be multiple non-void signs related to void and other non-void signs. Void as a sign forms the context of the non-void signs, and therefore, void relates to non-void, within the semiotic system; in other words, void forms difference. In applying the Peircian triadic framework, on the other hand, as shown on the right side of the figure, void would form part of the interpretant, as the *use* of the non-void signs. The dashed lines indicate the correspondences of the relata in each framework.

In [11], I further indicated how a sign whose content (i.e., the signified, or Peirce's immediate object) is defined through its use (i.e., within the Saussurian system, or through Peirce's interpretant) makes the two different models equivalent. A self-referential sign acquires its content through the use of itself; therefore, content and use become tightly coupled, because articulation requires reference to a complex unit operating as the *self* through a signifier. Void is yet another example of a self-referential sign to which such equivalence applies.

This reciprocal nature of void further suggests that it is something human and difficult to handle naturally within a computational information representation. Before going on to this aspect, however, it is interesting to see what kinds of void exist, through semiotic consideration of different kinds of sign.

3.2   Kinds of Void

If void can be considered as a sign, it should be classifiable in terms of semiotic classes. Such a conjecture could provide a better understanding of the nature of void. In the frameworks of both Saussure and Peirce, such sign classes have been proposed [7], for the former by Hjelmslev and the latter by Peirce himself. I discussed their correspondence in [11], at least through signs used in programming languages. Therefore, either framework should apply, given these discussions, and I have chosen to apply the most widely used sign classes framed by Peirce [8] (i.e., icon, index, symbol) to consider the nature of void. Peirce's definitions of the icon, index, and symbol are as follows [8]:

- An *icon* is "a sign which stands for something merely because it resembles it" [3.362], "partaking in the characters of the object" [4.531]. For example, a portrait of a person or a color sample of paint is an icon since it stands for something merely because it resembles the original.
- An *index* is "physically connected with its object; they make an organic pair, but the interpreting mind has nothing to do with this connection" [2.299]; "it is a 'reference'" [2.283]. According to Peirce, clocks, sundials, and door knocks are example of indexes, since each makes an organic pair with another fact. Moreover, uses of signs A, B, and C in a formal statement such as 'A and B are married and C is their child' are indexes [2.285].
- A *symbol* is a sign that "refers to the object that it denotes by virtue of law, usually an association of general ideas" [2.249] "Any ordinary word as 'give', 'bird', 'marriage', is an example of a symbol" [2.298].

Briefly, in the jargon of computer science, an icon represents an instance, an index represents a variable, and a symbol represents a type.

Void as icon corresponds to the specific blanks and spaces introduced for a representation, as instances of spacing. For example, a visual representation requires regulation of space before it is complete, and this could require modification applied to the general spacing rules governing the representation. Such adjustment is often due to optical illusions caused by the placement of non-void content. Another example could be a moment of silence in a musical performance. The best length depends on the context, as the performance, its speed and intensity, and every musical non-event moment constitutes an instance.

Void as index requires attachment of a secondary, unrelated meaning, according to Peirce's definition. An example was already shown in Figure 1, in which the space is not only a blank but also requires the viewer's imagination. Another temporal example is Cage's piece *4'33"*. The "performance" of silence in this piece provokes consideration of what is music, and such connotation is indexed through the void as silence. From this view, an artistically designed representation of void is deemed an index, with the difference from icon being whether the void adds a further connotation.

Lastly, void as Peircian symbol is deemed to indicate the typical types of spaces in a representation. We often refer to such voids in terms of *format*. A text format (such as the format for this paper, specified by the HCII Conference) defines spacing, or how void should appear together with text: the amount of space between lines, and the blank spaces framing the main text. The normal lengths of musical notes indicated in musical scores also define such a format, although the notes become icons once played (if played by a human).

Such discussion of void also supports the notion of how void could constitute a sign and be analyzed within a semiotic framework. Moreover, this discussion also shows another characteristic of having interest in void as index or icon, rather than as a Peircian symbol. Usually in semiotics as a science, the emphasis of such classification lies more in organization in the form of symbols, i.e., a typical group of signs appearing in a certain kind of representation. In contrast, the question of void governing a representation holistically seems to lie in how optimally the void is organized in every representation instance.

The important point here is that such a representation instance is realized through a mixture of icon, index, and symbol. For example, in a musical performance, the symbol is indicated first but then regulated at the level of individual play as an icon and completed as art in terms of index. This happens similarly for visual representations: first is regulation in terms of symbol, realized in an instance and completed in terms of index, in which void speaks eloquently.

4   Towards a More Human-Oriented Information Representation

The semiotic conjecture of void in the previous section highlights the following three points:

- The characteristics of void as a sign lie in its holistic nature.
- Void is a typical reciprocal sign, in which the frameworks of Peirce and Saussure become equivalent.
- Void presents signification more at the level of icon and index, which derive from other semiotic classes. This suggests the importance of optimal spaciotemporal placement of each instance of void.

What can these observations bring to HCI and UX?

Above all, with void being reciprocal and holistic, it is a non-trivial target for handling within computational information representation. In [11], I highlighted the difference in the semiotic natures of computer and human signs, in terms of *constructive* vs. *structural*. The difference derives from the different interpretive strategies for reflexive expressions in these two sign systems. Natural sign systems handle self-reference, including any problematic self-referential expressions, by leaving ambiguity as is. This interpretive mechanism generates a structural system in which the signification of signs exists in the holistic system and the whole sign system operates reflexively. In contrast, in computer sign systems, programs must be constructive, generated by a safe combination of signs that is guaranteed to halt, since self-reference directly concerns the halting problem[1].

---

[1] It has been logically proved that any computer based on a Turing machine is incapable of judging whether a given program halts [10].

Making computer sign systems structural holds the key to developing computer systems that behave in a more human-friendly manner.

Returning to the question raised in Section 1, of how semiotic consideration of void could provoke *better* information representation, here is a possible answer: by filling the gap between structure and construction for a more human-oriented information representation. Void is a typical sign of the structural type. Naturally, then, void does not conform well with computational handling, and synthesis has been made with the focus on the non-void aspects of information representation. Further, this could be one reason why all such synthesis remains mechanical, in contrast to human representation, which is always adjusted holistically through repeated, reciprocal consideration of non-void and void elements. For example, in automatic musical performance, every length of musical event must be recalculated according to a holistic strategy of how to represent an event and the subsequent void. Likewise, for an interactive system, the optimal spacing of interaction, including speed and silence, requires proper design depending on whom the system interacts with.

Consideration of void in semiotics therefore aids formulation of how signs should be holistically organized in a system—which concerns not only the non-void but also the sign system as a whole, including void. This helps fill the gap between structure and construction. How well a representation communicates to an audience depends on the organic handling of signs, including the design of void, which currently tends to be missing and ignored.

There are two possible paths to studying a more human-oriented computational representation:

- holistic analysis of human sign systems, and
- a computational optimization methodology oriented towards holism.

The first point derives from content processing within computer science. It entails construction of various corpora founded on analysis of the content. Such corpus construction, however, has placed the focus on non-void content. It could be possible to integrate void so as to form part of a corpus. This would require assembling a language for describing void, which could be generated through detailed categorical analysis of void and annotation of void by using language appearing in multiple cases of information design[2]. Better synthesis could become possible by using such a corpus as a gold standard.

Second, based on this understanding of void, proper computational handling methods for void must be reconsidered. This is the matter of global optimization of the semiotic system as a whole, including the design of void. Usually an optimization problem requires combinatorial calculation. At the same time, as seen in the previous section, since void has more signification at the level of icon and index, such optimization must be made individually for each instance of representation. Various optimization techniques would apply to synthesis of

---

[2] A good starting point could be borrowed from a corpus annotating metalanguage, including elements such as brackets, appearing in [12], in the sense that metalanguage also concerns signification at the semiotic system level.

computational design instances, and moreover, planning algorithms must be deduced from these techniques, in order to construct interactive systems with partially optimized void at each interaction point.

Such studies could highlight the underlying nature of human information. An endeavor towards a better, more human-oriented synthesis could possibly lead to a better man-machine interface.

References

[1] Casalis, M.: The semiotics of the visible in japanese rock gardens. Semiotica, 349–362 (1983)

[2] Cheng, F.: Vide et Plein. Seuil (1991) (in French)

[3] D'Amato, M.: The semiotics of signlessness: A buddhist doctrine of signs. Semiotica, 185–207 (2003)

[4] Köhler, W.: Gestalt Psychology. Liveright Publishing Corporation (1947) (reprinted in 1992)

[5] Maruyama, K.: Thoughts of de Saussure. Iwanami publishing (1981) (in Japanese)

[6] Minami, H.: A Study on Ma —A Japanese Aesthetic Representation. Kodansha (1983) (in Japanese)

[7] Nöth, W.: Handbook of Semiotics. Indiana University Press (1990)

[8] Peirce, C.: Collected Papers. Harvard University Press (1931)

[9] de Saussure, F.: Saussure's Second Course of Lectures on General Linguistics. Pergamon (1908-1909); from notebooks of Albert Riedlinger and Charles Patois (1998)

[10] Sipser, M.: Introduction to the Theory of Computation, 2nd edn. Course Technology (2005)

[11] Tanaka-Ishii, K.: Semiotics of Programming. Cambridge University Press (2010)

[12] Wilson, S.: The creation of a corpus of english metalanguage, pp. 638–646 (2012)

Of Hoverboards and Hypertext

Daniel Yule and Jamie Blustein

Dalhousie University
Halifax, Nova Scotia, Canada
{yule,jamie}@cs.dal.ca

Abstract. In 1968, Doug Englebart and his team at the Stanford Research Institute amazed the world with their oN-Line System (NLS), giving what has since been dubbed the "Mother of all Demos." The NLS system, later renamed Augment, was the first Graphical User Interface, the first Word Processor, the first Wiki, the first Hypertext system, essentially the first of many applications we think of as modern. Much of the progress in software of the last forty-five years can be seen as attempting to realize the vision first articulated by Englebart at the '68 Fall Joint Computer Conference.

However, it has only been recently, with the advent of HTML5 and related standards, that the entirety of the NLS/Augment system can be implemented in the browser in a standardized fashion. This article examines what has changed to finally allow the realization of a half-century old vision and investigates why it took so long.

We ask: where are we going next? More importantly, where *should* we be going?

1 Introduction

In the 1989 film "Back to the Future Part II," the protagonists Marty McFly and Doc Brown travel to the year 2015 and have a glimpse of the future. That future includes holographic movies, self-tying shoes and, most importantly, hoverboards. [1]

With 2015 only two years away, the hoverboards that seemed entirely plausible in the 1989 film are incredibly unlikely. In fact, it seems neither that hoverboards are going to arrive in the foreseeable future, nor that they would be especially useful if they did arrive. Despite this, in 2010, an artist created a hoverboard replica (that really floats) for installation in a museum.[1]

Hypertext finds itself in a similar, if somewhat more prolonged, situation. Early visionaries foresaw the future of computing over fifty years ago, and created its precursors not long after. Those early pioneer's visions still haven't been realized in their entirety, but the pieces that have are responsible for most of the innovations of personal computing. Hypertext researchers over the years have built on top of those early visions, but with few exceptions they see little use outside of labs, not much more useful than a hoverboard in a museum.

This paper argues that the problems faced by hypertext pioneers have indeed been realized, although not through scientific deliberation and standardization, but through

---

[1] http://vimeo.com/11968215

A. Marcus (Ed.): DUXU/HCII 2013, Part I, LNCS 8012, pp. 162–170, 2013.

a hodgepodge of academics, industry and government. Furthermore, if the hypertext community does not embrace the tumbling torrent of disparate actors and conflicting goals that define modern technology, we risk irrelevancy, as industry will surely step in to fill in the gap.

The essential concepts of hypertext are almost as old as text itself. The Talmud, Bible Concordances and the I Ching hold the fundamental characteristics of intertextuality and reader interaction that inform modern hypertext theory [2].

In papers such as this, it is customary to cite Vannevar Bush's "As We May Think" published in *The Atlantic Monthly 1945* [3] as the birth of modern hypertext, although he was preceded technically by Emmanuel Goldberg [4–6] and theoretically by Paul Otlet [7, 8]. However, in a premonition of what was to come, it was Bush's evocative, accessible description of his imaginary Memex machine, as opposed to the more technical and obscure writings of his forerunners, that inspired a generation of Computer Scientists who would go on to create the world's first computerized hypertext systems.

It was almost twenty years after Bush's article, in the early sixties, that his spark would finally flare into the systems that would become the first computerized hypertext. The first half of the decade saw the publishing of Doug Englebart's Conceptual Model for Augmenting Human Intellect [9], and Theodore Nelson's coining of the word 'hypertext.' [10, p. 13].

Later in the sixties, the Nelson inspired Hypertext Editing System (HES) [11] pioneered a new approach to documentation that would be used by the Apollo program [12], but it was Doug Englebart's oN-Line System (NLS) that would explode hypertext (among other ideas) into the wider academic consciousness. [13, p 144]

Following those projects were a parade of innovative systems straight through the late eighties, most notably: HES's successors - FRESS and DPS [12], The Aspen Movie Map, KMS, Hyperties, Symbolics Document Examiner, Intermedia, and the first runaway commercial hypermedia success, HyperCard [14]. But none of these are as grandiose and tragic as Xanadu. Xanadu is emblematic of hypertext systems in general: exceedingly clever, seemingly crucial systems that never see any widespread uptake. [15, 16]

For better or for worse it was Tim Berners-Lee's WorldWideWeb, as implemented by the NSCA's Mosiac web browser, that would finally set the world ablaze from the carefully laid kindling of the hypertext community.

The web, as it's come to be known today, has brought the world together in previously unimaginable ways, but members of the hypertext community lament its superficiality and lack of attention to the work that came before it, calling it variously 'Hypertext 0.5,' [17] 'prodigal' [18] and 'feral.' [19]

To determine what's missing from the web and why those elements are important to the community, we must first look back to the stated goals of one of the early pioneers of hypertext: Douglas Englebart.

2   NLS/Augment

Douglas Englebart's goal was "increasing the capability of a man to approach a complex problem situation, to gain comprehension to suit his particular needs, and to derive solutions to problems." [9]

Englebart's thought was to build a system which information workers, such as himself and his team at the Stanford Research Institute might use to become more efficient. As such, they were the primary users of the system they built, in a process Englebart called 'Bootstrapping.' [20].

When Englebart demonstrated the resulting system at the Fall Joint Computer Conference in 1968, he showed the audience the first word processor, the first wiki, the first graphical user interface and the first computerized hypertext, all within his oN-Line System. Englebart had given a glimpse of the hoverboard hypertext of the future, and the computing world would never be the same. [13]

Unfortunately, although the ideas presented defined personal computing for decades to come, that conference was a high point for the NLS system. As more people used the system, its complexity began to show. Englebart believed that a certain level of complexity was acceptable, reasoning that if people were willing to spend three years learning how to speak a language and ten years learning mathematics, they could afford to spend a few months learning to use a computer. [p. 245] [13] However, even with other computer experts, its complexity and rigid hierarchy did not sit well. Englebart's colleague, John MacCarthy, head of SRI's AI program, tried to write a paper using NLS and found it so difficult that he swore he'd never use it again [13, p 171].

Despite the excitement generated by the demo, work on NLS declined throughout the early seventies. Much of Englebart's team jumped ship to Xerox's new research institute, PARC. At PARC, Englebart's ideas found expression in the world's first personal computer, the Alto, but only at the cost of cutting out all of NLS's complexity and hierarchy.

Just as Goldberg and Otley's ideas didn't catch on until Vannevar Bush expressed them clearly in *The Atlantic Monthly*, Englebarts ideas only found expression after being refined and adapted for a wider audience than simply highly trained experts. [21]

3   WorldWideWeb

The World Wide Web is at once hypertext's killer app and its greatest disappointment. It has spun hypertext across the world, but done so at the cost of ignoring most of classical hypertext's richness, at least on the surface.

The original goal of Tim Berners-Lee's WorldWideWeb was to store information and documentation relating to research groups at CERN. But Berners-Lee recognized that the problem he was solving was more general. "Suppose all the information stored on computers everywhere were linked," he thought. "Suppose I could program my computer to create a space in which anything could be linked to anything." [22, p 4]

The WorldWideWeb was not the only hypertext system available, nor was it even the only internet based hypertext system. But it became the most successful. Exactly how and why this happened is a topic of debate and discussion, [23] but that it has happened is undeniable.

Berners-Lee and his associates had built a solid foundation, but it was the NSCA's Mosaic web browser that gave the web mass market appeal. Mosaic went from nothing to an estimated 93% browser share in one year, [24] in large part because its creator, Marc Andreessen, focused intently on what users wanted [25]. Following Mosaic's success, both Microsoft and Netscape (among others) released competing browsers, setting off the first "Browser Wars" in 1995 [26].

HTML, driven by industrial competition, was improved rapidly, moving from HTML 2.0 in 1995 to HTML 4 by 1997, before settling on HTML 4.01 in 1999. [27] Many of the essential tenets of the modern web were developed during that period: JavaScript (developed by Netscape) [28], CSS (developed by the W3C) [29], Asynchronous HTTP (developed by Microsoft) [30], and XML (developed by the W3C) [31], all made their debut during this time.

Microsoft's practice of bundling Internet Explorer with Windows won the first browser war, but it wasn't long before Mozilla [32] was joined by Apple and Google in creating powerful open source browsers, sparking the second browser war.

During the lull between the browser wars, the W3C worked on web related specifications, not demanded by the browser manufacturers, including XML and Semantic Web related technologies, such as RDF and OWL. Breaking with its tradition of standardizing already existing HTML implementations, or highly requested features, the W3C set about defining XHTML 2.0, a non-backwards compatible update to HTML 4/XHTML 1.0. This would prove to be a colossal mistake for the W3C.

Browser vendors completely ignored XHTML 2.0, and created their own group for the advancement of Web Standards, the Web Hypertext Application Technology Working Group (WHATWG). This group defined the HTML 5 standard, later dropping the number to have a so-called "Living Standard." Although the W3C has dropped their work on XHTML 2.0 and standardized HTML 5 instead, since the membership of WHATWG is made entirely of the major browser vendors (with the exception of Microsoft), that group is essentially the authority on web standards today, leaving the W3C completely behind. [33]

WHATWG's living HTML standard is more than just the markup language used for webpages. It has grown to include the Document Object Model, Cascading Style sheets and JavaScript, as well as various JavaScript APIs such as geolocation, offline storage and more. [34] With the fast pace driven by Microsoft, Google, Apple and Mozilla's battle for supremacy, new concepts and ideas are being constantly added and improved to the HTML5 collection of standards.

4   HTML5 Augment

The web has evolved far beyond Tim Berners-Lee's original vision. Indeed, right from the start, few web browsers outside of his own supported inline editing of webpages. Today, none do. Even his WorldWideWeb browser was less 'hypertext-y' than his original ENQUIRE browser, which had bi-directional, annotated links. [22] However, it is a testament to his design and leadership that the web has been able to evolve to what it has become today.

With the new power of HTML5 related standards, the web has become a platform in its own right. Google[2], Microsoft[3] and Zoho[4] all offer complete office software,

---

[2] http://docs.google.com
[3] http://office.microsoft.com
[4] http://www.zoho.com/

entirely in the browser. There are sophisticated games[5] which can be played entirely using HTML. Indeed, Mozilla plans to release a smartphone with nothing *but* HTML 5 and related technologies later this year. [35]

All of these things have been possible for many years, with system dependent machine code, Java or Flash. But, for the first time there is a completely open, hypertext based, standardized platform that has the power to build essentially any application. In fact, HTML5 and related technologies has the expressive power to re-create Douglas Englebart's Augment system in the browser.

Attached to this paper is a demonstration of some parts of Englebart's original Augment system as implemented in HTML 5[6]. The system allows for the creation of a hierarchy of items, the association of locations with those items, and the plotting of these locations on a map. This demo makes use of the Canvas element for drawing the map and the local storage API for storing the items between sessions. These are both new to HTML 5, and such a system could not be made using standards compliant code wholly in the browser until now. Indeed, much of the technologies necessary for a browser based NLS system (e.g. JavaScript and Asynchronous HTTP) were not created by academics, or even the W3C, but by commercial browser vendors.

But we needn't stop here! HTML5 and related technologies are powerful enough to re-create any classical hypertext system, from Intermedia to Xanadu. Indeed, many of today's web apps have direct analogues with hypertext systems from the seventies and eighties, such as Google Maps (Aspen Movie Map) and Wikis (Knowledge Management System). [14]

So, although the web is 'wild' and 'untamed', out of the chaos we can create the orderly systems of yesteryear. The question is, should we?

5   Grappling with the Future

One of the defining features of the web is that it imposes few constraints on its use, either technical or political. Users are able to organize what they want, link what they want and write what they want, subject to the laws of their resident country. This was by design, as Berners-Lee saw the repeated failure of documentation systems at CERN as they tried to impose organizational hierarchies onto researchers. [22, p 14]

The web is designed like a market economy: anyone can do anything, but there are a few conventions and procedures they must agree to, such as currency and rules for fair trading. [22, p 36]. This wide open space created an ecosystem in which anyone with an idea could try it out, and potentially create something great. Most of the innovations associated with the web did not come from Berners-Lee or even the W3C: they came from companies or individuals who had an idea.

On top of the web's wide open ecosystem, a powerful platform has emerged. The web is not like any platform that came before it. There is no one group in charge, it's completely open, it runs almost anywhere and is somewhat standardized. But compared to the hypertext systems envisioned and created by early hypertext pioneers, this is no

---

[5] See, for example, this 3D game rendered entirely using CSS transforms:
   http://keithclark.co.uk/labs/css3-fps/

[6] See http://web.cs.dal.ca/~yule/nls2/

closer to the hypertext hoverboard of the future than a skateboard with a fan taped on. If the explosion of the web was possible with "Hypertext 0.5," imagine what we might do with a full blown hypertext system!

But of course, the web *is* a full hypertext system. If we can implement full hypertext systems using the web, its power must be sufficient for anything under the sun. And the simple fact is, the world is not the same as it was when classical hypertext systems were proposed.

Douglas Englebart's stated goal with Augment was quite simply to augment human abilities to allow us to cope with the growing complexity of problems in the world [36]. The web has put the world no more than a URL away. Project Gutenburg and its commercial cousin Google Books have made a significant portion human literary output instantly available. Wikipedia and digital libraries have made factual knowledge accessible on an unprecedented scale. An emerging class of low cost electronics[7] is putting that information in the hands of billions of people. Human ability has been augmented: mission accomplished?

But, just as Englebart foresaw, in creating these tools, we have created additional complexity. In making information easier to process, we've raised the expectation in terms of how much information we're expected to handle[8].

Tools that were created to solve problems at the dawn of personal computing are no longer relevant. The problems have evolved, and so have the expectations of those who use them. The first generation of so-called 'Digital Natives' are entering adulthood. These people have grown up with the web, and it completely informs their ideas of how to interact with information. For them, instant access is the norm. Although the web has become an incredibly sophisticated system, for them, it just works [38].

Unfortunately for its moving forward, the history of hypertext has been one of complete disregard for usability. Englebart specifically believed that his system would be complicated to use, but that end users would learn it eventually [13]. Xanadu's excessive focus on clever technology in the back-end meant its creators never had an idea of how someone might actually use the system [15, 39]. A major stumbling block for the Web, until Mosaic came along, was the difficulty of installing and operating a browser [22]. Certainly designing systems that will serve the needs of information experts is necessary, but it is hardly sufficient.

This is not to say we should be only aiming for a replication of the web. As academics, it's our job to create esoteric and quixotic systems that push the boundaries of what's possible. But there are big problems out there to solve, which are just begging for the application of hypertext.

Academic publishing is a topic that has been touched on by every generation of hypertext scholars. Bush's article, Englebart's NLS and Berners-Lee's WorldWide Web were all aimed squarely at changing the way academics process and share information and yet after 68 years, the only difference in how we submit a paper to a conference is

---

[7] For example, the Aakash 2 Tablet recently launched in India is roughly 1/30 the price of an iPad [37].

[8] See http://informationoverloadresources.com/ for a list of resources on the rush of information, and how it affects us.

that we upload what is essentially an electronic duplicate of a printed page, containing no links, no annotation, and no multi-media beyond charts and graphs.

The hypertext community should be on the vanguard of new publishing technologies. Simply attaching a more hypertext-y version of a conference paper isn't good enough. The web has shown that we need to create a platform that is open, accessible and easy to use. It's embarrassing that in this day and age, the most sophisticated links possible between two papers is a citation at the end of a paper and the only annotations are footnotes[9]. The hypertext community should not wait around until a commercial vendor figures out how to take its ideas and exploit them.

Furthermore, although the web is the most obvious example of a widely used hypertext, story driven video games (Mass Effect, The Elder Scrolls, Final Fantasy, etc) have clear connections to ergodic literature, and thusly hypertext. In such a narrative based game, the choices the character makes affect not only the narrative but the entire world they live in. In the Mass Effect Trilogy, for example, narrative (not gameplay) choices made in the second game have consequences for the entire storyline of the third game, including which characters are still alive. Entire fields of study have sprung up to study various aspects of video gaming, from the sociological to the narrative, but the discussion of game as hypertext has been conspicuously absent, outside of their connection through Cybertext [40].

The hypertext community has built some incredibly [41] clever [42] systems [43] using a combination of web strategies and classical hypertext ideas. But these systems have yet to see widespread adoption.

5.1 Semantic Web

6 Conclusion

We are faced with a world suffocating with complexity and drowning in urgency. The tools inherited from the minds of the early hypertext pioneers have allowed us to meet the challenges of the modern world, but in doing so, created new ones. We need new tools and new approaches to confront the jungle of information we descend further into each day. We may dream of hoverboards, but until we can find a path through the information jungle, we're better off on foot. Furthermore, if we academics can't find our way out, we can be sure the business community will hack their way through with the machete of consumer satisfaction.

It took four decades, but we've finally managed to build a system on open standards that is roughly equivalent to the visions of the founders. We need new goals and a new vision going forward. Ideas such as adaptive hypertext [44] and the semantic web are clearly designed to solve a new set of problems. Indeed many of the ideas of adaptive hypertext have found expression in the behavioral advertising used by Google and Facebook, but surveillance by commercial entities is hardly the end goal of hypertext.

The web was built through dialogue and communication between academia and industry. The W3C had its greatest success leading from behind, allowing academia and industry to innovate, but ensuring all the players were speaking the same language. In this

---

[9] Like this one.

we can find a model for going forward. By no means should the hypertext community become fixated on creating products for the public. But that's not to say we shouldn't be aware of who might be interested in our ideas, and how they might expect to use them.

We propose new area of hypertext research, in addition to the three already in existence. Alongside theoreticians, designers and authors [45], we suggest a new category of researcher, implementers, whose responsibility is to think about how to bring the next generation of hypertext to the masses. This isn't about building a marketable product, it's about creating an ecosystem.

Many of the classical hypertext systems, from NLS to Xanadu to Microcosm [46] were an attempt to cultivate an orderly garden of information. But at this point, the only way to cultivate such a garden would be to clear-cut the Information Jungle, which is probably as poor an idea as clear-cutting real jungle. All we can do is create pathways through the jungle, and hope that we'll build tools such that where we're going, we won't need roads.

References

1. Zemeckis, R.: Back to The Future Part II (1989)
2. Landow, G.P.: Hypertext 3.0: Critical Theory and New Media in an Era of Globalization, 3rd edn. John Hopkins University Press (2006)
3. Bush, V.: As We Think. The Atlantic 176(1), 101–108 (1945)
4. Buckland, M.K.: Emanuel Goldberg, Electronic Document Retrieval, And Vannevar Bush's Memex. Journal of the American Society for Information Science 43(4), 284–294 (1992)
5. van den Heuvel, C.: Building Society, Constructing Knowledge, Weaving the Web: Otlet s Visualizations of a Global Information Society and His Concept of a Universal Civilization. In: Rayward, W.B. (ed.) European Modernism and the Information Society. Informing the Present, Understanding the Past, pp. 127–154. Ashgate Publishing Ltd. (2008)
6. Goldberg, E.: Statistical Machine (1931)
7. Rayward, W.B.: Visions of Xanadu: Paul Otlet (1868-1944) and hypertext. Journal of the American Society for Information Science 45(4), 235–250 (1994)
8. Otlet, P.: Traité de documentation: le livre sur le livre, theéorie et pratique. Editiones edn. (1934)
9. Engelbart, D.C.: Augmenting Human Intellect: A Conceptual Framework-1962. Technical report, Stanford Research Institute (1962)
10. Nelson, T.H.: A File Structure for the Complex, the Changing and the Interderminite. In: Proceedings of the 1965 20th National Conference, pp. 84–100. ACM Press, New York (1965)
11. Carmody, S., Gross, W., Nelson, T.H., Rice, D., van Dam, A.: A Hypertext Editing System for the /360. Technical report, Brown University, Providence, Rhode Island (1969)
12. van Dam, A.: Hypertext '87 Keynote Address.
13. Markoff, J.: What the Dormouse Said: How the Sixties Counterculture Shaped the Personal Computer Industry. Penguin Books, New York (2006)
14. Nielsen, J.: Multimedia and Hypertext: The Internet and Beyond. Academic Press, Inc., Cambridge (1995)
15. Wolf, G.: The Curse of Xanadu. Wired, 1–27 (June 1995)
16. Nelson, T.H.: Literary Machines, 1st edn. Mindful Press, Sausalito (1990)
17. Atzenbeck, C.: Interview with George P. Landow. ACM SIGWEB Newsletter, 1–4 (March 2009)
18. Goble, C.A.: The return of the prodigal web. In: Proceedings of the 18th Conference on Hypertext and Hypermedia - HT 2007, p. 2. ACM Press, New York (2007)

19. Rettberg, J.W.: Feral Hypertext: When Hypertext Literature Escapes Control. In: Hunsinger, J., Klastrup, L., Allen, M. (eds.) International Handbook of Internet Research, pp. 477–492. Springer, Netherlands (2010)
20. Bardini, T.: Bootstrapping: Douglas Englebert, Coevolution, and the Origins of Personal Computing. Stanford University Press, Stanford (2000)
21. Smith, D.K., Alexander, R.C.: Fumbling the Future: How Xerox Invented, then Ignored, the First Personal Computer. iUniverse (1999)
22. Berners-Lee, T., Fischetti, M.: Weaving the Web: The Original Design and Ultimate Destiny of the World Wide Web by Its Inventor, 1st edn., Number 1999. HarperCollins, San Francisco (1999)
23. Hall, W.: The Ever Evolving Web: The Power of Networks. International Journal of Communication 5, 651–664 (2011)
24. Pitkow, J., Recker, M.: Results from the First World-Wide Web user survey. Computer Networks and ISDN Systems 27(2), 243–254 (1994)
25. Wolf, G.: The (Second Phase of the) Revolution Has Begun. Wired (1994)
26. Sink, E.: Memoirs From the Browser Wars (2003)
27. Raggett, D., Lam, J., Alexander, I.F., Kmiec, M.: A History of HTML. In: Raggett on HTML 4, 2nd edn. Addison-Wesley Professional (1997)
28. Severance, C.: JavaScript: Designing a Language in 10 Days. Computer 45(2), 7–8 (2012)
29. Lie, H.W., Bos, B.: The CSS saga. In: Cascading Style Sheets: Designing for the Web, 2nd edn. Addison-Wesley Professional (1999)
30. Hopmann, A.: The Story of XMLHTTP
31. Bosak, J.: The Birth of XML (2001)
32. Mozilla: Mozilla Firefox 1.0 Release Notes (2004)
33. Anthes, G.: HTML5 leads a web revolution. Communications of the ACM 55(7), 16 (2012)
34. WHATWG: Web Hypertext Application Technology Working Group Specifications (2012)
35. Mozilla: Mozilla Gains Global Support For a Firefox Mobile OS
36. Adams, J., Lowood, H., Bardini, T.: Englebert Oral History Series: Interview 1 (1986)
37. The Times of India: President launches low-cost Aakash-2 tablet (November 2012)
38. Palfrey, J., Gasser, U.: Born Digital: Understanding the First Generation of Digital Natives. Basic Books (2008)
39. Raskin, J.: The hype in hypertext. In: Proceeding of the ACM Conference on Hypertext - HYPERTEXT 1987, pp. 325–330. ACM Press, New York (1987)
40. Aarseth, E.J.: Cybertext: Perspectives on Ergodic Literature, vol. 8. John Hopkins University Press, Baltimore (1997)
41. Smits, D., De Bra, P.: GALE: a highly extensible adaptive hypermedia engine. In: Proceedings of the 22nd ACM Conference on Hypertext and Hypermedia - HT 2011, p. 63. ACM Press, New York (2011)
42. Li, G., Uren, V., Motta, E., Buckingham Shum, S., Domingue, J.: ClaiMaker: weaving a semantic web of research papers. In: Horrocks, I., Hendler, J. (eds.) ISWC 2002. LNCS, vol. 2342, pp. 436–441. Springer, Heidelberg (2002)
43. Simko, J., Tvarozek, M., Bielikova, M.: Little search game. In: Proceedings of the 22nd ACM Conference on Hypertext and Hypermedia - HT 2011, p. 57. ACM, New York (2011)
44. Brusilovsky, P., Kobsa, A., Vassileva, J.: Adaptive Hypertext and Hypermedia. Kluwer Academic Publishers (1998)
45. Nürnberg, P.J., Leggett, J.J., Wiil, U.K.: An agenda for open hypermedia research. In: Proceedings of the Ninth ACM Conference on Hypertext and Hypermedia: Links, Objects, Time and Space—Structure in Hypermedia Systems Links, Objects, Time and Space—Structure in Hypermedia Systems - HYPERTEXT 1998, pp. 198–206. ACM Press, New York (1998)
46. Fountain, A.M., Hall, W., Heath, I., Davis, H.C.: MICROCOSM: an open model for hypermedia with dynamic linking, pp. 298–311 (January 1992)

User-Mobile Phone Interactions:
A Postphenomenology Analysis

Bin Zhang[1] and Hua Dong[2,3]

[1] University of Chinese Academy of Sciences, No. 19 Yuquan Road,
Shijingshan District, Beijing 100049, China
[2] College of Design and Innovation, Tongji University, 1239 Siping Road,
Shanghai 200092, China
[3] School of Engineering and Design, Brunel University, Kingston Lane,
Uxbridge UB8 3PH, United Kingdom
{zhangbin108}@mails.gucas.ac.cn,
Hua.Dong@brunel.ac.uk

Abstract. User-artefact interactions, to a great extent, are defined by their relations. On the other hand, different relations emerge from different interactions. In order to get a better understanding of this phenomenon, we start and focus on the relation studies. Based on the four human-artefact relations in postphenomenology, a framework was developed. Through applying the framework to a case analysis, we describe the dynamic user-mobile interactions in the use process. This paper provides a new perspective of the interactions between the user and the product. Theoretically, the framework offers a comprehensive picture of user-product relations; practically, designers can be inspired to think about the different kinds of relations from the very beginning of their design process and design for specific relations.

Keywords: interactions, relations, postphenomenology, framework, Village Phone Programme.

1 Introduction

Mobile phones have become an important part of our daily life, and there are more than 5.6 billion people using them every day[1]. The use of mobile phones has changed people's behaviours and habits, and also changed the world.

Mobile phones, especially the smart phone, contain both hard-technologies (e.g. materials technology, processing technology, communication technology) and soft-technologies (software design, graphical design, user interface design). For the user, the mobile phone is not only a kind of man-made product in his/her hands, but also a platform or a machine, providing and producing various software and services with different functions; for the designer, to design a mobile phone is to design and provide an experience of how to interact with it, not only with the hardware, but also with the

---

[1] Source: http://www.gartner.com/it/page.jsp?id=1759714

A. Marcus (Ed.): DUXU/HCII 2013, Part I, LNCS 8012, pp. 171–180, 2013.
© Springer-Verlag Berlin Heidelberg 2013

software. This interaction can be regarded as a dialogue between a person and a product, service, or system [1]. The design of this interaction needs to focus on providing end users with a rich and satisfying mobile-communication experience [2].

Existing studies show that the user-mobile phone interactions research is mainly focussed on industrial design, product design, accessible possibilities [3], user experiences [4-5], and design innovation [6]. Those studies often reflect the designers' and innovators' standpoints; they are featured by empirical, experimental or problem-solving natures.

Postphenomenology studies start from a variety of use contexts where users' perceptions and experiences are mediated by artefacts, while artefacts acquire their meanings during the using process. Four basic models of user-artefact relations exit, i.e. embodiment relations, hermeneutic relations, alterity relations and background relations [7]. Each model can be regarded as a different interaction in a different use context. Based on the existing research, the authors have developed a framework (see Figure 1) to describe the four relations in the use process, and demonstrated how the user-artefact relations change from one kind of relation to another.

The case analysed in this paper, the Village Phone Programme (VPP), is about renting calling time of mobile phones in the rural areas of Bangladesh. This programme becomes well-known because of the tiny loans to poor rural women, funded by the Grameen Bank. One of the offshoots of the Grameen Bank, the Grameenphone, provides mobile phones for the buyers to rent the calling time. There are more than 100,000 people who buy the phones and then rent out the calling time to other people [8].

Through applying the framework to the analysis of the VPP, the authors reveal that different ways of using mobile phones for different purposes in specific use contexts lead to different kinds of user-mobile phone relations. Different relations are established through different user-mobile interactions, which can be understood as a multi-relational and dynamic use process. By following this process, designers can either re-design the existing relations, or create new ones.

The paper provides a new perspective of the interactions between the user and the product, and it will be divided into three parts: The first part, introducing the four basic relation models as a framework in postphenomenology; the second part, describing and analysing the Village Phone Programme (VPP) case through using the framework, to show the user-mobile phone interactions in the dynamic use process; the last part, discussing the findings and results of the user-mobile phone interactions in VPP, and providing suggestions.

1.1   The Framework of Four Basic User-Artefact Relations

The four basic relation models are developed by researchers in the fields of postphenomenology and Science Technology Studies (STS):

Embodiment Relations. The user can get different, mediated experiences from the world *through* the artefact [7,9] e.g., wearing the glasses;

Hermeneutic Relations. The user can get experiences and information *with* the artefact. For the user, it is about "reading a text from something" [7: pp 80-97; 9: pp11-13] e.g., reading the thermometer;

In *alterity relations*, users relate positively or presententially *to* the artefacts. In these relations, artefact becomes an 'other' or "quasi-other" as focal entities of the user's experience [7: P107], e.g., interacting with robots;

Background relations, artefacts in these relations "remain in the background or become a kind of near-technological environment itself" [7: P108]. It is a 'technosphere' or becomes technological cocoons surrounding the user [7: P14], e.g., clothes, electric systems.

The imitation of these four relation models is that they are static, stable, and ideal conditions. They are the ultimate goals of the development of technology which will lead to harmony between human-technology-world. However, in daily life, when thinking about the relations of user-artefact, it is always in a use context, which is dynamic, with different types of relations. Thus, in a specific use context, the types of relation between the user and artefact may not be one, but several.

Based on these four models of user-artefact relations, we develop a coordinate system as framework to show the user-artefact relations in a dynamic use context, see Figure 1. Point A as an example represents a condition. The four different models of user-artefact relation can be considered as the results of different types of interactions. Through different interactions, relations can be built and created.

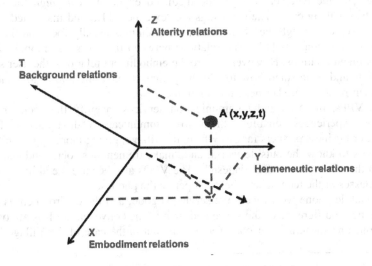

Fig. 1. A coordinate system of four relations

2   Case Analysis: The Village Phone Programme (VPP)

The case to be analysed is about renting the calling time in rural countries of Bangladesh, which is one of the poorest countries in the world. This programme becomes well-known because of the tiny loans to poor rural women, provided by the Grameen Bank[2]. In so doing, the founder of the bank Muhammad Yunus, won the 2006 Nobel peace prize.

The Grameenphone, an offshoot of Grameen Bank, provides mobile phones for the buyers to be rented the calling time, which are called the Village Phone Programme (VPP)[3]. There are more than 100,000 people who buy the phones and then rent out the time [8]. Most Village Phone participants are women living in remote areas[4].

For the Village Phones (VPs), there are two kinds of users: one is the phone's owners, who buy the phone form the Grameen Bank and sell the calling time. They are named as the Village Phone Operators (VPOs); the other is the local people, the users or potential users, who buy or will buy the service from the phone's owners [10]. The VPs also have three different conditions, which are making calls, incoming calls, and standby. The Bengalis people, the VPs, and the rural environment make the interactions between the different users and mobile phone more complex [11]. We shall apply our framework to anaylse the case, to describe the user-mobile relations, and to show the interactions during the use context.

2.1   Making Calls

The caller and the receiver will get the mediated experiences *through* the mobile phone, when making calls. Their hearings are 'extended' [12] and magnified to hear the other's voices through the phone, and their attentions usually focus on the voice and conversation contents [13]. The relations between the users and mobile phones are embodiment relations. However, before the embodiment relations, the user should firstly know and understand how to use the phone, to have the ability to 'read' the phone. Their relations are hermeneutic relations.

In the VPPs, the VPs and communication services magnify the users' bodily-perceptual experiences, enabling them to communicate with relatives, family members, or business partners far away from the village, giving more opportunities to the villagers to know the outside world, and "make tremendous social and economic impact in the rural areas of Bangladesh"[5]. The VPOs also acquire the ability through training classes or the technicians' help to operate the phones.

If the mobile phone works well, the service is good, and the environment is quiet, there will be no difference of the space and time to the conversation. It is almost like to hear someone speaking near one of your ears, but in the case of the Village Phone

---

[2] Source: http://www.economist.com/node/21543547
[3] Source: http://www.grameenphone.com/business/packages-information/gpvp
[4] Source: http://en.wikipedia.org/wiki/GrameenPhone#cite_note-23
[5] Source: http://www.grameenphone.com/business/packages-information/gpvp

Programme (VPP), the village phones (VPs) are used in a specific environment and used by different users (i.e. the VPOs and the buyers). Thus, there are two kinds of users in two different scenarios, one is for the VPOs, using the VPs themselves in their shops or homes, which is the same as the normal use of mobile phones as private products only for the owners; the other is for the buyers, other villagers paying money for the use of VPs, when the VPs are regarded as open resources and the shops as public areas.

The Calling/Using of VPOs. In the rural areas of Bangladesh, VPs are usually installed in the owners' small shops, nearby some small local markets. For the VPOs, when using the mobile phones by themselves, they can often find quiet places to get a better communication quality. The mobile phones become the means of communication, and are (semi-)transparent and withdraw into background during the calling [7:P24] [13]. The VPs extend the VPOs' experiences, while they also 'reduce' the users to voices, not the 'flesh' speakers with the absence of phone user's "multiple sensory dimensions of a face to face situation" [9:pp24-25].

Meanwhile, unlike the normal use of mobile phones, the VPOs have to make a short and quick call if they really need it, and then keep the VPs standby for renting or any incoming calls. Because the VPs in their hands are a mean of making money; they need to rent the calling time to customers, not only using by themselves. In this condition, for VPOs, the VPs become 'others' who can make money for them. The reduction and this alterity relation can change the VPOs' behaviours of using mobile phones, which are different from the face-to-face talking, e.g., it lets the VPOs speak fast to save time; worrying about the money let them become impatient with the people and conversations on the phone.

So the interactions between the owner and mobile phones lead to three kinds of relations: the embodiment relations, hermeneutic relations, and alterity relations, see the Figure 2. C1 in the figure represents Condition 1. Its coordinate is (x, y, z, 0), which means in this condition, the user and mobile phone has three kinds of relations.

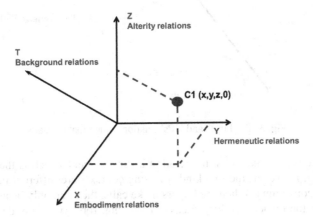

Fig. 2. The owner and VPs' relations when making calls

However, the two relations conflict each other: in embodiment relations, the VPs become the means of communication, and try to be (semi-)transparent and withdraw into background during the calling, while in alterity relations, the VPs turn to be focal entities of the VPOs' experience. For VPOs, this kind of contradiction happens in the whole using process.

The Call by the Buyers. For the buyers, because of the needs, they are willing to go to the shop where the VPs are located, and pay the calling time to make calls. The buyers' intentions lead to the interactions between the buyers and the VPs. In so doing, the VPs are experienced from absence to presence of the buyers' perceptions, from the background to the focal entities. The buyers' attentions will change from the mobile phones' appearance, shape to its performance and operation. At the beginning of the interaction, the VPs are 'others' for the buyers before being used. They are alterity relations.

However, the buyers' purposes are not to play with the VPs, but to communicate with other people far away from them. So the VPs quickly change their roles from 'others' to 'tools' and the relations are changed from alterity to embodiment. Besides, the buyers do not need to learn and know how to use the VPs. So in this condition, there are three kinds of relations between the buyer and mobile phone, see Figure 3.

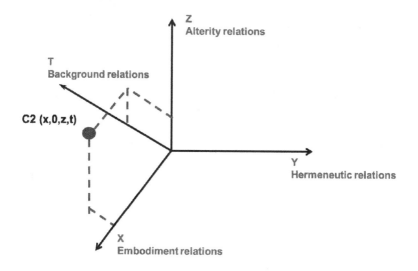

Fig. 3. The buyer and VPs' relations when making calls

When the buyers make calls, the relation is embodiment which is the same as the VPOs' calling. However, the two kinds of using contexts are different because of the different use constraints. When the buyers make calls, they can only be allowed to use the phones in the owners' sights, in case of stealing, robbery or any damages of the phone. If the buyers do not want anybody else to hear the conversation, the VOPs will offer the privacy through taking some measures to keep the VPs safe, e.g. using a hanging wire.

If the environments of the shop or rural markets are so noisy when making calls, it is difficult for the buyers to get a good communication through the mobile phones. They cannot hear each other clearly. It becomes a bad and ineffective interaction, not only with the people who they are talking with on the phone, but also with the VPs in their hands. The buyers will stop calling and the interaction will stop. The embodiment relations, which the buyers and VPs once build, disappear and the VPs thus become 'others' or "quasi-others" as focal entities. It turns out to be the alterity relations. This interruption for the buyers is a bad use experience, and cause a negative impact on the next time buying.

For the VPOs, the VPs in the buyers hands are 'others' for the VPOs, and they get the alterity relations. When the buyers make calls, the VPs cause them to concern the VPs and it changes their perceptions and behaviours. The VPOs have to pay more attentions to the VPs during the calling, making sure that the phones work well, the telecom's services are good, and the buyers are just the buyers, not thieve or robbers. They also have to change the behaviours to follow social etiquettes. When the buyers make calls, the VPOs should try to keep the environment quiet and make them unobtrusive in order not to interrupt or intervene in the buyers' affairs [11].

2.2   Incoming Calls

The mobile phone is also a receiver to get incoming calls and messages. In this case, there are two different kinds of the incoming calls: one is for the VPOs, and the other is for the villagers. For the VPOs, it is a same procedure as the calls they make (see Figure 2). The phone's owner will make short and quick answers if necessary and keep the VPs ready for renting or for villagers' incoming calls.

For the villagers' incoming calls, the VPOs will answer the phone and then have two options: One is to remember the important information of the calls, e.g., the callers' names, calling time, contents, and then tell the villagers or tell them to call back; the other option is to stay on the line, and send someone, e.g., family members or other nearby villagers, to inform the villagers to answer the phone immediately. These two kinds of situations also depend on the contents of the incoming calls, whether they are emergent, private, important or not.

These two options lead to different relations between the owner and the mobile phone. The first is embodiment relations, and it is the same as they have the incoming calls. When the calls are finished, the VPs begin to standby and go to backgrounds; The second option leads to the alterity relations. The VPOs have to keep the call online, and wait for the villagers to answer the phone. They will care about the calling times, worry about the batteries and the services' conditions. The VPs and services get the VPOs' intentions and attentions, and become 'others' and focal entities.

2.3   Standby

When mobile phones standby, the interactions between users and mobile phones seem to disappear, but it is a new form of interactions and relations. With the VPs, the small shops and the whole villages are changed from the rural areas to modern technical environments. The standby VPs, the services, and the communication systems are background relations to the VPOs and other local people.

For the VPOs, when there are no calls, the VPs are working in the background and become transparent for them. These background relations are non-continuous and can be easily changed to other relations, because the VPOs care about the renting times and how to make more money. They will check the VPs many times in a day, to make sure that the VPs are still working well, the services are good, and they did not miss any incoming calls. The VPOs usually hope that this 'silence' and the background relations can be broken and changed, either through the buyers or the incoming calls. The VPOs and VPs maintain a multi-stable relation during this process.

For other people in the village, including the buyers and the potential buyers, the standby VPs, the services, and the communication systems are not only a new way of communicating with other people outside the countries, but also a 'technosphere' surrounding them. They are add-ons and become part of their living environment whether they can perceive it or not. The VPs, services, and the system will keep absence, silence and transparency as backgrounds, before the villagers begin to think about them, talk about them, and use them. Thus, they emerge, appear and turn to focal entities, entering into the villagers' daily life as ideas to be thought about, topics to be discussed, and novel objects to be handled and used. The results of the interactions between the villagers and VPs are not only technical, but also entertaining and secular.

3   Discussions

The purpose of the VPP is on one hand to provide self-employment opportunity for the people in the rural areas of Bangladesh, on the other hand to let the villagers make calls easily and conveniently. Through using the framework, we analysed the relations between two kinds of users and village phones, and illustrated the dynamic interactions and multi-stable relations in the Village Phone Programme. It is clear that different use conditions have different interactions and relations which lead to users' and other stakeholders' different perceptions and behaviours. The users' experiences are mediated, while the VPs acquire the meanings during the using process, through the interaction with them.

According to our analysis, there are some problems in the Village Phone Programme which need to be improved:

This programme is not able to give more opportunities for the VPOs to 'read' the village phones. It is important for users to read various texts on the mobile phone, not only the short messages (SMS), but also the software applications. This kind of interactions will lead to hermeneutic relations between the user and the artefact.

In the VPP case, when there are no buyers at that time, there are many opportunities for the VPOs to use the VPs to send SMS to other mobile phone users or other VPOs. This information exchanges and social chats can give the VPOs more access to find new friends in a simple and easy way, and extend their social networks, or even build small communities.

There are two reasons for this problem: one is that the VPs' provider, the Grameenphone Company, merely provides one type of service and one single function of the phone; the other is the VPOs' lack of education and skills.

There are two potential solutions: for the provider, it can provide several VP models with different functions for the VPOs to choose. They can also improve the quality of the call, letting the VPs 'transparent and withdraw into background' through increasing the maximum of the handsets' volumes because of the noisy environment, adding the beep tone every minute when making calls to remind the user, finding ways to balance the buyers' privacy and VPs' safety, designing the VPs so that they are easy to use and maintain. They can also consult and invite the VPOs, the villagers to discuss and participate in the design process.

For the VPOs, building the hermeneutic relations requires basic knowledge of how to operate the system, type the words and send them to someone. In rural areas, there are many illiterates. This lack of knowledge and education lets the VPs rely heavily on technical professionals (most of them are male), "who are charged with keeping the phone systems operative and fixing malfunctioning equipment" [11].

Studies show that users, who have a long history with the mobile phone, or those who use mobile phones very often, can acquire strong habits. These habits develop users' new behaviours when using the mobile phones [13]. In this case, the VPOs behaviours are influenced and new social manners will be built through the calls not only by them, but also the buyers. For the governments or the communities, it is also a good chance and a new way to teach the VPOs and improve their education and technical skills through the use of mobile phones.

Building better relations and interactions can not only provide the poor people in rural areas the self-employment opportunity to earn money, but also give a chance for them to communicate with the outside world, to be educated and to acquire new skills.

Our framework proves useful in analyzing the complicated relations in the VPP case, and it has provided a new perspective of user-artefact relations, which we hope will inspire designers and innovators to better understand the user-product interactions and design according to different relations.

Acknowledgments. We thank the China Scholarship Council (CSC) for sponsoring the study.

References

1. Kolko, J.: Thoughts on Interaction Design. Brown Bear LLC, Buena Park (2007)
2. Subramanya, S.R., Yi, B.K.: Enhancing the User Experience in Mobile Phones. Computer 40, 114–117 (2007)
3. Lee, Y.S., Jhangiani, I., Smith-Jackson, T., Nussbaum, M., Tomioka, K.: Design Considerations for Accessible Mobile Phones. In: Proceedings of the Human Factors and Ergonomics Society 50th Annual Meeting, pp. 2178–2182. SAGE Publications Ltd., London (2006)

4. Taylor, A., Harper, R.: Age-old practices in the 'new world': A study of gift-giving between teenage mobile phone users. In: Proceedings of the SIGCHI Conference on Human Factors in Computing Systems, pp. 439–446. ACM, Minneapolis (2002)
5. Goodman, J., Brewster, S., Gray, P.: Older people, mobile devices and navigation. In: Goodman, J., Brewster, S. (eds.) HCI and the Older Population, HCI 2004, Leeds, pp. 13–14 (2004)
6. Steinbock, D.: Design and Mobile Innovation. Design Management Review 16, 55–87 (2005)
7. Ihde, D.: Technology and the Lifeworld: From Garden to Earth. Indiana University Press, Bloomington (1990)
8. Madeley, J.: Mobile phones - a way out of poverty? Appropriate Technology 34, 9 (2007)
9. Ihde, D.: Technics and Praxis. Reidel Publishing Company, Dordrecht (1979)
10. Bayes, A.: Infrastructure and rural development: insights from a Grameen Bank village phone initiative in Bangladesh. Agricultural Economics 25, 261–272 (2001)
11. Selinger, E.: Does Microcredit "Empower"? Reflections on the Grameen Bank Debate. Human Studies 31, 27–41 (2008)
12. Ihde, D.: Stretching the In-between: Embodiment and Beyond. Foundations of Science 16, 109–118 (2011)
13. Rosenberger, R.: Embodied Technology and the Dangers of Using the Phone while Driving. Phenomenology and the Cognitive Sciences 11, 79–94 (2012)

Part II
Usability Methods and Tools

Assessing Designs of Interactive Voice Response Systems for Better Usability

Siddhartha Asthana, Pushpendra Singh, and Amarjeet Singh

Indraprastha Institute of Information Technology
{siddharthaa,psingh,amarjeet}@iiitd.ac.in

Abstract. Interactive Voice Response Systems (IVR) have emerged as a popular medium to access information over phones. Despite the low usability of IVR systems, they are widely used by commercial organizations due to high reach of phones. Several studies have focused on improving the usability and design of IVR systems. An IVR can be designed in several ways which can have one or more features like touch-tone, speech recognition, content searching etc. However, selecting an appropriate design requires comparison of different designs. In this paper, we propose an information space with three dimensions to study the usability of IVR design as an Information System. We study two different IVR designs - real world deployment and controlled experiment. We further compare these with the traditional IVR design over the proposed dimensions of Information space.

Keywords: IVR, Information space, usability.

1 Introduction

Interactive Voice Response (IVR) technology is used for accessing information via phones. IVR systems automate the call handling and are used in customer care, call routing etc. and also as a medium for information dissemination [10]. High reach of telecommunication services and the need to automate information exchange and communication has made it imperative for the commercial organizations to use IVR systems.

Although IVR systems have been in use for some time, they are often considered as frustrating and time consuming [1]. The usability issues in IVR have drawn attention of the research community. Various improvements in design have been proposed. In particular, interface design, especially navigation [7,4], has received a lot of attention from the research community. Several system designs have been proposed which are specific either to an ethnic groups like illiterate [13], rural [9] etc. or to an application scenario like browsing web pages on voice interface, accessing health information on phones [14], etc.

A design which is focused on improving one aspect of usability may adversely affect the other. Prior studies suggest that an appropriate system design is highly contextual which involves knowledge of target user base and application scenario.

A. Marcus (Ed.): DUXU/HCII 2013, Part I, LNCS 8012, pp. 183–192, 2013.

Thus, for a known scenario and a user base, selecting an appropriate design requires comparing several designs on different usability aspects and understanding trade-offs among the usability aspects of each design. Though now automated tools [6] exist that allow testing of an IVR system before actual deployment, it is important to have design parameters which help in analyzing the usability of IVR systems as Information Systems.

To define design parameters that measure usability of an information system requires focus on information delivery mechanisms. The information delivery mechanism has access to a repository with information content that the system is expected to deliver. This amount of information in the repository can be termed as the information delivery capacity of the system. The next step requires gathering information need of the user which may be either selecting appropriate menu and sub-menu options or query formulation through speech utterances. After gathering the requirement of users information needs, the system must respond to the user with appropriate information content from the repository. Hence, the usability of information system depends upon the three factors:

- Information capacity of the system
- Time taken in expressing the information need of the user to the system
- The quality of information delivered to the user

Based on this, we propose an information space to measure the usability of an IVR system as an information system. The next section describes the information space in detail and explores the existing literature across the three dimensions of it.

2   Information Space

Perugini et al. [11] have studied different aspects (e.g. Interaction style, input modality) of IVR system's design through a 3-Dimensional conceptual design space. The dimensions of the design space in their work is focused on exploring the alternatives for different design aspects of IVR rather than analyzing its usability. In our work, we propose the concept of an information space to study usability aspects of different IVR designs. Information space is a 3-Dimensional space with each dimension measuring usability aspect of an information system as shown in Figure 1. The three dimensions of information space are as follows:

- **Information navigation time:** It refers to time spent on navigation to access information in IVR systems. Lesser the navigation time the quicker a user can access information.
- **Information relevance:** It refers to the relevance of information provided by the system as measured through standard metrics like precision and recall. Traditional IVR systems, provide relevant information as information content is prepared manually. However, automated technique as practiced by the upcoming system may result in providing irrelevant information.

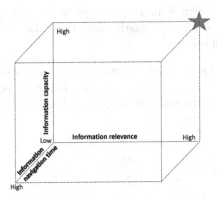

Fig. 1. Information space to measure the usability of information dissemination system

- **Information capacity:** It refers to the breadth of information content provided by the system for a variety of user queries. Traditional IVR systems provide limited information as browsing and navigating through large content is difficult on audio interfaces.

Ideally, a usable system should provide relevant information from large content and should have low navigation-time as shown by "⋆" in Figure 1. Prior work has shown to improve the usability of IVR in one or more dimensions of information space. Skip and Scan [12], ZAP and ZOOM [8] have tried to improve on navigation time. These techniques allow caller easily navigate back and forth through menus or jump directly to another location using shortcuts without first listening to all of the prompts for a particular menu. IVR systems with dynamic rearrangement of menu and use of information retrieval (IR) technique have been proposed to reduce navigation time and to increase the information capacity in voice based system [15,2,4,3]. In the next section we will study two system designs for IVR system that are based on dynamic rearrangement and automatic IR technique in detail through real world deployment and control experiment. Further, we will compare the system usage of IVR based on dynamic rearrangement and automatic IR technique with a traditional IVR system.

3 Experiment Design

We did our experiment in two phases. In the first phase we deployed two IVR systems in the real world and in a second phase, we conducted a controlled experiment.

IVR systems in the first phase were designed, developed and deployed to serve information to the applicants for admission in undergraduate and post-graduate courses at IIIT-Delhi (a state university in India). This deployment helped us to create real world usage of our system [4]. We designed a traditional static IVR system with static menu options. With the intent to reduce navigation time in the

IVR system, we also designed an adaptive system that dynamically rearranges
the menu options based on their relative popularity. Details of Traditional and
Dynamic IVR is given below:

- Traditional IVR: An IVR system with a static menu deployed in practice to
  provide information to applicants for admission to undergraduate and post-
  graduate courses in the institute. Figure 2 shows the various menu options
  available in IVR system.

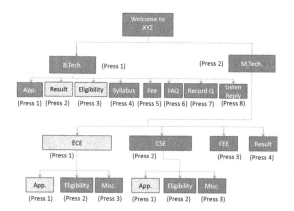

Fig. 2. Menu options in Traditional and Dynamic Rearrangement IVR

- Dynamic IVR: An IVR system deployed in parallel with traditional IVR
  but the menu sequence gets rearranged based on the relative popularity of
  menu options among the callers. The goal of this system design is to reduce
  the navigation time by decreasing the waiting time for the desired option to
  appear in menu sequence. In this IVR, nodes (menu options) at the same
  level are rearranged in descending order of the number of times a node
  has been accessed in the past by the users. The menu items placed at the
  same level were rearranged automatically without any manual intervention.
  Hierarchical scheme decides the new order of options based on the historical
  data of calls made to system.

In the second phase, we deployed an IVR (named IR-IVR) which was aimed
to address the inability of IVR system to serve large information content. The
menu structure of IVR grows with the increase in information content. Thus,
accessing information through a huge number of options in IVR becomes difficult. This is the primary reason for IVR being kept for delivering small amount
of information. Thus, to support information access in IVR from a bigger set
of information is a challenging task. To overcome this challenge we have used
Information retrieval (IR) techniques.

We built an information corpus from the text sources which were used in
audio recording of conventional IVR system. Results retrieved by IR component

of IR-IVR was compared against the text played in human recorded voice by the traditional IVR system. To assess the usability of the IR-IVR system, we conducted a controlled user experiment with 16 participants. The information corpus was the official website of IIIT-Delhi.

- IR-IVR: An IVR system using IR technique to automatically generate responses to the user query. The system was designed to achieve high information capacity in IVR system. This IVR was tested under controlled experiment as impact of using IR technique on information relevance was not known and inaccurate or irrelevant information may have had adverse effects in real world deployments. IR-IVR takes the speech input as user query and process this voice data to satisfy the information need of the caller. This allows user to make a free form query. It helped us to do away with menu-based navigation of traditional IVR system.

4   System Usage

Traditional and Dynamic IVR were up from 28th May to 7th July, 2012. In this duration we received 188 calls on both the systems. Calls were audio recorded and users were informed about this at the beginning of each call. We also logged the phone number, received as caller-ID information, with each call. Users of the system accessed various content on the IVR. Number of applicants for undergraduate course were higher than the number of applicants for postgraduate course and it was clearly reflected in system usage as well. Contents of B.Tech (Undergraduate equivalent to BS program) were accessed far more than the M.tech (Postgraduate equivalent to MS program). Among the B.Tech submenu as shown in Figure 2 Application process was all time favorite among the callers. B.Tech result saw a steep rise in number of times it is accessed after the announcement for the results of selected candidate as was expected. It is this dynamic nature of menu sequence that we wanted to capture through our menu rearrangement [4].

In the second phase, we conducted a controlled study in which participants engaged in an informational search task. We had 16 participants in our study. Twelve out of 16 participants were from IIIT-Delhi. These 12 participants had good information about the IIIT-Delhi. The rest 4 participant were from outside the institute and had no or little knowledge about the IIIT-Delhi. All the 16 participants were told to ask 4 queries on IR-IVR about IIIT-Delhi.Accuracy of speech recognizer used in IR-IVR in terms of Word-Error-Rate (WER) came out to be 0.267.We also found that WebScore of our system came out to be 59.8%. WebScore measures semantic quality of the recognizer. A higher value indicates better performance. It is calculated by measuring the number of times the search result as queried by the recognition hypothesis varies from the search result as queried by a human transcription. The average response time of IR-IVR for the queries came out to be 1.257 seconds. We measure the response time of IR-IVR as the time taken by it in fetching the results from information corpus. We also found that the average response length for words in the query response.

The average response length for our experiment came out to be 98.46 words. IR-IVR allowed user to make free form of query e.g. "What is the last date of application form submission". The query length is the length of query text in words. The average query length for our experiment came out to be 7.96 words. The longest query had 13 words in it. Higher values of query length shows the system was able to handle complex queries both in terms of recognition and retrieval. Table 1 represents system usage of each IVR system. We define user query as a expression of information need by the user response to which system gives specific information related to IIIT-Delhi admission. In menu based IVR (i.e. Traditional and dynamic) selection of menu and sub-menu options for which IVR system gives a piece of information is treated as 1 user query. On the other hand, in IR-IVR a user input given by speaking into the system is treated as 1 user query. Further, number of unique callers for menu based IVR is assessed based on number of unique caller-ID (i.e. received as phone number) received by us. In the case of IR-IVR, 16 participants are treated as 16 different caller to the system.

Table 1. Data collection of each IVR system

	Traditional	Dynamic	IR-IVR
User Queries	174	202	64
Unique callers	127	132	16
User type	All age group, across the India	All age group, across the India	Students in age group of 18-24 with different background
Remarks	1 month deployment for admission process	1 month deployment for admission process	Conducted a control experiment with 16 users

5   Results and Analysis

In this section, we will show that how different designs have performed on each dimension of information space. We will compare each system usability and will try to place them at correct position in information space.

5.1   Navigation

As defined earlier navigation time is the time spent on navigation to access information in IVR systems. In the menu based IVR, it is the time spent on the announcement and selection of menu and submenu options whereas in IR-IVR, it is the time taken by user to speak into the system followed by the time taken by system to recognize this speech. Based on this we calculated the average navigation time of each system as shown in Table 2.

Table 2. Average Navigation time (in seconds) of each system

System	Navigation Time
Traditional	51.59
Dynamic	44.41
IR	5.2

5.2 Relevance

Relevance of information delivered to the user is a subjective decision and requires human intelligence to assess it correctly. Traditional IVR and its contents were prepared manually. Hence they are assumed to be highly relevant. We are giving traditional IVR a normalized score of 1 (or 100% relevant information) and other system will be evaluated in comparison to this score for calculating their information relevance.

Similarly the content of Dynamically rearranging IVR was also prepared manually but they try to assess the information need of the user based on past system usage. This creates a chance for system to make error with some caller. We have found that repeated caller (i.e., the callers who had called to the system before) has tendency to select menu options based on their past interaction with the system. They often select a menu option before it is announced by IVR. But because menu changed from their last interaction to current interaction they end up in selecting wrong menu options. This effects the information relevance as the information needed by user is different from information delivered to the user. Hence a repeated user who has tendency to select menu ahead of its announcement is likely to get wrong information in dynamically rearranging IVR. In our experiment, Dynamic rearrangement IVR received 70 repeated calls. However, some of the repeated user who behaved like first time caller did not faced the problem of selecting wrong menu options but as soon as they get acquainted with the system they are likely to be more prone to such error. Hence, assuming that system will only provide relevant information to new callers. We evaluate information relevance by evaluating the following expression:

$$NewCaller/TotalCall = 132/202 = 0.65 \qquad (1)$$

This expression will tend to normalized score of 1 which shows dynamically rear-ranging IVR will perfect in the situation where system does not have any repeated caller.

In IR-IVR system we asked user to rate the retrieved response from IR-IVR on a of scale of 1 to 5. A score of 1 signifies the response were extremely poor and has no relevance to the query where as a score of 5 signifies the response generated by IR-IVR were extremely good and relevant to the user query. Here user were told to rate the responses they listen on Mega-IVR for its relevance to the query asked. We then computed the accuracy of information retrieval based on user relevance feedback as average score given by user. In our experiment we found that, the value for information retrieval accuracy as assessed by users came out to be 3.46 (out of 5) and a normalized score of 0.69.

5.3   Capacity

Increasing content on menu based IVR increases its menu size. As menu can not grow infinite so it imposes an upper limit on the size content of menu. In our experiment, Traditional IVR and Dynamic rearrangement IVR had 16 different information content out of which 12 are general content and other 4 were specific to the caller. The option specific to the callers are the option provided by system where human intervention is needed to answer the query e.g. user can record their voice message for admission authorities at IIIT-Delhi. Thus our menu based IVR is capable of answering 10 different queries Information content of IR-IVR system were prepared from FAQ available on IIIT-Delhi website. Information corpus had answers of 70 FAQ available on website. Similar to menu based IVR, IR-IVR can not have infinite information content in it. On increasing the information content on IR-IVR may result in low relevance of information as it increase the chance of error. On increasing the size of content a system need to increase the size of vocabulary used for speech recognition. Bigger the vocabulary larger are the chance of error in speech recognition. Similarly IR component of such system is also affected because increasing the size of information corpus increase the chance of selecting irrelevant content for a given user query. Thus for comparing IR-IVR with other systems for information capacity we gave it a normalized score of 1. Based on this relative capacity of menu based IVR which had capacity to answer 12 different user query in comparison to IR-IVR which can answer 70 different query had a information capacity score of

$$Query\ (Traditional\ or\ Dynamic)/Query\ (IR-IVR) = 12/70 = 0.171 \quad (2)$$

5.4   Analysis

Earlier, we have computed the values of each IVR design on different dimensions of Information space. We have measured navigation time in seconds. Information relevance is assumed to be highest when prepared information content is manually prepared. We gave the Traditional IVR maximum score on a scale of 0 to 1 as its content were manually prepared and placed in the IVR. We calculated information relevance of dynamic rearrangement IVR based on the number of time it is expected to deliver relevant information. We found that the dynamic rearrangement IVR may give wrong or irrelevant information to repeated callers. Hence relevant information is guaranteed only for new callers. Based on this we calculate the information relevance of dynamic rearrangement IVR. Information relevance of IR-IVR is directly assessed by the participants. The third dimension of Information space i.e. information capacity is measured in terms of ability to handle different user queries. A menu based IVR which gave different information about the admission process is assume to answer exactly one user query for each information. Similarly, IR-IVR was prepared from 70 FAQ so it is assumed to answer 70 different user queries. In Table 3 we show the score of each IVR system on different dimensions of information space. Improving a usability aspects affects other usability aspects. Figure 3 shows three system in Information

Table 3. Usability score of IVR system on each dimension

	Traditional	Dynamic	IR
Navigation	51.59	44.41	5.2
Relevance	1	0.65	0.69
Capacity	0.17	0.17	1

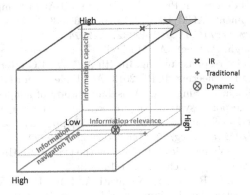

Fig. 3. Comparison of IVR design in Information Space

Space. This suggests that the techniques used for reducing navigation time or increasing the information capacity may result in low information relevance.

6 Conclusions

In this work, we have extended our initial work [5] and proposed and studied information space for identifying the usability of IVR systems. We also evaluated three system designs through real world experiment and controlled lab studies. The system designs were analyzed on different dimension of information space. We showed that improving a design for one usability aspect may affect other usability aspects of information system.

Our proposed information space may help in designing an IVR system based on desired usability on different dimensions.

Acknowledgment. We would like to thank Tata Consultancy Services for supporting this research.

References

1. Consumer Study Finds Overwhelming Dissatisfaction with IVR (June 2011), http://ibm-news.tmcnet.com/news/2011/06/23/5593905.htm
2. Asthana, S., Singh, P., Kumaraguru, P., Singh, A., Vinayak, N.: Tring! tring! - an exploration and analysis of interactive voice response systems. In: 4th International Conference on Human Computer Interaction, IndiaHCI 2012 (2012)

3. Asthana, S., Singh, P., Singh, A.: Design and evaluation of adaptive interfaces for ivr systems. In: CHI 2013 Extended Abstracts on Human Factors in Computing Systems, CHI EA 2013. ACM, New York (2013)

4. Asthana, S., Singh, P., Singh, A.: Exploring adverse effects of adaptive voice menu. In: CHI 2013 Extended Abstracts on Human Factors in Computing Systems, CHI EA 2013. ACM, New York (2013)

5. Asthana, S., Singh, P., Singh, A.: Exploring the usability of interactive voice response system's design. In: Proceedings of the 3rd ACM Symposium on Computing for Development, ACM DEV 2013, pp. 36:1–36:2. ACM, New York (2013), http://doi.acm.org/10.1145/2442882.2442924

6. Asthana, S., Singh, P., Singh, A.: Mocktell: Exploring challenges of user emulation in interactive voice response testing. In: 4th ACM/SPEC International Conference on Performance Engineering, ICPE 2013. ACM, New York (2013)

7. Asthana, S., Singh, P., Singh, A.: A usability study of adaptive interfaces for interactive voice response system. In: Proceedings of the 3rd ACM Symposium on Computing for Development, ACM DEV 2013, pp. 34:1–34:2. ACM, New York (2013), http://doi.acm.org/10.1145/2442882.2442922

8. Hornstein, T.: Telephone Voice Interfaces on the Cheap. In: Union Bank of Switzerland, UVK Informatik, Zurich, pp. 134–146 (1994)

9. Patel, N., Agarwal, S., Rajput, N., Nanavati, A., Dave, P., Parikh, T.S.: A comparative study of speech and dialed input voice interfaces in rural India. In: Proceedings of the 27th International Conference on Human Factors in Computing Systems, CHI 2009, pp. 51–54. ACM (2009)

10. Patel, N., Chittamuru, D., Jain, A., Dave, P., Parikh, T.S.: Avaaj otalo: A field study of an interactive voice forum for small farmers in rural india. In: Proceedings of the 28th International Conference on Human Factors in Computing Systems, CHI 2010, pp. 733–742. ACM, New York (2010)

11. Perugini, S., Anderson, T.J., Moroney, W.F.: A study of out-of-turn interaction in menu-based, IVR, voicemail systems. In: Proceedings of the SIGCHI Conference on Human Factors in Computing Systems, CHI 2007, pp. 961–970. ACM, New York (2007)

12. Resnick, P., Virzi, R.A.: Skip and scan: Cleaning up telephone interface. In: Proceedings of the SIGCHI Conference on Human Factors in Computing Systems, CHI 1992, pp. 419–426. ACM, New York (1992)

13. Sharma Grover, A., Stewart, O., Lubensky, D.: Designing interactive voice response (IVR) interfaces: localisation for low literacy users. In: Proceedings of Computers and Advanced Technology in Education, CATE 2009, St Thomas, US Virgin Islands (2009)

14. Sherwani, J., Ali, N., Mirza, S., Fatma, A., Memon, Y., Karim, M., Tongia, R., Rosenfeld, R.: Healthline: Speech-based access to health information by low-literate users. In: International Conference on Information and Communication Technologies and Development, ICTD 2007., pp. 1–9. IEEE (December 2007)

15. Sherwani, J., Yu, D., Paek, T., Czerwinski, M., Ju, Y.C., Acero, A.: Voicepedia: Towards speech-based access to unstructured information. In: INTERSPEECH 2007, pp. 146–149 (2007)

User Interaction Forensics

Detecting and Interpreting the User's Footprints during Touch Interaction

Kai Breiner

Fraunhofer Institute for Experimental Software Engineering IESE,
Fraunhofer-Platz 1, 67663 Kaiserslautern, Germany
Kai.Breiner@iese.fraunhofer.de

Abstract. The foundation of self-adaptive systems is sound elicitation of the input for the adaptation algorithm. If the input of the adaptation is not reliable, the resulting adaptation will not be reliable either. Especially if the aim is to adapt to the user, the information probably stems from unobtrusive measures but still needs to be reliable. Thus, this paper describes a controlled experiment conducted to investigate in four hypotheses how to make miscellaneous interaction information (which is available anyway) interpretable. These four hypotheses concern three aspects: precision of the interaction step, bias according to right-/left-handedness, and bias of the interaction element. A total of 33 participants were involved. All four hypotheses could be strengthened at a high level of significance.

1 Introduction

Traditionally, the interaction loop that describes human-computer interaction consists of a human action and the functional reaction of an information system. Approaches for self-adaptive systems (SAS, see Fig. 1) extend this model by adding the user's performance with which the particular action is performed and describe the behavior of the SAS as a non-functional reaction of the information system in order to adapt itself [1,10]. The trigger of the interaction is the user who has a specific intention. To implement this intention, the user possesses specific skills that are used as well as abilities that influence the quality of the execution. In combination, these result in a certain performance with which the action is then executed. Vice versa, by interpreting the performance, the idea is to draw conclusions about the user's skills and abilities.

SAS that adapt to the user already do exist, but they demand explicit information before they can perform the adaptation. Basically, there are two ways of how this can be done: (1) performing user tests and (2) using additional (obtrusive) sensors. A representative for the first case is SUPPLE++. Prior to the interaction, the user has to perform ability tests (e.g., concerning precision and performance), after which the user interface will be adapted accordingly [4,5,6,7]. A representative for the latter case is MyUI, where (in addition to user tests) additional sensors are used to

A. Marcus (Ed.): DUXU/HCII 2013, Part I, LNCS 8012, pp. 193–202, 2013.
© Springer-Verlag Berlin Heidelberg 2013

determine the user's characteristic [11]. The advantage is that sensors providing a high level of detail can be used. The disadvantage of both approaches is their obtrusiveness, since either users are directly exposed to their abilities, or they are aware of that there is surveillance and therefore act differently (i.e., the Hawthorne effect).

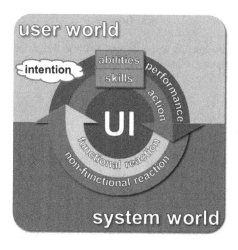

Fig. 1. Interaction loop distinguishing between functional action and non-functional action [1]

As motivated above, it is also possible to evaluate the data that can be observed during the interaction itself. To gain a better understanding, several models characterizing the performance of the user interaction need to be discussed. The available models can be described in three categories:

- **Conceptual models:** These models are used to describe and understand the human interaction itself (e.g., Model Human Processor [2]).
- **Constructive models:** The content of constructive models is the predicted or calculated behavior of the users. These models are used to simulate usage (e.g., based on keystrokes [3]).
- **Analytical models:** During runtime, these models are filled with data in order to analyze the interaction (e.g., MyUI [11], or skill models [8, 9]).

For our controlled experiment, analytical models are of interest. In current models, predefined information is collected. In the case of the skill model developed by Ghazarian and Noorhosseini, there are four metrics of interest: task completion time, pause, mouse motion, and interactor [8]. Since many metrics are strongly related to the interaction task to be performed, there is a need for more generic metrics that can be used in a broader context.

With regard to task-related metrics, there is the assumption that aspects such as precision can actually be measured. This leads to the hypothesis that the action is (with some variance) predictable. On the other side, interaction-design-related aspects can also impact the execution of the performance. A famous example is the influence of handedness on optimal design. At any rate, contextual influences need to be considered during the interaction, which can influence the result and explain the deviation of the results from the expectations. An example is the role of labels presented on the interaction objects – which impact precision.

2   Hypotheses

To investigate these assumptions, four hypotheses were constructed that will be explained in the following.

2.1   Hypothesis 1 – Precision

Overall, the user only interacts with a subset of the available interaction area. Additionally, the user will tend to always interact with almost the same area within the available interaction area. Therefore, the hypothesis is that all the measured interactions will be concentrated within a subarea $\mu_0 = 25\%$ of the available interaction area.

$$H1_1 : \mu < \mu_0$$
$$H1_0 : \mu \geq \mu_0$$

2.2   Hypothesis 2 – Handedness via Centroid

When considering the centroid of the cloud of interaction points within an interaction object, the centroid can be calculated. It can be assumed that users will execute a certain interaction in a cost-efficient way. Therefore, the hypothesis is that the centroid will be oriented towards the user's interacting hand. This means in case of right-handed test persons that the majority ($\mu_0 = 50\%$) of centroids will be located on the right side of the interaction object.

$$H2_1 : \mu > \mu_0$$
$$H2_0 : \mu \leq \mu_0$$

2.3   Hypothesis 3 – Handedness via Precision

It can be assumed that the precision of the interaction with available interaction objects will differ according to their position on the user interface in relation to the interacting hand. The hypothesis is that users interact more precisely the closer the interaction object is located to the interacting hand. In case of right-handed users, the relation of the interaction area used to the interaction area available is significantly higher on the left side of the screen than that of areas located on the right side of the screen.

$$H3_1 : \mu_{\text{left}} > \mu_{\text{right}}$$
$$E3_0 : \mu_{\text{left}} \leq \mu_{\text{right}}$$

2.4   Hypothesis 4 – Icon Bias

It can be assumed that the interaction is influenced by contextual factors, such as the interaction object itself. Thus, the hypothesis is that the label/icon of the interaction object has an influence on the location of the centroid. The distance between the label/icon is less than $\mu_o = 25\%$ of the diagonal of the interaction object.

$$EH4_1 : \mu < \mu_0$$
$$EH4_0 : \mu \geq \mu_0$$

3   Experimental Design

This section contains the description of the experimental design, which consisted of apparatus, participants, and expected validity.

3.1   Apparatus

Calculator software was used to conduct the experiment. This particular calculator is able to detect the exact point of interaction along with a time-stamp. Thus the interaction can be analyzed in every detail. Fig. 2 shows on the left side the calculator software as presented to the participants. It contains all the buttons of a simple calculator, and the participants were familiar with its functionality and layout and therefore did not need any training. Further, the tasks of the test were also quite simple, as they merely involved entering numbers and the corresponding mathematical operations. In total, 104 such tasks ensured an even distribution of interactions with every available interaction object. One concrete task always consisted of two three-digit numbers combined with one operation and the participants had to check their result against the one provided. In case there was a deviation, they were to repeat the task. Fig. 2 depicts on the right side a preview of the evaluation of the results as a visualization of the detected points of interaction.

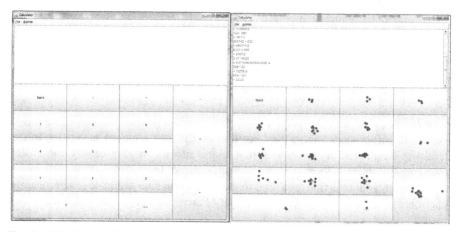

Fig. 2. Calculator software: (left) as presented to the participants, (right) visualizing the gathered point of interaction of each interaction object

The calculator runs on 10-inch tablet PCs (s. Fig. 3, various products of the vendor Paceblade equipped with a resistive touch screen). As shown in Fig. 3, during a test run the participants were sitting at a desk, with the tablet PC on the desk along with the list of tasks. The arrangement on top of the desk was their choice. This setup along with the tasks ensured that the participants were completely unaware of what was being tested.

Fig. 3. Participants executing the tasks: entering the list of mathematical calculations

Within the experiment, the following variables were of interest:

- **Control variables:** The calculator software as well as the list of tasks was always the same.
- **Independent variables:** The participants differed in terms of age, education, or impairments.
- **Context variables:** The participants were executing the tasks while sitting at a desk, with the tablet PC on top of the desk. Help was available during every test run (in terms of a tutor), but was not used. The participants were not confronted with anything that would have distracted from conducting the tasks.
- **Dependent variables:** Relation between the interaction area used and the total interaction area available, centroid of the interaction area used, timestamps, id of each interaction object.

3.2   Participants

Most of the participants were recruited at the computer science department of the University of Kaiserslautern, Germany. In total, 33 participants (all of them male) were recruited, aged between 18 and 51 years (s. Fig. 4, average 23, median 20). Out of the 33 participants, 25 were undergraduates (bachelor students), two of them were graduate students (master students), and four of them were scientists at the computer science department (PhD students). Also, two non-professionals were recruited who are related to one participant.

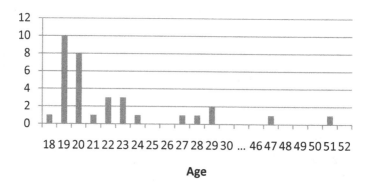

Fig. 3. Distribution of the participants with respect to their age

Only three of the 33 participants were left-handed, which led to the decision to omit hypotheses concerning left-handedness. The results concerning left-handed participants would have been without any statistical significance.

All cases of (minor) short- or farsightedness were compensated by glasses or contact lenses.

All the participants were tested for cases of impaired color perception. Actually, two participants were red-green blind, but this did not have any effect on the test or the interpretation of the results.

Only two of the participants were not familiar with touchscreens as they do not use such devices on a regular basis. But they did not have any problems using the calculator.

3.3   Validity

In order to be able to use the interpretation of the results, internal validity (according to the setup), external validity (according to the execution), and threats to validity need to be reflected on:

- **Internal validity:** No training was necessary, as all participants were familiar with calculators in general. Due to the setup, all of them were completely unaware of what was being tested. The implementation of the calculator also produced (mathematically) correct results.
- **External validity:** Most of the participants were within the same age group, but a few outliners were also included. They were not affected by anything that could have had an impact during the test. They did not ask for help, nor did they need any help to successfully execute the demanded tasks.
- **Threats to validity:** As mentioned above, there are two major threats: the entire test population was male, and there were only three left-handed participants.

4   Interpretation of the Results

The interpretation of the results will be clustered analogously to the structure of the hypotheses. Because of the expected string effect of the result and the number of the participants, a significance level of $\alpha = 0.01$ can be expected. All of the numerical evaluation was processed by SPSS.

4.1   Hypothesis 1 – Precision

After evaluating the measured values, the observed average is $\bar{X} = 0.075$ with a standard deviation of $\sigma = 0.0177$.

As a precondition for applying a one-sample t-test, the data needs to be normally distributed. This is shown by executing a Shapiro-Wilk test. On a significance level of $\alpha = 0.01$, the test result is $W_{critical} = 0.906 < 0.965 = W$, which indicates that the data is normally distributed.

The result of the one-sample t-test is $t = -56.622$ (df $= 32$). The corresponding p-value is calculated as follows:

$$p = N(-56.622; 32) < 0.001$$

Thus, $p < \alpha$ and the null hypothesis $H1_0$ can be rejected, which strengthens the hypothesis.

This means that there is a strong indication that users tend to activate a particular interaction object always in the (almost) same spot. There are various benefits of this knowledge. First, there is the possibility to use this data in general. Second, a change within precision over time may mean that the user's abilities have changed. Third, the knowledge of this pattern can be used to interpret available data in a more fine-grained manner, e.g., Hypotheses 2 and 3.

4.2   Hypothesis 2 – Handedness via Centroid

For this hypothesis, a one-sample binomial-test needed to be performed. The expectation was $p_0 = 0.5$. In 27 cases (out of 30 right-handed participants), the centroid was located on the right side of the interaction object ($m = 27$).

The result of the binomial test is as follows:

$$p = B_{n;p_0}(n - m) = 0.000$$

Thus, $p < \alpha$ and the null hypothesis $H2_0$ can be rejected, which strengthens the hypothesis.

This indicates that there is a strong relation between handedness and the position of the centroid, which means that users tend to execute interaction in a cost-efficient manner.

4.3   Hypothesis 3 – Handedness vial Precision

After evaluating the measured data, the mean of the relation between the interaction area used and the total interaction area of interaction objects on the left side of the screen is $\overline{\mu_{left}} = 0.082$ ($\sigma_{left} = 0.022$) and the corresponding mean for interaction objects on the right side of the screen is $\overline{\mu_{right}} = 0.067$ ($\sigma_{right} = 0.022$).

Both sets of samples need to be normally distributed in order to be able to apply a two-sample t-test. On a significance level of $\alpha = 0.01$, the Shapiro-Wilk test results for objects located on the left side of the user interface in $W_{critical} = 0.906 < 0.935 = W$- On a significance level of $\alpha = 0.05$, the Shapiro-Wilk test results for objects located on the right side of the user interface in $W_{critical} = 0.906 < 0.965 = W$. This indicates that both sets are normally distributed.

The two-sample t-test results in:

$$t = \frac{\mu_1 - \mu_1}{\sqrt{\frac{\sigma_1^2}{n} + \frac{\sigma_2^2}{n}}} = 2.768; \ df = 29$$

According to this, the p-value was calculated as follows:

$$p = 0.010$$

Thus, $p < \alpha$ and the null hypothesis $H3_0$ can be rejected, which strengthens the hypothesis.

This indicates that users tend to execute interaction more precisely the shorter the distance to the final destination.

4.4   Hypothesis 4 – Icon Bias

After evaluating the measured data, the calculated average is $\bar{X} = 0.092$ with a standard deviation of $\sigma = 0.032$.

As a precondition to applying a one-sample t-test, the data needs to be normally distributed. On a significance level of $\alpha = 0.01$, the Shapiro-Wilk test results in $W_{critical} = 0.906 < 0.918 = W$, which indicates that the underlying data is normally distributed.

The result of the t-test is:

$$t = -38.927; \ df = 32$$

According to this, the p-value is calculated as follows:

$$p = N(-38.927; 32) < 0.001$$

Thus, $p < \alpha$ and the null hypothesis $H4_0$ can be rejected, which strengthens the hypothesis.

This result indicates that there is a strong relation between an icon or text that is displayed on the interaction object and the position at which a user tends to trigger this interaction object.

5   Summary and Future Work

There is no need to obtrusively measure the interaction using tests or sensors in order to determine a user's performance. The overall hypothesis of this paper was that information that can be elicited during runtime without any further sensors can be interpreted in order to characterize the user.

Therefore, this paper described a controlled experiment that was conducted in order to evaluate whether:

- **Interaction is a matter of habit** – If the user always (or often) tends to activate an interaction object in the same position, indirect metrics such as precision can be measured and evaluated (especially over time). For instance, if decreasing precision is detected, this can be compensated by appropriate adaptation measures.
- **Handedness is detectable** – Due to further habits (e.g., economics of movement), handedness can be detected either via the shift within the position of the centroid or via the difference within the precision of the interaction according to the position of the interaction object. Once handedness can be detected (which can also change), the user interface, for instance, can be adapted to meet the basic requirements of efficient visual design (e.g., by replacing the navigation bar).
- **Interaction can be influenced** – In case there is an icon or label displayed on the interaction object, users tend to be distracted and it is more likely that the interaction object will be activated at (or in the general area of) the position of this icon or label. This implies that when interpreting information gathered during runtime, such influencing factors need to be considered within any calculation.

Overall, the controlled experiment that was conducted using 33 participants in the context of the University of Kaiserslautern was able to strengthen the four hypotheses at a high level of significance.

These are important findings in the field of user interaction forensics, which will allow more research into areas such as adaptation according to the user's preferences. There is still much to investigate, especially in terms of the gathered data. New hypotheses can be formulated and tested against the available data. Possible candidates are:

- There is a relation between the distance of two interaction objects and precision.
- There is a relation between time (beginning, middle, or end of the test) and precision.

In particular with regard to self-adaptive systems that are able to adapt to the performance of a concrete user, this adaptation can be measured precisely and it can be determined whether there is a positive effect on the overall performance. This will be shown in future experiments.

Acknowledgments. The results presented in this paper are part of the project GaBi (Generating task-oriented user interfaces for intelligent production environments), which was funded by the German Research Foundation (DFG, RO 3343/1-1,2).

References

1. Breiner, K.: AssistU - A framework for user interaction forensics. TU Kaiserslautern, Kaiserslautern. PhD-Thesis (2013)
2. Card, S.K., Moran, T.P., Newell, A.: The Model Human Processor: An engineering model of human performance. In: Boff, K.R., Kaufmann, L., Thomas, J.P. (eds.) Handbook of Perception and Human Performance. Wiley and Sons, New York (1986)
3. Esteves, M., Komischke, T., Zapf, S., Weiss, A.: Applied user performance modeling in industry – A case study from medical imaging. In: Duffy, V.G. (ed.) HCII 2007 and DHM 2007. LNCS, vol. 4561, pp. 576–585. Springer, Heidelberg (2007)
4. Gajos, K.: Automatically Generating Personalized User Interfaces. University of Washington, Washington. PhD-Thesis (2008)
5. Gajos, K., Czerwinski, M., Tan, D.S., Weld, D.S.: Exploring the Design Space For Adaptive Graphical User Interfaces. In: Proceedings of AVI 2006, Venice, Italy (2006)
6. Gajos, K., Long, J.J., Weld, D.S.: Automatically Generating Custom User Interfaces for Users With Physical Disabilities. In: ASSETS 2006, Portland, OR (2006)
7. Gajos, K., Wobbrock, J.O., Weld, D.S.: Automatically Generating User Interfaces Adapted To Users' Motor And Vision Capabilities. In: Proceedings of UIST 2007, Newport, RI, USA (2007)
8. Ghazarian, A., Noorhosseini, S.M.: Automatic detection of users' skill levels using high-frequency user interface events. In: Journal User Modeling and User-Adapted Interaction. Kluwer Academic Publishers, Hingham (2010)
9. Hernández, J. A., Larrabeiti, D., Strnad, O., Schmidt, A.: Prototype for user context management (2011)
10. Hess, S., Maier, A., Trapp, M.: Differentiating between successful and less successful products by using MAInEEAC - a model for interaction characterization. In: Jacko, J.A. (ed.) Human-Computer Interaction, Part I, HCII 2011. LNCS, vol. 6761, pp. 238–247. Springer, Heidelberg (2011)
11. MyUI - Mainstreaming Accessibility through Synergistic User Modelling and Adaptability, http://www.myui.eu/ (retrieved February 12, 2012)

The Conjunction Fallacy and Its Impacts in the User's Data Acquisition Process

Fábio Campos[1], Dino Lincoln[1], Maria Neves[2], Walter Correia[1], and Marcelo Soares[1]

[1] UFPE, Design Dept. Recife-PE, Brazil
[2] CESAR, Porto Digital, Recife-PE, Brazil
{fc2005,dinolincoln,wfmc10}@gmail.com,
marie@cesar.org.br, marcelo2@nlink.com.br

Abstract. There are moments within the process of creating an artifact, for instance at the initial requirements gathering or in the assessment phase, that users input data is collected. There may be an impact directly on the results of the analysis of this data if, for some reason, this data input is not accurate. This paper will focus on a specific phenomenon, known as the Conjunction Fallacy, which may lead users to commit errors of judgment that would impact directly in the accuracy of their evaluation of alternatives. In order to exemplify this issue, this paper presents experiments where, during the evaluation phase of the design of a product, it was verified the presence of the conjunction fallacy. It also presents a possible strategy to minimize the errors of judgment caused by the fallacy.

Keywords: evaluation of artifacts, conjunction fallacy, ergonomic assessment, usability evaluation.

1 Introduction

Collecting an accurate user's input is an important issue in many areas such as Design, Ergonomics and Usability. Assessing the usability of an artifact, the perception of comfort in an ergonomic analysis, or the decision making process of launching a new product, are some examples, among the wide range of applications, where this issue is involved.

Even when the experiment conditions seem to be all controlled, with the sample correctly dimensioned, and questions clearly formulated, users may incur into mistakes [5]. This paper will focus on a specific phenomenon, known as the Conjunction Fallacy [6], which may lead users to commit errors of judgment.

According to a basic principle of mathematics, the "rule of conjunction", the probability that two events occur together cannot be higher than the smallest probability of each event happening isolated. For instance, considering two events "A" and "B", the probability of occurrence of a conjunctive event, the occurrence of "A" and "B" simultaneously, which we will denote as "A & B", can never be higher than the lowest probability of the event "A" or "B" isolated occurring.

A. Marcus (Ed.): DUXU/HCII 2013, Part I, LNCS 8012, pp. 203–211, 2013.

For example, imagine that we have two dice, one black dice and one white dice. Considering that the event "A" happens when we throw the black dice resulting in number "5", and the event "B" happens when we throw the white dice and the result is number "3". If we throw the black and the white dice at the same time, then the probability of the event "A" happening is of 1/6 (since the dice has 6 faces and only one is a number "3"). The same way, the probability of the event "B" happening is of 1/6. However, the probability of these two events occurring together, "A & B" is 1/36 (since there are 36 possible outcomes and only one of them is "black dice = 5 and white dice = 3").

Thus, when there is a judgment or evaluation of conjunctive events, and the user assigns a higher probability of occurrence to a conjunctive event than to any of the isolated events, we say a "conjunction fallacy" had occurred.

The importance of discussing the conjunction fallacy permeates many areas of knowledge where there is a need for users to choose from alternatives, especially when the answers present conjunctive events [4]. In Design, these choices may happen at various points within the process of creating an artifact, either at the initial requirements gathering, in the assessment phase, or at any other moment [1]. An error of judgment arising from a possible conjunction fallacy would impact directly on the results of an analysis thus constituting itself as an important point to be studied [2].

In this sense, this paper presents, in Section 2, two experiments where, during the evaluation phase of the design of a product, it was verified the presence of the conjunction fallacy. One of the experiments used a digital data collection instrument, while the other did not. This procedure was adopted to avoid any influence in the results by the collection instrument. This paper also shows, in Section 3, another experiment where a strategy to minimize the errors of judgment caused by the fallacy was used. Finally, the conclusions and final considerations are shown in Section 4.

2   Case Studies Where the Fallacy Occurred

This section presents two case studies [3]. These case studies aimed to verify experimentally the occurrence of the conjunction fallacy. In both cases, the experiments consisted in exposing a problem to the user, followed by a set of isolated and conjunctive alternatives for the user to grade.

In order to isolate the data collection instrument variable, the first case study used a digital instrument, an online form, to collect the input data from the users, while the second case study used a paper version of a survey to collect the data.

For these experiments, there were chosen randomly 92 undergraduate students, from public and private universities in Brazil, and from different periods of design courses.

2.1   Case Study One

For the case study one, 50 of the 92 undergraduate students, which we will designate "Group 1", received a description of a problem followed by five possible alternative

Table 1. Questions and alternative answers for case study one

DINOTUNES is a website that sells music albums. This site received a bad user satisfaction review. The site users claim to find problems to buy the songs.
The website looks like a computer store
The website has usability problems
The website lacks presence in social networks
The website has too many buttons
The website lacks presence in social networks and has usability problems

solutions. They were asked to rank these alternatives from 1 to 5, in such way that the most likely alternative would receive the value of 1, the second most likely alternative would be assigned the value of 2, and so on. The table 1 bellow shows the question that was presented to the users followed by the 5 alternative answers:

The question was intentionally designed to represent a usability problem easily identifiable by designers. The answers were designed to represent four different alternatives for the users to chose, were each alternative represented an isolated event, and one alternative represented a conjunctive event. The table 2 bellow shows the events associated to each of the 5 alternative answers:

Table 2. Events and alternative answers for case study one

Event	Alternative answer
Isolated event A	The website looks like a computer store
Isolated event B	The website has usability problems
Isolated event C	The website lacks presence in social networks
Isolated event D	The website has too many buttons
Conjunctive event B&C	The website lacks presence in social networks and has usability problems

The respondents answered the survey on computers in the design lab of their college through the free software Survey Monkey [7]. The software was configured so that the user was only able to assign to each alternative a different value from 1 to 5. For example, it was not possible to have two or more alternatives with value 1.

In Table 3, there are the mean scores assigned by respondents for each alternative. The lower the value of the average, the higher the probability assigned by respondents, exactly as postulated by the Tversky & Kahneman procedure [6].

Table 3. Events, alternative answers and mean score

Type of event	Alternative answer	Mean score
Isolated event A	The website looks like a computer store	3.98
Isolated event B	The website has usability problems	1.92
Isolated event C	The website lacks presence in social networks	3.48
Isolated event D	The website has too many buttons	2.98
Conjunctive event B&C	The website lacks presence in social networks and has usability problems	2.64

It was expected the conjunctive event B&C to have less probability to occur than the isolated event B or the isolated event C . However, according to the data collected and presented on table 3, the conjunctive event B&C had a lower average value than the isolated event C, meaning for the users as a higher probability to happen, than the isolated event C.

2.2 Case Study Two

For the case study 2, in a posterior moment, another 42 of the 92 undergraduate students, which we will designate "Group 2", received a description of a new problem followed by another possible set of solution alternatives.

The same protocol was followed, however, this time a paper form (rather than an online form) was used to collect the user data. There were 6 alternatives instead of 5, as in case study one.

The users were asked to rank these alternatives from 1 to 6, in such way that the more likely alternative would receive the value of 1, the second most likely alternative would be assigned the value of 2, and so on (similar to case study one). The table 4 bellow shows the question that was presented to the users followed by the 6 alternative answers.

Table 4. Questions and alternative answers for case study two

Designers are designing the iCOPA, an application for smartphones that simultaneously presents relevant information about the World Cup. The prototype of the product has received many complaints from their appraisers such as getting lost in the interface.
The application presents a complex interface with many buttons
The application looks like a digital newspaper
The application lacks presence in social networks
The application does not provide a sports themed interface
The application lacks presence in social networks and presents a complex interface with many buttons
The application consists of an outdated technology

Again, the question was intentionally designed to represent a usability problem. The answers were designed to represent five different alternatives for the users to chose, where each alternative represented an isolated event, and one alternative represented a conjunctive event. The table 5 bellow shows the events associated to each of the 6 alternative answers.

Table 5. Events and alternative answers in case study two

Type of event	Alternative answer
Isolated event A	The application presents a complex interface with many buttons
Isolated event B	The application looks like a digital newspaper
Isolated event C	The application lacks presence in social networks
Isolated event D	The application does not provide a sports themed interface
Conjunctive event A&C	The presents a complex interface with many buttons application and it lacks presence in social networks
Isolated event E	The application consists of an outdated technology

The respondents answered the paper form survey, assigning to each alternative a different value from 1 to 6.

Table 6 shows the mean scores assigned by respondents for each alternative. Again, in this case study, the lower the value of the average, the higher the probability assigned by respondents.

Table 6. Events, alternative answers and mean score in case study two

Type of event	Alternative answer	Mean score
Isolated event A	The application presents a complex interface with many buttons	1.86
Isolated event B	The application looks like a digital newspaper	3.64
Isolated event C	The website lacks presence in social networks	3.90
Isolated event D	The application does not provide a sports themed interface	4.26
Conjunctive event A&C	The presents a complex interface with many buttons application and it lacks presence in social networks	2.48
Isolated event E	The application consists of an outdated technology	4.88

It was expected the conjunctive event A&C to have less probability to occur than the isolated event A or the isolated event C . However, according to the data collected and presented on table 6, the conjunctive event A&C had a lower average value, meaning for the users as a higher probability to happen, than the isolated event A.

3   Case Study 3: A Strategy to Minimize the Effect of the Conjunction Fallacy

The analysis of the results of case studies one and two, presented a possible solution to minimize error in judgment caused by the propensity to belief in conjunctive events. This solution was to reshape the procedure so that all alternatives were conjunctive. For instance, an alternative would be described as "A & B", while the following would be described "C & A", "B & C", and so on. In this experiment, the alternative "A & B" would represent an event more likely than any of the other events represented by the other alternatives "C & A", "B & C" etc.

3.1   Case Study Three

This section will present case study 3 [3] . This experiment shows a   strategy to minimize the errors of judgment caused by the fallacy was used.

In order to verify this approach, a group of 93 new students, that were not part of neither "Group 1" nor "Group 2", designated as "Group 3", received the same description of the problem as in the case study one, however followed by alternatives arranged according to the procedure described previously. The table 7 below presents the question and the alternatives presented to "Group 3":

Table 7. Questions and alternative answers for case study three

DINOTUNES is a website that sells music albums. This site received a bad satisfaction review. The site users claim to find problems to buy the songs.
The website looks like a computer store and presents usability problems
The website lacks presence in social networks and looks like a computer store
The website presents usability problems and has many buttons
The website has lots of buttons and lacks presence in social networks

Again, the question was intentionally designed to represent a usability problem. The answers were designed to represent different alternatives for the users to chose, however this time each alternative represented a conjunctive event. The Table 8 bellow shows the events associated to each of the 4 alternative answers:

Table 8. Events and alternative answers in case study three

Type of event	Alternative answer
Isolated event A1	The website presents usability problems
Isolated event A2	The website has lots of buttons
Isolated event B1	The website looks like a computer store
Isolated event B2	The website lacks presence in social networks
Conjunctive event A1&B1	The website looks like a computer store and presents usability problems
Conjunctive event B1 &B2	The website lacks presence in social networks and looks like a computer store
Conjunctive event A1 & A2	The website presents usability problems and has many buttons
Conjunctive event A2 & B2	The website has lots of buttons and lacks presence in social networks

Thus, it is expected that the conjunctive event combining "likely" alternatives, represented in this experiment as   Conjunctive event A1 & A2, would be ranked by the respondents as the most probable one. Also, the events that intentionally combine "likely" and "unlikely" alternatives ("A1 & B1" and "B2 & A2", not necessarily in that order) would receive lower probabilities. It would be also expected that the alternative combining the most improbable events "B1 & B2" be ranked as the least probable one (recalling that the events "B1" and "B2" are intentionally designed to be considered unlikely, as the events "A1 and "A2").

The respondents answered the paper form survey, assigning to each alternative a different value from 1 to 4.

Table 8 shows the mean scores assigned by respondents for each alternative. Again, the lower the value of the average means that the higher the probability assigned by respondents.

Table 9. Events, alternative answers and mean score in case study three

Type of event	Alternative answer	Mean score
Conjunctive event A1 & B1	The website looks like a computer store and presents usability problems.	2.45
Conjunctive event B1 & B2	The website lacks presence in social networks and looks like a computer store.	3.07
Conjunctive event A1 & A2	The website presents usability problems and has many buttons.	1.61
Conjunctive event A2 & B2	The website has lots of buttons and lacks presence in social networks	2.88

As expected, the results presented that the conjunctive event combining "likely" alternatives, conjunctive event A1 & A2, highlighted in table 9, was ranked as the most probable one, with mean score of 1.61. Also, as anticipated, the events that combined "likely" and "unlikely" alternatives, conjunctive event "A1 & B1" and "A2 & B2", with mean scores of 2.45 and 2.88 respectively, received higher probabilities than the alternative combining the most improbable events, the conjunctive event B1 & B2, with mean score of 3.07.

In contrast with the previous case studies presented in Section 2 of this document, the users chose the erroneous answered in only 17.2% of the cases. In other words, the users rated correctly, in 77 of the 93 interviews (82.8%), the most likely event, "A1 & A2", as more likely than the event "B1 & B2".

In summary, compared to case study one, presented in Section 2.1 of this paper, the results decreased from an average of 80.4% of bad choices (caused by the conjunction fallacy) to only 17.2% of bad selections.

4   Conclusions and Final Considerations

The idea of this paper was not to present a statistically valid demonstration but to verify if the occurrence of the conjunction fallacy is easily observed, also indicating a possibility of a solution to it.

In fact, the results of the experiments of case studies one and two were analyzed separately to verify the internal consistency of the experiment, and in both cases it was possible to find out that the fallacy had occurred. This was verified since a percentage of conjunctive events were considered more likely to occur than isolated events. In the case of "Group 1", a total of 76% of respondents judged erroneously the conjunctive event as more likely to occur than some isolated event. In the "Group 2", the event conjunctive was chosen erroneously as more possible that some isolated event by 85.7% of the sample.

The results of "Group 3" were that only 17,2% of the respondents incurred in an error of judgment when ranking the alternatives.   It seems that there was a reduction in the percentage of choices misjudged when comparing with the results obtained previously with the "Group 2", of 85.7%, and also when comparing with the results of "Group 1", of 76%.

In conclusion, although we may not assure that the solution proposed at case study 3 solves all the problems arisen by the conjunction fallacy, such knowledge contributes to the search for ways to minimize the error of probabilistic judgment arising out of such phenomenon and consequently to enhance the process of decision making.

References

1. Baxter, M.: Projeto de Produto: Guia Prático para o Desenvolvimento de Novos Produtos, 3rd edn. Editora Edgard Blücher Ltda, São Paulo (2011) (in Portuguese)
2. Figueiroa, D.L., Campos, F., Correia, W.: A Falácia da Conjunção no Processo de Design. In: P&D Design 2012 | 10° Congresso Brasileiro de Pesquisa e Desenvolvimento em Design, Anais do 10° Congresso Brasileiro de Pesquisa e Desenvolvimento em Design, São Luis (2012)
3. Figueiroa, D.L., Campos, F.: A avaliação de artefatos em Design e os problemas decorrentes da aleatoriedade. PhD Thesis. Universidade Federal de Pernambuco, Departamento de Design. Recife (2012) (in Portuguese)
4. Fox, C.R., Birke, R.: Forecasting trial outcomes: lawyers assign higher probabilities to possibilities that are described in greater details. Law and Human Behavior 26(2), 159–173 (2002)
5. Mlodinow, L.: O Andar do Bêbado – Como o Acaso Determina Nossas Vidas. Rio de Janeiro, Jorge Zahar (2009) (in Portuguese)
6. Tversky, A., Kahneman, D.: Extensional vs. intuitive reasoning: The conjunction fallacy in probability judgment. Psychological Review 90, 293–315 (1983)
7. Survey Monkey, http://www.surveymonkey.com

Remote Usability Evaluation Using Eye Tracking Enhanced with Intelligent Data Analysis

Piotr Chynał, Janusz Sobecki, and Jerzy M. Szymański

Wrocław University of Technology
{piotr.chynal,janusz.sobecki,jerzy.szymanski}@pwr.wroc.pl

Abstract. In this paper we present a new cost-effective method for usability evaluation using eye tracking enhanced with intelligent data analysis. In this method we propose application of a low-cost infrared camera and free Ogama software. Moreover we present how the standard data analysis, which is usually made manually by experts, may be enhanced by application of intelligent data analysis. We applied well known expert system, which is using fuzzy reasoning. To build such a system we should first define a model of "desired" eye tracking record for a given poster, or more general web page or the whole application.

Keywords: Usability, Eye Tracking, Human Computer-Interaction, Fuzzy Expert Systems.

1 Introduction

In today's world we are surrounded by all sorts of advertisements. They are the fuel that runs the economy, so all advertising agencies are doing their best to come up with good designs for new posters, billboards etc. After such new designs are created they are usually evaluated by a group of people in a focus group research [1], [2], [3]. However application of a focus group evaluation is not perfect because in a real life customer usually has only a few seconds to recognize and memorize the product, for example when they are looking at a billboard while driving a car [1]. This means that focus group evaluation is only good for situations where customer has a lot of time to look at the advertisements. We can of course show our test participants the designs for a short amount of time and ask them what have they remembered, but this method does not give a good overview of the most visible and invisible parts of the design. Because of that more and more companies start to use a technique called eye tracking for this purpose [4], [5], and [6]. This method enables recording the line of gaze of user during the test, so it is possible to see where users were looking while they were evaluating the design. However the biggest drawback of the eye tracking technology is its cost. The application of the commercial eye trackers is too expensive especially in the developing countries, so smaller marketing agencies cannot cover these costs. We tried to perform such research using low-cost eye tracking method that we have implemented. For our study we wanted to show three different designs of the same

A. Marcus (Ed.): DUXU/HCII 2013, Part I, LNCS 8012, pp. 212–221, 2013.

product to the testers, just for a few seconds, to record, using eye tracking equipment, which parts of those designs testers were able to notice. Such case study would also show can our low-cost eye tracking method provide valuable results for visual media evaluation.

The construction of this paper is following. In the following section we present the tools we have applied in the usability evaluation, then we describe the experiment. In the section 4 we present the results of the eye tracking experiments. In the section 5 we describe the application of the fuzzy expert systems for the gaze tracking data analysis and finally in section 6 we present the summary and the future work.

2   Tools Used in the Experiment

Having a lot of experience with performing low-cost eye tracking using web cam [7], [8] we used the similar method with new applications. In this research we performed eye tracking with and infrared A4-TECH PK-333E camera[1], and ITU GazeTracker[2] combined with Ogama[3] software.

A4-TECH PK-333E camera is a very cheap camera, equipped with seven LEDs so it enables night vision. It has high image quality and works without delay at 640x480 pixels video resolution.

ITU GazeTracker [9], [10] is an open-source application that enables gazetracking using an infrared camera. It supports two methods of operating – pupil tracking and glint tracking. We need to obtain a clear image of the eye in order to perform effective eye tracking. Both methods use corneal reflection created by infrared light sources.

Ogama software allows recording and analyzing eye and mouse-tracking data from slideshow eye tracking experiments. Ogama is a freeware and open-source project. Its main features include database-driven pre-processing and filtering of gaze and mouse data, the creation of attention maps, areas of interest definition, saliency calculation and many more. Nearly any eye tracking and/or presentation soft- and hardware recordings in ASCII format can be imported. Direct recording is possible with commercial tracking such as Tobii and it also enables recording from open-source applications like the ITU GazeTracker.

To perform recording of the gaze or mouse data in Ogama we must create a slide show at first. It is done in the Slide Design Module. We can place different types of media on those slides such as images, text and flash animations.

After creating the slideshow we can proceed to the recording module in which we setup the participants' data. After that we can calibrate the camera with ITU Gaze-Tracker and launch the slideshow and the application gathers the eye tracking data. After the test we can visualize these data. The visualization module can calculate Gaussian distributions of the fixation data and overlay it on the original stimulus image, so that we can see a landscape of seen and unseen locations on the stimulus. We can choose the subjects to include in the calculation and whether the calculation

---

[1] www.a4tech.com/product.asp?cid=77&scid=160&id=593
[2] http://www.gazegroup.org/
[3] http://www.ogama.net/

should be based only on the first or all fixations. Moreover Ogama allows to create Areas of Interest. Using this feature we can draw shapes on our slides and create areas that are most important to us. Using this option we can see the number of fixations and their total duration time, for one or many participants, in the given area of the poster.

The last tool that we used was Precision_test. We used this application to compare the precision of our eyetracking solution with the previous methods and a commercial ASL eye tracker [7].

3   The Eye Tracking Experiment

At first we needed to get several different designs for the same product. We decided to find some posters regarding social campaign instead of particular products, so we would not advertise any products. We decided to go with three posters of Polish "Speed kills" campaign – "Prędkość zabija"[4]. They all have the same structure. The main element is a picture of a particular situation. On the right site we have a slogan regarding the situation in the picture with reference to fast driving. At the bottom of each poster there is the main slogan and information about the campaign. All designs are showed in figure 1.

Fig. 1. Poster designs

---

[4] www.predkosczabija.pl

The first poster shows a lady which is in a hurry and the slogan says "Sometimes you race against time?". Second design is a man holding a young girl, probably his daughter, while going on a roundabout. The slogan says "Do you like spinning fast?". The third design shows a couple lying in the bed and the slogan which may be translated as "Are you Speedy Gonzales?"

The second step was to determine the areas in which we would expect the participants' gaze to spend the most time. Poster designers want to achieve specific goals by the means of visual patterns. The way in which viewers perceive posters, read and think about them depends on many factors. There are several general psychological rules of visual perception and many studies about text, web pages and digital banners contents visibility such as[11], [12], [13] were done. The usage of eyetracking in advertisements industry is well known [14], for example there is the rule of F-shaped pattern of gaze lanes made by web pages viewers [15]. In our experiment designers expectations about message transferred by a poster are more important than general principles. We have taken this presumption, as in the case of posters, it is important to convey specific information, in expected way. This is the basis for determining the real usefulness of the poster in achieving the assumed information functions.

Based on campaign materials we have elaborated sets of data, for each poster, including messages that they want to pass, so we were able to define essential areas, connected with corresponding message, that apply for all examined posters. General structure of examined posters is as shown in figure 2, where 1 - area showing people in strange situations, 2- short text area, 3 - slogan to remember, 4 - contact and reference for details.

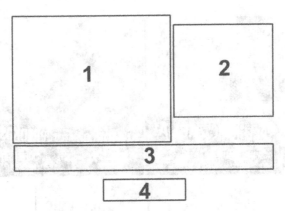

Fig. 2. Essential areas of interest for our posters

For this experiment we have taken a group of 20 people. The group consisted of 10 male and 10 female participants. They were all in a group age from 20 to 28 years old. Young people were the target group for this campaign because they cause the accidents according to the authors of "Prędkość zabija" ("Speed kills") campaign.

For the first part of the research we have taken all the participants individually in front of a computer and set them up with our eyetracking gear. After calibrating the ITU GazeTracker application we ran the precision_test application and we have recorded the results of it. Because of the rather poor optics in our camera we needed to move it very close to the eye of the participant so we used a tripod. First thing that we have noticed was that the correct set up of the elements of the eye was very easy and very fast. ITU GazeTracker was automatically finding the pupil with just a few adjustments to the light and other parameters. We did not need to repeat the calibration process for the most of the participants because after the correct eye set up, the calibration had very good results most of the time. After that we have shown the participants each of the designs (in random order for each participant) for 4 seconds using Ogama software, and asked them to browse it as they would normally do with an advertisement. It is a time that user has to recognize and memorize the advertisement message that is placed on a billboard, bus or another object which makes it impossible to look at this ad for a longer time. During this test we recorded the eye tracking data for each participant in Ogama software. The whole process of performing such tests in Ogama was very easy and intuitive and we managed to complete the whole experiment without any problems.

4   Results of the Eye Tracking Experiment and Their analysis

At first we present the results from eye tracking study. We obtained three heat maps for each participant. We combined all those heat maps into one to show overall heat map for each design for all participants. Those maps are shown in figure 3. The "warmer" the color the more time users gaze spend in the particular area. The Gaussian kernel size was set to 333 for best visibility of the results.

Fig. 3. Eye tracking heat maps for each design

In a short interview after the test each participant said that the red slogan is visible, but the lower part of the poster with a body bag and white slogan is not visible at all and the main slogan "Speed kills" should be at the top of the poster, maybe also in red color. Furthermore participants suggested that the picture should represent an accident or something more drastic to have an impact on people.

As for the precision test, the average precision for all participants was 81,25 pixels. Precision_test, which we have conducted in our previous research, on ASL Eyetracker and Logitech Quick Pro Webcam combined with Opengazer[5] gave average precision 47,65 pixels and 122,67 pixels accordingly [7]. Moreover calibration process using ITU GazeTracker was a lot easier and faster than while using both previously used eyetracking solutions.

Using Ogama software we were also able to determine the number of fixations and the total fixation time for our areas of interest, as shown on figure 4.

Fig. 4. Total fixation time for every participant in every area for the third design

First of all we will look at the generated heat maps. For picture 1 it is clearly visible that the good looking woman has overshadowed the slogans, so with such design it would be hard to get the overall idea what this poster represents in just a few seconds. The second heatmap shows that the main points of focus were the faces, but participants also noticed the red slogan and the white sign, so they had some idea what this poster represents. The third heatmap shows that participants looked at the man for the most time, and they also noticed the lady, red slogan and the white sign along with the zipper.

Those heatmaps show that the lower parts of the pictures were not visible to the participants. The most important slogans and web address were completely invisible.

First design was interesting for male participants because of the good looking woman. However this was in overall the worst design mainly because of the situation, which did not suggest that this is a poster for anti fast driving campaign. Participants also pointed out the bad coloring and the fact that the woman in the picture draws too much attention.

---

[5] http://www.inference.phy.cam.ac.uk/opengazer/

Second design was the most popular mainly because of the dynamics showed on this picture and also because it contained a scared child. Participants also liked the idea of the presented situation and the expressions on the faces of the father and daughter. The visual value of the picture was also the best in this poster.

The views on the third design were divided. Some participants insisted that the sexual subtext is a good thing that brings more attention to this design, while others insisted that this is a bit too vulgar and does not fit this campaign.

Generally all posters were rated poorly by the participants. First one and the third one should be used for advertisements of some other products and not for anti fast driving campaign. Second design was closest to what people expected, some dynamic and extreme situations showing the dangers of fast driving.

5   Applying the Intelligent Data Analysis

In our experiments only 20 participants took part, however for more reliable research also more participants is needed. But as a consequence we obtain more data for analysis, which in turn may be quite difficult. We propose to apply well known fuzzy inference systems [16] in usability verification based on gaze tracking data. Fuzzy inference systems are application of fuzzy logic and fuzzy set theory proposed by Lofti Zadeh in 1965. They are used to carry out very different tasks such as classification, diagnosis, process control or decision support, however they were also successfully applied in recommender systems [17].

The Mumdani model Of Fuzzy Rule Based System (FRBS) a is shown in Fig. 5, in this model the particular input characteristics is first mapped to the input membership functions (fuzzification), which then is mapped to rules that are mapped into a set of output characteristics and consequently to output membership function, which finally is mapped to a single-valued output associated with the decision (defuzzification).

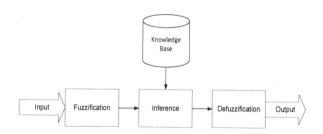

Fig. 5. Mamdani model of FRBS [18]

In our case we can select the following attributes concerning both the experiment participants' description such as: age, gender, education, place of living. The values of these attributes were used as the input to determine the membership function values of linguistic variables [16]. All the membership functions applied in the system have the trapezoid shape. The membership function values are defined as follows:

$$\mu_{trapezoid}(x) = \begin{cases} 1 & \\ \dfrac{x-a_1}{b_1-a_1} & , x \in [b_1,b_2] \\ & , x \in [a_1,b_1) \\ \dfrac{a_2-x}{a_2-b_2} & , x \in (b_a,a_2) \\ 0 & , otherwise \end{cases} \tag{1}$$

For example for variable x representing the participants' gaze time (in seconds) being short, we have the following values of $a_1=2$, $b_1=4$, $b_2=6$, $a_2=8$.

The attributes were used to construct fuzzy inference rules that for some assumptions expressed in so called linguistic values (eg. short time) assign conclusions concerning usability also expressed in the linguistic values. Depending on the complexity of the poster (number of the different regions) and the differences among the participants the system the number of the inference rules may vary from about 20 to over 60 in the following form:

If the age of the participant is medium and the gaze time at region 1 is long and the gaze time at the region 4 is short then the usability of the design is high.

Each rule has associated confidence factor ($cf \in [0,1]$) given by the expert, which expresses his or her confidence in the particular rule. The cf multiplies the membership function value of the outcome of the rule and by default this factor is set to 1.0.

The defuzzification process is based on a very simple method called Mean of Maximum (MOM) [16], which takes the mean value of the set with maximum membership grade. According to the fuzzy inference system we determine values that represent the usability of the particular design, for the particular experiment participant, particular group of participants, the all the participants or select the best design according to the highest usability value.

6   Summary and Future Work

In our experiment we have shown that this low-cost eye tracking method can be used to perform a professional visual media evaluation and can be an additional tool to standard techniques such as focus group research. ITU GazeTracker combined with infrared camera provides descent eye tracking precision in comparison to commercial ASL eyetracker. Furthermore this method provides better precision than previous methods that we have developed earlier and presented in works [7] and [8]. Also the setting up and the calibration process are easier and faster with this method comparing with the previous one. As for the Ogama software it provides a very efficient testing environment for eye tracking. It is easy to set up a slideshow and the camera with eye tracking. Generated heatmaps look very professionally and an option for generating heatmap based on the data from many participants is a very useful addition. The data gained from the areas of interest allowed us to perform the second part of our analysis

– intelligent analysis of the eye tracking data. Using eye tracking allowed us to precisely determine which areas of the design were visible and which were invisible to the participants in the first four seconds of their encounter with given media. It was a simulation of a real life situation in which recipients view a poster or a billboard just for a few seconds, and its design should give all the necessary information in this short time. Eye tracking allows evaluating any visual media this way. It gives more empirical information about the design than the discussion with participants of the focus group.

We have also presented how we can enhance the process of gaze tracking data analysis by application of fuzzy reasoning. The most important advantage of this method (besides low cost of eye tracking device) is that it may be used to analyze the data gathered for single user, several users or even hundreds of users, which will give the statistical significance. However one of the drawbacks of this method is necessity of definition or redefinition of set of rules for the different experiments. This problem may be solved by application of determining fuzzy rules out of experimental data [19].

This method that we presented can be used not only in evaluating posters, but also in many other types of media and also in website usability testing. Its precision was not as good as the precision of a commercial eyetracker, but for smaller companies it is a very good alternative for such tests.

Acknowledgement. The research was partially supported by Grant no. N N519 444939 funded by Polish Ministry of Science and Higher Education (2010-2013) and the European Commission under the 7th Framework Programme, Coordination and Support Action, Grant Agreement Number 316097, ENGINE - European research centre of Network intelliGence for INnovation Enhancement (http://engine.pwr.wroc.pl/).

References

1. Burke, R.R., Rangaswamy, A., Sunil, G.: Rethinking Marketing Research in the Digital World. eBusiness Researcher Center Working Paper 01, 13 (1999)
2. Krueger, R.A., Casey, M.A.: Focus groups: A practical guide for applied research, pp. 107–113. Sage, Thousand Oaks (1999)
3. Moyle, K.: Focus groups in educational research: using ICT to assist in meaningful data collection. MOY06634, 1–3 (2006)
4. Duchowski, A.T.: A Breadth-First Survey of Eye Tracking Applications, http://brm.psychonomic-journals.org/content/34/4/455.full.pdf
5. Duchowski, A.T.: Eye tracking methodology: Theory and practice, pp. 205–300. Springer-Verlag Ltd., London (2003)
6. Goldberg, H.J., Wichansky, A.M.: Eye tracking in usability evaluation: A practitioner's guide. Elsevier, Amsterdam (2003)
7. Chynał, P., Sobecki, J.: Comparison and analysis of the eye pointing methods and applications. In: Pan, J.-S., Chen, S.-M., Nguyen, N.T. (eds.) ICCCI 2010, Part I. LNCS, vol. 6421, pp. 30–38. Springer, Heidelberg (2010)

8. Chynał, P., Szymański, J.M.: Remote Usability Testing Using Eye tracking. In: Campos, P., Graham, N., Jorge, J., Nunes, N., Palanque, P., Winckler, M. (eds.) INTERACT 2011, Part I. LNCS, vol. 6946, pp. 356–361. Springer, Heidelberg (2011)
9. San Agustin, J., Skovsgaard, H., Mollenbach, E., Barret, M., Tall, M., Hansen, D.W., Hansen, J.P.: Evaluation of a low-cost open-source gaze tracker. In: Proceedings of the 2010 Symposium on Eye-Tracking Research & Applications, ETRA 2010, Austin, Texas, March 22 - 24, pp. 77–80. ACM, New York (2010)
10. San Agustin, J., Skovsgaard, H., Hansen, J.P., Hansen, D.W.: Low-cost gaze interaction: ready to deliver the promises. In: Proceedings of the 27th International Conference Extended Abstracts on Human Factors in Computing Systems, CHI EA 2009, Boston, MA, USA, pp. 4453–4458. ACM, New York (2009)
11. Rayner, K., Rotello, C.M., Stewart, A.J.: Integrating text and pictorial information: eye movements when looking at print advertisements. Journal of Experimental Psychology: Applied 7(3), 219–226 (2001)
12. Rayner, K., Miller, B., Rotello, C.M.: Eye Movements When Looking at Print Advertisements: The Goal of the Viewer Matters. Appl. Cogn. Psychol. 22(5), 697–707 (2008)
13. Li, M., Song, Y., Lu, S., Zhong, N.: The Layout of Web Pages: A Study on the Relation between Information Forms and Locations Using Eye-Tracking. In: Liu, J., Wu, J., Yao, Y., Nishida, T. (eds.) AMT 2009. LNCS, vol. 5820, pp. 207–216. Springer, Heidelberg (2009)
14. Nielsen, J., Pernice, K.: Eyetracking Web Usability. Pearson, Berkeley (2010)
15. Jakob, N.: F-Shaped Pattern For Reading Web Content. Jakob Nielsen's Alertbox (2006), http://www.useit.com/alertbox/reading_pattern.html
16. Jang, J.-S.R., Sun, C.-T., Mizutani, E.: Neuro-Fuzzy and Soft Computing: A computational approach to learning and machine intelligence. Matlab Curriculum Series. Prentice Hall (1997)
17. Sobecki, J., Babiak, E., Słanina, M.: Application of Hybrid Recommendation in Web-Based Cooking Assistant. In: Gabrys, B., Howlett, R.J., Jain, L.C. (eds.) KES 2006. LNCS (LNAI), vol. 4253, pp. 797–804. Springer, Heidelberg (2006)
18. Akerkar, R., Sajja, P.: Knowledge-Based Systems. Jones & Bartlett Learning (2010)
19. Guillaume, S.: Designing Fuzzy Inference Systems from Data: An Interpretability-Oriented Review. IEEE Transactions on Fuzzy Systems 9(3), 426–443 (2001)

Beyond Satisfaction Questionnaires:
"Hacking" the Online Survey

Andrea L. Evans

Oracle, Middleware User Experience, Redwood Shores, CA, USA
andrea.evans@oracle.com

Abstract. This paper presents a practical method of using online survey tools to gather formative user feedback on UI designs and interactions. It describes how online survey tools have been used to administer both unmoderated cognitive walkthroughs and progressive comparisons among colors in screen mockups. It also details the process by which an online survey tool has been used to allow the off-label ability to gather rich clickstream data: number, location and chronological order of clicks.

1 Introduction

As used throughout this paper, the term "hacks" indicates only that the survey tool is being used in a non-traditional way that is supported but not advertised. The survey tool itself is not modified in any manner.

1.1 Online Survey Tools

An ever-increasing number and variety of survey tools are available online: so many that a comprehensive review of their features and pricing models is beyond the scope of this paper. Fortunately for the researcher on a budget, many online survey tools have a free version, which is limited by time or functionality.

Even the free versions of survey tools can be used for other usability activities beyond standard questionnaires, which typically gather demographic information, satisfaction ratings, wishlists of desired features, or lists of pain points.

All the survey tool uses described in this paper are illustrated with real life examples from past user research activities conducted at Oracle, and they all have one aspect in common: the use of screenshots. The good news is that even free survey tools often allow images to be uploaded.

1.2 Content Hacks

Content hacking is the simpler of the two forms of survey tool hack, since no programming knowledge is required.

Two different categories of content hacks will be discussed below: design comparisons, and unmoderated cognitive walkthroughs.

A. Marcus (Ed.): DUXU/HCII 2013, Part I, LNCS 8012, pp. 222–231, 2013.

1.3   Software Hacks

Software hacks are more advanced, since as well as requiring the online survey tool to display static screenshots, they also require JavaScript and image maps to create interactive regions in the screenshot and capture click data from them. The section on interactive images will describe this procedure in detail.

Other practitioners, such as Tullis [1] have hacked online survey tools before: Tullis hacked SurveyGizmo [2] to gather task success and task time, as well as more usual ratings and comments. The hacks described in this paper differ from previously published hacks by capturing number, location, and chronological order of clicks.

2   Design Comparisons

As the name suggests, design comparisons are activities aimed at making cognitively straightforward choices between two or more alternative designs.

When presenting design mockups or screenshots to non-employees in situations where a confidential disclosure agreement cannot be obtained, it is crucial to keep these images as generic as possible, to avoid disclosure of proprietary information.

2.1   Simple Comparisons

Simple comparisons present static screenshots of two or more design alternatives and ask the participant to choose between them. The choice can be one of nonspecific, overall preference ("Which do you like better?"), or more targeted preference (e.g.; "Which is cleaner?" "Which is more modern?"), or, as in the case below, it can be a choice that shows how the participant interprets the meaning of the design.

Screenshots of two application pages (one containing an editable table and one containing a read-only table), were presented side by side on the same screen for ease of comparison, and a radio button question asked:

Which of These Pages Contains an Editable Table?

- Page A
- Page B
- Both pages
- Neither page
- Not sure

It is essential to randomize presentation order of screenshots, to avoid order effects. It is also vital to include all possible responses when writing response options.

2.2   Progressive Comparisons

Progressive comparisons are suitable for deciding among several alternative designs which vary along a single continuum by subtle degrees.

Unlike simple comparisons, which require only that the online survey tool can display static images, progressive comparisons also require that the tool has branch logic, which sends participants to different pages of the survey, depending on which answer they gave on the previous page.

Preliminary user feedback on the design of a released product had stated that the current background was "too dark". However, it was unknown how much lighter the background needed to be, to meet user approval. As a result, five mockups were evaluated. Their backgrounds were lighter than the current background, by very slightly different amounts.

Mockups were presented in pairs, because the differences in color were so subtle it was unrealistic to expect accurate comparisons if mockups were on different pages of the survey. Pairs of mockups varied systematically in the amount of difference between their backgrounds. The branch logic feature of the online survey tool was used to show progressively smaller differences within each pair of mockups.

First of all, to confirm the previous user feedback, the first page of the survey showed only the current design and asked:

What Do You Think about the Background Color of This Page?

- It's too light
- It's OK
- It's too dark

Then subsequent survey pages all showed pairs of mockups. Mockups varied very subtly in lightness: either 1, 2, 3, 4 or 5 steps lighter than the current design. All participants started off with the pair 1 & 5 (or 5 & 1: order of mockups varied on each page to prevent order effects). For each pair of mockups, participants were asked:

Which Background Do You Prefer?

- I prefer the first background
- I prefer the second background
- They both look about the same

Out of the 1 & 5 pair, if participants preferred 1, the next pair they saw was 1 & 4. If they preferred 5, the next pair they saw was 2 & 5. And so on, with each subsequent pair narrowing progressively in difference, by a single step each time. As soon as the participant said both members of a pair looked about the same, the survey ended.

Because of this progressively narrowing structure, there were large variations in the numbers of participants who saw specific pairs of mockups. Everyone saw the pair with the largest difference, but very few people saw any of the pairs which differed by only 1 step (1 & 2, 2 & 3, 3 & 4 or 4 & 5).

One way of comparing sizes of difference in preference across different pairs of mockups, is to calculate a score which is weighted to account for the large variations in the number of participants who see different pairs of mockups. The weighted preference score for each pair of mockups is the difference between the size of the preference for the more popular mockup in the pair, vs. the number of participants who couldn't distinguish between the mockups in the pair. The formula is

$$(P-S)*N/T \tag{1}$$

P = Preference size (= **M-L**)
M = number preferring the More popular mockup in that pair
L = number preferring the Less popular mockup in that pair
S = No Preference size (number thinking both mockups in that pair were the Same)
N = Number who saw that pair of mockups (= **M+L+S**)
T = Total participants

Usually, the greater the actual difference between members of a pair, the greater the weighted preference score. A negative score means that more participants couldn't see a difference between members of a pair, than could see a difference.

3   Unmoderated Cognitive Walkthroughs

Unmoderated cognitive walkthroughs – which use mockups and onscreen instructions to take the participant step by step through tasks [3] – are simple to implement in online survey tools, in the sense that they only require the online survey tool to display static images (though, as with design comparisons, the images must be kept generic if presented without a nondisclosure agreement).

However, unmoderated cognitive walkthroughs are complex in the sense that great care must be taken in the writing of the accompanying text. Question text must present each stage of the task in a manner that approximates as closely as possible the experience of working with live code, and the response options must be carefully crafted to cover all relevant alternatives.

Next are two examples of how online survey tools were used to walk participants through simple tasks.

3.1   Deciding on a Stateful or Stateless Selection Model

It was strongly believed that users would prefer a stateful selection model over a stateless model in places such as multi-tabbed dialogs; that users would expect their selections to persist as they navigate among tabs, even when they did not click an Apply button before changing tabs.

This question could be addressed by a standard questionnaire that simply asks participants about their preferences for selection persistence. However that approach has the problem that people do not always have perfect insight into, or memory of, their own work practices.

To avoid this problem, an online survey was used to walk participants through a sequence of screenshots with appropriate callouts, and then ask them for what they would expect to happen after the last screenshot in the sequence.

Imagine Yourself Interacting with the Following Three Screens, Then Choose Which Outcome You Would Prefer

Initially, the First Checkbox is Not Checked

Now, you Have Checked the First Checkbox

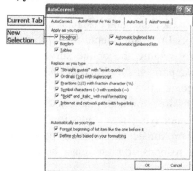

Now, you Have Switched Immediately to a Different Tab

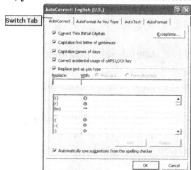

If you Switched Back to the Previous Tab, Which Would you Prefer to See?

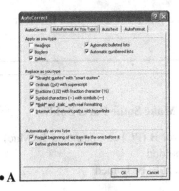

• A   • B

Presentation order of the last two images was randomized, to prevent order effects. Responses were restricted to a simple binary choice, because the only difference between the two options was whether or not a single checkbox was checked. In this specific case, it would not have been of much benefit to include an "I don't know" or "Other" option, because the possible responses were so restricted.

3.2 Evaluating the Usability of a Preliminary Design

Another online survey was run with early-stage design mockups. For each mockup, participants were asked how they would expect to interact with it to perform simple tasks. Two questions from this survey are below. Both questions were asked about the same screenshot.

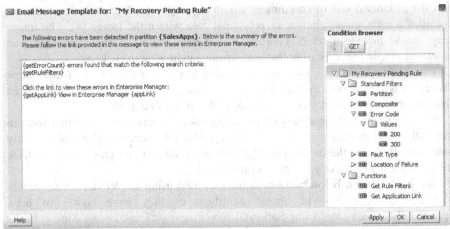

What do you expect will happen if you click on 200?

- errorCode=200 will be inserted in the message
- 200 will be inserted in the message

- errorCode=200 will be inserted in the empty field at the top of the Condition Browser
- 200 will be inserted in the empty field at the top of the Condition Browser
- Nothing will happen
- I don't know
- Other: [   ]

How Would You Edit the Message Text to Make Some Parts Bold?

- Select the text to be bolded and press Control-B (PC) or Command-B (Mac)
- Type <b> </b> tags around the text to be bolded
- Type <strong> </strong> tags around the text to be bolded
- I don't know
- Other: [   ]

These examples attempted to include all relevant response alternatives. Each question also included both an "I don't know" option, and an "Other" option. The "Other" option is particularly important, in case a response alternative exists which was not apparent to the survey author. If the online survey tool allows, it is best to set permissions so that if a participant selects the "Other" option, they are required to enter text in the accompanying text box.

4   Interactive Images

This is the only type of hack that requires any coding knowledge: specifically enough JavaScript to show alert popups and capture clicks from image maps. An image map is a list of labeled sets of coordinates within a <map> tag. Each set of coordinates specifies a rectangular, circular or polygonal area within the image [4]. The image map should include a set of coordinates for each control in the screenshot, and anywhere else in the screenshot that participants might want to click.

The interactive images hack is an off-label usage of survey tools. Most online survey tools – especially the free ones – do not advertise the ability to capture clicks from an image. But this doesn't always mean that it can't be done.

If, on inspection of the survey tool's image upload function, you find that you can manually insert an <img> tag into the survey, where the survey tool would normally automatically insert the image, then the odds are good that you may be able to hack the survey tool and make your images interactive.

The hacks shown below were both implemented using the Vovici online survey tool (vovici.com). With minor modifications they have both also been successfully implemented using SurveyGizmo (surveygizmo.com). Similar hacks should be possible in other survey tools that allow you to insert JavaScript, upload images, and use hidden questions.

Although this is the most demanding type of hack to implement, the result is a much higher fidelity experience than is possible with static images. With a thorough image map, it is possible to collect rich clickstream data, and for the participant the experience is not far short of interacting with a coded prototype.

4.1   Number of Attempts to Accomplish a Task

As well as an image map, this hack requires enough JavaScript knowledge to count clicks in correct and incorrect areas, and show alert popups which either warn that a click was incorrect, or show the total number of clicks taken to reach the correct area.

The JavaScript code for a simple demo of this functionality in Vovici is below.

To see this code in a working demo at Vovici, go to ow.ly/fRvWB

To see similar code in a working demo at SurveyGizmo, go to ow.ly/g5dar

In each working demo, use your browser's "View Source" feature to see the code.

```
<script type="text/javascript">var clickCount=0;function
planets(correct,planet)
{ clickCount++; if (correct)
   { alert("Correct! That took you " + clickCount + "
click(s)."); } else
   { alert("Incorrect: this is " + planet + "!"); }}
</script>
<p>
<map name="planets">
<area href="#" coords="68,186,6" shape="circle"
id="Mercury" onclick="planets(false,this.id)"/>
<area href="#" coords="101,180,12" shape="circle"
id="Venus" onclick="planets(false,this.id)"/>
<area href="#" coords="136,178,10" shape="circle"
id="Earth" onclick="planets(false,this.id)"/>
<area href="#" coords="175,175,8" shape="circle"
id="Mars" onclick="planets(false,this.id)"/>
<area href="#" coords="223,169,27" shape="circle"
id="Jupiter" onclick="planets(true,this.id)"/>
<area href="#" coords="285,170,14" shape="circle"
id="Saturn" onclick="planets(false,this.id)"/>
<area href="#" coords="357,160,15" shape="circle"
id="Uranus" onclick="planets(false,this.id)"/>
<area href="#" coords="449,154,11" shape="circle"
id="Neptune" onclick="planets(false,this.id)"/>
<area href="#" coords="513,142,4" shape="circle"
id="Pluto" onclick="planets(false,this.id)"/>
<img border="0"
src="/AppData/1885224700/users/256801141/User%20Media/
planets.png" usemap="#planets" />
</map>
```

4.2   Location and Chronological Order of Clicks

This hack is a direct expansion of the previous one, both in functionality and in the survey tool features required for its implementation. As well as the ability to insert JavaScript and an image map, this hack also requires that the online survey tool has hidden questions. Although hidden questions are not rendered in the survey UI, they can still be used to capture data from another question.

This hack uses a hidden question to capture the chronological order and location of each click. The location of each click is gathered in an array which has been added to the JavaScript [5]. The order of entry of locations into the array preserves the chronological order of clicks, and the full set of click locations in chronological order is passed into the hidden question after the participant clicks on the correct location.

The full JavaScript code for a simple demo of this functionality is below.

To see this code in a working demo at Vovici, go to ow.ly/aYLOU

To see similar code in a working demo at SurveyGizmo, go to ow.ly/g5dez

The hidden question is not hidden in the demo, so you can see the contents of the array.

```
<script type="text/javascript">var clickCount=0;var
clickArray=new Array;function planets(correct,planet)
{ clickCount++; clickArray.push(planet); if (correct)
{  document.getElementById("Q1").value=clickArray;  alert
("Correct! That took you " + clickCount + "
click(s)."); } else {  alert("Incorrect: this is " +
planet + "!"); }}
</script>
<p>
<map name="planets"><area href="#" coords="68,186,6"
shape="circle" id="Mercury"
onclick="planets(false,this.id)" />
<area href="#" coords="101,180,12" shape="circle"
id="Venus" onclick="planets(false,this.id)" />
<area href="#" coords="136,178,10" shape="circle"
id="Earth" onclick="planets(false,this.id)" />
<area href="#" coords="175,175,8" shape="circle"
id="Mars" onclick="planets(false,this.id)" />
<area href="#" coords="223,169,27" shape="circle"
id="Jupiter" onclick="planets(true,this.id)" />
<area href="#" coords="285,170,14" shape="circle"
id="Saturn" onclick="planets(false,this.id)" />
<area href="#" coords="357,160,15" shape="circle"
id="Uranus" onclick="planets(false,this.id)" />
<area href="#" coords="449,154,11" shape="circle"
id="Neptune" onclick="planets(false,this.id)" />
<area href="#" coords="513,142,4" shape="circle"
id="Pluto" onclick="planets(false,this.id)" />
```

```
<!--hack to stop Vovici corrupting img tag is to break it
over two lines--><img
border="0" src="/AppData/1885224700/users/256801141/User%
20Media/planets.png" usemap="#planets" /></map></p>
```

This code shows the type of workaround that is often necessary when hacking an online survey tool. In this case, unlike in the previous example, Vovici corrupted the `<img>` tag, and the code would not run unless the `<img>` tag was broken over two lines. This is very nonstandard behavior, as HTML should always be whitespace-agnostic.

5   Conclusion

These examples, all drawn from real life applications of online survey tools, show how such tools can be used to gather data beyond the scope of satisfaction polls and other standard types of questionnaire.

Online survey tools can be used to walk participants through a sequence of task steps and gather formative usability feedback about interaction behaviors, subtle differences in look and feel, and other facets of UI designs.

With an entry-level knowledge of JavaScript and image maps, online survey tools can sometimes be used to capture rich clickstream data, even when the survey tool providers themselves give no hint that such things are possible.

References

1. Tullis, T.: Creating an Online Study with SurveyGizmo,
   http://www.measuringux.com/SurveyGizmo.htm
2. Tullis, T.: "Rolling Your Own" Online Usability Study,
   http://www.measuringux.com/RollingYourOwnOnlineStudy.ppt
3. Polson, P.G., Lewis, C., Rieman, J., Wharton, C.: Cognitive Walkthroughs: A Method for Theory-based Evaluation of User Interfaces. International Journal of Man-Machine Studies 36(5), 741–773 (1992)
4. McDaniel, A.: HTML5 Your visual blueprint™ for designing rich web pages and applications, p. 349. Wiley, Hoboken (2011)
5. Wright, T.: Learning JavaScript: A Hands-On Guide to the Fundamentals of Modern JavaScript. Addison-Wesley, Upper Saddle River (2012)

A Component-Based Evaluation Protocol for Clinical Decision Support Interfaces

Alessandro Febretti[1], Karen Dunn Lopez[2], Janet Stifter[2], Andrew E. Johnson[1], Gail M. Keenan[2], and Diana J. Wilkie[2]

[1] Department of Computer Science, College of Engineering,
University of Illinois at Chicago (UIC), USA
[2] Department of Health Systems Science, College of Nursing, UIC, USA
febret@gmail.com

Abstract. In this paper we present our experience in designing and applying an evaluation protocol for assessing usability of a clinical decision support (CDS) system. The protocol is based on component-based usability testing, cognitive interviewing, and a rigorous coding scheme cross-referenced to a component library. We applied this protocol to evaluate alternate designs of a CDS interface for a nursing plan of care tool. The protocol allowed us to aggregate and analyze usability data at various granularity levels, supporting both validation of existing components and providing guidance for targeted redesign.

Keywords: component-based testing, cognitive interviewing, user-centric design, healthcare interfaces.

1 Introduction

Clinical Decision Support systems (CDSs) are software tools designed to support decision making in the clinical setting and facilitate the practice of evidence-based healthcare. CDSs have traditionally consisted of alerts and guidelines based on randomized clinical trials, systematic reviews and other sources of evidence. More recently developed CDSs are based on the characteristics of an individual patient that are matched to an electronic knowledge base and health record, to provide healthcare personnel with just-in-time, patient-specific recommendations.

The use of electronic health records in general and clinical decision support systems in particular has the potential of greatly improving care quality, but the adoption rate of these tools in the United States has been lower than expected. One of the main reasons for this delay is the lack of efficiency and usability of available systems [1].

Most CDS research and systems focus on identifying what information to show to users, but little has been done to find how to present complex patient data to support efficient decision making. Performing usability testing in the context of CDS design is therefore fundamental. CDS systems should drive healthcare

A. Marcus (Ed.): DUXU/HCII 2013, Part I, LNCS 8012, pp. 232–241, 2013.

personnel towards effective and targeted actions to improve patient outcomes. Poorly designed CDS features may confuse the user and lead to longer response times. Nursing staff often have strict time constraints and may also choose to ignore CDS features that are not easily accessible, or that do not provide clear information. Worse yet, inconsistent CDS features may drive healthcare personnel into making wrong decision about the patient's care.

Given the variety of forms in which clinical information can be transformed and presented, the overall organization of user testing is highly complex. For example, a single user may be exposed to multiple prototypes of the overall system, each one showing variants and compositions of CDS features in order to determine what is the best (i.e. fastest and clearest) interface. As the interface evolves and new evidence arises from practice or literature, features may be added, removed or redesigned and then evaluated in a new testing cycle.

In this paper we present a protocol that applies the principles of component-specific usability testing, quantitative content analysis and cognitive interviewing to the evaluation of a prototype CDS interface. The protocol has been applied to support the design of the next generation Hands-on Automated Nursing Data System (HANDS). In particular, we wanted to assess the accessibility, interpretability, satisfaction and value-to-practice of distinct CDS artifacts embedded in the interface. We wanted to compare variants of those artifacts across all those metrics. And we wanted to evaluate different compositions of those artifacts in the prototype.

2 Related Work

Usability testing of electronic health record (EHR) interfaces is not new and has been applied both for personal and clinical interfaces [2], [3]. Beyond usability capturing practice-based and literature-based evidence for CDS interfaces, it is also critically important to evaluate how the integration of this evidence into EHRs affects professional and organization practices [2].

Similar work has also been done in the context of CDS [4], but most of the work evaluates interfaces as a whole, have a priori defined tasks or do not consider compositional variations of multiple interface features. For these reasons, they typically lack a quantitative analysis of user response to specific features within the interface.

In [5], the authors underscore how traditional usability tests that capture usability for the application as a whole are less effective at capturing the inherent interaction between application components: evaluating the overall usability of an application also cannot inform the selection of right components, their composition into a system and the analysis of their value which includes human-factor issues.

A component-based testing methodology can drive the development of modular, usable interface artifacts for future use and helps in determining whether, for instance, the user interface provided by the various components do not rely on conflicting mental models. Our work represents a practical example of iterative, component-based testing applied in the context of CDS systems.

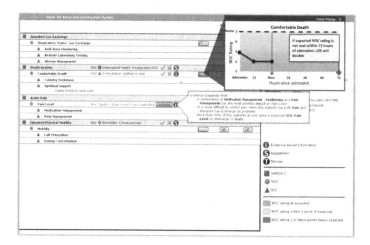

Fig. 1. An example of HANDS interface enriched with clinical decision support features. Shown here are quick actions, outcome trend charts with annotations, and evidence-based information tooltips.

3   Context: The HANDS System

The need for a component based evaluation protocol was driven by the need to integrate CDS into HANDS [6]. HANDS is an electronic tool that nurses use across time to enter data and track the patient's clinical history within a care setting, such as a hospital. A hospitalization includes all plans of care that nurses document at every formal handoff (admission, shift-change update, or discharge). HANDS uses a standardized nomenclature to describe diagnoses, outcomes and interventions.

Nursing diagnoses are coded with NANDA-I terms[7], outcomes are coded using terms and rating scales from the Nursing Outcomes Classification (NOC)[8], and interventions are coded with terms from the Nursing Intervention Classification (NIC)[9].

3.1   End-of-Life CDS

Of the 60 billion of Medicare dollars spent each year on care of the dying, $300 million are spent during the last month of life, including many millions for inappropriate treatments provided to hospitalized patients [10].

Until now, not enough standardized nursing care data was available, making it impossible to develop a set of CDS benchmarks that could be used to guide nursing actions for end-of-life patients. Recently, the HANDS system has been successfully used over a two-year period on 8 acute care units in 4 Midwestern hospitals, accounting for more than 40,000 patient care episodes. Data mining and statistical analysis on those episodes of care identified a set of benchmarks that related to end-of-life pain management and death anxiety. For instance, specific interventions, like patient positioning, were statistically more likely to achieve desired pain outcomes; pain control achieved at 24 hours predicted pain levels for the entire stay; and dealing with family coping in younger patients helped reduce death anxiety. These findings allowed us to prepare 6 distinct evidence-based-information (EBI) components that we wanted to add to the HANDS interface.

We therefore wanted to develop an evaluation protocol that would allow us to:

- Assess the interpretation, accessibility and value-to-practice characteristics of single CDS features
- Evaluate the effectiveness of feature compositions into full prototypes
- Track the evolution of features at different stages of the design

4   Methodology

Our proposed evaluation protocol is defined by three major elements: a component library, a user interview protocol and a data coding scheme.

4.1   Component Library

To effectively analyze usability data it is fundamental to keep track of CDS and non-CDS component versioning and composition. To address this challenge we developed a component library that associates unique names to components, lets the researchers visualize their different versions and track which version is used in which prototype. Figure 2 shows an example of a component library.

4.2   User Interview Protocol

User interviews are divided in two parts. During the first part of the interview, the user is introduced to the patient care scenario (in our context, an end-of-life patient history and current status). The user is then presented with the first of a series of prototypes exposing a set of pre-selected components and instructed to "think-aloud" as they interact with them.

It is important to underscore here that the user is not assigned to complete a specific task. Our users are health care professionals: we want them to take reasonable actions on the interface, depending on the patient status, history and on the presented CDS information. Defining tasks *a priori* is challenging and less meaningful in this context. We therefore take task completion to correspond to users verbally 'committing' their actions. For instance, after reading the patient information and CDS, and modifying the plan of care, the user could say he has done what was needed and is ready to move to the next patient. During this part of the interview, the user may go through multiple prototype versions.

Component / prototype matrix

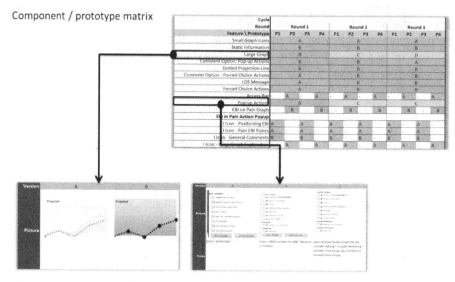

Component version database

Fig. 2. An example of a component library. The summary matrix identifies components used for each prototype iteration. Component names are linked to a database of images and notes, to simplify recalling the evolution of each feature.

Before each version, the prototype is reset to its initial state, and a few components are switched to different versions or turned on/off completely. The composition of features into tested prototypes depends on which research questions we wish to address for a group of subjects.

During the second part of the interview, the interviewer performs a cognitive interview [11], reviewing their actions, investigating why specific paths in the interface were taken (or not) and eliciting additional responses about interpretability and value to practice of CDS features.

4.3   Data Coding Scheme

Meaningful information is extracted from the interview using a qualitative approach. Qualitative analysis is advantageous in our setting, since it allows an expert reviewer to analyze the full context of user actions and utterances [12], [13]. In particular we are interested in evaluating the meaningfulness of user interaction (i.e., users correctly interpret presented evidence and take appropriate actions), levels of user confusion over specific components, or their considerations over the significance or display of information in the interface. A disadvantage of qualitative analysis is its subjectivity. Different reviewers may code user behavior in different ways, or the same reviewer may be inconsistent in interpreting it. The first problem can be mitigated by implementing inter-rater reliability practices as part of the protocol [14]. The second is addressed by the rigorous definition of a coding scheme.

For component-based CDS interface evaluation, we propose coding based on linking codes to components: Each code in the scheme identifies a unique component, as described in the component library. Therefore, each appearance of a code marks some meaningful user activity associated to a specific component. Codes are enriched with additional information: a category that identifies the type of user activity (accessibility, interpretation, or comments on component value or pleasantness); a three-category score (positive, negative, unclear); a component version and prototype identifier; and an optional comment by the reviewer that further defines the activity.

As an example, consider the following user activity with a 'chart' component in a nursing plan of care interface. A nurse tries to click on the chart and is surprised when nothing happens. After realizing the chart is static, she goes on and correctly interprets the information presented by the chart. Before moving on, she mentions that although she likes the chart she does not think her colleagues would use that in practice, since they are more used to simple tables. In our protocol a reviewer would code the previous activity using the four markers shown in Table 1.

Table 1. Markers used in the charting activity example

Component type	Category	Score	Prototype Id
Chart	Accessibility	Unclear	1
Chart	Interpretation	Positive	1
Chart	Likability	Positive	1
Chart	Value	Negative	1

A valuable feature of this coding scheme is that, while extracting data in a qualitative (but rigorous) manner, it supports quantitative analysis on interface components. The coding scheme is generic enough to allow for a great amount of flexibility in possible research questions. It also supports exploratory analysis of recording data, when researchers have no a priori theory to validate. Moreover, it allows the aggregation of multiple component scores into bigger modules to change the granularity of the analysis. The presence of reviewer comments allows for qualitative analysis of specific findings when needed.

5   Experiment

As mentioned in section 0, this protocol was implemented to test the introduction of CDS features into a prototype of the HANDS system. This is an ongoing research project. The total number of CDS features developed at the time of publication is 6. Together with ancillary user interface elements that we wanted to evaluate, we had a total of 16 distinct components, possibly with multiple versions each (up to 4).

We recruited a total of 25 nurses in different age groups, years of experience and education levels. We ran 4 interview rounds. Each pair of rounds was considered part of a design cycle: in each cycle we tested the introduction of EBI features relative to a specific end-of-life issue. The first cycle addressed EBIs related to pain, the second addressed pain and death anxiety. Minor prototype redesign were carried out between rounds in the same cycle. New components and major redesign of existing ones happened between the cycles based on component-specific usability data analysis.

Users were introduced to a fictional end-of-life patient that was assigned to their shift. The patient history, demographics and current plan of care were designed to elicit the activation of the CDS features that we wanted to test. Users were presented with a prototype of the plan of care interface. Once they considered their actions on the plan of care satisfactory, they would be presented with a new prototype: the initial patient plan of care would stay the same but some of the interface components would be switched to different versions.

The users were instructed to 'rewind' and observe this patient again through the interface, as if it was a new patient. We tested four prototype variations for each user. The order in which the prototypes were presented to the users was randomized. Cognitive interviewing would then be performed, and users were asked to choose their most and least favorite prototype versions before ending the interview.

6   Results

For the purpose of this paper we will present an example of analysis from our second design cycle. During this cycle we interviewed 15 users, collecting a total of ~1600 markers. Qualitative data analysis was performed by 4 separate reviewers. Inter-rater reliability was established through a tutorial coding run, and then by separately coding and comparing about 25 minutes of interview data. Coding agreement was measured at 80%. Most disagreement was represented by differing use of the negative and unclear scores.

The coded data were extracted from the coding software (Morae [15]) and preprocessed to extract data fields. The data were then pivoted / aggregated along several dimensions to perform analysis.

For instance, aggregating data by interview section along the user-id dimension, allowed us to perform a quick assessment of the data quality. Most subjects were coded consistently, except for two for which we collected a below average number of codes (3.5% compared to 7% average). Aggregating by component id along the prototype-id dimension was used to generate a component 'heat-map' (Figure 3) that could be used to quickly identify areas of interest for analysis.

Aggregating data by component along the score dimension provided an overview of score distributions for each component. This process allows us to quickly identify issues with specific components with high percentages of negative or unclear scores. For instance, one of our CDS features (a popup message related to pain management) had a low positive score of 25% (over 63 total component activations). Through the pivot table, we easily 'zoomed into' this specific component, to split percentages by category (Figure 5). We then assessed that the problem was not related to the component usability (i.e., finding and opening the popup), but interpretation scores were very low (16% positive).

Count of Event Row Labels	Column Labels Cognitive Interview	Prototype 1	Prototype 2	Prototype 3	Prototype 4	Grand Total
A (Pop-up Actions)	5.08%	11.38%	10.33%	11.35%	11.85%	9.21%
B (Dotted Projection Line)	2.26%	1.72%	0.47%	1.77%	0.74%	1.58%
C (Forced Choice Actions)	13.56%	13.79%	15.02%	15.96%	7.41%	13.18%
E (EBI – Under Red Flashing Alert)	8.10%	0.00%	3.29%	0.35%	0.37%	3.28%
F (Flashing Alert)	3.01%	6.90%	13.15%	14.54%	15.19%	9.21%
G (Gold Star)	3.01%	1.03%	0.00%	0.00%	1.11%	1.39%
H (I Icon - EBI Pain)	7.72%	2.76%	0.00%	2.84%	2.59%	4.04%
I (I icon - General Comments)	1.88%	3.79%	1.41%	4.96%	1.48%	2.65%
J (Mini POC)	1.69%	0.69%	1.41%	0.71%	0.37%	1.07%
K (Palliative Consult)	1.32%	0.00%	0.47%	0.71%	0.00%	0.63%
L (LOS Message)	5.27%	2.07%	0.47%	1.77%	3.70%	3.15%
M (i Icon - Large Graph Explanation)	2.07%	0.00%	1.88%	0.00%	1.48%	1.20%
N (I icon - EBI Positioning)	2.45%	1.03%	0.00%	2.13%	0.00%	1.39%
O (Field Notes/Observation)	6.59%	6.55%	2.82%	6.03%	6.30%	5.93%
P (Preliminary Design Ideas)	5.27%	3.79%	2.82%	1.42%	3.70%	3.72%
Q (Static Information)	0.94%	6.21%	3.29%	3.55%	7.41%	3.78%
R (Large Graph)	5.65%	8.62%	8.92%	6.38%	11.11%	7.69%
S (Small Graph Icons)	0.75%	4.83%	9.86%	7.45%	7.41%	5.04%
T (NNN Icons)	1.51%	14.14%	7.98%	3.55%	4.44%	5.55%
U (Comments Option - Forced Choice Actions)	0.94%	0.34%	0.47%	1.06%	0.37%	0.69%
V (Change Recognition)	4.71%	4.48%	7.98%	7.80%	5.93%	5.86%
W (Long Access Bar)	1.88%	0.00%	1.88%	0.00%	1.85%	1.20%
X (Bug)	0.75%	2.41%	2.82%	2.13%	1.85%	1.77%
Y (Comments Option - Pop-up Actions)	2.64%	2.07%	1.88%	1.06%	1.85%	2.02%
Z (General Prototype Comments)	10.92%	1.38%	1.41%	2.48%	1.48%	4.79%

Fig. 3. A 'heat map' view of the marker data using conditional coloring on marker percentages. Through this view it is possible to quickly identify particularly active components. In this interview cycle we identified five main active components.

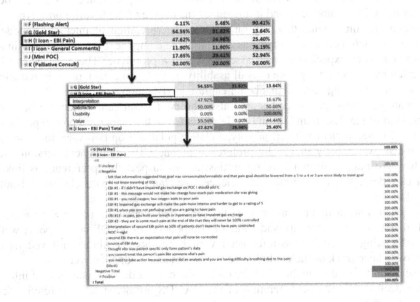

Fig. 4. Incremental zoom levels into the data

This means that the pain evidence we presented was formulated in an inconsistent or unclear way. We then further zoomed the view for negative scores, to access available reviewer comments and identify problem patterns across multiple users. Incrementally zooming into the data in this fashion was a very effective analysis tool. It allowed us to identify issues at a high level, hiding unnecessary information until needed.

Another fundamental tool for data analysis was the ability to quickly filter data along any dimension. It was used to identify hard-to-find or unused CDS components. One CDS feature in particular was not noticed by most users until the interviewer guided them to it during cognitive interview. We excluded the cognitive interview codes form the aggregate data: when users accessed this CDS component unassisted, they valued it positively (67%). For the next design cycle we then kept the content of this component, and moved to increase the likelihood of users accessing it.

7   Concluding Remarks

One issue we observed with this methodology is common to other component-based testing approaches. A usability assessment of single components does not automatically translate into an assessment of full interfaces. For instance, averaging likability scores for all the CDS features expose in a prototype did not necessarily lead to an estimate of overall prototype likability.

At the end of an interview we asked the user to choose most and least favorite versions of the HANDS CDS prototype. We observed that preference was usually tied to only one CDS component, and it influenced the choice of the favorite prototype.

Moreover, components that rely on different interpretation or interaction models may be considered clear or valuable as a stand-alone component but could result in an inconsistent user experience when assembled into a prototype. These issues can be mitigated by collecting separate overall usability or preference data, or by introducing markers in the coding scheme that better capture inter-component factors.

Regarding prototype preference, we also observed significant variability between users. During the design and testing cycle presented in this paper, no prototype out of the 4 tested was a clear winner: prototype choice polarized on two variations, and as mentioned, was mostly driven by preference of one CDS component version over another. We plan to further investigate this, as we suspect this preference is linked with user demographics (clinical experience, age, familiarity with electronic health record tools).

In conclusion, in its current version, the presented evaluation protocol performed well in assessing the usability and value of components of a CDS prototype. A well-defined coding scheme cross-referenced with a component library allowed us to effectively keep track of the evolution of prototypes and component versions.

The quantitative data gathered at the end of the current design cycle helped inform design decision for the next iteration of the HANDS prototype, and captured a few issues that did not emerge by inspection of prototypes, or by informal assessment of user performance. We plan to further use and validate this protocol in several future design and evaluation cycles of the HANDS CDS interface.

References

1. Belden, J., Grayson, R., Barnes, J.: Defining and testing EMR usability: Principles and proposed methods of EMR usability evaluation and rating. Healthcare Information and Management Systems Society, HIMSS (2009)
2. Haggstrom, D.A., Saleem, J.J., Russ, A.L., Jones, J., Russell, S.A., Chumbler, N.R.: Lessons learned from usability testing of the VA's personal health record. Journal of the American Medical Informatics Association: JAMIA 18(suppl. 1), i13–i17 (2011)
3. Hori, M., Kihara, Y., Kato, T.: Investigation of indirect oral operation method for think aloud usability testing. Human Centered Design, 38–46 (2011)
4. Cho, I., Staggers, N., Park, I.: Nurses' responses to differing amounts and information content in a diagnostic computer-based decision support application. Computers Informatics Nursing 28(2), 95–102 (2010)
5. Brinkman, W.-P., Haakma, R., Bouwhuis, D.G.: Component-Specific Usability Testing. IEEE Transactions on Systems, Man, and Cybernetics - Part A: Systems and Humans 38(5), 1143–1155 (2008)
6. Keenan, G., Yakel, E., Yao, Y.: Maintaining a Consistent Big Picture: Meaningful Use of a Web-based POC EHR System. International Journal of Nursing Knowledge (2012)
7. NANDA International, Nursing diagnoses: Definition and classification
8. Moorhead S, M.M.I., Johnson, M.: Outcomes Project. Nursing outcomes classification (NOC). Mosby (2004)
9. Dochterman, B.G., JM: Nursing interventions classification (NIC). Mosby (2004)
10. Zhang, B., Wright, A.: Health care costs in the last week of life: associations with end-of-life conversations. Archives of Internal Medicine (2009)
11. Beatty, P., Willis, G.: Research synthesis: The practice of cognitive interviewing. Public Opinion Quarterly (2007)
12. Patton, M.: Qualitative research & evaluation methods (2001)
13. Hsieh, H., Shannon, S.: Three approaches to qualitative content analysis. Qualitative Health Research (2005)
14. Armstrong, D., Gosling, A., Weinman, J., Marteau, T.: The place of inter-rater reliability in qualitative research: an empirical study. Sociology (1997)
15. Morae usability testing software from TechSmith,
    http://www.techsmith.com/morae.html

Human in the Loop: A Model to Integrate Interaction Issues in Complex Simulations

Stefano Filippi[1], Daniela Barattin[1], Francesco Ferrise[2], Monica Bordegoni[2], and Umberto Cugini[2]

[1] University of Udine - DIEGM Dept. - PIRG Group
Via delle Scienze 206, 33100 Udine, Italy
{filippi,daniela.barattin}@uniud.it
[2] Politecnico di Milano
Via La Masa 34, 20156 Milano
{francesco.ferrise,monica.bordegoni,umberto.cugini}@polimi.it

Abstract. Several activities of the product development process as for example ergonomic analyses, usability testing, and what is defined as User Experience - UX- design in general require humans to be involved as testers. In order to achieve a good effectiveness degree, these tests must be performed on prototypes as much as possible similar to the final product, and this is costly and sometimes difficult to obtain during the development process. This is especially true at the earliest stages of the process. Functional mock-up - FMU - methods and tools can be of great help, because they allow technological aspects of the products, as electronics, hydraulics, mechanics, etc. to be represented and managed in a simple and effective way. Mathematical equations allow product behavior to be determined, due to input values representing the application environment of the product. At the moment, an FMU model is great in simulating product behavior from the technological point of view, but concerns about user interaction issues are left apart. The research described in this paper aims at widening the coverage of FMU to user-product interaction issues. The goal aims at evaluating the possibility of substituting real users with a characterization of them, and to model and simulate interaction in a homogeneous way together with all the other product aspects. All of this makes the research activities very challenging, and the result is a sort of FMU-assisted interaction modeling. As an evolution of what is generally recognized as hardware and software-in-the-loop, this methodology will be referred as human-in-the-loop.

Keywords: Functional Mock-Up, Interaction, User Experience.

1   Introduction

Several activities during the product development process [1] require the involvement of real humans as testers. This is the case for example of ergonomic analyses that despite the recent interest toward the use of virtual humans in the industrial practice [2] still require some physical testing involving real users. It is also the case of any

A. Marcus (Ed.): DUXU/HCII 2013, Part I, LNCS 8012, pp. 242–251, 2013.

kind of usability testing [3], and what is defined as User Experience - UX - in general [4] especially concerning the testing of the emotional response of products. In order to achieve a good effectiveness degree, these tests must be performed on physical prototypes as much as possible similar to the final product, and this is costly and time-consuming [5]. This is especially true at the earlier stages of the process when only an idea of the product to-be is available.

Recent advances in virtual reality technologies and simulation algorithms suggest moving these testing activities from physical to virtual prototypes. Virtual prototypes can be used by humans through several sensory modalities, so as to reproduce the real interaction as best as possible. All these issues make real-time responses of simulation tools mandatory. Consequently, it comes out that simulation algorithms must be simplifications of the physical behavior of products, in order to be executed in real-time.

Functional mock-up - FMU - methods and tools can be of great help in this sense, because they allow technological aspects of the products, as electronics, hydraulics, mechanics, etc. to be represented and managed in a simple and effective way. Mathematical equations allow product behavior to be determined, due to input values representing the application environment of the product [6].

To date, FMU models have been used mainly to simulate the product behavior from the technological point of view. Mathematical descriptions of any kind of product components, from mechanical to control, are usually available in the FMU tools. However, less has been done for human behavior simulations. This implies that still the user must experience personally and physically the prototype when necessary, and this means a loss of time and higher costs by the companies. The challenge in simulating users is to be able to correctly predict all their possible behaviors, as a function of a certain phenomenon they must deal with. The user is not a machine that according to a given input always behaves in the same way. People have different needs and expectations concerning a product and they implement different ways to interact with it, according to their characteristics and abilities.

The research described in this paper aims at widening the coverage of FMU to user-product interaction issues. The goal is evaluating the possibility to substitute real users with a characterization of them, and to model and simulate interaction in a homogeneous way together with all the other product aspects. This aims at extending the concept of technological FMU to include interaction, in order to be able to simulate the characteristics and behavior of the user who turns out to be highly unpredictable and showing very different characteristics compared to the components of the current traditional FMU.

In this way real users are no longer required in the tests in which the FMU are involved, but their presence would be considered through the new component of the FMU dedicated to interaction.

All of this makes the research activities very challenging, and the result is a sort of FMU-assisted interaction modeling. As an evolution of what is generally recognized as hardware and software-in-the-loop, this methodology will be referred as human-in-the-loop.

The paper is structured as follows: Section 2 summarizes the main achievements in the field of virtual prototyping, focusing on the FMU tools; Section 3 describes the core activities of the research, the development of the FMU components devoted to interaction; Section 4 discusses the results and, finally, Section 5 draws the conclusions and plots some hints for future work.

2   Background

A mock-up, or prototype, is a product simulation used for a specific testing activity [5]. Several kinds of mock-ups or prototypes exist which are specifically built for different testing activities as for example product resistance, engineering performances, usability and UX, and they can be physical or virtual [7]. If the aim of the prototypes is to allow designers to test aspects concerning the product functionality, these are called Functional Mock-Up - FMU. Different tools exist that support the creation and use of Functional Mock-Ups. Modelica is a well-established language that allows the creation of technological FMU with particular attention to the models and simulation exchanges [8]. Modelica allows designers to simulate multi-physics and multi-domain problems in a unique environment. Many tools have been developed to simulate single, specific aspects of the product and they are currently used in the industrial practice (multi-body, FEM, etc.). More than often, product complexity requires many aspects to be simulated simultaneously; thus, recent researches aim at creating a standard FMU interface to allow different tools to communicate to each other [9]. Modelica-based tools do not still include simulations of the users in order to test the functioning of the products. In general, few human simulations are available; one example of them is used in testing the driving performance of cars. Another human simulation usually available is exploited in evaluating the thermal comfort in buildings. Anyway, these models are specifically built for companies and not generally available in open and commercial libraries. The research described in the paper aims at enlarging the domain of FMU to include the simulation of the human-machine interaction, applicable in a wide collection of situations and environments.

3   Activities

3.1   Definition of the FMU about Interaction

Real situations where user-product interactions happen are considered to highlight similarities with technological FMU. After that, the highlighted elements are analyzed and formally described, in order to make them suitable to be considered as part of future FMU.

Technological FMU simulate physical products. FMU about interaction - named hereafter FMUi - simulate the synergy between a user and a product during problem solving activities. This synergy is named situation here. Fifteen situations have been considered. Among them, there is the interaction with a photocell-driven door to access a security room, the management of the temperature in a room through a heater and the loudness control of radio equipment.

Technological FMU is made of blocks, corresponding to product components like valves, pumps, gears, etc. The predictable behavior of these components allows the corresponding mathematical equations to be defined and used in the simulation. Similarly, the FMUi should represent all the simple user-product interactions due to the user (unpredictable) and the product (predictable) behavior in every situation. Simple interaction is when only one action is involved (performed by the user or the product indifferently). For example, leveling the radio volume happens thanks to two simple interactions because the first action is to rotate the control knob (user) and the second is to change the volume level (product). Simple interactions are considered the blocks of the FMUi corresponding to the FMU ones.

FMUi blocks are characterized using two orthogonal dimensions. One sets the goal of the FMUi, the simulation of ergonomic vs. cognitive aspects. The second refers to the structure of the FMUi; it can be based on functions as for the technological ones but in some cases other formalisms, tools, etc. will be used for data processing. Once the nature of the FMUi blocks has been defined, it is the time to deal with their input, output, and structure, in order to perform a simulation of interaction as controlled and predictable as possible.

Input. The input of technological FMU is constituted by physical quantities, processed by flowing through the blocks simulating the product. These quantities are univocally measurable and this measurement is repeatable. All of this must be worth also for the FMUi. In order to simulate simple interactions, FMUi blocks need to know the characteristics that determine the user behavior, as well as the environmental conditions that could affect interaction.

User characteristics belong to three categories: ergonomics, skill and needs/expectations. Regarding the first one, height and sight are two examples, useful in dealing with the interaction with a photo-cell or with a display respectively. Memorability and dexterity are two examples belonging to the second category. They could be exploited in simulating the interaction with a teller machine (code to memorize and recall) or with a vending machine (accessibility of the delivered product). The last category could include the desired volume of a TV program or the type of linen and the ending time using a washing machine.

Thanks to this three-category characterization, users are described in the FMUi quantitatively and univocally, in order to be able to consider their description as repeatable in different situations.

Environmental conditions allow describing the context where the interaction takes place. They regard both the product itself (it is already described by the FMU but only from the technological point of view) and all the external elements it interacts with. Some examples are the height of a piece of furniture where a radio is placed on top, the color of a warning label and the darkness level in a room.

Since FMUi input is mainly related to user behavior, needs and expectations, its characterization is expressed using the user language. In this way, the generation of the FMUi can be seen as a co-design activity, where sample users are constructively involved. Consider for example the radio loudness control. Input will be the current level, the desired one and the maximum level allowed by the neighbors. Moreover, current noise level in the room must be considered. Measuring these parameters in decibel, especially the desired volume level and the room noise, would be scarcely useful because users do not get it. So, ranges are introduced. They are value intervals labeled in a user friendly way. For example, desired volume is represented by a four-value parameter: silent, corresponding to the interval 0 to 10 dB, whispers - 11 to 35 dB, talks - 36 to 65 dB and shouts - 66+ dB. In this way the user can directly associate the desired volume level to his/her need: hearing the actors' whispering in a movies, rather than having the TV set switched on just to hear some noise sometimes in the background.

Output. The output of the technological FMU is constituted by product performances evaluated thanks to the prototype. The FMUi output has a double-face nature.

From one hand, it has the same role and meaning as for the technological FMU. FMUi performances are the translation of user needs and expectations in order to make them measurable and comparable against target values. Considering again the example of the radio loudness, the output is the yes/no success of the volume leveling action performed by the user/product system given the surrounding conditions (users' and environmental).

From the other hand, FMUi output presents further aspects that mainly characterize the interaction in terms of evolution in time, and definitely distinguishes the FMUi from the technological FMU. FMUi blocks can generate numerical values, percentages, Boolean values, etc. that become known and available only at precise moments and thanks to precise interaction paths. These values can be used as input both for FMU and FMUi blocks and their timing and triggering conditions make them the personification of the simulation of interaction. For example, a FMUi block controlling the brakes of a car will generate as output both the yes/no flag of the pedal pressed and the current pressure in the braking system, available only if and when the pedal is pressed by a driver with specific characteristics and perceptions of the environment.

Structure. Technological FMU generate results starting from input data thanks to mathematical equations. Again, FMUi show the same characteristics from one hand, but they need more sophisticated tools in order to manage unpredictability and qualitative issues. If the output is a numeric value, mainly related to quantifications of ergonomic issues, etc., mathematical equations are involved. For example, if a FMUi block simulate the approaching of the user's hand/finger to the stop button riding a bus, the value indicating the distance between the hand/finger and the button is computed thanks to a mathematical equations based on anthropometric parameters (user's height, arm length, etc.). In case of Boolean or even more complex results, more articulated elaborations are required. They must be generic, repeatable and comparable as well. Results are obtained thanks to procedures exploiting logical expressions, conditional statements, etc. For example, consider a magnetic card lock system. Its interaction with the user can be simulated through an FMUi block that reads the card and opens the lock in case of success. The input is composed by the signal coming from the swipe sensor and the orientation of the card during the swiping action. The output consists of a success flag about the correct reading of the card and another value indicating the status of the lock (open/locked). The input and the statements used to compute the output are shown in table 1.

Table 1. Input and output of an FMUi block simulating a magnetic card lock system

INPUT	(Bool)swiping_in_progress, (Bool)card_orientation, (int)lock_number, (int)card_number

OUTPUT	(Bool)success(swiping_in_progress, card_orientation, lock_number, card_number)=
	 IF (swiping_in_progress AND card_orientation)
	 THEN
	     IF (lock_number=card_number) THEN success=1 ELSE success=0
	 ELSE
	     success=0

	(Bool)lock_status=NOT success

3.2   Experience in the Field

A first experience in the field has been conducted to test and validate the FMUi. The test case regards the hand washing using a faucet releasing water at a pleasant temperature thanks to a photo-cell, and with the temperature controlled by a notched knob. This situation counts on four simple interactions corresponding to the following FMUi blocks: B1 - hand positioning, B2 - automatic water release, B3 - water temperature evaluation and B4 - water temperature setting.

B1 - Hand Positioning. The user approaches the faucet with his/her hands. This action depends from user's height and washbasin dimensions. This block clearly refers to ergonomic issues and a simple function is enough to implement it. In this case the output is numeric but it does not represent a performance; on the contrary, it belongs to the category of output that characterizes interaction. In fact, the hand distance becomes known and available only if and when other interaction conditions happen (the approaching of a user showing specific characteristics). Table 2 summarizes the data processing inside block B1.

Table 2. Data processing in the FMUi block B1

INPUT	(cm)user_height, (cm)washbasin_height, (cm)washbasin_depth
OUTPUT	(cm)hand_distance(user_height, washbasin_height, washbasin_depth)= user_height-washbasin_height+wasbasin_depth

For example, a user 160cm tall, interacting with a washbasin placed one meter high from the floor and with a depth of 50cm (distance between the foremost surface and the wall), will have his hands 10cm far from the faucet.

B2 - Automatic Water Release. Given the distance of the user's hands from the faucet, the faucet can release the water or not. Here the only input is this distance. There is not any other variable, human or environmental, that could influence this action (except for hardware/system failure like water shortage, photo-cell breaks, etc., not managed here). Regarding the output, the water will flow only if the hands are less than 10cm far from the faucet. If yes, the temperature of the water spilling from the faucet is given. This value is known in the system because it corresponds to the aqueduct temperature at the beginning, and to the last use of the basing afterwards. So it is used both as input and output of this block. Otherwise, a N/A value is given. Table 3 shows the data processing in the FMUi block B2.

Table 3. Data processing in the FMUi block B2

INPUT	(cm)hand_distance, (°C)water_temperature
OUTPUT	(°C)water_temperature(hand_distance, water_temperature)=
	IF hand_distance<10
	THEN water_temperature=water_temperature
	ELSE water_temperature=N/A

B3 - Water Temperature Evaluation. This block simulates the user evaluation of the temperature of the water spilling from the faucet. The input consists of the current temperature and the user's desired one. It can have four values: scalding, hot, warm and cold. These are the four values used by the user to qualify the temperature using his/her language. They refer implicitly to the following intervals: equal or more than 50°C, 40°C to 49°C, 30°C to 39°C and less than 30°C.

Table 4 shows data processing in this block. Output consists of the success of the user evaluation and it also informs about the current water temperature in order to manage further iterations in case of success equal to 0.

Table 4. Data processing in the FMUi block B3

INPUT	(custom)water_temperature, (custom)user's_expectation
OUTPUT	(Bool)success(water_temperature, user's_expectation)=
	IF (water_temperature=user's_expectation)
	THEN success=1
	ELSE success=0
	(°C) water_temperature(water_temperature)=water_temperature

B4 - Water Temperature Setting. The last FMUi block focuses on the interaction between the user and the faucet, aimed at adjusting the water temperature. This block is involved in any case; if there is the need to adjust the temperature because the current one does not match the user's expectation some elaboration happens, otherwise no actions are taken. If the user feels uncomfortable with current temperature, he/she operates the knob to raise or lower it. In this case the input of the block corresponds to the knob change (number of notches), the success flag coming from the previous block and the water temperature. The output is the new water temperature, looped-back to the previous block for a new evaluation. The number of notches quantifying the user action determines the required variation in the water temperature. Each notch corresponds to two degrees Celsius. Table 5 shows the data processing inside the block B4.

Table 5. Data processing in the FMUi block B4

INPUT	(notches)knob_change, (°C)water_temperature, (Bool)success
OUTPUT	(°C)new_water_temperature(water_temperature, knob_change)=
	IF (success=0)
	THEN new_water_temperature=water_temperature+knob_change*2
	ELSE new_water_temperature=water_temperature

There is no success flag this time, because the action will be performed for sure and the outcome will be checked again in the block B3, as shown by the block layout in figure 1.

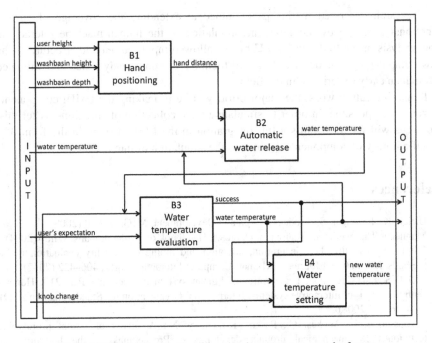

Fig. 1. FMUi simulating the interaction between a user and a faucet

4   Results and Discussion

The FMUi shown in Figure 1 simulates the interaction between a user and a washbasin currently installed in almost any public restroom. The input values can be changed as required by the prototyping situations. This model allows verifying different what-if situations and this satisfies the main reason for the FMU adoption. Regarding the pros, these early results show that user-product interaction can be simulated quite easily; moreover, the components used for this simulation appear to be compatible with technological FMU mainly because they have been generated just starting from these.

There are also some cons. FMUi blocks are scarce at the moment, regarding both the number and the definition refinement. They are too specific and the data processing suffers from two major drawbacks. The first refers to the discretization of the input values introduced by the ranges. These can determine lack of precision. Second, it is quite impossible to foresee - and consequently manage - all the combinations of input values and this could generate steady situations.

5   Conclusions

The research described in this paper aimed at extending the coverage of current functional mock-up by including the simulation of the human-machine interaction. The analysis of the traditional FMU blocks allowed input, output and structure of the new components to be defined. Some of them have been already tested and validated through an early experience in the field.

Regarding future work, the major effort will be in making the FMUi components as general as possible, in order to simulate a wide collection of situations. After this, the focus will move towards a full integration in the FMU, maybe in the form of a specific library of components devoted to the simulation of interaction.

References

1. Ulrich, K., Eppinger, S.: Product Design and Development. McGraw-Hill (2008)
2. Magnenat-Thalmann, N., Thalmann, D. (eds.): Handbook of virtual humans. Wiley (2004)
3. Filippi, S., Barattin, D.: Generation, adoption and tuning of usability evaluation multi-methods. International Journal of Human-Computer Interaction 28(6), 406–422 (2012)
4. ISO DIS 9241-210:2008. Ergonomics of human system interaction - Part 210: Human-centred design for interactive systems. International Organization for Standardization (ISO). Switzerland (2008)
5. Zorriassatine, F., Wykes, C., Parkin, R., Gindy, N.: A survey of virtual prototyping techniques for mechanical product development. Proceedings of the Institution of Mechanical Engineers, Part B: Journal of Engineering Manufacture 217(4), 513–530 (2003)

6. Ferrise, F., Bordegoni, M., Cugini, U.: Interactive Virtual Prototypes for testing the interaction with new products. Computer-Aided Design and Applications 10(3), 515–525 (2013)
7. Wang, G.G.: Definition and review of virtual prototyping. Journal of Computing and Information Science in Engineering(Transactions of the ASME) 2(3), 232–236 (2002)
8. Mattsson, S.E., Elmqvist, H., Otter, M.: Physical system modeling with Modelica. Control Engineering Practice 6(4), 501–510 (1998)
9. Blochwitz, T., Otter, M., Arnold, M., Bausch, C., Clauß, C., Elmqvist, H., Wolf, S.: The Functional Mockup Interface for Tool independent Exchange of Simulation Models. In: Modelica'2011 Conference, pp. 20–22 (2011)

Towards a Holistic Tool for the Selection and Validation of Usability Method Sets Supporting Human-Centered Design

Holger Fischer[1], Benjamin Strenge[1], and Karsten Nebe[2]

[1] University of Paderborn, C-LAB, Fuerstenallee 11, 33102 Paderborn, Germany
holger.fischer@c-lab.de, best@mail.upb.de
[2] Rhine-Waal University of Applied Sciences, Suedstraße 8, 47475 Kamp-Lintfort, Germany
karsten.nebe@hochschule-rhein-waal.de

Abstract. The establishment of human-centered design within system development processes is still a challenge. Numerous usability methods exist that aim to increase usability and user experience of a system. Nevertheless, the selection of appropriate methods remains to be difficult, as there exist many different factors that have a significant influence on the appropriateness of the methods in their context of use. This paper presents a new concept for the selection of usability methods. It focuses on a) the selection of appropriate usability methods with regard to their applicability in the various stages of system development and b) accounting for interdependencies between multiple methods by balancing them with respect to the usability dimensions effectiveness, efficiency and satisfaction.

Keywords: Human-Centered Design, Usability Engineering, Method Selection, Method Set Validation, ISO/TR 16982.

1 Introduction

Usability has been recognized as an important quality aspect in today's system development industry. However, the integration of usability activities and the establishment of human-centered design (HCD) as part of the development process is still a challenge. Therefore, various approaches have been developed to integrate usability activities in software development, e.g. [1], [2], [3], [4].

Today, many methods exist that aim on an increase of the system's usability using different strategies, e.g. Personas [5], Contextual Inquiry [6], Cognitive Walkthrough [7], etc. One can easily find more than 100 methods by just searching the web. However, a recent study in Germany shows that system development companies rarely use usability methods or only just use the same methods in almost every project due to missing knowledge about alternative methods [8]. Reasons for this lack of knowledge transfer from science to practice might presumably be the vast number of existing methods and lack of suitable support in selecting appropriate ones for a specific project. Some methods are unique but in many cases their divergence is

A. Marcus (Ed.): DUXU/HCII 2013, Part I, LNCS 8012, pp. 252–261, 2013.

minimal and they often make use of an incoherent terminology across the various authors.

The challenge addressed in this paper is to provide tool-based support for the selection of appropriate usability methods, not just by selecting formal and informal criteria (e.g. time constraints, access to test users etc.) but also by considering the applicability in the various stages of system development as defined in ISO/IEC 12207 [9] and interdependencies between multiple methods. The author's approach incorporates a method to validate whether the selected method set is sufficiently balanced with respect to the different dimensions of usability: effectiveness, efficiency and satisfaction.

The paper is structured as following: First, the authors present previous approaches regarding the selection of usability methods and highlight potential for improvements as well as further requirements for a selection concept. Then, the authors report on their proceedings and their method selection approach. Finally, an initial evaluation of the concept and future work is described.

2   Related Work

Several different tools for the selection of usability methods exist. Deliberately excluding static method catalogues, e.g. [10], [11], [12], [13], [14], the following section describes recent dynamic approaches

- 'UsabilityNet' [15],
- 'Usability Planner' [16],
- ISO/TR 16982 [17],
- 'UCD Toolbox' [18],

which differ primarily in terms of the used selection criteria.

2.1   Existing Approaches

Within the 'UsabilityNet' [15] project, 35 methods have been selected based on personal experience of the project partners. These methods are assigned to six system lifecycle steps, i.e. the five steps mentioned in the TRUMP project and a further sixth step of testing and measuring. The methods can be filtered based on three criteria (limited time/resources, no direct access to users, limited skills or expertise of the person executing the method). The selection procedure is therefore quick and easy, but at least one of the three criteria is disputable: There is no reference project for the definition of time and resources although this criterion depends on the complexity of a concrete project. Ten man-days can be very rare for implementing complex accounting software while this is a lot of time implementing a simple website with only six to ten subpages. Actually, 'limited time/resources' is a criterion that should in principle be always affirmed by a project manager because time and resources are always rare and should be minimized in nearly every project.

The 'Usability Planner' [16] is a tool, which enables the method selection based on project and organizational constraints. Aspects that have been taken into account are the person's background (usability expert or software developer), the project stage (e.g. requirements, design, evaluation) and project constraints (e.g. user involvement, task complexity). Methods are filtered by a set of predefined rules and ratings based on the authors' experiences from practice. This form of subjective rating by a few individuals causes a lack of transparency and may influence the reliability of the selection process.

The ISO/TR 16982 [17] (abbreviated with TR hereafter) includes extensive tables, which rate the appropriateness of several types of usability methods (e.g. 'document-based methods', 'model-based methods' and 'creativity methods') with respect to 18 separate criteria (rated on a scale with five dimensions from 'recommended' to 'not applicable'), such as user involvement, usability expertise, project constraints, lifecycle steps, task characteristics, and properties of the developed product itself. There are also two criteria named 'Very tight time scale' and 'Cost/price control', which can be disputed analogously to the abovementioned criterion 'limited time/resources' from the UsabilityNet method table.

For a given development project, the applicable criteria and the respective ratings for each method category must be determined. However, the TR does not specify how to assess or merge this set of several possibly different ratings for each method category into an overall rating. Due to the usage of categories of usability methods instead of concrete methods, this concept also requires a level of usability expertise, which is not necessarily available to all developers and decision-makers.

Weevers [18] developed an interactive website 'UCD Toolbox' on which the selection of methods is primarily based on four main selection criteria: product type (e.g. interface, tangible product), research goal (e.g. 'Learn about the context of use'), resources (e.g. time, budget, staff) and additional criteria (e.g. equipment, participants number). The authors of this approach focus on concrete methods instead of methods categories. This seems much easier to understand from a usability newcomers' perspective. Unlike 'UsabilityNet' [15], the methods' complexity is reasonably quantified in man-hours, but selection is done by filtering the list based on a fixed value of 1-5h. This yields methods that may be performed only isolated within that time.

The existing tools' different selection criteria reflect different approaches to modeling the real world. In order to choose appropriate usability methods, the development project's characteristics should ideally be captured by the criteria as precisely as possible. This is desirable to adequately rate the individual usability methods. However, due to reality's complexity it is impossible to determine a finite set of criteria, which cover every aspect. Furthermore, an extensive set of criteria would make the process of method selection very complicated.

2.2   Potential for Improvement and Requirements

The existing tools are useful to select single, decoupled methods for a project. However, the major flaw shared by these approaches is the missing continuity of the methods' usage in terms of a human-centered design process perspective. Usability should not be considered as a one-dimensional construct but rather as a result of many different properties of a system. In practice there is usually not one 'best' method [19], which is sufficient to satisfy all usability goals. Therefore, the outcome of a usability method selection process should strive to provide a set of methods that collectively cover all relevant aspects of a system's usability. It is therefore necessary to provide methods that act in concert by taking the correlations and interrelations of methods into account. Furthermore, the set of methods must actually be executable within the given project's constraints. Obviously, an important aspect is that the selected usability methods match the available project resources.

Apart from this, the knowledge transfer from scientific research into practical usage should explicitly be supported. It must be possible to easily add and consider new and so far unknown methods. The tool should provide enough information about these methods in order to enable usability specialists and developers to perform them with as little effort as possible. Furthermore, it must still be possible to quickly decide which methods to use from an extensive collection of usability methods.

3   Proceedings

The authors have analyzed the existing selection approaches presented previously. The aim was to create an overview of used selection criteria in order to decide about their relevance. Subsequently, the authors developed a concept consisting of several parts. A necessary basis for the selection of usability methods is to establish a collection of methods and adequately describe them. Therefore, a scheme was created for the description of methods based on the specified selection criteria and an initial paper-based collection of fifteen methods has been established. Secondly, the authors developed a concept for a selection tool that is meant to support extensibility of the method collection and the HCD process planning by taking resource requirements in terms of man-days into account. Afterwards, the authors established an algorithm for the validation of the selected method set. The goal was to ensure that the method set takes all dimensions of usability into account. Finally, the authors evaluated the method-rating with usability experts by asking them to select methods out of the initial collection with respect to different given descriptions of development scenarios out of ISO/TR 16982. The output has been compared with that of the simulated selection tool concept using spreadsheet analysis.

As a result, the approach was partially approved and seems to have potential for further research. The detailed proceedings will be described as follows.

3.1   Establishing the Method Collection

The fundamental approach is to enhance the concept of the TR in a way that the appropriateness of extensive collections of concrete usability methods can quickly be rated. Therefore, each concrete method has to be assigned to one of the TR's method categories. The method then inherits the category's ratings with respect to each selection criterion as stated in the TR and may be adjusted whenever research results suggest that the category's 'default' ratings are inaccurate for that method. Because a finite set of selection criteria can never cover all possibly relevant aspects, any additional relevant properties of a method, e.g. applicability constraints, should be provided in textual form. This allows the tool's user to manually take them into account. This is especially important concerning interdependencies with other methods.

Furthermore, the average amount of resources in terms of man-days required for a single execution of the method must be determined. The best way to do so is possibly to have a community-based implementation of the tool to collect as many values from real-life applications as possible and calculate an average. This contributes to replacing the TR's 'very tight time scale' and 'cost/price control', rendering these criteria dispensable.

The concept also incorporates a later validation of method sets to check whether the usability dimensions (effectiveness, efficiency, and satisfaction) are equally well considered (see Section 3.3). The concept therefore claims it is necessary to determine which of these three dimensions are addressed by each method. Such a mapping for some common usability methods can be found in [20].

Fig. 1 (left) shows a wireframe illustration of how a GUI for adding a method to the tool's collection might look like.

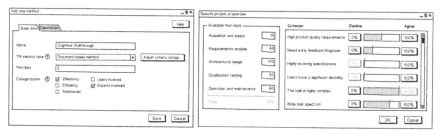

Fig. 1. Wireframes: Adding methods to the collection (left), Entering project characteristics (right)

3.2 Method Selection

To determine appropriate methods for a given development scenario, the project characteristics must be stated in terms of the selection criteria. To resolve the conflict between reality's complexity and usability of the selection tool, the authors adapted the set of criteria specified in ISO/TR 16982 because they are based on expert consensus and are comprehensive enough to enable accurate ratings. Fig. 1 (right) shows a wireframe of a possible GUI for entering this information. As another enhancement to the concept of the TR, the tool's user should not just be able to agree or decline any criterion in a 'binary' way, but state the degree of affirmation, e.g. from a scale of five values. This partially mitigates the issue that for several qualitative criteria of the TR (e.g. 'The task is highly complex') it is sometimes hard to decide whether to apply or to reject. Furthermore, the continuous characteristics of real-world projects can potentially be modeled more precisely this way.

In addition, the available resources (man-days) for each development phase must be entered.

For further calculations, the respective ratings for each criterion must be interpreted as appropriate numeric values (e.g. 'Recommended (++)' → 1; 'Appropriate (+)' → 0.75; 'Neutral' → 0.5; 'Not recommended (-)' → 0).

Based on this mapping, an overall appropriateness rating for each method can be determined by calculating the weighted average of all the ratings with respect to the degree of affirmation to the respective criterion. In the case that any criterion that (partially) applies to the project rates a method as 'Not applicable (NA)', the overall rating for that method must always be the lowest possible value, i.e. zero. This approach enables sorting an extensive collection of usability methods by the overall ratings.

It can then quickly be decided which (of the top-rated) methods to use. Fig. 2 shows an exemplary wireframe of a GUI, which allows the user to state how often each method should be used within each development phase. More than one application of a method within the same phase may for example be necessary when the (iterative) human-centred design process recurs several times within the same step of the system development lifecycle. The sum of man-days required for execution can then automatically be subtracted from the total available man-days. This facilitates the HCD process planning while still leaving room for manual decisions based on properties not directly regarded by the rating algorithm.

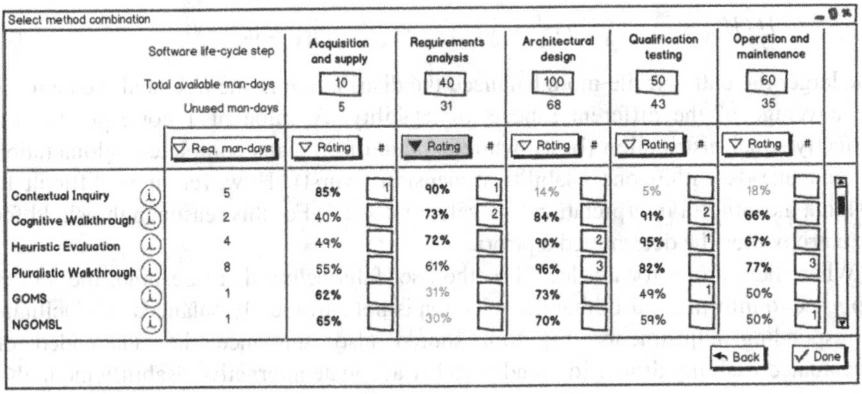

Select method combination						
Software life-cycle step		Acquisition and supply	Requirements analysis	Architectural design	Qualification testing	Operation and maintenance
Total available man-days		10	40	100	50	60
Unused man-days		5	31	68	43	35
	▽ Req. man-days	▽ Rating #	▼ Rating #	▽ Rating #	▽ Rating #	▽ Rating #
Contextual Inquiry ⓘ	5	85% [1]	90% [1]	14% [ ]	5% [ ]	18% [ ]
Cognitive Walkthrough ⓘ	2	40% [ ]	73% [2]	84% [ ]	91% [2]	66% [ ]
Heuristic Evaluation ⓘ	4	49% [ ]	72% [ ]	90% [2]	95% [1]	67% [ ]
Pluralistic Walkthrough ⓘ	8	55% [ ]	61% [ ]	96% [3]	82% [ ]	77% [3]
GOMS ⓘ	1	62% [ ]	31% [ ]	73% [ ]	49% [1]	50% [ ]
NGOMSL ⓘ	1	65% [ ]	30% [ ]	70% [ ]	59% [ ]	50% [1]

←ⁿ Back   ✓ Done

Fig. 2. Wireframe: Method set selection

3.3   Validation of Method Sets

Apart from the calculation of numeric overall ratings for concrete methods and replacing resource-related selection criteria with planning based on man-days, the second major conceptual improvement with respect to the TR is a subsequent validation of the selected method set. Following the above argumentation to illustrate the concept, the usability dimensions (effectiveness, efficiency and satisfaction) are

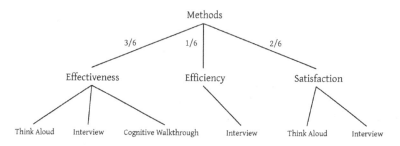

Fig. 3. Method categorization tree

exemplarily regarded as reflecting all aspects of usability as a complex construct. The selected methods can then be interpreted as leafs in a tree of this categorization. Fig. 3 shows an example where the selected method set consists of the methods 'Think Aloud', 'Interview' and 'Cognitive Walkthrough'.

The balance of distribution of the selected methods on the categories (i.e. usability dimensions) can be determined using an inequality metric, e.g. the normalized Shannon entropy

$$H/H_{max} = -\sum_{k=1}^{n} p_k \cdot \log_n p_k \tag{1}$$

with n = (number of categories). For the example in Fig. 3, this yields a value of

$$H/H_{max} = -(\tfrac{3}{6}\log_3\tfrac{3}{6} + \tfrac{1}{6}\log_3\tfrac{1}{6} + \tfrac{2}{6}\log_3\tfrac{2}{6}) \approx 0,9206 \tag{2}$$

The larger the entropy, the more balanced the distribution in the tree, and the better is the coverage of the different aspects of usability. A value of 1 corresponds to a perfectly equal distribution (best), while a value of 0 means complete agglomeration of all methods within one usability dimension (worst). However, it is difficult to assign a meaningful interpretation to a value $0 < x < 1$. For this reason, a threshold for the entropy must be determined a priori.

When the entropy for a selected method set falls below this threshold, the tool is supposed to inform the user that the selection is not sufficiently balanced. To facilitate corresponding adjustments, the tool should also announce the unattended or accentuated usability dimensions and possibly adequate alternative usability methods.

3.4   Evaluation with Usability Experts

Until now, two features of the method selection concept have been evaluated empirically: The numerical calculation of overall appropriateness ratings for concrete methods and the entropy-based validation algorithm. Thus, an initial collection of 15 representative usability methods was created, containing all of the abovementioned information relevant to assess the appropriateness and validity. A selection based on man-days is dependent on properties of real world projects, which can hardly be simulated for evaluation purposes. For this reason, that conceptual feature was excluded in the evaluation.

As a reference source for evaluation, five real-world development scenarios presented in ISO/TR 16982 Annex B ('Examples of in situ applications') have been used. Each consists of a short description of the project goals and constraints in natural language, and the corresponding set of TR selection criteria. Due to the fact that these given criteria must be regarded as 'fully agreed upon' with respect to the scenario (fully declining all other criteria), the concept of allowing the user to partially affirm a criterion did not come into play in this first evaluation.

The descriptions have been exempted from any specific hints related to the usability methods that had actually been used in the real projects. Then, the descriptions have been given to usability professionals unfamiliar with the selection tool concept. The experts were each independently asked to name the methods they would apply in each scenario.

Sometimes an expert stated to be unsure which of some alternative methods to use when several methods were recognized as appropriate. The preferred methods were then assigned the value '1', alternative methods were weighted with '0.75' (according to the abovementioned value for criteria with an 'Appropriate (+)' rating), and unused methods were given the value '0'. As can be seen in Fig. 4, there was a strong tendency of methods with a higher calculated overall rating also being chosen more likely by the usability experts.

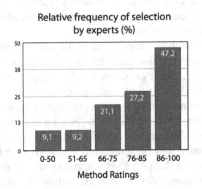

Fig. 4. Evaluation results

Surprisingly, there were also a few cases where methods have been rated '0' overall by the simulated tool, but still chosen by the professionals. This was probably due to the fact that the experts sometimes came to an intuitive understanding of the project characteristics based on the textual descriptions that differed significantly from the facts covered by the selection criteria.

Although man-days-based planning was not explicitly included in the evaluation, this concept interestingly got indirect support from the fact that all experts stated that the time frames specified in the scenario descriptions were in most cases highly important for their choices. Actually, the professionals mostly started with an analysis of how much time is available and which methods could possibly be used under this condition.

4   Conclusion and Outlook

In this paper, the authors presented a concept for the establishment of a community-based usability method collection as well as for the selection of an adequate method set for a user-specified project. A first evaluation of the basic method-rating concept was done using spreadsheet calculation and reviews from usability experts.

The author's analysis of existing approaches to the systematic selection of usability methods showed that usually a narrow angle is taken. In these approaches single methods are selected in isolation from the larger context of planning the development process is taken. Although usually several different methods must be used within one project, their interdependencies are not taken into account. To improve the knowledge transfer from science to practice, a selection tool's method collection should be extensible in an unproblematic and systematic way. Methods should be described in a way that HCI specialists as well as developers can easily understand and learn how to perform each method (suitability for learning).

The current status of our work on these issues is primarily a theoretical concept for method selections based on and extending the ISO/TR 16982. The approach allows calculating numeric overall ratings for the appropriateness of concrete usability methods based on a flexible and robust specification of project characteristics and other criteria. When a computer automatically does this calculation, it enables the user to easily assess extensive collections of usability methods. To facilitate the HCD process planning, the concept envisages quantifying available resources and the methods' requirements in terms of man-days.

In order to fortify the holistic consideration of all aspects of usability during a development project, the concept also provides an algorithm to validate selected method sets regarding their balance. The evaluation results suggest that the calculated overall ratings of concrete methods coincide with judgment from usability professionals. However, until now the low number of samples prohibits a definite conclusion.

Future work will contain further evaluations and an implementation of the concept in form of a conventional software tool or rich Internet application. Mechanisms for feedback from a community will be integrated and used to refine information in the methods repository. Such a loopback is expected to be especially beneficial to determine the man-days required for method executions but also for the categorization of methods and the adjustment of criteria ratings.

Finally, apart from practical applications, the concept presented in this paper could lead to further general theoretical discussions regarding method selection approaches, e.g. the ongoing revision of ISO/TR 16982 to ISO 9241-230.

References

1. Lallemand, C.: Toward a Closer Integration of Usability in Software Development: A Study of Usability Inputs in a Model-Driven Engineering Process. In: Proceedings of the 3rd ACM SIGCHI Symposium on Engineering Interactive Computing Systems EICS, pp. 299–302. ACM, New York (2011)
2. Fischer, H., Nebe, K., Klompmaker, F.: A Holistic Model for Integrating Usability Engineering and Software Engineering Enriched with Marketing Activities. In: Kurosu, M. (ed.) Human-Centered Design, HCII 2011. LNCS, vol. 6776, pp. 28–37. Springer, Heidelberg (2011)

3. Nebe, K., Zimmermann, D., Paelke, V.: Integrating Software Engineering and Usability Engineering. In: Pinder, S. (ed.) Advances in Human-Computer Interaction, pp. 332–350. InTech (2008)
4. Seffah, A., Desmarais, M.C., Metzker, E.: HCI, Usability and Software Engineering Integration: Present and Future. In: Seffah, A., Gulliksen, J., Desmarais, M.C. (eds.) Human-Centered Software Engineering – Integrating Usability in the Development Process, pp. 37–57. Springer, Heidelberg (2005)
5. Adlin, T., Pruitt, J.: The Essential Persona Lifecycle – Your Guide to 'Building and Using' Personas. Morgan Kaufmann, San Francisco (2010)
6. Holtzblatt, K., Wendell, J.B., Wood, S.: Rapid Contextual Design – A How-to Guide to Key Techniques for User-Centered Design. Morgan Kaufmann, San Francisco (2004)
7. Benyon, D.: Designing Interactive Systems: A comprehensive guide to HCI and interaction design, 2nd edn. Pearson Education Ltd., Harlow (2010)
8. Woywode, M., Mädche, A., Wallach, D., Plach, M.: Usability of Software Applications as a Competitive Factor for Small and Medium-Sized Enterprises. German Federal Ministry of Economics and Technology, BMWi (2012) (in German)
9. ISO/IEC 12207: Systems and software engineering – Software life cycle processes (2008)
10. Usability Body of Knowledge, http://www.usabilitybok.org/methods
11. Generic Work Process, http://project.cmd.hro.nl/cmi/hci/toolkit/index2.php
12. Usability Gov, http://www.usability.gov/methods
13. The Methods Lab, http://www.education.edean.org/pdf/Tool039.pdf
14. Ideo Method Cards, http://www.ideo.com/work/method-cards
15. Bevan, N.: UsabilityNet Methods for User Centred Design. In: Jacko, J.A., Stephanidis, C. (eds.) Human-Computer Interaction: Theory and Practice (Part 1), HCII 2003, vol. 1, pp. 434–438. Lawrence Erlbaum Associates, Mahwah (2003)
16. Ferre, X., Bevan, N.: Usability Planner: A Tool to Support the Process of Selecting Usability Methods. In: Campos, P., Graham, N., Jorge, J., Nunes, N., Palanque, P., Winckler, M. (eds.) INTERACT 2011, Part IV. LNCS, vol. 6949, pp. 652–655. Springer, Heidelberg (2011)
17. ISO/TR 16982: Ergonomics of human-system interaction – Usability methods supporting human-centred design (2002)
18. Weevers, T.: Method selection tool for User Centred Product Development. Master Thesis, Delft University of Technology (2011)
19. Wixon, D.: Evaluating Usability Methods: Why the Current Literature Fails the Practitioner. Interactions 10(4), 28–34 (2003)
20. Freymann, M.: Classification of User-Centered Evaluation Methods within the User-Centered Design Process. Diploma Thesis, University of Paderborn (2007) (in German)

VMUXE
An Approach to User Experience Evaluation for Virtual Museums

Bianca Gockel[1], Holger Graf[1], Alfonsina Pagano[2], Sofia Pescarin[2], and Joakim Eriksson[3]

[1] Fraunhofer Institute for Computer Graphics, Fraunhoferstr. 5, 64283 Darmstadt, Germany
bianca.gockel@gmail.com, holger.graf@igd.fraunhofer.de
[2] CNR-ITABC, Virtual Heritage Lab, Via Salaria, km 29, Monterotondo St., Roma, Italy
alfonsina.pagano@usi.ch, sofia.pescarin@itabc.cnr.it
[3] Lund University, Department of Design Science, Sölvegatan 26, 22100 Lund, Sweden
joakim.eriksson@design.lth.se

Abstract. This paper presents a new approach for the evaluation of User Experience (UX) aspects applied to virtual museums (VM) - VMUXE. A wide percentage of projects and applications for VMs are often "born and buried" in digital labs, without having been experimented and monitored with people. These "prototypes" are the result of experts, technicians, curators, combined together to give birth for multidisciplinary and avant-garde outputs. Earlier attempts to evaluate VM installations failed due to the lack of strategy facing the multidimensional complexity in studying and comparing digital applications in different installations using different devices and metaphors offering different UXs. As a conclusion "communicating" culture through the aid of advanced technology was not a technological issue, but an epistemological one. Setting up a good process of evaluation and analysis is therefore important for establishing next generation virtual museums (NGVM) aiming to reach certain goals such as knowledge exchange, cognitive improvement and heritage communication.

Keywords: User Experience Evaluation, Virtual Museums, (Non-) Instrumental Qualities, Digital Cultural Heritage.

1   Introduction

Today's rapid technological development provides a variety of new possibilities for the cultural heritage sector. In recent years, one major trend became visible as European endeavors aim to digitally master its vast and exclusive cultural resources and learning traditions as source for creativity and inspiration. Michaelis et al. [1] point out, that with the new communication models which are coming along with this evolution the understanding and access to cultural heritage can be enhanced essentially.

A. Marcus (Ed.): DUXU/HCII 2013, Part I, LNCS 8012, pp. 262–272, 2013.

One of the trends in digital cultural heritage (DCH) is dedicated to the design and implementation of virtual museums (VMs). The European Commission acknowledges this by funding the Network of Excellence V-MusT.net[1] in order to support this process. Though, no consent on a clear definition for VMs has been found up to now, the V-MusT terminology suggests their nature as being "various digital creations which acquire, conserve, research, communicate and exhibit, in a digital way, the tangible and intangible heritage of humanity and its environment" [2].

As the understanding and learning of our cultural background is inherently aligned to the applied communication models the focus on users' needs, perceptions and interests has to be ensured by a participatory software design. According to Carillo et al. [3] it is already prevalent practice for ICT developments, but not for the implementation of applications in the DCH sector. This needs to be reinforced!

In recent years, some evaluation studies in the DCH domain were conducted. However, those showed a significant fragmentation in their methods, e.g. Carillo et al. [3], Pescarin et al. [4], Micheal et al. [5]. Several authors used a diversity of approaches in different settings (lab vs. in-situ) focusing on certain aspects such as Usability tests using "Cognitive Walkthrough" methods, or considering degree of immersion, behavioral and social aspects, "Smileyometer" and "Again table" of the Fun Toolkit [6] with children to investigate engagement, endurability, and recurrences.

Pujol Tost & Ecounmou [7] predict that lab-based evaluations do not deliver reliable results as they do not take into account the natural environment of exhibitions. On contrary, Rodriguez-Echavarria et al. [8] claim that VM are not well defined as e.g. web application that profit from more standardized hardware and software interfaces and recommend user-based testing at labs. This diversity of opinions is quite predictable as there are specific challenges in the DCH domain.

Thus, the motivation of our paper is to provide a new approach on how we can evaluate the success of a virtual museum aiming for an enhanced user experience. Which are the criteria and quality parameters we can use as reference? What kind of method, if one exists, we should adopt? We present a holistic approach for the design and implementation of an evaluation for VMs – VMUXE. Its analysis will then provide a scaffold of design indicators required for NGVMs.

2   Methodology

2.1   Selection of UX Aspects

Due to the manifold of (non-)instrumental qualities, the selection has been based on "subjective" priorities for interactive VMs. We have been focussing on four selected aspects of UX proposed by the model of Thüring und Mahlke [9]: utility, learnability, efficiency and stimulation.

---

[1] http://www.v-must.net/ (aof February 2013).

Utility: Requirement analysis that contains the elaboration of user profiles and the contextual task analysis are often not realized in the DCH domain. Therefore, it is vital to examine, if the VM supports all required and desired functions.

Learnability: As users of VMs are often non-experts who only use these applications for example during a visit of a cultural site or even at a physical museum for a limited period of time, it is crucial to ensure an easy learnability of the interface.

Efficiency: As the user continues to use the VM a lack of efficiency might lead to a high level of frustration. Typical objective measures for efficiency are counting clicks or stopping the time for the fulfillment of tasks [10]. However, within this work the subjective perceived efficiency is investigated based on the users' satisfaction.

Stimulation: Although the instrumental needs are fulfilled, excitement and joy which captivate the user are not guaranteed. This term was introduced by Hassenzahl [11] who highlights that individuals strive after reinforcement of their personal development which can be given by providing new, interesting or even exciting content, functionality, presentation or interaction style. Consequently, stimulation as a "driving power" for interaction and learning of new skills and knowledge represents significant quality of VMs.

The focus of this evaluation is thus on the instrumental qualities.

2.2   Selection of Evaluation Methods

For the elevation of data a combination of two methods was chosen, as to achieve a holistic picture highlighted by Lehn et al. [12]. A written survey in form of a paper-based questionnaire was designed with the aim of collecting quantitative data that should be used to identify tendencies for the levels of maturity concerning the different selected UX aspects that are statistical significant. The questionnaire follows ensured structure:

1. *Part A - Demographic Data* that collects essential information about the users' characteristics (gender, age, origin, occupation and ICT knowledge)
2. *Part B - Feedback* that contains:
   (a) an extract from the User Experience Questionnaire (UEQ) [13] that summarizes the results of 12 pairs of contrasting attributes with a seven point scale to the terms perspicuity, efficiency and stimulation
   (b) several multiple choice questions to deliver concrete statements (see tab. 1)

As a completion, an *interview guideline* based on a questionnaire was developed in order to identify the motivation behind the users' reactions and deduce some suggestions for improvements for the concept of a VM, with a focus on qualitative data and is structured as follows:

Table 1. Written Survey: Part A - Feedback: Multiple choice questions

UX Aspect	Question	Answer Category
Utility	Q1: What do you think about the functions of the virtual museum?	AC1: All functions are useful and interesting to me AC2: The virtual museum contains some interesting functions, but also some unnecessary functions, namely:_____ AC3: No functions are useful and interesting for me
	Q2: Was every function available that you wish to have?	AC1: Yes AC2: No, I would like to add following function:____
Learnability	Q3: What do you think about the handling of the virtual museum?	AC1: It was hard to use the virtual museum, so I couldn't focus on the content. AC2: At first I had to fully concentrate to use the virtual museum, but after some time I could focus on the content. AC3: From the start I had no problems to use the virtual museum and could fully enjoy it.
Efficiency	Q4: What do you think about the time it took to use it?	AC1: I am satisfied with the time that took me to reach my goals and I could fully enjoy the content. AC2: Sometimes it took too much time, because the system reacted slowly. AC3: Sometimes it took too much time, because I had to perform unnecessary and/or inconvenient steps. AC4: It took me so much time, that I completely lost focus of the content.
Stimulation	Q5: What do you think about your experience with the virtual museum?	AC1: I experienced something totally new for me and got new insights. AC2: Experienced something I already know, but I could still enjoy AC3: Experienced something already known a lot and boring.

1. *Part A - Demographic Questionnaire* that is equal to the one of the written survey
2. *Part B - Demonstrator Use* that instructs the participant to accomplish tasks adapted to each VM while applying "Thinking Aloud" observed by the evaluator
3. *Part C - Final Questions* that is similarly structured as the multiple choice questions of the written survey, but   more broken-down and opened-up designed

3   Results

3.1   Practical Implementation

We conducted the evaluation during the Archeovirtual 2012[2] which offers showcases of various VMs from all over the world. 24 scientifically reviewed projects were allocated to 5 technological areas: Mobile, Touch, Computer Animation, Emerging Technologies, Natural Interaction and Desktop Virtual Reality. The written survey was applied to several presented 18 *interactive* VMs. 10 most innovative and interesting projects were chosen for a deeper evaluation in face-to-face interviews. Table 2 shows the total numbers that could be reached for the whole evaluation study.

Table 2. User Profile of the Archeovirtual 2012

		Written Survey (N = 301)	Interview (N = 81)
Gender	Female	157	34
	Male	144	47
Age	Range	11 – 70 years	7 – 63 years
Occupation	Composition	Other 33; ICT Expert 38; Tourism-expert 14; Student in Uni 38; 70 Student in School; 108 Expert in CH	Other 21; 21 CH Expert; ICT atpert 15; 9 Student in School; 9 Student at Uni; 6 Tourismexpert

Due to the scope of this paper, we decided to present the results of three VMs for a special technological domain that mirrors the results for the overall domain. The results for desktop based VR can be found in [14]. Several quantitative results were mapped onto a scale between -3 and 3. The neutral interval contains values between -0.8 and 0.8. Extreme values at the end of the scale either smaller than -2 or bigger than 2 are rated as "very poor" or "very good".

3.2   Area Mobile: Chartreuse Numérique

This VM offers an interactive 3D real-time visit for the iPad of the Charterhouse's church [3] of Villeneuve-lès-Avignon (Gard, France) based on panoramic photos obtained by superposition between virtual images (extracted from a 3D model) and images of the real space. A tap on an interactive map chooses a location inside the

---

[2] Archeovirtual – Embedded within Mediterranean Expo for Archaeological Tourism, in 2012: 15th-18th of November, Paestum, Italy, www.archeovirtual.it (aof February 2013).

[3] Project by Prof. Livio De Luca, MAP laboratory, UMR CNRS/MCC 3495, ENSA Marseille, France - http://www.chartreuse.org/16/337/espace-3d-chartreuse (aof February 2013).

church. By using a slider the panoramic picture is increasingly overlaid by the 3D reconstruction. Swiping on the touchscreen allows changing the perspective and tapping paintings zoom the user in. Further descriptive information about the paintings can be accessed by tapping on an icon located at the lower right corner (see fig. 1). 22 written survey and 7 interviews were carried out for the VM. Table 3 shows the quantitative data that could be achieved for perspicuity, efficiency and stimulation.

For *learnability* only an average result could be achieved. It was enhanced by simple map navigation, but also lowered by two main problems: First the 3D reconstruction could not be related to a specific historical time as the color concept of the interactive map was not clear and the time slider was not labeled. Second, the accessibility of the paintings is for the users not transparent as these hotspots are not specifically highlighted compared to other non-interactive parts. For *efficiency* a good result could be obtained with a tendency to very good as only 21% within the written survey detected inefficiencies. The *stimulation* values range between average and good, as the combination of content and functions appeared new.

Fig. 1. Chartreuse Numérique - Left: Interactive map as starting point, Mid: Location inside the church at present state or at past state, Right: Description about selected paintings

Table 3. Chartreuse Numérique - Scales

		Perspicuity	*Efficiency*	*Stimulation*
N	Valid	21	21	21
	Missing	1	1	1
Median		.75	1.50	1.00
Std. Deviation		1.19784	1.26220	.89642
Rating		Neutral	Good	Good

The *utility* of this VM was marked as very good. Within the written survey 91% of participants rated all available functions as useful. Only the transition from present to past by changing the opacity was criticized. A wish list does provide suggestions for further developments: More descriptions and storytelling, move from room to room without going back to the map, links between paintings, audio comments, more hotspots inside the church, e.g. windows.

3.3   Area Emerging Technologies: Bravo – BRAin Virtual Operator

The emerging technology area was dedicated to Brain-Computer Interfaces (BCI). BRAVO (BRAin Virtual Operator)[4] represents a user-centered and portable solution that applies BCI to e-learning. It is a tool for reading customisable eLearning courses and multimedia content using a BCI acquiring information about attention and relaxation levels (see fig.2).

While for the scale *perspicuity* a good level was achieved, *learnability* reached only an average level with a predisposition to good as to a large extent it required some time to understand how to use the VM (see table 4). *Efficiency* reached a good level with a tendency to very good as only 11% mentioned that the system reacted sometimes too slow.

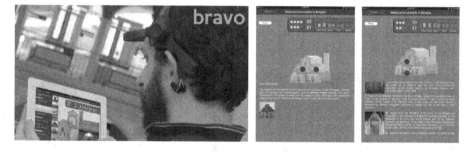

Fig. 2. Bravo - Left: Setting, Right: Screenshots of adapted content

Table 4. Bravo - Scales

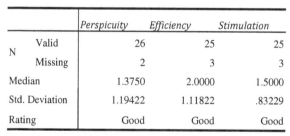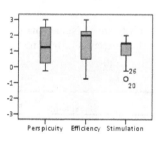

		Perspicuity	Efficiency	Stimulation
N	Valid	26	25	25
	Missing	2	3	3
Median		1.3750	2.0000	1.5000
Std. Deviation		1.19422	1.11822	.83229
Rating		Good	Good	Good

In addition, for *stimulation* a good result was achieved as it was for a majority of 79% a totally new experience to interact with such a VM. Nobody disliked the VM or felt bored. For *utility*, 96% of the participants rated that all available functions are useful and interesting to them. Suggestions for enhancements: A higher variety of media types and a more reliable auditing system.

---

[4] Project by Dr. Marco Marchesi, University of Bologna, DEIS Dept. of Electronics, Italy.

3.4   Area Natural Interaction: Rediscovering Vrouw Maria

Rediscovering Vrouw Maria[5] is an interactive, real-time, virtual reality simulation about the Vrouw Maria shipwreck that uses stereoscopic projection. The interaction is gesture based tracked by the Microsoft's Kinect Sensor. The user can navigate freely through the landscape and inspect a selection of the remains of the wreck displayed that can be chosen by moving through the particular info-icon (see fig.3).

Only an average result was obtained for *learnability* as it was decreased by initial problems to understand which gesture leads to which system reaction. After a short learning phase the gestures could easily be applied. For *efficiency* different results were obtained. While in the interview all participants were satisfied, within the written survey 32% detected inefficiencies. For *stimulation* a good result was reached due to the immersive environment that allows exploring the wreck in a new way. For *utility* all available functions were appreciated by 92% who participated at the written survey. Only one participant rated the selection of information by moving through an icon as not useful (see table 5). Enhancements: More objects/remains to investigate under the sea and audio, "swim" gestures, more contextual information.

Fig. 3. Rediscovering Vrouw Maria - Left: Scrennshot, Right: Person interacting with the VM by pointing with the hand

Table 5. Vrouw Maria - Scales

		Perspicuity	Efficiency	Stimulation
N	Valid	24	24	24
	Missing	0	0	0
Median		.75	1.00	1.00
Std. Deviation		1.50843	1.18793	1.00842
Rating		Neutral	Good	Good

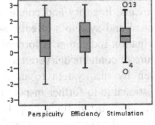

[5] Project by Prof. Lily Diaz-Kommonen, Aalto University School of Arts Design and Architecture, Aalto, Finland - http://sysrep.aalto.fi/vrouwmaria/ (aof February 2013).

4   Discussion

As all VMs presented at Archeovirtual 2012 faced a technological-based categorization, the subsequent discussion highlights general tendencies for the thematic groups and reveals weaknesses and strengths of VMUXE.

Mobile Area: VMUXE mainly revealed issues on the visibility of system's elements and content redundancy. This is obviously reflected in the usability of applications, leaving users disoriented by misleading information and confusing interfaces. The same visual and textual indicators (i.e. hotspots' accessibility) suffered from consistency and users' orientation, e.g. the paintings' accessibility within Chartréuse Numerique using highlights for non-/interactive parts of the church. Apart from this, VMs of this category were appreciated as involving and well structured.

Emerging Technologies: required a constant maintenance by the particular developers on site because of the necessity of a preliminary introduction to users (fitting of the BCI headset, explanation on the interaction). Here, the categories of learnability and efficiency resulted to be irrelevant for our study as the time needed to reach certain goals is planned to be a result of the applications not a parameter to be investigated. Also the easiness of the system turned to be a subjective datum, as user alone could not grab if he succeeded unless the developer explained it to him. In general, the two presented VMs are more suitable for visibility and aesthetical evaluations since interface and visual elements resulted the most interesting items highlighted by users (i.e. more multimedia functions, changes in icons, customization of characters).

Natural Interaction Area: all of the presented VMs were appreciated for their immersiveness, the natural atmosphere recreated, and good feedback of the system. Nevertheless, some efforts were suggested wrt. content redundancy (i.e. too much text in the Wreck objects' explanations), visibility of interface elements (i.e. orientation map of Vrouw Maria which indicated the position of the user in relation to the wreck were not clearly identifiable), and mapping between users' controls and system's effects. Again for this category, the presence of developers on site was essential.

In the end, speaking about UX aspects and what can positively influence their values, we can affirm that *utility* is founded on the consistency of interface's elements, linearity and conciseness of contents and a good mapping between users' control and system's effects; *learnability* sees connections with a good visibility of navigation indicators, affordance of visual and textual information and the consistent nature of contents delivered to users; *efficiency* takes advantages of the rapid feedback given by the system to users and the multiplicity of functions offered, yet, its questionable to further inspect this as users should be granted some time to explore a VM; *stimulation* finds help by the integration of media, which provides pleasant aesthetical features, the natural setting presented by the whole environment and the easiness of interaction.

5   Conclusion

One can certainly expect that NGVMs appearing in forthcoming years will have a wide variation in interaction techniques, as well as in the level of ambition regarding information/education. Thus, it is of course a challenge to use a uniform evaluation method for all these different applications.

With VMUXE, we propose an evaluation method that addresses both instrumental and non-instrumental qualities, and collects both quantitative as well as qualitative data. The case studies performed at Archeovirtual, showed that the method works well and is efficient, especially considering the special circumstances in field-testing on museum visitors, as opposed to how a controlled environment study could have been performed. When evaluating with VMUXE, there will naturally be some applications where certain questions may feel irrelevant to ask people, and some UX-aspects may feel of less importance, such as efficiency.

However, the generative approach provides the benefit to gradually build up some benchmark values, based on a larger number of investigations. It would then become easier to validate a new VM's status by comparing results with existing benchmarks.

Acknowledgements. The work is funded by the European Commission through the European Community's Seventh Framework Programme (FP7 2007/2013) under grant agreement 270404 – "V-Must.net".

References

1. Michaelis, N., Jung, Y., Behr, J.: Virtual Heritage to go. In: Proceedings of the 17th International Conference on 3D Web Technology, pp. 113–116. ACM, New York (2012)
2. Consortium of the V-MusT.net: Terminology, Definitions and Type for Virtual Museums. In: Deliverable Report: V-MusT.net – D 2.Version 3 (2013)
3. Carillo, E., Rodriguez-Echavarria, K., Heath, R., Arnold, D.: Effective user-centred design for the Vindolanda interactive multimedia application. In: Digital Heritage, Proceedings of the 14th International Conference on Virtual Systems and Multimedia, Short Papers, VSMM 2008, pp. 337–342. Archeolingua, Limassol (2008)
4. Pescarin, S., Pagano, A., Wallergård, H.W., Ray, C.: Archeovirtual 2011: An Evaluation Approach to Virtual Museums. In: Proceedings of the 18th Conference on Virtual Systems and Multimedia, VSMM 2012, pp. 25–32. IEEE Press, Milan (2012)
5. Michael, D., Pelekanos, N., Chrysanthou, I., Zaharias, P., Hadjigavriel, L.L., Chrysanthou, Y.: Comparative Study of Interactive Systems in a Museum. In: Ioannides, M., Fellner, D., Georgopoulos, A., Hadjimitsis, D.G. (eds.) EuroMed 2010. LNCS, vol. 6436, pp. 250–261. Springer, Heidelberg (2010)
6. Read, J., MacFarlane, S., Casey, C.: Endurability, Engagement and Expectations: Measuring Children's Fun. In: Interaction Design and Children, pp. 189–198. Shaker Publishing, Eindhoven (2002)
7. Pujol Tost, L., Economou, M.: Evaluating the Social Context of ICT Applications in Museum Exhibitions. In: Proceedings of the 7th International Symposium on Virtual Reality, Archaeology and Cultural Heritage, VAST 2006, pp. 219–228. Eurographics Association, Nicosia (2006)

8. Rodriguez-Echavarria, K., Morris, D., Moore, C., Arnold, D., Glauert, J., Jennings, V.: Developing Effective Interfaces for Cultural Heritage 3D Immersive Environments. In: Proceedings of the 8th International Symposium on Virtual Reality, Archaeology and Cultural Heritage, VAST 2007, pp. 93–99. Eurographics Association, Brighton (2007)

9. Thüring, M., Mahlke, S.: Usability, aesthetics, and emotion in human-technology interaction. International Journal of Psychology 42, 253–264 (2007)

10. Nielsen, J.: Usability Engineering. Morgan Kaufmann, San Francisco (1994)

11. Hassenzahl, M.: The thing and I: understanding the relationship between user and product. In: Blythe, M.A., Overbeeke, K., Monk, A.F. (eds.) Funology: From Usability to Enjoyment, pp. 31–42. Kluwer Academic Publisher, Dordrecht (2003)

12. Vom Lehn, D., Heath, C., Hindmarsh, J.: Video based field studies in museums and galleries. Visitor Studies Today! 5(3), 15–23 (2002)

13. Laugwitz, B., Held, T., Schrepp, M.: Construction and Evaluation of a User Experience Questionnaire. In: Holzinger, A. (ed.) USAB 2008. LNCS, vol. 5298, pp. 63–76. Springer, Heidelberg (2008)

14. Baldassari, G.L., Demetrescu, E., Pescarin, S., Eriksson, J., Graf, H.: "Villa di Livia": A case study for the devolution of large scale interactive "in-site" to "on-line" application. In: Proceedings of the HCI International 2013. LNCS. Springer, Heidelberg (2013)

Customer Recruitment:
Ethical, Legal and Practical Issues

Kristyn Greenwood and Angela Johnston

Oracle, Redwood Shores, CA
{kristyn.greenwood,angela.johnston}@oracle.com

Abstract. An often overlooked aspect of usability testing methodology is participant recruitment. Traditionally, test participants have either been independent users recruited by usability programs irrespective of their employer or they have been company representatives provided by product management or a sales team. However, there are drawbacks associated with these types of recruitment programs, which led our organizations at Oracle to create a standardized program of customer recruitment, instead. In this paper we describe the problems that we encountered when using the traditional methods of recruitment, how a new legal document and a customer recruiting process solved those problems, and what ethical considerations need to be made when recruiting customers.

Keywords: Participant recruitment, user research, customer recruitment, usability testing.

1 Customer Recruitment History

For over 20 years, Oracle has had an active user experience program, testing product designs with all types of users. Usability testing of Oracle products requires access to a broad range of users, who can work in departments such as HR, Finance, Sales, Procurement, IT, Development, Shipping & Receiving, and more. Last year alone, Oracle conducted over 320 usability activities. These activities engaged over 2000 participants, 75% of them employed by Oracle customers or partners. Participant recruitment is an essential component of the user experience program; however it has been fraught with difficulties. As noted by Sova and Nielsen [8], "The main obstacle to quick and frequent user testing is the difficulty of finding warm bodies."

1.1 Independent User Recruitment

Traditionally, we depended on the general public to test our products and prototypes. These individuals were recruited irrespective of who they were employed by. This "independent user" recruitment program required a special legal document (Individual Confidential Disclosure and Informed Consent Agreement) per participant, per activity and a large participant database for maintaining participant data and tracking participation. This program provided participants for usability research for many years.

A. Marcus (Ed.): DUXU/HCII 2013, Part I, LNCS 8012, pp. 273–282, 2013.
© Springer-Verlag Berlin Heidelberg 2013

1.2   Drawbacks of Independent User Recruitment

However, there are downsides to recruiting from the general public. These include: cost, time, paperwork and security.

- Recruiting from the general public is costly, whether you have an in-house recruiter or utilize a third-party agency. To entice a member of the general public to participate, you often need to offer competitive incentives. Some user types, such as highly skilled specialized users, require higher incentives.
- It can be very time consuming and difficult to recruit participants from the general public.
  − Certain user types may be hard to find, and using services like Craigslist, Meetup, or LinkedIn to find participants can lead to a bias towards more experienced computer users.
  − There is a tendency to re-use participants. Recruiting participants to participate in multiple activities reduced the time and effort needed for recruitment, but led to a lack of variety and diversity.
- Tracking participation and incentives requires a database or some other system.
  − The use of paid participants leads to increased paperwork as payments made to individuals need to be tracked for company accounting purposes and IRS compliance. Employees that work for government agencies are not eligible to receive incentives and therefore cannot be recruited.
  − Additionally, undesirable test participants need to be flagged so they are not recruited more than once.
- Security is also a concern. Remote usability testing with participants recruited from the general public can be risky as it is not possible to know who else might be watching. It is also impossible to know if the test participant is recording the session in any way. As discussed by Bartek et al [2], "Session security is another concern, particularly if the material is confidential. It is not always obvious that the participant has other people in the room observing; also, the participant could take screen captures of the user interface without the facilitator's knowledge".
- Another concern when recruiting from the general public is the risk of recruiting professional usability testers (scammers). These people will falsify their job title, employer, and often identity in order to better match what the tester is looking for, to qualify for a study that would earn them money. As a result, the validity of their data is questionable as is their adherence to the non-disclosure aspects of the confidentiality agreement that they signed.

1.3   Company Representative Recruitment

Approximately six years ago, Oracle's user experience groups started supplementing individual user recruitment with specially chosen customer representatives. These individuals were representatives of their companies and were typically supplied by the Product Management (PM) team. Customer representatives usually participated in the usability activities as part of a larger activity, such as a Beta program. The use of company representatives was less expensive than individual user recruitment because company representatives do not expect to be paid for their time and participation.

1.4   Drawbacks of Company Representative Recruitment

However, other drawbacks experienced during individual user recruitment such as paperwork, security and difficulty in recruiting still exist.

- It's hard to get past the "gatekeeper." Permission from the PM team has to be obtained every time we want to work with a customer. PMs can be very protective of their customers, and often want to send the UX activity invitation themselves; however they don't always know how to properly explain a UX activity (feedback session or usability test). Their explanations can mislead a customer and cause less interest in participation. Additionally, the PM team may recommend contacting specific customers only due to the customer mood or current situation and not due to their suitability for the study.
- It's difficult to find the right user. PMs only provide access to customer 'super users' who are using Oracle products regularly; specifically the products that the PM is managing. These users often know too much to provide new user feedback, and are not often suitable to represent potential customers because their expectations are based on their past experiences with the product.
- Security is also a concern. A signed Informed Consent and Confidential Disclosure Agreement (CDA) covers only one person and does not cover their office-mate, manager (potentially listening in to get a peek at a new product design) or IT staff who could, theoretically, capture or record the web conference being conducted on their company systems. Most customers have to participate in remote testing because they are not co-located with our engineering offices, but widespread across the globe.
- Tracking was difficult when we first started this program, because we were using multiple spreadsheets, which often contained duplicate information, or could be misplaced.
- Usability participants were often end-users (not the decision makers) and didn't feel comfortable signing an individual CDA or submitting this document to legal for review just to participate in one usability test.
- Customers often wanted to use existing legal documents instead of signing something new, specific to one activity. These existing documents did not often cover the use of feedback and were often specific to one product. Documents often referenced were: Development Collaboration CDA; Beta Trial License Agreement; NDAs for 2-way disclosure; and Software License & Services Agreement (SLSA).

2   Legal Documents

Unfortunately, most traditional legal documents between companies did not cover usability testing and the collection of feedback from customers. The Beta and Partner agreements that we used at Oracle sometimes covered usability activities and sometimes did not. Oracle's legal staff was concerned about whether we could use *any* product feedback provided to us under a Beta Agreement. Beta agreements are typically written in ways that limit the collection of feedback to current design of the product in Beta. However, these agreements often don't cover the collection of feedback that is peripheral to the product, such as how it would be used and what other products would it be used with, which is information that would aid future product design.

Instead of depending upon the Beta agreement, the UX department started using a company-standard document for working with customers; the Individual CDA and Informed Consent. This document was used solely for the purpose of UX activities and included coverage for one individual and was not between the customer company and Oracle, but the individual only. This document proved to be difficult to use because the usability participant was often uncomfortable signing this document. Another document that was occasionally used was the Development Collaboration CDA which is a company level agreement, but also specific to one activity or product. They would have to arrange for someone with signing authority to sign the forms for each activity that a company representative participated in (e.g. Procurement Customer Advisory Board, High Tech Industry Strategy Council, and Usability Test). Unfortunately, it was often difficult to obtain to obtain a Development Collaboration CDA for each activity when working with customers. Customers didn't like having to sign multiple agreements and this again, prompted customers to try and leverage other agreements that did not provide adequate protection to Oracle.

3   Our Solution: UX Customer Participation Program

Over time, it became apparent that utilizing company representatives at Beta events or mediated by a product manager was not a feasible long term solution but neither was recruiting from the general public. We decided that we needed to focus on usability testing with customers but that we needed to find a way to build our own relationships with them. There were two key elements to making this plan successful: a new (better) legal document to cover all customer feedback activities and a method of tracking customer participation at the company level.

First, we consulted with Oracle's legal team to have them draft a new legal document, the Customer Participation Confidentiality Agreement (CPCA). This document was designed to address confidentiality and feedback as covered by previous agreements and also meet the following requirements:

- Cover multiple development-related activities (customer advisory boards, councils, design reviews, and user experience activities)
- Bind the customer company, covering ALL employees
- Place the burden and determination of what information to share on the customer company and cover permission to use feedback that participants provide to us, allowing us to use it to improve our products.
- Create a perpetual master agreement that would be agreed upon and signed once. After that, projects and disclosure period could be defined as needed using a project attachment (or addendum)

Next, we created a database to track customer participation and the existence of a CPCA. We call it the Customer Participation Database or CPD. This database tracks participation in all development-related activities allowing us to look up a customer company and see what they are involved in from CABs to UX participation, the valid dates of the agreement, if they have completed the CPCA, and what activities are covered.

3.1   Legal Documents

The core of the customer recruitment program is the legal document. At Oracle, we call it the Customer Participation Confidentiality Agreement (CPCA). Legal documents used for customer recruitment should allow an organization to collect and *use* the feedback provided for product design and development. Many non-disclosure and Beta agreements do not cover this. The contents of such a document would need to be worked out with your legal teams and we do not aim to provide legal instructions as to the content of such a document for any organization. However, we can provide a short list of the elements of this document that we think are most important.

Key components of Oracle's Customer Participation Confidentiality Agreement are:

- Clear definitions of what is to be considered "company confidential information" and what is to be considered "participant confidential information"
- A clear definition of "feedback", as well as ownership of or a broad license to use that feedback in any way (eliminating limitations on how feedback may be incorporated into future products)
- An explanation as to how the information gathered from the participants may be used
- A statement that communicates that participant-confidential information should only be provided if and only if necessary in order to provide feedback – clearly noting that the primary intent is to collect feedback and not any participant-confidential information (this puts the responsibility on the participating company representatives to protect their information by simply not disclosing it)
- Sufficient flexibility so that the agreement can cover multiple activities, by a variety groups with the same general intent and goal, over a period of time
- Use of a "project attachment" (or addendum) to define new projects and a disclosure period whenever needed without having to draft a new CPCA and new legal terms

The CPCA is now a requirement for any Oracle development activity that involves collecting feedback from customers. So if a customer is a member of an existing customer advisory board or customer council at Oracle, their company should have already signed a CPCA. Once a signed CPCA is obtained from a customer company, any development organization within Oracle may leverage the same CPCA without having to obtain a new agreement, as long as the document was written to cover multiple activities. In the case that it was not written to cover multiple activities, only a new project attachment (addendum) would be required. This ability to use or modify an existing agreement drastically reduces the time required for recruitment for a specific activity. With an existing CPCA on file, an individual could theoretically participate in a user experience activity immediately.

3.2 Central Database or System

Equally important to Oracle's customer recruitment program is the Customer Participation Database (CPD). Originally, we kept track of the companies that signed the CPCA and participated in UX activities utilizing a spreadsheet (see Figure 1). However, it very soon became apparent that this was not feasible and required too much manual entry and too many separate, but related spreadsheets. It was determined that a single database was required. This database could track CPCA status, contact information and descriptive information for individuals at the company who had participated or were interested in participating in UX activities, a list of UX activities that each individual and company had participated in, and so on. The customer participation database would make it easy to identify user types who aren't necessarily interested in the product (such as end-users), but who may match the user profile that we are seeking.

Company	Name	Title	Location	Phone	Email	Product	Source	Notes
Company A	First & Last name	Senior Manager, Global Incentive Pay	Boston, MA	555-555-5555	email address	Enterprise, HCM Employee Self-Service	HCM Connect 2004	Expressed interest in participating in usability evaluations.
Company B	First & Last name	IT Solutions Specialist	Chicago, IL	555-555-5555	email address	Enterprise, HCM Employee Self-Service & Manager Self-Service	HCM Connect 2004	Area of interest: HCM
Company C	First & Last name	IT Solutions, HR	Santa Clara, CA	555-555-5555	email address	Enterprise, HCM (Employee Self-Service), & FMS	Bill Johnson (Oracle)	Upgrading from 7.5 to 8.8. Expressed interest in participating in usability evaluations.
Company D	First & Last name	Functional Analyst	Hyderabad India	555-555-5555	email address	FMS, HRMS, EPM, CRM, PeopleTools	UE Connect 2003	Expressed interest in participating in usability evaluations.

Fig. 1. Typical Information gathered in a spreadsheet

The Customer Participation Database makes it easy to search for and obtain contact information for users who aren't necessarily interested in the product from a technical perspective, but instead use a product or similar product every day as a part of their job. Obtaining contact data makes it easier to track down participants who match a user profile but who do not have a professional relationship with any other Oracle organizations. A key part of this process is to collect and store as much information about the company and its employees as possible (see Figures 2, 3, and 4).

Overview

Name : Angela's Company

HQ Address : 1234 Street
        Detroit Michigan 48048
        United States

HQ Phone : 555-555-5555

Website : http://www.angelascompany.com

Oracle Contact :

Participation/Projects :

CPP Member: Yes

Notes :

Customer/Partner : Customer

Type : Public Sector

Industry : High Tech

CPCA/PPCA Status : Signed CPCA

Gift Policy : Oracle logo gifts under $10 in value are permitted

Number of Employees : 1,000-4,999

Oracle ASM : John Stevens

Fig. 2. Company information gathered and displayed in CPD

Projects Covered	Customer/Partner Signee	Master Effective	Oracle VP	Expiration Date	Recording Option
CABs, Councils, Focus Groups, Guide Groups, Requirement, Validation & Design Reviews, Customer Feedback Sessions and UX activities.	Angela Miller, President & CEO	25-AUG-12	Bob Fubble	25-AUG-15	Yes

Fig. 3. CPCA details displayed in CPD

Name	Title	Email	Time Zone	Phone	Associated Projects	Contact Type	Oracle Contact	Newsletter	Notes	Interested in UX Activity
Kristina Wheeler	Procurement Analyst	kwheeler@angelascompany.com	Eastern	(w) 555-555-5551 (c) 555-555-5552	UX Procurement CIF Test (Nov 2012)	Procurement	John Davis	Yes	Also willing to test HR and Finance apps.	Yes

Fig. 4. Contact information gathered and displayed in CPD

4 Tips and Hints

The creation of a customer recruitment program is a company-specific process so there are lots of ways that it can be implemented. This section covers some of the elements that we think are most important to consider and develop plans for. However, this is not an instructional manual or even a checklist. You should only set up a customer recruitment program after discussions with your company's Legal and Product Management teams.

4.1 Practical

There are a number of practical issues that relate to the customer participation program. These are tips that we found useful for helping to find participants and keep track of their participation.

Create, Update and Maintain a Database: We continually work to keep information current and track all participation. We do our best to ensure that the information entered is as complete as possible (see examples above) and not just the information related to one activity, but all activities that fall under the CPCA. The CPD makes it easy to identify potential participants. However, this process only works if the information exists in the database.

Implement Quality Control for your Database: Once the database is established, it can be maintained by many organizations. This allows for the quick accumulation of data and the ability to share information. However, we find that some mechanism of quality control should be maintained, either through limiting the allocation of "administrator accounts" and by allowing a central administrator to review any changes before they are made permanent. It is practical to be consistent. We established processes and UI controls (i.e. using drop-down fields or radio buttons) allowing data to be entered consistently to allow for easy searching.

Start Recruiting Early: Customer recruiting starts long before UX activities are planned. Getting the CPCA signed can be time consuming as it may be difficult to find someone with the appropriate signing authority for the company and to answer all of their questions about the document. With this in mind, we actively attempt to have the CPCA signed by as many customer companies as possible prior to their being involved in a UX activity.

Publicize: We promote our customer participation program at conferences (user group events and Oracle conferences), attend customer advisory boards, and customer council meetings. We write a newsletter with on-going, current information about UX activities at Oracle. We invite customers to learn about UX and the ways that we are trying to work with customers. We are also partnering with Product Management and Marketing to help them understand how promoting UX to their customers can benefit their organizations.

4.2   Ethics

There are many articles about the ethics of user recruitment and participation in usability tests [6, 7] and there are a number of professional "codes of conduct" published by professional organizations such as the American Psychological Association [1] and the User Experience Professionals Association [9]. However, there are a few elements of customer recruitment which are unique and therefore may not covered in those documents.

Customers are NOT the General Public: The ethical guidelines and advice related to recruitment from the general public may not always apply to customers. Individuals at a company that has a CPCA on file may be asked by a manager or colleague to participate. Therefore, their participation in the UX activity is known by the company and is officially a part of their employment. As a result, articles related to usability testing with internal participants (employees) [3] will likely have more relevance than those articles & guidelines that assume participation by the general public [4].

Confidentiality of Nonparticipation: Customer representatives that are nominated for a user experience activity by their colleagues, manager, or upper management may feel unable to decline to participation. Participants should be informed that their participation is confidential and if they wish to decline participation, their management will not be informed of their decision.

Confidentiality of Participation: While it is common practice to explain to participants that they are not being tested but in fact are the evaluators themselves [5] participants may have concerns that their usability test data might reflect badly upon themselves. Participants should be clearly informed that the data collected is confidential and would NOT be shared with their manager or colleagues.

Scope of Data: A final consideration is the nature of the data collected. Because individuals are participating as representatives of their company and the participation is "blessed" by their employers, they may feel more comfortable providing data about their company practices. While legally, the burden of determining what they are allowed to communicate during the user experience activity is on the employee and their company, the UX practitioner should be considerate of the questions that they ask and how they handle the data collected.

Confidentiality: Anonymity of participants should be maintained so that only those who have a reason to view participant data or identifying information should be able to do so. This prevents PMs and Marketing teams from viewing confidential data that might impact their relationship with the customer company. "The usability engineer is responsible to adequately protect the privacy of their participants. Failing to protect their privacy, even from management within the testing organization is a breach of the contractual agreement entered into with the study's participants." [3].

Relationship Management: A final consideration is the relationship between your company and your customers may be affected by any confusion or concerns over ethics. Any *perception* of ethical misconduct or even simple misunderstandings could damage the relationship between the customer and your company. A company may expect to be provided information about their employee's participation that you feel that you cannot provide, as it violates your ethical guidelines. It is imperative that a clear description of what companies can expect and NOT expect should be provided.

Signing Authority: It is important to ensure that the appropriate individuals review and sign the CPCA. The individual who signs the CPCA must have the authority to bind their company and its employees. It is not your responsibility to understand the customer company's policies to determine who has the appropriate authority to sign the document, but ethically, you should make a good faith effort to ensure that you have the appropriate signature level. It is imperative that all communications (see Figure 5) with individuals at the company stress this requirement.

In preparation for your participation in the upcoming **Revenue Management & Billing CAB Meetings**, I have attached our Customer Participation Confidentiality Agreement (CPCA) for review. The next step is to have the CPCA signed and return it to us before the meeting/event. This document is required to cover participation in Oracle Activities when we are collecting feedback on Oracle products/services and to serve as an NDA when Oracle Confidential Information may be shared. Please have your organization's appropriate signatory review the CPCA and let me know if you have any questions. By signing the CPCA, the signee must represent that they have signatory authority to bind your organization to the terms of the agreement. Please return signed document to...

Fig. 5. Letter accompanying Standard CPCA

5 Conclusion

At this point, we are having great success with our customer participation program. As a result, last year we conducted over 320 UX activities, recruiting 75% of the participant base from customer companies. Our customer participation program has lowered our cost significantly, and protects Oracle's legal interests more effectively. In this paper, we've attempted to show how setting up a customer recruitment program can address some of the problems inherent in traditional methods of obtaining participants and the benefits of utilizing customers. We've also reviewed the elements that we think are essential (a good legal document and a database) to a customer recruitment program. Hopefully, you are now motivated to start your own customer recruitment program or to at least supplement your existing individual participant recruitment program.

References

1. Association for Computing Machinery (ACM) Code of Ethics and Professional Conduct, http://www.acm.org/about/code-of-ethics
2. Bartek, V., Cheatham, D.: Experience Remote Usability Testing, Part 1. In: IBM Developer Works (2003), http://www.ibm.com/developerworks/web/library/wa-rmusts1/
3. Burmeister, O.: HCI Professionalism: Ethical Concerns in Usability Engineering. In: CRPIT 2000 Selected Papers from the 2nd Australian Institute of Computer Ethics Conference (AICE 2000), pp. 11–17. ACS, Canberra (2001)
4. Dumas, J.S., Fox, J.E.: Usability Testing: Current Practice and Future Directions. In: Sears, A., Jacko, J. (eds.) The Human-Computer Interaction Handbook: Fundamentals, Evolving Technologies, and Emerging Applications, Lawrence Erlbaum Associates, New York (2008)
5. Dumas, J., Redish, J.: A practical guide to usability testing. Intellect Books, Portland (1994)
6. Minocha, S., Tzanidou, E.: Ethics in usability engineering. In: 2010/Interaction Design for International Development, pp. 20–24. Indian Institute of Technology, Bombay India (2010)
7. Molich, R., Laurel, C., Snyder, C., Quesenbery, W., Wilson, C.: Ethics in HCI. In: CHI 2001 Extended Abstracts on Human Factors in Computing Systems, pp. 217–218. ACM Press, New York (2001)
8. Sova, D., Nielsen, N.: How to recruit participants for usability studies (2003), http://media.nngroup.com/media/reports/free/How_To_Recruit_Participants_for_Usability_Studies.pdf
9. UPA Code of Professional Conduct (2005), http://ethics.iit.edu/ecodes/node/3139

Novel Method of Evaluating GUI Design
from the Viewpoint of Worker Experience

Central Control Systems for Social Infrastructure

Daiki Hama[1], Mai Kurioka[1], Mariko Kato[2], Ken Imamura[2], and Miwa Nakanishi[1]

[1] Keio University, Yokohama, Japan
hamadai@a3.keio.jp, miwa_nakanishi@ae.keio.ac.jp
[2] Hitachi, Ltd., Tokyo, Japan
{mariko.kato.kd,ken.imamura.fd}@hitachi.com

Abstract. In this study, the value of different experiences obtained from operations was defined as worker experience. From this viewpoint, we have developed a novel method to evaluate graphical user interfaces (GUI) for next-generation control systems for social infrastructure. Beyond the traditional concept of *ease of use*, this method aims to introduce a *sense of worth* gained by operations and instill some sense of motivation to work through the GUI design, which will provide GUI designers a new viewpoint. In this paper, this method was adapted to application software to use it more practically, and the GUIs of two different systems are evaluated.

Keywords: worker experience, GUI, design evaluation.

1 Introduction

It is extremely important that social infrastructure systems such as plant control systems and IT systems are efficiently and stably operated. Most operations are processed through interaction between operators and systems via computer screens. Therefore, the interface—the system's graphical user interface (GUI)—plays an extremely important role.

The GUIs of such systems have mostly been evaluated and implemented from the viewpoint of *ease of use* so that operators can avoid overlooking or misreading important parameters, spot alerts quickly and make decisions accurately. Because of these efforts, current GUIs realise a very high *ease of use*. However, the next-generation GUI is expected to enrich operators experience in work and enhance their motivation for the job and for teamwork. Thus, GUI designers are interested in the psychological effect of GUI on the operators.

In this study, we define these operators' experience as worker experience (WX) on the basis user experience (UX), the details of which are described in the next section. In addition, this study aims to construct a novel method to evaluate the GUI of a central control system for social infrastructure from the viewpoint of WX, which will support GUI designers in designing GUIs for systems that effectively give operators a good experience at work.

A. Marcus (Ed.): DUXU/HCII 2013, Part I, LNCS 8012, pp. 283–293, 2013.

2   Procedure to Evaluate a System's GUI from the Viewpoint of WX

UX is defined in ISO9241-210:2010[1] as a person's perceptions and responses resulting from the use and/or anticipated use of a product, system or service. This is a concept that includes all of the experience with respect to the use of products and services. This study applies the concept of UX and proposes the concept of WX—defined here as 'worker's perceptions resulting from a particular task'.

Evaluating systems or methods at work from the viewpoints of WX is, in other words, evaluating how systems or methods can increase the value of operators' experiences from work. In this study, we specially focus on a work environment where a large system is managed via a computer screen, then embody WX in this situation and finally build the process to evaluate the system's GUI from the viewpoints of WX.

As stated above, UX is a concept of including work experiences in which users use products and services. Similarly, WX is a concept of including experiences in which workers use the system's GUI. Therefore, in the evaluation processes, a wide range of factors has to be discussed at the same time. In order to do so, this study introduces the performance shaping factor (PSF) model, which is well known in human error research, into the evaluation of a system's GUI from the viewpoint of WX. The PSF refers to the various factors that influence human performance. In particular, human error researchers have focused on 'bad factors' which cause bad experiences for operators. In this research area, on the basis of the idea that the condition of the PSF can change the possibility of human error, a method to extract, analyses and control the PSF has been developed and applied in practical fields. Fig. 2 shows the structure of influence from PSF on human error.

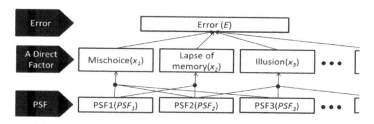

Fig. 1. Structure of influence of PSF on human error

On the other hand, there are also some 'good factors' that influence human performance. This study focuses on such factors and explores a method to extract, analyse and control the PSF that is a reason for good experiences of operators, based on the idea that the condition of the PSF can raise the expectation that the operators are motivated, delighted, confident and so on. Fig. 2 shows the structure of the influence of the PSF on WX.

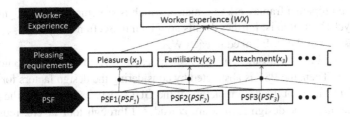

Fig. 2. Structure of influence of PSF on WX

On the basis of this structure, this study attempts to establish a method to evaluate the system's GUI from the viewpoint of WX. In this process, we adopt the GUI of an IT management system as a case study. Thus, the PSF corresponds to the design elements of the system's GUI that relate to the operator's good experience. The evaluation method enables an estimation to be made of the WX that is expected in the work of IT management by evaluating the state of each PSF. The perspective of this method is shown in Fig. 3. The specific process to establish the method is described below.

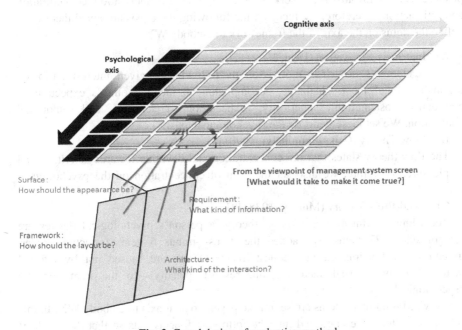

Fig. 3. Grand design of evaluation method

A) Embodiment of WX

First of all, it is necessary to identify what can be considered to be WX for the operator in a given situation. In order to embody WX from as many viewpoints as possible, we prepare a framework in a matrix which is structured by the cognitive axis and the psychological axis. Further details are given in Section 3.

B)   Abstract of the PSF linked to each WX

Second, we link the abstract of the PSF to each WX that was embodied in the previous step. Then, the PSF is abstracted by considering the design factors for realising each WX, such as what the design factors of the GUI satisfy or enhance in the particular WX. Furthermore, the design factors are considered through four layers: requirement, architecture, framework and surface. Further details are given in Section 4.

C)   Establishing the method to estimate WX from PSF scoring

Each PSF abstracted in the previous step is set as an item in the checklist, and it is used for evaluation. By determining whether the evaluation target GUI meets each item, the result, which is how much of WX will be realised by the GUI in the work, is estimated. Further details are given in Section 5.

3   Embodiment of WX

In order to effectively manage large systems, it is important that operators have positive feelings towards their work, such as high level of motivation, concentration and satisfaction. Therefore, we focus on the following three psychological theories to define the items on the axis of the framework to embody WX.

A)   Inntrinsic Motivation (Deci, 1972) [2]

As the elements of intrinsic motivation, the following are given: interest, curiosity, originality, amazement, challenge, accomplishment, meeting other's expectations, confidence, ostentation, superiority, expectation, attachment and emotional connection. We set these items on the psychological axis.

B)   Flow Theory (Csikszentmihalyi, 1990) [3]

The flow theory states that the concentration and devotion towards activities lead to pleasure. Therefore, we also set the item of concentration on the psychological axis.

C)   Need-Press Theory (Murray, 1938) [4]

According to Murray's need-press theory, a person's psychological desires are categorised in 27 items. We added the items—minus 6 items (structure, order, imitation, clarification, caring, request, reaction) that are caused not by internal factors but by external factors (pain, reward, penalty)—to the items on the psychological axis.

A revised total of 17 items are set on the psychological axis to embody WX. In this study, these items are classified into the following four aspects so that the result of evaluation can be easily understandable: pleasure, sense of worth, comfort, relationship (Table 1).

Table 1. 17 psychological aspects

Pshchological theory	Psychological item	Detail	Classification
Intrinsic Motivation	interest & curiosity	You can take an interest.	pleasure
	originality	You can feel an originality.	pleasure
	amazement	You can have an experience with amazement.	pleasure
	challenge & accomplishment	You can feel fulfilled.	sense of worth
	confidence	You can become more confident.	sense of worth
	ostentaion & superiority	You can superior to others.	sense of worth
	expectation	You can come up to my expectation.	comfort
	attachment	You can feel an attachment.	relationship
	emotional connection	You can enjoy a sense of togetherness.	relationship
	respondence to the expectations from others	You can respond to the expectations from others.	relationship
Flow Theory	enthusiasm & devotion & concentration	You can concentrate.	pleasure
Need-Press Theory	composition & tidying	You can feel a gathering.	comfort
	imitation	You want to imitate.	comfort
	elucidation	You can clearly explain.	comfort
	nursing	You can become eager to help.	relationship
	request	You can become eager to lean.	relationship
	reaction	You can feel the difference between you and others.	relationship

On the other hand, the 6 aspects, which are commonly seen in many noted cognitive models, are set on the cognitive axis. The details are shown in Table 2.

Table 2. 6 cognitive aspects

	Cognitive item	Detail
1	Receipt of an information	Ease of information acquisition
2	Checking of a memory	Making use of a past experience
3	Conception of a mental model	Ease of making the correct image
4	Action	Ease of behavior
5	Feedback on behavior	Ease of obtaining the response
6	Stock of a memory	Ease of learning

As a consequence, we prepare a framework to embody WX by using both psychological aspects and the cognitive aspects (Fig. 4).

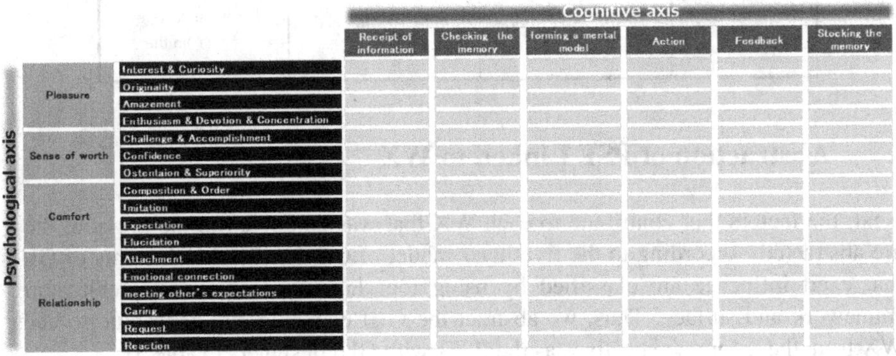

Fig. 4. Framework to embody WX

WX is embodied from several perspectives by filling in each cell of the matrix framework. This method also gives example sentences to appropriately and easily support embodying of each WX. Parts of example sentences are shown in Table 3.

Table 3. Example sentences to support embodying of WX

		Receipt of information	Checking the memory	forming a mental model
Pleasure	Interest & Curiosity	① You want to look (information, behavior).	①You want to associate current (event, action) and similar previous (event, action)	①You want to simulate an image of (my action).
		Action	**Feedback**	**Stocking the memory**
		①You want to perform (my action).	①You want to check the signal from (system, organization, others).	①You want to memorize an actual status because of what might happen ([similar experience])in the furure.

We embodied WX in the domain of IT management by using the framework. By filling in each cell of this matrix with the views of practical operators, a concrete WX was obtained as shown in Table 4.

Table 4. Embodied WX in the work of an IT management operation

		Receipt of information	Checking the memory	forming a mental model
Pleasure	Interest & Curiosity	① You want to look (the information from the screen).	①You want to associate current (system failure) and similar previous (system failure)	①You want to simulate an image of (my handling for server down).
		Action	**Feedback**	**Stocking the memory**
		①You want to perform (more effective system operation).	①You want to check the signal from (server).	①You want to memorize an actual status because of what might happen ([current handling for server down])in the furure.

4   Abstraction of PSF Linked to WX

Next, the factors that contribute to each WX that was embodied in the previous step are abstracted. According to the five-layer model of Garrett [5], the elements of GUI that exert influence are classified by using four layers: requirement, architecture, framework and surface. Thus, we abstract the GUI elements that contribute to each WX from these four perspectives as the PSFs with GUI designers (Table 5).

Table 5. Five-layer model

	layer	Details	Contents
1	Requirement	What kind of the method?	Function, Technique
2	Architecture	What kind of the interaction?	Medium, Exchange with the user
3	Framework	What kind of the process and the media content?	Flow, Content
4	Surface	What kind of the beauty and the senses?	Look and Feel, Stimulus to the senses

Table. 6. shows the abstracted PSFs for each layer that contribute to WX [You want to look (the information from the screen)].

Table 6. Extracted PSFs in evaluation of the GUI of IT management system

		Requirement	Architecture	Framework	Surface
Pleasure	Interest & Curiosity	· The attractive information I want to see.	· Understanding an explanation and a technical lunguage.	· Preferential access to prior information. · Momentary warning by pop-up or alarm in abnormal time.	· Tinting for only important information. · Tinting and sound for only a warning.

5   Development of the Evaluation Method

A checklist to determine whether the GUI meets each PSF is complied by using the PSFs abstracted in the previous step. Each item on the checklist is evaluatedand the evaluation result is computed. The result suggests which PSFs are satisfied, which aspects of WX could be realised, and how much of WX in total could be realised. Each item on the checklist is judged and quantified as follows. If a GUI satisfies a PSF perfectly, it is judged as 'Perfect'. If a GUI satisfies a PSF partially, it is judged as 'Partial'. And, if a GUI does not satisfy a PSF at all, it is judged as 'None'. This method outputs the following four indices as the evaluation result.

1) Index of sufficiency level of PSF

The index of sufficiency level of PSF suggests which PSFs are satisfied and to what degree they are satisfied. The result is visualised as shown in Table 7, in which the sufficiency levels are expressed in different colours. Thus, we can easily understand which of PSFs are satisfied absolutely or partially or never. This index shows the evaluation result in more detail than any of the other indices.

Table 7. Sufficiency level of PSF of the GUI for an IT management system

		Requirement	Architecture	Framework	Surface
Pleasure	Interest & Curiosity	· The attractive information I want to see.	· Understanding an explanation and a technical lunguage.	· Preferential access to prior information. · Momentary warning by pop-up or alarm in abnormal time.	· Tinting for only important information. · Tinting and sound for only a warning.

2) Index of satisfaction level of WX

The index of satisfaction level of WX suggests which WX can be realised by using the GUI in the work. This index is calculated by the following procedure. According to the evaluation of each PSF of four layers that contributes to a particular WX, the score is given as follows: the PSF judged to be 'Perfect' is given as 1.0, the PSF judged to be 'Partial' is given as 0.5, the PSF judged to be 'None' is given as 0.0. Moreover, when all the PSFs of the four layers are judged to be 'Perfect', a bonus score is added. The total WX score is calculated as follows:

$$WX = PSF_{Requirement} \times 20 + PSF_{Architecture} \times 20 + PSF_{Framework} \times 20 + PSF_{Surface} \times 20 + 20 \tag{1}$$

Accordingly, WX is estimated from 0 [%] to 100 [%]. This visualised result can be expressed as shown in Table 8. We can easily understand which WX has high expectations of being realised and which one could not be realised.

Table 8. Satisfaction level of WX at work using the GUI for an IT management system [%]

		Receipt of Information	Checking the memory	forming a mental model	Action	Feedback	Stocking the memory
Pleasure	Interest & Curiosity	50	30	100	60	100	50
	Originality	100	50	40	70	100	60
	Amazement	70	60	40	20	40	60
	Enthusiasm & Devotion & Concentration	100	70	60	100	100	60
Sense of worth	Challenge & Accomplishment	50	30	100	20	50	60
	Confidence	50	40	60	60	50	40
	Ostentaion & Superiority	70	30	40	30	40	30
Comfort	Composition & Order	70	70	70	70	60	40
	Imitation	70	60	70	50	20	60
	Expectation	60	60	70	40	60	100
	Elucidation	100	40	100	70	70	60
Relationship	Attachment	20	30	20	30	20	100
	Emotional connection	10	0	10	0	0	10
	Respondence to the expectations from others	0	0	100	50	50	60
	Caring	0	0	0	20	20	20
	Request	0	0	0	0	0	0
	Reaction	0	0	0	0	0	0

3) Index of satisfaction level of each aspect of WX [%]

The index of satisfaction level of each of the four aspects of WX suggests which aspect of WX is expected to be realised. This index helps us understand the evaluation result more easily. It is given by calculating the average of each WX score that belongs to a particular aspect (see Table 8). The result is expressed by the chart shown in Fig. 5. In this case, in which the GUI for IT management system is evaluated, we can understand from the result that the WX concerning pleasure, sense of worth and comfort has a high expectation of being realised. However, the WX concerning relationship has a low expectation of being realised by using the GUI. Thus, it is suggested that the GUI could be improved by focusing on this aspect, so that a higher level of WX could be achieved.

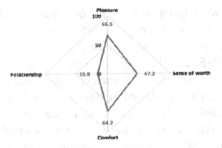

Fig. 5. Satisfaction level of each aspect of WX at work using the GUI for an IT management system [%]

4)   Index of total estimation of WX [%]

The index of total estimation of WX means to what degree the GUI can realise WX as a whole in the work. This index is given by calculating the average of all WX scores. In this case, in which the GUI for the IT management system is evaluated, the total estimation of WX is *48.36(%)*.

This evaluation method is implemented as a PC application as shown in Fig. 6 for practical use. By using this application, it is expected that GUI designers can discuss their development of a GUI from the viewpoints of WX.

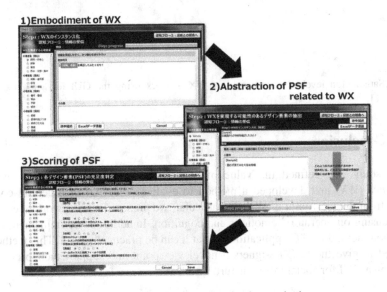

Fig. 6. Implementation of evaluation method

6   Verification of Applicability to Other Systems

In order to verify the possibility of applying the evaluation method to the GUI to another system, we evaluate the GUI of a plant control system by using this method.

As the same steps were taken as those in the case in which the GUI of an IT management system was evaluated, the WX in the work of plant control was embodied, after which the GUI element of the plant control system linked to each WX was extracted as a PSF, and then the WX scores were calculated by determining whether each PSF was designed to a sufficiently high level. As a result, the GUI for the plant control system was evaluated as shown in Fig. 7. In this case, in which the GUI for the plant control system is evaluated, we can understand that the WX concerning pleasure, sense of worth and comfort shows high expectations of being realised. However, the WX concerning relationship shows a low expectation of being realised by using the GUI. This result is similar to the result of the evaluation of the GUI for the IT management system. This suggests that the GUI for the plant control system should also be improved by focusing on the aspect of relationships, such as teamwork among the operators or communication with each other, so that higher level of WX can be achieved.

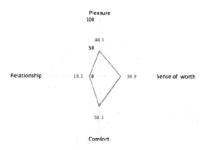

Fig. 7. Satisfaction level of each aspect of WX at work using the GUI for a plant control system [%]

7   Conclusion

In this study, we defined the value of experiences obtained in work as *worker experience (WX)* and developed a method to evaluate the GUI of a central control system from the viewpoint of WX. In particular, we prepared a framework to embody WX focusing on operators' emotions and cognition. In addition, we implemented the evaluation method for PC application so that it can be practically used. This method is expected to give the GUI designers a novel viewpoint and support their process of designing a GUI for social infrastructure systems.

Acknowledgement. We would like to thank Mr. Takashi Matsubara and Mr. Masahide Ban (Hitachi, Ltd.) who provided helpful comments and suggestions.

References

1. ISO9241-210:2010: Ergonomics of Human-System Interaction-Part 210: Human-Centered Design for Interactive Systems (2010)
2. Deci, E.L., et al.: Intrinsic motivation, extrinsic reinforcement and inequity. Journal of Perdonality and Social Psychology 22, 113–120 (1972)
3. Chilszentmihalyi, M.: Flow: The Pshchology of Optimal Experience. Harper and Row, New York (1990)
4. Murray, H.A., et al.: Explorations in Personality. Oxford, New York (1938)
5. Garrett, J.J.: The elements of User Experience (1990)

Understand System's Relative Effectiveness Using Adapted Confusion Matrix

Nan Jiang[1] and Haibin Liu[2]

[1] Software Systems Research Centre,
School of Design, Engineering and Computing
Bournemouth University, United Kingdom
njiang@bournemouth.ac.uk
[2] National Center for Biotechnology Information
National Library of Medicine
National Institutes of Health, United States
haibin.liu@nih.gov

Abstract. The effectiveness of a system refers to the accuracy and completeness with which users achieve specified goals. These two aspects are interpreted as errors and completion in the context of usability testing. However, a holistic view of effectiveness is not straight forward to establish in a comparative test because the two measures focus on different aspects of user outputs. In this paper, we propose a predictive method to measure a system's relative effectiveness based on its own performance prediction. We achieve it by using an adapted confusion matrix to establish a correlation model between the two measures. A real-world use case is provided to demonstrate the usefulness of our method in a comparative study of the two websites.

Keywords: Accuracy, completeness, errors, completion, confusion matrix.

1   Introduction

The definition of effectiveness considers two aspects with which users achieve specified goals: accuracy and completeness [1]. In usability testing, the two aspects are commonly interpreted by errors and completion respectively [2] and thus are often measured as error rate and task completion rate [3]. A practical understanding of effectiveness in the measurement is that the system should aim at low error occurrences and good task completions. However, there might exist other potential factors in a comparative study as the comparison is mainly done through using relevant usability metrics. Moreover, if a holistic view of effectiveness cannot be established, it will not be able to understand a system's relative effectiveness appropriately, leading to an inaccurate comparison.

A few approaches have been taken to address this issue. For example, ISO guideline introduced a single measure of effectiveness by multiplying accuracy and completeness (i.e., error rate × completion rate) but it also states that the formula only works when one measure can be traded off by the other. Alternatively, error-free rate,

A. Marcus (Ed.): DUXU/HCII 2013, Part I, LNCS 8012, pp. 294–302, 2013.

which is defined as the percentage of participants who completed the task without any errors, can be used to understand the "quality" of completion in the context of errors [6]. The downside is also obvious: this measure works better only when all systems in the comparison have achieved good task completions [4]. Otherwise, the results are not convincible. Moreover, it can also establish the understanding within a more generic context by considering all key usability metrics. For example, effectiveness can be measured in conjunction with efficiency and/or satisfaction measures through a single, summated metric [7][8][9]. Since this process is commonly achieved by summing up individual metrics via a weighting scheme, the success of this method relies on choosing the appropriate scheme. However, such parameters for optimized weighting scheme are not trivial.

In this paper, we propose a method to discover and measure a system's relative effectiveness based on its own performance prediction. First, a correlation model is defined and then presented by adapting confusion matrix in Section 2. A case study demonstrating the use of the method in practice is provided in Section 3. Section 4 presents results and discussion and Section 5 is the conclusion.

2   Methodology

2.1   Correlation for Relative Effectiveness

A holistic view of effectiveness is crucial for understanding a system's relative effectiveness in comparative usability test. In order to establish this, it needs to correlate the measurements of errors and completion first. The link between errors and completion is not always obvious because errors are varied in different contexts. In fact, there are many ways to categorize errors for identifying potential usability problems. We take a widely used approach [5] by classifying errors into critical and non-critical errors based on their impact on task performance. The main difference between the two groups is that only critical errors will result in task incompletion as they represent unsolved errors.

Let e represent an estimated upper bound of errors of a system and

$$e \in [0, Error_{max}]$$

where $Error_{Max}$ is the maximum number of errors happened when an individual user performs the task. If a system reported relatively the most task completions in $[0, e]$, it indicates that relatively the fewest critical errors were made in the same interval, too. Then the system's relative effectiveness can be considered as the performance it achieved with $[0, e]$. Moreover, when e is close to the lower boundary, it will also imply that most errors made by users are non-critical errors. In other words, the smaller e the system has, the better relative effectiveness it has achieved. Therefore, a system's relative effectiveness can be understood in two steps:

1. Predict the e for the system.
2. Measure the performance of the system at the e.

2.2   Adapted Confusion Matrix

Confusion matrix [10] is a predictive method widely used for understanding the performance of different classification algorithms (classifiers) in artificial intelligence, information retrieval and data mining. The core concept of this method is to compare the results of a classifier with established presets to understand how accurate the results are to these benchmarks. As illustrated in Table 1, this process is done by using a 2 × 2 matrix to visualize the differences between the true (presets) and predicted classes (classifiers).

Table 1. A common confusion matrix

		Prediction	
		Positive	Negative
Actual	Positive	*true positive cases (tp)*	*false negative cases (fn)*
	Negative	*false positive cases (fp)*	*true negative cases (tn)*

In this matrix, each row represents an actual or observed class while each column represents a predicted class. Then each cell can be used to count the number of samples in the intersection for those classes. Four terms are used here:

- True positive: true cases correctly identified;
- False negative: true cases mistakenly identified as false ones;
- True negative: false cases correctly identified;
- False positive: false cases mistakenly identified.

Once such a table is generated, it can easily visualize the performance of a classifier. Since it needs to find out at which e a system showed relatively the best effectiveness, it is clear that the classifier should be usability metrics used to measure errors. Here the number of errors is selected as it is one of the fundamental usability metrics. Moreover, since task completion is often determined with a binary measure, completion and incompletion can be used to present the concept of positive cases and negative cases. As discussed above, an adapted confusion matrix can therefore be established using the number of errors as classifiers and completion/incompletion as classes (Table 2).

Table 2. Adapted confusion matrix with an estimated upper error bound as classifiers

		Prediction	
		Completion	Incompletion
Actual	Completion	*true positive cases (tp)*	*false negative cases (fn)*
	Incompletion	*false positive cases (fp)*	*true negative cases (tn)*

For a specific task, the number of errors made by a user on the system always belongs to [0, $Error_{max}$]. In other words, classifiers can be decided by picking up representative numbers of errors or error rates made by users as upper bounds.

2.3   Measurement

The two standard terminologies used to analyze confusion matrix data are used with adapted interpretations.

Recall is the proportion of completion correctly identified, which is calculated as:

$$recall = \frac{tp}{tp + fn}$$

Recall represents how accurate predicted completions are found in the actual observation. It will grow when the upper error bound increases. This is because more completion in the observation will be included into the prediction. Therefore, for any given number of errors, the higher the recall, the more task completions were occurred.

On the other hand, precision is the proportion of predicted completions that were correct, which is calculated as:

$$precision = \frac{tp}{tp + fp}$$

It presents a different perspective as it considers how accurate the actual completions were predicted. For a given number of errors, the higher the precision, the less incompletion were found. Considering the fact that incompletion is mainly driven by critical errors, precision actually implies the proportion of critical errors found at the upper error bound.

In order to find out the e of a system where it showed relatively the best effectiveness, it needs to identity at which upper error bound (classifier) the system reported relatively the highest recall and precision. The reason is obvious: relatively most task completions (recall) with least critical errors (precision) are shown at this boundary. In addition, the smaller the upper bound is, the fewer non-critical errors were reported. However, precision does not follow a similar linear progression as shown on recall when the upper bound increases. That is to say, when the recall is the highest, the precision is not always the highest. Thus, a balancing mechanism is needed. F1 score, which represents the harmonic mean of two numbers, is commonly used to provide a balanced view of high recall and precision, which is defined as follows:

$$Fscore = 2 \times \left(\frac{tp \times fp}{tp + fp}\right)$$

Hence, the highest F1 score can be used to identify and measure the e of a system to find out its relatively best effectiveness performance for comparison.

3   Case Study

A case study to compare the effectiveness of Play.com and Amazon.co.uk using this adapted confusion matrix method is presented in this section. Two tasks were designed for reflecting some of the most common uses of e-commerce websites [11] with the consideration of task complexity as follows:

1. Search the website to find out the cheapest 16GB SD card on sale.
2. Browse the website to find out the best selling picture books for a 6 years old girl with a budget of 10 pounds.

Task 1 is a bargain hunting type of task for known item purchase while Task 2 is a browsing and inspiration type of task for unknown item purchase. Considering the task complexity based on possible user actions and results, Task 1 is close and simple while Task 2 is semi-open and complex.

3.1   Sample Size

A total of 194 first-year computing students with an age between 18 and 24 from Bournemouth University were asked to take participate in this study where all of them responded that they had online shopping experience before in the background survey. The detailed sampling for each task is shown in Table 3 (Fisher's Exact, $p > 0.05$).

Table 3. Task sampling for websites

	Task 1	Task 2
Play.com	55	53
Amazon.co.uk	46	40

3.2   Data Collection

Key performance data were collected and recorded by volunteer observers sitting next to a participant during the test using Google Docs.

3.3   Usability Metrics Defined

Errors were defined by following Sauro's approach [13]. That is, an error is considered as a user's attempt led by a mouse click which was not needed for error-free task completion with the minimal effort. Here the minimal effort was pre-determined by considering all possibilities of landing pages and it was measured as key 'checkpoints' based on task analysis . This is particularly important to Task 2 as users may choose different categories reflecting their personal interests to start browsing. Error rate was chosen as the usability metric to measure errors, which was defined as the percentage of these attempts made by participants during the process of task completion. For example, if the minimal efforts were 4 attempts while 5 attempts were taken by a user, the error rate will be 10%.

Completion was calculated in a binary measure [12]. That is, a completion (by a participant) was considered only when he/she achieved the correct outcome based on the success criteria. For example, if the expected product of Task 1 was found in the user test, it will be considered as a success (completion). It should note that there were a few products expected for Task 2 because Task 2 is a semi-open task with various landing categories. Then a completion was decided based on the user's landing category. In addition, task completion rate, which is defined as the percentage of participants who successfully completed the tasks, was also measured to provide an overview of completion.

3.4   Confusion Matrix Setting

For illustration purpose, error rates were used as the classifiers of the adapted confusion matrix and their upper bounds were set from 0% to 99%. Note that 100% error rate found in a task indicates the task was not completed so there is no point to include it in the confusion matrix.

4   Results and Discussion

An overall view of results related to effectiveness measurement is illustrated in Fig. 1 where CR stands for task completion rate and ER stands for error rate.

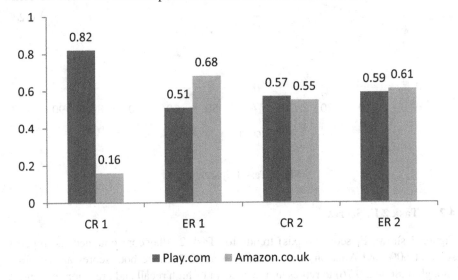

Fig. 1. An overall view of errors and completion

It is obvious that Play.com outperformed Amazon.co.uk in Task 1 as it achieved significantly lower error rate and higher task completion rate (82% and 51% vs. 16% and 68%). However, the two websites performed similarly in Task 2 which leads to a not straight forward justification. In detail, Play.com achieved 57% task completion rate with 59% error rate while Amazon.co.uk reported 55% with 61%.

4.1   Task 1 F_1 Scores

The F_1 score (y-axis) trends over the set of error rate bounds (x-axis) for Task 1 is illustrated in Fig. 2. The findings are in line with what we have found in the descriptive data as Play.com outperformed Amazon.co.uk at all error rate bounds. Moreover, both websites reported highest F_1 scores at 99% error rate (0.94 vs 0.28). Although Play.com obtained a significantly higher score, the error rate bound suggests that participants had to make more attempts on both websites in order to complete this task successfully. In addition, Play.com showed 0.29 at 0%, which means that error-free task completion was found on the website.

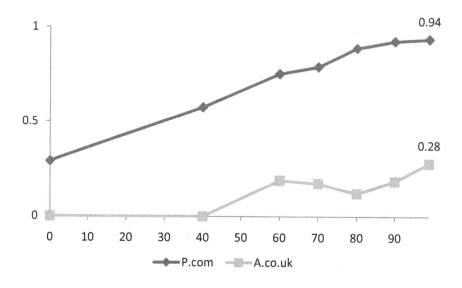

Fig. 2. Task 1 F_1 score trends

4.2   Task 2 F_1 Scores

Figure 3 shows F_1 score (y-axis) trends for Task 2. Play.com obtained the highest score at 60% and Amazon.co.uk obtained it at 90%. Since both scores are accurate enough (0.86 and 0.76) to represent the concept of high recall and precision, it suggest that Play.com has relatively better effectiveness than Amazon.co.uk as its upper error bound is lower. Again, Play.com showed error-free task completion (0%, 0.24) which was not found on Amazon.co.uk (0%, 0).

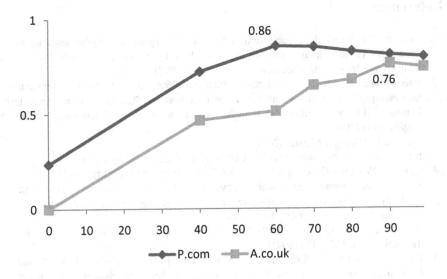

Fig. 3. Task 2 F_1 score trends

5   Conclusion

A predictive method has been described to measure a system's relative effectiveness in comparative studies by establishing a correlation between errors and completion and representing this concept with an adapted confusion matrix. It also uses F_1 score, which is a simplified single measure, to predict the system's relative effectiveness performance through a self-benchmarking process. Unlike other methods, this approach is more robust to the context and it does not require detailed error data recording. In fact, counting the number of errors or error rates will be sufficient with this method. This is particularly useful in remote, unmoderated testing environment. More importantly, the method is still based on the common understanding of effectiveness. It should note that the accuracy of measurement in the adapted confusion matrix relies on selecting an appropriate classifier. For example, error rates were chosen as classifiers in our case study rather than the number of errors because of the complexity of Task 2. In addition, when choosing referencing upper bounds, it should consider the representativeness of these values. Certainly, in order to generalize this method, more user studies focusing on different contexts (e.g., task difficulties) will be needed in the future.

Acknowledgements. The authors are grateful to Dr Amanda Schierz for providing advice on validating the method and to Dr John Beavis for suggestions and supports on statistics. Further thanks to all first year students in the 2011-2012 cohort at Bournemouth University for their participations. Thanks should also be given to a number of usability practitioners in UPA (Usability Professionals' Association) networks who shared their industrial experience and inspired the work. This research was supported in part by the Intramural Research Program of the NIH, NLM.

References

1. International Standards Organisation: ISO 9241-11 Ergonomic requirements for office work with visual display terminals (VDTs) - Part 11: Guidance on usability. Geneva. Switzerland: International Standards Organisation (1998)
2. International Standards Organisation: ISO/IEC 25062:2006 Software engineering - Software product Quality Requirements and Evaluation (SQuaRE) - Common Industry Format (CIF) for usability test reports. Geneva. Switzerland: International Standards Organisation (2006)
3. Nielsen, J.: Usability Metrics (2001), http://www.nngroup.com/articles/usability-metrics/
4. Sauro, J.: What is a Good Task Completion Rate? Measuring Usability (2011), http://www.measuringusability.com/blog/task-completion.php
5. Usability Test Plan Template (2012), http://www.usability.gov/templates/docs/u-test_plan_template.doc
6. Bevan, N., Macleod, M.: Usability Measurement in Context. Behaviour and Information Technology 13, 132–145 (1994)
7. Lin, H., Choong, Y., Salvendy, G.: A Proposed Index of Usability: A Method for Comparing the Relative Usability of Different Software Systems. Behaviour & Information Technology 16(4/5), 267–278 (1997)
8. Joshi, A., Tripathi, S.: User Experience Metric and Index of Integration: Measuring Impact of HCI Activities on User Experience. In: The First Workshop on the Interplay between Usability Evaluation and Software Development (I-USED 2008), Pisa, Italy (2008)
9. Sauro, J., Kindlund, E.: Using a Single Usability Metric (SUM) to Compare the Usability of Competing products. In: Annual SIGCHI Conference on Human Factors in Computing Systems, pp. 401–409. ACM, New York (2005)
10. Kohavi, R., Provost, F.: Glossary of Terms. Machine Learning 30, 2–3 (1998)
11. Nielsen, J.: E-Commerce Usability (2011), http://www.nngroup.com/articles/e-commerce-usability
12. Nielsen, J.: Success Rate: The Simplest Usability Metric (2001), http://www.useit.com/alertbox/20010218.html
13. Sauro, J., Lewis, J.R.: Correlations among Prototypical Usability Metrics: Evidence for The Construct of Usability. In: Annual SIGCHI Conference on Human Factors in Computing Systems, pp. 1609–1618. ACM, Boston (2009)

Development of a General Internet Attitude Scale

Mary Joyce and Jurek Kirakowski

School of Applied Psychology,
University College Cork, Ireland
{m.joyce,jzk}@ucc.ie

Abstract. This paper presents findings on the recently developed General Internet Attitude Scale (GIAS). Fundamental aspects of attitude in Social Psychological literature outlining appropriate definitions and theoretical frameworks are first presented. Previous issues in Internet attitude research are then reviewed with a focus on the validity of such proposed scales as measurement of attitude. The consideration of such issues in the development of the new attitude scale is then outlined, and the development process of the GIAS is summarized. Although studies with GIAS found difference between age groups, the effect sizes for differences between the genders were extremely small.

Keywords: Internet, Attitude, Measurement, Validity, Scale development, Gender differences, Age factors.

1   Introduction

Because the Internet has become so ubiquitous, the need to measure how individuals relate to the Internet has become an extremely important aspect of Human-Computer Interaction. However, the measurement of users' attitudes towards the Internet is a poorly researched topic. There have been few attempts at developing an Internet attitude scale in the last number of years [1-3]. These attempts have produced unsatisfactory means of measuring Internet attitudes and have raised issues that serve to obfuscate rather than clarify. Principal failings in the research to date stem from a lack of clarity regarding how attitudes in general are conceptualized. Issues include: the absence of a theoretical framework to measure attitudes; a lack of distinction between the terms 'attitude' and 'self-efficacy'; and inclusion of Internet *uses* as statements of Internet *attitude*.

The primary aim of this research was to develop a statistically reliable and psychometrically valid scale which accurately measures *attitudes* towards the *Internet*. In order to do so, guidelines for the development of attitude scales must be adhered to. With this in mind, this paper outlines briefly the fundamental background from Social Psychology attitude literature as it pertains to the development of the Internet attitude scale. Following this, the four main issues in previous Internet attitude literature are reviewed. The paper concludes with a brief outline of the newly developed General Internet Attitude Scale.

A. Marcus (Ed.): DUXU/HCII 2013, Part I, LNCS 8012, pp. 303–311, 2013.
© Springer-Verlag Berlin Heidelberg 2013

1.1   Definition of Attitude

Since the beginnings of attitude research, agreement on a definition of attitude has excited much debate amongst psychologists. Numerous definitions of attitude have been proposed since early characterizations of attitude at the beginning of the 20th Century. Fishbein and Ajzen's [4] description of attitude became the accepted definition for a considerable time, where they define an attitude as "a person's feelings toward and evaluation of some object, person, issue, or event" (p.12). Note the emphases on feelings toward and evaluation in their definition. In more recent times, Eagly and Chaiken [5] define an attitude more generally as "a psychological tendency that is expressed by evaluating a particular entity with some degree of favor or disfavor" (p.1). This research favors Eagly and Chaiken's more general definition of attitude and defines an Internet attitude as "a psychological tendency that is expressed by evaluating the Internet with some degree of favor or disfavor".

1.2   Theoretical Models of Attitude

Various models of attitude have also been proposed since the beginning of attitude research. These models have close connections to the definitions of attitude which have been proposed throughout the duration of attitude research. One, two and three component models of attitude have all been proposed by various researchers; the three component model being the dominant paradigm in attitude research for much of the last fifty years. The three component attitude model consists of *affect, behavior* and *cognitive* elements as first proposed by Katz and Stotland [6]. However, in recent times, Fishbein & Azjen [7] challenged the notion of the three-component model of attitude. The authors suggest that: "theory and measurement have converged on a unidimensional conception of attitude" (p.77). This unidimensional structure focuses on the "unitary evaluative dimension with respect to an object" (p. 76) [7]. However, there are arguments against such a position. Eagly and Chaiken [5] propose that while it may be the case that the proposed attitude components do not produce three separable omnipresent components of evaluation tendencies, an individual's experience with an attitude object might be *formed* or *expressed* on the basis of any one of three types of processes. Feelings, experiences and beliefs inform attitude; thus an individual's attitude to the Internet might be informed by their feelings towards it, their intended behavior to it, or what they think about it.

While it is possible to continue with theoretical propositions on the structure of attitudes, empirical evidence in the investigation of such theories is necessary. However, such evidence in support of these propositions has been minimal. Thus, it is imperative to empirically test the three-component model of attitudes to identify the underlying structure of attitudes.

This research favors Eagly and Chaiken's [5] position that affect, behavior and cognition ought to be considered in terms of the evaluative response that the attitude object elicits, and attitudes can be formed on the basis of any one, or a mix of the three types of processes involved. As a result, the three-component model is the theoretical framework applied to the development of the Internet attitude scale. Analyses of the scale will not only tell us information about the underlying structure of *Internet attitudes,* it should also provide suggestions about the underlying structure of attitudes in general.

2   Internet Attitudes

There have been a number of attempts at developing an Internet attitude scale since the turn of the twenty-first century. None of these studies have produced satisfactory means of measuring Internet attitudes. A number of issues have been identified with such attempts which include:

- lack of a theoretical framework for the measurement of attitudes
- inclusion of items which do not represent an attitude, or a component of an attitude
- lack of distinction and clarification between 'attitude' and 'self-efficacy'

The most significant issue identified in previous research has been the absence of a theoretical framework for the measurement of Internet attitudes.

2.1   Absence of Theoretical Framework

Some previous studies [1], [2], write statements for inclusion in their scale without reference to what (implicit) theories about the Internet and its usage were being held by the sources for the statements. More often than not, this has resulted in the inclusion of items which describe idiosyncratic *uses* of the Internet, rather than *attitudes* about the Internet. For example, the initial item pool for Morse et al's Attitudes Towards the Internet Scale (ATIS) [1] was created by identifying the most common uses of Internet technologies using five subject matter experts of Internet use. Instead of following a theoretical framework for attitude measurement on which items are based, common uses of Internet technologies were used to create statements for inclusion on the scale. The item pool resulted in 42 items encompassing seven general factors: general positive attitudes, general negative preferences and preferences for the following five activities: shopping, banking, information searching, entertainment, and communication. Examples of statements from two of the factors include: Shopping: 'I would rather shop online than in a physical store'; and Banking: 'I prefer to use the Internet to pay my bills rather than sending them by mail'. Such items represent uses of the Internet (indeed the authors do point out that items were developed through identification of the most common uses of the Internet!) rather than attitudes about the Internet. Consequently, Morse et al.'s questionnaire is really attempting to measure preference for use of Internet activities. Their failure to adhere to appropriate methodologies results in questionable validity of the items as measures of Internet attitude.

Similarly, Tsai et al.'s study [2] also failed to employ a methodology or theoretical framework for the development of attitude items for their Internet Attitude Scale (IAS). Tsai et al.'s IAS was developed through the revision of Selwyn's [8] Computer Attitude Scale (1997) with the addition of 11 new items following consultation with experts in Internet technology and technology education. The four subscales as initially proposed in Selwyn's Computer Attitude Scale and reiterated as appropriate for Tsai et al.'s study were (a) perceived usefulness – perceptions about the positive impacts of the Internet on individuals and society, (b) affection – feelings and anxiety when using the Internet, (c) perceived control – confidence about the independent control of Internet usage, and (d) behavior – assessment of actual practice and frequency of using the Internet. However, neither in Selwyn's original study, nor in Tsai et. al's study is it made clear as to how the four subscales were decided upon as being representative of attitudes. Although perceived usefulness may relate to the cognitive element of attitude and affection may relate to the affective element, it is difficult to see how perceived control and actual practice of using the Internet fit into an attitudinal model.

2.2   Inclusion of Non-attitude Items

In addition to the absence of a theoretical framework, the problem arises that proposed scale items may incorrectly represent components of an attitude. An example of this is the inclusion of the subscale 'behavior' which appears in some Internet attitude scales. Whilst behavior is proposed as one of the three components of attitude, attitude researchers have clearly outlined that the behavioral component of an attitude denotes the action *tendency* of the respondent to the object under investigation. It is well understood that very often, in the real, such a tendency to action may not be expressed in overt behavior, although it may persist over actual encounters.

Tsai et al.'s [2] statements for the subscale 'behavior' depict specific past behaviors in relation to the Internet. An example of one of these statements is 'I use the Internet regularly throughout school'. Tsai et al.'s behavior subscale consists of statements which assess students' practice and frequency of Internet use, instead of including items which refer to the intention to behave as recommended by attitude researchers. If veridically reported, actual behavior in the past may be a poor predictor of attitude toward and hence of attitude tendency at the present moment. One may have been forced to use the Internet through school, hated it, and therefore have an extreme aversion to ever using it in the future (although no doubt life will continue to inflict this painful experience over and over again in the 21st century.) As a result, such items inaccurately represent the proposed attitude components.

Additionally, statements which delineate specific past behaviors in relation to the Internet are evident in other Internet attitude scales. An example of one such item from Morse et al.'s study [1] is 'I like to sell items in Internet sites or Internet auctions'. Many items on these scales include statements which refer to specific uses of the Internet rather than attitudes about the Internet. Such statements tell us more about one's exposure to, and frequency of activity use on the Internet, rather than one's attitude about the Internet. Thus, the inclusion of such statements is unsatisfactory in attitude scales.

2.3   Lack of Distinction between 'Attitude' and 'Self-efficacy

A significant issue in past research is the lack of clarification and distinction between the terms attitude and self-efficacy. In Social Psychology, attitudes and self-efficacy are treated as separate constructs. An attitude is defined as "a psychological tendency that is expressed by evaluating a particular entity with some degree of favor or disfavor" (p.1) [5] whereas self-efficacy is described as "beliefs in one's capabilities to organize and execute the courses of action required to produce given attainments" (p. 3) [9]. Whilst attitude is concerned with an evaluation of some person or object; self-efficacy focuses on self-evaluation of personal capabilities in achieving goals.

Many studies which attempt to measure Internet attitudes include self-efficacy as a subscale, or a component of an Internet attitude. Why this should be is a mystery, especially as none of the authors who do so give any explanation of why they should expect to find self-efficacy as a component of an attitude. For example, Zhang [3] proposed an Internet attitude scale through adjustments made from a previous questionnaire used in Zhang, Dronet and VanMetre's [10] study which measured something other than Internet attitudes (although what is measured in this previous study is really unclear). Zhang explains that extensive changes were made to the previous questionnaire in an attempt to keep up with more recent technologies. Following a review of relevant literature, consultation with Internet professionals, reviews by experts in educational technology and professors who regularly use the Internet, the final version of the questionnaire consisted of forty items with ten items describing each of four proposed Internet attributes – Internet enjoyment, usefulness, anxiety, - and self-efficacy. It is unclear how these four attributes were decided upon for inclusion as subscales of the Internet attitude scale. A more cautious researcher might have attempted to find empirical evidence for the hypotheses generated by the reviewers. An Internet attitude refers to a person's *feelings,* likes and dislikes about the Internet whereas Internet self-efficacy focuses on the way a person evaluates their personal *capabilities* to achieve goals whilst using the Internet.

Self-efficacy and attitudes are constructs which are not interchangeable, and the difference between feelings and perceived capabilities indicate that self-efficacy should *not* be regarded as a component of an attitude. Therefore self-efficacy should not be included as a subscale of an attitude scale. Similarly, anxiety is not a component of attitude but is more representative of an emotion rather than an attitude. The implicit model of Zhang's reviewers of Internet experience is a psychological one, to be sure; but it is not a model that will find resonances in any mainstream theory in Social Psychology. As a result, the validity of the statements as measures of attitude in Zhang's Internet Attitude Scale is questionable.

Having identified the primary issues in previous Internet attitude measures was a salutary experience for the researchers as we started to address the development of the new Internet attitude scale. The development of this scale is now outlined.

3 Development of the General Internet Attitude Scale

As earlier outlined, the three component model of attitude is the framework which was followed for the development of the General Internet Attitude Scale (GIAS). The three components are briefly described as: *affect* - an emotion which charges the idea; a feeling which may be good or bad when thinking about the attitude object; *behavior* – the individual's predisposition to action in regard to the attitude object; and *cognition* – the beliefs and ideas a person has about the attitude object. The GIAS will consist of items relating to *Affect* (feelings, likes/ dislikes about the Internet), *Behavior* (behavioral tendencies to act a certain way on the Internet), and *Cognition* (beliefs and cognitions of individuals about the Internet).

An initial item pool of 97 statements was used in the first stage of scale development. Statements from four previous questionnaires which attempted to assess Internet attitudes were collated. These four studies were chosen as the basis for the item pool as these studies exemplified the best attempts at creating items depicting Internet attitudes in the past decade. It was decided that it was first important to address the earlier outlined issues with previous measures and statements which focused on specific Internet uses, or referred to feelings of confidence (self-efficacy) with the Internet, were deleted. When this was completed, the theoretical framework of attitudes employed by this research was applied to the final item pool. Each of the statements was examined in detail to identify whether or not the statement represented (or could represent) one of the three components of an attitude: affect, behavior or cognition. Following this step, the final scale ready for distribution, consisted of 27 items. There were 8 statements representing the 'affect' component, 8 statements representing the 'behavior' component, and 11 statements representing the 'cognition' component of an Internet attitude. Examples of statements representing each of the three attitude components are outlined in table 1.

Table 1. Examples of Statements in the General Internet Attitude Scale

Subscale	Statement
Internet Affect	I feel intimidated by the Internet
	I feel at ease using the Internet
Internet Behavior	The less contact I have with the Internet, the better
	I would like to stay on the Internet for as long as I can
Internet Cognition	The Internet makes life more efficient
	The Internet lessens the importance of people's jobs

4 Results

The scale was distributed to participants on four different occasions for which a total of 2,600 participants completed the scale. Exploratory factor analyses were carried out on the data and revealed the presence of four underlying factors. The four factors were named as *Internet Affect, Internet Exhilaration, Social Benefit of the Internet,* and *Internet Detriment*. The original three-component model of attitudes was not replicated in the Internet attitude scale. This in itself is a significant finding, given that the researchers attempted over and over again to include behavioral disposition items into the earlier versions. However, some interesting trends emerged. Previous literature in general attitude theory advocates that behavioral elements of attitude ought to address the *intention to behave* with the attitude object. As a result, this guideline was followed in the development of items for the current scale. Nonetheless, it seems that such items still did not hold significance for participants in the domain of Internet attitudes. So although some intention to behave items remain there is no behavior subscale per se. Intention to behave thus enriches the scope of the Affect and Cognitive factors but does not constitute a factor in its own right.

4.1   Examination of the Attitude Components

As can be deduced following the naming of the subscales, the subscale *Internet Affect* consisted of only 'affect' items which were proposed in the original version of the scale. However the subscale *Internet Exhilaration* contained 'affect' items and one 'behavior' item. Thus a positive attitude towards the Internet may not always be accompanied by an exhilaration component towards it – and indeed, vice versa. The exhilaration component possibly involves an intended action.

With the exception of one 'behavior' item, both the *Social Benefit of the Internet* and *Internet Detriment* subscales consisted solely of cognitive statements. We may wish to view these two scales as positive and negative beliefs about the Internet, noting that it is perfectly possible, since these factors are moderately orthogonal, that a person may at any one moment entertain both kinds of beliefs about the Internet.

What was of particular interest over the four stages of scale development was the manner in which 'behavior' items fell out during the analyses. Following numerous analyses, the original scale which had consisted of 27 items was reduced to 21 items. The majority of deleted items were 'behavior' statements which achieved unsatisfactory loadings during factor analysis or did not fit semantically on the factor on which they loaded. In the final version of the GIAS, only two 'behavior' items remain. These findings are in line with previous concerns regarding the 'behavior' element of attitudes.

4.2   Gender Differences

Much literature in the area of gender and the Internet suggest that there may be a gender gap in technology. Studies which attempted to develop Internet 'attitude' scales in the past did indeed *find* gender differences in Internet attitudes. However, as earlier outlined, previous measures of Internet attitudes are insecure and possibly invalid as a result of the failure to follow well-established methodologies for attitude measurement. It is unclear what the scales in these studies are actually measuring; thus while such studies claim to have found gender differences in Internet attitude, the results ought to be interpreted with caution.

The results of the analyses in the present studies found *no* significant differences in Internet attitudes between the males and females. Effect sizes for the differences between the sexes are so small as to be negligible.

4.3   Age Differences

While there is much speculation about gender differences in Internet attitudes, little research investigated *age* differences in Internet attitudes. This research hypothesized that older participants may have less positive Internet attitudes than younger individuals as the Internet is a relatively recent phenomenon about which older generations would have known little about until later in life. Age differences in Internet attitude *were* found in the current analyses. Participants aged *25-34 years* obtained the highest scores on Internet attitudes while participants aged *55-64 years* obtained the lowest scores on Internet attitudes. The differences between the groups were significantly different. What was surprising was the low Internet attitude scores achieved for the youngest age group (*<18 years*). However, the number of participants in the sample for this age group was extremely small ($n = 11$) so these results must be interpreted with caution. Further exploration of Internet attitudes in this age category is thus necessary.

5   Conclusion

Following extensive testing and iterative analyses of the GIAS, the current scale consists of 21 items with four subscales: *Internet Affect, Internet Exhilaration, Social Benefit of the Internet,* and *Internet Detriment.* Confirmatory factor analyses of the final scale achieved excellent goodness-of-fit of the current model and demonstrated excellent reliability with Cronbach Alpha coefficients ranging from .67 to 87 for the four subscales and a value of .86 for the overall scale. The construct validity of the questionnaire is at least positively commendable and the authors hope that other researchers interested in Internet attitude will be challenged enough by our results to want to adopt our scales in their research.

References

1. Morse, B.J., Gullekson, N.L., Morris, S.A., Popovich, P.M.: The development of a general internet attitude scale. Computers in Human Behaviour 27(1), 480–489 (2011)
2. Tsai, C.-C., Lin, S.S.J., Tsai, M.-J.: Developing an Internet attitude scale for high school students. Computers and Education 37(1), 41–51 (2001)
3. Zhang, Y.: Development and validation of an internet use attitude scale. Computers and Education 49, 243–253 (2007)
4. Fishbein, M., Azjen, I.: Belief, attitude, intention and behavior: an introduction to theory and research. Addison-Wesley, Mass. (1975)
5. Eagly, A.H., Chaiken, S.: The advantages of an inclusive definition of attitude. Social Cognition 25(5), 582–602 (2007)

6. Katz, D., Stotland, E.: A Preliminary Statement of a Theory of Attitude Structure and Change. In: Koch, S. (ed.) Psychology: A Study of a Science, vol. III, McGraw-Hill, New York (1959)
7. Fishbein, M., Azjen, I.: Predicting and changing behaviour: the reasoned action approach. Psychology Press (Taylor & Francis), New York (2010)
8. Selwyn, N.: Students' attitudes toward computers: validation of a computer attitude scale for 16-19 education. Computers and Education 28(1), 35–41 (1997)
9. Bandura, A.: Self-efficacy: the exercise of control. W. H. Freeman, New York (1997)
10. Zhang, Y., Dronet, V., VanMetre, S.: /2000). Louisiana teachers' learning and adopting the Internet through inservice training. Lousisiana Education Research Journal 25(1), 3–18 (1999)

The Usability Perception Scale (UPscale): A Measure for Evaluating Feedback Displays[*]

Beth Karlin[1] and Rebecca Ford[2]

[1] School of Social Ecology, University of California, Irvine,
202 Social Ecology I, Irvine, California, 92697-7075
bkarlin@uci.edu
[2] Centre for Sustainability, University of Otago, P.O. Box 56, Dunedin, 9054, New Zealand
rebecca.ford@otago.ac.nz

Abstract. This paper proposes and tests the Usability Perception Scale (UPscale), developed to evaluate the perceived usability of eco-feedback. This tool builds on previous system usability scales and includes sub-scales for ease of use and engagement. The scale was tested via an online survey of 1103 US residents. Factor analysis supported a two-factor solution, supporting subscales for ease of use and engagement. Reliability tests revealed high levels of internal consistency for the overall scale and both subscales. A test of criterion validity with behavioral intention found significant correlations with both subscales, suggesting that usability is a key mediator for behavior change. Finally, ANOVA results found differences between randomly assigned images, suggesting the scale has sufficient sensitivity for use in experimental research. Future research is suggested to test abbreviated versions as well as to further assess this scale with actual behavioral pilot studies.

Keywords: evaluation, scale, energy, feedback, usability, user experience.

1 Introduction

Residential energy use is a significant and rising contribution to carbon emissions and recent studies suggest potential savings up to 25% through conservation behavior [1], [2]. As the use of electricity in the home is "abstract, invisible, and untouchable" [3], the provision of information about energy use, also known as eco-feedback, has been hypothesized to serve a vital function in making this energy use visible and interpretable to the consumer. Decades of research support the effectiveness of eco-feedback [4], and advances in sensing and energy metering technology now allow the collection and provision of real-time data to consumers via a multitude of in-home and web- or mobile-based displays [5]. Despite this promise, eco-feedback products have not yet taken a strong hold in the marketplace and the results of empirical studies vary significantly, suggesting that the effectiveness of eco-feedback may depend on both what information is given to consumers and how it is presented [6].

---

[*] Both authors contributed equally to this work.

A. Marcus (Ed.): DUXU/HCII 2013, Part I, LNCS 8012, pp. 312–321, 2013.
© Springer-Verlag Berlin Heidelberg 2013

As the goal of eco-feedback is reducing environmental impact, most field studies have relied on energy usage data (measured in kWh) as the dependent variable for evaluation [7], [8]. Although this is vital to assess overall effectiveness, additional information about the subjective experience of using eco-feedback could add significantly to our understanding about not only *whether* different types of feedback work, but *how* they work. At it's core Human Computer Interaction (HCI) is focused on applying scientific methodology to further knowledge about how people interact with computers, and how computers may be designed so that they are "easy, efficient, error free – even enjoyable" [9]. As eco-feedback becomes increasingly pervasive, HCI is well placed to offer useful contributions to improve the evaluation and design of display interfaces. Measure such as preference, usability, and satisfaction, central to HCI, can yield useful insights for effective design [10], [11].

Although eco-feedback research dates back to the 1970s [6], its inclusion in the HCI literature is more recent, with over 90% of HCI papers on eco-feedback published since 2008 [7]. A review comparing environmental psychology and HCI approaches to eco-feedback [7] found that HCI studies have been primarily lab-based or qualitative with an emphasis on "understandability, aesthetic, and perceived usefulness"; the few field trials conducted were relatively brief (1-4 weeks) and used small samples (average 11 participants). On the other hand, research studies from psychology (as well as industry) have focused on field trials to assess behavioral outcomes of feedback compared to a control condition and/or pre-treatment baseline. The average sample size is 6,108 participants and average study length is 9 months [8]. Data collection in these studies is typically quantitative, with energy usage data as the most common variable collected. The review concludes that both approaches are valuable and suggest efforts toward greater integration [7].

One way to integrate these approaches is to include subjective measures of users' experience and perceptions of eco-feedback displays into larger scale field trials, to understand their impact on behavioural outcomes. As qualitative data is cumbersome to collect and analyze for larger samples, the development of a quantitative instrument would be ideally suited. Past work in HCI has led to the development of multiple scales assessing the user experience of computer systems, but this work has yet to be applied within the eco-feedback literature.

In addition, it is vital that such an instrument be designed with specific intention. Although questions assessing a person's gender or age may be fairly objective, questions about perceptions and attitudes are often subjective in nature and therefore care must be taken in question design. Psychometrics is a branch of psychology that addresses this issue through the development of methods for creating and assessing the quality of variables used to measure subjective human experience [12].

This paper introduces a new instrument, the Usability Perception Scale (UPscale), designed to measure users' perceptions of eco-feedback displays. After reviewing past HCI research on usability, assessment, and limitations of current measures for eco-feedback evaluation, the UPscale is introduced and tested against four types of psychometric properties: factor structure, reliability, validity, and sensitivity. It concludes with suggestions for future research to both refine and use the UPscale in field studies.

2   Literature Review

A key function of HCI research is to assess the subjective user experience of computer systems, programs, and interfaces [9]. As such, a great deal of effort has been spent defining and determining the key characteristics of usability. Although the definition of usability is sometimes simplified to "ease of use", a more comprehensive definition takes into account several characteristics related to user experience [13]. The ISO 9241 standard definition of usability is "the extent to which a product can be used by specified users to achieve specified goals with effectiveness, efficiency, and satisfaction in a specified context of use". Additional work has defined several characteristics of usability within the above definition. Although variations abound, a common definition of usability includes five key characteristics: effectiveness, efficiency, error tolerance, ease of use, and engagement [13]. Effectiveness, efficiency, and error tolerance all refer to the users' ability to complete tasks with the system or interface. Effectiveness refers to overall ability to accomplish the task, efficiency refers to the speed an accuracy of completion, and error tolerance refers to the ability to minimize errors. They are typically measured objectively via usability studies in which subjects complete a task and metrics related to overall performance (effectiveness), time to completion (efficiency), and number of errors (error tolerance) are evaluated [14].

Ease of use refers to the ability of a user to learn and use a system or interface; it is sometimes broken into sub-characteristics of learnability and memorability [15]. Engagement refers to the whether a system or interface is pleasing and satisfying to use. As both ease of use and engagement are inherently subjective, self-report is the primary form of data collection for these characteristics. These two variables have been determined to be particularly important in predicting the degree to which people accept and use particular information technologies [11].

2.1   Usability Assessment in HCI

A number of survey instruments have been developed to evaluate the usability of a system or interface, assessing a number of characteristics related to usability, including perceived efficiency, learnability, and satisfaction. A list of these scales is presented in Table 1. These scales have been shown to predict similar responses for user satisfaction; the System Usability Scale (SUS) has been found to correlate with both the Software Usability Measurement Inventory (SUMI) (r=0.86) and the Usability Metric for User Experience (UMUX) (r=0.96) [19].

Among them, the System Usability Scale (SUS) is by far the most commonly cited and utilized scale in the HCI literature [20], [21]. It consists of 10 likert-scale items which ask respondents to agree or disagree with given statements on a 5-point scale. Odd-numbered items are worded positively and even-numbered items are worded negatively. SUS has proven popular and cost effective for evaluating usability across a wide variety of systems including cell phone equipment, modems, voice response systems, and websites [20]. It has been shown to outperform other scales at small sample sizes, has been found to be easy to administer and score, and is the only scale that addresses the whole system rather than a particular feature of the system [20].

Table 1. Commonly cited usability scales in HCI literature

Scale	Items	Dimension assessed
After Scenario Questionnaire (ASQ) [14]	3	User satisfaction with system usability
Post-Study System Usability Questionnaire (PSSUQ) [14]	19	User satisfaction with: 1) system usefulness; 2) information quality; 3) interface quality
Computer System Usability Questionnaire (CSUQ) [14]	19	User satisfaction with: 1) system usefulness; 2) information quality; 3) interface quality
Questionnaire for User Interface Satisfaction (QUIS) [16]	27	1) Overall reaction 2) learning; 3) terminology & information flow; 4) system output; and 5) system characteristics
System Usability Scale (SUS) [17]	10	Perceived system usability and learnability
Software Usability Measurement Inventory (SUMI) [18]	50	1) Global usability plus perception of: 2) affect; 3) efficiency; 4) learnability; 5) helpfulness; and 6) control
Usability Metric for User Experience (UMUX) [19]	4	Perceived usability (efficiency, effectiveness, and satisfaction)

No psychometric analyses on SUS were initially published and it was originally thought to be a unidimensional scale [17]. Subsequent researchers assessed the measure [20], [21], [22] and found "inconsistent results regarding the factorial structure of its items" [22]. Both Lewis and Sauro [21] and Borsci et al [22] identified two factors, which they termed usability (8 items) and learnability (2 items).

2.2   Limitations of Current Usability Scales

The SUS and other usability scales provide much instructional value for the design of an eco-feedback usability scale, but two primary limitations suggest the need for a new instrument targeted to this purpose.

First of all, current usability scales have been designed primarily to evaluate products or systems rather than info-visualizations such as those provided via eco-feedback displays [22]. Although in some cases simple wording changes from system/product to image/information are possible, this is not always the case. Additionally, there are items measured by the SUS, and included in the total score, that are not relevant when evaluating usability of info-visualizations, e.g. SUS item 5: "I found the various functions in this system were well integrated" [18].

Additionally, as user interface design progresses from functional (i.e. pre-defined tools designed for fixed tasks) to experiential (i.e. interactive interfaces designed for sociability and pleasure), alongside an increasing selection of technology options, the metrics used to evaluate subjective user responses must also progress [23]. Operational interfaces were appropriately assessed with metrics primarily associated with ease of use, such as learnability and the efficiency with which tasks could be carried out. However, experiential interfaces, should also be evaluated with metrics that account for continued engagement, as a good interface design may result in increased time on task and this can't be captured by ease of use metrics [23].

As such, no instrument has yet been developed that (1) addresses the unique needs of eco-feedback displays (as opposed to systems or products), and (2) incorporates psychometrically validated sub-scales for both the ease of use and engagement characteristics of usability. The current study is designed to meet this need.

3   Method

The present study introduces and tests the Usability Perception Scale (UPscale), which was designed to measure the user experience of eco-feedback displays. UPscale builds from previous system usability studies published in the HCI literature, but was designed to be different from the work reviewed above in that the UPscale questions were designed to: (1) measure information received from a feedback graph or other info-visualization and (2) incorporate and distinguish between hypothesizes subscales for ease of use and engagement.

3.1   Participants and Procedure

The scale was tested via an online experimental survey of 1103 US residents. Participants were recruited via Amazon Mechanical Turk and paid $0.31 for survey completion. After excluding incomplete responses as well as those who completed the survey in less than 5 minutes or answered a trick question incorrectly, 1103 responses remained for analysis. Table 2 presents summary data on demographic variables for the survey sample compared to U.S. Census data (2010).

Table 2. Demographic characteristics of the sample (n=1103) compared to US Census data

Demographic variables	Sample	Census
Gender	47% Male	49% Male
Average age[*]	31.3 Years	36.8 Years
Race	78% White	79% White
Average education[*]	14.6 Years	13.3 Years
Average income[**]	$52,940	$67,609

[*] Sample and census significantly different based on independent t-test ($p < .01$)

3.2   Measures

Data analyzed in this study were collected as part of a larger online survey, which was designed to address three major topics with the eco-feedback literature: (1) perception of graphical displays based on information density, (2) the role of message framing in behavioral intention, and (3) measuring subjective appraisal of user experience. The current paper presents results related to the third goal; measures examined in this study are described below.

UPscale. The Usability Perception Scale (UPscale) consists of eight likert-scale items, which ask respondents to agree or disagree with given statements on a 5-point scale. Odd-numbered items are worded positively and even-numbered items are worded negatively. It includes four questions designed to test for ease of use attributes, including complexity, interpretation, and learnability. An additional four questions test engagement attributes, which include relevance, usefulness, and intention to use. Questions included in the UPscale are listed in Table 3.

Table 3. Questions included in the UPscale

Ease of Use Questions:	Engagement Questions:
1. I am able to get the information I need easily.	5. I gained information from this image that will benefit my life.
2. I think the image is difficult to understand.	6. I do not find this image useful.
3. I feel very confident interpreting the information in this image.	7. I think that I would like to use this image frequently.
4. A person would need to learn a lot in order to understand this image	8. I would not want to use this image.

Note: responses are scored on a Likert scale from "strongly agree" to "strongly disagree"

Experimental Design. Participants were randomly shown one of four images depicting energy use by time, or one of four images depicting energy use by appliance. Figure 1 shows example images from each of these groups. Participants were then presented with the 8-item UPscale and asked to respond to each statement using a 5 point Likert Scale. Negatively worded items 1, 2, 6 and 8 were recoded for use in analysis.

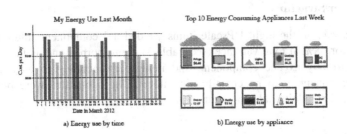

a) Energy use by time   b) Energy use by appliance

Fig. 1. Example of energy use by time and use by appliance images shown to participants

Behavioral Intention. As the goal of eco-feedback is to reduce environmental impact via individual behavior, two questions were included which asked participants about their intention to change their behaviour based on the information presented to them. These questions were intended to serve as a proxy for actual behaviour and were tested for criterion validity of the instrument.

Demographic Variables. Demographic questions were included to determine the representativeness of the sample and to test for the sensitivity of the instrument.

Traditional demographic data included gender, age, race, income, and education. Since the study was concerned with pro-environmental behavior, a single item measuring environmentalism (Do you consider yourself to be an environmentalist?) was also included.

3.3   Analysis

Statistical analyses were conducted to test for four key aspects of psychometric quality commonly utilized in the HCI community: factor structure, reliability, validity and sensitivity [14]. Factor structure refers to naturally occurring groups of items that arise from multiple items. A scale may have just one or several factors, depending on the questions included. Factor structure is generally measured using factor analysis; factors include all the items with loading scores above a set point (generally .40).

Reliability refers to the internal consistency among the items within the scale. Once factors are established or confirmed, each factor, as well as the overall scale, is tested for reliability. Reliability is generally measured using Cronbach's co-efficient a; if a is sufficiently high (> 0.70), items can be combined to produce a scale.

Validity refers to whether an instrument measures what it claims to measure. One of the main forms of validity, criterion validity, compares the scale to other indicators of a construct to assess any relationships. Validity is generally measured using Pearson correlation coefficient r. Sensitivity refers to how much the scale varies based on different users or independent variables. Sensitivity is typically measured using t-tests for binary variables or analysis of variance (ANOVA) for categorical variables.

4   Results

4.1   Factor Structure

Factor Analysis on the eight UPscale items yielded a 2-component solution, which accounted for 68% of total variance (see Table 3). Items corresponding to ease of use clustered strongly as one component, and items corresponding to engagement as another component, with no cross-loading items. The sub-scales were both tested separately but no additional sub-factors emerged.

4.2   Reliability

Reliability tests revealed high levels of internal consistency for the overall scale ($\alpha=.85$), and for both the ease of use ($\alpha=.84$) and engagement ($\alpha=.83$) subscales.

4.3   Validity

Validity was tested by correlating UPscale scores with self-reported behaviour change intention scores. Results suggest evidence of predictive validity, with significant correlations ($p<.001$) for the overall scale ($r=.536$) as well as both subscales: ease of use ($r=.213$), and engagement ($r=.685$).

Table 4. Factor Structure of UPscale

Item	Factor 1 Ease of Use	Factor 2: Engagement
1. I am able to get the information I need easily.	**.696**	.368
2. I think the image is difficult to understand.	**.830**	.180
3. I feel confident interpreting the information in this image.	**.791**	.219
4. A person would need to learn a lot in order to understand this image.	**.818**	.045
5. I gained information from this image that will benefit my life.	.113	**.793**
6. I do not find this image useful.	.309	**.751**
7. I think that I would like to use this image frequently.	.031	**.828**
8. I would not want to use this image.	.349	**.710**
Explained Variance	50%	18%

Note. Values in bold indicate which items load to each factor.

4.4 Sensitivity

Image Type. A one-way analysis of variance (ANOVA) was run to assess the sensitivity of UPscale scores across the different images. Results indicated a significant effect of image type on the full scale ($F=3.616$, $p=.001$) and ease of use subscale ($F=6.411$, $p<.001$), and a marginally significant effect on engagement subscale ($F=1.744$, $p=.095$). This suggests that UPscale is reasonably responsive to different image properties.

Demographic Variables. ANOVAs were run test the sensitivity of the UPscale and its two subscales across the demographic variables: gender, age, race, income, education, and environmentalism. Results revealed that age ($F=2.624$, $p=.004$) and environmentalism ($F=11.092$, $p=.001$) had a significant effect on the overall scale, while gender ($F=4.082$, $p=.044$), age ($F=6.169$, $p<.001$), environmentalism ($F=18.635$, $p<.001$) and income ($F=2.117$, $p=.026$) all had a significant effect on the engagement subscale. No tested variables display significant effects on ease of use.

5   Discussion

The UPscale, building on insights from existing usability measures, was developed to evaluate user perceptions of information visualizations such as those provided by eco-feedback displays. It incorporates and psychometrically evaluates questions relating to the ease of use (complexity, interpretability, and learnability) and engagement (relevance, usefulness, intention to use) characteristics of usability.

The psychometric properties of the UPscale point to its reliability and validity. Factor analysis supported the two theoretically derived subscales for ease of use and engagement. Both the overall scale as well as both subscales were found to be high in internal consistency, proving reliability. These two tests are vital for instrument validation, as they indicate that the questions can be summed and/or averaged into a single variable "item" for statistical analysis. As such, the UPscale can be used as a single eight-item scale, and the two four-item sub-scales for ease of use and engagement can also be used on their own.

The overall scale and both subscales also correlated with behavioral intention, suggesting criterion validity with energy savings. These results indicate that perceived ease of use and engagement may be key mediators of feedback effectiveness, though there are limitations with this method, as behavioural intention does not always accurately predict actual behaviour. Further research testing this hypothesis with actual behavior would be beneficial to explore this hypothesis more fully.

Finally, the UPscale was found to be sensitive to experimental manipulation, which suggests it can be used successfully to determine differences in usability among feedback types. As the scale was also sensitive to demographic variables (gender, age, income, environmentalism), it is highly recommended that they be included and controlled for in analysis to account for variability in subsequent findings.

As eco-feedback becomes more common, the need to ensure that it is useful and engaging to consumers is paramount. Programs like the U.S. Green Button Initiative [24], as well as the 200+ feedback products and services that have emerged on the market [25], are based on the idea that consumers will be engaged with and transformed by access to energy information. Attention to the usability of such eco-feedback displays is a key step toward this goal and the UPscale provides an instrument that can be used at scale in the hundreds of field trials planned in the coming months and years.

Acknowledgments. Part of this research was supported by the Calit2 California Plug Load Research Center (CalPlug) at the University of California, Irvine. The authors thank Haley Herrera for assistance with survey development and implementation, and Nicole Sintov for valuable input on previous drafts.

References

1. Granade, H.C., Creyts, J., Derkach, A., Farese, P., Nyquist, S., Ostrowski, K.: Unlocking energy efficiency in the U.S. economy. Technical Report, McKinsey (2009)
2. Dietz, T., Gardner, G.T., Gilligan, J., Stern, P.C., Vandenbergh, M.P.: Household actions can provide a behavioral wedge to rapidly reduce US carbon emissions. Proceedings of the National Academy of Sciences 106, 18452–18456 (2009)
3. Fischer, C.: Feedback on household electricity consumption: A tool for saving energy? Energy Efficiency 1, 79–104 (2008)
4. Darby, S.: A Review for Defra of the literature on metering, billing, and direct displays.Technical Report, Environmental Change Institute (2006)
5. Darby, S.: Smart metering: what potential for householder engagement? Building Research & Information 38, 442–457 (2010)
6. Ehrhardt-Martinez, K., Donnelly, K.A., Laitner, J.A.: Advanced metering initiatives and residential feedback programs: a meta-review for household electricity-saving opportunities. Technical report, ACEEE (2010)
7. Froehlich, J., Findlater, L., Landay, J.: The Design of Eco-Feedback Technology. In: Proc. CHI 2010, pp. 1999–2008. ACM Press (2010)

8. Karlin, B., Zinger, J.: Residential energy feedback: A meta-analysis and methodological review (manuscript submitted for publication)

9. Card, S.K., Moran, T.P., Newell, A.: The Psychology of Human-Computer Interaction. Lawrence Erlbaum Associates (1983)

10. Toomim, M., Kriplean, T., Pörtner, C., Landay, J.A.: Utility of human-computer interactions: Toward a science of preference measurement. In: Proc. CHI 2011, pp. 2275–2284. ACM Press (2011)

11. Davis, F.D.: Perceived usefulness, perceived ease of use, and user acceptance of information technology. MIS Quarterly, 319–340 (1989)

12. Kline, P.: Handbook of Psychological Testing. Routledge, London (2000)

13. Quesenbery, W.: What Does Usability Mean: Looking Beyond 'Ease of Use'. In: Proceedings of the 48th Annual Conference, Society for Technical Communication (2001)

14. Lewis, J.R.: IBM computer usability satisfaction questionnaires: Psychometric evaluation and instructions for use. International Journal of Human-Computer Interaction 7, 57–78 (1995)

15. Nielsen, J., Hackos, J.T.: Usability engineering. Academic Press, San Diego (1993)

16. Chin, J.P., Diehl, V.A., Norman, K.L.: Development of an Instrument Measuring Human-Computer User Satisfaction Interface. In: Proc. CHI 1988, pp. 213–218. ACM Press (1988)

17. Brooke, J.: SUS - A quick and dirty usability scale. In: Jordan, Thomas, Weerdmeester, McClelland (eds.) Usability Evaluation in Industry, vol. 189, pp. 189–194 (1996)

18. Kirakowski, J., Corbett, M.: SUMI: The software usability measurement inventory. British Journal of Educational Technology 24, 210–212 (1993)

19. Finstad, K.: The Usability Metric for User Experience. Interacting with Computers 22, 323–327 (2010)

20. Bangor, A., Kortum, P.T., Miller, J.T.: An Empirical Evaluation of the System Usability Scale. International Journal of Human-Computer Interaction 24, 574–594 (2008)

21. Lewis, J., Sauro, J.: The factor structure of the system usability scale. Human Centered Design, 94–103 (2009)

22. Borsci, S., Federici, S., Lauriola, M.: On the dimensionality of the System Usability Scale: a test of alternative measurement models. Cognitive Processing 10, 193–197 (2009)

23. De Angeli, A., Sutcliffe, A., Hartmann, J.: Interaction, Usability and Aesthetics: What Influences Users' Preferences? In: 8th ACM Conference on Designing Interactive Systems, pp. 271–280 (2006)

24. Chopra, A.: Modeling a green energy challenge after a blue button, http://www.whitehouse.gov/blog/2011/09/15/ modeling-green-energy-challenge-after-blue-button

25. Karlin, B., Ford, R., Squiers, C.: Energy Feedback: A Review and Taxonomy of Products and Technologies (manuscript submitted for publication)

System for Evaluating Usability and User Experience by Analyzing Repeated Patterns

Young Bin Kim[1], Shin Jin Kang[2], and Chang Hun Kim[3]

[1] Interdisciplinary Program in Visual Information Processing, Korea University, Korea
zulzin@korea.ac.kr
[2] School of Games, Hongik University, Korea
directx@korea.ac.kr
[3] Department of Computer and Radio Communications Engineering, Korea University, Korea
chkim@korea.ac.kr

Abstract. In this paper, a new system for evaluating interface usability through the analysis of repeated patterns is proposed. The system can be a valuable tool for verifying interfaces and in evaluating their usability by users, both of which are necessary stages in the development and operation of software. This paper concentrates on the repeated patterns that occur when users use an interface. Extracting these repeated patterns and analyzing them could enhance the development and usability of interfaces. Through experiments that applied the proposed system to several kinds of software, it was confirmed that problems with interfaces can be understood, and usability can be improved without requiring complicated analyses of user logs.

Keywords: Usability Methods and Tools, Analyzing Repeated Patterns.

1   Introduction

Evaluating usability is regarded as an essential element in the development of software. Such usability evaluation enables the software to be used more easily and efficiently, with users achieving their objectives and being satisfied. Moreover, by evaluating usability during development, any problems with the usability or functionality of the software can potentially be solved at an early stage.

Recently, many studies on the evaluation of usability have been undertaken. These studies mainly involved confirming the completeness and practicality of web designs or evaluating game interface designs [1, 2, 7]. The approach was usually to analyze the data obtained from surveys or log files, which recorded the activity of users, or to use technology such as user eye tracking [3-6]. Studies based on surveys have the advantage of easy and convenient measurement, but there is a possible problem in that subjects can distort the results, consciously or unconsciously. In contrast, observation of the reactions of a living body using eye tracking is advantageous for obtaining objective data, but the requirement to wear a special apparatus may cause unnatural behavior in subjects.

A. Marcus (Ed.): DUXU/HCII 2013, Part I, LNCS 8012, pp. 322–329, 2013.

In this paper, we propose a new system that automatically analyzes users' input log data to measure usability. The suggested system offers the advantage of collecting data naturally from many users and analyzing them automatically. This system mainly studies the aspects of the user interface that users focus on and the repetitive patterns that occur when the system is used. If a repetitive pattern exceeds a certain length, it indicates a poor user experience with the interface, or it warns designers that the specification of the interface should be improved. Our system analyzes sequences of user input data, visualizes them, generates tables of character-string patterns, and identifies repetitive patterns. We are able to evaluate the usability and the completeness of the application interface automatically via this system.

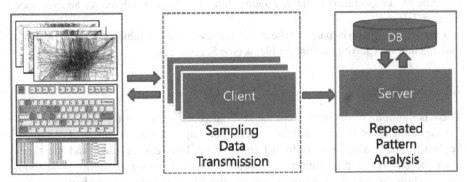

Fig. 1. System overview. Collect user input data from mouse and keyboard (Left). Transmit the received data from client to server (Middle). Conduct the usability evaluation by analyzing patterns repeated by the user (Right).

2   System

2.1   System Overview

The proposed system is based on a client–server architecture. It deals with sequences sent to the server during fixed periods while the users are generating mouse and keyboard input data (see Figure 1). The system has four main parts, a sampling part to collect the data from users, an identification part to find repeated patterns in the collected data, a visualization part that presents various pieces of information visually, and an analysis part to analyze the repeated patterns found.

First, in the sampling part, we collect data from the users' mouse and keyboard input over a fixed period of time and save it for repetitive-pattern identification analysis. For the mouse input, we classify the direction of movement as one of sixteen directions. For the keyboard input, we save the users' input as a continual sequence. In addition, we classify repetitive patterns as repetitive keyboard input sequences, repetitive mouse movements, or repetitive sequences based on a mixture of keyboard and mouse data   (see Section 2.2).

Second, to search for repeated patterns in the keyboard and mouse input sequences, we use a method that updates a simple form of string-pattern table. We choose a minimum pattern length for pattern verification, and we are able to identify repetitive patterns that are above that minimum pattern length. In addition, by storing the coordinate values for these repeated patterns, they can then be visualized, enabling repeated patterns to be confirmed visually (see Section 2.3).

Third, the visualization part is designed to identify those aspects of the interface that users mainly focus on when they use the application. The input values from the mouse and keyboard are both visualized. For the mouse, its path and speed of movement are presented visually. This visualization enables understanding of what aspects of the system users tend to concentrate on. In addition, we found a way to identify the interface's utilization by marking the keyboard inputs following mouse movements. The duration of input standby times was also visualized for analysis (see Section 2.4).

Finally, the analysis part is where the repeated pattern table is used to identify patterns that may have potential problems (see Section 2.5).

2.2   Sampling

There is sampling of the input from the keyboards and mice of users. The sampling of the keyboard input is implemented in terms of sequential input values. For typical keyboard input sequences, additional (modifying) keys can be used, and the times when these keys are in operation are separately sampled. This gives information about the weight to give to the keys used, and enables identification of periods when many keys are used simultaneously.

As mentioned, the mouse input is classified in terms of sixteen directions, and this direction of movement is sampled. Here, we use directions that are pre-learned based on the Hidden Markov Model method, which minimizes the error values in mouse directivity. The keyboard input is sampled at the same rate for all input conditions, but the mouse input sampling is variable. An appropriate sampling rate will depend on the environment of the software to be evaluated. In this paper, software involving much mouse manipulation has a sampling period of 30 ms; for other software, sampling occurs every 50 ms.

Incorrect repeated patterns can be generated in mouse usage areas moving from work space to interface (ex: movement to one direction only). To solve such problems, the part where simple movement occurs mainly after data gathering has to be identified. In this paper, a region including more parts moving faster than others was set as the movement part.

.In addition, the input standby time and the number of keyboard and mouse operations per minute are sampled and made available for use if necessary.

2.3   Repeated Pattern Table

By analyzing the sampled data, repeated patterns are found. Because the amount of sampled data can become large over time, resulting from an accumulation of users, it can be difficult to extract useful data. Recently, many studies in the data-mining field have involved this concept of "big data".

Sequential pattern-matching techniques are used to search for mutual correlation among items occurring in sequences by adding the concept of time to the association rules. GSP and SPADE are examples of these algorithms [8]. Such algorithms aim to find frequent sequences in a database.

However, it is difficult to use algorithms such as these for the extraction of sequential patterns in a normal software-development environment. In such an environment, identical and restricted keyboard input is used repeatedly and there is much repetitive mouse movement. Repetitive and tautological key values are often taken as sequences, which is a drawback to using the existing algorithms.

In this paper, a method that creates and updates a repeated pattern table is used. The method is advantageous because it can extract frequently occurring repeated patterns efficiently, and at low cost. An algorithm for creating a repeated pattern table is as follows:

```
1. Initialize the pattern table to contain all strings of
length one.
2. Take initial pattern with length 2 or more.
3. Add pattern to dictionary.
4-1. If pattern already exists, add next sequence to
pattern.
4-2. Else initialize a new pattern from second sequence
of previous pattern with length 2 or more.
5. Iterate 3 to 4 until the input sequence is exhausted.
```

If the client sends the sampled data to the server regularly, this algorithm enables the repeated pattern tables to be continuously updated and managed. Also, by managing the pattern tables, using a basic data compression algorithm, the time and memory space were not greatly affected.

2.4   System Visualization

The visualization part of the system allows you to identify those parts of the application that users tend to concentrate on and any problems in using the interface. This was inspired by IOGraph software [9], which was visualized using the movement and standby time for users' mice. The movement of the mouse of users is visualized in terms of its weighted speed. Weighting the speed is helpful in understanding where the users are concentrating their attention. In the system described in this paper, a speed of at least 30 pixels per second is weighted. If a heat map is used for all of the mouse movements, there is the problem of separating movements related to the work of the users from movements caused by an object of interest. To identify the degree of concentration on the user interface, a color map showing mouse movement speed is available (see Figure 2). An additional heat map was created and visualized for keyboard input.

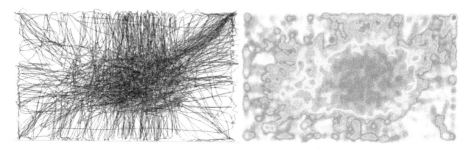

Fig. 2. The color map of mouse movement speed (Left) and the mouse movement's heatmap (Right)

2.5 Analyzing Repeated Patterns

In creating a repeated pattern table, it is important to understand what patterns have potential problems. In the present system, repeated patterns are analyzed in two stages. First, in the server stage, the sequences of all users are put together to identify repeated patterns. Second, in the client stage, the repeated patterns of particular users are analyzed. The repeated patterns for all users can indicate a problem with the interface on many occasions.

Through the system visualization, we can see that there are places where users are concentrating on their work using the mouse and places where there are simple movements.

3   Experiment

3.1 Experiment Design

A major experiment was carried out to evaluate the usability of a program currently being developed. To evaluate the completeness and usability of the interface of the software being developed, its usability was evaluated using the proposed system. The pieces of software used in the experiment are editing tools for general-purpose multimedia, used mainly for image and audio editing. This software supports numerous functions and most work is carried out using the movement and clicking of a mouse and the keys on a keyboard. Identifying problems with its interface could allow us to enhance its usability. The evaluation of this program was divided into three experimental periods, with the software being modified after each period. We confirmed that an improvement in actual usability was possible after the survey in each experiment. In addition, the usability of a commercial image-editing program was evaluated using our system.

3.2 Experiment Process

Experiment was carried out two times as a whole. In the first stage, the interface was improved using a repeating pattern table; in the second stage, usability evaluation by comparison between the interfaces before and after improvement was carried out. 4

participants were present at each experiment. They were all postgraduate students, recruited on campus, and were familiar with image processing, audio processing, and mouse and keyboard interfaces. They were given proper compensation for the participation.

The first experiment involving software under development lasted nine days. The software, with its prototype interface, was freely used for three days. From the results of the pattern table generated, the interface to the software was modified, and then the experiment was repeated for another three days. The basis of interface change was that of removing repetitive patterns. Shortcut keys were created for mainly appearing patterns or the relevant actions were placed on the top menu bar. The interface was again modified, and the process repeated for a third time.

In the second stage, the participants were instructed to perform specific tasks using the modified interface and asked the following (all measured in the 7 Likert scale) [10] :

- Learnability – Was there any difficulty in learning the interface?
- Ease of Use – How convenient was it to use the interface?
- Efficiency – How efficient was it to perform the specified task using the interface?
- Satisfaction – Was the interface satisfactory as a whole?

4   Result

4.1   Experiment Result

Through the experiment of the first stage, the locations of bottlenecks for the users of the software were identified, and the interface was modified appropriately. The figure 3 illustrates the survey result through the two test stages. We could verify that the users' satisfaction improved gradually with use of the modified interface.

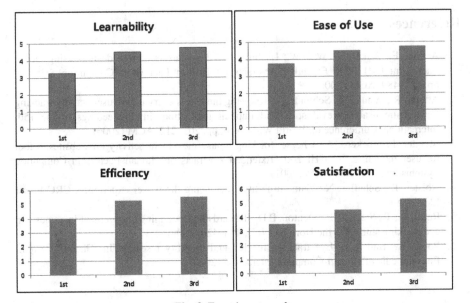

Fig. 3. Experiment results

Additionally, when particular users produced many repeated patterns or movements of the mouse, we could suggest ways for users to improve their usability.

4.2   Limitations

Because the experiment was undertaken with software under development, sufficient participants for a suitable evaluation of usability could not be recruited [11]. However, because of its server-client structure, it may be possible to obtain data for numerous users in the future. In addition, we plan to apply this system on software of various areas.

5   Conclusion

In this paper, we have analyzed input log data from various users and proposed a system that measures usability. The main advantages of this system are that it reduces the time required to investigate all log data and conducts usability evaluations effectively. Moreover, the proposed system is suited to the analysis of large datasets, and it will help improve user-interface designs. We believe this system will improve the evaluation of software usability in a variety of fields.

Acknowledgment. This research was supported by the Basic Science Research Program through the National Research Foundation of Korea (NRF) and was funded by the Ministry of Education, Science, and Technology (NRF-2012R1A1A1012895).

References

1. Arroyo, E., Selker, T., Wei, W.: Usability tool for analysis of web designs using mouse tracks. In: CHI 2006 Extended Abstracts on Human Factors in Computing Systems, pp. 484–489. ACM (2006)
2. Atterer, R., Wnuk, M., Schmidt, A.: Knowing the user's every move: user activity tracking for website usability evaluation and implicit interaction. In: Proceedings of the 15th International Conference on World Wide Web, pp. 203–212. ACM (2006)
3. Mueller, F., Lockerd, A.: Cheese: tracking mouse movement activity on websites, a tool for user modeling. In: CHI 2001 Extended Abstracts on Human Factors in Computing Systems, pp. 279–280. ACM (2001)
4. Isbister, K., Schaffer, N.: Game usability: Advancing the player experience. CRC PressI Llc (2008)
5. Renshaw, T., Stevens, R., Denton, P.D.: Towards understanding engagement in games: An eye-tracking study. On the Horizon 17(4), 408–420 (2009)
6. Poole, A., Ball, L.J.: Eye tracking in HCI and usability research. In: Ghaoui, C. (ed.) Encyclopedia of Human-Computer Interaction (2006)

7. Kjeldskov, J., Stage, J.: New techniques for usability evaluation of mobile systems. International Journal of Human-Computer Studies 60(5), 599–620 (2004)
8. Agrawal, R., Srikant, R.: Mining sequential patterns. In: Proceedings of the Eleventh International Conference on Data Engineering, pp. 3–14. IEEE (1995)
9. IOGraphica, http://iographica.com/
10. Nielsen, J., Hackos, J.T.: Usability engineering, vol. 125184069. Academic press, San Diego (1993)
11. Hwang, W., Salvendy, G.: Number of people required for usability evaluation: the 10±2 rule. Communications of the ACM 53(5), 130–133 (2010)

A Color Model in the Usability of Computer Interface Applied to Users with Low Vision

Cínthia Costa Kulpa, Fábio Gonçalves Teixeira, and Régio Pierre Da Silva

Federal University of Rio Grande do Sul, Porto Alegre, Brazil
{cinthia.kulpa,fabio.teixeira,régio}@ufrgs.br

Abstract. This paper presents the results of a research on the usability of computer interfaces through colors for Low Vision users. It describes the methodology used, the 3 web interfaces tested for usability with the users in question, showing the results for the development of a prototype interface with colors as the main aspect. The prototype developed is presented with the usability test carried out with it. As a result of the work, a proposed color model is presented that includes Low Vision users in the construction and upgrading of computer interfaces, aimed at the usability of web interfaces.

Keywords: Color, Usability, Low Vision.

1 Introduction

The current guidelines for the design and redesign of computer interfaces, which consider Universal Design requirements and are applied to users in general, does not ensure that all users are equally benefited in the same manner by those requirements. It occurs due to the great diversity of the requirements demanded by the disabled and non-disabled population [3].

Among those with disabilities in Brazil [5], a number of 35 million of people with Low Vision are users of web facilities in some way to obtain information, knowledge and interact with friends. Those users need specific tools that stimulate their skills and permit social inclusion without reducing or limiting their actions. Such tools are used in order to increase their functional view, enable them to increase visual efficiency and are applied to a range of countless possibilities.

From this perspective, this paper introduces a study aiming to propose a color model to assist web designers in developing interfaces for users with low vision. This study demonstrates the difficulties faced by users with low vision to navigate virtual environments. A usability test was carried out on three web interfaces with 10 low vision users with the use of color as a facilitator in the process of understanding, reading, identifying and memorizing information.

In order to identify the three most accessed websites by users, two open questions were applied in unstructured interviews. Participants who had adequate functional vision were chosen to navigate the web without the aid of voice programs. This enabled the researcher to identify eventual difficulties, problems and characteristics common to participants in the survey.

A. Marcus (Ed.): DUXU/HCII 2013, Part I, LNCS 8012, pp. 330–339, 2013.
© Springer-Verlag Berlin Heidelberg 2013

After selecting the websites to be used in the study, a usability test was carried out using a questionnaire with 10 questions to identify the efficiency of the websites in carrying out some tasks; the efficiency of colors to assist in carrying out some tasks; the use of colors to reduce mistakes; and the contribution of the colors to: identify participant perception of the website function, learn some website functions, and memorize information in the website though color layout. The survey was carried out in an information technology laboratory where it was possible observe and film participant behavior.

As a result, prototype website was designed in order to validate and identify the contrasts of colors which would improve the usability of web interfaces. The results of the survey shows the categorization of the color contrast considering efficiency as the first characteristic most voted by respondents, followed by facility of reading, memorization, feeling of safety, and assistance in reading for users with light sensitivity and other characteristics.

It was necessary to analyze the color combinations separating them in the following components: main menu, submenu, heading, body of text and footnotes. This approach was used to design a contrasting color model which improved interface usability for the user and the website. In addition, this approach also improved the accessibility of users with low vision, enabling them to navigate in virtual environments with functional view comfortably and satisfactorily without the aid of any assistive technology.

Below we present the Low Vision disability in order to provide a better understanding of the development of this research.

2 Low Vision Disability

According to Faye [4], the term Low Vision (LV) is usually applied to define a situation in which the eye has had one of its visual impulse carrying paths irreversibly altered, where the loss of sight represents an obstacle for the development of a person's normal life and requires special correction. Carvalho [1] and Vanderheiden & Vanderheiden [12] state that this disability includes problems such as darkening of vision, blurred vision, mist or film over the eyes, vision only of objects that are extremely close objects or loss of distant vision, color distortion or color blindness, visual field defects, tunnel vision, lack or peripheral vision, abnormal sensitivity to light or brightness and night blindness..

LV uses or is potentially capable of making use of vision to plan or execute certain tasks [2]. The main characteristic for a person to be diagnosed as having LV is related to the visual capacity a person has between 20/40 and 20/200 after correction. This means that a person with 20/200 vision can see an object from a distance of 20 feet, while a person whose vision is considered normal can see the same object from a distance of 200 feet. It is also described as the degree of visual weakening that results in incapability and visual performance reduction.

Due to those issues, Paschoal [8] states that LV is in an intermediate position between the reality of people who can see normally and total visually disabled people.

They is not treated as people with normal vision, as they feature limitations that do not allow to perform certain functions, and are not treated as blind, as they have residual vision that allows to execute some tasks perfectly. This borderline condition leads to difficulty in adjusting to society and the consequent exclusion at a higher level than the exclusion of people who are blind or have normal vision.

Despite the difficulties faced with LV, the factor that best determines vision quality lies in the brain's ability to capture, codify, select and organize the images perceived by the eyes. This way, Sá [11] points out that visual efficiency takes place through the quality and efficient use of the visual potential according to the conditions of stimulation and activation of the visual functions, which means that emotional factors, environmental conditions and life contingencies of the person interfere directly in the potential use of vision.

Thus, it is understood that LV needs specific tools that stimulate its possibilities and bring social inclusion, without reducing or limiting the person's actions, with the functional vision of that person resulting in an increase of their visual efficiency and leading to a variety of possibilities.

Even with the constant creation of technologies that allow for better accessibility to the web environments by the disabled in general, there are no guidelines for the development of interfaces aimed specifically at LV. This makes evident the search for research and development of products and resources that stimulate those persons' visual stimulation, with colors carrying great importance in this relation due to the possibility they offer in calling attention, indicate aspects of the interface, make memorization easier, create back planes, direct reading and making it possible for it to designate meaning and value to those interfaces according to their interpretation [6].

3   Methodology

To make use of colors as facilitators in the process of understanding, reading, identifying and memorizing of a web interface with LV, we have established the usability test as an assessment method that is user-centered.

According to Cybis et al. [3], the usability test focuses on the assessment of the quality of interaction between users and system. The objective of this test is to ascertain problems found, measure their impact on the interaction and identify causes on the interface. It involves actual users of the system carrying out certain tasks in a real context in order to reflect the general behavior of the target population.

To take part in the usability test, we selected 10 LV users [3], regardless of each one's diagnostic and etiology, considering only the functional vision required to navigate the web without voice programs to make it possible to identify problems and positive points common to all participants.

To identify the three sites mostly accessed by the participants, an initial interview was made, with two open questions (Table 1), to collect primary data.

Table 1. Questions about the sites mostly accessed

1.	What are the sites you want to navigate without the use of voice programmes, but can not? Give three examples:
2.	What problems do you find with the sites listed when you use them? Please describe the problems in detail if possible:

The analysis of the answers provided resulted in search sites: Google (Fig. 1), information sites: Zero Hora Newspaper (Fig.2) and bank sites: Banco do Brasil (Fig. 3), since the majority of LV use these sites to make payments, check account statements, among others.

Fig. 1. http://www.google.com.br   **Fig. 2.** http://zerohora.clicrbs.com.br

Fig. 3. http://www.bb.com.br

3.1   Usability Testing of the Three Sites

The usability test was done in an information technology laboratory (APADEV); carried out in a questionnaire form with questions based on the usability aims and resulting from user experience [9]. A term of consent was produced through which the participants agree to take part in the test and authorize the disclosure of the results in the scientific medium, which allowed the data to be filmed individually.

The questionnaire was based on usability aims with 10 questions such as: the effectiveness of the sites to do what was expected of them; how efficient were the colors in aiding the accomplishment of tasks; the safety provided by the colors reducing errors and mistakes; the site function perceived through colors; how the colors contributed in their quick learning of how to use the sites; and memorization of the information laid out on the sites through colors.

The simplicity of the Google site helped in searches and the user of larger fonts, in bold or highlighted with more space "between letters" and *sans serif* contributed directly in the efficiency of colors for identification, learning, memorization and the easiness to read the site contents. The lack of the option for inverted contrast of the site's interface (dark background with light colored letters) made it impossible for participants who are highly sensitive to light to navigate it.

On the Zero Hora Newspaper site, the importance was perceived of the high contrast between the background colors and the letter colors adequately. However, the use of high contrast by the site did nor assure the expected usability, because the use of many colors on the interface resulted in difficult memorization and slowed down the visual adaptation by a LV user to the change from one color to another.

The Banco do Brasil site presented a lot of disorderly content, directly interfering in participant navigating, resulting in delays, tiredness and even giving up trying to access the page. The text contrast in bold, dark blue text (larger letter) with the strong yellow background and the white background on the site were perceived by all participant users as being the "best contrast. The contrast of the text in bold, dark blue with the white background made it possible for them to identify and read information with any letter size.

Throughout the test, both the interest and the motivation from the participants to contribute in the identification of the positive and negative characteristics of each one of the three sites were determining to obtain the results presented.

3.2   Prototype Site

From the results obtained in the above described test, it was possible to develop a prototype site and carry out the same usability test to confirm the contribution of colors in the usability of web interfaces.

Five interface variations were established with combinations of distinct colors placed as links on the heading. The combinations below were based on factors such as: allowing to read from a distance, call attention, direct the vision, make searching easier, memorize the layout of contents, prevent errors and surprise the user.

Fig. 4. Interface Prototypes with different color contrasts

This usability test was carried out using the same criteria, participants, information technology laboratory (APADEV) and questionnaire that were created to test the three existing sites. By analyzing the results, we observed that interface 1 contrast was the most efficient, being the one that best transmitted safety for navigating was the most perceived, did not generate difficulty in understanding or reading the texts with any font size. Compared with the other contrasts, it was possible for participants to read at a greater distance and for longer, in addition to these users qualifying this contrast as pleasant and rewarding.

Interface 5 contrast, in turn, was the most adequate to indicate the active window and helping to locate the links to the other interfaces, acting as an indicator. Thus, we reached the conclusion that this contrast option may be used for the main menu and submenu and inform about links that lead to more extensive texts. However, according to observations by the participants, the text font seemed to reduce visually in size, which in fact did not occur. This way, it can be stated that this contrast should not be used when the text fonts are small and thin, as it visually reduces their size, hampering text comprehension.

The contrast with red background and bold, white text on interface 3 submenu shoed to be efficient for reading and was well accepted by all.

The use of few colors on the same interface helped with user appreciation, generated interest to explore the page and showed how important colors are for the general context. These combinations brought to evidence the difficulty of LV to identify different color hues. They perceived the difference between the primary color and other variations, and managed to read the content when it was adequate, but could not identify what the variations of the primary color were precisely. In interface 2 main menu, some named the medium violet color as "pink", "lilac" and even "light blue", as with the orange color heading as "yellow".

It should be stressed that such observation did not prevent them from reading the contents, nor did those colors assist in the interface usability. Simplification of tone variations in color composition favoring LV navigating is not an essential and indispensable requirement if the interface is adequate in other ways.

4   Color Model

The result from the test analysis led to a categorization of color contrasts where efficiency was placed first, followed by easiness to read, to memorize, conveying security, assistance in reading for light sensitive users and other characteristics. It was necessary to analyze the color combination separating them into the following elements: main menu, submenu, heading, text body and footnote.

The objective of this color model is to indicate to web designers good practices for creating or adjusting interfaces with the use of colors that make possible for LV to navigate through the virtual environment with just their functional vision in a comfortable and satisfactory fashion without the aid of assistive technologies.

- Contrasts that are more efficient for reading (Figure 5)
- Contrasts that reach several types of LV diagnostics (Figure 6)
- Contrasts more esthetically appreciated (Figure 7)
- Contrasts that allow for the use of other combinations in the same interface (Figure 8)
- Contrasts that better indicate and assist in the identification of icons, topics and titles (Figure 9)
- Contrasts that assist reading by light sensitive users (Figure 10 and Figure 11)
- Contrasts deemed to be discreet (Figure 12)
- Contrasts that make reading easier of long texts with small lettered fonts, but make reading more difficult for light sensitive users (Figure 13)

All these proposed color combinations were tested by LV users who collaborated with the research. Next to each color contrast there is a brief comment suggesting which situation it may be used.

With this, we intend to assist web designers in the choice of contrasts that seek to include specific qualities on each site in pursuit of defined objectives. The character of this color model is innovative and concerns the limitations those users have, but does not prevent other people from being included.

Fig. 5. Contrastes mais eficientes paraler

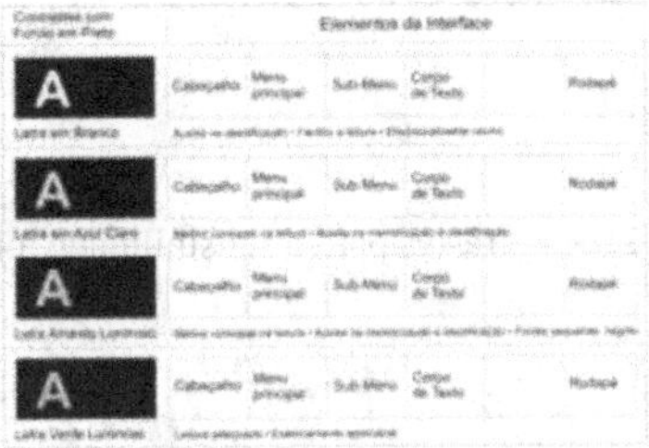

Fig. 6. Contrastes p/ diversos tipos BV

Fig. 7. Contrastes mais percebidos

Fig. 8. Contrastes Neutros

Fig. 9. Contrastes que melhor sinalizam

Fig. 10. Contrastes para a sensibilidade à luz

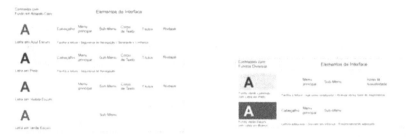

Fig. 11. Contrastes para a sensibilidade à luz   **Fig. 12.** Contrastes considerados discretos

Fig. 13. Contrastes que facilitam a leitura de textos longos

5   Final Considerations

Despite the advances in computing, there is still a significant portion of people who are still outside of this reality. Understanding and making use of guidelines that include users with different characteristics in the development of a site, as simple as it may be, helps in a considerable increase in building awareness to ensure adequate accessibility and usability without distinction.

Comprehension of the interaction between user and computer system through the interface leads us to knowledge of usability as a quality attribute related to easy use of an interface and determine it as the basis to carry out experiments for researching. In that relation, we perceived that color definition has a direct influence in the quality of presenting the information conveyed by any means of communication. Thus, it is necessary to know about the Low Vision disability in order to attain a comprehension of its actual difficulties.

The result obtained from this research show that colors are the visual element with the strongest influence in interface usability, establishing that when colors are used in the construction of a user interface following certain criteria and taking into consideration the limitations of Low Vision users can positively assist in the usability of that interface. We suggest that the color model created and presented in this article be used and commented on by web designers, allowing Low Vision users to enjoy those facilities and validate the research carried out and assisting in the disclosure of this knowledge among professionals in the design & technology area.

References

1. de Carvalho, J.O.F.: Soluções tecnológicas para viabilizar o acesso do deficiente visual à Educação a Distância no ensino superior. Unicamp, Originalmente apresentada comoTese de Doutorado, São Paulo, SP (2001)
2. Carvalho, K.M., Gaspareto, M.E., Venturini, N.H.: Visão Subnormal: Orientaçãoao Professor do Ensino Regular. Unicamp, Campinas (1992)
3. Cybis, W., Betiol, A.H., Faust, R.: Ergonomia e Usabilidade: Conhecimento, Métodos e Aplicações. Novatec, São Paulo (2007)
4. Faye, E.E.: El Enfermo com Déficit Visual – experiênciaclínicaemadultos y niños. Editorial Científico – Médica, Barcelona (1972)
5. IBGE (InstitutoBrasileiro de Geografia e Estatística). CensoDemográfico 2010: Resultados Gerais da Amostra. Rio de Janeiro: Ministério do Planejamento, Orçamento e Gestão (2012)
6. Kulpa, C.C.: A contribuição de um Modelo de Cores na Usabilidade das Interfaces Computacionais para Usuários de Baixa Visão. Originalmente apresentada como Dissertação de Mestrado. Faculdade de Arquitetura, Universidade Federal do Rio Grande do Sul, Porto Alegre, RS (2009)
7. Nielsen, J.: Usability Engineering. Morgan Kaufmann, San Francisco (1993)
8. Paschoal, C.L.L.: Educação visual. Instituto Benjamin Constant, Área da Deficiência Visual: Originalmente apresentada como Dissertação de Mestrado, Rio de Janeiro, RJ (1993)
9. Preece, J., Rogers, Y., Sharp, H.: Design de Interação: além da interação homem-computador. Bookman, Porto Alegre (2005)
10. Rocha, H., Baranauskas, M.C.: Design e Avaliação de Interfaces Humano-Computador. Unicamp/Nied, São Paulo (2003)
11. Sá, E.D., de Campos, I.M., de Silva, M.B.C.: Deficiência Visual: formaçãocontinuada a distância de professores para o atendimento educacionalespecializado. Ministério da Educação/SEESP/Brasil (2007)
12. Vanderheiden, G.C., Vanderheiden, K.R.: Acessible design of consumer products. Guidelines for the design of consumer products to increase their accessibility to the people with disabilities or who are aging. Center at the University of Wisconsin, USA (1991)

Usability of Virtual Worlds

Haind Lu, Tobias Brockmann, and Stefan Stieglitz

University of Muenster, Department for Information Systems, Muenster, Germany
{haind.lu,tobias.brockmann,stefan.stieglitz}@uni-muenster.de

Abstract. In recent years virtual worlds left their origins driven by new technologies. As a consequence 3D-based environments moved into business related domains and are used e.g. to support virtual meetings or product presentations. However, enterprises have to consider that a large share of companies' employees still fits to the definition of so-called digital immigrants. While younger employees are familiar with the usage of 3D-based environments, navigating in virtual rooms might be challenging for digital immigrants. This could limit the usage of virtual worlds for business related contexts. We therefore conducted usability tests with digital immigrants in virtual worlds and analyzed their experiences. Our results show that in fact digital immigrants face problems when using virtual worlds. Based upon our study we discuss how to improve the usability of virtual worlds for this group of users.

Keywords: Virtual worlds, usability, digital immigrants.

1 Introduction

In the last decade, virtual worlds (VW) faced a tremendous media hype, primarily focused on Second Life, which has been followed by a strong decline of interest. Widely unrecognized, platforms like HabboHotel now have more than 200 million users and outpace pioneers such as Second Life or Twinity. Moreover, open source solutions were developed, which begin to solve major problems of virtual worlds such as high access barriers and outdated graphic engines.

Generally, virtual worlds are characterized by social interconnectedness and generation of content by users [1, 2]. Virtual worlds differ from other social media platforms by embedding those properties in a virtual 3D-context and by extending them through a wide range of interaction possibilities (bridging of geographical and physical barriers) [3–8]. Although literature does not provide a single definition for VWs, contemporary VWs are generally characterized as graphical, persistent and immersive environments which facilitate interaction among users who are represented as avatars [9-12].

People that are located at different geographical places can use virtual worlds as a platform to collaborate with each other in a common environment, e.g. for purposes of business [13] or learning [14, 15]. The users act through avatars in three-dimensional spaces [11]. Compared to other social media applications, VWs impose higher requirements to the technical skills of users due to the navigation in

A. Marcus (Ed.): DUXU/HCII 2013, Part I, LNCS 8012, pp. 340–348, 2013.

three-dimensional spaces. Social media applications and therefore also virtual worlds increasingly emerge in everyday work to a certain degree and are thus not solely used by technophile persons (digital natives) but also increasingly by digital immigrants or visitors being dependent on an efficient usage during their work. The usage, or respectively the usability of VWs as well as of other software systems, constitutes an important criterion for the acceptance by users and eventually the successful usage [16].

In this article we address the question to what extent user guidance in VWs is suited for the target group of digital immigrants. Therefore, we evaluated an exemplarily virtual world and conducted usability tests. We considered the level of knowledge of the participants and identified problems participants faced when navigating in this virtual world [17–19].

The remainder of the paper is structured as follows. First, we provide a literature review concerning digital immigrants. Afterwards in chapter 3 we describe the research design. In chapter 4 the results of the usability test are discussed. The article ends with a conclusion and discussion of following research.

2   Technology Skills of Digital Immigrants

Prensky used the terms "digital native" and "digital immigrant" in an article about the differences between various age groups and their interactions with technology [20]. He proposes that younger people tend to be digital natives due to their exposure to information and communication technology from an early age on. As a result these young individuals require multiple streams of information, prefer inductive reasoning and want frequent and quick interactions with content. In contrast, older people, even those remaining current with technological advances, are labeled as digital immigrants. Methodologically, digital immigrants prefer consecutive, step-by-step instructions rather than parallel information channels with random access. This general division through age is challenged by other scholars, arguing that it is simplistic and problematic. Despite growing up in a society with digital technology being highly integrated into everyday life, a significant proportion of young people is not adept with technology [21, 22].

White provides an alternate differentiation, redefining digital natives and digital immigrants as "residents" and "visitors" [23]. This categorization is based on motivation rather than age. Residents shift a proportion of their social life into the digital environment by maintaining profiles on social networking platforms. Visitors, on the other hand, view technology as a tool to attain their goal, such as information research, rather than as a communication platform to express themselves. They are however not averse to using e-mail or instant messaging. White emphasizes that the distinction between residents and visitors is gradual rather than binary [23]. Individuals may be able to place themselves at a particular point along this continuum rather than in one of two boxes.

According to Oblinger and Oblinger, one of the defining characteristics that separates digital natives from digital immigrants is that the natives are more comfortable in image-rich environments and have advanced visual-spatial skills through the influence of computer games [24].

Previous studies conducted to examine the usability and likeability of educational virtual reality games concluded that issues, such as false handling of user interfaces or navigational problems, mainly affect novice users. However, these issues did not discourage them from playing the game. Moreover, the likeability of a virtual reality game was found to be proportional to the level of sophistication of that game [25].

Usability tests in virtual worlds using the constructivist theory identified several usability issues. The three main problems concerned lag time, which prohibited complex tasks, inconvenient avatar maneuverability, which affected new users in particular, and unhelpful sounds, which represented a distraction to the user. Additionally confusing messages as well as irreversible actions constituted problems [26].

3   Usability Test

Methodologically, the measurement of usability and user skills in our study is based on empirical research. In 2011 we investigated the behavior of 5 digital immigrants using the virtual world Second Life (as a representative for virtual worlds). A survey has been conducted before and after the usability test to gain demographic information, to measure the technology skills of the participants concerning social media and 3D-environments, and to observe usage behavior of the participants based on specific tasks that had to be fulfilled. The results were documented via an audio recording as well as a screen capture of each participant. The user-tests were conducted with the same PCs and the viewer. The test for each participant was performed separately in a quiet room. In a first step a method to evaluate the usability in dependency of the skills of digital immigrants was chosen. In a second step, based on the DIN EN ISO 9241 specification, concrete task for the usability test were created.

3.1   Methods

In literature several methods for empirical usability research are discussed. One of the most common methods is known as *thinking-aloud*. The basic principle is that participants solve tasks on the system to be examined, while continuously speaking out their thoughts. The verbalization of thoughts gives insight into the perspective of the user and developers have the possibility to identify misinterpretations [27, 28].

Another method is *constructive interaction*, sometimes also referred to as *co-discovery learning*. It has similarities to the *thinking-aloud* approach, however, participants elaborate on the tasks as a team while exchanging their thoughts. In contrast to the *thinking-aloud* method, people find this approach more natural since they have a counterpart to speak to. As a downside, different problem solving strategies may conflict with each other. Moreover, this method requires at least twice the amount of participants, thereby raising the costs of the entire procedure [29].

Traditionally, the test conductor remains neutral and does not interfere during testing. The *coaching method*, though, encourages participants to ask questions to the conductor, who in return responds with appropriate instructions. By hearing typical user questions, problems are identified and help documentation can be designed accordingly [30].

Websites and interfaces are often only briefly noticed. Therefore the view has to be quickly drawn to the relevant aspects. *Eye-tracking* is a method of analyzing the attention span that a user gives to these aspects. Based on measurements of the viewing directions and movements, user interfaces can be evaluated according to the distribution of attention. However, due to the technical complexity it is rather seldom implemented, but nevertheless a very insightful method [31].

This usability test was conducted based on the methods *thinking-aloud* in conjunction with the *coaching method*. This combination was chosen in order to gain insight into the actions of the users while at the same time discovering information needs. Afterwards a discussion was held between the test conductor and the participants, in which the participants evaluated their experiences retrospectively.

3.2   Conception of Tasks

The usability test was designed according to criteria based on the DIN EN ISO 9241 (ISO 9241). The ISO 9241 generally deals with aspects of human-computer-interaction. Its origins, though, are rooted in applications for office work and have evolved historically. The norm comprises seven principles that act as guidelines for the design of dialogues between humans and information systems:

- Suitability for the task: the dialogue is suitable for a task when it supports the user in the effective and efficient completion of the task.
- Suitability for learning: the dialogue is suitable for learning when it supports and guides the user in learning to use the system.
- Suitability for individualization: the dialogue is capable of individualization when the interface software can be modified to suit the task needs, individual preferences, and skills of the user.
- Conformity with user expectations: the dialogue conforms with user expectations when it is consistent and corresponds to the user characteristics, such as task knowledge, education, experience, and to commonly accepted conventions.
- Self-descriptiveness: the dialogue is self-descriptive when each dialogue step is immediately comprehensible through feedback from the system or is explained to the user on request.
- Controllability: the dialogue is controllable when the user is able to initiate and control the direction and pace of the interaction until the point at which the goal has been met.
- Error tolerance: the dialogue is error tolerant if despite evident errors in input, the intended result may be achieved with either no or minimal action by the user. (DIN EN ISO 9241, 1992 - 2006)

The transferability of all criteria to virtual worlds had to be carefully examined, since certain characteristics of a virtual world, such as the freedom of scope for players, differentiated them strongly from conventional applications that were developed for a specific task. Standardized questions concerning individualization were not suitable for this usability test and were therefore excluded.

Generally, there are many aspects to consider in the development of tasks. The tasks should have a high relation to the real deployment. It is recommendable to include all relevant areas into the task creation. The first task should be kept simple, whereas the rest should not be too trivial and manageable in a reasonable time [30]. Tasks are frequently chosen according to the following criteria:

- First impression (look and feel of the program)
- First tasks (to determine whether a user considers the program generally as easy or difficult to use)
- Most executed activities
- Critical tasks (even if executed infrequently)
- Specific problem areas (usually identified by customer or through heuristic evaluation)
- New functions that were added to a program or changed from previous versions (including changes based on previous usability tests) [32]

Under consideration of these criteria 10 tasks were developed, which covered basic movements, orientation in the virtual environment, communication, interaction with objects within the VW, and adjustment of the avatar's appearance. The tasks started with relatively simple instructions so that users would get acquainted with the navigation of the avatar and get a feeling of movement within the VW. The subsequent tasks instructed them to locate other avatars in their vicinity and communicate to them via chat. Further tasks involved teleportation to different locations, interaction with objects, such as using elevators, and adjusting the appearance of the avatar either through changes in clothing or the body.

4   Results

4.1   Knowledge of Participants

The test persons had no prior experiences with virtual worlds. Moreover, participants were selected that showed typical characteristics of a digital immigrant. The first questionnaire acquired demographic information and determined the computer skills. The average age was 35 (min: 23 max: 48). All of the participants were employees working in office jobs. It was also noted in the questionnaire that on average the participants spent 2 hours a day on the computer in their leisure time. Main activities included communication and news as well as general information research. Online shopping and photo and video editing were also relevant use cases. Games, on the other hand, were hardly played.

4.2   Evaluation of the System

The questionnaire we conducted afterwards, contained questions that were linked to the criteria of the ISO 9241. We analyzed raw data by measuring the mean value and the standard deviation of each question of a criterion. The scale ranged from 1 to 7. A higher score indicated a better performance of the software in that category. The results are summarized in the graph below (see Table 1.)

Table 1. Evaluation of the virtual world according to ISO 9241

ISO-Criterion	Mean	Standard deviation
Suitability for the task	4,50	1,18
Self descriptiveness	3,27	1,62
Conformity with user expectations	4,00	1,37
Suitability for learning	4,40	1,60
Controllability	4,60	1,21
Fault tolerance	3,95	1,41
Total	4,12	1,40

Generally, the virtual world was assessed as being neutral to positive. The category self descriptiveness, however, is characterized by a low mean. The conformity with user expectations as well as the fault tolerance was also rated as relatively low. These categories are further analyzed in the next section.

4.3   Usability Issues

Our analysis shows that participants misinterpreted or ignored certain functions in the menu repeatedly due to their insufficient labeling. E.g. the term "IM (Instant Messaging)" was not understood by most of the participants or a "click to chat"-box remained unused despite its prominence in the menu. Participants tried to chat via the "speak" function instead, which turned out ineffective since this function concealed the voice-speak feature. The meaning of a profile and its comment function was misinterpreted as chat.

In the navigational menu, which was controlled via mouse, it was only apparent that an arrow had to be clicked but not that while holding down the mouse button several arrows could be simultaneously activated which would have enabled a smoother movement.

A more critical issue was revealed when it came to changing the avatar's appearance. The menu for changing the appearance was found quickly and seemed easy to use at first. Within the main menu there were several submenus, which had a similar look but different functions which were not intuitive. Clicking with the left mouse button often led to no effect. In order to open the respective options menu several clicks were needed. Furthermore, objects in the list for clothing were shown which could not be deployed. Through respective icons, such as the "+"-symbol, however, participants mistakenly assumed they were immediately deployable.

Limited server capacities resulted in delayed loadings. Some clothes did not load until a long time into the test which irritated users. Also some objects were not rendered any longer when the distance was too far. This became a problem when an avatar was flying in a certain height and all of its reference points vanished.

Furthermore, no mechanisms were provided to intercept mode errors. If a user has activated a specific function, such as the chat, and tries to navigate the avatar through his keyboard, the action will remain ineffective since the keyboard only works within the chat. The same issue appears once the map is opened. All keyboard commands are directed to the menu of the map. The user only realizes this when his actions have false results. The results of the usability test with respect to prior knowledge are depicted summarizing in the following:

- Problems to find menu bars despite daily usage of software and the Internet.
- Motivation for usage was high and potentials for distributed teams were recognized, mechanisms of the classical web could be transferred to virtual worlds.
- The movement and navigation was perceived as being easy and intuitive (some of the participants already had experiences with video games).
- High correlation between the regular usage of social media elements and the communication in virtual worlds has been identified (IM, VoIP).
- Breaking geographical and physical laws (e.g. flying) gives participants pleasure despite no prior experiences.
- Rapid movements were perceived as being unpleasant.

5   Conclusion

In summary we can state that digital immigrants are used to use traditional web features but lack skills in using game-based functionalities in virtual worlds. Despite the limited gaming experiences, the users quickly adjusted to the navigation via keyboard buttons. After a short learning phase they had acquired the proficiency to control their avatars fluently. The control via mouse (by clicking on direction arrows) on the other hand caused more problems. The avatar's motions were more abrupt and took more time to handle. When using the first-person-perspective the mouse reacted very sensitively resulting in rapid movements in the perspective. These were perceived as unpleasant and criticized by most users.

In contrast to this, the breaking of geographical and physical laws (e.g. flying or teleportation) gave participants pleasure despite no prior experiences. However, flying too high resulted in the loss of orientation points on the ground which caused the avatar to get lost. The same problem occurred when avatars got teleported to unknown locations far away from their origin. Without any hints of how to return to their original position, users were left confused.

Interesting is that, although the digital immigrants have experiences in using 2D-based software systems, they had problems to find menu bars in Second Life. This became apparent in particular when trying to find and communicate to other users. Nonetheless, participants learned how to control several functions within a short period of time and were highly motivated in the execution of the tasks.

It has to be mentioned that, based on the data, certainly no general statements can be concluded. Future research activities could be based on a bigger sample size. The research discussion profits from a first juxtaposition of skills and requirements for the usage of virtual worlds by digital immigrants. For practice, on the one hand, implications for the design of 3D-environments could be derived. Based on our results, companies could decide more differentiated whether the use of virtual worlds can generate advantages based on the available human capital. This can be validated based on the target group profile in this study and the skills of the employees.

References

1. O'Reilly, T.: What is Web 2.0: Design patterns and business models for the next generation of software. Communications & Strategies (2007)
2. McLoughlin, C., Lee, M.: Social software and participatory learning: Pedagogical choices with technology affordances in the Web 2.0 era. In: ascilite, Singapore (2007)
3. Poian, M., Cagnina, M.R.: Business Models and Virtual Worlds: The Second Life Lesson. SSRN Electronic Journal, 1–24 (2010)
4. Arora, V., Khazanchi, D.: Sense of Place in Virtual World Learning Environments: A Conceptual Exploration. In: MWAIS 2010 Proceedings (2010)
5. Warburton, S.: Second Life in higher education: Assessing the potential for and the barriers to deploying virtual worlds in learning and teaching. British Journal of Educational Technology 40, 14–426 (2009)
6. Bartle, R.: Designing virtual worlds. New Riders (2004)
7. Castronova, E.: Synthetic worlds: The business and culture of online games. University of Chicago Press (2005)
8. Davis, A., Murphy, J.: Avatars, People, and Virtual Worlds: Foundations for Research in Metaverses. Journal of the Association for Information Systems 10, 1 (2009)
9. Cahalane, M., Feller, J., Finnegan, P.: Investigating Collaborative Development Activities in a Virtual World: An Activity Theory Perspective Investigating Collaborative Development Activities in a Virtual World: An Activity Theory Perspective. In: ICIS 2010 Proceedings (2010)
10. Bell, M.: Virtual Worlds Research: Past, Present & Future. Journal of Virtual Worlds Research 1 (2008)
11. Messinger, P., Stroulia, E., Lyons, K.: Virtual worlds—past, present, and future: New directions in social computing. Decision Support Systems 47, 204–228 (2009)
12. Stieglitz, S., Lattemann, C., Fohr, G.: Learning Arrangements in Virtual Worlds. In: 43rd Hawaii International Conference on System Sciences (2010)
13. Stieglitz, S., Brockmann, T.: Virtual Worlds as Environments for Virtual Customer Integration. In: 45th Hawaii International Conference on System Sciences, pp. 1013–1020 (2012)
14. Stieglitz, S., Lattemann, C.: Experiential Learning in Second Life. In: 17th Americas Conference on Information Systems, Paper 238, USA, Detroit (2011)
15. Lattemann, C., Stieglitz, S.: Challenges for Lecturers in Virtual Worlds. In: 20th European Conference on Information Systems, Paper 243, Barcelona, Spain (2012)
16. Zerfaß, A., Zimmermann, H.: Usability von Internet-Angeboten: Grundlagen und Fallstudien. Fachhochschule Stuttgart - Hochschule der Medien (2004)

17. Kaplan, A., Haenlein, M.: The fairyland of Second Life: Virtual social worlds and how to use them. Business Horizons 52, 563–572 (2009)
18. Enright, A.: How the second half lives. Marketing news (2007)
19. Hemp, P.: Avatar-based marketing. Harvard Business Review 84, 48–57 (2006)
20. Prensky, M.: Digital natives, digital immigrants. On the Horizon 9 (2001)
21. Bennett, S., Maton, K., Kervin, L.: The 'digital natives' debate: A critical review of the evidence. British Journal of Educational Technology 39, 775–786 (2008)
22. Margaryan, A., Littlejohn, A., Vojt, G.: Are digital natives a myth or reality? University students' use of digital technologies. Computers & Education 56, 429–440 (2011)
23. White, D.S., Le Cornu, A.: Visitors and Residents: A new typology for online engagement. First Monday 16 (2011)
24. Oblinger, D., Oblinger, J.: Is It Age or IT: First Steps Toward Understanding the Net Generation. Educating the Net Generation 29 (2006)
25. Virvou, M., Katsionis, G.: On the usability and likeability of virtual reality games for education: The case of VR-ENGAGE. Computers & Education, 1–22 (2008)
26. Slone, D.: A methodology for measuring usability evaluation skills using the constructivist theory and the second life virtual world. Journal of Usability Studies 4, 178–188 (2009)
27. Nielsen, J.: Usability inspection methods. In: Conference Companion on Human Factors in Computing Systems, pp. 413–414 (1994)
28. Virzi, R.: Refining the test phase of usability evaluation: How many subjects is enough? Human Factors: The Journal of the Human Factors and Ergonomic Society 34, 457–468 (1992)
29. Nielsen, J.: The usability engineering life cycle. Computer (1992)
30. Sarodnick, F., Brau, H.: Methoden der Usability Evaluation. Verlag Hans Huber (2006)
31. Scheier, C., Heinsen, S.: Aufmerksamkeitsanalyse - Usability praktisch umsetzen, pp. 154–167. Carl Hanser, München (2003)
32. Dragg, C.M.: Usability Testing and Research. Longman Pub. Group, Barnum (2001)

Assessing Perceived Experience
with Magnitude Estimation

Mick McGee[1], Misha Vaughan[2], and Joseph Dumas[3]

[1] EchoUser, San Francisco, USA
mick.mcgee@echouser.com
[2] Oracle Corporation, Applications User Experience, Redwood Shores, USA
misha.vaughan@oracle.com
[3] Dumas Consulting, Yarmouth Port, USA
joe.dumas99@gmail.com

Abstract. Professionals who develop and evaluate the interaction between people and systems have broadened their interests beyond ease of use and learning to higher-order concepts, such as "user experience." "Excellence," "delight" and other emotion-driven experiences are becoming more central to product and company success. In three case studies, we explore and demonstrate how the psychophysical Magnitude Estimation Technique (MET) can be used to quantify complex subjective experiences. We hypothesize that MET can be used to assess *any* user experience that can be defined. We describe studies that apply MET to three different contexts and perceived experience definitions: (1) the riding experience in a public transit system, (2) the effectiveness of a sales presentation, presented online vs. live, and (3) the safety and usability of cancer radiation equipment. In all three situations, participants were able to comprehend the definitions of and assign numeric values to the intensity of their experience. Those judgments were used in combination with other measures to assess the strengths and weaknesses of the overarching user experiences.

Keywords: user experience, usability, magnitude estimation, measurement.

1 Introduction

As technologies mature and business strategies adapt, the demand for differentiating user experience has increased. Making products simple and easy is now the minimum threshold; qualities such as excellence and delight are now expected [1]. Competitive advantage comes from well-designed experiences that have an engaging emotional impact. Synthesizing these engaging experiences into products requires that we enhance the way that we assess such qualities.

Usability measures of task completion rate, assists, time, and errors are still extremely useful and remain a fundamental part of our product development toolkit. Additionally, subjective ratings remain an effective way to assess usability "satisfaction". Our expanded interest goes beyond usability to other aspects of user experience such as 'fun,' 'delight,' and 'engagement,' across devices, formats, and contexts.

A. Marcus (Ed.): DUXU/HCII 2013, Part I, LNCS 8012, pp. 349–358, 2013.
© Springer-Verlag Berlin Heidelberg 2013

The quantification of the "user experience" construct is still in a formative stage. "The key argument hinges on the meaningfulness, validity and usefulness of reducing fuzzy experiential qualities such as fun, challenge and trust to numbers [2]." Recently there have been a number of studies on the partitioning of user experience into some of its components, especially the interaction between aesthetics and usability [3,4]. These studies have used a variety of traditional measurement techniques, though most have used Likert scales. While Likert scales have the advantages of being both quick to administer and familiar to most end users, they have at least two limitations: they are closed ended, which results and floor and ceiling effects, and their equal-interval scale properties have been questioned [5].

In recent projects, to meet changing business demands and keep users at the center of design processes, we have explored methods to capture experiences and emotion-driven responses. We pursued measures that (1) assess a holistic experience rather than its components, (2) are open ended and have equal interval properties, (3) present the results in an easily interpretable metric, and (4) are flexible enough to accommodate widely differing contexts. We have had success applying a technique from psychophysics, the Magnitude Estimation Technique (MET) [6].

In previous studies, MET has proven flexible and robust enough to scale multifaceted perceptions with complex underlying physical stimuli. This capability is particularly compelling with perceptions that do not have a physical analog, especially when produced from multidimensional stimuli that are difficult to measure. For example, Gescheider [7] cites successful uses of magnitude estimation in a variety of contexts: trial evidence (physical stimulus) with guilt (perception); life events with emotional stress; and psychiatric symptoms with judgments of the severity of mental disorder. McGee [8] demonstrated that MET can measure usability on a variety of platforms: desktop browsers, handheld devices (PDAs and cellular phones), and interactive-voice applications. Rich and McGee [9] further demonstrated that MET is effective at assessing both expectations and actual usability, which can allow practitioners to more meaningfully prioritize usability issues.

2   Our Objective

We set out to explore the hypothesis that MET can be used to measure any novel user experience that can be clearly defined to participants. For example, McGee, Rich and Dumas [10] created an empirical definition of the concept of "usability." They asked 46 respondents to fill out a survey containing adjectives that described 64 potential usability characteristics. The respondents rated how integral each characteristic was to their concept of usability. A cluster and factor analysis was used to create a definition:

> Usability is your perception of how consistent, efficient, productive, organized, easy to use, intuitive, and straightforward it is to accomplish tasks within a system.

Currently in our profession there is no clear context-free definition of "user experience" [2]. Consequently, we wanted to start by sampling a wide variety of contexts in which we could create tailored definitions of an experience that end-users could then use to judge the quality of the experience. We report in this paper on case studies of perceived experience for:

- The quality of the public transit riding experience.
- The effectiveness of a sales presentation using two different formats.
- The safety and usability of medical equipment.

In each of the studies we followed a similar basic MET procedure but with some modifications to explore variations of the method.

3   MET Mechanics

Historically MET began as a way to determine simple relationships between physical intensity, such as decibels, and psychological intensity, such as perceived loudness. Participants in those studies were asked to assign a number to a tone that represented its perceived loudness. Through an initial training session participants were taught to make ratio judgments about loudness. For example, a tone assigned the value of 50 should be perceived as twice as loud as a tone assigned the value of 25 [11]. While each participant is allowed to assign his or her own numbers, magnitude estimation scaling transforms them into a common scale.

As described above, researchers have learned that people can assign reliable judgments to much more complex qualities and experiences. MET can be used within any evaluation that assesses tasks, settings, environments, etc. Participants perform a number assignment procedure across items of interest based on their subjective perception of the defined experience. The outcome is a ratio scale that can be used to make a variety of summary judgments about whatever is being evaluated.

In our three studies, we followed a similar basic procedure. Participants were:

- Given an introduction to the study and that they would be rating an experience.
- Given a definition of the quality of the experience, and provided with an example of a ratio judgment. The definition of quality was developed empirically in some studies and by user experience and subject matter experts in others.
- Given a short reference exercise in which they were asked to assign ratio values to contextually comparable experiences such as the usability of sample web pages.
- Asked to assign ratio values to the primary subject of the study such as the quality of urban transportation experiences, or the quality of a sales presentation, or the usability and safety of medical hardware and software.

These case studies explore magnitude estimation as a metric for measuring users' holistic experience in a variety of different settings and complex user experiences. In each case, we were able to create custom definitions of the quality of experience that participants could understand. Furthermore, by including reference tasks, we were able to assess the quality of experiences in comparison with relevant benchmarks.

4   Case Study I: The Quality of an Urban Transportation Riding Experience

The purpose of this study was to provide the management of the Bay Area Rapid Transit (BART) system with insight into user experience issues through a series of "ride-along" sessions. BART was particularly interested in riders that had a "choice," such as tourists, shoppers, and occasional riders.

We began this research by observing people at BART transit stations and bus stops. The actions of the riders were observed and recorded, especially positive and negative experiences. Once we recorded the main rider activities and notable events, several riders were approached (with a permission letter created by the BART board) for feedback on what characteristics contributed to a positive transit riding experience. The participants either answered brief interview questions or completed a similar survey to that described in [10]. Through that work the following definition of "riding experience" was created:

> *A good public transportation experience is a cost-effective way of reliably, conveniently, and safely getting me to my intended destination on time.*

For the main study, fifteen BART riders were recruited and accompanied through their entire ride. They rode a subway train and/or bus. Upon meeting the participant at their desired location, a facilitator explained the purpose of the study and provided them with training on how to make ratio judgments for the riding experience. They were then given the above definition of rider experience and asked if they understood it or if there were any questions.

For the reference experience, they were given a description of a poor experience that included difficulties buying a ticket and having to stand in a crowded vehicle. They were told to assign that experience a value of 10 and to use that value as a baseline to rate their following ride-along experiences. We used a negative experience because we wanted to set the same lower limit for each rider, which in our experience, makes it easier to use the scale.

We could not control the order of tasks that each participant performed in their specific trip; each rider executed their trip as they normally would. Instead, we had a pre-made set of possible events and, as they occurred, participants provided ratings for that specific event. This "event-based" procedure had seven different possible activities, including waiting for the vehicle (train or bus), riding it, and getting off. Participants were also asked to think aloud to the facilitator about the experience as it was happening. Additional broad questions were asked between events as time permitted, such as rating seating and ride comfort. At the conclusion of the trip, participants made one final rating of the overall experience.

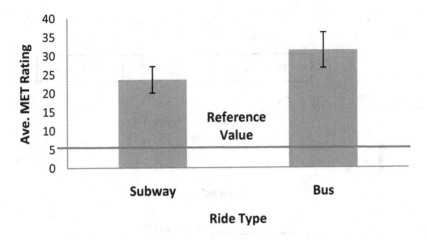

Fig. 1. Average MET ratings for 15 Bart riders

The results of the magnitude estimation ratings of the overall experience for bus and subway rides are shown in Figure 1. The y-axis shows the average rating value provided by the riders.

The scale on that axis had no upper limit as riders where allowed to assign any positive number to their experience. The reference value line represents the poor transit scenario, set at a value of 10. Both the BART bus and subway ride experiences were rated better than the reference experience and the bus rides were rated higher than the subway rides. We did not compute inferential statistics on the averages, but the confidence interval bars indicate a good deal of variability. The think aloud protocol indicated that factors such as the crowding, lack of cleanliness, and higher cost lowered the ratings for the subway.

Participants were also asked to rate their expectations for the experience before each of the events. Figure 2 shows the expected versus observed ratings for four bus ride (AC) events. The results are plotted by scaled expected versus actual user experience per event. For example, the "getting off AC" value shows the average expected usability (x-axis) against the average actual usability (y-axis) for all riders of the event of getting off the bus. The diagonal line (from bottom left to top right) represents where expectations are exactly met. The line from the bottom right to the top left represents where satisfaction is met exactly. The graph shows that the time waiting for the bus fell below expectations (a Fix it issue), but that getting off the bus was well above expectations (a Promote it opportunity). In contrast, settling into the bus seat and riding the bus approximately met expectations (either an opportunity to try and push actual experience above expectations, or information that resource investment may not be worthwhile, compared to other more urgent concerns).

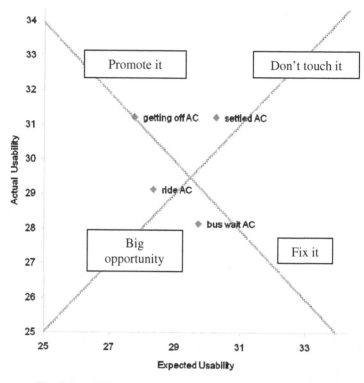

Fig. 2. Bus (AC) user experience expected vs. actual usability

5   Case Study II: The Quality of a Presentation Format

The objective of this study was to determine whether the quality of a presentation about a new product would be perceived as more effective live or in an online video.

We created a presentation about Oracle's next generation of applications. The participants were Oracle customers. Our goal was to make both presentation formats high quality. The presentations were given by the same Oracle VP. The slides for the live version were created with professional graphics and animations. The online presentation was in the form of a movie, which was professional quality, the same presenter's voice and slides.

We ran the session with eight Oracle customers in a group, a new variation of MET. We wanted to see if we could increase the sample size by running group sessions and we wanted to use MET in a setting in which participants normally experience a stimulus in groups. The session began with an introduction to the study and explanation of magnitude estimation. The customers were then asked if they understood the definition and it was discussed further when there were questions.

To establish a baseline for comparison, the participants were given three divergent multimedia scenarios to rate: negative, positive, and neutral:

- Think about an online video that is hard to hear, dimly lit, and boring (negative)
- Think about a podcast that is short, lively, easy to follow, with a clear concept and easy-to-hear voices (positive)
- Think about a blog post that is long and a bit boring, with too many ideas, but with a clear concept and clear and relevant pictures (neutral)

The live presentation was given in a room by the VP. The pre-recorded online movie was then shown projected on a screen. The participants rated the overall quality of each section of the presentation and, at the end, the overall presentation. Because this was a group session, we could not counterbalance the order of the formats.

The results are shown in Figure 3. The three lines represent the average ratings for the baseline definitions. The y-axis is the average quality rating for the eight participants for each format. The scale is open ended so there is no upper limit. Both formats were rated as higher quality than the neutral baseline, which suggests that our goal to create professional presentations was at least partially met. The fact that both formats fell below the positive experience indicates that they could do more to meet customers' expectations.

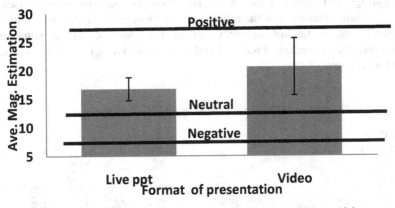

Fig. 3. Average MET ratings for live and video formats by eight participants

Collecting the data in a group setting presented no difficulties. The video presentation format was rated higher than the live presentation in perceived quality, which suggests that that format may be more effective for Oracle customers. The confidence intervals, however, show a large amount of variability. We also realize that we had no independent measure of quality and the live format was seen first. We do see the potential for having two different presenters give the same presentation and measuring the difference in the quality of the experience for the audience.

6   Case Study III: The Perceived Usability and Safety of Medical Equipment

In response to new FDA requirements, a medical equipment manufacturer requested help with creating a method for assessing both the safety and usability of complex hardware and software. Incorporating safety with usability in one unified scale was a challenge. We devised a definition with medical experts:

You will be rating user and safety experience. This is your perception of how easy to use, well designed, productive and safe the interface is for conducting tasks. "Safe" is how free an environment (including devices, software, facilities, people, etc.) is from danger, risk, and injury.

Participants were asked if they understood the definition and if there were any questions. The test participants were physicians and technicians who did not have experience with the models being tested. The participants appeared to perceive safety as critical and integral to the overall 'user experience' and had no issues with the definition.

Reference comparisons for these studies were made against both generic and product specific safety-related tasks, from a common household "safety" task (e.g., using cleaning supplies) to representative tasks related to the products tested (e.g., a patient-management task).

The study consisted of evaluations of two products using this methodology. One product was a hardware medical treatment device; the second was a software application suite of patient management tools.

Comparing MET results between the two products, participants who used the hardware system rated most of the actual task experiences better than they expected, while participants of the software-only test rated the majority of the actual experiences worse than expected. Figures 4 and 5 show the average expected and actual ratings for each task.

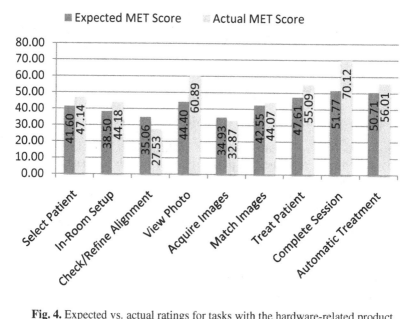

Fig. 4. Expected vs. actual ratings for tasks with the hardware-related product

The rating was open-ended so the y-axis has no upper limit. Notice that in Figure 4, most of the lighter bars (actual rating) are higher than the darker bars (expected rating). In Figure 5 the order is reversed.

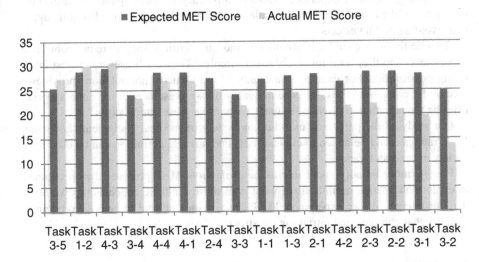

Fig. 5. Expected vs. actual ratings for tasks with the software-related product

Participants using the hardware system did spontaneously comment on safety mitigators that were in place, which they may not have expected. However, issues identified by participants using the software system, which, in our view, had safety concerns far less critical than the hardware system, seemed to focus on traditional usability problems. Perhaps for software-based products, the usability component of the definition becomes dominant. Objective data collected across the two studies did not show the same dichotomy as the holistic, subjective MET results.

Overall, testing for the two products showed successful integration of safety and usability into overall user experience. The results show that even experiences that are not inherently similar can be successfully assessed the same way as long as the measureable construct is the same and the definition of quality is clear to the raters.

7   Discussion

These case studies explored magnitude estimation as a metric for measuring users' holistic experience in a variety of different settings. In each case, we were able to create custom definitions of the quality of experience that participants could understand. Furthermore, by including reference tasks, we were able to assess the quality of experiences in comparison with relevant benchmarks. Additional method variations that we explored included, (1) event-based tasks across an extended transit trip, (2) using MET in a group setting, and (3) combining two perceptual concepts, safety and usability, into one definition.

Once a definition of the quality of the experience was created, the method was relatively easy to administer to participants with a few minutes of training. Participants could make their ratings without interfering with the experience itself. The concept of rating a holistic experience seemed to be easy for participants to grasp. Furthermore, unlike a traditional Likert scale, the MET scale is not bounded at its upper end, avoiding ceiling effects.

Because these case studies were done in industry settings, they were not controlled experiments and they used relatively small samples. They do, however, suggest interesting possibilities. For example, our study of the industry presentations provides a method for comparing the difference in quality of two presenters of the same material, offering the potential to provide feedback to improve presentation skills.

Our study of the perceived usability and safety of medical equipment shows that MET ratings could be added to clinical trials and a single definition can be used for a variety of product types.

Finally, more broadly applicable to the profession, MET provides the opportunity to explore alternative definitions of what is meant by holistic concepts. As we broaden our interest in user experience, MET can provide one tool to help us to begin to quantify that complex and intriguing construct.

References

1. Calacanis, J.: The age of excellence, http://www.launch.co/blog/the-age-of-excellence.html
2. Law, E.: The Measurability and Predictability of User Experience. In: Proceedings of the 3rd ACM SIGCHI Symposium Engineering Interactive Computing Systems EICS 2011, pp. 13–16. ACM, Pisa (2011)
3. Mahlke, S.: Understanding Users' Experience of Interaction. In: EACE 2005 Proceedings of the Annual Conference of the European Association of Cognitive Ergonomics, pp. 251–254 (2005)
4. Hartmann, J.: Assessing the Attractiveness of Interactive Systems. In: Proceedings of CHI 2006, Doctoral Consortium, Montréal, Québec, Canada, pp. 755–1758 (2006)
5. Badia, P., Runyon, R.P.: Fundamentals of Behavioral Research. Random House, New York (1982)
6. Stevens, S.S.: Psychophysics: Introduction to its Perceptual, Neural, and Social Prospects. John Wiley, New York (1975)
7. Gescheider, G.A.: Psychophysics: The Fundamentals, 3rd edn. Lawrence Erlbaum Associates, Publishers, Mahwah (1997)
8. McGee, M.: Usability Magnitude Estimation. In: Proceedings of the Human Factors and Ergonomics Society 47th Annual Meeting, pp. 691–695 (2003)
9. Rich, A., McGee, M.: Expected Usability Magnitude Estimation. In: Proceedings of the Human Factors and Ergonomics Society 48th Annual Meeting, pp. 912–916 (2004)
10. McGee, M., Rich, A., Dumas, J.: Understanding the Usability Construct: User-perceived Usability. In: Proceedings of Human Factors and Ergonomics Society 48th Annual Meeting, pp. 907–911 (2004)
11. Stevens, S.S.: The Direct Estimation of Sensory Magnitudes—Loudness. The American Journal of Psychology 69, 1–15 (1956)

SINGRAR Usability Study

Isabel L. Nunes[1,2] and Mário Simões-Marques[3]

[1] Faculdade de Ciências e Tecnologia - UNL, 2829-516 Caparica, Portugal
[2] UNIDEMI, Faculdade de Ciências e Tecnologia - UNL, 2829-516 Caparica, Portugal
[3] CINAV, Portuguese Navy, BNL/Alfeite, 2810-001 Almada, Portugal
imn@fct.unl.pt, mj.simoes.marques@gmail.com

Abstract. Usability is a very important issue that affects the effectiveness and success of systems. Such importance becomes particularly critical when systems are complex, and when the accuracy and timeliness of operation is decisive to the system outputs. Naturally, the usability of decision support systems used for emergency management is of utmost relevance. The present paper addresses a usability study performed to the Portuguese Navy SINGRAR system.

Keywords: emergency management system, usability study, SINGRAR.

1 Introduction

SINGRAR is the acronym of the Priority Management and Resource Assignment Integrated System. This system is a distributed expert system used on board of Portuguese warships, to compile information about the status of the platform, equipment and personnel, supporting the management of emergency situations (e.g., fires, floods) and giving advice about recommended courses of action (e.g., damage control, equipment repair priorities). SINGRAR is an emergency management system (EMS) used in combat and emergency, situations in which users may have to wear personnel protective equipment, e.g. gloves, anti-flash gear or masks. This equipment presents a challenge in the operation of the system [1].

The importance of usability becomes particularly critical when systems are complex, and the accuracy and timeliness of operation is decisive to the system usefulness. Naturally, the usability of EMS is of utmost relevance.

Usability is a critical aspect to consider in the development cycle of software applications, and for this purpose, user-centered design and usability testing must be conducted. The design and testing cannot ignore the context of use of software, whose knowledge is essential. Usability of a system is characterized by its intuitiveness, efficiency, effectiveness, memorization and satisfaction. Good usability allows decreasing the time to perform tasks, reducing errors, reducing learning time and improving system users' satisfaction [2].

Usability assessment can be done based on objective and subjective evaluations. Objective evaluation of performance, measures the ability of users to operate the system. The subjective assessment of users' preferences evaluates how much users like the system. ISO 9241 - Part 11 refers that usability is measured as a function of the degree to which the goals of the system are achieved (effectiveness), of the resources

A. Marcus (Ed.): DUXU/HCII 2013, Part I, LNCS 8012, pp. 359–368, 2013.

(such as time, money, or mental stress) that must be spent to achieve the objectives (efficiency) and of the extent to which users of the system find it acceptable (satisfaction) [3]. Therefore, effectiveness, efficiency and satisfaction are criteria that have to be considered when evaluating the usability of a system. To assess these criteria, it is necessary to consider sub-criteria, which are measurable.

There is a wide range of tools and methodologies for identifying and evaluating the usability of a system, thus contributing directly or indirectly, for its improvement. The selection of these tools and methodologies depends on the objective to achieve, which usually is related to the development phase the system is in. Some approaches are better suited to the design stage (e.g., analysis of context of use and task analysis), while others are more suited to early stages of development and prototyping (e.g., brainstorming, prototyping) and others for the evaluation and testing (e.g., analytical and heuristic evaluations, SUMI). A compilation of methods can be found in [4].

For instance, SUMI is a rigorously tested and validated questionnaire based method to measure software quality from a user's perspective [5]. This tool is supported by an extensive reference database and embedded in an effective analysis and reporting tool, has been applied to a great number of projects.

The goal of the study was to identify the usability factors affecting operators' performance, recommend potential solutions to improve SINGRAR, and assess the gains achieved by the implementation of improvements introduced during the study period.

2   SINGRAR Characterization

SINGRAR is used to generate a common operational picture of the ship and their systems; support the decision making regarding courses of action and human resources allocation in critical combat and emergency situations; and support the flow of information between the different technical and operational areas of the ship. The compilation of a consolidated picture is made by operators from different technical areas, and information is automatically shared among the EMS terminals connected to a local area network.

Figure 1 illustrates examples of interfaces that combine graphical, tabular and text information used to characterize the environment, the status of the ship and their equipment and to support the decision-making process.

Despite some complexity of the interfaces, the operation is relatively intuitive for users who are familiar with the tasks that the system supports. The system was designed to maximize compatibility with existing procedures and the previously existing manual recording media, to allow a simple transition from one method to the other.

Users - SINGRAR is used by military personnel onboard Portuguese Navy ships. Users can be categorized into two groups, decision makers (Captain and Heads of Department) and technicians.

Tasks - Tasks performed with SINGRAR depend on the profile of users, which are related to their responsibilities within the organization on board. Usually the operating requirements are inversely proportional to the user level within the chain of command. That is, the activity performed by the Captain is low, increases slightly for the other decision makers, and is maximal for the technicians.

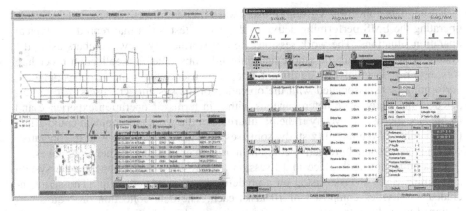

Fig. 1. SINGRAR - examples of interfaces

Operational environment - SINGRAR can be used in all degrees of readiness of the ship, from the ship moored alongside to Battle Stations. The number of workstations required increases as the ship readiness evolves towards Emergency or Battle Stations, which is the highest.

SINGRAR is installed mainly in desktop computers, but runs also in portable computers. Portable computers are used, for example, in Damage Control command posts. In these posts operators are standing and working in a confined area that usually does not allow the use of a mouse or a trackball. These workstations are not suitable for an extended operation of the system. Desktop based workstations are more suitable since they allow a more comfortable use of the computer, a factor which is very important to ensure an efficient, effective and satisfactory use of any type of application.

3   SINGRAR - Usability Evaluation Methodology

The usability study was prompted after users of the EMS advanced prototype reported some difficulties in inputting data at an adequate pace. These difficulties were experienced especially when dealing with high tempo incidents while training demanding operational and emergency scenarios.

The EMS was developed from the very beginning with usability concerns, particularly because the system is operated using a quite high number of interfaces, some of them presenting a high density of information which is complex in nature. In fact, the use of critical applications, developed based on information technologies, such as the EMS, had an exponential increase in recent years. However, their development is challenging considering that these systems are required to have high reliability and their users have to be able to use them effortlessly, with minimal training and that the tasks have to be performed in the shortest time possible. Thus, it is extremely important to ensure that usability is taken into consideration since the early stages of the development of such systems.

The methodology of the usability study considered three phases: data collection, results analysis and recommendations.

During data collection a group of users was observed directly by the analyst while operating the EMS performing activities defined in test script that reproduces typical operation situations. The work sessions were performed by crew members using the system both in a simulator ashore and onboard ships. The data collection procedure was designed to involve a significant sample of users within the target population, performing tasks associated with the operation of the system. The users that participated in the study were heterogeneous, either in terms of operation experience and technical expertise. To verify if the peculiarities of the work environment could affect the reliability of the usability study, some sessions were performed with the operators wearing the personnel protective equipment used in emergency, namely the gloves.

Data collection took place in 12 sessions, where users had to operate the system performing a set of tasks listed on a predefined and validated script. The script included 9 activities composed of 10 tasks each. The data collection procedure was designed to evaluate the efficiency, effectiveness and satisfaction of system operation and also to compare different operational methods (Table 1). The first two characteristics were assessed using objective data collected during usability tests. In addition, users answered the Portuguese version of SUMI [6], providing measures regarding the intuitiveness and ease of memorization of the application.

To collect and process the subjective data it was used the SUMI method, which employs a metric to assess the overall satisfaction or overall usability of software. The evaluation of the software quality from the users' point of view is based on a questionnaire with 50 statements, which was answered by the users at the end of each session.

Table 1. Characteristics assessed in the SINGRAR usability study

| | SUMI Questionnnaire (Subjective Data) | Activity Analysis | |
		Objective Data	Parameters
Effectiveness	X	X	Number of user errors Number of tasks finished in a given period of time
Efficiency	X	X	Number of actions performed Average, maximum and minimum time for performing the activity tasks
Satisfaction	X		-
Intuitiveness	X		-
Ease of memorization	X		-

For the analysis of objective data it were considered, first, the recording of the data inserted by each user and, second, the video recordings of the session in order to understand the circumstances in which the session evolved, and the reason for any disparate performance (e.g., long execution times and errors). The observation of the video recordings was particularly useful in isolating aspects of the procedures adopted to pass information to the users and of the methods of operation that proved to be problematic or, on the other hand, which constitute good practices to follow.

The records of the Event Logs exported from the EMS were processed to extract the main data elements (e.g., duration of each task), to detect errors in the input of the information defined by the script, and also to compare the progression of events with the desired state.

The video recording involved two video cameras and was intended to support the analysis of data collected, documenting the actions, comments and attitudes of users towards the application. The first recorder was placed in a fixed position perpendicular to the operator, and recorded actions, facial expressions and body posture of the users. The second camera was mobile collecting images of the computer screen, and recorded the actions performed by the users during the procedure.

Individual data were later aggregated in order to have a perception on the use of the system considering a broader set of users. In general, the data aggregation was based on average, minimum and maximum functions, which can identify trends and variability in performance. Processing the data as a whole allowed identifying the events, procedures or methods that revealed to be more problematic for the users.

4   Results and Discussion

4.1   SINGRAR Usability Analysis Using the SUMI Method

SUMI method was applied to 13 users. All users answered the questionnaires correctly and their opinions were used to generate the results presented in Figure 2, in terms of Median and Upper and Lower Confidence Limit, for each of the five dimensions of usability (efficiency, affect, helpfulness, controllability and learnability). These results are synthesized by the Global usability assessment.

The analysis of the results allows concluding that users have a positive opinion about the system, i.e. equal to or greater than the commercial standard (the reference level 50), with some degree of dispersion in all dimensions of usability. The Global assessment with a value 60 and a small standard deviation indicates that the EMS is a software with high usability, better than the standard. Therefore, users were satisfied with the system, and to improve it only ad hoc corrections were needed. With the exception of items related to Control that were assessed as medium (controllability = 50), all items were assessed above the reference standard. The EMS is perceived by users as being very useful (helpfulness = 60), satisfactory (affect = 56), efficient (efficiency = 55) and relatively easy to learn (learnability = 54). The fact that the group of users who responded to the questionnaire is sufficiently large ensures that the analysis results are relevant.

Besides the general evaluation of the system's data, it was also performed an Item Consensual Analysis (ICA). The results related with 7 items (items 4, 6, 14, 22, 27, 29 and 41) of the SUMI questionnaire departed significantly from the pattern of response expected on the basis of the SUMI standardization database. In this set of items, four reflected a positive perception by users (items 6, 22, 27 and 41) and three reflected a negative perception (items 4, 14 and 29). The last three items were the ones that deserved special attention by the analysts, together with the software development team.

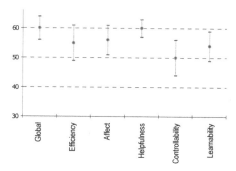

Fig. 2. SUMI Global Usability evaluation

The most important issues relate with the perception on the speed of the software (item 29) and to unexpected stops of the software (item 4). These issues were consistent with the concerns previously expressed by the users to the development team, and they were the main reason for the study. In fact, the main problems reported by users were related to the speed of data entry and to episodes of the software freezing.

Item 14 (related to the controllability of the system) was another area that deserved attention. Item 14 statement reads "I feel safer if I use only a few familiar commands or operations". The results most probably reflected a lack of training on how the software works, and the recommendation of the study regarding this issue was that all operators should receive training, not to feel insecure when using the system.

The results for all other items addressed by the ICA indicate that the observed values did not differ substantially from the expected values, and the usability of the software components was not very different from the usability characteristics recorded in the SUMI database. There were several items where the software analyzed ranked better than standard, for example, items 12, 13, 24, 37 or 48. However, an example of items that were rated poorly is item 46, which is also an indicator of lack of knowledge about the system, which reinforces the previous recommendation on the need to increase education and training.

The use of the SUMI method offered a very good perspective about the level of quality of the EMS usability, and pointed to the need of implementing some minor modifications in the system, particularly in the domain of system control. In fact, this analysis together with a detailed interface and functionality analysis, allowed the identification of specific areas for improvement by the development team, that are discussed below. After these adjustments some gains in terms of system's efficiency and effectiveness were obtained, which were evaluated and validated based on the objective analysis that is presented at the end of this section.

4.2 Dynamic Analysis of the Application

In order to analyze the aspects regarding the effectiveness and efficiency of EMS use, several sessions of objective data collection were conducted.

As referred, the measurements taken were obtained primarily from processing the Event Log files exported from the EMS at the end of each session. The analysis of these logs allowed, for example, obtaining data about the time spent to perform each task, and detecting the errors in inputting the events defined in the script. The analysis was complemented by the visualization of the videos recorded, enabling the review of the circumstances in which users performed the tasks, their comments and attitudes.

The processing and analysis of data collected in each individual session allowed understanding the circumstances that led to the specific results, in terms of time spent to perform the tasks and number of errors. This analysis allowed isolating aspects of the application, of the procedures associated with data entry and of the operation methods that proved problematic, or that were good practices to adopt. For instance it was possible to find that the way information was reported to users for data entry may significantly affect the amount of time spent to input it in the EMS and the number of errors, therefore affecting users' performance. Figure 3 illustrates this situation depicting the time spend to input data regarding a series of events. When the data is uniquely coded the time spent is consistently small. When the information is passed in a descriptive format the time required to process it presented high variability. This issue will be further discussed later in this sub-section.

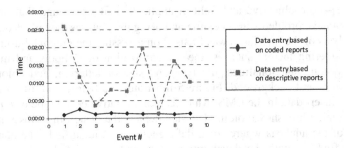

Fig. 3. Differences in data entry performance depending on the reporting procedure

On a second step the data were processed as a whole in order to identify how the events, procedures or methods imposed by the script affected the generality of the users group. This aggregation of individual data made possible identifying whether there were trends or variability in performance.

The operators engaged in the study presented different levels of experience, so that it was possible to evaluate if this factor affected in any way the user performance. The results demonstrated that experience was not significant in terms of the proficiency in data entry. It was observed that some of the users that were supposed to be more experienced presented levels of performance worse than the inexperienced users. The causes identified for this finding related mainly with the adoption of deficient procedures for using the system. Figure 4 illustrates the level of performance that could be reached by inexperienced users after the introduction of some improvements in the software and in the data input procedures, by comparing it with the output of the experienced user with best performance obtained in the tests done before improvements.

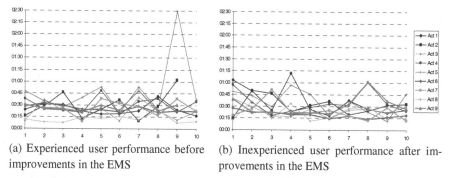

(a) Experienced user performance before improvements in the EMS

(b) Inexperienced user performance after improvements in the EMS

Fig. 4. Comparison of performance in data entry before and after improvements in usability

4.3   Analysis of Interfaces and User Interaction

The general arrangement of the interfaces was assessed considering the specificity of the context of use. Despite some complexity of the interface, the system was designed for a very specific objective and field of application. It was found that, in general, users did not have problems in accessing and using the features they needed.

The analysis of the interfaces was focused on assessing the graphical user interface (GUI), considering factors such as, the standardization of symbols and methods of accessing system functionalities, the type and size of lettering, and color contrast between letters and background. Figure 5 illustrates the before and after of a dialog box used to insert data in the EMS, which is representative of the type of intervention done. The dialog box shown on the left side depicts the design that was found in the beginning of the analysis where some deficiencies were identified. The analysts discussed the findings with the development team and some details were modified to improve interaction. The modified dialog box is depicted in the right side of the figure. Four modifications are highlighted in the figure, which will be discussed below as examples of the intervention that resulted from the usability analysis.

Considering the image contrast there were screens lacking adequate contrast between the background and the label letters, making it difficult to read, for example, white letters over a gray background (see 1, 2 and 3 in Figure 5). The symbology adopted failed to adhere consistently to common standards. Sometimes the icons chosen might lead users to make mistakes or were hard to relate to the functions they were associated with (see 4 in Figure 5). Similarly, the use of captions in the buttons was not consistent, since the terminology was not always the same. It was further observed that the operators tended to assume the existence and tried to use some mouse actions common in Windows environment (e.g., double-click), which were not always programmed, reducing efficiency and user satisfaction. The use of standard mouse forms of interaction such as double-click was recommended.

For experienced users the fastest way to access the features of a program is through the keyboard, for example using shortcut keys. This option was not systematically considered in the interface design, which limited the user's efficiency, since operation often required to take the hand out of the keyboard and to use the mouse to position the cursor over a button and to click. The use of shortcut keys was recommended.

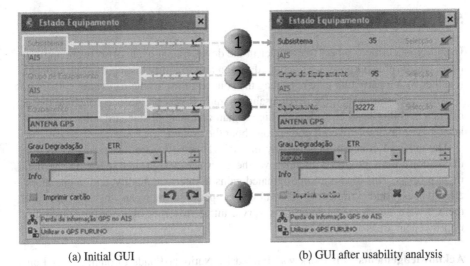

(a) Initial GUI   (b) GUI after usability analysis

Fig. 5. Examples of interface characteristics that were improved after the usability analysis

Data entry was often followed by the clicking of a command button (e.g., "OK"). Setting this button as the default button, improves user performance since it allows the operator to hit the "Enter" key in the keyboard, without having to handle the mouse. The use of default buttons was recommended for non-critical operations.

In order to expedite the selection of equipment for data entry, the "Equipment Code" (illustrated as 3 in Figure 5) became editable using a text box that allows writing directly the code of equipment. This solution avoided the need to manipulate other types of interfaces to select the equipment, saving significant amounts of time.

After finishing the entry of data regarding one event the software always closed the window presented in Figure 5. However this form is used repeatedly to input data. A new option was offered to users, which was to save the changes resulting from the entry of data of one event and to proceed with the introduction of data from a new event, without closing the window (see new icon in 4 of Figure 5). Besides this new feature, the cursor was also positioned automatically in the text box where the operator usually starts writing, thus avoiding the need to use the mouse to position the cursor. The implementation of these minor modifications significantly improved the efficiency in the entry of data of multiple events.

One issue that also had big influence on the systems effectiveness related with the performance of the search tool that was already available for finding equipment based on a textual descriptor. Although the algorithm worked properly, the Knowledge Base was not designed in a way that supported the system to recognize alternative acronyms (i.e., synonyms), making it difficult to find equipment that could be referred in the reports using multiple names or abbreviations. This limitation was noticed and the EMS Knowledge Base was updated, resulting in a major reduction of the time spent by users trying to locate equipment based on an equipment description.

5   Conclusions

Usability is a critical aspect to consider in the development cycle of software applications, and for this purpose, user-centered design and usability testing must be adopted, together with a particular care regarding the context of use of the software.

After performing the SINGRAR usability study it was possible to conclude that it offers a usability level considerably higher than commercial standard software. Users have a very favorable overall perception about the system.

The areas of concern identified by the SUMI method were analyzed and recommendations were produced to improve the interface design and speed up the data input process. This intervention originated gains in interface quality, and in operators' effectiveness and efficiency. The close cooperation between the analysts and the software development team was very fruitful in terms of identifying usability improvement areas and solutions.

Acknowledgements: This work was funded by National Funds through FCT - Fundação para a Ciência e a Tecnologia under the scope of project PEst-OE/EEI/UI0066.

References

1. Simões-Marques, M.J., Pires, F.J.: SINGRAR - A fuzzy distributed expert system to support Command and Control activities in Naval environment. European Journal of Operational Research 145(2), 343–362 (2003)
2. Nielsen, J.: Usability Engineering. Academic Press (1993)
3. ISO9241, Ergonomic requirements for office work with visual display terminals (VDTs) - Part 11: Guidance on Usability. International Organization for Standardization (1998)
4. Simões-Marques, M., Nunes, I.L.: Usability of Interfaces. In: Nunes, I.L. (ed.) Ergonomics - A Systems Approach, pp. 155–170. InTech (2012), doi:10.5772/37299
5. Kirakowski, J.: The Use of Questionnaire Methods for Usability Assessment (1994), http://sumi.ucc.ie/sumipapp.html (accessed December 2012)
6. Nunes, I.L., Kirakowski, J.: Usabilidade de interfaces – versão Portuguesa do Software Usability Measurement Inventory (SUMI) [Interfaces Usability – Portuguese version of the Software Usability Measurement Inventory (SUMI)]. In: Arezes, P., Baptista, J.S., Barroso, M.P., et al. (eds.) Occupational Safety and Hygiene (SHO 2010), SPOSHO, Guimarães - Portugal, pp. 389–393 (2010)

Development and Validation of an Instrument to Measure the Usability of Educational Artifacts Created with Web 2.0 Applications

Tihomir Orehovački and Nikolina Žajdela Hrustek

University of Zagreb, Faculty of Organization and Informatics
Pavlinska 2, 42000 Varaždin, Croatia
{tihomir.orehovacki,nikolina.zajdela}@foi.hr

Abstract. The emergence of Web 2.0 applications has provided new opportunities for all participants in the educational process. Students are encouraged to create and share educational artifacts and thereby actively contribute to the development of knowledge repository. On the other hand, teachers are enabled to publish lecture resources, communicate with students, comment on shared and integrated artifacts, and evaluate completed educational e-activities. Considering that usability represents a necessary condition for an effective learning, it affects the adoption and use of created artifacts in e-learning settings. Although Web 2.0 applications are widely used for educational purposes, a consolidated methodology for the assessment of artifacts resulting from their use is still not available. The work presented in this paper is the first step towards a comprehensive framework for evaluating the usability of educational artifacts created with Web 2.0 applications. Following the standard procedure for instrument development, we conducted an empirical study during which specific pedagogical and technical attributes that capture certain usability facets of educational artifacts created with Web 2.0 applications were identified.

Keywords: Web 2.0, Usability Evaluation, Educational Artifacts, Study Results.

1 Introduction

Web 2.0 refers to a shift from the read-only paradigm of static web pages where users were passive recipients of published information towards user-centered web applications that support different kinds of interaction among users [16]. Orehovački et al. [18] distinguish eighteen types of Web 2.0 applications with educational potential that support communication and collaboration among students and enable them to create, organize, share, and integrate various artifacts. Results of two consecutive studies [17][20] pointed out that blogs, social networks, video podcasting services, and wikis are most commonly used types of Web 2.0 applications in the e-learning environment. In addition, findings of a study conducted by Bubaš et al. [4] suggest that integration of educational artifacts created with Web 2.0 applications into wiki, blog, or e-portfolio enables students to create personal learning environment and become active members of a learning community.

A. Marcus (Ed.): DUXU/HCII 2013, Part I, LNCS 8012, pp. 369–378, 2013.

Usability plays an important role in the assessment of Web 2.0 applications and artifacts created by their use. In educational environment, usability is composed of two different but rather complementary concepts. While technical usability deals with the evaluation of pragmatic aspects of Web 2.0 applications, pedagogical usability consists of the assessment of educational benefits gained while using created artifacts. The latest research related to Web 2.0 applications has mainly focused on modeling their adoption [8][25] as well as on their assessment from either the objective [1][5] or the subjective [3][14][16][22] perspective, or both [15][19]. Literature related to the usability evaluation in the educational settings offers diverse frameworks [2][26][27], guidelines [10][23], and instruments [12][28]. Nevertheless, research on evaluation of educational artifacts created with Web 2.0 applications has not attracted enough attention from the HCI community. With an aim to overcome the set forth gap, we initiated a research on the development of a framework that would enable the assessment of various usability facets in the context of educational artifacts created by means of Web 2.0 applications. As a first step towards this goal, we present results of an empirical study carried out to validate an instrument aimed for measuring technical and pedagogical usability dimensions of educational artifacts.

2   Related Work

Current research on usability evaluation in the educational context deals with the development and application of questionnaires, heuristics, and methodologies. The scope of this section is to provide concise overview of their most prominent representatives.

Questionnaires have been widely used in the usability evaluation of e-learning systems and educational artifacts. For instance, Nokelainen [12] developed self-rating Pedagogically Meaningful Learning Questionnaire (PMLQ) composed of 92 multiple-choice items meant for concurrent usability evaluation of a learning management system and digital learning materials. The PMLQ includes ten most widely applied technical usability dimensions (accessibility, learnability and memorability, user control, help, graphical layout, reliability, consistency, efficiency of use, memory load, and errors) as well as ten pedagogical usability criteria (learner control, learner activity, cooperative learning, goal orientation, applicability, added value, motivation, valuation of previous knowledge, flexibility, and feedback). By conducting two empirical studies, Zaharias and Poylymenakou [28] introduced questionnaire-based evaluation method for e-learning applications. The final version of questionnaire contained 49 items grouped into seven separate categories: self-assessment and learnability, interactivity, accessibility, navigation, visual design, learning and support, and content.

Heuristic evaluation is usability inspection technique in which expert evaluators examine the system and determine to what extent it conforms to recognized set of usability principles known as heuristics. Ssemugabi and De Villiers [23] adapted initial set of Nielsen's heuristics [11] on general interface usability (visibility of system status; match between designer and user model; learner control and freedom; consistency and adherence to standards; prevention of peripheral usability-related errors; recognition rather than recall; flexibility and efficiency of use; aesthetics and minimalism in design; recognition, diagnosis, and recovery from errors; and help and documentation) to the e-learning context. They also suggested additional heuristics related to educational websites (simplicity of site navigation, organization and structure; and relevance of site content to the learner and the learning process) and learner-centred instructional design (clarity of goals, objectives, and outcomes; effectiveness of collaborative learning; level of learner control; support for personally significant approaches to learning; cognitive error recognition, diagnosis and recovery; feedback, guidance and assessment; context meaningful to domain and learner; and learner motivation, creativity and active learning). Drawing on prior research, Mehlenbacher et al. [10] proposed a set of heuristics for the design of e-learning environments. The outlined set of heuristics was based on following dimensions of instructional situations: learner background and knowledge (accessibility; customizability and maintainability; error support and feedback; navigability and user movement; and user control, error tolerance, and flexibility), social dynamics (mutual goals and outcomes; and communication protocols), instructional content (completeness; examples and case studies; readability and quality of writing; and relationship with real-world tasks), interaction display (aesthetic appeal; consistency and layout; typographic cues and structuring; and visibility of features and self-description), instructor activities (authority and authenticity; and intimacy and presence), and environment and tools (help and support documentation; metaphors and maps; organization and information relevance; and reliability and functionality).

Existing methodologies intended for the assessment of e-learning applications represent a synthesis of different usability evaluation methods. For example, Milano-Lugano Evaluation method (MiLE) [26] is an experience-based inspection framework that combines scenario-driven and heuristic-based techniques in the evaluation of e-learning web applications. Ardito et al. [2] employed Systematic Usability Evaluation (SUE) [9] methodology that suggests coupling of inspection and user-testing activities thus enabling evaluation of four usability dimensions (presentation, hypermediality, application proactivity, and user activity) of e-learning platforms. MiLE+ [27] presents an evolution of MiLE and SUE into structured usability evaluation framework that is more convenient for novice evaluators than its predecessors.

3   Methodology

3.1   Participants

A total of 102 Information Science students enrolled in the Data Structures course took part in the study. The sample was composed of 81.37% male, and 18.63%

female students. They ranged in age from 19 to 23 years (M = 20.23, SD = .843). At the time the study was carried out, the majority (85.29%) of participants were second-year undergraduate students.

3.2   Procedure

With an objective to validate an instrument for measuring usability of educational artifacts created with Web 2.0 applications, we adopted scale development process proposed by Straub et al. [24]. As a starting point, an initial pool of 47 items was drafted based on the questionnaires, heuristics, and methodologies outlined in previous section. We then conducted a pilot study [21] to explore the appropriateness and perceived meaning of generated pool of items. Drawing on collected data, ten distinguishable usability facets of educational artifacts (completeness, usefulness, availability, learning flow, content quality, added value, adaptability, presentation quality, memorability, and learnability) were identified. In the follow-up to the aforementioned steps, initial pool of items was supplemented with statements inspired by
authors' practical experience in use and evaluation of Web 2.0 applications. Subsequently, an online questionnaire comprising 120 items was designed. Answers to the items were given on a five-point Likert scale ranging from 1 (strongly agree) to 5 (strongly disagree).

Prior to data collection, each student had to solve four different programming problems by completing following educational e-activities: (a) use mind mapping service to illustrate the decomposition of the programming problem; (b) employ diagramming application to create a flowchart that depicts the algorithmic solution; (c) develop a solution to the programming problem; (d) use screencasting service to narratively explain the main parts of the code and demonstrate how it works; (e) post the snippets of the code on the social network aimed for collaborative programming thus enabling teacher, experts in the field, and other students to provide constructive feedback; (f) integrate all the aforementioned artifacts or links to their locations on the wiki page together with a concise explanation on completed e-activities; and (g) use created artifacts when learning for the midterms. Students' reflections on usability of created and disseminated educational artifacts were obtained by administering an online questionnaire at the end of the semester.

The psychometric properties of the online questionnaire were evaluated in terms of construct validity and reliability. Construct validity determines the extent to which items capture the essence of the underlying construct. In this study, construct validity was established through convergent and discriminant validity. The former is the degree to which items of the underlying factor are in agreement while the latter refers to the extent to which items of different factors are distinct. Convergent and discriminant validity were assessed by means of a principal component analysis (PCA) with equamax rotation and Keiser normalization. They were both verified by observing correlations between items of the extracted factors. The Kaiser-Meyer-Olkin test of sampling adequacy and Bartlett's test of sphericity were examined to check that the requirements for factor extraction were met. An eigenvalue greater than 1 was used as a criterion to determine the number of factors. Only items with factor loadings above .40 and cross-loadings below .40 were retained [7]. Reliability refers to the extent to which a strong mutual association exists among items assigned to the same factor. This study employed Cronbach's Alpha reliability coefficient for measuring internal consistency of extracted factors. Considering a minimum value of .40 [6] the item-total correlation was used to improve the levels of Cronbach's Alpha coefficient.

4   Results

The Kaiser-Meyer-Olkin measure of sampling adequacy (KMO = .693) and Bartlett's test of sphericity ($\chi2 = 2275.114$, p = .000) both confirmed that the data satisfied the requirements for carrying out the principal component analysis (PCA). After the first PCA iteration, items that did not meet the loading cut-off or loaded on more than one factor were dropped. The remaining items were then subjected to another round of PCA. The process was continued until a meaningful factor structure had been reached. A total of 81 items were eliminated after 27 PCA iterations. In addition, 7 items were removed because their item-total correlation was below the .40 threshold. The final PCA iteration uncovered 11 distinct usability dimensions of educational artifacts created with Web 2.0 applications. They accounted for 82.032% of the sample variance. All 32 retained items had a factor loading greater than the .50 cut-off [7]. The communalities ranged from 0.666 to 0.900 with an average value of 0.820, indicating that yielded factors explained an acceptable amount of the variance in each of the items. Cronbach's Alpha values for all extracted factors exceeded the .70 threshold [13]. Since all reported results were above the cut-off values for exploratory research, they provided support for the validity and reliability of identified factor structure.

As a follow-up to afore discussed findings, factors that determine the usability of educational artifacts created with Web 2.0 applications were defined. The first one, *learnability* appeared to be the most important because it explained the largest portion (9.174%) of the total variance after the equamax rotation. It consisted of 4 items meant for measuring ease and pace of learning from the educational artifacts. The second factor, *productivity*, explained 8.432% of the variance. It had 3 items that addressed students' productivity in solving programming problems. The third factor, *content quality*, accounted for 8.146% of the variance. It employed 3 items for evaluating the credibility, truthfulness, and accuracy of the content included in the educational artifacts. The fourth factor, *learning performance*, represented 7.958% of the variance and consisted of 3 items measuring students' learning effectiveness and efficiency. The fifth factor, *consistency*, explained 7.914% of the total variance. It was assessed with 3 items aimed for measuring the extent to which terminology, structure, and layout of the educational artifacts are consistent. The sixth factor, *satisfaction*, explained 7.672% of the variance and used 3 items for evaluating the degree to which the educational artifacts meet students' expectations and needs. The seventh factor, *availability*, accounted for 7.349% of the variance. It applied 3 items to measure the extent to which the educational artifacts are continuously available. The eighth factor, *added value*, represented 7.226% of the total variance. It encompassed 4 items for evaluating pedagogical benefits of the educational artifacts created with certain types of Web 2.0 applications. The ninth factor, *usefulness*, accounted for 6.517% of the variance. It employed 2 items for assessing the degree to which the educational artifacts affect existing students' knowledge and are valuable for learning theoretical course concepts. The tenth factor, *adaptability*, represented 6.105% of the variance and consisted of 2 items measuring the extent to which the educational artifacts are customized to students' learning style and pace. The last factor, *learning flow*, explained 5.540% of the total variance and consisted of 2 items that addressed students' concentration when learning from the educational artifacts.

It should be noted that learnability, content quality, consistency, satisfaction, availability, and adaptability are technical usability aspects while productivity, learning performance, added value, usefulness, and learning flow are pedagogical usability facets of the educational artifacts created with Web 2.0 applications. The summary of the study findings is presented in Table 1 (see Appendix).

5   Conclusion

The work reported in this paper was motivated by the need to address the specificities of measuring the usability of educational artifacts created with Web 2.0 applications. Therefore, we initiated a study on the development and evaluation of a multi-dimensional scale. The results of the empirical validation revealed six technical and five pedagogical usability dimensions and provided evidence for the validity and reliability of the 32-item instrument.

As with most empirical studies, our work has some limitations. The employment of a homogenous group of students as study participants represents limitation to the generalizability of the results. Heterogeneous sample of students may have decidedly different attitudinal structure with respect to usability dimensions of created educational artifacts. Another limitation is the applicability of the results to educational artifacts created by means of Web 2.0 applications in general. It is likely that the type of Web 2.0 application is moderating the relationships between generated artifacts and their perceived usability.

In spite of study limitations, this paper provides valuable guidelines for assessing educational artifacts created with Web 2.0 applications. Teachers of the programming-related courses can use the developed instrument to examine and improve the usability of created educational artifacts. In addition, the validated instrument adds to extant body of knowledge by establishing a basis for further advances on evaluating educational artifacts created with Web 2.0 applications. Given that this paper presents results of an on-going research, our future work will be focused on modeling the interplay among identified usability dimensions of educational artifacts created by means of Web 2.0 applications.

References

1. Almeida, J.M., Gonçalves, M.A., Figueiredo, F., Pinto, H., Belém, F.: On the Quality of Information for Web 2.0 Services. IEEE Internet Computing 14(6), 47–55 (2010)
2. Ardito, C., Costabile, M.F., De Marsico, M., Lanzilotti, R., Levialdi, S., Roselli, T., Rossano, V.: An approach to usability evaluation of e-learning applications. Universal Access in the Information Society 4(3), 270–283 (2006)
3. Brown, A., Jay, C., Chen, A.Q., Harper, S.: The uptake of Web 2.0 technologies, and its impact on visually disabled users. Universal Access in the Information Society 11(2), 185–199 (2012)
4. Bubaš, G., Ćorić, A., Orehovački, T.: The integration of students' artifacts created with Web 2.0 tools into Moodle, blog, wiki, e-portfolio and Ning. In: Proceedings of the 34th International Convention MIPRO, pp. 1084–1089. IEEE Press, Opatija (2011)
5. Cappiello, C., Daniel, F., Koschmider, A., Matera, M., Picozzi, M.: A Quality Model for Mashups. In: Auer, S., Díaz, O., Papadopoulos, G.A. (eds.) ICWE 2011. LNCS, vol. 6757, pp. 137–151. Springer, Heidelberg (2011)
6. Churchill, G.A.: A paradigm for developing better measures of marketing constructs. Journal of Marketing Research 16(1), 64–73 (1979)
7. Hair Jr., J.F., Black, W.C., Babin, B.J., Anderson, R.E.: Multivariate Data Analysis, 7th edn. Prentice Hall, Englewood Cliffs (2009)
8. Hartshorne, R., Ajjan, H.: Examining student decisions to adopt Web 2.0 technologies: theory and empirical tests. Journal of Computing in Higher Education 21(3), 183–198 (2009)
9. Matera, M., Costabile, M.F., Garzotto, F., Paolini, P.: SUE Inspection: An Effective Method for Systematic Usability Evaluation of Hypermedia. IEEE Transactions on Systems, Man, and Cybernetics – Part A: Systems and Humans 32(1), 93–103 (2002)
10. Mehlenbacher, B., Bennett, L., Bird, T., Ivey, M., Lucas, J., Morton, J., Whitman, L.: Usable E-Learning: A Conceptual Model for Evaluation and Design. In: Proceedings of the 11th International Conference on Human-Computer Interaction, pp. 1–10. Lawrence Erlbaum Associates, Las Vegas (2005)
11. Nielsen, J.: Heuristic evaluation. In: Nielsen, J., Mack, R.L. (eds.) Usability Inspection Methods, pp. 25–62. Wiley & Sons, New York (1994)
12. Nokelainen, P.: Conceptual Definition of the Technical and Pedagogical Usability Criteria for Digital Learning Material. In: Cantoni, L., McLoughlin, C. (eds.) Proceedings of World Conference on Educational Multimedia, Hypermedia and Telecommunications 2004, pp. 4249–4254. AACE, Chesapeake (2004)
13. Nunnally, J.C.: Psychometric Theory. McGraw-Hill, New York (1978)
14. Orehovački, T.: Proposal for a Set of Quality Attributes Relevant for Web 2.0 Application Success. In: Proceedings of the 32nd International Conference on Information Technology Interfaces, pp. 319–326. IEEE Press, Cavtat (2010)
15. Orehovački, T.: Development of a Methodology for Evaluating the Quality in Use of Web 2.0 Applications. In: Campos, P., Graham, N., Jorge, J., Nunes, N., Palanque, P., Winckler, M. (eds.) INTERACT 2011, Part IV. LNCS, vol. 6949, pp. 382–385. Springer, Heidelberg (2011)
16. Orehovački, T.: Perceived Quality of Cloud Based Applications for Collaborative Writing. In: Pokorny, J., et al. (eds.) Information Systems Development – Business Systems and Services: Modeling and Development, pp. 575–586. Springer, Heidelberg (2011)

17. Orehovački, T., Bubaš, G., Konecki, M.: Web 2.0 in Education and Potential Factors of Web 2.0 Use by Students of Information Systems. In: Proceedings of the 31st International Conference on Information Technology Interfaces, pp. 443–448. IEEE Press, Cavtat (2009)

18. Orehovački, T., Bubaš, G., Kovačić, A.: Taxonomy of Web 2.0 Applications with Educational Potential. In: Cheal, C., Coughlin, J., Moore, S. (eds.) Transformation in Teaching: Social Media Strategies in Higher Education, pp. 43–72. Informing Science Press, Santa Rosa (2012)

19. Orehovački, T., Granić, A., Kermek, D.: Exploring the Quality in Use of Web 2.0 Applications: The Case of Mind Mapping Services. In: Harth, A., Koch, N. (eds.) ICWE 2011. LNCS, vol. 7059, pp. 266–277. Springer, Heidelberg (2012)

20. Orehovački, T., Konecki, M., Radošević, D.: Web 2.0 technologies in university education. In: Proceedings of the 31st MIPRO International Convention on Computers in Education, pp. 269–273. MIPRO, Opatija (2008)

21. Orehovački, T., Žajdela Hrustek, N.: Towards a Framework for Usability Evaluation of Educational Artifacts created with Web 2.0 Applications: A Pilot Study. In: Proceedings of the 36th International Convention MIPRO, pp. 691–696. IEEE Press, Opatija (2013)

22. Pang, M., Suh, W., Hong, J., Kim, J., Lee, H.: A New Web Site Quality Assessment Model for the Web 2.0 Era. In: Murugesan, S. (ed.) Handbook of Research on Web 2.0, 3.0, and X.0: Technologies, Business, and Social Applications, pp. 387–410. IGI Global, Hershey (2010)

23. Ssemugabi, S., De Villiers, R.: Usability and Learning: A Framework for Evaluation of Web-Based e-Learning Applications. In: Montgomerie, C., Seale, J. (eds.) Proceedings of World Conference on Educational Multimedia, Hypermedia and Telecommunications, pp. 906–913. AACE, Chesapeake (2007)

24. Straub, D., Boudreau, M., Gefen, D.: Validation Guidelines for IS Positivist Research. Communications of the Association for Information Systems 13(1), 380–427 (2004)

25. Suki, N.M., Ramayah, T., Ly, K.K.: Empirical investigation on factors influencing the behavioral intention to use Facebook. Universal Access in the Information Society 11(2), 223–231 (2012)

26. Triacca, L., Bolchini, D., Botturi, L., Inversini, A.: MiLE: Systematic Usability Evaluation for E-learning Web Applications. In: Cantoni, L., McLoughlin, C. (eds.) Proceedings of World Conference on Educational Multimedia, Hypermedia and Telecommunications 2004, pp. 4398–4405. AACE, Chesapeake (2004)

27. Triacca, L., Inversini, A., Bolchini, D.: Evaluating Web usability with MiLE+. In: Proceedings of the 7th IEEE International Symposium on Web Site Evolution, pp. 22–29. IEEE, Lugano (2005)

28. Zaharias, P., Poylymenakou, A.: Developing a Usability Evaluation Method for e-Learning Applications: Beyond Functional Usability. International Journal of Human-Computer Interaction 25(1), 75–98 (2009)

Appendix

Table 1. Summary of the study findings

Items	Loading	Mean	SD
Learnability (Cronbach's α = .886)			
Students learn easier from the educational artifacts than they do from the course-related books.	.831	2.10	1.067
Students learn faster from the educational artifacts than they do from the course-related books.	.806	2.10	1.058
Students learn faster from the educational artifacts than they do from the resources published on the LMS*.	.787	2.85	.938
Students learn easier from the educational artifacts than they do from the resources published on the LMS*.	.765	2.97	.959
Productivity (Cronbach's α = .926)			
The educational artifacts increase students' effectiveness in solving the programming problems.	.898	2.29	.918
The educational artifacts increase students' productivity in solving the programming problems.	.880	2.35	.971
The educational artifacts increase students' efficiency in solving the programming problems.	.843	2.24	.869
Content Quality (Cronbach's α = .905)			
The content of the educational artifacts is trustworthy.	.917	1.82	.604
The content of the educational artifacts is true.	.909	1.76	.632
The content of the educational artifacts is accurate.	.839	1.83	.646
Learning Performance (Cronbach's α = .877)			
The educational artifacts enhance students' learning effectiveness.	.884	2.09	.785
The educational artifacts enhance students' learning efficiency.	.862	2.09	.834
The educational artifacts enhance students' learning productivity.	.832	2.17	.759
Consistency (Cronbach's α = .849)			
The terminology used in the educational artifacts is consistent.	.856	2.17	.661
The educational artifacts have consistent structure.	.854	2.11	.659
The educational artifacts have consistent layout.	.829	2.13	.792

* Learning Management System

Table 1. (*Continued.*)

Items	Loading	Mean	SD
Satisfaction (Cronbach's α = .884)			
The quality of the educational artifacts is satisfactory.	.836	2.11	.782
The content of the educational artifacts meets students' expectations.	.833	2.24	.811
The manner in which the educational artifacts present the course topics meets students' needs.	.731	2.23	.819
Availability (Cronbach's α = .846)			
Students can access the educational artifacts whenever they want to do so.	.883	1.52	.521
The educational artifacts are available when students need them.	.859	1.62	.527
The educational artifacts are continuously available.	.842	1.61	.566
Added Value (Cronbach's α = .846)			
Shared code snippets help students to develop their own solution to the programming problem.	.775	2.02	1.062
Mind map helps students to understand the relationship between the programming problem and its solution.	.709	2.15	.999
Screencast helps students to understand the relationship between theoretical and practical aspects of the course.	.687	2.34	1.039
Flowchart helps students to design the logical structure of the solution to the programming problem.	.681	2.04	.964
Usefulness (Cronbach's α = .868)			
The educational artifacts are advantageous for learning the data structures concepts.	.876	1.97	.777
The educational artifacts alter existing students' knowledge.	.824	1.91	.810
Adaptability (Cronbach's α = .815)			
The educational artifacts are adapted to the students' learning pace.	.821	2.61	.881
The educational artifacts are adapted to the students' learning style.	.817	2.86	.890
Learning Flow (Cronbach's α = .750)			
When learning from the educational artifacts, students are not aware of any noise.	.881	3.43	.939
When learning from the educational artifacts, students do not realize the time elapsed.	.869	3.36	1.124

Ergonomic Evaluation of Usability with Users – Application of the Technique of Cooperative Evaluation

Marcelo Penha[1], Walter Correia[2], Marcelo Soares[2],
Fábio Campos[2], and Marina Barros[2]

[1] Unibratec – Recife-PE / Brazil
marcelopenha.unibratec@gmail.com
[2] Post-Graduate Program in Design / Federal University of Pernambuco
Centre for Arts and Communication - Cidade Universitária – Recife-PE / Brazil
{ergonomia,marinalnbarros}@terra.com.br, marcelo2@nlink.com.br,
fc2005@gmail.com

Abstract. This paper presents the application of a cooperative evaluation, technical evaluation performed ergonomic usability with users in the Learning Management Systens (LMS) used at the Instituto Federal de Pernambuco (IFPE). The data collected in the assessments were analyzed with users from Nielsen usability heuristics. The results showed that the environment has evaluated a large number of usability problems.

Keywords: Cooperative evaluation, usability, Learning Management Systems.

1 Introduction

The e-learning is characterized as an educational modality in which mediation didactic and pedagogical processes of teaching and learning occurs with the use of media and information technologies and communication with students and teachers developing educational activities in different places or times (MEC, decree No. 5.622/05).

According to Moran [1], in the teaching / learning between teachers and students of e-learning used mainly telematic technologies, such as the Internet.

To mediate the interaction between those involved in the process of e-learning, Araujo Junior [2] states that may be necessary to use a Learning Management Systens (LMS). A LMS for its features and tools available, is a tool of interaction in the learning process, based on the features available on the Internet.

Interaction tools must be very efficient, allowing your users to be highly productive in their work [3]. According to Cybis [4], unsuccessful interactions not only annoy users and cause for frustration and loss of self esteem.

In order to obtain a good interaction, it is necessary that the tool has good usability, which is defined by ISO 9241 as "the ability of a product to be used by specified users to achieve specified goals with effectiveness, efficiency and satisfaction in a specified context of use ".

A. Marcus (Ed.): DUXU/HCII 2013, Part I, LNCS 8012, pp. 379–388, 2013.
© Springer-Verlag Berlin Heidelberg 2013

Preece [3] list many technical usability evaluation which can be used in different ways and in different patterns. Among these techniques, the cooperative evaluation.

2   Theoretical Framework

This topic explains, from literature, the theoretical foundation of the issues relevant to meet the objective of the research, a cooperative evaluation of the virtual environment IFPE.

2.1   Learning Management Systems

With the support of the Internet and communication technologies that enabled more effectively, especially from the 90s, the distance has been improving as a teaching modality capable of meeting the difficulties of geographic distance and time between students and teachers.

According to Martin-Brabero [5], with the technological resources we have to learn a new method and this task is made much more wealth by the computer.

A LMS can be defined in the user's perspective, as an environment that simulates face learning with the use of information technology [2]. Equivalently to-face classrooms, Learning Management Systems constitute themselves as a place to carry out educational activities. In virtual environments, we can publish, store and distribute educational materials, but also realize the communication between students and support staff. All these processes must be mediated by the interaction between people, content and tools involved.

The term Learning Management Systems refers to the concept of space resulting from the learning opportunities available through information technologies, characterized by Valentini [6], as a space where cognitive-social interactions occur, enabled by the GUI.

Franco [7] points out four strategies were followed in the development of the first virtual environments in the mid-90s:

- Incorporating elements already available on the web, such as electronic mail and discussion groups;
- Add elements to specific activities of computer, managing files and backups;
- Create specific elements of the educational activity, such as modules for content and assessment;
- Add elements of academic administration of courses, students, evaluations and reports.

Through these strategies were created the first LMS seeking a specific use in learning activities.

Currently available are various Learning Management Systens such as Moodle, Teleduc, AulaNet, among others, developed both by educational institutions and by public and private companies, each with its particular characteristics, with each institution to conduct a contextual analysis identify the most important variables that may constrain or promote particular learning process.

Communication Tools. According to Cabral [8], the process of interaction between students and teachers is accomplished through communication tools. There are two groups of these tools:

- Synchronous tools: are those that enable communication between those involved in real time, with a "resemblance to the classroom, because they constitute a more spontaneous, which leads us to use language more relaxed and closer to the student" [8]. Examples include chat rooms, teleconferencing, instant messengers. The asynchronous tools have a more immediate, leading those involved to equity reflected or less superficial.
- Asynchronous tools: this group, the message sent by a participant is received and answered later by others, ie, those involved need not be connected at the same time so there is interaction. Examples are the bulletin board, discussion forums, e-mail. The asynchronous tools promote a more critical and reflective of the participants, since there is "more time" to think what will be placed at each entry. One purpose of these tools is the socialization, stated by Cabral and Cavalcanti [8].

2.2   Usability

Usability is defined by ISO 9241 as "the ability of an artifact to be used by specified users to achieve specified goals with effectiveness, efficiency and satisfaction in a specified context of use". The effectiveness with which the user will achieve their goals means he is able to perform the task successfully. The (lower) time this task is performed with regard to efficiency. The satisfaction, in turn, defines how the system is acceptable to the user [4]. Consisting of objective aspects, such as productivity in the interaction, and subjective, such as user satisfaction in their experience with the artifact, the definition of ISO proves to be quite flexible.

Usability can also be defined as a synonym for ease of use of something [9]. Greater ease in learning and memory, faster task completion, lower error rate and higher user satisfaction with the system are a reflection of a greater usability of an interface.

Having easy to learn, allowing efficient and have few errors are aspects that return the user a perception of good usability [9].

Usability Evaluation of Interfaces. According to Preece [3], the evaluation of an artifact helps to ensure that it will satisfy user needs. Cybis [4] states that the evaluation techniques and ergonomics are based on diagnostic checks and inspections of interfaces looking for problems of interaction between the user and the system.

For carrying out the evaluation of usability of the interface of a system, a technique that can be used is cooperative evaluation [3].

This technique, based on notes, audio, video and interaction logs, search for information related to how the user behaves in its natural environment and identification of errors during the use of the interface routes. Penha [10] divides this technique in four steps: Recruitment, where he must recruit one or more users similar to user type system, Task List, where the appraiser must specify the tasks to be performed by users; Conduct of sessions, where the assessor will observe and take notes, and briefing, where the assessor will talk to users after the completion of tasks, looking for more information.

Usability Heuristics. Several researchers in usability and human-computer interaction, in recent decades, have established lists of principles for design of interfaces and software systems for web environment, also called ergonomic criteria, from experiments and scientific methods. These criteria are used in the classification of the problems encountered in assessing the usability of interfaces.

Penha [10] puts ten fundamental principles that must be met by an interface so that it offers good usability:

> H1-Visibility of system status
> H2-Compatibility between the system and the real world
> H3-Freedom and control to the user
> H4 Consistency and standards
> H5-Support for the user recognize, diagnose and recover from errors
> H6-Error prevention
> H7-Recognize instead remind
> H8-Flexibility and efficiency of use
> H9-Design aesthetic and minimalist
> H10-Help and documentation

Nielsen's heuristics are widely used in research related to the process of man-machine interaction, and thus the usability. According to Santa Rosa [11], in an paper on research on mapping the design of interaction in e-learning in the international arena, it was found that Nielsen is a common references used in the research, part of 60% of cases.

3   Object of Research

The IFPE offers courses in the distance on the technical level, higher and postgraduate. The evaluations performed on this cooperative research were carried out using the environment of the graduate in Environmental Management. The virtual environment has the IFPE MOODLE platform software.

In this environment, students have the following features at your disposal:

- Contact: e-mail address to support the environment.
- News: Local users to post announcements.
- Messages: access tool for communication among the participants of the environment that are part of the student's contact list.
- My Courses: A list of the disciplines in which the student is enrolled, allowing access to specific content thereof.
- Users Online: Access the list and profile of the course participants connected and option for sending messages.
- Administration: Access to the table notes, reports and student profile.
- Participants: List of participants accessed the course.
- Activities: Access to specific types of activities undertaken in the discipline (chats, forums, surveys, questionnaires, resources and tasks).
- Calendar: Indications for major events such as exams and due jobs dates.

All options described above are common to all students and follow a standard content, except for the agenda of the course that will have its content varies according to discipline. For students enrolled in the same discipline, the agenda of the course will present the same content.

4   Cooperative Environmental Assessment DEAD / IFPE-PE

The evaluation was performed cooperative with eight users. Instructions for completion of the evaluation, and a list of tasks were previously transmitted to users. Cybis [4] states that this technique is primarily useful for obtaining qualitative data.

The tasks to be performed by users should be as follows:

1. Access the virtual environment IFPE: http://dead.ifpe.edu.br/moodle/
2. Log into the environment from the user specified;
3. Edit your profile (change image, insert description, change password);
4. Access the Course "Sistemas de Informações Geográficas ";
5. Access the Course Calendar and find out the commitments of the month of May;
6. Access the Material "Aulas 1 e 2";
7. Perform the deployment of Task "Envio de arquivo 6";
8. Enter a post on the sixth week, the topic Classroom attendance;
9. Enter a message in the Chat online tutoring, one week;
10. Send a Message to Tutor Carlos Viana;
11. Visit the Notes;
12. Log off.

Before the evaluation the users were informed that the evaluation focus would be directed to the interface [10].

With respect to age, users concentrated in the range 24-35 years. According to Santa Rosa [11], there is no set age for students in distance courses.

The degree of training of participants was divided equally into high school and college. On the issue of computer experience, the majority uses the computer daily and surfing the internet for over three years.

Finally, regarding the past use of MOODLE, only two users had used the environment of other institutions, but sporadically. Most users of the research participants (75%) used the environment for the first time conducting the evaluation.

The observations made by users and difficulties encountered by them in carrying out tasks stipulated in the report were recorded by the researcher. According to Preece [3], observations can be made in a controlled environment (laboratory) or natural (field), which can occur anytime, anywhere. This research was conducted in the natural environment of each user.

Completed the evaluation, users were free to express their opinions about the usability and user interface environment.

The reports were subsequently analyzed for patterns or significant events [3], is also highlighted unexpected behavior, subjective comments from users about the interface and the heuristics of Nielsen violated in each task.

4.1   Analysis of Cooperative Assessments

The average time spent by users to perform the proposed tasks was 25 minutes. The two users who said they have used MOODLE previously carried out the assessment in times similar to other users.

After analyzing the problems identified from the assessments carried out by cooperative users, it was observed that only heuristic H10 was not violated. Some tasks presented problems that fall in more than a heuristic.

- Task: Login to the environment

Most users could accomplish the task quickly, but it was necessary to roll the home in search of the field access. One of the users confused the banner help with the field access and clicked on it several times until I realized I was on a banner.

In contrast, several participants were in doubt whether they were actually logged as none found any visual clue indicating the success of the operation. Only those that rolled all found the confirmation page, located at the bottom of the layout.

User reviews: "Why is log into this position?"

"Normally the log is over."

"I think that I have accessed the system. We did not see was logged. "

"He entered? Where the user name?"

Heuristics violated: H1 / H4 / H7 / H9

- Task: Edit profile

One participant was unable to perform the task. All others had difficulty in accomplishing this task. In general, participants sailed several times by the home environment for a link to edit profile without success. Most users could access the profile editing page by chance, by clicking on the name of the logged in user. None of them could change the profile picture. One of the participants in the search for some way to make the change of image, which had lost the description entered. One user complained that it did not understand the meaning of the options available on the "Edit Profile" to be very technical.

User reviews: "My God, how to change that picture?"

"I'm not able to find."

Heuristics violated: H3 / H5 / H8 / H9

- Task: Access course

From the homepage of the environment, all participants were able to perform the task without difficulty. However, none of them used the option group "My Courses". All rolled down the page to find the course content.

To return to the course after accessing other pages, most used the browser's back button. One participant clicked on the course code available in the path of the page accessed, but it certainly was right.

User reviews: "I think it's here." (Trying to return to the course)

Heuristics violated: H4 / H8 / H9

- Task: Access Calendar

Only two users quickly found the feature "Calendar", located on the right side of the screen. Most searched initially in the left hand menu interface. To get to the month requested the task, all using the navigation arrows, which is month to month.

User reviews: "You can not enter the month you want?"

"It takes time to come."

Heuristics violated: H3 / H5

- Task: Access material

Some users sought for materials primarily a link from the menu on the left corner of the layout. So many of these, like others, have managed to successfully access the material, but some were in doubt whether they had successfully done because the material is slow to load was not given any information about the charging status.

Heuristics violated: H1 / H8

- Task: Submit Job

All participants were able to access the page to send the task quickly through the "Tasks" menu located on the left of the Layout. Some users were in doubt whether the file was actually being sent because the system does not display the progress of the process. The confirmation is provided only after completion of the transmission.

Heuristics violated: H1

- Task: Enter a message in the forum (week 6)

Most users accessed the page quickly through the forums link "Forum", located on the left side menu of the Layout. When accessing the forum indicated, however, some participants made the wrong choice, because the name of the forums does not match the week indicated. The forum 6 is on the fifth week (Figure 1).

Heuristics violated: H7

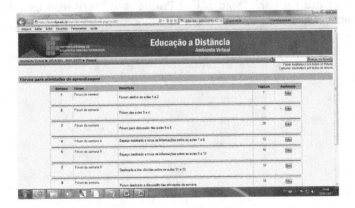

Fig. 1. Screen Forums

- Task: Enter a message in chat

In general, participants accessed the chat through the "Chat" located at the left side menu of the Layout and performed the task successfully. But for this it was necessary to return to the homepage of the environment. One user questioned the lack of a link that allows direct access of the forum page of the task prior to the chat page.

User reviews: "It has the menu on this screen?"
Heuristics violated: H8

- Task: Send a message

Most users first tried the "Messages" menu on the left side of the layout. After several visual search, the block "Messages" was located. Some tried to locate the tutor Carlos Viana via the link "Participants", but were unsuccessful because this function only lists the users in the course that is currently active in the research. Those who could, at first thought they had made a mistake, for it displayed an error message (Figure 2).

User reviews: "It was hard. The group is isolated."
"He mistake?"
Heuristics violated: H1 / H2 / H5 / H6

- Task: Access notes

All participants performed the task successfully and without difficulty.

- Task: Logging off

Most users tend to search for the "Exit" button at the top of the layout. Only after rolling the page were a few times, the job was located. Some users complained about the font size of button.

User reviews: "It's hard to find out because he is down there."
Heuristics violated: H4 / H9

The figure 3 shows the number of heuristics violated in each of the tasks performed by users. Note that the tasks "Sign", "Edit Profile" and "Send message" showed the largest number of heuristics violated, each with four.

Fig. 2. Error Message Screen

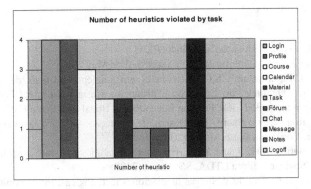

Fig. 3. Number of heuristics violated by task

With respect to frequency, the heuristics H1, H8 and H9 are those with the highest number of occurrences, each in four different tasks, as shown in figure 4.

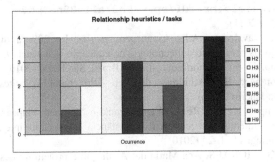

Fig. 4. Relationship heuristics / tasks

5   Conclusions

The chosen technique for usability evaluation was effective in pointing out many usability problems. It also proved possible, considering that the number of members required to obtain good results is not high.

The evaluation was a cooperative and active participation of users, who at times showed to be very excited to be able to weave their views and were happy to contribute to research.

The results obtained from the tests applied in the case study showed that the virtual environment has enjoyed usability deficiencies, creating an interplay of low quality and, at times, unpleasant for the students. Some of the tasks posed ended up not being made by some participants.

Overall, the results pointed to the lack of basic principles of design and usability, content as too long and sometimes unnecessary, lack of standard layout, inappropriate language and messages in inconsistent placement of some features.

References

1. Moran, J.M.: O que é educação à distância (2011), http://www.eca.usp.br/prof/ (accessed on May 2011)
2. Araujo Jr., C.F., Marquesi, S.C.: Atividades em ambientes virtuais de aprendizagem: parâmetros de qualidade. In: Educação a distância: o estado da arte / Fedric M. Litto, Marcos Formiga, pp. 358–368. Pearson Education do Brasil, São Paulo (2009)
3. Preece, J., Rogers, Y., Sharp, H.: Design de interação – Além da interação homem-computador. Bookman, Porto Alegre (2005)
4. Cybis, W., Betiol, A.H., Faust, R.: Ergonomia e Usabilidade, conhecimentos, métodos e aplicações. Novatec Editora LTDA, São Paulo (2007)
5. Martin-Barbero, J.: Cultura y Nuevas mediaciones tecnológicas. In: Martinbarbero, Jesús. América-latina: otras visiones de La cultura, CAB, Bogotá (2005)
6. Valentini, C.B.: SOARES, Eliane Maria do Sacramento. Aprendizagem em ambientes virtuais: compartilhando ideias e construindo cenários. Educs, Caxias do Sul (2005)
7. Franco, M.A., Cordeiro, L.M., Fonseca del Castillo, R.A.: O ambiente virtual de aprendizagem e sua incorporação na UNICAMP (2003), http://www.scielo.br/pdf/ep/v29n2/a11v29n2.pdf (accessed on May 2011)
8. Cabral, A.L.T., Cavalcante, A.F.: Linguagem escrita. In: 20% a distância: e agora: orientações práticas para o uso de tecnologia de educação a distância / Alda Carlini, Rita Maria Tarcia, pp. 53–80. Pearson Education do Brasil, São Paulo (2010)
9. Nielsen, J., Loranger, H.: Usabilidade na Web - Projetando Websites com Qualidade. Campus, Rio de Janeiro (2006)
10. Penha, M., Campos, F.: CORREIA, Walter Franklin Marques. Mapeamento da pesquisa sobre design de interação na educação a distância no cenário internacional. Revista Científica Tecnologus 5, 1–24 (2010)
11. Santa Rosa, J.G.: MORAES, Ana Maria de: Avaliação e projeto no design de interfaces. 2AB, Rio de Janeiro (2008)

Using Eye-Tracking to Test and Improve Website Design

Anna Prisacari and Thomas Holme

Human-Computer Interaction Program, Iowa State University, Ames, IA 50011, USA
{annacari,taholme}@iastate.edu

Abstract. In developing a website, it is essential to test its design. For example, users may look at a certain image or text paragraph without paying attention to what designers may consider being the most essential information or the users may erroneously interpret its design and get confused. If users don't interact with the website as designers anticipate, the design of website becomes dubious. In our eye-tracking study we invited 11 undergraduate students from an introductory chemistry course to test the usability of newly developed website on climate change. The results show that animated features draw more attention regardless of strength of relationship to content. Based on quantitative and qualitative data, we present possible recommendations how to improve the design of the website and how to enhance user's overall experience.

Keywords: eye-tracking, usability, web site design.

1 Introduction

One of the more challenging characteristics associated with the development of educational web sites is the wide array of experience and proclivity of those who carry out the work. Particularly for college-level target audiences, the people who envision and oversee development are often more likely to be content experts than they are design experts. Thus, educational materials development for the web has a wide range of probable effects on target audiences, and estimating the actual impact of these materials provides an important avenue for usability. Academic development efforts seldom include funding for usability testing while sites are being built, so empirical studies that investigate active sites developed in academic settings are an important mechanism for determining how to promote good design characteristics in web site development.

While this premise could be applied within any academic discipline, an overall interest in educational efforts within Science, Technology, Engineering and Mathematics (STEM) suggests that efforts to consider usability of educational materials for the web in these areas are particularly important. An emerging emphasis on interdisciplinary efforts within STEM education, in particular, provides additional motivation to consider web sites related to topics such as Climate Change, which are not only important in a global policy sense, but challenging because of the fundamental interdisciplinary nature of the topic. The study reported here considers the usability of an academically produced site about the chemistry aspects of climate change as an example of the type of empirical data that can be considered within this topic from the perspective of human-computer interactions.

A. Marcus (Ed.): DUXU/HCII 2013, Part I, LNCS 8012, pp. 389–398, 2013.

2   Literature on Usability and Eye-Tracking

Studies in human-computer interaction that probe usability of web site and factors of design that affect usability have become increasingly common. These studies have become more important in the academic environment as the number of students in higher education with reasonable information technology (IT) access continues to grow [1]. One key area of concern for academic uses of IT and internet information resources lies in how well students can locate needed information, a type of task that is strongly associated with the concept of information architecture [2,3]. Within this area, the concept of the depth of information processing undertaken, in particular, plays a prominent role in the manner in which students in academic environments use web sites [4]. Specific studies of the role of navigation elements compliment the concept of depth of information and information architecture conceptualizations of the challenge of presenting high information content density in web environments [5]. More recently, the interplay between practical usability and aesthetic design concepts have been noted as well [6,7], studies that may inform some aspects of the presentation of visually oriented information content in the sciences, for example.

Sites designed for students to engage in STEM materials are often infused with visual elements that scientific experts use to organize and summarize large amounts of information. Studies that focus on this type of visual representation are increasingly considering the challenges students face in digesting the information in these environments [8,9], particularly when the learning is self-directed or only lightly scaffolded, such as is common when students visit web sites. Indeed, this level of interest is taken even further in studies directed towards understanding behavior in virtual learning environments [10], but for the purpose of the work reported here, emphasis will remain on more traditional web-delivered information.

Considering the use of eye-tracking studies to look at web site usability, there are several previously reported studies of note. First, it's important to note that some methods related to eye-tracking can be powerful, and powerfully misleading if incorrectly applied. Thus, Bojko argues [11] that heatmaps of behaviors such as fixation counts of subjects looking at the site, must be carefully defined and methodologies chosen wisely to meet the desired level of data reliability and utility. Similarly, Siirtola and Räihä [12], propose data analysis methods for eye-tracking data that reduces the voluminous data produced by such studies into categories of (1) fixation heatmaps, (2) time spent in areas-of-interest (AOIs) and (3) transitions between AOIs. Results from previous eye-tracking usability studies have emphasized the interaction of users with navigation capabilities [13]; the visual appeal and structure of design elements of the site [14]; and the role of simultaneous think-aloud protocols as a research methodology [15]. All of these studies find that the data provided from eye-tracking can provide important insight into how usability is influenced by various elements commonly found in web environments.

It is also important to recognize that within an academic environment, the means by which students are encouraged to obtain information from the web can play a role in how they interact with the resources there. Considerable interest has accrued to the question of student motivation in on-line courses where retention rates are often low [16, 17]. Recently, attempts to formalize student behaviors in terms of cognitive theory have suggested factors that may influence student persistence [18]. Importantly, the nature of the motivational drivers, internal or external, appear to play a key role in how well students learn in on-line environments [19]. Thus, there have been a variety of studies that provide information about how web site usability can be considered. In the work reported here a combination of usability and eye-tracking methodologies are applied to a web site on chemistry concepts related to climate change.

3   Methodology

The web-site studied in this work was developed by a collaboration of scientists associated with several scientific societies. The site URL is www.explainingclimate change.ca and it was developed by faculty and students associated with the King's Center for Visualization in Science at The King's University College in Edmonton, Alberta. Ultimately, the science content is broken into nine lessons, most of which include interactive elements in addition to didactic textual material. There is an initial page on the site that provides overall introductory information, followed by navigation page where the nine lessons are enumerated and can be accessed by clicking on the appropriate icon/link. While the level of information contained in each lesson is broad, this navigation page also has mouse-over information indicating more specifics about the contents within each lesson.

The aim of this laboratory experiment was to study (1) the ease of understanding the layout of the website including its functions and content; (2) the simplicity of use of the website; and (3) the speed and accuracy of locating needed information. Eye-tracking measures were predicted to reveal that most or all students would exhibit similar patterns of interaction. In particular, it was expected that students would take more time to understand the operation of interactive tools on the site, such as the Earth's Atmosphere learning tool.

3.1   Participants

Eleven students who participated in this study were recruited from a chemistry course designed for non-science majors at a large Midwestern University. The course includes formal study of key chemical concepts in climate change, such as the greenhouse effect of atmospheric gases. Thus, the participants in this study were aware of fundamental science, but did not have a particular penchant for studying scientific topics. Subjects received extra credit for their class and provided informed consent. Due to poor eye calibration, one participant was excluded, thus resulting in n=10 participants (5 males and 5 females; 4 freshmen, 3 sophomores, 1 junior, and 2 seniors; age mean age = 20.4.)

3.2   Tools and Materials

During the study, both the researcher and the participant were present in the same room. The researcher's computer was separated by a divider from the participant's computer and monitored the participant's eye-movement and task progress, allowing researcher to take notes and provide assistance when needed. Eye movements were recorded with a VT2 Eye-tracker [20]. The hardware for this system was located below the participant's computer screen and unobtrusively captured the respondent's eye movements. The accuracy of eye fixation was +/-0.5 degree (0.5 degree of visual angle amounts to approximately 0.5 cm on the screen at a 50 cm distance). This level of accuracy of recordings was satisfactory for the inferences about usability patterns made here. Eye-tracking data were recorded with iMotions software [21].

Another tool that was incorporated in the design of this project was UserZoom [22] - an online usability testing tool that allowed several advantages including; (1) the randomization of questions; (2) posting of instructions for participants to reference at the bottom of the screen; (3) time management for each task – timing out students when a pre-set limit was reached; and; (4) participant navigation through the tasks. Figure 1 illustrates how UserZoom was used and intergraded in our design.

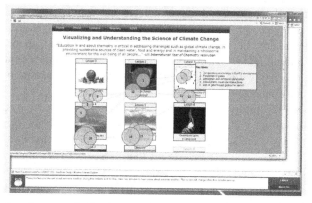

Fig. 1. A gaze plot of one user's fixations. This participant looked at the image and lesson title areas. The bottom window depicts how instructions were presented during the task. Participants were provided an opportunity to move to the next task by clicking on "I did it" button signaling task completion or "Move On" button signaling task fatigue.

By itself, eye-tracking is only able to determine where users look. A pure count of fixations cannot tell researcher whether users are productive, happy, or confused when they look at some elements of the website and ignore others. Thus, to augment the data from eye-tracking, both quantitative studies (such as measuring time spent on each task or the average time per task for a participant) and qualitative studies via personal interviews, were used to collect additional insights.

3.3   System Usability Scale

There are numerous instruments available to assess the usability of a website. One of the most robust and low-cost tools in evaluating the interface types is the System Usability Scale (SUS). Multiple studies confirm that the SUS is highly reliable ($\alpha = 0.91$) and can be applied in evaluating the interfaces of a variety of products and services including websites [23]. It consists of ten equally balanced questions that ask participant to indicate the degree of agreement or disagreement with the statement on a 5-point scale ranging from *Strongly Disagree* to *Strongly Agree*. SUS is generally used shortly after the subject has interacted with the product, but before discussing it with the researcher. Instructions given to participants emphasize that they complete all items and mark the first answer that stands out rather than think about questions for a long time.

SUS score ranges between 0 and 100, 90 and above indicating that a product is exceptional, the score ranging in the 80s – good, and in 70s - acceptable [24, 25]. Negatively worded statements are reversed scored in obtaining the overall SUS score reported here. Initially responses are recorded as ranging from 1 to 5, but for positively worded items, a value of 1 is subtracted from the response value so they range from 0 to 4. For negatively worded items the user response value is subtracted from 5. Finally, all responses are summed and that value is multiplied by 2.5 to achieve the 100 point scale [24].

3.4   Task Procedures

All participants performed five tasks: (1) explore the website; (2) learn more about extreme weather; (3) learn when chlorofluorcarbons were invented; (4) locate and use Earth's Atmosphere learning tool; and (5) explore the definition of ocean acidification. The time allowed for the completion of any task was intentionally quite limited, varying from 2 to 5 minutes depending on level of interaction as judged by results from pilot study efforts using chemistry graduate students who were expected to be more familiar with the basic science associated with the site. Before proceeding with the task, participants were given the instructions (what the participant needed to do and how much time was allocated to the task.) Only after clicking the "Start" button, was the participant presented with the main menu page of the site (which occurs after an introductory page) and could start working on the task. Throughout the task, the instructions were available at the bottom of the page so participant could revisit them, if needed (Fig.1).

When subjects arrived, they were first introduced to the study and asked to sign consent forms. Then the experimenter gave a quick overview of eye-tracking system and asked participants to complete a short eye-calibration exercise followed by a brief demographics survey. After the survey, participants were instructed to complete five tasks. For each participant the first task was exploratory so that the participant would be able to become more familiar with the basic ideas of the website within two minutes. Participants were then introduced to four tasks that were presented in random order. After the experiment participants were asked to complete online System Usability Scale survey and to participate in a brief interview with the researcher. The interviews were audiotaped and included the video of desktop activity. All sessions were conducted on an individual basis and lasted between 50 and 60 minutes.

4   Results

4.1   Site Navigation and Eye-Tracking

A number of usability variables were measured including; the ease with which the site layout was understood by participants; the perceived simplicity of the site; the accuracy with which participants completed the tasks; and the speed of task completion. (Speed of task completion is derived from three quantitative measures that are often employed in usability work: average task time for both success and non-success groups, success score, and the number of clicks).

Table 1. Summary of success/non-success. Exploratory task #1 is not included. Number in each column represents number of participants. Number in braces indicates the mean time spent on the task. Numbers in brackets indicate information on clicks [min-max; mean].

Task	Participant indicated actions			Predetermined metric	
	Task success	Task non-success	Abandoned	Task success	Task non-success
2	3 {1:31} [2-11; 6]	7 {2:00} [9]	0	5	5
3	1 {0:59} [2-2; 2]	9 {2:00} [16]	0	5	5
4	3 {2:34} [0-10; 5]	6 {5:00} [18]	1 {0:38} [2]	4	5
5	1 {2:39} [14-14; 14]	9 {3:00} [12]	0	0	10

Table 1 shows a summary of the success or non-success on the final four tasks by all participants. (Task 1 is not included as it was strictly to explore the site, and all participants were able to do so.) Participants indicated success by clicking on a button "I did it". As depicted, the success indicated by participants did not match the actual results, as determined when the task was constructed. For example, while one participant has indicated that he was successful on Task 3 (when were CFCs invented) completion, a total of 5 participants were successful at this task, in that they arrived at the page where the information was available. This data suggests that while participants are able to navigate the site reasonably well, they are not always certain they have found the correct information in the short time frames allowed in this study. Note that the site has a relatively large amount of textual information, so when students arrive at the correct location, they still need to read material, so they may not have had time to click the "completed" button despite arriving at the page with the needed information. Overall, the non-success rate is still somewhat high (50% for 3 tasks and 100% for 1 task), so the usability for finding specific information about content related to the chemistry of climate change appears to be subject to issues of the grain size of the information content in the navigation aides relative to the tasks assigned in this study.

Another way to assess student navigation of the web site is to analyze the pages visited or "clicked through". For example, in task 2 students were asked to learn more about extreme weather as an impact of climate change using this website and its links and given two minutes. Participants exhibited little difficulty locating the correct initial lesson page (in this case Lesson 5), and interviews confirm that the mouse over information on the lessons navigation page assist significantly in this component of the task completion. The click through data for this task revealed that on average participants spent 1:31 minutes on the task (st. dev. 0:13 min), minimum time = 1:15 minutes. Three students indicated successful completion by moving to the next task. However, two students from non-success group have also completed this task successfully, in that they arrived at the specific page (within lesson 5) that describes the issue of extreme weather. Figure 2 illustrates the diagram of click path for Task 2. It demonstrates that 70% of participants visited the correct initial page - Lesson 5. Nonetheless only 30% of participants who visited Lesson 5 reported success (highlighted in green color) before time ran out. 30% of all participants visited, however, incorrect pages (highlighted in yellow) and showed relatively limited amount of exploration.

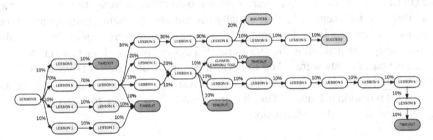

Fig. 2. Diagram of path measured in clicks for Task 2. Blocks highlighted in red show timeout, green blocks indicate success rate, and yellow blocks indicate incorrect route.

For the navigation oriented tasks described thus far, eye-tracking information tends to corroborate that students are using the intended navigation features of the site. The place where eye-tracking reveals important additional information is Task 4. In this task, students were asked to interact with an interactive feature on the site. This applet allows the participants to move an object that looks like a weather balloon up and down to explore features of the atmosphere, such as average temperature as a function of altitude. Directions for the use of the tool are presented on an introductory page and were not present on the page where the tool actually resided. In addition, designers of the tool used animations of meteors falling in the upper parts of the atmosphere or a plane flying through the sky. These animations occur at random times and as might be expected, eye-tracking shows that the movement strongly attracts student attention when they are using the tool. As a result, in general students' performance on Task 4 was affected by animated distracters. Figure 3 shows the eye gazing for participants 6 and 10.

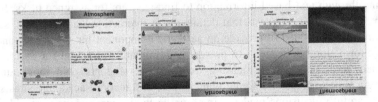

Fig. 3. A closer look at the images on the Task 4 page. Moving objects such as flying plane and falling meteors distracted participants from completing the task.

4.2   Participant Impressions of Usability

The key quantitative tool used to measure overall impressions of the site was the SUS. The calculated average SUS score over the 10 participants was 77.75 which indicates that users find the usability acceptable, but that there are ways that usability could be improved.

To hone in on ways to consider improving usability, interviews provide key quantitative data about users' subjective perspective of the overall site. During the interview, participants were asked to indicate what changes in design they would suggest. The top recommendation that 8 out of 10 students mentioned was to re-design the "green boxes" referring to the mouse-over boxes on the lessons navigation page (Fig.1). These mouse-overs were informational only, so navigation was in some sense directed by them, but not actually facilitated by them. Participants have suggested adding the links to content within the mouse-overs would dramatically improve navigation and allow the user to reach a desired page with just one click.

Because participants were asked to perform a variety of search activities, 7 out 10 suggested during the interview that including a search tool to the toolbar would be an important navigational feature. This feature would allow a user to faster locate the page that contains needed information.

5   Conclusions

This study looked at an academic web site with a relatively high level of information, including extensive text and interactive tools for understanding the chemistry associated with climate change, an arguably complex scientific topic. The tasks utilized in the study were devised to mimic activities that one might anticipate a teacher would ask a student to do given access to this site, or that a student who finds this site while doing self-directed research, might be trying to find. The tasks were intentionally designed to be short in time duration because there are many sites with information on climate change, and typical user behavior would be to move to a different site if information is difficulty to find or seems to take the user too long. The usability data tend to suggest that students are able to navigate easily through the website and find needed content relatively quickly. Thus, the main navigational features of the site, in particular the division of information into nine "lessons" appears to mesh with student-user experience for finding information. Interactive tools, not surprisingly, result in more detailed user interaction than tasks that involve navigating through text-based information to find answers for assigned tasks. Indeed, eye movement analysis suggests that details about interactive learning tools, such as animations that are added to provide an aesthetic component but do not advance the content information per se, tend to present a significant distraction for users. In the case noted here, rather than focusing on the task, students paid more attention following a shooting star or a flying plane. Thus, designers of academic sites should consider carefully decisions made to improve aesthetic impressions to decide if the gains from the added element are worth more than the possible distractions they can cause. Additionally, minor changes in design to existing navigational aids such as adding the links within mouse-over information and a search tool, can considerably improve the usability of an academic site.

Some of the basic results of this usability study have already been incorporated into improvements on this site. For example, the animations that provided distractions in the interactive tool have been removed. The usability study will be carried out again to determine if these adjustments and other improvements in navigation (such as replacing the word "glossary" with "definitions" on the glossary link) will enhance the SUS score from users. The generalizability of these observations will be further tested as well, by carrying out usability studies with other sites about this topic to see how variation in navigational aids and other features lead to different impressions by users and different success rates for specific tasks, such as those explored here.

Acknowledgments. Funding for this project was provided by the National Science Foundation under grant DUE-102292. Assistance from J. Raker, and K. Linenberger including helpful comments and pilot testing of tasks assigned to participants is gratefully acknowledged. Technical support for the use of the eye-tracking system from A. Peer was instrumental to the progress of this project.

References

1. Smith, S.D., Caruso, J.B.: The ECAR Study of Undergraduate Students and Information Technology. Educause, Louisville (2010)
2. Rosenfeld, L., Morville, P.: Information architecture for the World Wide Web. O'Reilly, Campbridge (1998)
3. Jacob, E.K., Loehrlein, A.: Information Architecture. Ann. Rev. Inform. Sci. & Tech. 43, 147–186 (2009)
4. Boatright-Horowitz, S.L., Langley, B.A., Gunnip, M.: Depth-of-Processing Effects as College Students use Academic Advising Web Sites. Cyberpsychology & Behavior 12, 331–335 (2009)
5. Fang, X., Holsapple, C.W.: An empirical study of web site navigation structures' impacts on web site usability. Decision Support Systems 43, 476–491 (2007)
6. van Schaik, P., Ling, J.: The role of context in perceptions of the aesthetics of web pages over time. Int. J. Human-Computer Stud. 67, 79–89 (2009)
7. Tuch, A.N., Roth, S.P., Hornbaek, K., Opwis, K., Bargas-Avila, J.A.: Is beautiful really usable? Toward understanding the relation between usability, aesthetics, and affect in HCI. Comp. in Human Behav. 28, 1596–1607 (2012)
8. Schonborn, K.J., Anderson, T.R.: A Model of Factors Determining Students' Ability to Interpret External Representations in Biochemistry. Int. J. Sci. Educ. 31, 193–232 (2009)
9. Kramer, I.M., Dahmani, H., Delouche, P., Bidabe, M., Schneeberger, P.: Education Catching Up with Science: Preparing Students for Three-Dimensional Literacy in Cell Biology. CBE-Life Sci. Educ. 11, 437–447 (2012)
10. Persky, S., Kaphingst, K.A., McCall, C., Lachance, C., Beall, A.C., Blascovich, J.: Presence Relates to Distinct Outcomes in Two Virtual Environments Employing Different Learning Modalities. Cyber Psychology & Behavior 12, 263–268 (2009)
11. Bojko, A(A.): Informative or Misleading? Heatmaps Deconstructed. In: Jacko, J.A. (ed.) HCI International 2009, Part I. LNCS, vol. 5610, pp. 30–39. Springer, Heidelberg (2009)

12. Siirtola, H., Räihä, K.-J.: Using Gaze Data in Evaluating Interactive Visualizations. In: Ebert, A., Dix, A., Gershon, N.D., Pohl, M. (eds.) HCIV (INTERACT) 2009. LNCS, vol. 6431, pp. 127–141. Springer, Heidelberg (2011)
13. Leuthold, S., Schmutz, P., Bargas-Avila, J.A., Tuch, A.N., Opwis, K.: Vertical versus dynamic menus on the world wide web: Eye tracking study measuring the influence of menu design and task complexity on user performance and subjective preference. Comp. Human Behav. 27, 459–472 (2011)
14. Djamasbi, S., Siegel, M., Tullis, T.: Generation Y, web design, and eye tracking. Int. J. Human-Computer Studies 68, 307–323 (2010)
15. Gerjets, P., Kammerer, Y., Werner, B.: Measuring spontaneous and instructed evaluation processes during Web search: Integrating concurrent thinking-aloud protocols and eye-tracking data. Learning & Instruction 21, 220–231 (2011)
16. Morris, L.V., Finnegan, C., Wu, S.-S.: Tracking student behavior, persistence, and achievement in online courses. Internet and Higher Education 8, 22–231 (2005)
17. Hart, C.: Factors Associated with Student Persistence in an Online Program of Study: A Review of the Literature. J. Interactive Online Learning 11, 19–42 (2012)
18. Lee, M.-C.: Explaining and predicting users' continuance intention toward e-learning: An extension of the expectation-confirmation model. Comp. & Educ. 54, 50–516 (2010)
19. Lee, M.K.O., Cheung, C.M.K., Chen, Z.: Acceptance of Internet-based learning medium: the role of extrinsic and intrinsic motivation. Information & Management 42, 1095–1104 (2005)
20. Eyetech, http://www.eyetechds.com/research/vt2
21. iMotions, http://imotionsglobal.com/
22. UserZoom, http://www.userzoom.com/
23. Brooke, J.: SUS: A "quick and dirty" usability scale. In: Jordan, P.W., Thomas, B., Weerdmeester, B.A., McClelland, I.L. (eds.) Usability evaluation in industry, pp. 189–194. Taylor & Francis, London (1996)
24. Bangor, A., Kortum, P., Miller, J.: Determining what individual SUS scores mean: Adding an adjective rating scale. Journal of Usability Studies 4, 114–123 (2009)

The Dimensions of Positive and Negative User Experiences with Interactive Products

Gabrielle Provost and Jean-Marc Robert

École Polytechnique de Montréal
Department of Mathematics and Industrial Engineering
P.O. 6079, St. Centre-Ville, Montréal, Québec, H3C 3A7
{gabrielle.provost,jean-marc.robert}@polymtl.ca

Abstract. This study aims to identify and define the dimensions of User Experience (UX) with interactive products, measure the frequency of their presence and their strength. We conducted an empirical study with 25 subjects who were asked to describe a positive and a negative experience with an interactive product, and explain why it was positive or negative. Then, they had to complete an evaluation grid about the dimensions. Three judges listened to the UX stories in order to extract the dimensions and point out those that were the most important. Results show that 10 dimensions can account for any UX. The psychological, functional and usability dimensions are present in a large number of UXs (90%, 88%, 88%), followed by the cognitive, informational and perceptual dimensions (74%, 70%, 66%). Results also show that the same dimensions can be used to describe positive and negative UXs and that positive UXs include a larger number of dimensions than the negative UXs.

Keywords: User Experience, Interactive products, UX Dimensions, UX Evaluation.

1 Introduction

Despite the conceptual complexity of User Experience (UX), there is a craze for the subject among researchers and practitioners in the HCI and interaction design communities. This enthusiasm can be explained by the fact that UX refers to a rich, broad and inclusive reality that focuses on the end of an interaction with a product rather than the means to get there [8]. "UX has emerged as an umbrella phrase for new ways of understanding and studying the quality-in-use of interactive products." [1] However, it is generally accepted that UX is an extension of the concept of usability, implying the existence of additional dimensions to be considered for its modeling and evaluation [5]. Since UX is an end, the challenge for researchers and practitioners is to understand how to create a positive experience among users of interactive products. To face this challenge, we need to be able to evaluate it. Thus, this study aims to identify and define the dimensions of UX with interactive products, to measure the frequency of their presence, and to assess their strength in order to lay the ground for

A. Marcus (Ed.): DUXU/HCII 2013, Part I, LNCS 8012, pp. 399–408, 2013.

the construction of a UX evaluation tool. UX dimensions can be defined as categories of elements that have an impact on a user when this user interacts with a product to do an activity in a given context.

2   Definition and Characteristics of UX

ISO9241-210 [6] defines UX as "a person's perceptions and responses that result from the use and/or anticipated use of a product, system or service." UX includes all the users' emotions, beliefs, preferences, perceptions, physical and psychological responses, behaviors and accomplishments that occur before, during and after use and that is influenced by the interactive system, the user and the context of use. Robert & Lesage [10] add that UX is also influenced by the activity. Indeed, since there is an interaction with a system, there must be an activity that involves a place, a time, inputs/outputs, etc. If the activity is poorly understood or considered out of context, the system, however effective, would not ensure a positive UX.

Based on a literature review and their own work, Robert & Lesage [12] extracted the following characteristics of UX: it is concerned with every aspect of the interaction with a system, related artifacts, the services, and the company; it is subjective; it is multidimensional and holistic; it is an overall effect on the user (it cumulates the effects experienced at each point of contact with the artifacts); it spans in and over time (it is not static); it depends on four basic elements: the *User* interacting with a *System* for doing an *Activity* in a *Context*; it is situated in a context (or is context-dependent); it can be considered at different granularity levels; it applies to an individual as well as to a team.

3   UX Dimensions

Since UX is not fully understood yet, it is a challenge to look into UX dimensions. UX models are not well established scientifically and do not all have the same level of granularity. Moreover, authors use different terms to refer to things about UX that are similar, close or different from each other, for instance: attributes [3], levels [2], components [12], aspects [7], elements [13] and dimensions [10] [11]. Dimension is the term that is preferred by [1] to incorporate the views on more than fifty studies on the dimensions of UX and it is the one we adopt in this work. In this study, we briefly discuss different models of UX and highlight the dimensions identified by various authors:

- Thüring & Mahlke [12] present a model according to which the user perceives two components: instrumental qualities and non-instrumental qualities. These two components influence a third one, i.e. the emotional reactions. The three components of UX lead to the establishment of an overall assessment of the quality of the system.
- Kort et al. [7] base their model on three aspects: composition (usability and pragmatic/behavioral characteristics), aesthetics and meaning. Each aspect is expressed through a set of design elements and combined to create the UX that evolves through a process of sense formation. The three UX aspects lead to emotions.

- Hassenzahl [3] believes that when a user comes into contact with a product, s/he perceives its characteristics and constructs a personal version of the product character. This character consists of pragmatic and hedonic attributes and leads to a judgment on the product's appeal and to emotional and behavioral reactions. Hedonic attributes are divided into two categories: stimulation and identification.
- Roto & Rautava [13] argue that a company can define a unique set of UX elements (between four and eight) that reflects its mission and objectives. There can be high-level elements for all products and lower-level elements for subcategories of products. For Nokia, four elements were divided into two groups: utility and usability in the pragmatic group; and social value and pleasure in the emotional group.
- According to Garrett [4], the secret to designing a positive UX lays in a fundamental duality of the product, that is to say, the functional and informational aspects.
- Robert & Lesage [11] argue that UX is formed by one or more dimensions whose relative weight varies depending on the user's perceptions. They suggest six dimensions: functional, physical, perceptual, cognitive, social, psychological and two meta-levels: sense-making and aesthetics. Sense-making is a basic requirement for every other dimension because users give meaning to everything they do and aesthetics acts as higher octave of one or several dimensions at a time as some users refer to it as an expression of their overall UX.

In light of the literature, it is possible to describe a UX through a small number of dimensions that would apply to the vast majority of products. The dimensions of Robert & Lesage [10] [11] represent a good starting point.

3.1   Two Empirical / Analytical Studies of UX Dimensions

Robert & Lesage [10] [11] observed (and interviewed in two cases) six individual users or groups of users who had been using different systems in various contexts. Their goal was to better understand the characteristics of UX and their effects on users, and to identify UX dimensions. They reported results of their interviews and observations in the form of short stories. They extracted six UX dimensions: functional, psychological, cognitive, perceptual, physical, and social.

Robert & Larouche [9] brought the project one step further: and conducted a questionnaire-based survey on UX with 52 respondents. Their results confirm that all of the UX dimensions below, with the exception of the cultural dimension, can capture the characteristics of UX with interactive systems.

1. **Functional:** the respondent discusses the importance of the product's capacity (or power), robustness, rapidity, reliability, usefulness, accessibility, usability, etc. S/he talks of the functionalities, novelty, type of technology, and of their impact on the realization of his/her activities. S/he also talks of duration of batteries.
2. **Perceptual:** the respondent talks of the importance of his/her perceptual contact with the object, through vision, audition, smell, or touch. S/he talks of the aura of the product, of its aesthetics.

3. **Physical:** the respondent talks of the product's weight, size and noise, of the physical effort s/he must make and of the fatigue or pain s/he might feel.
4. **Cognitive:** the respondent talks of the cognitive load related to the interaction with the product. S/he talks of learning, understanding, decision-making, development of his/her abilities, competence, and situation awareness.
5. **Psychological:** the respondent talks of the emotions generated by the interaction with the product, of the impact of the product on his/her attitudes, opinions, motivations, identity, satisfaction. S/he discusses the underlying values of the product in relation with his/her own emotions.
6. **Social:** the respondent talks of the importance of others (e.g., parents, friends, work colleagues, etc.) and his/her relations with them when s/he uses the product. S/he talks of the impact of different representatives of enterprises on his/her relation with the product (e.g., customer service).
7. **Informational:** the respondent talks of the quantity, quality, reliability, completeness, precision, and up-to-date of the information provided by a product (e.g., Web site). S/he talks of the quality of writing, spelling, and syntax.
8. **Contextual:** the respondent talks of elements which are outside the usage of the product but determinant for his/her global satisfaction: for instance, publicity, documentation, quality-price relation, his/her experiences with other products, etc. S/he also talks of different points of contact with the enterprise and their impacts on the appreciation of the product usage.
9. **Cultural:** the respondent talks of the way the product contributes to defining and reinforcing his/her cultural identity: for instance, language, culture, music, food.
10. **Temporal:** the respondent discusses the time spent doing the activity and the impact of the frequency of use of the product. S/he also talks of his/her perception of time s/he saves or looses when using the product.

In Robert & Larouche's study [9], the functional and psychological dimensions are present in almost all UX stories (96% and 90%), followed by the cognitive (80%), contextual (79%), and informational dimensions (74%). There are no differences between positive and negative UX stories when one looks at the dimensions that are present in them. There are no differences between the three groups of respondents (different ages) when one looks at the presence of dimensions in their UX stories.

4   Methodology

This section describes the methodology of the empirical study we conducted on UX. It includes a description of the subjects and the procedure with them, of the judges and the procedure with them, and of the analysis grid that was used to identify the UX dimensions.

Subjects. Twenty-five (N=25) subjects participated in a semi-structured telephone interview. Subjects were recruited from the personal contacts of the researcher. Of the 25 subjects, 12 (48%) are men and 13 (52%) are women. The distribution of subjects according to age goes as follows: 18-29 years (N = 8; 32%), 30-39 years (N = 6; 24%), 40-49 years (N = 6; 16%), 50 years and over (N = 6; 24%). The occupations are highly diversified among subjects. Participation was voluntary and the subjects were not paid.

Procedure for the Subjects. Interviews were conducted between July and August 2012. Interviews lasted approximately 30 minutes, were conducted with Skype and recorded. The subject's participation consisted of the following activities: read and sign the "Information and Consent Form"; provide demographic information; describe a positive and a negative experience with an interactive product; complete a UX evaluation grid

- **UX Description.** The subjects were asked to describe their positive experience with an interactive product and explain why it was positive. The exercise was then repeated with the negative experience. No other instructions were given to minimize the influence on their responses.

- **UX Evaluation Grid.** Subjects first had to read the grid that included a short definition of the nine following dimensions: functional, informational, perceptual, physical, cognitive, psychological, social, contextual, and temporal. Subject had to indicate on a scale of 0 to 5 if each of the dimensions had contributed to make his/her experience positive (0= no contribution; 5= great contribution). The exercise was repeated for the negative experience using a scale of 0 to -5. For each rating, subjects were encouraged to briefly justify the scores. All answers were given orally.

Judges. Three independent judges listened to the UX stories and evaluated them. Their qualifications were as follows: a woman with a bachelor's degree in mechanical engineering and a master's degree in ergonomics; a man with a bachelor's degree in computer science, a master's degree in software ergonomics and one year of experience as an interface ergonomist; a woman (the first author of this paper) with a bachelor's degree in marketing communications and a master degree in ergonomics in progress.

Analysis Grid. The analysis grid is a modified version of the UX evaluation grid described above, and aimed to facilitate judges' work. Dimensions were classified into two poles: the product pole (including the following dimensions: functional, usability, informational, physical characteristics, external characteristics, other) and the user pole (including the following dimensions: perceptual, cognitive, psychological, social, physical, other). Indeed, for some aspects of the UX, subjects mainly describe the qualities of the product and use objective terms, whereas for other aspects of the UX, they describe how they lived the experience and use personal terms. This classification of the dimensions has strong face validity and goes in the same direction as the distinction between the dimensions that relate to pragmatism and those that goes beyond it. Moreover, "other" was added to the user pole and the product pole to write down users' statements not belonging to any dimension identified so far; usability was added to separate it from the functional dimension; the physical dimension was split in two; the contextual dimension was renamed to avoid any confusion with "context of use"; the temporal dimension was removed because it overlapped with the notion of efficiency in the usability dimension.

Procedure for the Judges. The judges systematically extracted subjects' statements corresponding to the UX dimensions: they listened to the interviews, wrote down subjects' statements and associated them with one of the 10 UX dimensions (or "other") in the analysis grid. Then, judges' notes were pooled and transcribed into a new grid that the three judges agreed on. Finally, the judges had to determine the most important dimensions in each UX story in order to calculate the strength of the dimensions. The selection was based on the number of statements contained in a dimension, the frequency of each statement or synonyms, the time spent discussing a statement, and the expressions or the tone of subject' s voice.

5   Results

Frequency corresponds to the percentage of times (on a total of 50) a dimension is considered present in a UX and strength corresponds to the percentage of times a dimension is considered important in a UX.

Interviews. On average, an interview with a subject lasted 29.3 min (SD = 7.4 min; Min = 19 min ; Max = 53 min). Skype turned out to be an excellent method for collecting data because participants far away could easily be reached, they did not have to write or travel, we could ask questions of clarification, and we could collect the voice tone.

Products. Products chosen by the subjects can be grouped in seven main categories: Web sites (8); smartphones, tablets and their applications (10); computers and software (9); small electronic devices (10); cars, motorbikes and their components (6); furniture (3); and Bixi, a public bike service in Montreal. The participants had used most products quite recently: 92% (N = 23) of positive UXs and 68% (N = 17) of negative UXs had occurred during the week preceding the meeting.

Number of Dimensions Per UX. On average, positive UXs contain 8.8 dimensions (SD=1.5) and negative UXs contain 6.7 dimensions (SD=2.0) out of a total of 12 dimensions. Therefore, a positive UX contains on average 2.1 more dimensions than a negative UX. Because positive UXs are characterized by a greater number of dimensions, it leads us to believe they are richer and complete. It is also possible that several positive elements are needed to form a positive UX, while only one or a few negative elements are sufficient to form a negative UX.

Frequency of UX Dimensions. When all UX are combined, the three most frequent dimensions are psychological (90%), functional (88%) and usability (88%) (see Table 1). These three dimensions are also more frequent when positive UXs and negative UXs are taken separately. Since they are part of a greater number of UXs, it is possible that these three dimensions are more universal than the others. This result is consistent with those of Robert & Larouche [9], which is not surprising since the functionality is the reason why a person uses a product, the usability makes the interaction possible, and the psychological dimension, which includes fun, emotions, attitudes, values, is the user's response towards a product.

On average, dimensions are present in 73.7% of the positive UXs and in 56% of negative UXs (see Table 1). So positive UXs tend to be characterized by a greater number of dimensions than negative UXs. This difference is particularly marked for the perceptual, social, and external characteristics dimensions: they contribute more often to make a UX positive than to make it negative.

Table 1. Frequency of UX dimensions

Dimensions	Positive UXs	Negative UXs	Difference	Total of UXs
Product Pole				
Functional	92%	84%	8%	88%
Usability	100%	76%	24%	88%
Informational	84%	56%	28%	70%
Physical characteristics	48%	36%	12%	42%
External characteristics	72%	40%	32%	56%
Other	56%	40%	16%	48%
Mean	**75.3%**	**55.3%**	**n.a.**	**65.3%**
User Pole				
Perceptual	92%	40%	52%	66%
Cognitive	76%	72%	4%	74%
Psychological	88%	92%	-4%	90%
Social	76%	32%	44%	54%
Physical	40%	40%	0%	40%
Other	60%	64%	-4%	62%
Mean (User Pole)	**72.0%**	**56.7%**	**n.a.**	**64.3%**
Total				
Mean	**73.7%**	**56.0%**	**17.7%**	**64.8%**
Total	**N=25**	**N=25**	**n.a.**	**N=50**

Contribution of the UX Evaluation Grid. The results show that the UX evaluation grid leads subjects to discuss their UX with a larger number of dimensions. The dimensions that are most often forgotten by the subjects are the cognitive and the psychological. They are both related to the user pole. In fact, people forget to mention dimensions at the user pole three times more often than dimensions at the product pole. The reason might be that people have more difficulty talking about subjective dimensions (e.g., thoughts, emotions, perceptions, etc.) than about objective dimensions. The UX evaluation tool we are constructing will have an advantage over interviews or observations, since it will directly ask questions about all the dimensions.

Strength of the Dimensions. Four dimensions get higher scores than the others: usability (60%), psychological (44%), informational (38%) and functional (34%). Dimensions at the product pole are considered important almost two times more often than dimensions at the user pole. Moreover, there seems to be a relationship between the frequency of a dimension and its strength since the psychological, the functional and the usability dimensions emerge in both cases.

Table 2. Strength of UX dimensions

(N.B.: the percentage represents the number of times, out of a total of 50, a dimension is considered important in the UX stories)

Dimensions	Positive UXs	Negative UXs	Total of UXs
Product Pole			
Functional	40%	28%	34%
Usability	60%	60%	60%
Informational	44%	32%	38%
Physical characteristics	12%	20%	16%
External characteristics	12%	4%	8%
Other	16%	12%	14%
Mean	**30.7%**	**26.0%**	**28.3%**
User Pole			
Perceptual	12%	8%	10%
Cognitive	12%	16%	14%
Psychological	36%	52%	44%
Social	8%	4%	6%
Physical	20%	20%	20%
Other	0%	0%	0%
Mean	**14.7%**	**16.7%**	**15.7%**
Total			
Mean	**n=25**	**n=25**	**n=50**
Total	**22.7%**	**21.3%**	**22.0%**

Composition of UX Dimensions. Data analysis has allowed us to make a list of all users' statements related to each dimension. Subjects often used a variety of words to express the same thing, for example, "beautiful appearance", "beautiful object", "pretty", "visually appealing", "enhanced visual" "cute", "wow", etc. In such cases, words were grouped under a single term and only the most frequent words were reported. Moreover, some statements were grouped under a single label: for example, when subjects outlined a series of product features, it was summed up by "Includes many features." Because of space constraints, the complete lists of users' statements are not presented in this paper; we rather present a summary (Table 3). These words and statements can be considered as sub-dimensions and will be useful when building a subjective evaluation tool of UX.

Table 3. Users' statements for each dimension

Product Pole	User Pole
Functional: Utility and needs' satisfaction; Functionnalities and options	**Perceptual:** Aesthetic; Presence and quality of multimedia; Stimulation of the five senses
Usability: Simplicity and ease of use; Speed and efficiency	**Cognitive:** Comprehension; Concentration and reflection; Attention and memory; Stimulation, discovery and learning
Physical characteristics: Weight, size and dimension; Adjustments (including dis/assembly)	**Psychological:** Fun / Frustration; Motivation; Expectations (satisfaction and disappointment); Values, meaning and evocation
Informational: Presence and relevance of information; Quality of information	**Social:** Presence of others and quality of interactions; In/dependence on other; Obtaining information about others
External characteristics: Product ecosystem (products complementing each other); Customer service and brand	**Physical:** Physical activity; Transportation, movements and gestures; Dis/comfort
Other: Accessibility and availability; Reliability and durability; Security	**Other:** Productivity (time); Profitability (money)

6   Conclusion

This study showed that the 10 dimensions presented in this paper can be used to characterize UX with a large number of products. The same dimensions can be used to describe positive and negative UXs. However, results indicate that positive UXs tend to be characterized by a larger number of dimensions than negative UXs. The psychological, functional, and usability dimensions seem to play the most decisive role in the evaluation of UX by the subjects. There seems to be a relationship between the frequency of the dimensions and their strength as the most frequent dimensions are usually strong. Finally, the study has made possible to extract sub-dimensions of each dimension.

Next steps of our research will consist in doing the following activities: evaluate the independence or interdependence of the dimensions with statistical analysis to see if some can be merged together; confirm the validity of grouping the dimensions around the product pole and the user pole; refine the analysis of the UX sub-dimensions in order to have the most representative ones for each dimension; build, test and validate the prototype of a new UX subjective evaluation tool.

References

1. Bargas-Avila, J.A., Hornbæk, K.: Old wine in new bottles or novel challenges: a critical analysis of empirical studies of user experience. In: Proceedings of the 2011 Annual Conference on Human Factors in Computing Systems, pp. 268–2698. ACM, New York (2011)
2. Desmet, P., Hekkert, P.: Framework of product experience. International Journal of Design 1(1), 57–66 (2007)

3. Hassenzahl, M.: The thing and I: understanding the relationship between user and product. In: Blythe, M., Overbeeke, C., Monk, A.F., Wright, P.C. (eds.) Funology: From Usability to Enjoyment, pp. 31–42. Kluwer Academic Publishers, MDordrecht (2003)
4. Garrett, J.J.: Customer Loyalty and the Elements of User Experience. Design Management Review 17(1), 34–39 (2006)
5. Hassenzahl, M., Tractinsky, N.: User Experience – a Research Agenda. Behaviour and Information Technology 25(2), 91–97 (2006)
6. ISO 9241-210.: 2008. Ergonomics of Human System Interaction– Part 210: Human-centered design for interactive systems (formerly known as 13407). International Organization for Standardization (ISO), Switzerland (2010)
7. Kort, J., Vermeeren, A.P.O.S., Fokker, J.E.: Conceptualizing and Measuring User eXperience. In: Law, E., Vermeeren, A., Hassenzahl, M., Blythe, M. (eds.) Towards a UX Manifesto, COST294-MAUSE Affiliated Workshop, pp. 57–64. COST, Lancaster (2007)
8. Robert, J.-M.: Vers la plénitude de l'expérienceutilisateur. In: Proceedings of the 20th International Conference of the Association Francophone d'Interaction Homme-Machine, pp. 3–10. ACM, New York (2008)
9. Robert, J.M., Larouche, A.: The dimensions of user experience with interactive systems. In: Proceedings of IADIS International Conference - Interfaces and Human Computer Interaction 2012, pp. 89–96 (2012)
10. Robert, J.-M., Lesage, A.: Designing and evaluating user experience. In: Boy, G.A. (ed.) Handbook of Human-Computer Interaction: A Human-Centered Design Approach, Ashgate, U.K, pp. 321–338 (2011a)
11. Robert, J.-M., Lesage, A.: From usability to user experience with user interfaces. In: Boy, G.A. (ed.) Handbook of Human-Computer Interaction: A Human-Centered Design Approach, Ashgate, U.K, pp. 303–332 (2011b)
12. Thüring, M., Mahlke, S.: Usability, aesthetics and emotions in human-technology interaction. International Journal of Psychology 42(4), 253–264 (2007)
13. Roto, V., Rautava, M.: User experience elements and brand promise. In: International Engagability & Design Conference, in Conjunction with NordiCHI, Lund, Sweden (2008)

Participatory Design and Usability: A Behavioral Approach of Workers' Attitudes in the Work Environment

Dierci Marcio Cunha da Silveira

Universidade Federal Fluminense – UFF - Industrial Engineering Department, Brazil
dsilveira@metal.eeimvr.uff.br

Abstract. The present exploratory study on design and usability was developed to understand the user's participation in the design process, the concept of attitude and its outcomes (as a result of a participative process) and positioned in a contextual framework. The main focus was to explore the link between workers' participation and attitudes when design improvements are introduced in the workplace. Participants in the study were 15 oil drillers working in offshore drilling rigs and engaged in oil and gas exploration and production (E&P). They completed a set of tools covering the nine attitude dimensions, and five scales of satisfaction. The results showed a low level of participation within the two groups involved and attitude toward their participation and the outcomes of the engineering design intervention.

Keywords: participatory design, usability, behavior, attitude, oil industry.

1 Introduction

One of the goals of this exploratory study on design and usability originated with a feeling that to understand the user's participation in the design process, the concept of attitude and its outcomes (as a result of a participative process) should be positioned in a contextual framework [1]. The primary motivation for this research is to develop an understanding of how the workers' participation may influence their attitudes, intentions and behavior towards the technical system. The potential effects of participation stem from the assumption that the component structure of the attitude construct conceived at individual and organizational level.

The attitude and trust toward an object, system or environment depends upon the ways in which the individual interacts with and acquires information about it [2]. The information accumulated by the individual may come from a close relationship with the object or past environmental exposure and has a selective but direct effect on the individual's attitude. That is, the individual is more likely to make use of that which as learned in the past to confer trust and interpret the object or setting of concern.

2 Literature Review

The literature review has identified that the concept of attitude, as a dimension, based on social and psychological field should be considered carefully and is of direct

A. Marcus (Ed.): DUXU/HCII 2013, Part I, LNCS 8012, pp. 409–416, 2013.

relevance when applied to technical and engineering design matters. The starting point is the model of *Attitude to Act* developed by Fishbein [3] also Fishbein and Aj-zen [4]) and the model of *Trust in Machines* proposed by Muir [5], [6]. In order to translate attitude and trust from their models into the design field, with an emphasis on the participatory approach and ergonomics, a review was undertaken in order to identify possible contributions from other research. The design of complex systems, which requires the involvement of many individuals with different backgrounds and knowledge, demands the integration of technical information and systems require-ments at each stage of the design process for design decisions [7]. The technology-centred approach of reducing, in a static way, the interaction's effects of the specific task environment, the workload and the social and organizational environment, gives little attention to the behavioral component ([8], [9], [10]. Fortunately, two works following the groundwork developed on the problem of trust in machines [6], were developed by Lee [11] Lee and Wei [12] . Given that the concern of this research is about the problem of workers' attitudes in a changing work environment by the intro-duction of new devices and equipment for automation, the issue of personal beliefs or trust in machines is highlighted. From the original concept of trust as a sociological construct, Muir ([5], [6] formulated a hypothesis which states that trust is an impor-tant factor in determining user's behavior whilst interacting with automated systems.

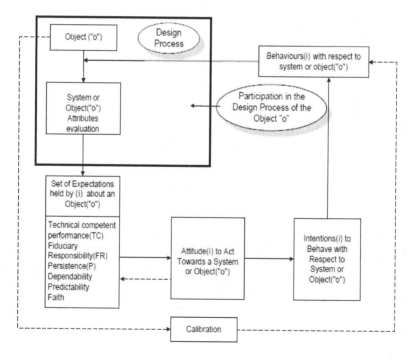

Fig. 1. Attitudes and Participation in the Design Process (Source: Silveira,1999b)

Among some possible questions posed in this area is: *How does the user's participation and involvement level in design influence the user's attitude to act towards a new technical system design?* A hypothetical model is proposed to be tested by assuming that participation as an external variable influencing attitudes and behavior, through a set of expectations and an evaluation of consequences. As the participation influence may change over time and from one group of concern to another, the effects of participation can enhance the understanding of a given behavioral situation [1].

3   Materials and Methods

Participants in the study were 15 oil drillers working in offshore drilling rigs and engaged in oil and gas exploration and production (E&P) involved in the redesign and operational upgrade in two offshore drilling platforms. They completed a set of tools covering the nine attitude dimensions, and five scales of satisfaction. The approach was accomplished through the remaining research instruments applied such as survey results, informal feedback and verbalizations of the subjects involved in the present study.

The factors observed were age, job experience, length of experience within the company, length of experience in the oil rig, as well as the confrontation between the groups of the drillers working within two different platforms (Group I: Platform PETROBRAS 10 and Group II: Platform PETROBRAS 23), which adopted distinct approaches for the design intervention. Three different questionnaires were applied to collect data regarding demographic background of the samples, to assess satisfaction with participation and to evaluate attitudes within two groups of users. The data were analyzed using descriptive statistics, cross-tabulations with the SPSS for Windows version 8.0 program.

4   Results

Both groups responded to an identical questionnaire to assess outcomes such as satisfaction with participation and attitudes. The overall mean value for age of the subjects was 42.2 years (SD±1.03 years) with a range of 37-49 years. The 37-45 years age range accounted for more 75% of the sample. The drillers' skills and knowledge in oil drilling operation may be characterized by the experience acquired along their career path. It highlights the importance of the background that they possess for contributing with suggestions towards design improvements in the workplace. The average for length of job in the oil rig was 8.6 ± 4.15 years, while the mean value for job experience as a driller was 9.41 ± 6.03 years. The data collected is shown in Table 1 below.

Table 1. Demographic Data: Job Experience (Group I and Group II)

		N	Mean	Std Deviation	Std Error	95% Confidence Interval for Mean		Min.	Max.
						Lower Bound	Upper Bound		
	PETROBRAS-23	8	18.67	2.44	.86	16.63	20.72	15.50	23.50
Job length in the company	PETROBRAS-10	7	18.07	2.40	.90	15.90	20.27	13.60	21.00
	Total	15	18.39	2.35	.61	17.10	19.70	13.60	23.50
	PETROBRAS-23	8	7.59	3.01	1.10	5.07	10.11	2.30	10.00
Job length on the rig	PETROBRAS-10	7	9.73	5.20	1.95	4.95	14.51	2.50	16.00
	Total	15	8.60	4.15	1.07	6.30	10.90	2.30	16.00
	PETROBRAS-23	8	9.82	6.50	2.30	4.40	15.26	.40	18.00
Work experience in the job	PETROBRAS-10	7	8.94	5.92	2.24	3.46	14.42	1.10	14.50
	Total	15	9.41	6.03	1.56	6.07	12.75	.40	18.00

With respect to training the demographic information collected through the *Questionnaire I* the results reveal that the totality of drillers received training for exerting their jobs. The same pattern was not verified regarding specific training for operation computer-based drilling systems.

4.1   Satisfaction with Participation: Results and Data Analysis

The dimensions considered in the *Questionnaire II* addressed the level of satisfaction with participation. *Selected dimensions* of satisfaction with participation included in the present study give emphasis to the salient results obtained in the field study. The first dimension *workplace design involvement (Questions 1.1 to 1.6 in Questionnaire II)* provided some insights. The subjects expressed equal desire for participation. The drillers in the Group I scored fairly their desire for participation even if they did not receive promotion or recognition to their contributions (*Question 1.1*). Being involved in initiatives for design improvements in the workplace was the highest scored aspect (*Question 1.2*). Figure 2 below shows the results.

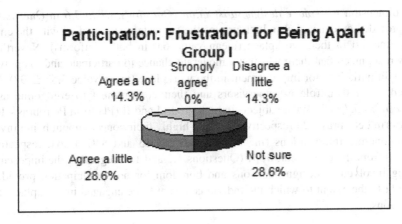

Fig. 2. Frustration for being apart of design decisions/Group I

The drillers among those working within Group II scored highly their desire for participation. To them, being involved in design decisions for improvements in the workplace and their desire for participation were the highest scored factors (*Question 1.2*). They expressed their concern in giving opinions and suggestions for workplace improvements. These results are shown in Figure 3 below.

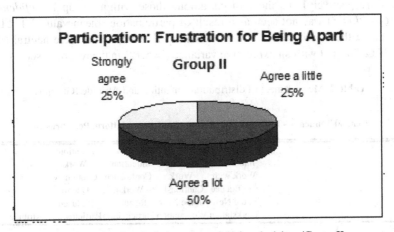

Fig. 3. Frustration for being apart of design decisions/Group II

It was observed that being involved in improvements in the design of the workplace was equally scored in both groups (*Question 1.2*) within the Group I and Group II (mean value 6.42±.53 and 6.37±.52, respectively). When confronting the scores concerning satisfaction levels if the subjects were apart of design modifications in their own workplace (*Question 1.3*), the subjects gave more importance to this factor among those individuals within the Group II (mean value 6.12 ± .83) than among those individuals within the Group I (mean value 4.14±1.8. The results from the dimension *workplace design satisfaction* (*Questions 3.1 to 3.6* in *Questionnaire II*) provided evidence that in both groups the subjects were satisfied with the changes implemented in their workplace (mean value 6.0 in both platforms). Nevertheless, they recognized that there was just a moderate chance to participate and to apply their skills in initiatives for improvement in the workplace (mean value 3.57 ± .97). When asked about their role as supervisors and their commitment to ergonomic aspects (*Questions 5.1 to 5.6*); the subjects in both group I and II (Platform Petrobras - 10 and Platform Petrobras – 23 respectively) rated highly their concern about being involved in ergonomic interventions (mean value 6.0 ± 1.15 and 5.87 ± .64, respectively). Scores from the *Questionnaire II* (Questions 1.2 and 1.4) regarding the importance of being involved in design decisions and boredom for non-participation provided an insight to the extent to which the individuals want to be engaged in workplace design decisions.

4.2   Attitudes: Results and Data Analysis

The first dimension considered in the attitude assessment was 'intention' (*Questions 1 to 4*). The individuals working within both platforms scored highly their intentions to work with confidence (*Question 1*) in the new driller's workstation (mean value 3.0±.00 and 2.0±2.07, respectively). The subjects in both groups felt that they should work cautiously (*Question 2*) in the new workstation (mean value 2.71±.50 and 2.25±.90, respectively). To the subjects among those within Group I *confidence to work* (*Question 3*) was not seen as a result of participation (mean value 1.14±1.57), while among those individuals within the Group II the opinions were neutral (mean value .37±2.70), but with an expressive variance ($'= 5.12$) in the response scores.

Table 2. Measurement of distribution: Intention and Attitude (Group I)

Central Tendency - Intention and Attitude Statistics - platform Petrobras 10

		Intention : Work with Confidence in the New Workstation	Intention: Work Cautiously in the New Workstation	Intention: Confidence to Work as a Result of Participation	Intention: Work Cautiously Due to Reduced Participation	Attitude
N	Valid	7	7	7	7	7
Mean		3.0000	2.7143	1.1429	1.1429	.8571
Mode		3.00	3.00	.00[a]	.00[a]	1.00
Std. Deviation		.0000	.4880	1.5736	1.7728	1.0690
Skewness			-1.230	.037	.205	-.772

[a.]Multiple modes exist. The smallest value is shown

Table 3. Measurement of distribution: Intention and Attitude (Group II)

Central Tendency - Intention Statistics - Platform Petrobras 23

		Intention : Work with Confidence in the New Workstation	Intention: Work Cautiously in the New Workstation	Intention: Confidence to Work as a Result of Participation	Intention: Work Cautiously Due to Reduced Participation	Attitude
N	Valid	8	8	8	8	8
Mean		2.0000	2.2500	.3750	.7500	1.5000
Mode		3.00	3.00	3.00	2.00	3.00
Std. Deviation		2.0702	.8864	2.2638	2.3755	2.0000
Skewness		-2.576	-.615	-.226	-.714	-1.071

The dimension *'beliefs'* (*Questions 19 and 20*) was aimed at the elicitation of salient beliefs. The results have shown that the subjects within the Group II (platform Petrobras-23) did not associate *'beliefs'* to a positive participation's effects towards their confidence (*Question 19*) to engage in a new work situation (mean value -.12±2.16), while among the individuals within the group I (platform Petrobras-10) was reported a neutral score (mean value 0.0±1.73). These scores highlighted their predisposition to keep performance even without participation in the design intervention (mean values 6.28±.49 and 6.25±.71, respectively). Table 4 below summarizes these results for Group I.

Table 4. Measurement of distribution: Normative Beliefs and Motivation (Petrobras 10)

Central Tendency - Normative Beliefs and Motivation to Comply Statistics - Platform Petrobras 10

		Normative Beliefs: Past Experience	Normative Beliefs: Supervisor and Managers Opinion	Motivation to Comply: Management Expectations	Motivation to Comply: Co-workers Expectations	Motivation:Keep Performance Even Without Participation
N	Valid	7	7	7	7	7
Mean		1.5714	1.8571	6.1429	6.2857	6.2857
Mode		2.00	2.00[a]	6.00	6.00[a]	6.00
Std. Deviation		2.0702	1.7728	.6901	.7559	.4880
Skewness		-2.351	-2.215	-.174	-.595	1.230

a. Multiple modes exist. The smallest value is shown

5   Conclusions

Since the beliefs related to technical systems deals with prescribed expectations such as technical competence, persistence and predictability, trust in the technical systems may be influenced by the participation in the design improvements. The effects of a participative role in workplace improvements played by the users may influence their behavioral intentions and satisfaction levels. Further research should be conducted to amplify the present research.

References

1. Silveira, D.M.C., Stubbs, D.A.: Participation, attitudes, and the design of technical systems: Testing a model in an oil rig. In: Hanson, M.A., Lovesey, E.J., Robertson, S.A. (eds.) Contemporary Ergonomics 1999, pp. 505–511. Taylor & Francis, London (1999b)
2. Silveira, D.M.C., Ferreira, P.R., Stubbs, D.A.: Oil Driller's Workstation: Assessment on Ergonomic Design Requirements for a Deepwater Driilling Rig. In: Proceedings of Offshore Mediterranean Conference 1999. OMC, Ravenna (1999a)
3. Fishbein, M.: Readings in Attitude Theory and Measurement. John Wiley, New York (1967)
4. Fishbein, M., Ajzen, I.: Belief, Attitude, Intention, and Behaviour: An Introduction to Theory and Research. Addison-Wesley, Reading (1975) ISBN- 0-201-02089-0
5. Muir, B.M.: Trust between human and machines, and the design of decision aids. International Journal of Man-Machine Studies 27, 527–539 (1987)
6. Muir, B.M.: Operators' trust in and use of automatic controllers in a supervisory control task. Doctoral Dissertation, University of Toronto, Canada (1989)
7. Czaja, S.J.: Systems Design and Evaluation. In: Salvendy, G. (ed.) Handbook of Human Factors and Ergonomics, 2nd edn., pp. 17–40. John Wiley, New York (1997)
8. Silveira, D.M.C.: Physiological Assessment of Petroleum Drilling Tasks. In: Proceedings of 12th Triennial Congress of the International Ergonomics Association, vol. 3, p. 365. HFAC/IEA, Toronto (1994a)
9. Silveira, D.M.C.: Petroleum Drilling Work: Ergonomical and Physiological Approach. In: Proceedings of 12th Triennial Congress of the International Ergonomics Association, vol. 3, p. 366. HFAC/IEA, Toronto (1994b)
10. Silveira, D.M.C.: Oil Drilling Workstation: Participatory Assessment on Ergonomic Design Requirements for an Oil Rig. In: Chatfield, R., Kuhn, S., Muller, M. (eds.) Proceedings of PDC 1998, Participatory Design Conference, November 12-14, vol. 5, CPSR, Seattle (1998)
11. Lee, J.D.: Trust, self confidence, and operators' adaptation to automation. Doctoral dissertation. University of Illinois at Urbana-Champaign, Illinois (1992)
12. Wei, Z.: Mental Load and Performance at Different Automation Levels. Doctoral Thesis, Deft University of Technology (1997) ISBN 90-370-0164-5

Merging Methodologies:
Combining Individual and Group Card Sorting

Robert L. Thomas and Ian Johnson

Liberty Mutual, Personal Insurance, Boston, MA
{robertl.thomas,ian.johnson}@liberty.mutual.com

Abstract. This paper presents a case study detailing how we combined individual card sorts with focus groups and group card sorting to improve the content hierarchy and organization of www.libertymutual.com, the personal insurance website of Liberty Mutual, which customers can visit to get an insurance quote, service their insurance policies, or find insurance-related information. We analyzed quantitative and qualitative data from 26 participants, on which we based our recommendations for a new hierarchy and site structure. Our paper will show how the results from the individual and group sorts differed, how the individual exercise informed the group exercise, and how the group exercise informed the recommendations. We believe this combination of individual sorting, group sorting, and focus group discussion makes this methodology unique.

Keywords: Card sorting, design methodology, information architecture, usability testing, user-based testing, content hierarchy, content organization.

1 Introduction

1.1 Background

The Liberty Mutual web site, www.libertymutual.com, had progressed from a small site with limited content to a large site with multiple lines of business as well as supporting information, insurance resources, and tools. The navigation suffered from having a limited number of options. It did not have a traditional navigation bar with drop-down options; it simply displayed nine categories in the top right corner of each page (see Figure 1). Four of those nine categories took users to a different website. We were also unsure whether some of the options, such as Member Rights, were top-level items that users would most gravitate toward.

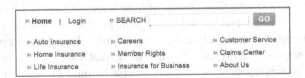

Fig. 1. Navigation from previous www.libertymutual.com website

A. Marcus (Ed.): DUXU/HCII 2013, Part I, LNCS 8012, pp. 417–426, 2013.
© Springer-Verlag Berlin Heidelberg 2013

1.2   Goals

We needed to create a new navigational hierarchy that would enable our users to more easily find specific options under main categories, and enable our team to provide new categories for supporting information. Our high-level objectives were to:

- Determine how current content hierarchies and labeling met users' needs
- Make the navigation labels understandable
- Make content discoverable
- Make the site attractive to users

In terms of visual hierarchy, we knew from our usability tests that participants scrolled down the page as they completed tasks and ignored the main nine links on the top right of each page.

1.3   Method Selection

A *card sort* is a categorization exercise, where participants group physical or virtual cards together based on their relationship to one another. By definition, an open card sort would allow our participants to name each of the categories they grouped together, thereby exposing where users would expect to find information, and what category names users would look for.

Various card sort methodologies have been implemented in the user experience field, including:

- Repeated card sorting
- Delphi and modified Delphi card sorting
- Focus group card sorting

Repeated card sorting is a "variation on open card sorting that involves the repeated sorting of a set of items to understand underlying dimensions or characteristics of a product or service" [1]. While this methodology intrigued us, we were not as interested in cataloging dimensions such as trustworthiness/untrustworthiness and attractiveness/unattractiveness as we were interested in how our users would group information into different categories.

Paul has done work on *Delphi* and *modified Delphi card sorting*, in which "participants build on the results from previous card sorts; instead of asking each participant to start from scratch, participants iteratively improve a proposed hierarchy, which may or may not be started by a subject matter expert" [6]. While Paul successfully reduced "the time to conduct the study and analyze the results" and also "lowered the costs of conducting a study" [6], we were not inhibited by these factors. We were also concerned that having subsequent participants work on modifying a card sort organized by others before them would color their own categorization and organizing principles. Finally, we did not think that running a card sort with a recommended participant pool of "8 to 10 people" would generate enough data to support a major overhaul to the site navigation, because user experience research experts recommend using at least 15-20 participants for a card sort to generate enough data to substantiate findings and recommendations [5, 9, 10]. However, Tullis & Wood used "a modified version of WebSort to look at random sub-samples of different sizes from [a] full dataset of 168 participants," and concluded from their research "that it may not be cost effective to spend resources to gather information from more than 20-30 participants in a card-sorting study" [10].

Hawley ran *focus group card sorting*, inviting "8–15 participants who are representative of the target audience to a conference room, with a computer for each person... First, ask participants to complete the card sort individually. Then, lead a discussion with participants, regarding the organizational strategies they used during the card sort" [3].

Of all the new card sort methodologies we researched, focus group card sorting provided innovative ways for us to combine quantitative and qualitative data. As Hawley states, "...with an online study, designers may miss out on the insights and comments users can provide in person. Interpreting users' intentions from the data they submit online can be challenging. A focus group card sort is a method that leverages the best of both online and in-person techniques" [3].

This idea intrigued us. As far as we knew, no one had invited up to 15 participants to do an individual card sort *and* followed it up with a group card sorting activity. If Nielsen recommends 15 participants in a card sort study, and Tullis up to 30, we could satisfy the higher criteria for number of participants (25-30), and employ a new methodology, to get the quantitative data we needed as well as rich qualitative data that an individual online sort could not provide.

1.4   Tool Selection

Card sorts are typically conducted in one of two ways: by having users interact with physical index cards, which get sorted into stacks; or by using online card sort applications (for example, WebSort and OptimalSort), which allow users to group items into lists or clusters. We had used physical index cards when running card sorts in the past, but that format presented issues when analyzing the data. We had to input the data ourselves into unsupported programs such as USort, which we knew could not analyze more than 50 labels, and we had 79 labels.

We had recently used an online card sort application, WebSort, and found it saved us from the tedious task of manually entering data from participants, and also provided data that could be downloaded and analyzed in an Excel spreadsheet. However, we were concerned that some participants might have difficulty in using the WebSort interface, and that confusion would color the data. To mitigate that effect, we created a five-minute demo that enabled participants to do a mini card sort and thus learn how to use the WebSort interface.

2   Methodology

After our survey of tools and techniques, we employed a methodology that combined online card sorting, physical card sorting, and focus group card sorting. We came up with 79 labels for the open card sort, based on primary and secondary content that our customers frequently accessed; we also included labels for content that we knew would be added to the site in the near future. As recommended by Donna Spencer [8], we wanted to watch out for "overuse of a particular word." We rewrote many of the labels (for example, "Auto Insurance Coverages," "Car Insurance in Your State," "Senior Driving Information") so that participants would not automatically group together labels that used the same terminology.

We conducted the card sort at a neutral off-site facility in September 2010, so that none of the participants knew the company conducting the card sort. We recruited 30 participants; 26 showed up. We recruited a mix of customers and non-customers, following standard Liberty Mutual recruiting criteria. We conducted one session with 13 participants in the morning and a second session with another group of 13 in the afternoon. Each person was provided a laptop for the individual sort, and sat at a table with 3 or 4 other participants with whom they would complete the group sort. We staffed each table with its own facilitator and note taker. Each session lasted two hours.

2.1   Individual, Online, Unmoderated, Open Card Sort

During the first hour, our participants used their laptops to complete an online, unmoderated, individual card sort, using WebSort. We provided a 5-minute demo of an open card sort that our participants completed on WebSort so that they could first learn how to use the online application. They then proceeded to complete the online open card sort with our 79 labels using WebSort (see Figure 2). There were also open-ended follow-up questions that our participants completed online after they finished the open card sort. All participants completed their work within 45 minutes.

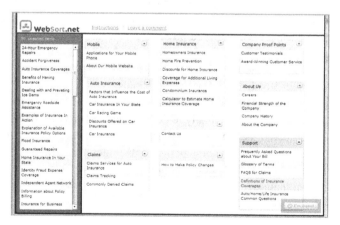

Fig. 2. Screenshot from WebSort. The dendrographs are M MODERATOR GUIDE] taking notes. front of them during teh eing captured.e results on WebSort and validated

2.2   Team-Based, Physical, Moderated, Open Card Sort

During the break, we removed the laptops and laid down brown paper to cover each of the tables. Then we brought our participants back in and asked them to sit at the same tables they were at before. Next, we evenly distributed, among participants in each group, a number of Post-It Notes that had printed on them the same 79 labels we used in the individual card sort. We asked participants at each table to work together and complete an open card sort as a team: that is, to organize the labels into groupings that made sense to them, and then to provide a name for each group of labels. As each team worked together, our facilitators moderated each team's activity: to encourage discussion, to ensure all members of the team were contributing to the conversation and activity, and to ensure no one person or persons were dominating the conversation and activity. Each table also had an assigned note taker to capture qualitative feedback and group discussion.

We asked each team to give a short presentation after they finished, in which a spokesperson for the group explained how and why they organized the information the way they did. We photographed the results of the Post-It Notes exercise for each group, and afterwards manually entered each group's results into WebSort.

2.3   Focus Group Discussion

We then followed up with questions to each group to facilitate a discussion. The moderator asked specific questions. Participants sat in their original seats, with the completed group card sort results still in front of them during the discussion. Supporting research team members (note takers and facilitators) were standing on the sides of the room, taking notes. These were the discussion topics for each group:

- How do you like to have your information organized (for example, by subject, process, business group, information type)?
- How many categories should there be? How many are too many? Too few?
- Were there any items that were difficult to categorize?
- What groups of items did you have difficulty naming?
- Were there any items you did not understand?

3   Analysis and Results

Our 26 participants created 210 unique category labels during their individual sorts. Our 6 groups of 4-5 participants used the same cards for the group sorts, and created 46 unique category labels. Some participants and groups used the same labels for categories (for example, "About Us," "Types of Insurance"), while others used different labels for similar concepts ("Resources," "Insurance Tips," "Helpful Tips & Suggestions," "Educational Tools").

After the 26 individual and 6 group card sorts were completed, we began analyzing the data. Three members of our team analyzed the individual card sorts, and three other members analyzed the group card sorts. As suggested by Spencer [7], we first standardized the main categories and applied consistent naming conventions. We gave categories with similar names or concepts a consistent name and combined groups where participants used the same basic concept but a slightly different label.

Second, each member of each team separately combined similar standardized categories. Each member then presented and explained their categorization, and then each team agreed upon and arrived at our totals of standardized categories (see Tables 1 and 2).

Table 1. Final list of 19 online, individual standardized categories

Standardised category	Sorters who used this	Total cards in this category	Unique cards	Agreement
Miscellaneous	38	266	79	9%
FAQs	18	174	49	20%
Types of Insurance	29	265	44	21%
About the Company	26	289	47	24%
Advice/Tips	21	189	35	26%
Mobile	11	35	12	27%
Testimonials & Customer Feedback	7	37	19	28%
Video/Interactive	11	49	16	28%
Insurance 101	6	20	11	30%
Billing	10	51	16	32%
Benefits/Perks	8	85	33	32%
Your Policy	5	49	28	35%
Claims	18	128	20	36%
Home/Property Insurance	14	158	26	43%
Life Insurance	6	17	6	47%
Agent	10	19	4	48%
Savings	4	23	10	58%
Auto/Car Insurance	15	197	22	60%
Careers	3	3	1	100%

For example, in the individual sorts, participants put an average of 13 cards (197/15) into the "Auto/Car Insurance" category and used 22 different cards. This category has an agreement number of 0.6, meaning that 60% of participants put the same 13 cards in this category.

Table 2. Final list of 11 in-person, group standardized categories

Standardised Category	Sorters Who Used This	Total Cards in This Category	Unique Cards	Agreement
Customer Service	9	72	29	28%
Tools & Resources	8	66	30	28%
Coverages & Benefits	4	34	22	39%
Insurance Products	6	80	30	44%
Interactive Media	4	30	16	47%
About Us	8	65	16	51%
Home Insurance	3	26	14	62%
Claims Center	6	45	11	68%
Find a Local Agent	4	11	4	69%
Auto Insurance	3	40	18	74%
Insurance Basics	1	5	5	100%

For example, in the group sorts, participant groups put an average of 13 cards (40/3) into the "Auto Insurance" category and used 18 different cards. This category has an agreement number of 0.74, meaning that 74% of participant groups put the same 13 cards in this category.

We saw differences between individual and group card sorts as we compiled the standardized categories. While individuals tended to create a greater number of minor categories, the groups tended to unite the minor categories into much broader categories. This difference might have been a product of analyzing fewer data points from the group vs. individual card sorts, or learned behavior and group think as individuals moved into the group card sort exercise. However, during the group card sorts and follow-up discussions, we discovered that the individual card sort exercise informed the group card sort exercise.

The group card sort exercise provided a forum for participants to discuss those items and categories that were confusing or unclassifiable to them, and enabled participants to relegate these previously unclassifiable items to defined categories, instead of bucketing them to their own minor categories such as those identified in Table 1 ("Advice/Tips," "Benefits/Perks," "FAQs," "Mobile," "Savings," "Testimonials & Customer Feedback," and "Video/Interactive"). This was a beneficial insight from the group card sort. Groups stated to us that their discussion and give-and-take enabled them to reach agreement on major categories to put these cards into.

Third, we compared the grouping of labels between the online, individual studies and the in-person group studies to detect any patterns. WebSort uses participant data to perform cluster analyses and generate "tree diagrams" or dendrograms [2], which display not only the relationship between items but the strength of that relationship, or how frequently the items are associated. The dendrograms showed differences between the individual and group results. The dendrogram for the group results showed closer relationships between content grouped together, but that could be an artifact of having a fewer number of groups (6) than number of individuals (26). The individual results showed weaker relationships between content grouped together.

Both individuals and groups wanted to separate information from tasks. For example, the Auto Insurance (or Auto/Car Insurance) category was focused on tasks, such as our label for "Tool to Estimate Car Insurance Coverage." Information on benefits and features – such as our labels for "24-hour Emergency Repairs," "Accident Forgiveness" and "New Car Replacement" – were isolated into a separate category, "Coverages & Benefits" (or "Benefits/Perks"). This revealed a key finding that both the individuals and the groups organized the content by task (for example, "Tool to Estimate Car Insurance Coverage") *and* by information (for example, "Accident Forgiveness").

Next, we created site maps to organize the results from the individual and group card sort exercises. What this visualized was that individuals had sorted items into a narrow and deep hierarchy. The site map created from the individual card sorts consisted of 3 major categories – Our Company; Policy, Billing, and Advice; Insurance; and 2 utility categories – Careers and FAQs. However, what the group card

Table 3. Group card sort categories and our final navigational categories

Group Card Sort, Major Categories	Our Final Navigational Categories
About Us	About Us (moved to shared navigation)
Auto Insurance	Auto Insurance
Home Insurance	Home Insurance
Insurance Basics	Insurance Resources
Insurance Products	
Claims Center	Claims Center
	Customer Service
	Life Insurance
Group Card Sort, Utility Categories	**Our Utility Bar Options**
Life Insurance	
Online Account	Customer Login
Find a Local Agent	Find a Local Agent

sort revealed was that our groups had sorted items into a medium navigational hierarchy, with 6 major categories, or double what our individual card sorts showed us – About Us, Auto Insurance, Home Insurance, Insurance Basics, Insurance Products, and Claims Center – and 3 utility categories: Online Account, Find a Local Agent, and Life Insurance, as shown in Table 3.

As a result, we created a 6-option navigational bar (see Figure 3). We moved About Us into a top-level navigation bar that all Liberty Mutual websites share. We moved Life Insurance to the same level as Auto Insurance and Home Insurance, based on the objectives of both our participants and our stakeholders, who wanted all insurance products at the same categorical level. We also created a utility bar above the 6-option navigational bar, which included Online Account (Customer Login) and Find a Local Agent.

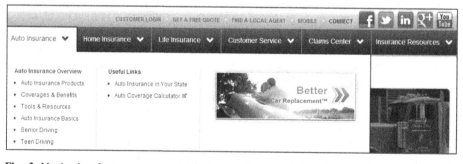

Fig. 3. Navigation from current www.libertymutual.com website, showing the utility bar and drop-down options for one category, Auto Insurance

4   Lessons Learned

One of the drawbacks of our study, and an opportunity for future studies, would be to have a better mechanism for collecting qualitative feedback from the smaller group card sorts and the larger group discussion. While our methodology included having a facilitator and a note taker for each group, the documentation of the raw, qualitative data was limited. The following factors could have contributed to it:

- The close proximity of the three groups per session and the groups having to talk over one another made it difficult for the note taker to listen
- The close proximity of the tables made it difficult for the note taker to navigate around the table to hear all participants in the group

Some solutions that could have improved the collection of the quantitative data include the following:

- A larger research room (or separate breakout rooms for the group sorts) would allow note takers and facilitators to walk around and avoid cross-talk from other groups
- Audio and/or video-recording equipment to record the conversations for each group would allow the research team to perform a content analysis of the raw data after the sessions

5   Conclusion

In conclusion, the combination of individual card sorts, group card sorts, and focus group discussions allowed us to obtain qualitative and quantitative data in one day with a large sample size but without a major investment in research budget or time. While the final recommendation for the new LibertyMutual.com site navigation largely followed the content organization from the group exercises and the focus group discussion, the individual card sort activity established a baseline of knowledge for each participant, aiding in productive negotiations and discussions for the group exercises. Also, by having the individual results, we were able to validate the differences between the results of the post-group exercise discussions with the quantitative similarities and differences of the individual and group card sort results.

Two years later, the site navigation has had a positive effect on the business. Key performance indicators and website analytics demonstrate that customers are actively using the new navigation to complete their tasks, rather than ignoring it as they did in the earlier version. In multiple usability testing studies since the navigation was updated in 2011, participants have commented positively on the website navigation, rating it as being one of the best attributes of the site. Third-party research panels have also favored the new site navigation: in its 2012 Insurance Website Evaluation Study[SM] Best Practices guide, J.D. Power and Associates commented that "Liberty Mutual provide[s] menus that include upper-funnel and lower-funnel shopping tools," allowing shoppers to easily find relevant shopping tools on any page [4].

References

1. Curran, M.J., Rugg, G., Corr, S.: Attitudes to Expert Systems: a Card Sort Study. The Foot 15(4), 190–197 (2005)
2. Dong, J., Martin, S., Waldo, P.: A User Input and Analysis Tool for Information Architecture. In: CHI 2001 Extended Abstracts on Human Factors in Computing Systems, pp. 23–24 (2001)
3. Hawley, M.: Extending Card-Sorting Techniques to Inform the Design of Web Site Hierarchies. In: UXmatters (2008),
   `http://www.uxmatters.com/mt/archives/2008/10/`
   `extending-card-sorting-techniques-to-inform-the-design-of-`
   `web-site-hierarchies.php`
4. Power, J.D., Associates, 2012 Insurance Website Evaluation Study^{SM} Best Practices. The McGraw-Hill Companies, Inc. (2012),
   `http://www.jdpower.com/content/press-release/xRjzSrq/`
   `2012-insurance-website-evaluation-study.htm`
5. Nielsen, J.: Card Sorting: How Many Users to Test (2004),
   `http://www.nngroup.com/articles/`
   `card-sorting-how-many-users-to-test`
6. Paul, C.L.: A Modified Delphi Approach to a New Card Sorting Methodology. Journal of Usability Studies 4(1), 7–30 (2008)
7. Spencer, D.: Card Sort Analysis Spreadsheet (2007),
   `http://rosenfeldmedia.com/books/cardsorting/`
   `blog/card_sort_analysis_spreadsheet`
8. Spencer, D.: Card Sorting: Designing Usable Categories. Rosenfeld Media, Brooklyn (2009)
9. Spencer, D., Warfel, T.: Card Sorting: A Definitive Guide (2004),
   `http://boxesandarrows.com/card-sorting-a-definitive-guide`
10. Tullis, T., Wood, L.: How Many Users Are Enough for a Card-Sorting Study? In: Proceedings, Usability Professionals Association (UPA) 2004 Conference, Minneapolis, MN (2004)

Engaging Citizens with UX Design

Kate Walser

CX Insights, a division of Tritus Technologies, Inc.
4800 Chucks Place
Gainesville, Virginia 20155 USA
kwalser@cxinsights.com

Abstract. This paper addresses the user experience (UX) design of open government initiatives. It provides an overview, definitions, and examples of open government, or government 2.0, that countries hope will engage citizens in democratic processes. The paper outlines different user experience design perspectives and describes design elements that agencies should consider to engage citizens. The paper concludes with examples of open government initiatives that apply these design elements.

Keywords: usability, user experience, government, open government, gov 2.0, web 2.0, social media, mobile, UX, design, participatory, citizen-centric, crowdsourcing, democracy, plain language, Challenge.gov, Iceland, Constitution, ImproveSF.

1 Introduction

With the adoption of social media, data standards, and open source tools, government agencies around the world are embracing the idea of participatory government. However, wanting citizens to engage in government initiatives is different from motivating them to engage. Critical to this effort is the user experience (UX). If agencies consider what motivates citizens to engage and factor those aspects into the user experience of their initiative, they can increase the likelihood that citizens will act. This paper suggests different user motivations and user experience design facets that address them, with examples from open government success stories. User experience designers can use these suggested approaches when designing and implementing their next government initiative, via website, mobile application (app), or other channel, to increase the participation rate with citizens.

2 What Is Open Government?

Government agencies around the world have a critical role in protecting citizen safety and well-being through missions and programs that range from the environment and transportation to healthcare and education. With the advent of social media, countries – from Iceland to the United States, Brazil to the New Zealand – have ventured into

A. Marcus (Ed.): DUXU/HCII 2013, Part I, LNCS 8012, pp. 427–436, 2013.

the world of open government. By partnering with citizens, agencies believe they can provide better services, improve strategic planning, and crowdsource innovation. [1]

Yet, wanting citizens to engage with government is different from actually moving them to action. A late 2009 Pew Research Center study showed that 61% of the 2,258 American adults surveyed visited a government website in the previous year, specifically to find needed information or complete a task. Agencies have an added challenge in that search engines are a large draw in bringing citizens to their websites and apps – citizens do not frequent agency websites. [1]

Open government holds tremendous potential if agencies can harness the energy of constituents through effective designs that engage them. User experience (UX) design, focused on all aspects of the citizen's experience as they interact with an agency and public servants, is core to this collaboration. Several user experience design perspectives exist, with related design criteria that agencies can use as design guideposts.

3   User Experience Design Perspectives

Several different perspectives exist for engaging citizens. Each serves as a lens for seeing what design considerations an agency must make in creating an engaging UX design for citizens. The perspectives suggested below are based on observation of public relation and gaming models. Agencies can and often should weave several perspectives into their initiative, giving more weight to the perspective that most closely aligns with the agency's objectives. Agencies can then see which user experience design aspects matter most in converting citizens into partners. The suggested perspectives include:

- Ease of use factor
- Social factor
- Competition and rewards factor
- Good story factor
- Fun factor
- Altruism factor

3.1   The Easy to Use Factor

The minimum requirement in engaging citizens is ease of use. It must be easy for a citizen to engage for them to do so. As an example, consider an initiative that asks citizens to sift through massive amounts of data to spot new opportunities or create a new solution. If the citizens have no means – such as visualization tools or suggestions for how to mine the data – to explore the data, the barrier for participation will be too high for them to engage.

Contrast that with a clear call to action, with an easy path and way for citizens to participate. The easier it is for citizens to know what the initiative entails and how to participate, the more likely they will be to engage with the agency in the initiative.

Ease of use can be addressed on websites and apps by using:

- Clear and immediate calls to action, so the initiative purpose and sponsor are obvious
- Plain language and clear labels that are easy to understand despite native language and reading level
- Simple instructions and tools to enable citizens to participate
- Familiar widgets, such as buttons, links, form fields, and other means to interact with information and tools

3.2   The Social Factor

Facebook, Twitter, YouTube, and other social media tools provide a way for people to connect (and reconnect) with friends and family. While most organizations offer websites and tools that serve some purpose – provide information, conduct transactions, contact someone – a subset of citizens crave the social component. The opportunity to be social and discover new networks of people and content drive these types of users to engage in opportunities.

Agencies can make their initiative a social one by including:

- Integration with social tools like Twitter, Facebook, and YouTube
- Resources for citizens to spread the word, such as "Like" and "Share" buttons
- Statistics about how many citizens participate in the initiative and how many ideas or resources exist
- Ways for citizens to discuss and respond to others' ideas and responses

3.3   The Competition and Rewards Factor

Some citizens are driven by competition and rewards they may earn. Consider the Foursquare mobile app audience. Using Foursquare, users can note their location on a map. The value may not be inherently clear, yet users remain loyal to the product. Users who check in the most times at a particular location earn a "mayor" title and their picture is shown for that venue's web page. The points and titles mean little outside the context of the app, but provide a reason for users to engage and keep using the app.

Agencies who want to attract this audience must consider what rewards, titles, point system, or other tangible opportunities that citizens can earn by engaging. Agencies can address the competition and rewards factor through:

- Chance to form teams with friends or other citizens to compete with others
- Countdown to deadline for participating
- Offers of rewards – money, goods, points that can be redeemed, or even contrived titles (*e.g.,* Idea Master, Idea Apprentice)
- Voting and reactions to ideas
- Words such as "Win," "Compete," "Chance," and "Prizes"
- Images that reinforce competition and rewards, such as calendar icons to indicate deadlines, trophies or badges to reflect prizes, and polls or scales

3.4   The Good Story Factor

People are intrigued by a good story. It can be as simple as a story with an unexpected twist or a great outcome. For government agencies, the unexpected twist can be something as simple as showing a sense of humor or human side.

The United States Internal Revenue Service (IRS) created its own buzz factor by showing it has a human side. As the International Business Times article[1] put it, "the IRS is not known for being very understanding when it comes to accepting excuses." The article described how a California couple wrote to the IRS asking for forgiveness of a tax penalty as they recently had a baby. The IRS provided a very unexpected reply, forgiving the penalty and even parroting back the parents' "the adult brain turns to jello those first few months raising a baby" excuse as a valid reason to forgive the penalty.

For a design, it can be something simple – an unexpected yet intuitive navigation option; a color scheme that is appealing to visitors, yet that does not look "bureaucratic." In the end, the good story component can help convey a sense of humor and humanity that makes citizens want to engage more than if they were interacting with a lifeless, humorless entity.

For the United Kingdom Patient Opinion website, the good story is what visitors share. The website invites UK citizens to provide feedback on their experiences with health services, provided by the government, through stories. [2] These stories then provide the material that serves as the "good story," drawing other citizens into the website and encouraging them to share their own story.

To offer a good story, try:

- Quick and simple numbers that tell how many people the initiative could help
- Human interest, by including names, pictures, or audio and video clips
- Surprising twists, such as civic leaders doing things that citizens would not expect
- Memorable interaction techniques, such as subtle movement, changes in imagery, and other elements to make the interaction more intriguing

3.5   The Fun Factor

In close relationship with the "good story" factor is the "fun" factor. Fun things can hook people quickly. The Rovio game Angry Birds[2] has been a runaway success with the simple concept of users launching birds – via slingshots – at green pigs. None of these elements individually would be that exciting, but the combination – the personalities, sounds, simple slingshot action, and colors employed – provides a fun factor that hooks users from the moment they first use it.

---

[1]   Tree, O. "IRS Refund: Tax Man Accepts Mother's 'My Brain Turned to Jello' Excuse, Wiping $2522 Fine," *International Business Times*. 01 February 2012.
http://www.ibtimes.com/irs-refund-tax-man-accepts-mothers-%E2%80%98my-brain-turned-jello%E2%80%99-excuse-wiping-2522-fine-404282

[2]   Angry Birds is a registered trademark of Rovio Entertainment Ltd.

If they perceive the initiative to be a task or work that does not offer some element of entertainment or fun, many citizens will pass. If design elements make it seem fun or at the least, like a pleasant distraction from everyday tasks and work, the likelihood that citizens will participate increases.

To make the initiative seem more fun to citizens, include:

- Humor, such as showing an agency leader has a fun side by using poetry, song, music, and even dance to capture citizens' attention and invite them to participate
- Widgets and design elements that veer from more traditional interactions, such as manipulative ones like gauges or buttons and widgets that "respond" even by slight movement to a user's interaction or visualization tools that enable citizens to create pictures of data
- Colors that are less typical of the country's government organizations and provide a fresh, less traditional perspective on the agencies

3.6   The Altruism Factor

Some citizens who have the opportunity to collaborate with government will do so for purely altruistic reasons. These citizens tend to be satisfied just with the opportunity to improve government. For many agencies, the assumption that citizens will participate just because they can correlates with the altruistic component. While this may be a legitimate reason that citizens choose to engage, it will probably be the least reliable motivator for citizen participation.

In countries with strong patriotism, addressing the altruistic side of citizens can be powerful. To use this approach in the design, consider:

- Words such as "Help," "Make a difference," "Improve," "Citizen-driven change," "How can we," and other words and phrases that reinforce change potential
- Rewards and recognition from government leaders, such as e-mail, letters, or even mention of citizen names in responses to ideas
- Images, video, and even music that evoke strong reactions in users, such as country heroes and images or video clips of country-defining moments (*e.g.*, founding)
- Colors that blend with the national flag and logos

4   Government Agencies Applying UX Design Factors

Agencies that weave the user experience design themes into their initiatives will engage more citizens. Example of successful initiatives include:

- **Challenge.gov,** a US-based online site that invites citizens to offer innovative solutions to various problems in exchange for various prizes [3]
- **Iceland's crowdsourced Constitution,** an online exercise inviting ideas and feedback from citizens for a major update to the Constitution [4] [5]
- **ImproveSF,** a site benefitting San Francisco, California, by inviting anyone to offer ideas for problems facing the city and earn points that can be redeemed for rewards [6]

These initiatives and the themes suggested translate into user experience design principles and elements.

4.1   Challenge.gov

Challenge.gov invites citizens to offer innovative ideas to challenges facing United States federal agencies. [3] With Challenge.gov, the impact can be felt on a larger, national scale, with a variety of impacts – economic, environmental, health, nutrition, energy, defense, economic, and others. With its name alone, Challenge.gov resonates with those who thrive on competition.

Fig. 1. The United States Challenge.gov website invites citizens to participate in challenges, offering rewards in exchange for top ideas

The design of Challenge.gov uses several techniques to engage citizens:

— **Ease of use** – Clear calls to action through labels and large, obvious buttons invite participation.
— **Social** – On pages describing each challenge, visitors can share the information with others by tweeting, liking on Facebook, or e-mailing the challenge to a friend.
— **Competition and rewards** – Each challenge lists the potential rewards participants could win, deadlines, and uses trophy icons to reinforce prizes.
— **Altruism** – Calls to action use words like "the public and government can solve problems together" and "Government challenges, your solutions."

4.2   Iceland Constitution

When it was time for Iceland to update its Constitution, the Constitutional Council of just 25 citizens drafted the revised articles and invited public comments. [4] The twist to the usual invitation to respond was that the comments were collected and discussed through social media tools. [5] The Council established a website[3] in the country's native language and integrated it with various social media tools citizens were using – Facebook, AOL, Yahoo, and Hotmail – to make it easy for citizens to post feedback and others to respond through comments or "Like" and "Share" votes.

The website's design incorporates user experience design facets such as:

— **Ease of use** – Large, clearly labeled elements guide users who speak Icelandic to read various sections of the Constitution, see others' comments, and post thoughts and reactions.
— **Social** – Integration with Facebook makes the initiative social and lets citizens engage with other citizens while discussing potential revisions and reactions.
— **Altruism** – The site ties in design elements including colors associated with the national flag, use of the native language, and other elements that reinforce patriotism.

Fig. 2. Iceland used a simple, clean and easy to use design for their website. Clear calls to action and use of colors that complement the country's flag reinforce an invitation to citizens to participate. The site's integration with Facebook and other social tools let citizens comment, discuss, and vote on the revised Constitution. [5]

---

3   Iceland Constitution website, http://stjornlagarad.is/english/

4.3   ImproveSF (San Francisco, California) (ImproveSF.com)

To gather more ideas about how to improve city services and access to various basic resources such as food, San Francisco government leaders established the ImproveSF website. City agencies post challenges to the website and invite the public to post suggestions. In exchange, the innovators suggesting ideas earn points that they can redeem for various rewards such as a voicemail recorded by the San Francisco mayor or cooking lessons with a well-known chef. [6]

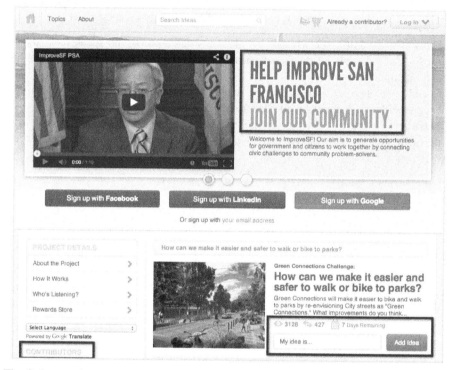

Fig. 3. ImproveSF engages visitors immediately by including clear and obvious calls to action (ease of use), ways to link to Facebook, Google, and LinkedIn and chances to interact with other contributors (social), point and reward opportunities as well as calendar icons and number of views to reinforce deadlines (competition and rewards), and words like "Help Improve and "how can we" (altruism). [6]

The site uses several UX perspectives and corresponding design elements to engage visitors:

- **Ease of use** – On the home page, visitors can immediately see the purpose ("Help improve...") and options through clear text and labels and widgets that let them interact (*i.e.*, "My idea is..." and "Add idea" button).
- **Social** – Users can participate through Facebook, Google, or LinkedIn accounts. They can see a list of contributors and see and discuss ideas, as well as vote on them.

Fig. 4. ImproveSF includes short, simple instructions in the home page slider to reinforce that it is easy for citizens to participate and that they can make a difference

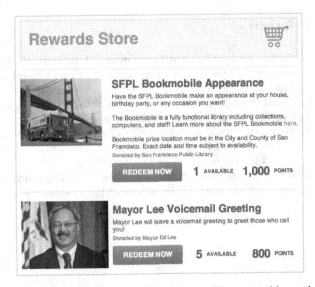

Fig. 5. The contributor rankings, points, and Rewards Store give ImproveSF a competition and rewards perspective. Bookmobile appearances, where the Public Library visits the participant's home or party, and other rewards such as a personalized voicemail greeting recorded by the mayor offer good story and fun elements. [6]

— **Competition and rewards** – Participants can earn and redeem points in the "Rewards Store" with rewards such as public library bookmobile appearances at the participant's home or business, cooking lessons, or even a personalized voicemail greeting recorded by the mayor.

— **Good story, Fun** – The Rewards Store offers the good story and fun elements of the initiative. Participants have a chance to win personalized, unique experiences such as having the public library bookmobile visit them or the Mayor record a personalized voicemail greeting that anyone who calls the participant can hear.

- **Altruism** – The calls to action use words like "Help improve," "Make a difference," and "How can we" that reinforce the initiative's potential impact on the community and the participants' role as community members.

5   Conclusion

The six UX design perspectives described above provide guideposts for government organizations to consider as they plan and build initiatives to engage citizens. The examples demonstrate their application to websites. These concepts can be expanded to apply to civic activities that include in-person town hall meetings, mobile applications, telephone-based activities, and others that include more citizens than just the tech-savvy crowd. Further research is needed to determine how the facets relate to audience demographics.

References

1. Walser, K.: Usability and Government 2.0. In: Buie, E., Murray, D. (eds.) Usability in Government Systems: User Experience Design for Citizens and Public Servants, Elsevier, Teddington (2012)
2. Patient Opinion, https://www.patientopinion.org.uk
3. Challenge. gov., http://challenge.gov
4. Morris, H.: Crowdsourcing Iceland's Constitution, NY Times (October 10, 2012), http://rendezvous.blogs.nytimes.com/2012/10/24/crowdsourcing-icelands-constitution/
5. Iceland Constitution website, http://stjornlagarad.is/english/
6. ImproveSF (Improve San Francisco), http://www.improvesf.com

Part III
Design Processes, Methods and Tools

Eliciting User Requirements and Acceptance for Customizing Mobile Device System Architecture

Katrin Arning[1,*], Bianka Trevisan[2], Martina Ziefle[1], and Eva-Maria Jakobs[2]

Human-Computer-Interaction Center, RWTH Aachen University
[1] Theaterplatz 14, 52062 Aachen, Germany
[2] Templergraben 83, 52066 Aachen, Germany
{arning,ziefle}@comm-rwth-aachen.de,
{b.trevisan,e.m.jakobs}@tk.rwth-aachen.de

Abstract. Mass customization is a popular approach in product design and manufacturing, where customers can configure standard products according to their individual preferences. Applied to the technical customization of mobile device system architecture (e.g. smartphones), an empirical multi-method approach was applied in order to elicit user requirements and acceptance. First, in a text mining analysis with n=80.995 blog comments relevant components and properties of cell phones were identified. Second, an online-survey with n=48 participants was conducted, which quantified user requirements and acceptance of the customization approach. The consecutive combination of text mining and survey provided valuable insights into user perceptions and acceptance. Customization was perceived positively, although the willingness to pay was low. Customizable technical characteristics in mobile device system design such as battery life, speech quality, memory capacity and connection quality as well as user profiles were identified.

Keywords: mass customization, acceptance, user requirements, survey, textmining.

1 Introduction

Today, customers prefer products, which are individually designed according to their personal ideas and preferences. A popular approach in product design is *Mass Customization*. Mass customization refers to the production of goods and services for a (relatively) large market that meets the diverse needs of each individual consumer of these products [1]. Thereby, customers can configure standard products according to their specific wishes, ideas and needs by choosing from a range of possible product components and designs. From the perspective of the manufacturer, it is possible to achieve a high efficiency of production and distribution in spite of individualization, which comes close to (mass-) standard products. Thus, the customized products are offered at prices that correspond to the willingness of buyers of (mass-) standard

---

* Corresponding author.

A. Marcus (Ed.): DUXU/HCII 2013, Part I, LNCS 8012, pp. 439–448, 2013.

products. Accordingly, customers can create and purchase a product individually to fair prices. Manufacturers of different products have proved the approach already, especially in the context of apparel manufacturing [2], a famous example of mass customization is the Nike shoe [3].

Although the demand for personalization of mobile devices is undoubtedly large, the customization approach is not yet applied to the technical customization of mobile devices (e.g. smartphones). Up to now, customization or personalization options in mobile devices are restricted to design factors of the interface or cell phone housing such as background images, ringtones, protection covers or the set-up of usage profiles (e.g. airplane mode) are available. However, the potential of customization of mobile device system architecture has not been explored yet, even though technical solutions for a flexible adaption of the system configuration to customers' needs already exist [4]. Recent research on mass customization almost exclusively focused on economic aspects, i.e. how mass customization can be efficiently delivered by manufacturers [5]. Aspects of mass customization acceptance have been rarely considered, even though customers' acceptance is a decisive factor for the market success of product. The issue of acceptance – especially in the context of technology acceptance – has become a key concept in the design and rollout of products. A product has a higher probability to be accepted by customers, if it is perceived as useful and easy to use [6]. Both criteria, usefulness and ease of use, are the central determinants of the Technology Acceptance Model [7], which was developed in the 80ies in order to explain the acceptance of job-related computer usage. However, apart from other critical objections [8], the TAM and its successors [9] are too generic to provide concrete guidelines for the design of customization approaches. Therefore, in a first step, it is necessary to investigate user perceptions in terms of relevant customizable technical features, as well as individual benefits and barriers related to the customization approach. In our paper, we present user requirements and an acceptance evaluation of the customization of mobile device system architecture. First, we identified technical components, which are perceived as relevant for customization by users (e.g., voice quality, camera or weight) und can variably be set up by manufacturers. Second, we quantified user preferences of relevant customizable technical components, and third, we assessed users' acceptance of the customization approach with regard to perceived drivers and barriers. A multi-method approach based on text mining and a survey was applied in order to assess user requirements and acceptance data.

2   Method

An empirical multi-method approach was applied in order to elicit user requirements and acceptance with regard to the customization of mobile device architecture. Two methods were applied sequentially: (1) A text mining analysis with n=80,995 blog comments was performed with the aim to identify relevant components and properties of cell phones. The results of the text mining were used for the selection of relevant technical features in the survey. (2) An online-survey with n=48 participants was conducted, which assessed user requirements regarding mobile device system architecture and users' acceptance regarding the customization approach.

2.1   Text Mining

Text mining refers to the (semi-)automatic content analysis of weakly structured or non-standardized contents (= texts), such as e-mails, newspaper articles or web comments in large text corpora, using statistical (quantitative) and linguistic (qualitative) methods of Information Retrieval (IR), Information Extraction (IE) and Natural Language Processing (NLP) [10], [11], [12]. Thereby, the application of text mining to web texts is called *Web Mining*. The aim of the methodology is to identify key-topics, topic relations and topic evaluations. The method is adapted from market and opinion research, where it is mainly used for product reviews.

Text Analysis. The study focused on the identification and analysis of evaluation-relevant cell phone components. Therefore, an explorative text analysis was performed using the software PASW Modeler 13. The blog comments were analyzed in a two-step procedure: (1) for frequency, to identify the most often mentioned items, (2) for co-occurrence or sentiment, to determine how the as relevant identified items are evaluated.

1. As a result of the frequency analysis, 25 relevant cell phone components were identified that were discussed and evaluated often in the respective comment corpus. These items are: battery life, camera, connection quality, connection stability, data rate, design, device size, display readability, display reflection, display resolution, display size, energysafe mode, exchangeability of the battery, Internet access, latency, memory capacity, radiation (SAR), reliability of the data transfer, robustness, speech quality, standby time, synchronization with PC, throughput, touchscreen, weight.

2. For each of the 25 items it was analyzed, how often they are evaluated positively or negatively in the Web comment corpus. For this purpose, the corpus is searched and analyzed based on allocation rules. The allocation rules (see example (1)) consist of a) relevant words of the semantically related word field (e.g. for the item battery life the synonym battery runtime) and b) links to word lists which contain positive and negative connoted words. For this analysis, iPhone as a synonym of cell or smart phone has been excluded. The rule states that the terms cell phone, battery and life must occur together in a sentence and have a negative sentiment.

$$(1) \quad \text{<cell phone>} \, \& \, \text{<negative>} \, \& \, \text{<battery>} \, \& \, \text{<life>}$$

Corpus. For the present study, a corpus of a topic-specific German blog dealing with MCS was selected and blog comments from the year 2009 elicited. In total, the corpus contained 80.995 blog comments. In a number of preprocessing steps, comments are bowdlerized from enclosing webpage elements and html-tags and corresponding meta information, e.g. user name is extracted and added as meta data to the comment. Table 1 illustrates some statistics about the corpus collection, particularly in terms of covered users and their blogging frequency.

Table 1. Comment corpus statistics

	Data 2009
Articles	1.289
Comments	81.831
Users	9.509
#Comments per article	63
#Comments per user	9

As commonly known, the blog *Heise.de* is a playground for high-potential users. Here, users interact with each other; these users are very familiar in the area of mobile communication systems. Users, who want to find out about pros and cons of a mobile device, search for information in this blog.

Statistical Analysis. The identified cell phone components or items were sorted and ranked descending automatically according to positive and negative polarity. The ranking demonstrates which item was discussed most frequently in which manner by bloggers. High listed entries dominate the bloggers talk.

2.2   Survey

Surveys are one of the most extensively used empirical research methods in information systems and technology acceptance research [13]. Based on the findings of the text mining study and on expert input, a user survey was conducted in order to identify and quantify the most relevant technical characteristics of mobile devices and customization acceptance from the users' perspective.

Questionnaire. The questionnaire was structured as follows: the first part assessed demographic characteristics (age, gender, profession, mobile communication equipment and usage behavior (duration, frequency)), the second part asked for purchase-relevant technical characteristics of mobile devices, the third part assessed participants' customization acceptance as well as drivers and barriers of customization acceptance. Questionnaire items had to be confirmed or denied on a six-point Likert scale ranging from "1 = totally unimportant" to "6 = extremely important" (for the preference ratings of purchase-relevant technical characteristics, questionnaire part 2) and "1 = totally disagree" to "6 = totally agree" (for customization acceptance, questionnaire part 3).

Sample. A total of n = 48 mobile phone and smartphone users between 23 - 62 years (M = 34.0, SD = 11.22, 52% female) took part in the survey. The educational level was comparably high (79.2% held an university degree). Asked for mobile communication equipment and usage behavior, the majority (89%) reported to own and use a mobile phone and/or a smartphone. Almost the half (49%) reported to predominantly use a mobile phone, and 51% reported to mainly use a smartphone. Regarding usage behavior, participants had on average 10.52 years of mobile device usage experience

(SD=3.71). Asked for the usage frequency of their mobile device, 50% reported to use it several times a day, 14.3% use it daily, 4.8% use it 2-3x per week, and 11.9% reported to use it 1x per week. Considering the high experience of using mobile devices in the sample we assume that the participants were able to give valid statements concerning the issue under study.

Statistical Analysis. Descriptive statistics as well as univariate and multivariate analyses of variance were employed. The significance of the omnibus F-Tests in the MANOVA analyses were taken from Pillai values. The level of significance was set at 5%. Due to the sample size, results on a alpha < 0.1 level are reported as marginally significant. In order to study the effects of mobile device type, the sample was divided into two groups according to the mainly used device type: mobile phone users (n=27, 55%) and smartphone users (n=21, 45%).

3   Results

3.1   Text Mining

Relevant Technical Characteristics of Mobile Devices. The results show that the items (1) *memory capacity* and (2) *battery life* are evaluated most frequently (Fig. 1). Regarding item (1), users evaluated the provided memory capacity by the manufacturer as sufficient or positive (n_p=347); contrarily, the other half of the blogger believes that sufficient memory capacities can only be maintain by capacity expansion. They evaluate the provided memory rather negative (n_n=304).

The second highest rated item is (2) battery life. The bloggers evaluate the duration (in hours) of cell phone batteries under normal use (average of calling, Internet usage, etc.) in relation to the battery charging time. Here, a charging time of 3 hours for a 1050 mA battery is classified as "inopportune". Overall, however, the battery life is rated mostly positive (n_p=174, n_n=147).

Moreover, other high-scored items are touchscreen (n_p=56, n_n=13), camera (n_p=22, n_n=52), battery exchangeability (n_p=54, n_n=52), display resolution (n_p=61, n_n=47) and speech quality (n_p=65, n_n=41). Overall, all items are usually equally often evaluated positively or negatively.

3.2   Survey

Relevant Technical Characteristics of Mobile Devices. Based on participants' preference ratings of purchase-relevant characteristics, the most important technical components of mobile devices were battery life, speech quality, connection stability and connection quality. The least important features were latency, camera, radiation (SAR) and brand (Fig. 2).

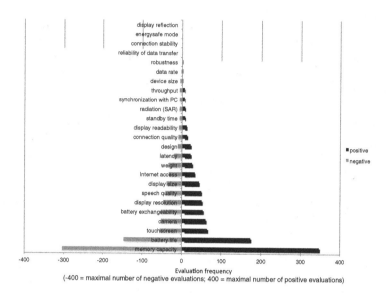

Fig. 1. Relevant technical characteristics of mobile devices (n=80.995); left side: negative polarity, right side: positive polarity

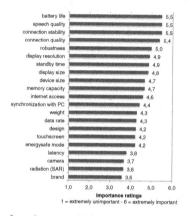

Fig. 2. Importance ratings for relevant technical characteristics of mobile devices (n = 48)

Customization Acceptance. The analysis of customization acceptance revealed a positive perception of the customization approach. Perceived usefulness of customization was M = 4.44 (SD = 1.17, max = 6) and perceived advantageousness was M = 4.29 (SD = 1.09). Participants liked the idea of customizing their mobile device (M = 4.40, SD = 1.35) and to adapt it to own preferences (M = 4.49, SD = 1.38) and usage situations (M = 4.60, SD = 1.46). However, participants clearly prefer one single optimal configuration profile (M = 4.11, SD = 1.29) instead of changing between situation-specific optimal configuration profiles (SD = 3.81, SD = 1.42).

The major *driver* of customization acceptance was improved efficiency (especially for job-related mobile phone usage (M = 5.49, SD = 1.31) and gaming (M = 5.22, SD

= 1.78). Further drivers were the improvement of mobile device performance (M = 5.06, SD = 1.03) and ease of use during the configuration process (M = 5.11, SD = 1.03). In contrast, the potential of reducing mobile devices' radiation was not perceived as a major advantage of customization (M = 3.98, SD = 1.50).

Main *barrier* of customization acceptance were additional costs (M = 2.43, SD = 1.19), i.e. users willingness to pay for customized mobile devices was rather low.

User Profiles. Moreover, different *user profiles* were identified according to mobile device usage characteristics. A user-profile (mobile phone users vs. smartphone users) specific analysis of preference ratings of relevant technical characteristics showed that smartphone users reported significantly higher demands regarding the performance of their mobile device (Table 2). We assume that the differences were caused by "data-driven needs": Smartphone users access the Internet via their mobile device more often and use it for data-oriented functions.

Table 2. Differences in preference ratings relevant technical characteristics of mobile devices for mobile phone and smartphone users

	mobile phone users (n = 27)		smartphone users (n = 21)		
	M	SD	M	SD	p
internet access	3.6	1.6	5.6	0.9	p < 0.01
data rate	3.2	1.3	5.3	0.7	p < 0.01
display size	4.3	1.1	5.3	0.7	p < 0.05
display resolution	4.6	1.1	5.2	0.8	p < 0.01
PC-synchronization	3.7	1.5	5.1	0.8	p < 0.01
memory capacity	4.3	1.4	5.0	0.9	p < 0.05
touchscreen	3.7	1.5	4.7	1.3	p < 0.05
latency	3.0	1.4	4.5	1.4	p < 0.01

Customization acceptance also significantly differed according to user group. Smartphone users perceived a significantly higher usefulness (F(1,44) = 6.37; p < 0.05) and advantageousness (F(1,44) = 5.35; p < 0.05) of customization (Fig. 3.).

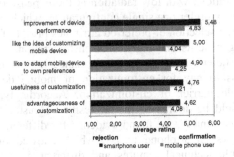

Fig. 3. Differences in customization acceptance for mobile phone and smartphone users

Regarding drivers and barriers of customization acceptance further user group-specific differences were found: General acceptance, measured by perceived usefulness ($F(1,43) = 3.23$, $p < 0.1$) and advantageousness ($F(1,43) = 3.39$, $p < 0.1$), as well as drivers of customization acceptance (improvement of device performance ($F(1,43) = 5.16$, $p < 0.05$), like the idea of customizing ($F(1,43) = 7.26$, $p < 0.01$) and adapting ($F(1,43) = 2.94$, $p < 0.1$) the device to own preferences) were stronger pronounced in smartphone users than in mobile phone users.

4   Discussion

The present study investigated user requirements and acceptance of the mass customization approach in the context of mobile device system architecture. Understanding user requirements and acceptance patterns is essential for a successful design of customization approaches. The following section therefore contains a discussion of results and of our methodological approach, as well as recommendations for a customization approach of mobile device system architecture.

4.1   User Requirements and Acceptance of Mass Customization

In general, we found a positive perception of mass customization, which indicates a high potential of this approach in the context of mobile device system architecture. Moreover, valuable insights into user requirements were gained, which provide a starting point for the design of customization approaches of mobile device system architecture. Relevant customizable technical features from the users' perspective, which were found in both empirical approaches (text mining and survey), were battery life, speech quality, memory capacity and connection quality. Future customization activities in system architecture design should therefore focus on these technical characteristics. Interestingly, users rejected the idea of changing between several system configuration profiles depending on specific situations (e.g. a "gaming configuration" with a high memory and processing capacity at the expense of battery runtime or a "healthy configuration" with low radiation at the expense of low data throughput). Instead of that they prefer one single configuration, which matches the customization approach, i.e. the selection of preferred attributes prior to fabrication far better. Regarding underlying benefits and barriers of customization, users emphasized aspects of improved efficiency and device performance improvements. On the other hand, the willingness to pay for customization of mobile devices was low and represented the single barrier of customization. Accordingly, these acceptance-relevant motives should be addressed in the design of customization systems and in marketing activities. Finally, we found evidence for different user profiles in the survey-data (mobile vs. smartphone users), which showed different preferences regarding customizable technical features and different customization acceptance patterns. The group of smartphone users expressed stronger preferences for a higher data throughput and showed a higher customization acceptance. Compared to that, the text mining data did not allow to extract which users have commented specific technical features. Taking into account comments from different blogs (balanced corpus), might show more concise results about user opinions due to a greater distribution across age and user groups. The shortcomings of the present study are apparent regarding the relatively equal feature evaluation (positive vs. negative, Fig. 1). Therefore, we assume that in a balanced corpus the weighting of cell phone characteristics is more evident. Nevertheless, our studies revealed valuable insights into the users' requirements and acceptance of customizing mobile device system architecture.

4.2 Methodological Approach

The combination of two empirical research methods, i.e. text mining and survey, in the context of eliciting user requirements and acceptance was proven to be successful. Regarding the identification of "top customizable features", both methods provided comparable results (e.g. significance of battery lifetime), which can be interpreted as mutual validation of measurement. On the other hand, both methods also had their specific strength and weaknesses. In the text mining study, for example, it was quantitatively determined which device characteristics are evaluated positively or negatively. More information about users opinions on device characteristics should provide an in-depth analysis, e.g., information on relevant rating scales, characteristic weights, etc. However, an in-depth analysis requires manual data annotation. For this purpose, small and user-specific corpora are needed. Looking at our research approach, we recommend a consecutive application of both methods as most advantageous in the context of acceptance research: The text mining approach is optimal for detecting acceptance-relevant trends in a natural and open environment such as the Internet. The survey, subsequently, which has a more closed and guided focus, is especially suited for taking up previously identified issues, as well as validating and quantifying them.

4.3 Limitations and Future Research

Finally, some limitations and future research directions based on our findings are discussed. One limitation of the text mining method is, that it does not allow yet to derive user profiles. Compared to surveys, where users can be asked for demographic data, user profiles of bloggers stay hidden. However, without demographic data, the circle of involved users cannot be determined exactly. Up to our knowledge, approaches that aim to fix this situation do not exist yet. One way to close this methodological gap could be to guess by some indicators the demographic profile of users, e.g., by metadata (nickname, posting periods) or by comment text (specific expression types). For instance, the nickname can provide hints on users gender (*Bill09*); expression specifics can give information about the educational background (*Cool stuff!*). We consider that an analytical framework for determining user profiles should include analysis categories such as *posting frequency* (allows for the identification of the activity type, active vs. passive user) or *linguistic profile* (refers to users formulation style, colloquial vs. standard style). Future work will deal with the solving of this problem, particularly. Useful methods and techniques can be borrowed from computational linguistics; its usefulness for identification of user profiles has been sketched by Neunerdt et al. [14] already.

A second aspect refers to further steps in the development of customization systems for mobile device architecture. In order to reach broader customer groups for mass customization (e.g. technically inexperienced customers) we suggest the development and evaluation of concrete system configuration profiles (e.g. the aforementioned gaming profile). Moreover, trade-offs between technical system characteristics from the user perspective need to be determined (an example can be found in [15]), in order to support engineers in the development of chip design, which forms the technical basis for the customization of mobile device system architecture.

Acknowledgments. This work was funded by the Project House HumTec at RWTH Aachen University, Germany.

References

1. Tseng, M., Jiao, J.: Mass Customization. In: Salvendy, G. (ed.) Handbook of Industrial Engineering, New York, pp. 684–709 (2001)
2. Lee, S.-E., Kunz, G.I., Fiore, A.M., Campbell, J.R.: Acceptance of mass customization of apparel: Merchandising issues associated with preference for product, process, and place. Cloth. Text. Res. J. 20, 138–146 (2002)
3. Piller, F., Moeslein, K., Stotko, C.M.: Does mass customization pay? An economic approach to evaluate customer integration. Production Planning & Control: The Management of Operations, Special Issue Mass customization 15, 435–444 (2004)
4. Schliebusch, O., Kammler, D., Chattopadhyay, A., Leupers, R., Ascheid, G., Meyr, H.: JTAG Interface and Debug Mechanism Generation for Automated ASIP Design. In: Proceedings of the Global Signal Processing Expo &Conf. (GSPx), Santa Clara, CA, USA (2004)
5. Hedge, V.G., Kekre, S., Radiv, S., Tadikamalla, P.R.: Customization:Impact on product and process performance. Prod. Oper. Manag. 14, 388–399 (2005)
6. Adams, D.A., Nelson, R.R., Todd, P.A.: Perceived usefulness, ease of use, and usage of information technology: A replication. MIS Quarterly 16, 227–247 (1992)
7. Davis, F.D.: Perceived Usefulness, Perceived Easeof Use, and User Acceptance of Information Technology. MIS Quarterly 13(3), 319–340 (1992)
8. Benbasat, I., Barki, H.: Quo vadis, TAM? Assoc. Inf. Syst. 8(4), 211–218 (2007)
9. Venkatesh, V., Morris, M.G., Davis, G.B., Davis, F.D.: User acceptance of information-technology: Toward a unified view. MIS Quarterly 27(3), 425–478 (2003)
10. Hotho, A., Nürnberger, A., Paaß, G.: A Brief Survey of Text Mining. Zeitschrift für Computerlinguistik und Sprachtechnologi 12, 19–62 (2005)
11. Mehler, A., Wolff, C.: Einleitung: Perspektiven und Positionen des Text Mining. Journal for Language Technology and Computational Linguistics (JLCL) 20, 1–18 (2005)
12. Heyer, G., Quasthoff, U., Wittig, T.: Text Mining: Wissensrohstoff Text. Konzepte, Algorithmen, Ergebnisse. Herdecke BochumW3L (2006)
13. Fowler Jr, F.J.: Survey Research Methods, 2nd edn. Sage, Thousand Oaks (1993)
14. Neunerdt, M., Trevisan, B., Mathar, R., Jakobs, E.-M.: Detecting Irregularities in Blog Comment Language Affecting POS Tagging Accuracy. International Journal of Computational Linguistiscs and Applications 1, 71–88 (2012)
15. Kowalewski, S., Arning, K., Minwegen, A., Ziefle, M., Ascheid, G.: Extending the engineering trade-off analysis by integrating user preferences in conjoint analysis. Expert Systems with Applications 40, 2947–2955 (2013)

User Experience Starts at the Keystroke Level: The Model of User Experience (MUX)

Stefan Brandenburg[1], Marlene Vogel[2], and Uwe Drewitz[3]

[1] Technische Universität Berlin, Germany
[2] Research Training Group prometei, Germany
[3] Deutsches Zentrum für Luft- und Raumfahrt, Germany
stefan.brandenburg@tu-berlin.de,
mvogel@zmms.tu-berlin.de, uwe.drewitz@dlr.de

Abstract. In the last years the emotional impact of artifacts became more and more interesting to the field of human-computer interaction research. Despite many models that describe factors of user experience (UX), most of them are of a descriptive nature. In contrast, we propose a theoretical approach, the model of user experience (MUX) that offers an explanation for the emergence of UX starting from the very first interaction steps. Additionally, we present empirical results that support these assumptions of our theoretical approach that were under investigation. In detail we found that affordances as well as standard signals foster users performance on a small time scale (up to 3 sec.). However, these small changes affected peoples UX. Hence we conclude that it is a fruitful approach to start investigating UX on a keystroke level.

Keywords: user experience, theoretical model of user experience, user experience design.

1 Introduction

The research focus of human-computer interaction (HCI) has shifted from usability research towards user experience (UX) in the recent decade (e.g. [1]). However, the concept of (UX) is still hard to capture (e.g. [1], [2]). Literature presents numerous theoretical models that consider many aspects of UX like instrumental as well as non-instrumental interaction aspects [3], hedonic and pragmatic qualities of products [4], levels of interactions [5] or stages of HCI [6]. However, most of these models are quite abstract when it comes to processes that yield UX. They rather describe drivers, factors, contexts etc. that might contribute to an understanding of the construct. In contrast to these approaches, we suggest that studying UX does not need to exclusively focus on high-level descriptions. Numerous well-known psychological concepts from different domains can be deployed to describe how features of the environment relate to user behavior and experience. The Model of User Experience (MUX) integrates such concepts into one comprehensive framework. Moreover, it defines whether its constructs are applied to the environment or the person. In addition, the model proposes possible measures for each of the implemented concepts. Focusing on

A. Marcus (Ed.): DUXU/HCII 2013, Part I, LNCS 8012, pp. 449–458, 2013.

the instrumental qualities of an artifact, the MUX emphasizes the relation between system properties and two central aspects of UX, Ease of Use [7] and Joy of Use (e.g. [8]). In fact, the MUX is based on the assumption that there are features of a technical artifact like affordances (e.g. [9], [10]), constraints [10], the attraction of attention [11] or mappings [10] that trigger cognitive processes which in turn evoke Immediate Interactive Behavior [12] and Ease of Induction [13], both yielding positive UX. Integrated in the MUX, these single concepts connect to a theoretical chain that attaches the design of technical devices on one hand with important aspects of UX on the other. Thereby, the MUX proposes that the very first interaction steps (i.e. actions of about 300ms to 3 sec.) already elicit UX. So far, several empirical investigations have shown support for the theoretical assumptions of the Model of User Experience (e.g. [13-15], [11]). However for one aspect of the MUX (i.e. affordances) no clear statement about the model assumptions was reached (cf. [15]). Therefore, the present research addresses this concept and investigates whether affordances elicit Immediate Interactive Behavior (IIB) as proposed by the MUX. In turn, if more IIB is observable subjects should report more positive user experience.

1.1   Affordances and Signals

Gibson suggested that we do not focus on single object properties when perceiving an object in real life [9]. Instead, one perceives what the object affords to oneself. Following Gibson "An affordance is an invariant combination of variables [...]" like color, surface structure or shape ([9], p.134). To specify affordances one needs to consider specifications of the environment and the observer (e.g. background knowledge). Hence an affordance relates properties of the environment to perceived action possibilities for the observer [9]. Based on Gibsons work, Norman transferred the concept of affordances to the human-computer interaction domain (cf. [10]). In line with Gibson, Norman proposed that affordances provide knowledge to the operation of things. However in contrast to Gibson, Norman stated that affordances are on hand if users of technical artifacts are enabled to apply their previously gained knowledge to the current interaction [10]. Maybe the most prominent examples for the role of affordances in interface design are Norman doors. Using different types of door handles, Norman pointed out that the ease of use regarding the operation of doors mainly depends on the application of affordances [10]. For example, in case the door needs to be pushed and the door handle affords pushing, people could easily operate the door. In line with Norman, we think of affordances as pointed out by Greeno: "In any interaction involving an agent with some other system, conditions that enable that interaction include some properties of the agent along with some properties of the other system. [...] The Term affordance refers to whatever is about the environment that contributes to the kind of interaction that occurs." ([16], pp. 338). In line with the Gibsonian idea of affordances [9], we assume that affordance congruent behavior is fast and unconscious.

Till now, affordances have been intensively studied and successfully implemented in design (e.g. [17]). For example, based on the Model of User Experience (MUX) Vogel et al. varied the affording character of a graphical user interface (high vs. low affording in terms of the goal of the task) and quantified subjective experience, usability (subjective, objective), utility and acceptance regarding two systems [11]. They found that an interface that strongly afforded behavior, which was leading to the goal accomplishment, resulted in higher ratings of subjective usability and utility as well as a more positive mood. In contrast to affordances, artificial indicators are conveyed culturally and their symbolic meanings have to be learned explicitly. Artificial visual indicators are often described as signs or symbols [18]. Following Petocz, signs are arbitrary cues that convey a pre-defined message [18]. Thus, signs and symbols are not affordances [19]. "They are examples of the use of a shared and visible conceptual model, appropriate feedback, and shared, cultural conventions." ([19], p. 41). Arrows are one type of symbols, defined as a line with one end marked, inducing an asymmetry (cf. [20]). Arrows have a diversity of semantic roles, e.g. moving direction, physical change, labeling, focusing attention, which have to be learned and distinguished in a given situation [20].

1.2   Immediate Interactive Behavior (IIB)

The concept of IIB "[...] entails all adaptive activities of agents that routinely and dynamically use their embodied and environmentally embedded nature to support and augment cognitive processes." ([21], p.33). That means the users' interaction with the environment utilizes simple interaction routines (i.e. tapping or pressing) which are fast (1/3 to 1 second), interaction-intensive and without cognitive effort [21]. Their application alters the cognitive system as well as the environment the agents are acting in [21]. Hence, the occurrence of IIB shows the expansion of cognition in real time. Its application impacts subjects' motivation due to the experience of their ability to make progress. Furthermore people have feelings of competence based on the successful application of their knowledge [14]. Empirical evidence from cognitive psychology and cognitive ergonomics support the assumptions of Neth et al. [21] with respect to IIB [12]. For example Neth and Payne investigated whether interaction fostered the resolution of counting tasks (i.e. counting coins) [12]. Subjects that were able to touch and move the coins were faster and more accurate in solving the counting task, compared to subjects that were only allowed to look at the arrangement of coins. In cognitive ergonomics Drewitz and Brandenburg published the Model of User Experience (MUX), embedding IIB as key concept [14]. This model lists factors that structure the environment in a way that it is likely to afford IIB. As shown in figure 1, the MUX proposes that the ideal environment is structured to support IIB, which conceptually captures the interaction of people with their environment on a very small time scale (see also [14]). However, the ideally structured environment always depends on the interaction goal.

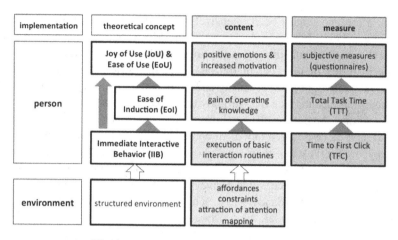

Fig. 1. The model of user experience (MUX)

1.3   Research Objectives

So far, empirical investigations did not yet deliver clear evidence for the aspect of affordances (see [15]). Therefore the present study investigates the role of affordances for the emergence of UX on a multi-touch table. Based on the MUX it can be assumed that the presence of affordances does facilitate subjects' performance and lead to more positive UX compared to their absence. To demonstrate that affordances do affect IIB and UX more than standard signals, we included the presence or absence of arrows as standard signals in the experiment as well (see also [15]). Since arrows are a somewhat well learned signal, their presence should increase IIB and thus elicit a more positive UX compared to their absence. However, the positive effect of affordances should be larger than the effect of signals. Including both factors in a 2x2 between subjects design, it was possible to test the single and joint effects of both types of information on subjects' performance and experience.

2   Method

2.1   Subjects and Material

A total of N = 48 multi-touch table novices (age: M = 30.5, SD = 9.2, 27 female/21 male) voluntarily participated in the experiment. The multi-touch interface consisted of a text box presenting the actual task, a working environment and three blue squares on the right hand side (see Fig.2). These three objects had to be manipulated using different gestures. Subjects' task was to execute the right gestures for rotating, scaling and cutting a blue square (see Fig.3). In the experiment, all subjects saw (light) touch areas indicating where they had to place their fingers. The arrows were presented to the subjects in the corresponding group, only. Affordances were defined as an initial movement of the object into the direction of gesture execution. For example, for scaling a blue object, subjects put their fingers in the lighted corners of the blue square.

As soon as both fingers were placed in opposite corners, the object started to gradually enlarge itself to 130 percent of its original size. Then it shrunk back to the original size. This movement was repeated as long as participants started to execute the gesture.

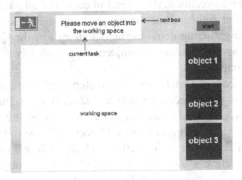

Fig. 2. Experimental environment presented on the multi-touch table

Additionally, participants were asked to fill in two questionnaires, the NASA-TLX [22] and the QUESI [23] to assess their subjective experience. The NASA questionnaire assesses subjective stress and strain, whereas the QUESI indicates feelings of ease of use.

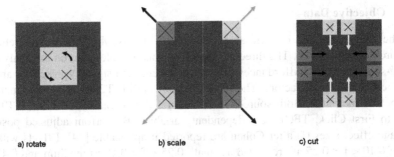

a) rotate   b) scale   c) cut

Fig. 3. Visualization of the three gestures. In the experiment, all subjects saw (light) touch areas. The arrows were presented to the subjects in the corresponding group, only. Crosses are shown for visualization purposes.

2.2   Procedure and Experimental Design

First of all, subjects familiarized themselves with the multi-touch table in an exercise trial. In this first trial, participants tested the movement of objects and the multi-touch surface sensitivity. Therefore, subjects were asked to move one of the three squares from the right hand side (see Fig.1) into the working space. Now participants received the instruction that their task was to execute the three different gestures: rotate, scale and cut (see Fig. 3a-c) three times. Hence each subject accomplished three trials, each of them containing all three gestures. The mapping of gestures to objects was randomized over subjects and trials. Hence it was impossible to associate an object with a special gesture. For each manipulation of a square, participants dragged one of them into the middle of the working space. Then, they read the current task in the interfaces text box. If participants felt that they understood the task, they pressed the start button and initiated the gesture execution. At the end of each trial all participants filled in the NASA-TLX [22]. After finishing the experiment they were also asked to complete a general questionnaire gathering demographic variables and the QUESI [23]. The entire experiment took about 30 minutes. Subjects were randomly assigned to one of the four experimental groups.

In total, two independent variables with two steps each were manipulated in a between-subjects design: affordances (present and absent) and signals (present and absent). Moreover three gestures (rotate, scale, cut) as well as three trials (T1, T2, T3) were manipulated as within-subjects factors. Objective (Time to First Click, TFC and Total Task Time, TTT) as well as subjective (NASA-TLX and QUESI) data was assessed. Time to first click was defined as period between subjects pressing of the start-button and the recognition of both fingers in the respective highlighted areas of the object (see Fig.3). Total task time was operationalized as time between participants pressing of the start-button and the automatic disappearance of the object after task completion.

3   Results

3.1   Objective Data

For the analysis of the behavioral data a mixed effects MANOVA with repeated measures was computed. The three gestures (cut, rotate, scale) entered the analysis as within-subjects factor. Affordances (present or absent) and signals (present or absent) were between-subjects factors. The three time points (T1, T2 and T3) were included as repeated measures. Both sources of behavioral data (Total Task Time, TTT and Time to First Click, TFC) were dependent variables. Bonferroni adjusted post-hoc tests and effect sizes (f) after Cohen are reported if applicable [24]. Effects with the size of $0.10 < f < 0.25$ are regarded as small, $0.25 < f < 0.40$ as medium and $0.40 < f$ as large. Due to limitations of space, the presentation of results will focus on most important effects only.

Regarding the results of the analysis, we found medium and large main effects of gesture (TFC: $(2,88) = 3.81$, $p = 0.02$, $f = 0.29$; TTT: $F(2, 88) = 7.91$, $p < 0.001$, $f = 0.42$) and time (TFC: $F(2,88) = 46.33$, $p < 0.001$, $f = 1.02$; TTT: $F(2, 88) = 9.69$, $p < 0.001$, $f = 0.46$) on both measures. With respect to the gestures, subjects showed a tendency to be slower in executing the cutting gesture compared to the other two gestures (TFC & TTT: $ps < 0.10$). Times did not differ for rotate and scale (TFC: $p = 1.00$; TTT: $p = 0.93$). In addition, participants significantly decreased in TTT and TFC for the first to the second trial (TFC & TTT: $ps < 0.01$). Further improvement from trial two to trial three was only significant for TFC ($p < 0.01$). With respect to the hypothesis, analysis revealed no main effects for affordances and signals (TFC & TTT: Fs < 1.52, ps > 0.22). However, the joined effect of both factors significantly impacted TFC ($F(1, 44) = 7.19$, $p < 0.01$, $f = 0.40$) and showed a tendency for TTT

(F(1, 44) = 3.02), p < 0.08, f = 0.25). As shown in Figure 3a, participants were fastest (regarding TTT) if both cues (affordances and signals) were present. This effect was not as strong for TFC (see Fig.3b). Here, two combinations revealed fastest TFCs: affordances and signals present and both absent.

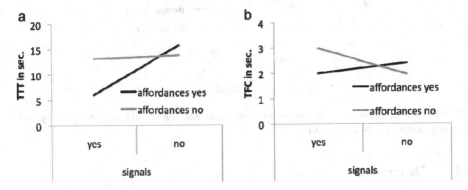

Fig. 4. Results regarding a) Total Task Time (TTT) and b) Time to First Click (TFC) in sec. for all combinations of affordances and signals

3.2   Subjective Data

Due to different points of measurement for the NASA-TLX (T1, T2, and T3) and only one point of measurement for the QUESI, two analyses of variance were computed for the subjective data. First, an ANOVA with repeated measurement over all trials was performed revealing the effects of affordances, signals and time (T) on subjective demand and effort (NASA-TLX). Second, an ANOVA was computed analyzing the influence of affordances and signals on intuitive use of the system (QUESI). Due to the massive amount of significant results, only data that are relevant for the hypothesis are reported in detail. With respect to subjective demand and effort (NASA-TLX), analysis revealed significant effects of affordances on the general score (F(1, 43) = 4.38, p = 0.04, f = 0.31) as well as on the subscales mental and temporal demand (Fs > 3.48, ps < 0.07, fs > 0.29). In contrast, signals only showed a tendency for the NASA-TLX subscale mental demand (F(1,43) = 3.09, p = 0.09, f = 0.29). Moreover, in line with the objective data the interaction of both factors effected the NASA – TLX general score (F(1,43) = 4.66, p = 0.04, f = 0.33) as well as the subscales mental demand, frustration and performance (Fs > 3.47, ps < 0.07). Figure 4 visualizes the main effect of affordances and the interaction effect of both factors on the general NASA-TLX score. It is visible that the presence of affordances lowers subjective feelings of strain. Moreover, subjects indicated lowest stain values if affordances and signals were present. In accordance with the impact of affordances on the scores of the NASA-TLX, analysis revealed tendency of affordances on the QUESI subscale goal attainment (F(1,43) = 3.30, p = 0.08, f = 0.27). Moreover the interaction of both factors impacted the general QUESI score (F(1,43) = 8.87, p < 0.01) as well as the subscales, goal attainment, learning effort, familiarity and subjective error rate (Fs > 4.79, ps < 0.02).

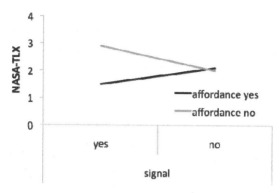

Fig. 5. Significant two-way interaction of affordances and signals and its effect on subjective feeling of demand (NASA-TLX)

4   Discussion

The aim of this study was to empirically demonstrate which form of assistance (affordances or signals) helps users the most and elicits highest UX ratings while interacting with a novel technical device. Results demonstrated, that there was no clear-cut advantage of either form of help. Instead, performance data coherently suggested an interaction of both factors. Thus the effect of affordances is not independent from the effect of signals. Based on the performance data, one could conclude that affordances and signals might be instances of the same category, which are operational clues. Another explanation might be found in the type of signals that were used in the experiment. Arrows that indicate a direction to move something are one of the most common hints in modern computer programs. Therefore subjects might have over learned their semantic meaning. If this is the case, natural indicators like affordances and well-learned signals might elicit the same behavior of subjects, although this behavior relies on different mechanisms. In the present work, affordances were implemented as object movements that corresponded to the execution of the gesture. Therefore these movements might have fostered subjects gesture execution on a natural basis. Participants might just have followed the objects movement that was already started. However, in terms of the arrows it is plausible to assume that these over learned symbolic cues triggered procedural knowledge, which is fast as well (cf. [25]). Hence, the group that saw both manipulations was able to rely on two different mechanisms. Thus, this group was fastest. Subjective data mainly supports this interpretation. As for the objective data, most subjects indicated less strain and more intuitive use if both, affordances and signals were present. Nevertheless, we also obtained main effects for affordances and signals on the mental demand subscale of the NASA-TLX. Hence the presence of each of them increases subjective wellbeing. Comparing the effects of affordances and signals, there is no clear picture favoring either one of them. However affordances showed a slightly larger impact on subjective measures than signals.

To sum up, the results partially support the assumptions of the Model of User Experience (MUX, [14]). As expected, affordances did enhance performance and fostered positive UX. However their effect was dependent of signals being present. The persistent interaction of both factors replicates results of Zinn and Brandenburg [15]. In their study subjects also indicated most positive UX if affordances and signals were presented at the same time. In addition, some limitations of the current experiment might have contributed to the results. Firstly we used a very simplistic experimental setting. Executing simple gestures with blue squares does not resemble real world tasks and might have channeled subjects' attention to the few things that were visible to them. Secondly large effects of gesture and time indicate that peoples' performance strongly changes over time and gesture familiarity (see also [15]). Of course ANOVA analysis revealed the effects across the experiment. Still, results might become clearer, if subjects gather more experience with the device. Thus upcoming experiments should go on to more realistic settings and tasks.

References

1. Hassenzahl, M., Tractinsky, N.: User experience – a research agenda. Behavior and Information Technology 25, 91–97 (2006)
2. Hassenzahl, M.: User Experience und Experience Design – Konzepte und Herausforderungen. In: Brau, H., Diefenbach, S., Hassenzahl, M., Kohler, K., Koller, F., Peissner, M., Petrovic, K., Thielsch, M., Ullrich, D., Zimmermann, D. (eds.) Usability Professionals, pp. 233–237. Fraunhofer Verlag, Stuttgart (2009)
3. Thüring, M., Mahlke, S.: Usability, aesthetics and emotions in human-technology interaction. International Journal of Psychology 42, 253–264 (2007)
4. Hassenzahl, M.: The thing and i: understanding the relationship between user and product. In: Blythe, M., Overbeeke, C., Monk, A., Wright, A. (eds.) Funology: From Usability to Enjoyment, pp. 31–42. Kluwer, Dordrecht (2003)
5. Norman, D.: Emotional Design: Why we love or hate things. Basic Books, New York (2004)
6. Pohlmeyer, A.E., Hecht, M., Blessing, L.: User Experience Lifecycle Model ContinUE [Continuous User Experience]. In: Lichtenstein, A., Stoessel, C., Clemens, C. (eds.) Der Mensch im Mittelpunkt technischer Systeme. 8. Berliner Werkstatt Mensch-Maschine-Systeme, pp. 314–317. VDI, Düsseldorf (2009)
7. Davis, E.D.: Perceived Usefulness, Perceived Ease of Use, and User Acceptance of Information Technology. Management Information Systems Quarterly 13, 319–340 (1989)
8. Norman, D.A.: Emotion & Attractive. Interactions: New Visions of Human-Computer Interaction 9, 36–42 (2002)
9. Gibson, J.: The Ecological Approach to Visual Perception. Houghton Mifflin, Boston (1985)
10. Norman, D.A.: The Psychology of Everyday Things. Basic Books, New York (1988)
11. Vogel, M., Brandenburg, S., Drewitz, U.: Zur Gestaltung graphischer Benutzungsschnittstellen: Einflussfaktorenfür das Nutzererleben. In: Eibl, M. (ed.) Mensch & Computer 2011: überMEDIEN|ÜBERmorgen, Oldenbourg, München (2011)
12. Neth, H., Payne, S.J.: Interactive coin addition: How hands can help us think. In: Carlson, L., Hölscher, C., Shipley, T. (eds.) Proceedings of the 33rd CogSci, pp. 279–284 (2011)

13. Brandenburg, S., Drewitz, U., Thüring, M., Minge, M., Brune, T.: Touch me if you can - Immediate Interactive Behavior alsBedienkonzeptfürMultimediageräte. In: Lichtenstein, A., Stößel, C., Clemens, C. (eds.) Der Mensch im Mittelpunkt technischer Systeme. 8.BerlinerWerkstatt Mensch-Maschine-Systeme, vol. 22, pp. 105–106. VDI Verlag GmbH, Düsseldorf (2009)

14. Drewitz, U., Brandenburg, S.: From design to experience: Towards a process model of user experience. In: Lin, J.C., Lin, D.M., Chen, H. (eds.) Ergonomics for all: Celebrating Ppcoe's 20 years of excellence: Selected papers of the Pan-Pacific Conference on Ergonomics, pp. 117–122. Taylor & Francis, London (2010)

15. Zinn, J.M., Brandenburg, S.: Support of Gesture Learning for MultiTouch Interfaces. In: Schmid, S., Elepfand, M., Adenauer, J., Lichtenstein, A. (eds.) Reflexionen und Visionen der Mensch-Maschine-InteraktionAus der Vergangenheitlernen, Zukunftgestalten 9. Berliner Werkstatt Mensch-Maschine-SystemeZMMS Spektrum Band, vol. 33, pp. 134–142. VDI Verlag, Düsseldorf (2011)

16. Greeno, J.G.: Gibson's Affordances. Psychological Review 101, 336–342 (1994)

17. Galvao, A.B., Sato, K.: Affordances in product architecture: Linking technical functions and users' tasks. In: Proceedings of DETC. University of Michigan, ASME (2005)

18. Petocz, A., Keller, P.E., Stevens, C.J.: Auditory warnings, signal-referent relations, and natural indicators: Re-thinking theory and application. Journal of experimental psychology: Applied 14, 165–178 (2008)

19. Norman, D.A.: Affordance, conventions, and design. Interactions 6, 38–43 (1999)

20. Kurata, Y., Egenhofer, M.: Semantics of Simple Arrow Diagrams. In: Barkowsky, T., Freksa, C., Hegarty, M., Lowe, R. (eds.) AAAI Spring Symposium on Reasoning with Mental and External Diagram: Computational Modeling and Spatial Assistance, pp. 101–104. AAAI Press, Palo Alto (2005)

21. Neth, H., Carlson, R.A., Gray, W.D., Kirlik, A., Kirsh, D., Payne, S.J.: Immediate Interactive Behavior: How Embodied and Embedded Cognition Uses and Changes the World to Achieve its Goals. In: McNamara, D.S., Trafton, J.G. (eds.) Proceedings of the 29th Annual Conference of the Cognitive Science Society, pp. 33–34. Texas, Austin (2007)

22. Hart, S.G., Staveland, L.E.: Development of NASA-TLX (Task Load Index): Results of empirical and theoretical research. Human mental workload. In: Hancock, P.A., Meshkati, N. (eds.) Human mental workload - Advances in psychology, vol. 52, pp. 139–183. North-Holland, Amsterdam (1988)

23. Mohs, C., Hurtienne, J., Scholz, D., Rötting, M.: Intuitivität - definierbar, beeinflussbar, überprüfbar. In: Useware 2006 - VDI Berichte, Nr. 1946, pp. 215-224. VDI-Verlag, Düsseldorf (2006)

24. Cohen, J.: Statistical power analysis for the behavioral sciences. Erlbaum, Hillsdale (1988)

25. Anderson, J.: KognitivePsychologie. Spektrum Akademischer Verlag, Heidelberg (2001)

Designing iDTV Applications from Participatory Use of Patterns

Samuel B. Buchdid, Roberto Pereira, and M. Cecília C. Baranauskas

Institute of Computing, State University of Campinas, Av. Albert Einstein N1251,
Campinas-SP, Brazil
{buchdid,rpereira,cecilia}@.ic.unicamp.br

Abstract. Interactive Digital TV (iDTV) is an emerging technology in Brazil, with inherent characteristics that must be addressed and which demand technical resources and references to support the design and development of interactive applications. This paper presents a design activity that reports and discusses the use of specific design patterns combined with prototyping tools and techniques inspired by Participatory Design in the design of applications for iDTV. Results are presented and discussed focusing on: the advantages of using design patterns in a participatory design, the main difficulties the groups had during the design activities, the importance of tools to support the design of iDTV applications.

Keywords: Interactive Digital TV, Design Patterns, Participatory Design, HCI.

1 Introduction

In 2003, the Brazilian government created the Brazilian Digital Television System with the aim of promoting democratization of information [5]. The analogical television is present in over 97% of Brazilian homes [10] and can be considered the main source of communication and entertainment in Brazil. Considering the major indexes regarding social and economic inequalities in the country, iDTV presents itself as a promising vehicle for the dissemination of information and education [20], and it may contribute to social and digital inclusion by reducing barriers that prevent the participatory and universal access of Brazilian citizens to knowledge: one of the 5 Grand Challenges of research in Computing in the country [2].

iDTV presents some challenges inherent to its technology that must be considered in the design of an interactive application. For instance: i) interaction (limited) by a remote control; ii) limited processing and memory capacity; iii) the physical distance between the user and the television; iv) the limitations in terms of input and output devices (keyboard and mouse); v) the diversity (cognitive, physical, socioeconomic, cultural) of users; vi) the usual presence of other viewers in the same place; and vii) the population's lack of experience in interacting with television content [6, 11, 18]. In fact, only recently standards were approved and receptors became able to receive the iDTV applications [4]. Hence, in Brazil there are still few applications available, and few users have access to interactive contents.

A. Marcus (Ed.): DUXU/HCII 2013, Part I, LNCS 8012, pp. 459–468, 2013.

Considering the lack of technical artifacts and tools specific to the iDTV context, this paper presents and discusses the experience of using Design Patterns articulated with techniques inspired by Participatory Design [14] and prototyping tools (e.g., Balsamiq® and CogTool®) for supporting the design of iDTV applications. The discussion of the paper is situated within a practical context of design in which eight different applications were designed by prospective designers to support social interaction through iDTV. The focus of this contribution is on the effectiveness of design patterns and its use in participatory practices to face the lack of support and technical resources, and to establish a first contact with the new technology. As a contribution, we are going to present and discuss: the patterns that were (and were not) used from the selected pattern collection; the main difficulties participant groups had during the design activities; the importance of technical resources to support the design; the benefits of articulating the usage of design patterns with techniques from the participatory design; important aspects that must be taken into account when designing iDTV applications for a wide audience (e.g., privacy, autonomy, accessibility); and suggestions for an authoring tool to support inexperienced designers in the iDTV context.

The paper is organized as follows: section 2 presents the main concepts related to design patterns and their relationships with emerging technologies; it also presents the collection of patterns for iDTV used in this study. Section 3 describes the case study in which the patterns for iDTV were used; it also presents and discusses the results of the case study based on an assessment by the participants. Finally, section 4 presents the final considerations about the work and directions for future research.

2   Design Patterns

Design patterns were originally proposed by the architect and urban planner Christopher Alexander in the 1970s. The main concept brings the idea of capturing the essence of successful solutions to recurring problems of architectural projects in a given context [1].

In addition to their use in the field of architecture, design patterns has been used in fields, such as Software Engineering [8] and Human-Computer Interaction (HCI) [3] and other contexts, such as Ubiquitous Computing [7], Web [13] and iDTV [11].

Compared to other forms of design guidance for interactive applications, such as guidelines, design principles and style guides, design patterns are slightly more extensive and therefore require more time to be understood and used. However, as Kunert [11] and Chung *et. al.* [7] discuss, design patterns have advantages: i) they are distributed in a hierarchical structure, which makes it easier to locate and differentiate between patterns of different granularity, which are situated at different levels of structure; ii) they are proposed in a language that is simple to those who use them; and iii) they incorporate references that may indicate other forms of design guidance, etc.

2.1 Patterns for iDTV

Studies that involve design patterns and report on experiences of success that could inspire other social contexts, such as that of Brazil, are still scarce. Some authors have previously identified a list of usability patterns for specific iDTV interactive tasks [19]. The pattern collection used in this work was proposed by Kunert [11] with a focus on interaction design for iDTV applications and special attention to usability issues. The patterns are divided into 10 groups. See Table 1.

Table 1. Groups of Patterns. Adapted from Kunert [11]

Name	Description
Group A: Page Layout	This group of patterns defines the layout types to be used in the application (e.g., overlay, full-screen with video, full-screen without video) and when to use each of them. It also determines the distribution of navigation elements, video and content.
Group B: Navigation	Defines what types of navigation are to be used in the application, ideally, after choosing the layout (Group A). For example: menus, index tabs.
Group C: Remote Control Keys	Defines the main keys of the remote control (e.g., colorful, numerical, arrow) and how they should be used in the whole application. For example: the color keys are usually used when only a key press is needed. Use color keys for choices that have to be efficient and for choosing an item in a menu.
Group D: Basic Functions	Highlights the basic functions that should be considered in the design of interaction and describes how to start, load, exit and hide an application, among other tasks.
Group E: Content Presentation	Determines the basic elements that form an application, such as text design (e.g., size, color and type), paging, content box, content update indication, etc.
Group F: User Participation	Describes how the interaction project on specific tasks should occur, i.e., the multiple types of user participation, such as voting and multiple-choice questions. It also describes how to conduct the approval for connectivity when the application needs to use the return channel and when the user's consent is required.
Group G: Text Input	Defines the multiple ways to input text (e.g., on-screen qwerty or alphabetical keyboard, mobile phone keyboard), when to use each, and how to use them in an application
Group H: Help	Defines the types of help (e.g., help section, on-screen instruction) and how provide them in an appropriate way to users according to the context of use.
Group I: Accessibility & Personalization	Deals with accessibility and personalization issues. For example: font size, subtitles, sign-language interpreter, audio feedback, option settings, etc.
Group J: Specific User Groups	Illustrates patterns for specific user groups (e.g., children). For example, how to define the menu, the remote control keys, etc.

Each of the 10 groups describes and illustrates first-level problems that are divided into new design problems of second and third levels. On the second level, there are 35 interaction problems; for each one, there is a corresponding pattern. For example, to define the application layout (first level: "Group A: Page Layout"), designers should choose from 3 different types of layout according to the constraints of the application being designed: "A2 Overlay", "A3 Full-Screen with Video" and "A4 Full-Screen without Video". On the third level, there are more specific problems that guide the solutions of the first and second levels. Regarding "Group A", these types of problems are characterized by the position and size of the application that is layered over the video, the position and size of the video, transparency issues, the application audio competing with the audio of the video, etc.

A pattern must follow a structure that is inherent to the purpose of the language or to the set of patterns on which it is inserted [3]. Kunert's iDTV patterns [11] are characterized by: 1. Reference: a unique identifier in the pattern collection ("A4"). 2. Name: usually describes the effect of using the pattern ("Full-Screen without Video"). 3. Examples: ways to use pattern (e.g., images that illustrate the pattern being used in practice). 4. Context: introductory paragraph contextualizing the use of the patterns. 5. Problem: shows the forces involved in the use of the pattern, aspects to be considered, etc. 6. Solution: different and generic ways of solving the problem. 7. Evidence: references and usability tests used to demonstrate the viability of the proposed solutions. 8. Related Patterns: patterns that influence and/or are influenced by the pattern in question.

In the next section, we present a case study in which the patterns presented were used to support the design of iDTV applications.

3   Case Study

The case study was conducted from August to December, 2011, and involved 38 prospective designers that were attending a Computer Science discipline for the "Design of Human-Computer Interfaces". The participants were divided into 8 groups: G1 (formed by the prospective designers: D1, D2, D3 and D4), G2 (D5-D9), G3 (D10-D14), G4 (D15-D19), G5 (D20-D23), G6 (D24-D28), G7 (D29-D33) and G8 (D34-D38). From the 38 participants, only D15 had already had some contact with the design of iDTV applications, but had no experience with Design Patterns. The other participants were aware of the existence of iDTV applications, but had never designed or even experienced them as end users.

The project developed by the groups was related to the design of "sustainable and social applications for iDTV". From the 8 groups, G2 designed a game to teach the concept of sustainability to children. G3 presented the prototype of an application for promoting social interaction during soccer matches on TV. G4 and G5 designed applications related to social networks for iDTV. G6 designed a social application to promote sustainable behavior in users. G7 designed an application to support an online chat, and G8 designed an application that complements educational courses via iDTV. At the end of the course, groups had to present an interactive prototype of their applications and share the results with each other.

After the course was finished, groups were asked to voluntarily answer an online questionnaire in order to evaluate the activities. At this time, groups were asked for their permission to use all the material they produced during the course and their answers to the questionnaire. G1 opted not to answer the evaluation questionnaire and is not included in the analysis presented in this paper.

Before using the iDTV patterns, groups conducted activities that favored problem clarification, analysis, and requirement refinement and organization. Artifacts from and based on the Organizational Semiotics [12] were used to support the identification of the stakeholders involved in the project, their cultural aspects, values, problems and ideas, and requirements to be considered in the design. In such applications, the concern with the culture and values of the different stakeholders were mandatory. The problem clarification and evaluation based on culture and values can be found in detail in [16] and [17], respectively.

Before starting the design activities, the pattern collection and examples were presented and discussed with the groups in a lecture. As support material, each group received a summary of the 10 groups of patterns presenting the name and a general description for each group, as well as all the patterns placed in each group, including their names, references, problems (description, advantages and disadvantages) and solutions. Generic patterns were incorporated into specialized patterns in order to simplify the activity and reduce the number of patterns to be analyzed.

The activity with Design Patterns for iDTV was organized into 3 steps:

1. In the first step, participants selected the patterns that would be used in their applications. With the list of patterns provided to support the activity, participants needed to justify their choices based on the scope of their applications and the inherent forces of each pattern.
2. For the creation of the first interface prototypes, participants were involved in participatory design activities (Brain Drawing [14] adapted) guided by the design patterns for iDTV. Participants received paper, pencils and pens to draw their ideas, respecting the design constraints and the previously selected patterns. As a result, each group created several interface proposals constructed by each participant and consolidated into a final proposal.
3. The material produced in the step 2 was used as a basis for designing the interface and for producing the first interactive version of the system prototype. Fig. 1 shows some examples of prototypes designed by G2, G3 and G8. The Balsamiq® tool was suggested to design interfaces and the CogTool® was used to model the tasks and create the interactive prototypes.

Fig. 1. Prototypes of Groups G2, G3 and G8

Other tools specific to the iDTV context were analyzed during the project – for instance: JAME Author®, iTVProject®, Composer®, Batuque® and BluTV®. However, none of them was viable for the project due to the need to acquire licenses, and sometimes due to the project's discontinuity or to the impossibility of obtaining the tool at the time of the case study. Participants were also encouraged to use emulators (Ginga-NCL [9] and Open Ginga [15]) with the NCL Eclipse® plug-in, but none of the groups chose this option due to the lack of time and the difficulty of learning a new programming language while developing the project.

3.1   Results and Discussion

All the initial layouts produced by the groups contained the design patterns that were kept in the final prototype. Fig. 2 illustrates the prototype created by G3 at three different design moments: 1st: after participatory design; 2nd: in an intermediate step; and 3rd: after the project was finished.

In Fig. 2, it is possible to see that higher level patterns, such as "A3 Full-Screen with Video", "B2 Menu" and "B6 Tabs" remained present at the different prototypes' stages. More specific patterns, such as "C2 Arrow Keys", "C3 OK-Key", "D4 Exiting", "H1 On-Screen Instruction" and "H2 Help Section" were incorporated into the prototypes as the design evolved.

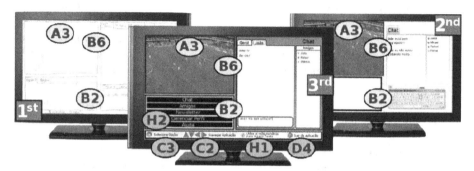

Fig. 2. Evolution of G3's Prototype since Brain Drawing Activity with Indicated Patterns

Considering the final prototype from each group, it was possible to make a mapping of all the patterns used in the activity (see Table 2). Each row of Table 2 corresponds to a pattern present in the summary given to the participants and each column represents the groups and their projects. Cells are labeled according to the following legend:

- "✓" - indicates that the pattern was identified in the final prototype of the corresponding group and was used in accordance with its proposal.
- "✗" - indicates that the pattern was not in accordance with its proposal (e.g., G3 used the pattern "A2 Overlay" in an application that requires high cognitive effort and did not provide a reason for the choice).
- "C" - indicates that there is a conflict among the patterns used (e.g., G5 used all the existing layouts). Preferably, the application should use the same layout across its different interfaces in order to keep the application's identity.
- "?" - Indicates that the pattern should have been used according to the television context (e.g., "D1 Initial Call to Action" or "D4 Exiting"), or according to the design requirements identified (e.g., "I1 Accessibility"), but, for different reasons, they were not used.
- The cells that do not have marks indicate that the patterns were not identified in the project, and have no direct implications in the final prototype.

Table 2. List of Patterns Used in Final Prototypes

Padrão	G2	G3	G4	G5	G6	G7	G8
A2 OVERLAY		x		C			
A3 FULL-SCREEN WITH VÍDEO				C	✔	C	C
A4 FULL-SCREEN WITHOUT VÍDEO	✔		✔	C		C	C
B2 MENU	✔	✔	✔	✔	✔	✔	✔
B4 INDEX						✔	✔
B5 PAGE NUMBERS				✔			
B6 TABS		✔		✔		✔	
C2 ARROW KEYS	✔	✔	✔	✔	✔	✔	✔
C3 OK-KEY	✔	✔	✔	✔	✔	✔	✔
C4 COLOUR KEYS	✔	✔		✔		✔	✔
C5 NUMBER KEYS		✔				✔	✔
C6 SPECIAL KEYS							
D1 INITIAL CALL TO ACTION	?	?	?	?	?	✔	?
D2 STARTING	?	✔	?	?	?	✔	?
D3 LOADING INDICATION	?	?	?	?	?	✔	?
D4 EXITING	?	✔	✔	✔	?	✔	✔
D5 HIDING APPLICATION	?	✔	?	✔	?	✔	?
D6 GOING ONE LEVEL UP	✔	✔	✔	✔	✔	✔	✔

Padrão	G2	G3	G4	G5	G6	G7	G8
E1 TEXT DESIGN	✔	✔	✔	✔	✔	✔	✔
E2 CONTENT BOX	✔	✔	✔	✔	✔	✔	✔
E3 PAGING			✔				
E4 SCROLLING			✔		✔	x	✔
E5 SWITCHING BETWEEN CONTENT ITEMS	✔	✔	✔	✔	✔	✔	✔
E6 SYNCHRONISED CONTENT		✔	✔	✔		✔	
F2 VOTING AND MULTIPLE-CHOICE QUESTION					✔		x
F3 ALLOCATION OF ITEMS							
F4 TEXT COMPLETION							
F5 APPROVAL FOR CONNECTIVITY	?	?	?	?	?	?	?
G2 ON-SCREEN QWERTY OR ALPHABETICAL KEYBOARD			x	✔	✔	?	
G3 MOBILE PHONE KEYBOARD						?	✔
H1 ON-SCREEN INSTRUCTION	✔		✔	✔	✔	✔	✔
H2 HELP SECTION	✔	✔	✔	✔	✔	✔	✔
I1 ACCESSIBILITY	?	?	✔	?	?	?	?
I2 PERSONALISATION	✔		✔	✔		✔	
J1 CHILDREN	x						

According to Table 2, the majority of patterns were used as proposed by Kunert [11]. This is an indication that participants paid attention and recognized the patterns as a reference for their projects. The participants had no previous experience in the use of patterns, so this is a positive indication of the patterns' ease of learning and their use in a practical context.

It was also possible to identify problems with the use of some patterns. G2, for example, used colorful ("C4 Colour Keys") and numerical ("C5 Number Keys") keys to design a game for children. However, these patterns are not compatible with the pattern "J1 Children", created especially for this audience. The "E4 Scrolling" (Scrollbar) was used improperly by groups G6 and G8. G6 did not indicate how to interact properly with the scrollbar and, as G8, did not show the correct status, or percentage, of the scrollbar along the body of the document. Just like G5, G7 and G8 also used more than one layout type in their applications, which may disperse the user's attention. Moreover, G8 did not use the pattern for multiple choices correctly ("F2 Voting and Multiple-Choice Question"), replacing the Arrows and OK ("C2 Arrow Keys" and "C3 OK-Key") keys by the numeric ("C5 Number Keys") keys to select few alternatives in a question. Once the number of choices was not greater than four, the use of arrows and OK keys would require less visual and cognitive effort.

In addition to the mentioned examples, some patterns could only be perceived when analyzing the interactive prototype (e.g., "D6 Going One Level Up" and "E5

Switching Between Content Items") because they represent dynamic transactions among the prototype's screens. The CogTool® proved to be effective in identifying these patterns, because it allows the modeling of tasks and the generation of interactive prototypes. Specific patterns for iDTV context, such as "D1 Initial Call to Action" and "D2 Starting", were not considered by most groups, which may indicate lack of contact with iDTV applications. The "D4 Exiting" pattern, which is essential for the user to return to the main television content, was neglected by G2 and G6. This may be a consequence of the inexperience of designers and the lack of contact with television applications.

An important pattern for the Brazilian economic context, "F5 Approval for Connectivity", was neglected in all the projects. Usually, there is a cost associated with connection and data transmission, so ignoring this aspect can trigger problems related to the user experience and also to legal and economic issues. Another important pattern that was neglected was "I1 Accessibility". This pattern was considered by G4, but was overlooked by the other groups preventing people with disabilities to use the application.

3.2   Preliminary Evaluation

The responses to the evaluation questionnaire indicated that the design patterns were actually useful in assisting the groups in designing their prototypes. For example, G2 mentioned that "iDTV is still an equipment that few people have access to. The patterns approximate of iDTV most of the participants".

Regarding the use of patterns, groups were asked about the usefulness and contribution of patterns to support the design of application prototypes. Two groups answered that the patterns contributed strongly and were fundamental to project development; four groups answered that they contributed moderately, and in one group, there was disagreement among the participants and the response of the group was classified as indifferent. No group answered that the patterns did not contribute or made the activity difficult.

The groups were also asked to express why and how the patterns were (or were not) important for designing the prototypes. Of the seven groups, only the participant of G7 who reported no contribution of patterns in the previous question did not provide a positive response. For G2, "the patterns were important, because it is hard to think of a project without knowledge about the technology". In this same sense, G6 added that "patterns contributed by providing ideas on how to design the prototype", and G3 mentioned that "the patterns served as inspiration" and "they were not restrictive, because it was possible to identify different ways of presenting the application's content". Similarly to G3, G5 mentioned that "the iDTV patterns supported design choices, but creativity and planning are also important". G4 said that "patterns served to maintain the cohesion of the designed content". Finally, G8 emphasized that "patterns were crucial for explaining the features and limitations that the group would face during the design".

The lack of concern regarding accessibility in the prototypes is critical. Considering the television in a context of high diversity, which is the case in Brazil, ignoring accessibility issues means imposing barriers on inclusion and directly impacting values that are of emotional and affective nature (e.g., autonomy, well-being, satisfaction), as well as on the right of access to knowledge and the exercise of citizenship.

Asked about the possibility of an authoring tool specifically for iDTV, two groups answered that an authoring tool would contribute strongly, and five groups said it would contribute moderately. None of the groups said they would be indifferent, did not contribute or made the activity difficult.

Finally, the groups were asked to leave suggestions and ideas for an authoring tool for iDTV applications. G2 and G6 suggested a graphical tool that incorporates predefined patterns for iDTV, similar to Balsamiq®. In this tool it would be possible to easily distribute and exchange elements of graphics (e.g., layout, menus, buttons, etc.). Additionally, G7 and G8 envisioned a tool similar to CogTools®, which could make the transition between different application screens in a storyboard style, but which would also allow the design of individual layouts. For G3 and G4, it would be interesting to have a tool with an easy-to-use graphical module (beginner mode), but that also generates code and is usable in programming mode.

4   Conclusion

Both the use and creation of iDTV applications are still a distant reality for many people as well as for designers involved with the creation of interactive systems. Unlike a PC or Web application, an iDTV design requires some special care due to the lack of specific tools and references for creating applications.

In the case study presented in this paper, the participants, with no previous contact with iDTV applications, used a pattern collection, prototyping tools and techniques inspired on participatory design to support the prototyping of iDTV applications. The results showed that the patterns were widely accepted by the participants and helped to establish a first contact with iDTV design. The misuse of some patterns may indicate the lack of contact with the technology and may also suggest that the patterns must not be taken in isolation. The results obtained from the case study also indicated that the use of an adapted version of the Brain Drawing, combined with the design patterns, was adequate in guiding the designers in the first stages of developing their prototypes. The technique contributed by encouraging participants to outline their views on the project, while the patterns helped to guide their ideas.

Finally, the lack of techniques and specific resources for iDTV makes it difficult to create prototypes or applications. Incorporating design patterns in authoring tools is potentially an important subject for further work.

Acknowledgment. The authors thank the participants of the case study who voluntarily collaborated and authorized the use of their project documentations in this paper. This research is partially funded by CNPq through the EcoWeb Project (#560044/2010-0).

References

1. Alexander, C.: The Timeless Way of Building. Oxford University Press, Oxford (1979)
2. Baranauskas, M.C.C., Souza, C.S.: Desafio 4: Acesso Participativo e Universal do Cidadão Brasileiro ao Conhecimento. Computação Brasil VII(23), 7 (2006)
3. Borchers, J.: A Pattern Approach to Interaction Design. John Wiley & Sons Ltd, England (2001)
4. Brazilian Forum for Digital Television, http://www.forumsbtvd.org.br
5. Brazilian Presidential Decree No 4.901, http://www.planalto.gov.br/ccivil_03/decreto/2003/d4901.htm
6. Cesar, P., Chorianopoulos, K., Jensen, J.F.: Social Television and User Interaction. Computers in Entertainment 6(1), 1–10 (2008)
7. Chung, E.S., Hong, J.I., Lin, J., Prabaker, M.K., Landay, J.A., Liu, A.L.: Development and evaluation of emerging design patterns for ubiquitous computing. In: 5th Conference on Designing Interactive Systems: Processes, Practices, Methods, and Techniques, pp. 233–242. ACM Press, New York (2004)
8. Gamma, E., Helm, R., Johnson, R., Vlissides, J.: Design Patterns: Elements of Reusable Object-Oriented Software. Addison-Wesley, Boston (1995)
9. Ginga-NCL, http://www.gingancl.org.br
10. IBGE (National Survey by Household Sample), http://www.ibge.gov.br/home/download/estatistica.shtm
11. Kunert, T.: User-Centered Interaction Design Patterns for Interactive Digital Television Applications. Springer, New York (2009)
12. Liu, K.: Semiotics in Information Systems Engineering. Cambridge University Press, Cambridge (2000)
13. Montero, F., Lozano, M., González, P.: A First Approach to Design Web Sites by Using Patterns. In: Second Latin American Conference on Pattern Languages of Programming, pp. 137–158. Microsoft Business Solution, Denmark (2002)
14. Muller, M.J., Haslwanter, J.H., Dayton, T.: Participatory Practices in the Software Life-cycle. In: Helander, M.G., Landauer, T.K., Prabhu, P.V. (eds.) Handbook of Human-Computer Interaction, 2nd edn., pp. 255–297. Elsevier, Amsterdam (1997)
15. Open Ginga, http://gingacdn.lavid.ufpb.br/projects/openginga
16. Pereira, R., Buchdid, S.B., Baranauskas, M.C.C.: Keeping Values in Mind: Artifacts for a Value-Oriented and Culturally Informed Design. In: 14th International Conference on Enterprise Information System, pp. 25–34. SciTePress, Portugal (2012)
17. Pereira, R., Buchdid, S.B., Miranda, L.C., Baranauskas, M.C.C.: Considering Values and Cultural Aspects in the Evaluation of Interactive Systems Prototypes. In: International Conference on Information Society, pp. 395–400. IEEE Press, New York (2012)
18. Piccolo, L.S.G., Baranauskas, M.C.C.: Desafios de design para a TV digital interativa. In: VII Brazilian symposium on Human factors in computing systems, pp. 1–10. ACM Press, New York (2006)
19. Sousa, K., Mendonça, H., Furtado, E.: Applying a multi-criteria approach for the selection of usability patterns in the development of DTV applications. In: VII Brazilian symposium on Human factors in computing systems, pp. 91–100. ACM Press, New York (2006)
20. Waisman, T.: Usabilidade em Serviços Educacionais em Ambiente de TV Digital. Doctoral thesis, 201 p. School of Communication and Arts, University of São Paulo (2006)

Design Process and Knowledge Searching Model Based on User Creativity

Chia-Ling Chang[1,*] and Ding-Bang Luh[2]

[1] Department of Creative Product Design and Management, Far East University
49, Zhonghua Rd., Xinshi Dist., Tainan City 74448, Taiwan (R.O.C.)
[2] Department of Industrial Design, National Cheng Kung University
1, University Road, Tainan City 70101, Taiwan, (R.O.C.)
{idit007,dingbangluh}@gmail.com

Abstract. With the rising of the open innovation notion, satisfying user's creative needs of has become a focus in new product development. Products that facilitate user's creativity can be regarded as a kind of creative platform. Extending the concept of user innovation, this study explored two issues based on "user creativity orientation". First, a design process based on user's creativity platform (UCP) is proposed for designers and enterprises, which includes eight steps: (1) explore user's creativity needs, (2) classify functionality of the product, (3) develop primary and secondary components, (4) design a creativity-friendly interface, (5) prototype components, (6) examine UCP product features, (7) evaluate user's creation experience, and (8) assess the potential creativity of the user's outcomes. Through the process, a set of school-aged toy allowing user successive design are developed for children. The proposed model is feasible and effective and can elevate the idea of design from the level of pure product design to a creative platform and experience design, assist industries in developing platform products and meeting the users' needs for self-accomplishment. Additionally, in order to explore the user's search behavior for design knowledge in self-design activity, this study proposes a methodology and tools and takes the highly-involved LEGO players as the subjects to construct a "model of user's search behavior for design knowledge". With the proposed method, the users can be categorized by length of involvement and breadth of experience content into four kinds of status types of users, and nine essential knowledge attributes and eight key search approaches can be gained. According to the constructed model, the enterprise's role as enabler and users' role as designer can be further explored in design research and marketing strategy of products. The design knowledge and skills of highly-involved users will advance form a few individual hobby to a creative experience industry. It is also anticipated to offer enterprises with effective applications of users' design resources and create new energy on knowledge economy.

Keywords: User Creativity-Oriented, User Involved Design, Design Knowledge, Search Behavior.

---

* Corresponding author.

A. Marcus (Ed.): DUXU/HCII 2013, Part I, LNCS 8012, pp. 469–478, 2013.
© Springer-Verlag Berlin Heidelberg 2013

1   Background

As the course of the economic evolution follows the changes of consumption, from the previous agricultural economy, industrial economy and service economy to the age of experience economy, the gradual progress of economic value is divided into four stages: commodities, goods, services, and experiences. Users are getting more and more interested in "the involved experience and emotion gained from the interaction with products" instead of the products themselves. It is increasingly common for user's participation or involvement in new product and new service development (Morrison, Roberts, and von Hippel, 2000). E. von Hippel (1998, 2005) pointed out that users have become a major source of innovation in the process of product innovation.   The wide variety of information available has sparked a lot of creativities in the new generation of users. Users often have creative ideas in their daily lives and want to design and show individual unique creativity through themselves creations. Therefore, Luh and Chang (2007) proposed the concept and characterization of "user creativity-oritented" and called "User Successive Design (USD)". "User creativity-oriented design" gradually becomes one of the key points of product and service innovation (Holbrook, 1996, Thomke and von Hippel., 2002, Moreau and Dahl, 2005) and many entrepreneurs start to learn to trust, opening up part of the right of design and creation to the users.

Some highly-involved users possess design techniques and knowledge to redesign the appearance and function of products, gradually, users' creativity and design knowledge is increasingly discussed as the potential and ideal resources to design new product and develop new service (Szmigin and Carrigan, 2000, Ulwick, 2002, Kristensson et al., 2004, Chu and Chan, 2009, and Essén and Östlund, 2011). The roles users play are from simply consumers upgrade to contributors for creativity and design knowledge.

According to the above literature review, the products which facilitate user's creativity can be viewed as a creativity platform. Users can create and recreate new products to a certain degree and become a successive product designer. At this moment, one of the most feasible ways to achieve users' own creativity is for designers to develop the platformizaton products, which can then direct the user to freely create and successively design. Due to the lack of a design process and methodology for explore how user search for design knowledge that concerns users' creative needs, this study proposes two potential issues to meet the above expectations.

Extending the concept of user innovation, this study explored two issues based on user's creativity-oriented. As the platformization of products has become the trend, first, this study targeted at physical products and proposed a design process of platform. Incorporate the concept of assessment rarely seen in general product design models, and add evaluation items, criteria and methods into the development steps. Second, we proposed the methodology to explore the user's search behavior in self-design activity. Figure 1 illustrates the relevance of two user creativity-oriented issues.

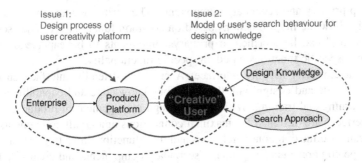

Fig. 1. The relevance of two user creativity-oriented issues

2   A Design Process of User Creativity Platform

User creativity platform is combined with different units rather than with a completed product. The process of User Creativity Platform (UCP) consists of eight steps (Fig.2), the resulting designs allow users to successively design and control part of the right to further re-invent the forms and functions of the product. Following the design process of User Creativity Platform, a school-aged toy is successfully developed.

Step 1	Step 2	Step 3	Step 4	Step 5	Step 6	Step 7	Step 8
Explore user creativity needs	Classify functionality of the product	Develop primary and secondary component	Design creativity-friendly interface	Prototype component	Examine UCP product features	Evaluate user's creation experience	Assess creativity potential of user's outcomes
Method: •observation, •Interviews, •Questionnaire, •Product Analysis, ... Define creativity need Set design target	Common → functionality Specific → functionality	Primary component Secondary component	Physical interface Cognitive interface	•3D rendering •Rough model •Function model	**Who:** Design expert **What:** UCP product **Criterion:** Four features of UCP	**Who:** Target user **What:** User's creation process **Criterion:** •User-friendliness •Accomplishment of Targets •Self- satisfaction	**Who:** Domain expert **What:** User's outcome **Criterion:** •Originality •Flexibility •Fluency •Elaboration
Development stage					Evaluation stage		

Fig. 2. A design process of user creativity platform

1. Explore user's creativity needs: Conventional design analysis methods, including user observation, questionnaires, product analysis, in-depth interviews, and ethnography, among others, can be applied to define user's potential creativity needs for future products. Design targets of products can be set accordingly.
2. Classify functionality of the product: Based on degree of shared abilities, functionality of a product can be classified into two categories. The "common functionality" refers to functionality that can simultaneously achieve more than two design targets. The "specific functionality", however, can only suit specific targets.

3. Develop primary and secondary components: The "primary components" can individually show the main functions based on common functionality. The "secondary components" can be attached to primary components to be capable of showing their own specific functions based on specific functionality.

4. Design a creativity-friendly interface: A creativity-friendly interface encourages users to create and design with their previous knowledge and capabilities without extra learning and training. With proper design management of product semantics, the interfaces are designed for maximal connections among all components so that users can redefine component relations and their functionalities to greatest extent.

5. Prototype components: The primary, secondary components and creativity-friendly interfaces are prototyped for further testing. They can be in form of a functional model for operation testing or an appearance mockup for perception validation.

6. Examine UCP product features: Inviting design professionals to check whether the product conforms to the requirements, namely reconfigurable components, creativity-friendly interfaces, open right design, and tolerance of unerror (Chang and Luh, 2009). If any of them is unmet, return to Step 2.

7. Evaluate user's creation experience: Target users are invited to successively design the product then evaluate the friendliness of the product interface, the degree of accomplishment of targets and self-satisfaction. This assessment should be according to user's own cognition and experience during the creation process of redesigning the product.

8. Assess creativity potential of user's outcomes: Domain experts compare the creativity potential of the user's outcomes from the developed UCP product and from other products with similar functionalities. In theory, a UCP should stand out in at least one of the four common creativity aspects of originality, flexibility, fluency and elaboration (Torrance and Orlow, 1984).

Based on the above UCP process, an innovative toy design was developed. Prototypes of the new design were tested by 20 pre-school kids. From their creative works, advancement of the proposed process can be seen. The toy can not only support 2D and 3D form designs, but also 4D form creations, for instances, wearable features and interactive functionalities.

3   A Model of User's Search Behavior for Design Knowledge

The study qualitatively proposes a feasible method to establish a framework which explores the user's search approaches for the needed design knowledge in the "design by user-self" process. The method can be applied to modular products with the "user's creativity-oriented" characteristic such as handicraft products, system furniture, assembled toy, and so on. The LEGO players are used as subjects for explanation. Following this method, a model of highly-involved users' searching approaches for design knowledge can built. The practice contents of methodology are introduced as follows:

1. Identification of design attributes and search approach: Identification of design attributes and search approach: Through KJ method, design knowledge stated by related studies are categorized into Product knowledge, Technique knowledge, Thinking knowledge, Experience knowledge, and Inspiration knowledge. Similarly, based on current information communication channels about LEGO, four aspects of information searching and searching approaches were identified.
2. Questionnaire development: Based on the characteristics of the LEGO bricks and LEGO players' cognition, the Design Knowledge Questionnaire (Table 1) and the Information Search Questionnaire with encoded items were developed (Table 2).

Table 1. Design Knowledge Questionnaire

Category	Design knowledge attributes
Product knowledge	A1.Component shape
	A2.Component color
	A3. Component size
	A4. Component material characteristic
	A5. Component price
Technique knowledge	B1.Component connection method
	B2.Component connection step
	B3.Object construction technique
	B4. Auxiliary tools application method
	B5. Structure constitution principle
Thinking knowledge	C1. Freehand sketch presentation method
	C2. 2D CAD presentation
	C3. 3D presentation method
	C4. Form esthetics concept
	C5. Color scheme skill
	C6. Design development step
	C7. Design thinking method
Experience knowledge	D1. Object operation intuition
	D2. Personal practice experience
	D3. Fellows' experience exchange
	D4. Expert instruction
Inspiration knowledge	E1. Intentional inspiration
	E2. Unintentional inspiration

3. Items Convergence: Three highly-involved users without institutional design educations were invited to do pre-test to increase the validity of the questionnaires and to converge the items.
4. Subject selection: The ideal subject has to meet the basic requirements with at least continuous five years of LEGO creation experiences and one of the following four qualifications: having LEGO works approved by peers, having LEGO works exhibited in public, having managed LEGO related groups or organizations, and having received LEGO creative contest awards.
5. Categorization of status type of subject: According to the above four qualifications, the statuses of highly-involved users were classified into four types: (1) Junior Expert (JE), who has works admired by peers, (2) Exhibition Participator (EP), who has works exhibited in public, (3) Business Manager (BM), who has managed LEGO related organizations, and (4) Award Winner (AW), who has received LEGO related creative contest awards. If a subject has two or more experience qualifications, only the most unusual one will be selected as his/her status type.

Table 2. Approach of information search

W. Self-learning	X. Fellow group	Y. Enterprise and society resource
W1. Instructional manual	X1. Joining fellow group	Y1. Themed books published by enterprise
W2. Related books	X2. Visiting exhibition held by fellow group	Y2. Regular magazine
W3. Newspaper and magazine	X3. Themed books published by fellow group	Y3. Membership club
W4. Internet knowledge searches	X4. Fellow group's electronic bulletin board	Y4. On-line simulation
W5. Physical store/online store	X5. On-line interactive forum (e.g. facebook)	Y5. Electronic newspaper
W6. Expert's blog	X6. On-line work exhibition	Y6. Contest sponsored
W7. Related television program	X7. Personal communication	Y7. Training course
W8. Advertisement	X8. Group gathering	Y8. Expert on-site demonstration
W9. Personal past experience	X9. Regular magazine published by fellow group	Y9. Expert on-line teaching
W10. Leisure activity		Y10. Upload system of enterprise
		Y11. Themed exhibitions
		Y12. Themed museum
		Y13. Themed park

6. Sampling: Three local professional LEGO users were taken as the initial subjects in snowball sampling. Each subject was asked to recommend at least two qualified subjects for each of the four status types as the next subjects, and the recommendations continued until two or more subjects in the same status type do not add or modify any opinion. Consequently, each of the four status types had four valid subjects when the information was saturated.

7. Interview with questionnaires: In the Design Knowledge Questionnaire, each subject was asked to select twelve comparatively important design knowledge attributes out of twenty-three. In the Information Search Questionnaire, the subject was asked to choose the effective search approaches. Each subject was interviewed about the reasons behind their answers in accordance with the results after finishing all questionnaires.

8. Content confirmation: The items selected by majority were regarded as the representative design knowledge attributes in a status type. For items selected by less than majority, the interviews about the subjects' answers were reviewed to determine if the items should be excluded.

9. Information integration: The results of design knowledge attributes selected by each user status type were illustrated via the Venn diagram (Fig 3). Based on the convergence number of user status type, four design knowledge gradations were identified: Essential Knowledge (EK), Main Knowledge (MK), Secondary Knowledge (SK), and Peculiar Knowledge (PK). Applying the same procedure, the distribution of search approaches selected. The search approaches selected by all status types of users were regarded as key search approaches which serve as the threshold for becoming highly-involved, consisting of eight items.

10. Matrix integration: the matrix of design knowledge gradation and search approach of highly-involved users was established. For simplification, duplications were merged (Table 3. Clearly, nine EK attributes and eight key search approaches are shared by all four user status types.

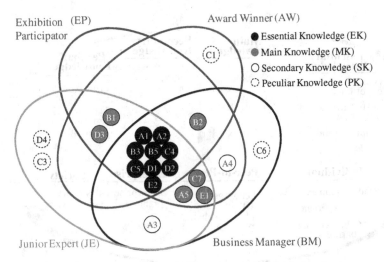

Fig. 3. Distribution of knowledge attributes for the highly-involved users

Table 3. Matrix of design knowledge and search approach of highly-involved users

Knowledge gradation		Status type of user			
		Junior Expert	Exhibition Participator	Business Manager	Award Winner
Peculiar	Attribute	C3, D4	n/a	C6	C1
Knowledge	Approach	n/a	n/a	n/a	n/a
Secondary	Attribute	A3	A4	A3, A4	n/a
Knowledge	Approach	n/a	Y4	n/a	n/a
Main	Attribute	A5, B1, C7, D3, E1	A5, B1, B2, C7, D3, E1	A5, B2, C7, E1	B1, B2, D3
Knowledge	Approach	n/a	W6, X7	W6, X9	X6, X9, Y6, Y11
Essential	Attribute	A1, A2, B3, B5, C4, C5, D1, D2, E2			
Knowledge	Key approach	W1, W4, W5, W9, X1, X2, X5, X8			

11. Concept generalization: Regards all status types of highly-involved users as a whole, based on the "Matrix of design knowledge and search approach for highly-involved user" (within the "attribute" column of the same knowledge category, merge the knowledge attributes that have similar meaning and propose an integrated conceptual name. Applying the same procedure, generalized concepts of search approaches were obtained. (Not listed, due to the exceeding amount of information.)

12. Framework construction: At knowledge gradation, four kinds of gradations were placed from its left to right based on their levels of importance. The generalized concepts of design knowledge attributes were sequentially filled in according to their knowledge gradations. At search aspects, them were put along relations with users between self and communities from left to right. The generalized concepts of search approaches were filled in proper positions. Consequently, a framework of searching design knowledge of highly-involved users can be established in Fig 4.

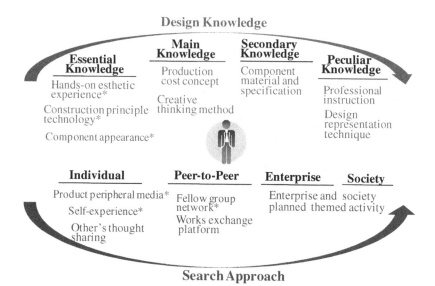

Fig. 3. The model of highly-involved users' searching approaches for design knowledge

4   Discussion and Implication

4.1   Meaning of UCP Design Process

Compared with the original site-simulation assembly toys of the manufacturer, the components of UCP toys developed by the study possess higher sharability, and the creativity interface is highly user-friendly. Users' creation outcomes are not only rich in design and functionality, but also go beyond the scope of the site-simulation. The proposed UCP design can help the manufacturers in opening new product lines, developing innovative products that meet users' creativity needs, and eventually elevating the innovation value of the enterprises.

The UCP design process elevates the idea of design from pure product design to the level of creativity platform and experience design, creates new value of design, assists industries to develop platform products, and meets the users' needs for self-accomplishment.

4.2   Implication of the Model of Highly-Involved Users' Searching Approaches for Design Knowledge

From the design knowledge in Figure 4, it can be found that level of the Essential Knowledge is the most important due to design knowledge with the most "*". Hands-on esthetic experience, Construction principle technique, and Component appearance are the most fundamental design knowledge that highly-involved users adopt first.

These can be regarded as the main principles for evaluating the maturity of user's design ability. In Main Knowledge, Creative thinking method helps group brainstorming and arouses diversified creative inspirations; whereas Production cost concept helps estimate product development time and costs from the design inspiration stage to the completion stage. As for Peculiar Knowledge, Design presentation technique can help users not only record creative ideas and construction steps, but also express ideas to other. When users provide design consulting services to others or enterprises by utilizing personal design knowledge and skills, their works and individual values also upgrade. The user innovation model may gradually replace professional model and users have the potential of personal brand.

The proposed model demonstrates the process difference between users and designers in applying design knowledge chain. The application value of this model can be described from three aspects: (1) Enhancing the importance of user innovation mode, (2) Helping establish the companionship between enterprises and users, and (3) Developing creative resources of industries and design knowledge chain.

5   Conclusions

As a result, a model of highly-involved users' searching approaches for design knowledge was established. The highly-involved LEGO is taken as the subjects to verify the feasibility and usefulness of proposed methods and tools, and this can be regarded as a fundamental study on exploring users' design knowledge.

13. Introduce the concept and four features of user creativity-oriented products: open design rights, tolerance for unerror, reconfigurable components, and creativity-friendly interfaces. Conceptually speaking, acceptance of "unerror" is greater than the allowance of error in essence.
14. The design process effectively develops toys more advanced than other products of the same category in the aspects of allowing innovation of the outcomes, improving interpersonal interaction, and the high sense of ownership.
15. The proposed research method and tools are feasible in exploring the user's search behavior for design knowledge. Following the method and tools, a model of highly-involved users' searching approaches for design knowledge can be established.
16. Hands-on esthetic experience, Construction principle technique, and Component appearance are found the most essential knowledge attributes, and Product peripheral media, Self-experience, and Fellow group network are identified as core search approaches for highly-involved users.

Acknowledgement. This paper is partially sponsored by National Science Council, Taiwan (NSC 101-2410-H-006-067-MY2). Moreover, we would like to thank designers Li-Yu Lin, Tzu-Husan Yu, and Yi-Ying Hsieh for assisting the product case development.

References

1. Chang, C.L., Luh, D.B.: A Study on Users Search Behavior for Design Knowledge: the LEGO Players as Example. Journal of Convergence Information Technology 7(17), 25–35 (2012)
2. Chu, K., Chan, H.: Community Based Innovation: Its Antecedents And Its Impact On Innovation Success. Internet Research 19(5), 496–516 (2009)
3. von Hippel, E.: Economics of product development by users: The impact of sticky' local information. Management Science 44(5), 629–644 (1998)
4. von Hippel, E.: Democratizing Innovation: Users Take Center Stage. MIT Press, Boston (2005)
5. Essén, A., Östlund, B.: Laggards as Innovators? Old Users as Designers Of New Services & Service Systems. International Journal of Design 5(3), 89–98 (2011)
6. Holbrook, M.B.: Customer Value - A Framework For Analysis And Research. Advances in Consumer Research 23(1), 138–142 (1996)
7. Krippendorff, K., Butter, R.: Product Semantics: Exploring the Symbolic Qualities of Form. Innovation 3(1), 4–9 (1984)
8. Kristensson, P., Gustafsson, A., Archer, T.: Harnessing The Creative Potential Among Users. Journal of Product Innovation Management 21(1), 4–14 (2004)
9. Luh, D.-B., Chang, C.-L.: From Novice to Expert - User's Search Approaches for Design Knowledge. In: Kurosu, M. (ed.) HCD 2009. LNCS, vol. 5619, pp. 501–510. Springer, Heidelberg (2009)
10. Luh, D.B., Chang, C.L.: The Concept and Design Process of User Successive Designing. Journal of Design 12(2), 1–13 (2007)
11. Luh, D.B., Chang, C.L.: Incorporating Users' Creativity in New Product Development via a User Successive Design Strategy. International Journal of Computer Applications in Technology 32(4), 312–321 (2008)
12. Moreau, C.P., Dahl, D.W.: Designing the Solution: The Impact of Constraints On Consumers'; Creativity. Journal of Consumer Research 32(1), 13–22 (2005)
13. Morrison, P.D., Roberts, J.H., von Hippel, E.: Determinants of User Innovation and Innovation Sharing in A Local Market. Management Science 46(12), 1513–1527 (2000)
14. Szmigin, I., Carrigan, M.: The Older Consumer As Innovator: Does Cognitive Age Hold The Key? Journal of Marketing Management 16(5), 505–527 (2000)
15. Thomke, S., von Hippel, E.: Customers as Innovators: A New Way to Create Value. Harvard Business Review 80(4), 74–81 (2002)
16. Torrance, E.P., Orlow, E.B.: Torrance tests of creative thinking streamlined manual (revised). Book, Scholastic Testing Service, Inc. (1984)
17. Ulwick, A.W.: Turn Customer Input into Innovation. Harvard Business Review 80(1), 91–97 (2002)

Activity-Based Context-Aware Model

Yuanyuan Chen, Zhengjie Liu, and Juhani Vainio

Sino-European Usability Center, Dalian Maritime University, Dalian, China
{chenyy,liuzhj}@dlmu.edu.cn, hci.juhani.vainio@gmail.com

Abstract. Context awareness is an important part of mobile and ubiquitous computing research. Most of the existing studies have concentrated on technical implementations. There is a considerable gap between systems context-aware actions and human expectations. We made an Activity-based Context-Aware Model based on Activity Theory and human situation awareness theories. Activity-based Context-Aware Model based on Activity Theory describes human context awareness within activities, which could offer more accurate understanding of human context awareness and help the development of context-aware technology. This paper defines the Activity-based Context-Aware Model based on Activity Theory, and presents a case study of shopping activity, which initially verifies the validity of the model.

Keywords: Context-aware, Activity Theory, Situation awareness, Activity-based Context Awareness Model.

1 Introduction

Just like a friend who knows certain things about you and can offer assistance when in need, a context-aware computer can gather contextual information and then provide 'right services' for people at the 'right time' and 'right place'. According B. Schilit, 'Context-aware systems adapts according to the location of use, the collection of nearby people, hosts and accessible devices, as well as to changes to such things over time. A system with these capabilities can examine the computing environment and react to changes to the environment.'[1]. Research on context-aware computing have been carried out in context information acquisition, context modeling, context reasoning and systems architecture [2], in the fields of education, health care, tourism, smart home, shopping, entertainment among others.

The majority of context-aware system design and implementation are based on a more technical point of view. The most common and the simplest services powered by context awareness are location-based services (LBS). Most of the LBS can obtain fairly accurate location data by GPS or CellID, but positioning techniques indoors still have many of limitations for wide usage. Some context-aware systems can integrate many sensors, such as Myexperience, a context-aware experience sampling tool, that can take advantage of multiple device and sensory multimedia data, calendar, Bluetooth, GPS etc., but the users have to predefine the sensors as in what information is to be collected and in what conditions [3].

A. Marcus (Ed.): DUXU/HCII 2013, Part I, LNCS 8012, pp. 479–487, 2013.
© Springer-Verlag Berlin Heidelberg 2013

If an ideal context-aware system should be like a friend, with similar abilities as humans do, a major problem within current context-aware systems is the gap or mismatch between people's expectations and context system behaviors. This affects user's trust, acceptance and user experience of context-aware systems [4]. Thus, reducing this gap or mismatch is an important issue for research within context awareness. There are two main reasons for this problem. As already mentioned, the majority of existing studies in context-aware systems design and implementation are focusing on technical implementation, and there is a lack of understanding of human context awareness, as in how do we form our awareness of context. It is a combination of perception, memory and experience, which gives us the ability to make decisions in complex situations. This mental process is very complex, and it makes the context-aware systems design and implementation a challenge.

The design and implementation of context-aware systems should try to reduce the awareness mismatch between the user and the system. For reducing the gap, a thorough and systematic understanding of human context awareness, and models and methods for describing it are needed. This paper explores the characteristics of human context awareness and looks for ways to improve the user experience of context-aware systems. Based on human activities and related context elements, we propose our Activity-based Context-Aware Model (ABCAM). We have preliminary verified the validity of the model by a case study examining human shopping activities in a supermarket for analyzing the process of human context awareness.

This paper is organized as following. The second part describes the related theories; activity theory and theories of human situation awareness. In the third part, the ABCAM is proposed and introduced in detail. The fourth part introduces the case study of human context-aware processes of shopping activities. The last part describes the research conclusions and our future work.

2   Related Theories

ABCAM is built on activity theory and theories of situation awareness.

2.1   Activity Theory

Activities are fundamental components of human's daily life. Soviet psychologist Vygotsky proposed activity theory as a common conceptual framework to understand and analyze human activities in 1920s[5]. Activity theory describes the basic elements of an activity including subject, object, tools, community, rules and division of labor. The basic structure of activity theory is show as Fig. 1.

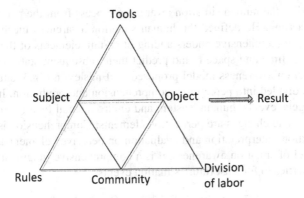

Fig. 1. Activity Theory diagram

An activity is the basic analysis unit in activity theory. An activity has three levels; purpose, functionality and reactivity. An activity is determined by subject's motivation and composed by actions. Actions are goal-directed and conscious. Different actions are executed by operations. Operations are unconscious or automatic. When some conditions are met, operations could be completed. Activities, behaviors and operations could change and transfer to each other dynamically. (As Fig.2)

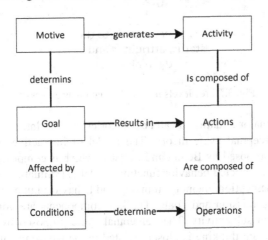

Fig. 2. Activity hierarchical structure

2.2   Theories of Situation Awareness

An important aspect of human cognition is situation awareness. Some of the earlier studies on human situation awareness were carried out on the industries related with aviation and control, emergency response, military command, and fuel and nuclear management. The tasks for the people operating in these industries are usually high on accuracy and time pressure, which demands good situation awareness to deal with some complex operations.

Endsley studies the human situation awareness process from the perspective of information processing. He defined the human situation awareness mechanism as [6]: "perception and comprehensive understanding of certain elements of the environment within a range of time and space t, and predict their subsequent status changes." According to situation awareness model proposed by Endsley in Fig.3, situation awareness process is divided into perception, comprehension and prediction. In the stage of perception, targets, events, human, system and environmental factors, and the related state, properties, and changes are perception elements; Comprehension is a process of pattern recognition, interpretation and evaluation on perceived elements; Prediction is the highest level of situation awareness, it is a comprehensive judgment according to states and properties to forecast future situation events.

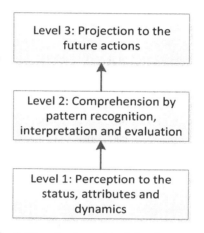

Fig. 3. Three levels model of situation awareness

The other two major situation awareness theories are the interactive sub-systems theory and the perceptual cycle theory. The model of interactive sub-systems is a theory of activity proposed by Bedny and Meister, which is composed of eight function blocks, and is a directed behavior function model [7]. Situation awareness is not the processing of perception, memory, thinking and behavior; but a process according to the nature of the mission and goals. The key components are conceptual model, goals and individual subjectivity. The perceptual cycle proposed by Neisser claims that the way people are thinking is closely related to the environment. In a particular environment, existing knowledge might lead to some expectations for the information and direct some behaviors of choosing and explanations of information [8].

3   Activity-Based Context Awareness Model

A system that is context aware should consider abundant contextual information and relations between them, and therefore we need methods to construct context awareness models describing the complexity [9] [10]. For to guiding the human situation awareness research, we propose a model of context awareness based on human activity, which describes and analyses human activities and human context awareness. The Activity-Based Context-Aware Model is based on combining the human situation awareness theories and activity theory, describing activities and contexts and the relation between them. According to activity theory, human activities can be divided into different behavioral phases and each behavioral phase is formed by several operations. Contextual factors related to subject, tool, physical environment, social environment and operation objects are included in an activity. A behavioral phase determines what context factors are active within the phase. The active context factors can be matched under rules and trigger behaviors when certain conditions are fulfilled or operations have occurred, as shown in Fig. 4. Subject, tool, object and environment related context elements exist within a specific activity (perception). A specific activity could be decomposed into different action phases, and each action phase is composed of several operations. Different action phases also have different active context elements and different trigger rules (comprehension); when these rules are satisfied, they may trigger behaviors (projection).

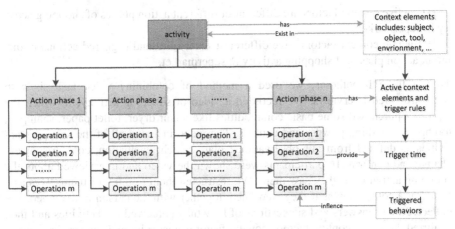

Fig. 4. Activity based context-aware model (ABCAM)

4   Case Study

A study to verify this model was conducted by examining normal supermarket shopping activity. We describe shopping as an enjoyable experience and an activity where customers can make decisions about what to buy. We think that if new technologies are introduced into the activity related to shopping, the purpose of them should be to make the experience more enjoyable rather than interruptive [11].

For confirming our activity-based context-aware model in a supermarket scenario, we needed to find out about and understand shopping activity. We did this by using activity theory by analyzing different behavioral phases of activities. The next thing we need to identify was the corresponding active context factors in different behavioral phases. After these steps, we analyzed the condition of active context factors and triggered actions. We then examined the process of human situation awareness within shopping activity in a supermarket including the division of action phases, active context factors in different behavioral phases, trigger rules and triggered actions.

Normally shopping behavior includes phases like planning, choosing and buying. We conducted field observations in a supermarket, and by using our Activity-Based Context-Aware model, we defined six action phases within shopping activity as plan, search, evaluate, compare, exchange and confirm. The operations within phases included look, touch, hold, release etc.

4.1   Experiment Design

Based on the normal customer behaviors and our field observation of active context factors in each behavioral phase, trigger rules of active context factor and triggered actions, we formed two basic hypotheses about action phases within shopping activity in a supermarket. The two basic hypotheses were:

H1: active context factors are different in different action phases of shopping activity in supermarket.

H2: active context factors have different trigger rules and triggered actions in different action phases of shopping activity in supermarket.

To test these hypotheses, we used a method of combining video analysis with semi-structured interviews. We recorded a video of shopping activity, in which the customer purchased some basic commodities like a hair dryer, toilet paper, shampoo, toothpaste, washing powder and cookies. The video included all of the shopping activities as defined from our observations: plan, search, evaluation, comparison, exchange and confirm. 16 participants were shown the video and interviewed about the shopping activities as they saw them. We instructed them to think of themselves as a friend or a companion as if they were there together with the person in the video. We collected their answers and suggestions of how they perceived the activities and then analyzed the active context factors, context factor trigger rules and triggered actions.

4.2   Results of the Experiment

1. Different action phases have different active context factors. (As Fig. 5)

Context factors can be divided into three categories in a shopping activity: purchaser-related, commodity-related and circumstance-related context factors. Commodity-related context factors include production attributes (brand, weight, material quality, level, etc.), sales attributes (price, sales volume, etc.) and use attribute (date of manufacture, packaging, etc.). Purchaser-related context factors include personal characteristic (gender, age, family, etc.), lifestyle (income, hobby, value, etc.) and purchase preference (brand or price preference, requirements for quality, etc.). Circumstance-related context factors include physical environment around (season, promotion, etc.) and social environment (friends experience suggestions, news reports, etc.)

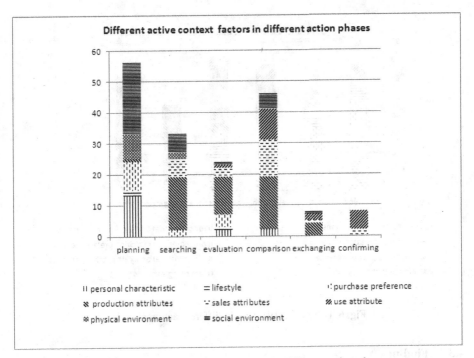

Fig. 5. Different active context factors in different action phases

2. As a shopping companion, the participants of the experiment suggested to offer different kinds of assistance to the person in the video or talk about different topics in different action phases.(As Fig. 6)

In the planning phase, the participants would provide advice or one's own shopping experience, including reminding about promotion information that could be suitable, offer sales information of a commodity or recommend brands according to the customers' preferences etc.

In the searching phase, the participants suggested to help finding commodities to match the needs of the customer.

In the evaluation phase, the participants suggested to evaluate the selected commodity and talk about whether it is suitable for customer preferences.

In the comparison phase, the participants suggested comparing two or more commodities and talk about which one is better or more suitable for the customer.

In the exchange phase, the participants suggested selecting a better one for the customer, and to get more detailed information about the preferences.

In the confirming phase, participant suggested paying more attention to the shelf life (expiration dates etc.) of a commodity and package, and to make sure about the price.

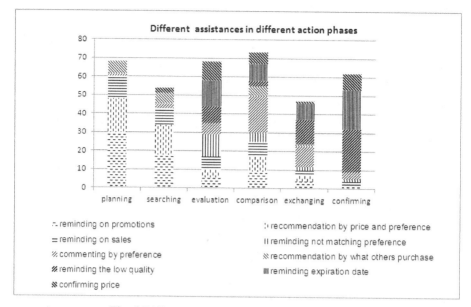

Fig. 6. Different assistances in different action phases

4.3   Findings

The result of this experiment verified our model of activity based context awareness. In a shopping activity, context factors can be divided into three parts: purchaser-related, commodity-related and circumstance-related context factors. In different action phases of shopping activity, there are different active context factors to help purchaser make decisions. The participants were aware of the different activities and suggested different assistance in different action phases. Through this experiment, the six action phases defined from the field observations were verified indirectly. The experiment was an initial test of accuracy and effectiveness of the Activity-Based Context-Aware Model.

5   Conclusion

Understanding human context awareness is a key point in designing context-aware system. This paper proposes our Activity-Based Context-Aware Model, which is based on activity theory and theories of human situation awareness. We have initially confirmed the rationality and validity of this model through field observation, video analysis and semi-structured interviews about shopping activity. Based on this model and experiment, our future work will seek to further optimize the model, and to continue to design and evaluate context-aware systems.

References

1. Schilit, B., Theimer, M.: Disseminating Active Map Information to Mobile Hosts. IEEE Network 8(5), 22–32 (1994)
2. Hong, J., Suh, E., Kim, S.-J.: Context-aware systems: A literature review and classification. Expert Syst. Appl. 36(4), 8509–8522 (2009)
3. Froehlich, J., Chen, M.Y., Consolvo, S., Harrison, B., Landay, J.A.: MyExperience: A system for in situ tracing and capturing of user feedback on mobile phones. In: Proceedings of the 5th International Conference on Mobile Systems, Applications and Services (MobiSys 2007), pp. 57–70. ACM, New York (2007)
4. Lim, B.Y., Dey, A.K.: Assessing demand for intelligibility in context-aware applications. In: Proceedings of the 11th International Conference on Ubiquitous Computing(Ubicomp 2009), vol. 204, pp. 195–204. ACM, New York (2009)
5. Kaptelinin, V.: Activity theory: Implications for human-computer interaction. In: Nardi, B. (ed.) Contexts and Consciousness. Activity Theory and Human-Computer Interaction, pp. 103–114. The MIT Press, Cambridge (1996)
6. Endsley, M.R.: Design and evaluation for situation awareness enhancement. In: Proceedings of the Human Factors Society 32nd Annual Meeting, pp. 97–101. Human Factors Society, Santa Monica (1988)
7. Bedny, G., Meister, D.: Theory of Activity and Situation Awareness. Int. J. Cognitive Ergonomics 3(1), 63–72 (1999)
8. Niesser, U.: Cognition and Reality: Principles and Implications of Cognitive Psychology. Freeman, San Francisco (1976)
9. Kaenampornpan, M., O'Neill, E.: Modelling context: an activity theory approach. In: Markopoulos, P., Eggen, B., Aarts, E., Crowley, J.L. (eds.) EUSAI 2004. LNCS, vol. 3295, pp. 367–374. Springer, Heidelberg (2004)
10. Bardram, J.E.: Activity-based computing for medical work in hospitals. ACM Transactions on Computer-Human Interaction (TOCHI) 16(2), 10 (2009)
11. Chu, M.: Natural and Implicit Interaction Systems. Computer 42(8), 109–111 (2009)

Satisfying Consumers' Needs through Systematic Empathic Design Model

Ming-Hsuan Hsieh[1,*], Ding-Bang Luh[2], Cheng-Yong Huang[3], and Chia-Hsiang Ma[2]

[1] Department of Industrial Engineering and Management, Overseas Chinese University,
Taichung City, Taiwan, ROC
[2] Department of Industrial Design, National Cheng Kung University,
Tainan City, Taiwan, ROC
[3] Department of Arts and Design, National Dong Hwa University,
Hualien County, Taiwan, ROC
mhhsieh@ocu.edu.tw, {luhdb,yufen}@mail.ncku.edu.tw,
yong@mail.ndhu.edu.tw,

Abstract. Customer-oriented customized design has become the key success factor in the process of product development. However, designers are typically unable to identify the actual demands of consumers to conduct customized designs because of numerous limitations. These limitations include consumers' lack of expressive abilities to clearly highlight their demands and designers' lack of measures and methods to effectively integrate consumer opinions. Thus, based on the proposed systematic empathic design model, the primary purpose of this study is to identify consumer demands. These demands can be identified by initially conducting participant observations to describe phenomena and applying the laddering method to obtain information. Then, the implication matrix was employed to facilitate analysis and the hierarchical value map was used to ensure the formulation and setting of the guidelines for demand. Finally, mind mapping was used to develop conceptual prototypes of the products. Through this combined process, customer satisfaction is achieved. This study contributes to the design industry by providing designers with a closely coordinated and clearly visible set of procedures for the initial stages of design process. This study endeavors to effectively satisfy the implicit demands of consumers and develop prototypes of customized products.

Keywords: Systematic Empathic Design Model, Customization, Consumer Demand, Concept Prototype.

1 Introduction

The current economic model has shifted from a production-oriented to a consumer-oriented model. Novel product development concepts have also evolved from highlighting production capacity enhancement, new techniques development, and better management methods formulation in the past, to the development of methods based

---

* Corresponding author.

A. Marcus (Ed.): DUXU/HCII 2013, Part I, LNCS 8012, pp. 488–497, 2013.
© Springer-Verlag Berlin Heidelberg 2013

on consumer demands that endeavor to identify and satisfy consumers' feelings towards products. Thus, under fixed constant variables, products that are co-manufactured with the participation of consumers gain greater preference among consumers [1]. The process of developing novel products is categorized into 4 stages, specifically, opportunity identification, development, optimization, and launch. Subsequently, successful novel product development is significantly influenced by whether opportunity identification accounts for the unmet needs of consumers [2]; thus, "listening to consumer aspirations" and "satisfying consumer needs" are focal topics that are vigorously discussed in modern product design. However, consumers' product demands typically change dynamically, are abstract and ambiguous, and are even unclear to the consumers themselves; therefore, methods to identify and convert these demands into approaches for design development have become key issues in the product development process. In other words, to truly achieve customization value, issues of specifying consumer satisfaction through design and identifying consumer needs should first be addressed; subsequently, demand trends should be anticipated prior to consumer recognition and applied in product design.

Consumers primarily take interest in certain products when these products retain specific significance to them. This significance originates from cognition, and is also the assessment criterion that determines purchase intention [3]; however, a gap exists between the cognitive models of designers and consumers [4]. In an age of product diversity, designers should extend beyond their trained and internalized thinking patterns when analyzing the consumer demands and preferences. Empathic design is a consumer-oriented design procedure that emphasizes the detailed observation of various phenomena that occur during the consumers' use of products. Consequently, by analyzing and understanding the produced affective viewpoints, customized products can be provided to individual consumers. However, the implementation of empathic design demands experiences and is extremely time consuming. Unlike traditional surveys, empathic design highlights the observation of consumers' daily lifestyles to collect five types of information otherwise difficult to obtain [5], specifically, data regarding triggers of use, interactions with the user's environment, user customization, intangible attributes of the product, and unarticulated user needs. Despite the general consensus regarding the importance of consumer demand and the various survey techniques that have been developed [6, 7, 8]; a specific method incorporating empathic design into product customization has yet to be established in the design industry. Thus, this study proposed the systematic empathic design model. This model was initially used to identify consumer opinions. These opinions were then analyzed and used to confirm consumer demands and formulate a product pre-development design orientation that expedites a product development trend capable of satisfying consumers.

2   Literature Review

2.1   Customization in Product Design

To obtain correct consumer demands, and subsequently tailoring these demands, is the first step in executing customization. In addition to considering market trends in the development of customized products, the planning and design of individual demands should be specifically incorporated into the numerous stages of design, manufacturing, and delivery [9]. Subsequently, adopting one-on-one methods to obtain customization demands is not only uneconomical, but also ineffective; thus, incorporating consumer preferences into product design is the primary challenge that is presented during customization processes. Customization elements should be considered in the design stage of a product to provide an entry point for consumer participation in product customization [10]. Based on practical observations, the customization can be sequentially categorized into four superficial to detailed dimensions, specifically, cosmetic, adaptive, collaborative, and transparent [11]. Customization demonstrates competitive advantage by diversifying products, changing products according to consumer demands, rapidly reflecting market shifts, and providing consumers with personalized products.

2.2   The Laddering Technique, Implication Matrix, and Hierarchical Value Map (HVM)

Products are stored as hierarchical structures of significance in one's cognitive memory; that is, the cascade process of product attributes, consumption consequences, and personal values. Consumers place greater value on attributes that are linked upwards to a more abstract value hierarchy [3]. These links can further be further categorized into six sub-hierarchies, specifically, physical characteristics, abstract characteristics, functional, psychosocial, instrumental-external, and terminal-internal [12]. The laddering technique is the most commonly applied qualitative method to collect means-end chains (MECs), which executes direct eliciting interviews to uncover the underlying values of consumers [13]. The main advantage of this technique is that it is able to retain the terms participants have selected during their descriptive decision-making process. This is particularly important because of the rapidly-changing use of language by present-day young people [14]. Pilot tests that were based on the categorization method proposed by Olson and Reynolds (1983) have found that the majority of consumers were unable to clearly describe the physical characteristics, abstract characteristics, instrumental-external, and terminal-internal hierarchies, but were able to clearly describe the functional and psychosocial hierarchies. In addition, numerous study results based on the laddering technique [14, 15, 16,] clearly suggested that the linking relationships in the MEC consequences hierarchy were significantly more intricate. Thus, this study retained the attributes and values hierarchies, but further categorized the consequences hierarchy into functional and psychosocial hierarchies.

The implication matrix was used to bridge the gaps in the qualitative and quantitative data; that is, to determine the relationship among the quantified elements [17]. The column-items stand for means and the row-items stand for ends. There are two ways to construct an aggregated Implication Matrix. (1) Through summing up the number of direct and indirect relations between all the pairs mentioned by subject; (2) Applying five-point scale questionnaire that asks the respondents to score the associations between two elements.

The development of a HVM was to graphically represent the analytical results of the implication matrix. Depicting all the element relationships within the matrix onto the HVM would be excessively complicated and the significant chains would be vague; thus, a HMV formulated using an aggregation approach must meet the following two criteria [18]: (1) elements that are included in the HVM must be proposed by 1/3 of the participants; and (2) the relationship of the direct link between two elements must be proposed by 1/4 of the participants. Subsequently, if a 5-point scale was used to measure the implication matrix data, the correlation between two elements are significant when the mean value of the two elements is greater than 3.60 [19].

2.3   Mind Mapping

Mind mapping is a structured radial mode of thinking that organizes messages based on hierarchies and categories [20]. The appearance and contours of a mind map comprises a core topic with many associations extending outward from the core topic. Each extending association formulates its own center point where sub-associations are subsequently generated and extended. Mind mapping is a visualized technique that presents the mental knowledge, ideas, concepts, and their mutual relations of an individual across a 2D plane [21]. Using mind mapping to generate ideas is extremely effective and useful, and facilitates the connection of each idea to other ideas and concepts [22]. The application of mind mapping not only assists designers in reorganizing past views, but also initiates unlimited creative ideas. This consequently creates a novel thinking framework.

3   Systematic Empathic Design Model Construction

Empathic design highlights the application of field observations and in-depth interviews to identify the problems and demands that consumers are unable to clearly express. However, during actual operations, this survey method is time-consuming and necessitates the surveyor to possess comprehensive experience and professional competency. Therefore, this study proposes a progressive model to systematically assist designers in satisfying the specific demands of individual consumers in varying environments. This further facilitates designers in providing suitable customized products that are customer-oriented. The proposed systematic empathic design model uses the participant observation method and the laddering technique to identify consumer demands, the implication matrix and HVM to analyze and confirm these demands, and mind mapping to satisfy these demands.

3.1   Understanding Consumers' Demands

Participant observation physically allocates surveyors into the observation group, and is a method that allows for the direct interaction between surveyor and consumer to effectively observe activity from within the group. The procedures in which this method is executed comprise the following: (1) surveyors select observation targets based on theme, arrange the observation schedule, and formulate observation items; (2) after acquiring participants' consensus, surveyors physically enter the observation environment, in which they engage in interpersonal interaction and employ strategies;

(3) when interacting with participants, surveyors must demonstrate cautious, honest, and unbiased attitudes to establish and maintain positive interactive relationships; (4) when conducting observations and collecting data, surveyors must uphold the key principles of "unfocused" observations; (5) surveyors must track all consumers' interactions with a specific product, during a service, or in a space, subsequently outlining their usage behaviors; and (6) surveyors must summarize the underlying responsive phenomena of the descriptive event, presenting these data on a phenomenon card. Phenomenon cards are composed of a group of images taken by the surveyors compensated by a set of descriptive text. These cards are then used as intermediaries during the laddering interviews to facilitate the focus group in linking the significance of their subconscious hierarchy.

Subsequently, the laddering method was employed to infer and allocate the observed phenomena into the 4 hierarchies of the means-end chain (e.g., as shown in Fig. 1). The procedures for the laddering method are as follows: (1) a group of designers were placed to a focus group; this group was instructed to select phenomenon cards they perceived as important or interesting prior to interviews; (2) initially, to link "phenomena" to "attributes," the question, "What is needed to improve it?" was asked; (3) then, the question, "Why is this important to you?" was asked; (4) content analysis was used to categorize the collected data into attributes, functional consequences, psychosocial consequences, and values hierarchies, simplifying, merging, and coding identical or similar significances; (5) Steps (1) to (4) were repeated and the next focus group was interviewed until no additional elements were added by the focus groups; consequently, this denoted that the elements have achieved representation. From the most physical phenomena to the most abstract values, this process facilitates consumer data to be more coherent and to demonstrate clearer causal relationships. In addition, the process of this stage facilitates interviewers to infer underlying cognitive structures that could not be observed.

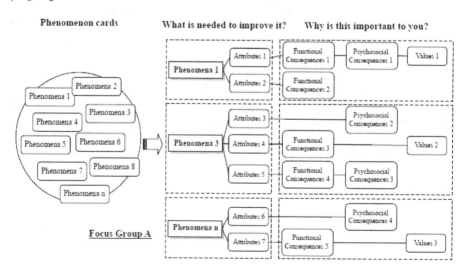

Fig. 1. Observing the phenomena → Laddering the cognition

3.2   Analyzing and Determining Consumers' Needs

Following the categorization and encoding of all the elements provided by the focus groups, the elements must then be converted into questionnaire form to allow target consumers to express the degree of relation between paired elements in different hierarchies. In this study, the 5-point scale was adopted as the scoring scale (e.g., as shown in Fig. 2). This type of implication matrix included weighted concepts that not only demonstrated relation and the differences in agreement levels, but could accurately reflect consumers' viewpoints.

Moreover, the data proved by the target consumer group was used to establish a summarized implication matrix. For example, the equation to calculate the association weight of each unit in the AF implication matrix was as follows:

$$\overline{A_i F_j} = \frac{\sum_{(i,j)=(1,1)}^{(24,13)} A_i F_j}{N} \tag{1}$$

where i is the number of attributes, ranging from 1 to 24; j the number of functional consequences, ranging from 1 to 13; N the number of consumers.

The A-F-P-V implication matrix can be converted into an HVM image, which can be used as a reference during the collective discussions of design teams. Based on the method proposed by Nielsen (1993), chains with mean values greater than 3.60 were illustrated. The thickness of the connecting lines represents the degree of relation between the paired elements (Fig. 3).

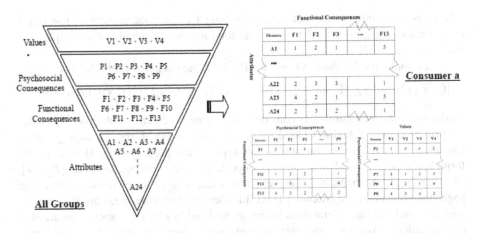

Fig. 2. Laddering the cognition → Implicating the matrix

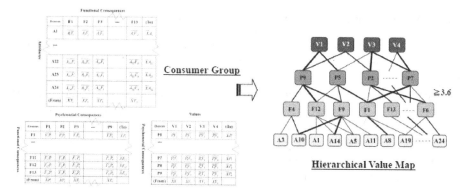

Fig. 3. Implicating the matrix → Hierarchy of the AFPV

3.3   Satisfying Consumers' Needs

Using HVM as the guidelines for product design is still overly complex. The From and To values of the various elements can be summed to further determine the strength of each complete chain and identify the several key chains for a simplified HVM. In Fig. 3, $\overline{X}_{A_i}$ denotes the means-association rating of attribute i, and can be calculated using the following equation:

$$\overline{X}_{A_i} = \frac{\sum_{j=1}^{13} \overline{A_i F_j}}{n} \qquad (2)$$

where i is the number of attributes, ranging from 1 to 24; j the number of functional consequences, ranging from 1 to 13; n the total number of functional consequences, with the value of 13.

For example, for the chain A1→F12→P9→V1, the strength of this chain is:

$$[0+\overline{X}_{A_1}(To)]+[\overline{X}_{F_{12}}(From)+\overline{X}_{F_{12}}(To)]+[\overline{X}_{P_9}(From)+\overline{X}_{P_9}(To)]+[\overline{X}_{V_1}(From)+0]$$

Designers can predominantly consider the stronger chains. Subsequently, after confirming design guidelines based on the streamlined HVM, mind mapping can be employed to develop the conceptual prototype of the product (Fig. 4). During the formulation of the mind map, several important basic skills are required [23, 24], specifically, (1) the theme must be presented in text or as an image in the center of the page; the core ideas are extended from this theme; these core ideas are the "conse-quences" and "values" hierarchies in the streamlined HVM; (2) associations are free and uncritical; (3) each supporting idea extending from the core idea should only illustrate 1 key image or keyword; the first supporting hierarchy extends possible products and service; the second supporting hierarchy extends the provided function or effect; (4) all supporting ideas must form a node structure; the line thickness for core and supporting ideas must vary; (5) during thinking gaps, several blank links can be added from a keyword (or an image) to stimulate thinking; (6) brain flow and brain bloom can be applied as the thinking methods; and (7) symbols, color, or images can be added to key opinions. The majority of investigatory research highlights the physical functions of products or services, and the immediate psychological satisfaction that these functions have on consumers; however, these studies neglected to examine the empathic benefits that these products or services provide, consequently failing to grasp the implicit opinions, experiences, feelings, and underlying context of the consumers. Thus, designers must focus on the "consequences" and "values" hierarchies when engaging in innovative product design.

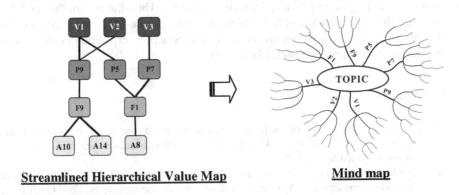

Streamlined Hierarchical Value Map   **Mind map**

Fig. 4. Hierarchy of the AFPV → Developing the concept prototype

4   Conclusion

In a time where consumers are demonstrating greater self-awareness, customization has inevitably become a key challenge for product designers. In this study, the proposed systematic empathic design model initially conducted a series of planned observations and monitoring on individual consumers using participant observation to obtain underlying consumer phenomena. Subsequently, the laddering method was employed to interview focus groups. These interviews facilitated interviewers to identify the implicit A-F-P-V linking network behind these phenomena. The implication matrix was used to conduct demand analysis by providing consumers with a scaled questionnaire. The consumers used this questionnaire to express their opinions on the relationship level of paired elements. The HVM was used to highlight and confirm the consumer market. The crucial customization demands obtained through the HVM facilitates designers in formulating design guidelines. Finally, mind mapping assists designers in developing a conceptual prototype of the product that is capable of satisfying consumers. In the systematic empathic design model, consumers play an extremely crucial role. They facilitate designers in developing customized products based on actual market needs. The primary value of the proposed model is as follows: (1) Clear definitions and connections are provided between each procedure. This not only allows consumers to effectively participate in product design, but also shortens the design process. (2) The phenomenon-attribute-functional consequence-psychosocial consequence-value connection process effectively guides and stratifies consumer demands, and facilitates designers in their idea formulation stages to implement customization. (3) Mind mapping assists designers in maintaining a balance between logical and imaginary thinking during conceptual design. This stimulates the designers to exert their full potential. In summary, the purpose of this study is to primarily introduce the systematic empathic design model, and the ways in which it effectively facilitates designers in satisfying the product demands of target consumers. Through the execution of this model, enterprises can more easily and rapidly adjust their product design orientation during market changes, and simultaneously take into account the key opinions provided by main consumers. Thus, the goal of this model is to ensure that designers not only focus on product functions and characteristics, but also provide consumers with a higher level of satisfaction, expediting consequences and values hierarchies of consumer behaviors.

References

1. Kramer, T.: The effect of preference measurement on preference construction and responses to customized offers. Unpublished Doctoral Dissertation, Stanford University, California, United States (2003)
2. van Kleef, E., van Trijp, H.C.M., Luning, P.: Consumer research in the early stages of new product development: A critical review of methods and techniques. Food Quality and Preference 16(3), 181–201 (2005)
3. Gutman, J.: A means-end chain model based on consumer categorization processes. Journal of Marketing 46(2), 60–72 (1982)
4. Chuang, M.C., Chang, C.C., Hsu, S.H.: Perceptual factors underlying user preferences toward product form of mobile phones. International Journal of Industrial Ergonomics 27(4), 247–258 (2001)
5. Leonard, D., Rayport, J.F.: Spark innovation through empathic design. Harvard Business Review 75(6), 102–113 (1997)
6. Henson, B., Barnes, C., Livesey, R., Childs, T., Ewart, K.: Affective consumer requirements: A case study of moisturizer packaging. Concurrent Engineering: Research and Applications 14(3), 187–196 (2006)
7. Maletz, M., Blouin, J.G., Schnedl, H., Brisson, D., Zamazal, K.: A holistic approach for integrated requirements modeling in the product development process. In: The Future of Product Development: Proceedings of the 17th CIRP Design Conference, pp. 197–207 (2007)
8. Kouprie, M., Visser, F.S.: A framework for empathy in design: Stepping into and out of the user's life. Journal of Engineering Design 20(5), 437–448 (2009)
9. Jagdev, H., Browne, J.: The extended enterprise a context for manufacturing. Production Planning and Control 9(3), 216–823 (1998)
10. Pine, B.J.: Making mass customization happen: strategic for the new competitive realities. Planning Review 21(5), 23–24 (1993)
11. Gilmore, J., Pine, J.: The four faces of mass customization. Harvard Business Review 75(1), 91–101 (1997)
12. Olson, J.C., Reynolds, T.J.: Understanding consumers' cognitive structures: Implications for marketing strategy. Lexington Books, Lexington (1983)

13. Chiu, C.-M.: Applying means-end chain theory to eliciting system requirements and understanding users perceptual orientations. Information & Management 42(3), 455–468 (2005)
14. Gutman, J., Miaoulis, G.: Communicating a quality position in service delivery: An application in higher education. Managing Service Quality 13(2), 105–111 (2003)
15. Fotopoulos, C., Krystallis, A., Ness, M.: Wine produced by organic grapes in Greece: Using means-end chains analysis to reveal organic buyers' purchasing motives in comparison to the non-buyers. Food Quality and Preference 14(7), 549–566 (2003)
16. Kuisma, T., Laukkanen, T., Hiltunen, M.: Mapping the reasons for resistance to internet banking: A means-end approach. International Journal of Information Management 27(2), 75–85 (2007)
17. Veludo-de-Oliveira, T.M., Ikeda, A.A., Campomar, M.C.: Discussing laddering application by the means-end chain theory. The Qualitative Report 11(4), 626–642 (2006)
18. Christensen, G.L., Olson, J.C.: Mapping consumers' mental models with ZMET. Psychology and Marketing 19(6), 477–502 (2002)
19. Nielsen, J.: Usability engineering. Academic, Boston (1993)
20. Budd, J.W.: Mind maps as classroom exercises. The Journal of Economic Education 35(1), 35–46 (2004)
21. Evrekli, E., İnel, D., Balım, A.G.: Development of a scoring system to assess mind maps. Procedia Social and Behavioral Sciences 2(2), 2330–2334 (2010)
22. Johari, J., Wahab, D.A., Sahari, J., Abdullah, S., Ramli, R., Yassin, R.M., Muhamad, N.: Systematic infusion of creativity in engineering design courses. Procedia Social and Behavioral Sciences 18, 255–259 (2011)
23. Buzan, T.: How to mind map: The ultimate thinking tool that will change your life. Thorsons, London (2002)
24. Reed, W.: Mind mapping for memory and creativity. Forest, Tokyo (2005) (in Japanese)

How to Observe, Share and Apply in Design Process?

Focusing on International Design Workshops as a Case Study

Namgyu Kang and Hidetsugu Suto

116-2 Kamedanalano, Hakodate, Hokkaido, 014-8655, Japan
kang@fun.ac.jp

Abstract. These days, many people in design field make a great point of observing a user with regard to the user's circumstances. From the background, there are many researches in User Centered Design field about the role and value of the observing in design process. However, there have been a few researches about how to observe users and how to share and apply the observed results to design process more effectively. The purpose of this research is to clarify the following hypothesis: 'Observing "Physical factor", "*Kansei* factor" and "Cultural factor" from different viewpoints, and visualizing and sharing the observed results does not helps only to understand users' needs but also to apply the observation results to design process.' Therefore, in this research, we discuss 1) the role of observing from different viewpoints, 2) the validity of the following three factors, Physical factor, Emotion factor and Culture factor as the subjects of observation and 3) the reconfirming "TTS method" to visualize and share the observed results, based on several international design workshops as a case study. As the results, the observation from different viewpoints is effective to find out users' needs including a potential needs which is difficult to be found out through the questionnaire survey. And the method to observe Physical factor, *Kansei* factor and Cultural factor helps to understand users' situation and needs. Moreover, sharing the visualized observation results with TTS method becomes easy to understand others' thinking, and easy to apply the observed results to design process.

Keywords: Observation, Culture, Sharing, Design process.

1 Introduction

A questionnaire survey is one of the most commonly used research methods by researchers when they try to explore a user's opinions and needs. However, it is difficult to find out the user's potential needs with the questionnaire survey. Observation in a design process is a useful method to know the user's various types of needs including potential needs. *Matsunami* and *Merholz*'s research teams emphasized the importance of observation in users' experiments in their daily life. Regarding the importance of observation, *Kelly* of IDEO noted "Seeing and hearing with your own eyes and ears is a critical first step in improving or creating a breakthrough product." *Kang*'s research group also indicated that observation is one of the most powerful methods to find out a user's potential needs that is hard to be verbalized.

A. Marcus (Ed.): DUXU/HCII 2013, Part I, LNCS 8012, pp. 498–505, 2013.

Consistent with these previous studies, there are many other studies that discuss the role and value of the observation in the design process (especially User Centered Design (UCD) field). However, there has been a lack of research that explored how to observe, how to share (part of reason is that most cases of design works are conducted as a team or group work.), and how to apply the shared observation results to design process effectively. In other words, we, designers, should consider not only "Relationship between designer side and user side," but also "Relationship between design team members" for better design.

Based on the mentioned backgrounds, *Kang* conducted several design workshops and found out that "Different viewpoints on observing process" helps to find out the user's various needs, including potential needs from his/her daily experiences. Each participant has a different nationality and major. It means that each one has a different viewpoint from their different experiments. There are many new discoveries on the observation process through different viewpoints.

However, many participants in the design workshops could not conduct an observation effectively. Kelly of IDEO said that a designer should give a "Deep Dive" into the observing process. To borrow Kelly's phrase, many participants give a "Shallow Dive" into their observing process, even though they used much time in observing users. Furthermore, although some groups in the design workshop had obtained rich information from their observation, they couldn't share the observation results and apply the shared results to their design processes. Despite the fact that they had known the value of observing, they didn't know specifically how to observe, share, and apply to their design process effectively.

The purpose of this research is to explore the method of how to observe, share the observation results, and apply the shared results to design process effectively through some international design workshops as a case study.

2   Literature Reviews

2.1   Different Viewpoint on Observation

UCD involves careful observation of users' experience in order to facilitate appreciation of their viewpoints. The process helps designers to create a new idea to solve a problem in our daily life. According to *James,* different viewpoint in observation is very important in a creative process. *Brown* emphasized the observation with multidisciplinary team in design process. *Ashikawa*'s research team reported that personal characteristics influence the process of knowledge activation in creativity work. The different viewpoint in observation process finds out the unexpected users' needs. However, the personal viewpoint, which is formed through one's various experiences, is hard to change suddenly. The design team of IDEO is composed of various experts in different fields. It means that each of the different viewpoints can facilitate appreciation on their creative design process. These previous researches and examples highlighted the importance of different personal viewpoints in the observing process.

2.2   ADT Model

According to the *Suto*'s Alethic/Deontic/Temporal (ADT) model that was developed based on the relationship with an artifact, the designer, and users, there are 3 layers in the design model: 1) Main layer reflects the user's possible states and operations, 2) Top layer reflects the designer's intentions, and 3) Base layer reflects physical laws. It means that the user's behaviors are affected by physical laws and are restricted by designer's intention. We designers need to observe the relationship between cause and effect in design. In other words, designers need to observe the user's experience based on the relationship with physical laws and the user's behavior.

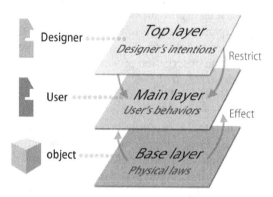

Fig. 1. ADT Model

2.3   *Kansei* and Culture on Design

Mark emphasized that we designers should more focus on user's feeling (=Kansei) than on user's opinion during the observation process. *Kansei* has a comprehensive meaning including feeling, emotion, and creativity etc,.). *Kansei* appears in different evaluations results in different cultures. To understand one's *Kansei,* designers need to understand the culture that had influenced the user's attitude and behavior. According to *Nagamatchi*, the *Kansei* included are the district's culture and history that should be implemented in the design. *Trevor* emphasized the reasons why emotion (*Kansei*) has a profound influence on the success of a design [9]: 1) Emotion is experience, 2) All design is emotional Design, 3) Emotion dominates decision making, 4) Emotion commands attention and affects memory, and 5) Emotion communicates personality, forms a relationship, and creates a meaning.

From the previous research, designers have to understand not only the relationship between physical laws of designed item and users' behavior but also users' *Kansei*, when they interpret and use the designed item. Moreover we have to understand the culture as a common value in design.

2.4   Visualizing and Sharing and TTS Method

According to *Suwa*'s research, visualization as Meta-recognition is very important in perceiving an idea in the design process. Meta-recognition means recognizing through the visualized one's cognition such as Idea sketch, note and photo. To borrow *Suwa*'s expression, the visualizing of one's idea is not only an expression tool but also a cognition tool. *Ikekawa* addresses the objective visualization of design process. In addition, *Takano* and *Saitou* proposed a tool of conception support using the visualized languages of adjective, noun, and mimetic word in a group. Visualizing helps to share others with their opinions and ideas. In addition to visualizing, conversation (language exchange) is one way to share others with their opinions and ideas. Sharing with conversation does not need any tools for sharing work. However, the conversation is likely be influenced by time series and is hard to conduct as a simultaneous work. Moreover, unless all participants have a common language, it is difficult to understand and share immediately, even though each one has a good idea. In contrast, using the visualized information such as photo, sketch, and note are not affected by time series, is able to be conducted as a simultaneous work in the same time without a common language.

Based on the previous research about visualizing, our research team proposed the Turning Thinking Sheet (TTS) method. The TTS method (Fig. 2) is a way to share with the visualized each other's opinion, experience, and idea, based on the role of Meta-recognition. The TTS method was composed of the following five steps to create new design: 1) Each participant visualizes a user's needs using several keywords from the observed user's experience on the first TTS method sheet (Step 1), 2) Each participant expresses one's similar experience about the keywords on the second TTS method sheet (Step 2), 3) Each participant expresses one's idea or proposal for fulfilling the user's needs on the third TTS method sheet (Step 3), 4) Each participant expresses a similar example with each of the created idea or proposal on the fourth TTS method sheet (Step 4), and 5) Each participant expresses one's feeling if he/she uses the created idea on the fifth TTS method sheet (Step 5). Every participant has to express one's opinion, experience, and idea on each sheet and return each sheet to all participants in his/her own team.

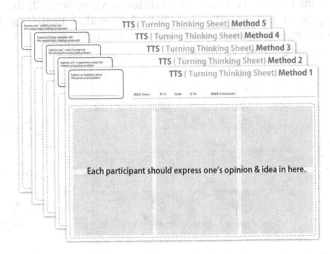

Fig. 2. TTS method sheets

Fig. 3. Example of using the TTS method sheets

2.5 Summary

From the review of previous research, the interdependence of cause and effect in design has to be observed in the design process. The interdependence of cause and effect is related to the designed subject, users, users' *Kansei*, and circumstances including culture. Consequently, in this research, we extend the base layer of the ADT model to the following three factors: 1) Physical factor: Artifact (Mental model, Affordance) , 2) *Kansei* factor: User's feeling (Emotion, Feeling), 3) Cultural factor: Circumstances surrounding human and artifact (Custom, Culture). It means we have to observe the relationships among users behavior, designers' intention, and the Physical *Kansei*, and Cultural factor as the base layer. Fig 6 shows the Extended ADT model.

In this research, the following hypothesis is drawn based on the review of the previous literature: "Observing physical factor, *Kansei* factor, and culture factor with different viewpoints, and visualizing and sharing the observation results not only helps to understand a user's needs including a potential need but also helps to apply the observation results to a design process."

The purpose of this research is to clarify the hypothesis, based on the results of some international design workshops as a case study. Therefore, in this research, we discuss 1) the role of observation with different viewpoints, 2) the validity of the following three factors: 'Physical factor,' 'Emotion factor,' and 'Culture factor' as the subjects of observation and 3) the reconfirming TTS method to visualize and share the observation results.

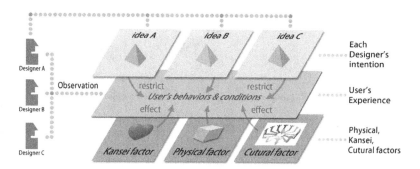

Fig. 4. Extended ADT model

3   Case Studies

3.1   Case Study 1: Portable Chair for Tourist (Theme: Asianism)

In Beijing, China, our research team that was comprised of students from Japan, Korea and China conducted observation as a part of the international design workshop process. During that time, each member observed the three factors: *Kansei*, Physical, and Cultural factors. As a result, they obtained the following four *Kansei* factors: 1) A tourist wants to enjoy their sightseeing, although it is bad weather (too hot), 2) A tourist wants to seat when he/she is tired (most tourists walk a lot to enjoy their sightseeing), 3) To seat on the ground without a chair is shame, and 4) Tourist does not want a heavy item for sightseeing (most tourists bring many items like a camera, a guidebook, some drink, etc.). In addition, they obtained the following five Physical factors: 1) A chair is to heavy to bring to the sightseeing point, 2) Ground is dirty to seat on without chair, 3) A flyer sheet has a role to protect dirty (=Affordance) when a tourist uses it for seating, 4) A raised spot of garden has a role to seat (=Affordance), and 5) There are only few trash cans in the historical place. Finally, they obtained the following four Cultural factors: 1) The Chinese like to talk with others, 2) Many Chinese seat on the ground, even though there is a historical place like the *Tiananmen*, 3) Many Chinese do not clean up the flysheet used for seating, 3) Summer of Beijing is too hot, and 4) There are too many chances to get a flysheet in front of the historical place.

Then, they shared their opinion and thinking with each other using the TTS method, and created a new design. Figure 5 shows the design processes based on the extended ADT model. The designed portable chair for tourists is small, light, and easy to carry, but it is strong due to the honeycomb structure, even though it is made from paper (Fig.6).

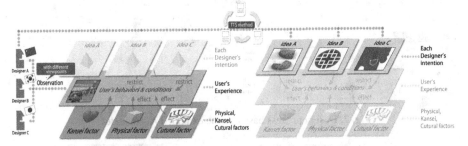

Fig. 5. Design process based on the extended ADT model

Fig. 6. Portable chair for tourist

3.2   Case Study 2: Dining Items for Party in Korea (Theme: Eating)

In Seoul, South Korea, our research team that was comprised of students from Japan, Korea and China, conducted observation as a part of the international design workshop process. During that time, each member observed the three factors: *Kansei*, Physical, and Cultural factors. As a result, they obtained the following three *Kansei* factors: 1) A tourist tries to eat different foods on one´s journey, 2) Everyone does not want to spoil their pleasure when they drink with others, and 3) Party with friends or family is always pleasant. They obtained the following three Physical factors: 1) The volumes of glasses for *Soju* are almost the same as those in Korea, 2) Many plates of side dishes need a lot of space on a table, 3) The chopstick set across plate of side dish are easy to fall into the table. They also obtained the following seven Cultural factors: 1) The Koreans share the food with others, 2) There are many side dishes in Korean food, 3) Koreans like to drink chugalug *Soju* using a small glass 4) It is difficult for Koreans to turn down alcohol drinks when he/she drinks with seniority, 5) The Koreans do not show their drinking figure to seniority, 6) The Koreans use chopsticks in their eating, and 7) Sticking chopsticks into the food is considered rude behavior in Korea.

Then, they shared their opinion and thinking with each other using the TTS method, and created a new design. Figure 7 shows the design processes based on the extended ADT model, and figure 8 shows the designed dining items for party in Korea. When you drink Soju with seniority, you can control the volume of glass of Soju. It means you do not feel any stress of overdrinking without spoiling your pleasure. The chopsticks and bowl are designed for sharing in party of Korea. The top of chopsticks is made with magnet. So if you want to take some side dishes, you connect the front part and take some side dishes to one's plate, and return the front part to original position.

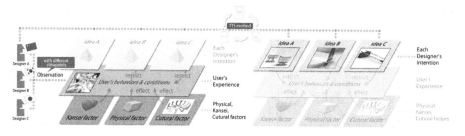

Fig. 7. Design process based on the extended ADT model

Fig. 8. Dining items for party in Korea

4   Conclusion

In this paper, we dealt with the way to observe, share and apply the results to design process. Therefore, we proposed TTS method and the extended ADT model based on 'Physical factor', 'Emotion factor' and 'Culture factor'. And we conducted both international design workshops using these methods. As the results, the method to observe 'Physical factor', 'Emotion factor' and 'Culture factor' helps to understand a user's situation and needs. And the observing with the three factors is effective to find out user' needs including a potential needs. This type of user's needs is difficult to be found out with the approach based on the questionnaire survey. And Moreover, as visualizing and sharing the observation results with TTS method become to easy to understand each other's thinking and opinion, and easy to apply the observation results to design process.

References

1. Yamaoka, T.K.: Observation Engineering. Kyoritsu publish (2008)
2. Mark, G.: Brandjam –Humanizing Brands Through Emotional Design. Jean V. Nagger Literary (2007)
3. Suto, H.T.: Media Viotope: Media Designing Analogous with Biotope. International Journal of Computer Information System and Industrial Management Applications 3, 264–270 (2011)
4. Kang, N.G.: Study on the Value of Sharing and Visualizing Observation Results through Multi-cultural Collaboration. DRS (2012)
5. Trevor, V.G., Edie, A.: Design for Emotion. Morgan Kaufmann publish (2012)
6. Nagamachi, M.T.: Kansei engineering as a powerful for product development. Applied Ergonomics 33(3), 289–294 (2002); consumer-oriented technology

Modelling User Behaviour and Experience – The R2D2 Networks Approach

Amela Karahasanović and Asbjørn Følstad

SINTEF IKT
Oslo, Norway
{Amela.Karahasanovic,Asbjorn.Folstad}@sintef.no

Abstract. The rapidly increasing importance of multimedia services delivered over telecommunication networks has heightened the need for technologies that adapt efficiently to users' needs. It is of particular interest to understand users of such services. This paper proposes a unified approach to modelling users' behaviour and experiences in the context of new multimedia services. Static information on users' behaviour is integrated with users' real-time feedback about their experiences. A unified user profile is used for implementation of a media-aware, user-dependent, self-adaptive network resource manager. Our first experience shows that such a unified approach might be beneficial for network and service providers. The tool for gathering real-time user experience, we propose, might also be useful in other contexts, such as personalised content recommender systems.

Keywords: Quality of Experience, User Experience, User Profiles, Multimedia Services, User Feedback.

1   Introduction

The use of multimedia services delivered over telecommunication networks is becoming increasingly widespread. With triple-play services (IPTV, IP-telephony, and Internet), households have all their services delivered through a single broadband access link. Household members expect all of their services to work perfectly all the time, in spite of technical limitations. The R2D2 Networks project aims to make this possible by developing media-aware, user-dependent, self-adaptive networks [1]. To enable development of a self-adaptive network that dynamically changes in accordance with user behaviour and satisfaction, we need: (i) to gather knowledge on users, their behaviour, and experiences both a priori and in real-time, and (ii) to communicate this knowledge to the network manager. More specifically, we impose the following requirements on the information on users and usage:

- Usefulness. The provided information should be useful for different stakeholders in the telecom and media industry, including customers, market researchers, network planners, system managers, and service/content providers.
- Usability. The provided information should be in a format that is easy to use by humans and/or to transform into machine-readable forms.

A. Marcus (Ed.): DUXU/HCII 2013, Part I, LNCS 8012, pp. 506–515, 2013.
© Springer-Verlag Berlin Heidelberg 2013

- Comprehensiveness. The provided information should describe different characteristics of users and types of their behaviour, such as answering the questions: who they are, where they are, which services they are using, etc.
- Granularity. The provided information should describe users' behaviour within different time spans (per hour, per day, per week, per year).
- Openness. The provided information should describe the events outside the network that might influence users' behaviour, such as the Olympic games.
- Correlation. The provided information should describe correlations between its different dimensions, e.g., types of services used by different age groups.
- Promptness. The provided information should capture real-time changes in user behaviour.

Whereas our previous work describes the studies we have conducted to understand users' behaviour [2, 3], this paper proposes a unified user profile, called the R2D2 Unified User Profile, as a means for communicating knowledge about users to the network manager.

This paper is organised as follows. Section 2 describes related work done in the area of modelling user behaviour. Section 3 proposes the R2D2 Unified User Profile. Section 4 describes the tool we developed for collecting real-time user experience, and Section 5 concludes and proposes future work.

2   Modelling User Behaviour

Modelling users' behaviour patterns has been done in several research areas. It originates from marketing research and aims to provide input to marketing strategies and product design. One widely applied technique is to segment customers by statistical and data mining techniques. It has been pointed out that many studies on user behaviour classify users based on demographic and background data and not on their actual behaviour, although a priori grouping of users is far from being exhaustive [4]. Within media and HCI research, several categorisations of users into distinct user types, called typology of users, have been proposed. In his survey of the field, Brandtzæg [5] analyses 22 media user typologies published from the year 2000. Based on this analysis, the author proposed a classification of user behaviours according to the following dimensions:

- Frequency of use (no use, low, medium, and high use)
- Variety of use (no variety, low, medium, and high variety)
- Content and activity preferences (non-users, sporadics, lurkers, entertainment users/socialisers, debaters, instrumental users, and advanced users)

This user typology is claimed to be universal across different cultures and stable over the time. It might therefore be a valuable framework for cross-country studies and studies of user behaviour over time.

In his study of user behaviour within the context of search engines, Stenmark [6] used log files to identify similar groups of users based on their actual search behaviour. In his research, he identified the following groups: unsophisticated users, occasional users, fact seekers, interactive users, knowledgeable users, and intensive searchers. Although conducted in a different application domain, this research can provide some input in studies of triple-play and over-the-top services, as there are some similarities in user behaviour. The users of these services can, for example, browse meta-information on TV programmes to decide what they want to watch, or they might want to read a newspaper article behind a video they watched.

Aghasaryan et al [7] propose an architecture for multi-source profiling and multi-application personalisation consisting of three layers: service domains, enablement layer and content personalization applications. This architecture enables a holistic approach to service personalization by offering a means to gather users' behavioral data from several sources in real time.

In the study of P2P IPTV systems, Hei et al. [8] collected numerous statistics, such as: evolution of total numbers of peers in the PPLive network, distribution of peak number of peers among all channels, trend numbers of participating users, peer arrival and departure evolution of a popular movie channel, and peer download and upload video traffic. In their study of video-on-demand over IP, Yu et al. [9] analysed user access over time (hourly, daily, and weekly access patterns), user arrival distributions, session lengths, popularity distribution, rate of change in user interests, etc.

In studies conducted to investigate patterns of ICT users' behaviour in Europe, network traffic data and questionnaires from more than 270,000 individual users and households were analysed [3]. User accesses over time, as well as users' habits, preferences, and motivations, were identified. The results indicated that the daily and weekly profiles are determined, in general terms, by two factors: type of user (residential, academic, employee) and type of access, which basically considers whether it is fixed or mobile and the available bandwidth. Furthermore, the results indicated the stability of users' behaviour across countries and over time, and differences among the access types. The information on user behaviour, based on the network statistics and surveys, allowed the identification of current trends in terms of applications and content being used, as well as the demand for bandwidth.

3   R2D2 Unified User Profiles

A user profile is a collection of personal data associated with a specific user. Such profiles are typically related to usage of a particular web-based application such as Amazon or Google AdWords. Development of a self-adaptive network manager requires more complex user profiles that will take into account use of different services as well as users' experiences with them. We therefore propose the R2D2 Unified User Profile, which integrates a priori and real-time information on users, their behaviour, and their perceived Quality of Experience.

3.1   Data Acquisition

Data about users can be collected at different times, at different places, and by different means. In this context, we find it useful to distinguish between a priori and real-time data collection. We also make a distinction between collection of information provided by users (explicit data collection) and collection of information by unobtrusive monitoring tools (implicit data collection).

We collect the following information:

- Information about users stored in companies' customer/user database. This includes:
  - Demographic data. This data comes from the customer databases. Although this information might be known on the individual or the household level, it is more appropriate to use the aggregate information about different segments of users (younger, older, males, females, and so on) as is typically done in market research.
  - Data related to their subscription to a service. This data also comes from the customer databases, and describes the types and characteristics of the contracted services. It is used on the individual or household level.
- Information coming from the content provider on events that may influence users' behaviour and network traffic, such as very popular sports events.
- Information about users and usage, either explicitly provided by users or deduced from their ICT usage. This includes:
  - General information about usage of Information Communication Technology (ICT) and media. This information is based on statistics of usage for a particular country or countries. Users are grouped in segments/user types based on their typical behaviour. These types describe users according to their frequency of use, variety of use, typical activities, and typical platform. Examples of such types are: non-users, sporadic users, entertainment users, instrumental users, and advanced users. Based on a simple questionnaire, users are placed in one of these categories.
- Self-defined user profiles. Users can provide information about themselves, their preferences, content they usually consume/produce, and the context of use. Users can update these profiles whenever they want.
- User feedback on Quality of Experience. Users provide their feedback on their perceived quality of experience. This information can be quantitative and qualitative. Whereas quantitative information, such as 'satisfaction with the sound' on a scale from one to five will be used for immediate adaptation of network parameters, qualitative information will be used for understanding the context of performance degradation and priorities related to QoE.
- Information about users and usage deduced from network traffic information. Users are categorised in different groups based on the traffic volume, applications used, and their daily and weekly traffic profiles.

3.2 Overall Architecture

Information about users and usage is used by the Network Manager to adapt the network in accordance with user behaviour and preferences, as well as relevant events. An adaptive system consists of two phases: user modelling and adaptation.

During the user modelling phase, one collects information about users, their usage and context of use, and transforms this knowledge into user profiles. During the adaptation phase, user profiles are used to derive policies that can be included in the subscription profiles: this means that requirements drawn from user profiles are mapped into parameters that can be understood by the network elements. The enforcement of these policies is implemented as a part of the Network Manager and is not described here.

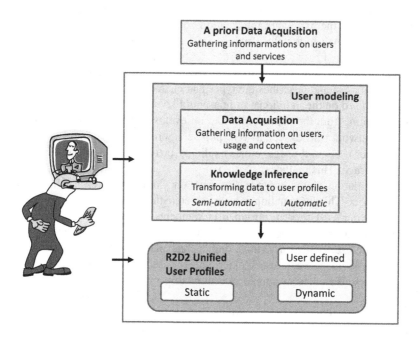

Fig. 1. High level model of R2D2 user modelling and user profiles

Figure 1 gives more details. We distinguish between data collection before usage of a particular service (A priori Data Acquisition) and data collection during the usage of a particular service/application. During the knowledge inference phase, we transform the collected information into user profiles. This can be done semi-automatically or automatically. The user profile consists of three parts: user-defined information, and static and dynamic information. User-defined information will typically be information on preferences and context given by users, such as 'football fan' or 'watching TV at home'. Static information is information that is relatively stable, such as a contracted Service Level Agreement. Dynamic information is information that changes in real-time, such as perceived QoE. User preferences and patterns of usage change over time and users may, for example, move from being sporadic users to being advanced Therefore, their profiles will have to be updated accordingly on a regular basis.

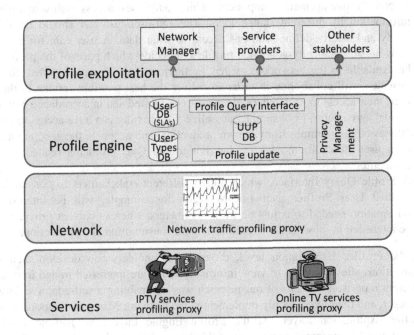

Fig. 2. High level model of R2D2 user modelling and user profiles

Figure 2 presents the R2D2 profiling architecture. We propose collection of data on users and usage at all points of the content journey from content providers to end-users, and exploitation of this information by different stakeholders; the architecture is designed to enable this. At the service layer, we have service profiling proxies that collect information on service usage for each service we are considering. At the network layer, we have a network traffic profiling proxy. It collects network traffic data that will be used for generating Unified User Profiles. At the profile engine level, we have:

- Two databases (User DB and User Types DB) populated by the a priori collected data on users and usage
- A Unified User Profiles DB, which is a central component of the profile engine. This is a temporal DB that consists of relevant information from the above-described databases and tables describing real-time users' behaviour
- Profile update component, which is a set of algorithms for real-time and regular updating of user profiles. This component will, for example, analyse daily network traffic profiles for a user once a week and update his category accordingly. For example, it might include a statement such as: 'if average downlink daily traffic > 3700 MB and number of applications > 20 then user_type := "advanced user"'. It will also respond to users' feedback on QoE in real-time and update the relevant information. For example, it might include a statement such as: 'if sound quality < 4 and video quality < 4 then QoE_action := "immediate intervention"'.

- A privacy management component, which addresses access rights to different information by different stakeholders. The end-user/customer should be able to easily and clearly define who has access to what data. A user can, for example, view his automatically-generated profile and decide which parts of the profile will be available to the network provider. Furthermore, as we envisage that different providers will collaborate in order to deliver the best possible service to the end user, their access to each others' data has to be limited and in accordance with their mutual agreements. For example, an online-TV provider can have access to the top 10 viewed programmes from its own production, and access to the general interests of a user (football, movies…), but not to the QoE problems related to their competitor.
- A Profile Query Interface, which allows different stakeholders to consult R2D2 Unified User Profiles. Network Manager, for example, will be interested in information needed to adjust network parameters, whereas content providers will be interested in information related to content consumption and production.

At the Profiles Exploitation level, different stakeholders can develop their own applications allowing them to view information they are interested in and to produce different reports. The focus of our research was on enabling a self-adaptive network manager, and therefore we only implemented the Network Manager component of the Profile Exploitation Layer. At the Profile Engine Layer, we had no need for the Privacy Management component at this stage of the project. More details on the implementation and evaluation of the network manager and its evaluation can be found in [10].

4   Real-Time Quality of the Experience Collection Tool

To collect Quality of Experience (QoE) as experience by users in real-time, we needed a tool that can do it in a way that allows users to continue with their activities, such as watching TV. Furthermore, we wanted to collect this data in vivo. The approach we have used could be considered a form of experience sampling [11] and feedback collection [12]. The basic principle is that users of a service are asked for their feedback on QoE at different times while using a service. Each such request for feedback is called a probe. Users might be asked general questions such as 'What do you think about the quality of Service X?' or more specific questions such as 'Do you now have better video quality?' Users might answer by rating the quality of the service on a scale from one to five or by describing their experience. Users may also see and comment on the feedback given by other users and by the Network Manager. Depending on the goal of QoE evaluation, the probes can be: i) triggered at random points, ii) triggered at regular intervals, iii) user driven (users provide feedback whenever they have a problem or feel it is appropriate), or iv) event/manager driven (users are asked to provide feedback if something specific happens, such as assigning them extra broadband or fixing problems they experience). The tool enables users to be in dialogue with each other and with their network/service providers.

Fig. 3. Example of QoE probes

The tool is currently implemented as an app for iPhone and iPad (Figure 3), available at the Apple AppStore. All feedback collected through the app is stored on a dedicated server for the tool. The feedback is then made available to the R2D2 Network Manager via an XML feed.

5   Conclusions and Future Work

The purpose of this document is to propose an architecture enabling collection and usage of information on users' behaviour and experiences in a common framework: the R2D2 Unified User Profile, and a four-layer enabling architecture. Within our model we collect:

- information about users stored in the companies'/user database, including demographic and subscription data
- information coming from the content provider about events that might influence users' behaviour
- information about users and usage either explicitly provided by users or deduced from their ICT usage, including general knowledge on Information Communication Technology usage, self-defined user profiles, and user feedback on Quality of Experience
- information about usage deduced from network traffic information

We propose a general architecture (R2D2 profiling architecture) where data on users and usage are collected at all points of the content journey from content providers to end-users, and exploited by different stakeholders. At the service layer, we collect information on usage of each service we are considering. At the network layer, we collect network traffic data. At the profile engine level, we have databases populated by relevant information on users and their behaviour, including a Unified User Profiles DB, a profile update component responsible for updating user profiles, a profile query interface, and a privacy management component. At the profile exploitation level, different stakeholders will develop their own applications enabling presentation of the relevant information.

The architecture we propose is similar to the architecture proposed by Stenmark [7]. However, our approach has several novelties: including (a) real-time feedback on QoE, (b) information on usage of services including typology of users based on statistics of ICT usage in Europe and (c) integration of this information with the network traffic information and the subscription profiles. The purpose of the implementation is to test these concepts, and only some parts of the database will be implemented. Other available methods and tools for collecting user experience when using services, such as myServiceFellow [13], or collecting longitudinal user experience over time, such as iScale [14], can easily be integrated with the proposed architecture.

Our future work will include implementation and validation of the proposed model of user behavior and experience, as well as its improvement and refinement.

Acknowledgements. This research was conducted within the CELTIC research project R2D2 Networks. We would like to thank our project partners. R2D2 Networks was supported by the VERDIKT programme of the Research Council of Norway (contract nr. 193018, 2009-2012). The publication and presentation of this paper was conducted within Customer Care 2015, supported by the BIA programme of the Research Council of Norway (contract nr.219800, 2012-2016).

References

1. Areizaga, E., et al.: A Road to media-aware user-dependent self-adaptive Networks. In: IEEE International Symposium on Broadband Multimedia Systems and Broadcasting, BMSB 2009, pp. 1–6. IEEE Press (2009)
2. Karahasanovic, A., Heim, J.: Understanding users of web-TV. In: Adjunct Proceedings EuroITV 2010 - 8th European Conference on Interactive TV and Video, June 9-11, pp. 96–98. Tampere University of Technology, Tampere (2010)
3. Karahasanovic, A., et al.: Insights in usage of multimedia straming services. IADIS International Journal on WWW/Internet 10(1), 105–121 (2012)
4. Chen, H.M., Cooper, M.D.: Using clustering techniques to detect usage patterns in a web-based information system. Journal of the American Society for the Information Science and Technology 52(11), 888–904 (2001)
5. Brandtzæg, P.B.: Towards a unified Media-User Typology (MUT): A meta-analysis and review of the research literature on media-user typologies. Computers in Human Behaviour 26(5), 940–956 (2010)

6. Aghasaryan, A., et al.: Personalized Application Enablement by Web Session Analysis and Multisource User Profilling. Bell Labs Technical Journal 15(1), 67–76 (2010)
7. Stenmark, D.: Identifying Clusters of User Behaviour in Intranet Search Engine Log Files. Journal of the American Society for Information Science and Technology 59(14), 2232–2243 (2008)
8. Hei, X., et al.: A Measurement Study of a Large-Scale P2P IPTV System. IEEE Transactions on Multimedia 9(8), 1672–1687 (2007)
9. Yu, H., et al.: Understanding User Behaviour in Large-Scale Video-on-Demand Systems. In: 1st ACM SIGOPS/EuroSys European Conference on Computer Systems 2006. ACM, Leuven (2006)
10. Florez, D., et al.: R2D2 Final report on tests and demontrations, Deliverable D521. In: R2D2 Project report, D. Florez, Editor. Celtic Office (2012)
11. Larson, R., Csikszentmihalyi, M.: The experience sampling method. New Directions for Methodology of Social and Behavioral Science 15, 41–56 (1983)
12. Karahasanović, A., et al.: Collecting Feedback during Software Engineering Experiments. Journal of Empirical Software Engineering 10(2), 113–147 (2005)
13. myServiceFellow, http://www.myservicefellow.com/ (accessed February 25, 2013)
14. Karapanos, E., Martens, J.-B., Hassenzahl, M.: Reconstructing experiences with iScale. Int. J. Human-Computer Studies 70, 849–865 (2012)

Community Participation Support Using an ICF-Based Community Map

Satoru Kitamura[1,2], Koji Kitamura[1], Yoshifumi Nishida[1], Ken-Ichiro Sakae[3], Junko Yasuda[4], and Hiroshi Mizoguchi[2]

[1] National Institute of Advanced Industrial Science and Technology, 2-3-26 Aomi, Koto-ku, Tokyo 135-0064, Japan
[2] Tokyo University of Science, 2641 Yamazaki, Noda-shi, Chiba 278-8510, Japan
[3] Tekiju Rehabilitation Hospital, 2-11-32 Hanayama-cho, Nagata-ku, Kobe, Hyogo 653-0876, Japan
4: Japan No Lifting Association

Abstract. Social participation is essential for health promotion, but it requires that participation is designed considering each individual's health status, capabilities, and desires, which vary greatly. In particular, a person with a disability may require a detailed individualized plan. In this study, we present a system for supporting the rehabilitation of patients through promoting their community participation. The system has a function for using a smartphone to create a community map based on the codes designed by the World Health Organization - International Classification of Functioning, Disability, and Health (WHO-ICF) [1]. It also has a function that recommends walking routes that take into consideration the patients' physical function and how they wish to participate in their communities. This study describes our practice at Nagata, Kobe, Japan and assesses the effectiveness of this system.

Keywords: Social participation, International Classification of Functioning, Disability, and Health (ICF), person with disability.

1 Introduction

The aging of the population is increasing worldwide. With an aging population, the number of people with a disability increases. Social participation, which means involvement in daily activities and social roles in communities (World Health Organization, 2001), is considered to be one of the best ways to promote health, especially in seniors. However, mental and physical functions tend to be reduced as a person ages, and this can lead to a decrease in social participation. Moreover, lack of social participation results in further reduction of both mental and physical functions. This negative cycle can cause disuse syndrome [2]. To solve this problem and improve the individual's quality of life, there is a need for new technology that supports rehabilitation and daily life, and aides the desired types of social participation.

A. Marcus (Ed.): DUXU/HCII 2013, Part I, LNCS 8012, pp. 516–524, 2013.
© Springer-Verlag Berlin Heidelberg 2013

2   Concept of an ICF-Based Community Map Based on Canonicalization

Personalization of social participation requires technology that not only matches a person's needs to the locally available social services but also accumulates reusable data on the social participation of many people. Both personalization and reusability are important, since otherwise one person's knowledge of what is good or bad practice cannot be utilized by others. To realize canonicalization, this study uses the code set of the World Health Organization - International Classification of Functioning, Disability, and Health (WHO-ICF) [1], which contains over 1,400 codes. Recently, research using WHO-ICF has been carried out on obesity [3], patients with chronic conditions [4], rheumatoid arthritis from the patient perspective using focus groups [5], and psychosocial features of depression [6]. In contrast to the above research, this paper deals with social participation support for the person with life functions decline by applying by WHO-ICF to a geographic information system [7]. Figure 1 shows the concept of the ICF-based community map. The figure shows the mechanism by which the map created for Place A or Person A can be utilized in Place B or Person B, through canonicalization using the ICF code. For example, Person A is a man who likes playing gateball, which is one of the most popular sports among old people in Japan, and he cannot walk on a steep slope because the range of movement of the joints in his foot is limited. His occupational therapist can recommend the most suitable route for walking to the field where he plays gateball, and the therapist can use the community map to record that route, along with information such as his life

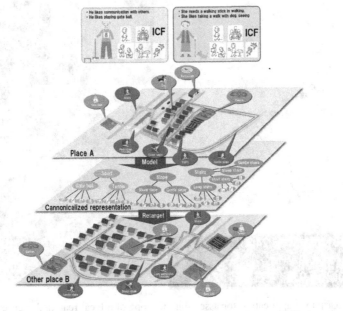

Fig. 1. ICF-based community map (canonicalized for reusability)

functions (physical, daily, and social function), the steepness of the road, and the location of the social event (e.g., a field for gateball). This information is canonicalized using the ICF code and its extension and registered in a geographic information system (the community map system).

Registered data can then be used in a different place by fitting the data into the circumstances of the other place. We call this function "retarget," which is the word used in the field of computer graphics to indicate that 3D motion data of a person has been fitted to a character with a different bone structure. In this research, we retarget life related data via the ICF code in place of a bone structure.

3   ICF-Based Community Map Creation System Using a Smartphone

3.1   Development of an Environmental Information Measuring Application for a Smartphone

In this study, as the first step in building the above community map, we developed a smartphone application for quantitatively measuring and registering environmental information, such as the steepness and distance of a road in the map system.

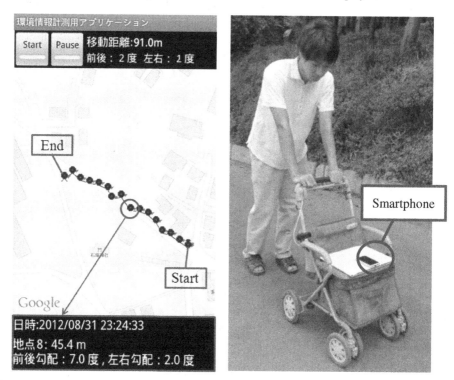

Fig. 2. Smartphone application for assessing the slope of a local road and registering facilities for social participation

The software we developed works in any Android standard smartphone that has a Global Positioning System (GPS) receiver, a three-axis accelerometer, and a digital compass. This system measures and registers not only information such as the steepness and distance traveled on a road, but also facilities for social participation such as hospitals, restaurants, hair salons, supermarkets, convenience stores, cultural centers, and bus stops. Figure 2 shows our smartphone application and a picture of the actual use of the smartphone with the software.

3.2 Evaluation of the Developed Application

To determine the effectiveness of the map system and the feasibility of a community map, we measured an actual community in Nagata Ward, Kobe, Hyogo, Japan in

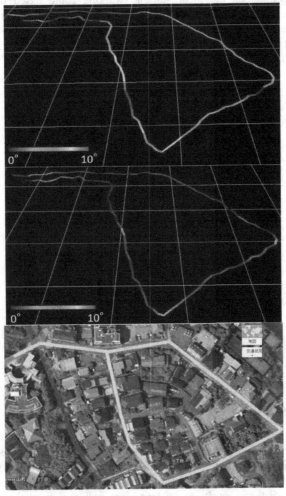

Fig. 3. Example of visualization of the steepness of the slope of a local road. (The top panel shows the steepness of the direction of travel, i.e., pitch, and the middle panel shows the steepness of the crossways direction, i.e., roll.)

cooperation with the Tekiju Rehabilitation Hospital. Figure 3 shows examples of measured and registered road data. The top panel in Fig. 3 shows the steepness of the direction of travel (pitch), and the middle panel of Fig. 3 shows the steepness of the crossways direction (roll). We have thus far measured six walking routes that are used as training routes in the hospital and in the roads that neighbor patients' homes.

4   Development of Walking-Route Recommendation System

4.1   Walking-Route Recommendation System

As a part of the service that we conducted, we developed a route recommendation system that recommends the most suitable walking route based on the patient's desires and circumstances after discharge from the hospital. Figure 4 shows the developed system. This system can recommend a walking route once it has been provided with 1) a walking route used as training in the hospital, 2) start and goal locations, and 3) the range of total vertical distance (patient's burden).

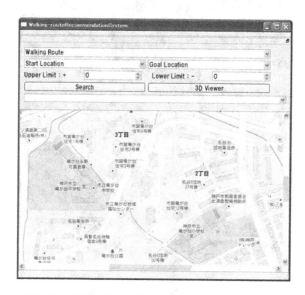

Fig. 4. Walking-Route Route recommendation system

4.2   Algorithm for Walking Route Recommendation

We developed a search algorithm for a walking-route recommendation system. In the algorithm that we developed, we adopted a back-track method that uses a branch-and-bound method. The algorithm considers all route candidates that satisfy the condition for total vertical distance, which is the sum of the absolute values of the altitude differences. The distance works as an important indicator to evaluate the patient's burden in a walking route. Figure 5 shows an example of our algorithm. In this

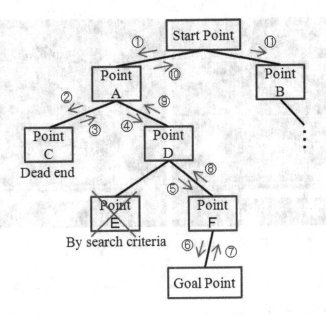

Fig. 5. Example of the search route algorithm

example, the algorithm searches for the ways to begin at "Start Point" and travel to "Goal Point." During the search, when a dead end is reached, the algorithm returns to the previous point and then continues to search the other candidates. If there are more than two candidates that satisfy the conditions, the present point moves to other candidates.

4.3   Evaluation of Walking-Route Recommendation System

Figure 6 shows an example of a route recommendation. In the case of Fig. 6, the condition are 1) Hanayama1-Chome_1 (total vertical distance: 22.6 [m]), 2) Start

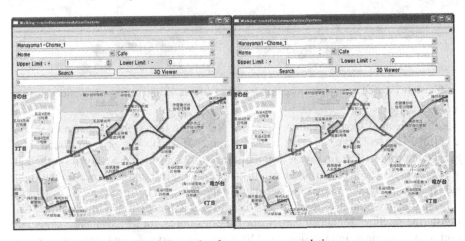

Fig. 6. Example of a route recommendation

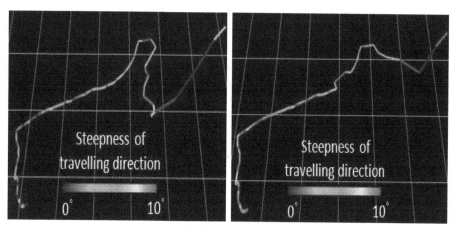

Fig. 7. Steepness in the direction of travel

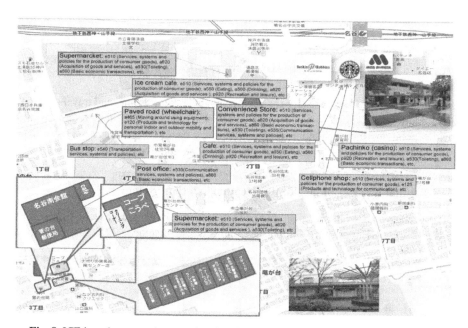

Fig. 8. ICF-based community map that describes various facilities for social participation

Location: Home, Goal Location: Cafe, 3) Range of total vertical distance: 22.6–23.6[m] (Upper Limit: +1 [m], Lower Limit: -0 [m]). The system found two acceptable routes. The first route has a distance of 22.8 [m] and is shown on the left side of Fig. 6. The second route has a distance of 23.0 [m] and is shown on the right side of Fig. 6. Figure 7 shows the steepness in the direction of travel.

Using this system, it is possible for a user to add ICF-code-based information after registering facilities for social participation. For example, for a convenience store, the user can add such information as 510 (services, systems, and policies for the production of consumer goods), a620 (acquisition of goods and services), a860 (basic economic transactions), a530 (toilet), e535 (communication services, systems, and policies) [8]. This kind of information is useful for planning a walking route that improves social participation. Figure 8 shows examples of the registered facilities for social participation around a patient's house.

5   Inquiring Survey on the Usefulness of the Developed System from Physical Therapist of Rehabilitation Hospital

We asked physical therapists at the Tekiju Rehabilitation Hospital about the usefulness of this route recommendation system. The therapists pointed out three advantages. First, the system allows the therapist to conduct a quantitative evaluation of the vertical distance of a walking route. Conventionally, the therapist had to make a walking route based on intuition and experience. Second, this system allows a therapist to conduct a subsequent evaluation of the social participation of a patient after discharge. For example, it can help a therapist understand the reason why a patient may fail to accomplish the intended social participation. In particular, a therapist can determine if a problem is due to a lack of physical ability or if it is due to a lack of commitment. Finally, the system allows a therapist to judge which assistive device is required because the map has information such as road steepness. Here, assistive devices include wheelchairs, ankle foot orthoses (AFOs), and other types of equipment. It is difficult for a wheelchair user to travel on a road that has a large degree of steepness in the crosswise direction (roll). An AFO limits ankle motion, so it is necessary for the therapist to judge the adequacy of the supplementary harness.

6   Conclusion

To prevent disuse syndrome and improve the quality of life of individuals, we developed a walking-route recommendation system that supports rehabilitation and the type of social participation that a patient wishes. We also developed a smartphone application for measuring and registering environmental information, such as the steepness of a road and the distance traveled on a local road. The application has a function that allows a user to create an ICF-based community map using the registered environmental information. To examine the effectiveness of our developed application and system, we measured environmental information in cooperation with a rehabilitation hospital. Experimental results show the feasibility of our walking-route recommendation service, which is based on the ICF-based community map.

In the future studies, we plan to accumulate additional information for the community map and evaluations of recommended routes, in cooperation with a rehabilitation hospital and patients.

References

1. WHO: International Classification of Functioning, Disability and Health (2001)
2. Yayoi, O., Shigemi, N., Minako, K., Satoshi, U.: Anevidence-based construction of the models of decline of functioning. Part 1: two major models of decline of functioning. International Journal of Rehabilitation Research 32, 189–192 (2009)
3. Armin, S., Peter, D., Michaela, F., Alarcos, C., Erika, H., Richard, A., Nenad, K., Gerold, S., Jörg, R.: ICF Core sets for obesity. J. Rehabi. Med. Suppl. 44, 107–113 (2004)
4. Alarcos, C., Thomas, E., Berdirhan, Ü., Somnath, C., Nenad, K., Gerold, S.: Development of ICF Core Sets for patients with chronic conditions. J. Rehabi. Med. Suppl. 44, 9–11 (2004)
5. Michaela, C., Alarcos, C., Tanja, A.S., Edda, A., Barbara, K., Gerold, S.: Validation of the International Classification of Functioning, Disability and Health(ICF) Core Set for rheumatoid arthritis from the patient perspective using focus groups. Arthritis Research & Therapy 8, R84 (2006)
6. Maria, C., Blanca, M.-M., Carla, S., Alarcos, C., Jerome, B., Jose, L., Ayuso, M.: Psychosocial features of depression: A systematic literature review. Journal of Affective Disorders 141, 22–33 (2012)
7. Heywood, I., Cornelius, S., Carver, S.: Geographical informationsystems, 3rd edn. Pearson Education Limited, England (2006)

Pragmatic Approach to Cost Benefit Analysis of User Centered Design

Izumi Kohno, Hiroko Yasu, Satoshi Sugawara, and Masahiro Nishikawa

NEC Corporation, Japan
{kohno@ay,h-yasu@ax,s-sugawara@iu,m-nishikawa@cd}.jp.nec.com

Abstract. User-centered design (UCD) is an effective method for understanding users' needs and improving usability. Introducing UCD to the existing development process increases new development activities, so it is important to analyze the cost benefits of UCD, but it is not clear how to measure the effectiveness of these benefits for actual projects in companies. It is not clear which analysis is more appropriate, quantitative or qualitative. We propose a pragmatic approach to analyzing the cost benefits of UCD. We analyzed the effectiveness of 22 projects in our company using this approach.

Keywords: UCD, cost benefit, quantitative analysis, qualitative analysis.

1 Introduction

User-centered design (UCD) is an effective method for understanding users' needs and improving usability. Introducing UCD to the existing development process increases new development activities, so it is important to analyze the cost benefits of UCD. Previous research clarified the cost benefits of UCD, such as a reduced need for resources, increased customer satisfaction, reduced product support cost, and increased productivity [1]. However, it is very difficult to measure the effectiveness of these benefits for actual projects in companies. Because it is not clear how to measure this, it is also not clear which analysis is more appropriate, quantitative or qualitative. We propose a pragmatic approach to analyzing the cost benefits of UCD.

2 Important Perspective for Cost Benefit Analysis

2.1 Clarifying Relationship between Activities and Benefits

(Hypothesis 1) Developers and managers generally do not know much about UCD activities. Therefore, it is necessary to clarify the activities, investment in UCD, and kinds of benefits. It is also important to clarify the relationship between activities and benefits, which is an input-output relationship. The benefits should be categorized as those for the customers and end users and those for the company. The following items should be clarified.

A. Marcus (Ed.): DUXU/HCII 2013, Part I, LNCS 8012, pp. 525–534, 2013.

<Activities>

1. What kinds of UCD activities did they do?
2. How much did the UCD activities cost?

<Benefits>

1.   Who received the benefits from the UCD activities?
2.   What kind of benefits did they obtain?

2.2   Combination of Quantitative Analysis and Qualitative Analysis

Quantitative analysis is important to clearly show the benefits of UCD and make developers and managers recognize the benefits. But not all benefits can be measured quantitatively, and numerical data on its own is not persuasive. Therefore, we think it is important to combine quantitative analysis and qualitative analysis.

(Hypothesis 2) It is difficult to measure and compare the development time and costs of real projects that used UCD and did not use it under the same conditions. Therefore, we think it is important to obtain estimates of development cost benefits.

(Hypothesis 3)   We think it is important to make tentative benefit lists in advance and draw out developer's and customer's opinions that they are not aware of.

Quantitative Analysis

1.Benefits to development organization

- Increased sales volume and profits

This benefit is the most attractive for managers. The investment in UCD and the order amount or sales volume of the products can be shown as quantitative data. However, various factors aside from UCD activities contribute to receiving a lot of orders, so qualitative analysis such as interviews should be added.

- Reduced product development cost

Measuring the reduction in the development cost quantitatively is difficult because comparing using UCD and not using it is impossible for the same project. Therefore, we make developers estimate the reduction in the development cost by using UCD. We ask developers questions such as, "How much would the cost be in terms of development time and cost to obtain the same quality of output if you had not used UCD for the project?" and compare the estimate cost and real cost of the project. We also ask developers the reason for the difference. It is a combination of quantitative analysis and qualitative analysis.

- Improved quality of product

Usability is improved by executing UCD. The usability metrics are effectiveness, efficiency, and satisfaction. These metrics can be shown in user test experiments, for example, operation time and number of errors are measurable. Therefore, we can measure the part of benefits that improved product quality as quantitative data.

2. Benefit to user's organization and end users
- Improved operational efficiency

The reduction of operation time and number of errors improves the operational efficiency of the user's organization. The cost of operation can be simulated using the number of people involved in the operation, working hours, unit price, and the reduction of operation time and number of errors. Therefore we can measure the part of benefits that improved operational efficiency as quantitative data.

Qualitative Analysis

We ask project-related people such as developers, planers, UCD professionals, and users about the benefits for qualitative analysis. The contents of the hearing are contribution to receiving a lot of orders, actual feelings about development costs, or feelings of satisfaction about the system, but the project-related people are often not thoroughly aware of the benefit. It is important to make tentative benefit lists in advance and draw out developer's and customer's opinions that they are not aware of by using tentative benefit lists. We selected the benefit items related to IT solutions that are related to our company's area and made specific tentative benefits for every item. The contents of quantitative and qualitative analysis are shown in Table1.

Table 1. Quantitative and qualitative analysis

Benefits		Quantitative analysis	Qualitative analysis
Benefits to development organization	Increased sales volume and profits	Order amount or sales volume	Contribution to successfully receiving orders
	Reduced product development cost	Reduction of development cost (estimated value)	Actual feelings about development costs
	Improved quality of product	Operation time or number of errors	Actual feelings of satisfaction about system
Benefits to user's organization and end users	Improved operational efficiency	Business efficiency (simulated value)	Actual feelings of satisfaction about system and job

3 Proposed Method of Measuring Cost Benefit

3.1 Making Case Sheet and Hearing

This proposal is related to hypothesis 1. To clarify the relationship between activities and benefits, we propose making a case sheet and hearing. In this method, first UCD professionals write what kinds of UCD activities, processes, and tentative benefits occur in their project on a case sheet. It can clarify the activities. Next, a cost benefit analyst and project- related people such as developers, planers, and UCD professionals share information on the UCD activities and processes using the case sheet, and then a cost benefit analysts asks project related people about the benefit of each UCD activity and process. This can clarify the relationship between activities and benefits.

3.2   Obtaining Estimates About Development Cost

This proposal is related to hypothesis 2. To clarify quantitative data about the reduction in development cost, we propose obtaining estimates. In this method, first a cost benefit analyst asks developers about what development process proceeds smoothly by using UCD compared to not using UCD and then asks about the development time and cost of the relevant development process in some past projects not using UCD. The past projects are simulated ones that require the same output quality. This data consist of estimates. The development process is broken down from the UCD process in order to make estimates close to the correct data. Therefore,. Examples of questions are shown below.

<Examples of questions for quantitative analysis>
Q: What items did you have success with when using UCD?

1.   Creating concrete usage scenarios
2.   Creating ideas
3.   Creating concepts
4.   Extracting and organizing customer's needs
5.   Setting persona
6.   Specifying the context of use
7.   Evaluating usability problems
8.   Making prototypes
9.   Creating UI guidelines, patterns,   or templates (software)
10.   Creating mockups (hardware)
11.   Complying with standards such as accessibility

Q: How much would the cost of the items you checked be if you did not use UCD?

- man-hours (   )
- costs (   )
- Impossible if UCD is not used

3.3   Making Tentative Benefit Lists

This proposal is related to hypothesis 3. To draw out the developer's and customer's opinions that they are not aware of, we propose making tentative benefit lists in advance. We referred to some previous research [1-6] and discussed the benefits of UCD that were shown in our company's past projects. We selected the benefit items that were related to IT solutions as shown in Table1, and then wrote down the specific benefits for every benefit item. We asked relevant people in the project which benefit lists apply to their project. Examples of questions are shown below.

<Examples of questions for qualitative analysis>
(1)Benefits to development organization
Q: What benefit did you obtain in your project?
i)   Increased sales volume and profits

- Proposal support
  E.g. you can meet mandatory requirements such as Section 508 of the US Rehabilitation Act.
- Customer satisfaction
  E.g. you can obtain some positive comments from customers.

ii) Reduced cost in product development

- Drawing out latent user needs
  E.g. you can draw out customer's needs that they are not aware of.
- Reducing agreement process
  E.g. you can adjust opinions and agree goals smoothly among developers.
  E.g. you can adjust opinions and agree goals smoothly with customers.
- Reducing development cost by making standards
  E.g. you can reduce the burden of development by using UI standards.
- Improving developer's motivation
  E.g. you can be motivated to develop functions since you can understand usage situation and need for these functions.
- Reducing backtracking
  E.g. you can reduce serious risks of demanding design changes at last phase because prototype images were agreed with customers.

iii) Improved quality of product

- Differentiation
  E.g. you can create appealing and unique concepts.
- Brand
  E.g. you can create consistent UI.
  E.g. you can create consistent appearance design.
- Usability
  E.g. you can improve usability, and learnability of your products.
  E.g. you can improve usability, and efficiency of your products.
  E.g. you can improve usability, and memorability of your products.
  E.g. you can improve usability, and reduce errors of your products.
  E.g. you can improve usability, and satisfaction of your products.

(2)Benefit to user's organization and end users
Q: What benefits did customers obtain?
i) Improved operational efficiency

- end user's operational efficiency
  E.g. users (end users) can reduce working time.
  E.g. users can reduce learning time.
  E.g. users can reduce number of errors.
- end user's satisfaction
  E.g. users increase job satisfaction.
- user's organization's efficiency
  E.g. user's organization can reduce training costs.
  E.g. user's organization can hire lower-level staff.
  E.g. end user's organization can decrease maintenance costs and inquiries.
- user's organization's satisfaction
  E.g. brand image of user's company is improved by usability or design.

4 Analyzing Actual Projects

4.1 Applied Projects

We analyzed the effectiveness of 22 projects that executed UCD in our company using this approach. The 22 projects were selected from various development processes, and UCD seemed to be effective in these projects. Some projects were selected from the upper phase such as system proposal or product planning, and some projects were selected from the requirement definition phase or development phase. The types of products were selected in accordance with our company's business domain, software, hardware, or IT solutions.

4.2 Procedures

The cost benefits of 22 projects were measured following orders as shown in Fig. 1. First, UCD professionals and cost benefit analysts made a case sheet as shown in Fig.2 in advance. The case sheets include: 1) abstract, 2) purpose of applying UCD, 3) list of UCD processes and related member's role, 4) activities of each UCD process, 5) benefits to user's organization and end users, 6) benefits to development organization, 7) cost and schedule of UCD. The purpose and activities were written in accordance with actual projects. Benefits were written by referring to the benefit list as shown in 3.3, and benefits were also written by referring comments of developers or customers provisionally. The cost and schedule of UCD were written to estimate which UCD costs is worth bearing.

User evaluation experiments were executed for some projects in advance. User interfaces were improved in these projects. The operation time and number of errors before improvement and after improvement were compared in these experiments. The reduction of operational time and cost a year were simulated by using them. We wrote down the reduction data as benefits to the user's organization and end users on a case-sheet.

Next, the UCD professional and cost benefit analysts interviewed project-related persons using the case sheet. Project-related persons mean developers or planners who are in charge of UCD in the development division, and project managers who are person in charge of budget control and progress management.

In the interview, first cost benefit analysts explained the purpose of the interview and confirmed the contents of 1) abstract, and 2) purpose of applying UCD on the case sheet to project-related persons.

Second, the UCD professional explained and confirmed 3) list of UCD processes and related member's role and 4) activities of each UCD process on the case sheet to project related persons. They also asked developers planners, or project managers how they felt about UCD and the different and advanced points of UCD compared to the traditional development process. We could collect the benefits related activities, because we confirmed their UCD activities and asked about the benefits of each activity.

Third, cost benefit analysts confirmed 6) benefits to development organization that were written provisionally to project-related persons, UCD professionals and then corrected the benefits reflected in the early part of the interview under participants' agreement.

For the last part of the interview, cost benefit analysts asked about benefits to project related persons using a questionnaire. The questions in 3.2 and 3.3 were collected in the questionnaire as shown in Fig. 3. Cost benefit analysts asked each question, and if the answer for the question had been determined before, analysts wrote the answers themselves. They asked the rest of the questions and discussed the benefits related to the questions. Before the questions for quantitative analysis, the analysts explained the intention of the questions, which is these questions should be answered in their heads, and it should be assumed the project requires the same output quality as the past project. If the project related persons did not know the numerical value in the interview, these data were supplied later.

The interview took about two hours. The participants were 1-4 developers, planners or project managers, 1-2 UCD professionals, and 1-4 UCD analysts. Case sheets were refined by the result of interview, and they were outputs for cost benefit analysis.

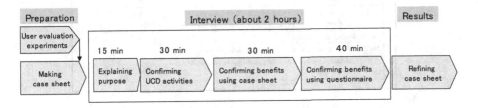

Fig. 1. Procedure for analyzing cost benefits

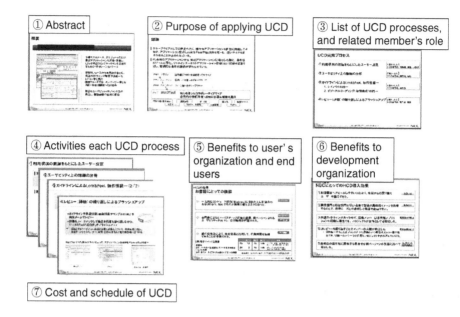

Fig. 2. Example of case-sheet

What benefit did you obtain in your project?

◆ Drawing out latent user needs	Answer	Apply
No.11. You can draw out latent customer's needs that they are not aware of.	☐Yes ☐No	☐Yes ☐No
◆ Reducing the agreement process	Answer	Apply
No.12. You can adjust opinions and agree goals smoothly with customers.	☐Yes ☐No	☐Yes ☐No
No.13. You can adjust opinions and agree goals smoothly among developers. project-related member's role ( )	☐Yes ☐No	☐Yes ☐No
◆ Reducing development cost by making standards	Answer	Apply
No.14. You can reduce the burden of development by using UI standards.	☐Yes ☐No	☐Yes ☐No
◆ Improving developer's motivation	Answer	Apply
No.15. You can be motivated to develop functions since you can understand usage situation and need for these functions.	☐Yes ☐No	☐Yes ☐No
◆ Reducing backtracking	Answer	Apply
No.16. You can reduce serious risks of demanding for design changes at last phase, because prototype images were agreed with customers.	☐Yes ☐No	☐Yes ☐No

Fig. 3. Questionnaire sheet

5   Results and Discussion

We clarified the benefits of UCD for 22 projects. We wrote down several benefits for the user's organization and end users and several benefits for the development organization of each project. Typical benefits that we obtained are shown below. Some concrete numerical data is hidden because it is confidential.

- Increased sales volume and profits
  In one project, which was a system proposal, UCD methods such as observation were used, and then the problems of the end-user's perspective were found. UCD professionals and planners in our company proposed a concept about their customer's facilities and system. Because the concept was a proposal to increase the customer's business value, our company could receive an order. The customer's present system was built by other companies, so the competition was challenging but we won. We wrote the order amount as quantitative benefits and the customer's comments in which they recognize the concept made by UCD activities as qualitative benefits.
- Reduced cost in product development
  In one project which was a user interface development for a major system renewal, UCD methods such as visualization for organizing customer's demand were used. The product development cost was reduced about the cost that 10 people worked for 2~3 months. This number was estimated by developers of this project. We found the developers felt the benefit of reduced cost in development very much.
- Improved quality of product and operational efficiency
  In one project, the user interface of one application was improved by unifying with some other applications and operating it intuitively. The operation time of sending and organizing e-mails of the application was expected to decrease by 8 seconds by our experiment. If 1000 people operate this application, the working time would be decreased by about 800 hours a year in the user's organization. We wrote the reduction of working time for business efficiency as quantitative benefits for the user's organization.

Our proposed method for measuring the benefits of UCD is effective as below.

- Benefits related to UCD activities are very persuasive to developers or managers.
- We could obtain some numerical data on reducing product development cost.
- UCD professionals could describe the benefits that they were not aware by using the questionnaire. We could also obtain various benefits from developers, planners, or project managers through the interview and questionnaire. This approach is effective for thoroughly obtaining benefits.

6   Conclusion

We proposed a pragmatic approach to analyzing the cost benefits of UCD. Our method is the combination of quantitative analysis and qualitative analysis. We described the procedures and results of applying this method to 22 projects in our company. We will study the difference in cost benefits and methods among various types of products in the future.

References

1. Rajanen, M.: Usability Cost-benefit models – Different Approach to Usability Benefit Analysis. In: Proceedings of 26th Information System Research Seminar In Scandinavia (IRIS26), Haikko, Finland
2. Ehrlich, K., Rohn, J.: Cost Justification of Usability Engineering: A Vendor's Perspective. In: Bias, R., Mayhew, D. (eds.) Cost-Justifying Usability, pp. 73–110. Academic Press (1994)
3. Bevan, N.: Cost Benefit Analysis TRUMP report (September 2000)
4. Karat, C.-M.: Cost benefit and business case analysis of usability engineering. In: Tutorial presented at the ACM SIGCHI Conference on Human Factors in Computing Systems, New Orleans, LA, April 28-May 2 (1993)
5. Mayhew, D., Mantei, M.: A Basic Framework for Cost-Justifying Usability Engineering. In: Bias, R., Mayhew, D. (eds.) Cost-Justifying Usability, pp. 9–43. Academic Press (1994)
6. Harrison, M., Henneman, R., Blatt, L.: Design of a Human Factors Cost-Justification Tool. In: Bias, R., Mayhew, D. (eds.) Cost-Justifying Usability, pp. 203–241. Academic Press (1994)

Innovative Behavioral Intention and Creativity Achievement in Design: Test of an Integrated Model

Chia-Chen Lu[1] and Ding-Bang Luh[2]

[1] Department of Industrial Design, Tunghai University, Taiwan
cclu@the.edu.tw
[2] Department of Industrial Design, National Cheng Kung University, Taiwan
luh@mail.ncku.edu.tw

Abstract. Accumulating creative achievements is a way to represent design ability and competitiveness for design students. This study proposes to employ the theory of planned behavior to predict creative achievements and augments it with personal intrinsic and extrinsic relative benefits, significant others' expectation and evaluation, self-efficacy, and facilitating conditions that are believed to influence students' innovative behavioral intention. The hypothesized model was validated empirically using data for 277 students from industrial and visual designs. The results confirmed that both innovative behavioral intention and perceived behavioral control affect student's creative achievements significantly. Subjective norms and perceived behavioral control were significantly related to the intention to exhibit innovative behavior, but attitude was not. Additionally, self-efficacy exerts its influence on students' perceived behavioral control more significantly than other antecedent variables. This paper presents an integrated model that provides a direction to help design students to increase their creative achievements accumulation in a school environment.

Keywords: Theory of Planned Behavior (TPB), Innovative Behavioral Intention, Creative Achievements.

1 Introduction

Creativity is a key factor determining competitive ability in the design field. In addition to domain knowledge and skills learning, design students are more encouraged to engage in specific design activities in practice. The goal is to enhance the design ability of the students so that they can accumulate creative works, design awards or design experiences for evidences of creativity in design ability when pursuing future careers. These creative outcomes which were accumulated in a period of time are defined as creative achievements by Carson, Peterson, and Higgins in 2005. Yang, You, and Guo (2010) interviewed the design students in relation to their employment situations after they graduated, and found that most of the interviewees pointed out that the design companies were not concerned with their educational background but with their design ability instead. The results revealed that the students who had more evidences about their design ability at school had more advantages and

A. Marcus (Ed.): DUXU/HCII 2013, Part I, LNCS 8012, pp. 535–544, 2013.

a higher degree of adaptation in their new careers. Hsu, Chang, and Yang (2007) investigated business recruitment methods and found that, in addition to interviews, 97% requested portfolios, 38% wanted tests, and 16% asked to have practical experience. Above methods such as the portfolios and practical experience are also related to creative achievements. Accumulating creative achievements from taking part in design activities not only made easier for students to understand the design position and reduce the gap between school and the workplace, but also provided an opportunity to accumulate the evidences of design ability.

However, accumulating creative achievements cannot be administered in a compulsory way. Jong and Hartog (2010) found that a positive relationship exists between innovative working behavior and innovation outcomes. It appeared that the students' willingness to actively accumulate creative achievements could depend on their behavioral intention. Ajzen (1985) proposed the theory of planning behavior (TBP) to explain the personal intention and to predict behavior. In the TPB model, an individual's behavior is directly affected by the behavioral intention and perceived behavioral control and indirectly affected by three variables, namely, attitude, subjective norms, and perceived behavioral controls (Ajzen 1991; Fishbein and Ajzen 1975). And these three factors are also affected by external variables, for example, beliefs structures (Chu and Chiu 2003), contextual forces (Bock et al. 2005), or personality (Ajzen 1989). This theory had been examined repeatedly by many studies and has been applied in various domains such as knowledge sharing (Cheng and Chen 2007), the usage of information technology (Taylor and Todd 1995), e-learning (Lee 2010), and training in participation behavior (Maurer et al. 2003; Ho et al. 2010). Compared with creativity and design education research, despite some studies indicating that innovative behavior can effectively predict innovative outcomes (Scott and Bruce 1994; Jong and Hartog 2010), there are no studies integrating the TPB model into their research. The attitudes, subjective norms, and perceived behavior controls of TBP, and the antecedents of the three factors have not examined and integrated in a model for predicting creative achievements yet, though they are crucial not only in academic but also in practice. Our study seeks to understand better how these factors combine to influence design students in their creative achievements.

The main goal of this study was to explore the determinants that increase students' tendencies toward innovative behavioral intention and to predict the creative achievements based on the TPB. Since innovative behavior appears to be facilitated by personal motivation (Amabile 1983) and the climates for innovation such as the support for innovation or the resource supply (Scott and Bruce 1994). This paper add intrinsic and extrinsic motivations, significant others expectation and evaluation, self-efficacy, and facilitating condition are integrated with theory of planning behavior (TBP).

2 Integrated Model of Design Creative Achievements

Behavior refers to the actions of the individual. The behavioral intention is the extent to which an individual intends to engage in some behavior (Fishbein and Ajzen 1975). Innovative behavior is defined as individual actions directed at the generation, introduction and application of beneficial novelty at any organizational level (Kleysen and Street 2001). Such beneficial novelty includes the development of new product ideas or technologies, and changes in administrative procedures to improve work relations, or the application of new ideas or technologies to significantly enhance the efficiency and effectiveness of work processes (West and Farr 1989; Kleysen and Street 2001). This study defines the innovative behavioral intention as referring to an individual who has a high tendency to innovate and achieve a status of innovative behavior. Scott and Bruce (1994) pointed out that the ratings for innovative behavior assessed by supervisors are positively and significantly associated with the numbers of inventions on the part of the employees. Other studies have also confirmed the close relationship between behavioral intention and actual behavior (Maurer et al. 2003; Fielding et al. 2008; Smith et al. 2008).

In the TPB model, behavioral intention is affected by attitude, subjective norm and perceived behavioral control (Taylor and Todd 1995; Chu and Chiu 2003; Maurer et al. 2003; Cheng and Chen 2007). The behavioral intention of individuals tend to be strong when they have a positive attitude, they support subjective norm, and there is strongly perceived behavioral control. According to expected-value theory, an attitude is a position regarding an individual's continual like or dislike of people and things. Studies showed that a personal positive attitude influences behavioral intention (Bock et al. 2005; Ryu et al. 2003; Smith et al. 2008). A subjective norm relates to the feeling of social pressure when the actor is engaging in a particular form of behavior. The social pressure comes from the reference group which is a person or a group that affects the decision of the actor (Ajzen 1985; 1989). The values, attitudes, behaviors and norms of the reference group are related to the evaluation, behavior and expectations of the actor (Blackwell et al. 2001). Perceived behavioral control (PBC) refers to a person who can control the extent of their resources or opportunities, such as time, money, ability, and personal knowledge (Ajzen 1989). PBC can directly affect behavioral intention (Ryu et al. 2003), and Ajzen (1985) pointed out that PBC directly affects actual behavior when personal PBC is close to actual behavior, and that PBC can influence the behavior in direct and indirect ways, as long as the actors increase their control over their behavior, the possibility of behavior will increase.

Attitude had been divided into two variables that are related to the personal relative benefit and social relative benefit. The former refers to rewards and the sense of achievement, while the latter is conducive to the overall public interest. Motivation comes from two directions, intrinsic and extrinsic (Amabile et al. 1994), both of which can positively predict the innovative behavior in the workplace (Tsai and Kao, 2004). Hence, the personal intrinsic benefit factors include the accomplishments and the satisfaction, and the personal extrinsic benefit factors include the rewards and the other s' approval. The subjective norm is determined by variables regarding the extent to which significant others want the individual to exhibit a certain type of behavior (Rivis and Sheeran 2003). Chang and Chiang (2008) indicated that both the evaluation and expectations of superiors were related to the creativity performances of individuals. In terms of significant others' expectation, Tierney and Farmer (2004) found that the supervisor who had higher expectations for the employee was perceived as being more creatively supported by the employee. Ramus (2001) pointed out that the employee liked to try to work creatively when the employee was encouraged and supported by the system or policy. In terms of significant others' evaluation, Yuan and Zhou (2008) found that an individual who expected an external evaluation exhibited greater ability in improving idea appropriateness during the selective retention. Shally (1995) noticed that an individual who had the goals of creativity and work independence in an expected evaluation environment would generate the highest creativity. Ajzen (1985) noted that an individual who had strongly perceived behavioral control had higher self-efficacy, which reflected the strength of confidence of the actor and the probability of succeeding. Several studies (Taylor and Todd 1995; Chu and Chiu 2003) have shown that both self-efficacy and facilitating condition affect perceived behavioral control. The former refers to the degree of confidence which the individual has in one's own ability to finish the task (Bandura 1977). The latter refers to the degree of resources needed when the decision maker engages in some behavior (Taylor and Todd 1995; Chu and Chiu 2003). Tierney and Farmer (2002) pointed out that creative self-efficacy had a significantly positive effect on employee creativity. Amabile and Gryskiewicz (1987) found that sufficient resources, such as facilities, equipment, information, and funds, contribute to the creativity of R&D scientists. To sum up, we propose the following hypotheses (HP):

HP 1: The innovative behavioral intention (IBI) is positively related to the creative achievements (CA).
HP 2: The positive attitude (AT) is strongly related to the IBI.
HP 3: The strong subjective norm (SN) is positively related to the IBI.
HP 4: The strong perceived behavioral control (PBC) is positively related to the IBI.
HP 5: The strong PBC is positively related to the CA.
HP 6: The personal intrinsic benefit (PIB) is positively related to the attitude (AT).
HP 7: The personal extrinsic benefit (PEB) is positively related to the attitude (AT).
HP 8: The significant others' evaluation (SOE) is positively related to the SN.
HP 9: The significant others' expectation (SOX) is positively related to the SN.
HP 10: The self-efficacy (SE) is positively related to the PBC.
HP 11: The facilitating condition (FC) is positively related to the PBC.

3   Methods

3.1   Sample Plan and Data Collection

The sample used in this study was taken from design students from northern, central and southern Taiwan. After considering that the main programs of the freshman and sophomore years involved studying a foundation course and accepting less practical training, this study focused on junior and senior undergraduate students as well as graduate students to collect samples using two approaches: to paste the questionnaire website with prize drawing on relevant pages of the design school, its blog and Facebook; to collect the email addresses of participants and send emails with the questionnaire website and prize drawing to the participants.

The internet questionnaire was first constructed based on the literature and then the content was reviewed and modified by two experienced experts for proper expressions. Owing to innovation being an abstract concept, we added an annotation (i.e., "Innovation" means that you put your design ideas into action) at the beginning of each part of the questionnaire as reminder. From a pilot-test with convenient sampling of the design students before formal survey, a total of 74 complete responses were collected for internal consistency analyses. The results showed that Cronbach's alpha values were ranged from .73 (for significant others' expectation) to .92 (for innovative behavior intention), which were higher than the suggested alpha value of 0.7 (Nunnally and Bernstein 1994). For formal survey, a total of 359 responses were received, in which 277 were valid. In terms of the gender, 33.6% (n=93) were boys and 66.4% (n=184) were girls. In year of study, 49.1% were in their junior year, 31.4% were seniors, and 19.5% were in their master's program.

3.2 Measurement

Creative achievement was measured by the creative achievement questionnaire, CAQ (Carson et al. 2005). This study used two fields, i.e., "visual arts (painting, sculpture)" and "inventions" from the second part of the CAQ. A slight modification was made without changing the original meaning in the inventions field. Participants responded based on the facts by multiple choices. There were totally 16 items in these two fields. The items in each field were rank-ordered and assigned ascending weights from 0 to 7 points. Thus, the highest score was 28 and the lowest score was 0 in each field. In short, higher score indicates higher creative achievement.

Innovative behavior intention was adapted from the innovation behavioral questionnaire (Scott and Bruce 1994). All 6 items were modified to measure the degree of intention to put in practice for searching new knowledge, new skills, and new product ideas during a student's time at university. Attitude, subjective norm and perceived behavioral control determined the intention in the TPB. The attitude involved using semantic differential scales with 7-point scale for measurement such as "I think innovation is good, beneficial, and valuable", and all three items were adapted from Ajzen (2002). The three items of subjective norm and three items of perceived behavioral control were adapted from Taylor and Todd (1995) and Lee (2010). Attitude was determined by personal intrinsic benefit and personal extrinsic benefit for which the definitions of both variables were based on the views of Amabile et al. (1994), Chu and Chiu (2003), and Bock et al. (2005). The Work Preference Inventory was used which included intrinsic and extrinsic motivation from Amabile et al. (1994) and which had been transferred to the Chinese version by Chiou (2000). The subjective norm was determined by the evaluation of significant others and others' expectations for which the items were developed using the definition based on the comprehensive views of Chang and Chiang (2008), Ramus (2001), Shally (1995) and Taylor and Todd (1995). The perceived behavioral control was determined by self-efficacy and facilitating condition for which the items were developed using the definitions of both variables from the viewpoints of Ajzen (2002), Bandura (1977) and Taylor and Todd (1995).

4   Results

Using LISREL8.8 and MLE estimates, all factor loadings of items were between .62 and .93, and that all factor loadings were significantly higher than the standard .5 (Hair et al. 1998). The composite reliability (CR) was between .60 and .89, and thus higher than the recommended value of .6 (Fornell and Larcker 1981). The average variance extracted (AVE) of most variables were between .51 and .68, and higher than the recommended value of .5 (Fornell and Larcker 1981). Except for the significant others' expectation (AVE=.47), which is close to the recommended value. Judging from the above, the results exhibited a certain degree of internal reliability and convergent validity, and showed that all values for the correlations of variables were lower than the values of the square roots of the average variance extracted, revealing that all variables had good discriminant validity.

The structural equation model includes model fitness analysis and the overall path coefficients and their significance analysis. In terms of model fitness, the ratio of the chi-square and degrees of freedom was χ^2/df =2.32 which was lower than .3. Other indices such as RMSEA=.069<.08 (Browne and Cudek 1993), CFI=.96, NNFI=.95, NFI=.93, and IFI=.96 were all greater than .90 (Hair et al. 1998). However, GFI=.81 and AGFI=.77 were lower than .90 and .80(Scott 1994), respectively.

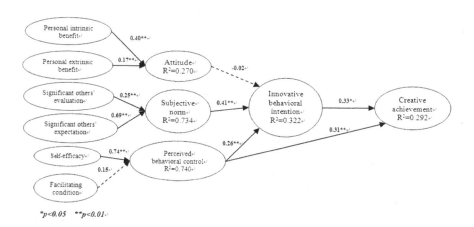

*p<0.05   **p<0.01

Fig. 1. Structural Model Analysis

Overall, the results indicated that the model was acceptable. The path coefficients and their significance for the 11 hypotheses of the integrated model are presented in Figure 1. The model shows that the coefficient of determination (R^2) of each latent variable was 27% for attitude, 73.4% for subjective norm, 74% for perceived behavioral control, 32.2% for innovative behavioral intention, and 29.2% for creative achievements.

5   Discussion

According to the analysis results, the creative achievements of design students are affected by perceived behavioral control and innovative behavioral intention. Ajzen (1985; 1989) pointed out that the behavior is dependent on the personal volitional control, for when people have more behavioral control such as enough ability, opportunity, and resources, the more they engage in such particular behavior. Thus, perceived behavioral control affects behavior directly when the behavior needs enough ability to perform in a particular way. Amabile (1983) described creativity as the confluence of task motivation, domain-relevant knowledge and abilities, and creativity-relevant skills. The second variable emphasized the importance of the ability and knowledge in a specific domain. The study results support the viewpoints of both scholars. While the innovative behavioral intention can explain the creative achievement, the perceived behavioral control also can explain the creative achievements.

Based on the results for the three variables of TPB, the influence of the subjective norms on the innovative behavioral intention is the strongest, the perceived behavioral control follows, but the attitude is not related. The results based on the mean and standard deviation of attitude indicate that many design students described the attitude toward the innovation trend as good, beneficial, and valuable. However, for students to have a good attitude toward innovation does not mean the students will exhibit a stronger innovative behavioral intention. When contrasted with subjective norms and perceived behavioral controls, the approach that consisted of guiding students to have higher creative achievement to increase the significant others' evaluation and expectation or enhance the innovation ability, opportunities and resources for actors was more effective in improving the creativity achievement of the students.

In terms of the antecedent variables, first of all, personal intrinsic benefit and personal extrinsic benefit can both positively affect the attitude of students toward innovation in which case the influence of personal intrinsic benefit is higher than that of personal extrinsic benefit. This result is the same as that of Amabile (1994) who investigated the WPI scale and found that when an individual leaned toward intrinsic motivation, he or she would continue to produce creative works. Besides, our results are similar to those by Tsai and Kao (2004) in that personal extrinsic benefits facilitated creativity improvement, yet the effect of personal extrinsic benefit was lower than that of personal intrinsic benefit. Secondly, significant others' expectation and evaluation both affected the subjective norm, in which the others' expectations were higher than the others' evaluation. Therefore, regardless of the expectations from teachers or students, both can encourage their students or peers to innovate. In addition, our results are similar to those for Yuan and Zhou (2008), Shally (1995), Fodor and Carver (2000), and Tierney and Farmer (2004), for which the results showed that the pressure from the expectations of others effectively influenced the creativity results when students engaged in their creative work. Thirdly, the perceived behavioral control was affected by self-efficacy but was not affected by facilitating condition, in which the self-efficacy was more important than the facilitating condition. The research indicated that the design students needed time, mental effort, and money to develop ideas, for sketches, modeling, and presenting work at different steps (Yang et al. 2003). However, even if it was possible to provide enough facilitating condition for the students, the self-efficacy that was the key factor for creativity. The results indicated that self-efficacy was able to explain the perceived behavioral control as in the studies by Tierney and Farmer (2002) and Hung et al. (2008). The former research showed that the creative efficacy of employees predicted creative outcomes. The latter research showed that the creative efficacy of 636 students predicted creative life experiences.

6   Conclusion

From above analyses and discussions, the hypothesized model was validated empirically using data for 277 students from industrial and visual designs. The results confirmed that both innovative behavioral intention and perceived behavioral control affect student's creative achievements significantly. Subjective norms and perceived behavioral control were significantly related to the intention to exhibit innovative behavior, but attitude was not. Self-efficacy exerts its influence on students' perceived behavioral control more significantly than other antecedent variables.

This study belongs to a cross-sectional study in which all the data for the variables were collected at the same time, yet this research design may confuse the cause with the effect. However, to resolve this problem, we could consider collecting the data on independent variables and dependent variables from different times, but two problems arise. First, creative achievements take a long time to accumulate. Even if data are collected at separate points of time, future achievements will cover the previous accumulation that is difficult to explain at this point in the relationship between cause and effect. Second, data collection at two points in time might cause a large number of participants to suffer loss and make the collection of data difficult. That is why studies predicting innovative behavior and creativity outcomes always collected data at the same time. Thus, according to the study of Jong and Hartog (2010), this study has used innovative behavior to predict creativity outcomes which reveal that our argument is reasonable.

The attitude variable was no significant affect on innovation behavior intention in the model used in this study. Students have a good attitude toward innovation does not mean the students will exhibit a stronger innovative behavioral intention. However, the descriptive statistics reveal that design students described the attitude toward the innovation trend as good, beneficial, and valuable which means that most students have a positive attitude and support innovation. It seems that the attitude might be affected by social expectations that might cause the participant to select a higher point. Therefore, the items regarding attitude have been improved. The relationship between attitude and innovation behavior intention needs to be carefully investigated in further research.

Acknowledgments. This work was partially supported by the National Science Council (NSC 101-2410-H-006-067-MY2) of Taiwan.

References

1. Ajzen, I.: Attitude structure and behavior. In: Pratkanis, A.R., Breckler, S.J., Greenwald, A.G. (eds.) Attitude Structure and Function, pp. 241–274. Lawrence Erlbaum Associates, Hillsdale (1989)
2. Ajzen, I., Madden, T.J.: Prediction of goal-directed behavior: Attitude, intention and perceived behavioral control. J. of Experimental Social Psychology 22, 453–474 (1986)
3. Amabile, T.M.: Children's artistic creativity: Detrimental effects of competition in a field setting. Personality and Social Psychology Bulletin 8, 573–578 (1982)
4. Amabile, T.M.: The Social Psychology of Creativity. Springer, New York (1983)
5. Amabile, T.M., Gryskiewicz, S.S.: Creativity in the R&D laboratory. Technical Report, No. 30, Greensboro, N. C.: Center for Creative Leadership (1987)
6. Amabile, T.M., Hill, K.G., Hennessey, B.A., Tighe, E.M.: The work preference inventory: Assessing intrinsic and extrinsic motivational orientations. Journal of Personality and Social Psychology 66(5), 950–967 (1994)
7. Bandura, A.: Social Learning Theory. Prentice-Hall, Englewood Cliffs (1977)
8. Blackwell, R.D., Miniard, P.W., Engel, J.E.: Consumer Behavior, 9th edn. Harcourt, Inc., Fort Worth (2001)
9. Bock, G.W., Zmud, R.W., Kim, Y.G., Lee, J.N.: Behavioral intention formation in knowledge sharing: Examining the roles of extrinsic motivators, social-psychological forces, and organizational climate. MIS Quarterly 29(1), 87–111 (2005)
10. Browne, M.W., Cudeck, R.: Alternative ways of assessing model fit. In: Bollen, K.A., Long, J.S. (eds.) Testing Structural Equation Models, pp. 136–162. Sage, Newbury Park, CA (1993)
11. Carson, S., Peterson, J.B., Higgins, D.M.: Reliability, validity, and factor structure of the creative achievement questionnaire. Creativity Research Journal 17(1), 37–50 (2005)
12. Cheng, C.M., Chen, L.J.: A study on the knowledge sharing of health technology for technological college students' mobile learning. International Journal of Education and Information Technologies 1(1), 24–29 (2007)
13. Chiou, H.: Intrinsic and extrinsic working motivation: An quantitative study of motivational orientations for Taiwanese and American undergraduates. Research in Applied Psychology 7, 221–251 (2000) (in Chinese)
14. Chu, P.Y., Chiu, J.F.: Factors influencing household waste recycling behavior: Test of an integrated model. Journal of Applied Social Psychology 33(3), 604–626 (2003)
15. Fielding, K.S., Terry, D.J., Masser, B.M., Hogg, M.A.: Integrating social identity theory and the theory of planned behavior to explain decisions to engage in sustainable agricultural practices. British Journal of Social Psychology 47(1), 23–48 (2008)
16. Fishbein, M., Ajzen, I.: Belief, Attitude, Intention, and Behavior: An Introduction to Theory and Research. Addison-Wesley, Reading (1975)
17. Fornell, C., Larcker, D.F.: Evaluating structural equation models with unobservable and measurement error. Journal of Marketing Research 18(1), 39–50 (1981)
18. Hair, J.F., Anderson, R.E., Black, W.C.: Multivariate Data Analysis, 5th edn. Prentice Hall International, UK (1998)
19. Ho, Y.Y., Tsai, H.T., Day, J.D.: Using the theory of planned behavior to predict public sector training participation. The Service Industries Journal 31(5), 771–790 (2011)
20. Hsu, Y., Chang, W.C., Yang, K.H.: The implication of designer recruitment methods and working performance in design education. The International Journal of Arts Education 1(5), 93–109 (2007) (in Chinese)

21. Hung, S.P., Huang, H.Y., Lin, S.S.J.: Do significant others' feedback influence one's creative behavior? - Using structural equation modeling to examine creativity self-efficacy and the creativity motivation mediation effect. Bulletin of Educational Psychology 40(2), 303–322 (2008) (in Chinese)
22. Jong, J.D., Hartog, D.D.: Measuring innovative work behavior. Creativity and Innovation Management 19(1), 23–36 (2010)
23. Kleysen, R.F., Street, C.T.: Toward a multi-dimensional measure of individual innovative behavior. Journal of Intellectual Capital 2(3), 284–296 (2001)
24. Lee, M.C.: Explaining and predicting users' continuance intention toward e-learning: An ext. of the expectation-confirmation model. Computers & Education 54, 506–516 (2010)
25. Maurer, T.J., Weiss, E.M., Barbeite, F.G.: A model of involvement in work-related learning and development activity: The effects of individual, situational, motivational, and age variables. Journal of Applied Psychology 88(4), 707–724 (2003)
26. Nunnally, J.C., Bernstein, I.H.: Psycho-metric Theory, 3rd edn. McGraw-Hill, New York (1994)
27. Ramus, C.A.: Organizational support for employees: Encouraging creative Ideas for environmental sustainability. California Management Review 43(3), 85–105 (2001)
28. Rivis, A., Sheeran, P.: Descriptive norms as an additional predictor in theory of planned behavior: A meta-analysis. Current Psychology 22(3), 213–233 (2003)
29. Scott, S.G., Bruce, R.A.: Determinants of innovative behavior: A path model of individual innovation in the workplace. Academy of Management J. 37(3), 580–607 (1994)
30. Shally, C.E.: Effects of coactions, expected evaluation, and goal setting on creativity and productivity. Academy of Management Journal 38, 483–503 (1995)
31. Taylor, S., Todd, P.A.: Understanding information technology usage: A test of competing models. Information Systems Research 6(2), 144–176 (1995)
32. Tierney, P., Farmer, S.M.: The pygmalion process and employee creativity. Journal of Management 30(3), 413–432 (2004)
33. Tsai, C.T., Kao, C.F.: The relationships among motivational orientations, climate for organization innovation, and employee innovative behavior: A test of Amabile's motivational synergy model. Journal of Management 21(5), 571–592 (2004) (in Chinese)
34. West, M.A., Farr, J.L.: Innovation at work: Psychological perspectives. Social Behavior 4(1), 15–30 (1989)
35. Yang, M.Y., You, M.L., Lin, S.H.: Preliminary study of learning situations and career issues for university ID students. Journal of Design 8(3), 75–90 (2003) (in Chinese)
36. Yang, M.Y., You, M.L., Guo, C.Y.: A preliminary study on industrial design graduates' employment in Taiwan. Journal of Design 15(2), 73–94 (2010) (in Chinese)
37. Yuan, F., Zhou, J.: Differential effects of expected external evaluation on different parts of the creative idea production process and on final product creativity. Creativity Research Journal 20(4), 391–403 (2008)

A Design Process for New Concept Development

Ding-Bang Luh, Frank (Ming-Hung) Chen, and Vincent (I-Hsun) Ku

Department of Industrial Design, National Cheng Kung University
No.1, University Road, Tainan City 701, Taiwan (R.O.C.)
luhdb@mail.ncku.edu.tw, frank0624_88@hotmail.com,
vincentqp@gmail.com

Abstract. A rise in service industry has allowed the service provider to realize the importance of service innovation. However, there are different sequences of design method which can generate a different result. Service innovation approaching from having the "least" complains within a service, may still result in customers' dissatisfaction. This research developed a new service design method approaching from satisfying the customers' "wish" instead of complains. This design method can generate an innovative solution that can be beyond customers' expectation, which create a higher impact on overall value that the customer may perceive. This service design method will be named as "wish-guided" service design method. It will transform the information gathered from service process, from complains to wishes. By knowing customers' wishes, the "value" of the design problem can be increased greatly.

Keywords: wish, expectation, service innovation, design method, value.

1   Introduction

Over the last century, the service industry has been a boom to the economy around the world. Industrial countries have begun to shift their focus of profit from manufacturing oriented to service dominated (Ostrom et al., 2010). From tangible products to intangible service, scholar Moritz (2005) describes the current marketing as "the service provider cannot no longer generate profit just from the physical product itself but the service it comes along." Even though service providers have noticed the importance of service innovation, the service providers have a difficult time using the current service design method available. Current service innovation tends to focus on the current service process to find the "least complains" from the customers as a solution, instead of focusing on the innovative fixation of the service. An ideal service innovation should be satisfying the customers' "wishes", to create a value that are beyond the customers' expectation; becoming the "highest satisfying" solution.

"Services, we maintain, are produced by means of a process" (Edvardsson& Olsson, 1996). It can be recognized as how the service provider "delivers" the service to the service receiver and how the service receiver "receives" the service. Even though there are different characteristics of service: intangibility, heterogeneity,

A. Marcus (Ed.): DUXU/HCII 2013, Part I, LNCS 8012, pp. 545–553, 2013.
© Springer-Verlag Berlin Heidelberg 2013

inseparability, and perishability, service itself by any means is still delivering the "quality" to the customer.

Scholar Lovelock & Yip (1996) described the range of service sector may be broken down into three sections: People process service, possession process service, and Information based Service. The service sector may be different, but it is still about the process of receiving service. The research from scholar Matthing & BodilSandén & Edvardsson (2004) mentioned the services today are interactive, technology intensive, and embedded in relationships. Even though service providers have noticed the importance of service innovation, the service providers have a difficult time using the current service design method available. If the service providers were able to apply a service process concept development for different types of service, the success rate would greatly be increased.

Even though there are different categories and characteristic within services, service itself by any means is still delivering the "quality" to the customer. Scholar Edvardsson and Gustavsson(1990) proposed a service system framework; the service system has four components: customer, staff, physical/technical environment, and organization and control. These four components will need to co-exist in order to deliver a proper service.

New Service Development (NSD) refers to "the overall process of developing new service offerings (Johnson et al., 2000), from idea generation to launch or implementation (Cooper et al., 1994)." The reason why there are so many types of NSD for the service provider to choose from is because the result of the current service design method is not able to achieve what the customers need, wish, and expect. Needs are basic, different customers look to satisfy their needs in different ways (Edvardsson & Olsson, 1996). Wishes refer to the way in which the customer wants to satisfy a specific need (Edvardsson& Olsson, 1996). Expectations are linked with a phenomenon or object, a specific service or a certain company. Expectation is based on the customer's needs and wishes but it is also influenced, often to a considerable extent, by the company's image or reputation on the market, the customer's previous experience of the service company, the service company's marketing, and so on (Edvardsson & Olsson, 1996).

The concept behind NSD is build upon service development, service operation, and service improvement. Service development: the service development phase develops a new service concept (what to deliver) and service delivery system (how to deliver it) (Kim & Meiren, 2012). Service Operation: the developed service is delivered and evaluated (Kim & Meiren, 2012). Service improvement: if a service failure occurs, service recovery is pursued. In case immediate service recovery is insufficient and fundamental improvement in the service is necessary, the service improvement phase is activated. It is in this phase that the problem is defined and the root causes are identified (Kim & Meiren, 2012).

The most important reasoning to create a new service is to create value. Therefore, the design process tempts to identify the value of service and to seek for an opportunity to gain advantages in the competitive field. Value itself can be defined differently on the goal or the subject, as well as being perceived differently. In this research, value will be defined as, "value is the consumer's overall assessment of the utility of a product based on perceptions of what is received and what is given (Zeithaml 1988, p. 14)."

Scholar Woodruff (1997) described the desired customer value as, "a maximum value can be generated if the service full-fill what the customer want." The service will tend to seek to achieve what the customers really want from the customer's perspective, which will be related to customer's process and activity within a service.

Current service providers tend to lean towards solving the issues with the current service instead of satisfying the need, wish, or expectation for the service receiver, which may result in a less innovative solution, as the result is not what the service receiver fully-wanted. The ultimate goal is to allow different background participants to use this design method in different industry, as well as having a proactive thought in mind while using this design method.

2   Process

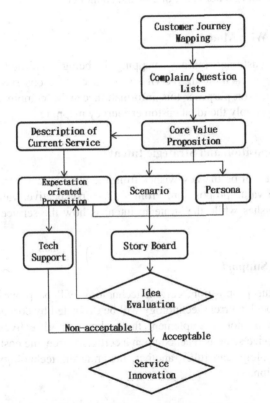

Fig. 1. Process of Wish-Guided Design Method

2.1   Customer Journey Mapping

The first step for Wish-Guided service design method is customer journey mapping. By listing out customer journey mapping, the subjects will be able to gather the information on processes that the customer will have to go through within the service. The motivation and purpose for each of the activities will be found.

2.2   Complain/Question Lists

After the listing out the customer journey mapping, the subjects will be able to analyze the questions and problems the customer may encounter within that step of process. Urgency and importance will be used to evaluate which questions and problems are the first priority, using urgency as the first priory at all time.

2.3   Binary Customer Journey

Once complains have been identified, these information can be transformed from complains to wishes. The ideal customer journey mapping can be express as a character, time, place, object, and an incident, in a binary sequence. For example, may and may not, need and do not need, or can and cannot etc.

2.4   Proposed Wish Model

When the ideal customer journey mapping is being identified, motivation and connection between each of the service process can be observed. If there is an identical motivation or purpose, this information can be combined and rephrased, which can help to simply the ideal customer journey mapping.

2.5   Value Proposition and Strategic Intent

Value proposition will be the key wishes from the wish model. Strategic Intent is to conceptualize the value proposition. From another perspective, value proposition is the customers' wishes while the strategic intent is how the service provider fulfills customers' wishes.

2.6   Technical Support

Based on the value proposition, current technology will be proposed to fulfill the proposed wish model. Current technology will be evaluated by cost and effectiveness, to judge whether or not to implement the technology. Effectiveness will be the priority, as the service scale is reached upon a certain degree, the cost will be reduced. Last, if one technology can fulfill another, integrate the technology to increase the chances of execution.

2.7   New Ideal Customer Journey Mapping

Synthesizing previous steps, a new ideal customer journey mapping will be constructed including the following: supporting technology, service interface, and customers' activity. The new customer journey mapping will be used towards later on for scenarios.

2.8   Persona, Scenario, and Storyboard

A persona will be chosen based on second most challenging customer for the service provider. The reason why choosing the second most challenging customer instead of the most extreme is because it will be able to represent majority of the customers' within the current service while having the most complains. If these customers' can be satisfied, it will be sufficient enough to meet the customers' wish. A scenario will be chosen upon where customers' activity will happen. A storyboard may be written or drawn, to describe the new customer journey mapping.

2.9   Concept Evaluation

Based on the result of the storyboard, the result will be evaluated to determine if the wish model will need to be revised. It will still be evaluated based on the cost and effectiveness, to judge if it idea is reasonable or not; keeping the ideas that has a higher effectiveness. Once the wish model has been adjusted, the steps will need to be reviewed and re-evaluate, as it will create a different innovation result.

2.10   Qualitative Interview

Qualitative interview will be used to gather the subjects' past experience on service design method. The interview questions will involve with their experience and problem the subject have encountered when using Wish-Guided service design method, as well as the subjects' opinion and perspective on the overall value proposition of the design method. These information and data will be use towards on revision of the Wish-Guided service design method in the future.

3   Verification

This research will host workshops with 20 subjects on their experience and opinion on the Wish-Guided service design method. 20 subjects will be divided into three different groups. Within these three groups of subject, there will be one experienced facilitator in each of the group as an interpreter and analysis. The facilitator will be recording all the process, questions, and problems etc. that the team has faced. The workshop process will follow the process of Wish-Guided design method based on figure 1.

Using one of the design topics from the workshop as an example, one of the team worked on the topic "postcard".

The subjects first listed out the customers' journey mapping: looking for a shop → looking for a postcard → looking for a shop that sells stamps → asking for the costs to mail the postcard → writing the content on the postcard → looking for a place to mail the postcard → mail the postcard → make sure the postcard arrive.

The intention of these steps are: to share travel experience, to pick a style that they like, it requires stamps to mail the postcard, to share the experience and send messages, to mail the postcard, and to make sure the person gets the postcard and the sharing experience.

The questions the customers may ask themselves within these steps are: where can they purchase the postcard and stamps? Is there a postcard that I like? Can it be a private content? When will it arrive? Is the address correct? Etc.

The complains the customers may have are: language barrier, dislike the style of the postcard, does not know where to purchase or to mail the postcard, does not know the mailing address, does not know when the postcard arrives etc.

Then integrating the questions and complains to identify the main question and complains that the customers may face within the service process. The main questions the customers will ask are is the mailing address correct? Does it have a commemorate value? While the main complains for the customer are: there is not a style of a postcard that the customers like and does not know the mailing process (postage, stamps, location). If the customer does not know the mailing address, then the whole mailing process cannot be completed within the current mailing service system.

The binary steps of the service process is first by listing out the worst case scenario of the current service: I do not know where to purchase the postcard, may not like the style, may not have the commemorate value, I do not know the mailing process, I need to go to different location, I need to know the mailing address, content may be restricted, public content, does not have information of the postcard after mailing. Then switching these service process as a binary sequence: I know where to purchase the postcard, will like the style, have the commemorate value, I know the mailing process, I d not need to go to different location, I do not need to know the mailing address, content will not be restricted, content may be private, have update on the mailing postcard. This new sequence will be proposed wish model for the postcard services.

After knowing the proposed wish model, the subjects will need to consider the value proposition of the service from a customers' perspective. The quote for the value proposition is "Will like the style, guaranteed arrival". Then strategic intent is how the service provider will need to achieve the value proposition. The strategy is "Persona and exclusion gift to the door".

The technical support is the technology will be able to achieve the proposed with model. Different technology will be looked into and then integrating a similar technology into one. The technology that is required to achieve this postcard service may be postage calculation, digital information, packaging, tracking system, text messages, email etc. After the team integrate all the technology, it came to a conclusion that these three current technologies will be able to satisfy all the needs of the postcard service: digital work station, customization and packaging, and electronic tracking system.

The new ideal customer journey mapping for the service process for the postcard will be: go to service location, pick a personal photo, the postcard can be physical or digital, it can be private or not, purchase stamps and mailing it at the store, provide tracking information, complete mailing.

After choosing an ideal persona and scenario for the service, the team tried the new postcard service system with the following storyboard: Alex went to a gift shop to use the digital work station → Alex chooses a language that he is familiar with → choose a photo from his camera during his vacation → the postcard has a serial number of #0004392 (meaning this is the 4392th postcard that is being made from this service), Alex chooses to print physical postcard instead of a digital version → Alex also chooses to upload a video clip on his vacation to the server so his grandchild can download it off when they receive the postcard → because Alex remembers the mailing address so he does not require to do a second time mailing from the post office in his country → the system calculated prices of postage → Alex pays the postage and mail the postcard at the gift shop → Alex receives a tracking number for his postcard where he can receive the status of the postcard in mobile application or email.

Last, the team review and evaluate the concept to examine if there may be a problem for the new postcard service system. The team believes that the postcard service is achievable in the real-world.

Throughout the workshop, the subjects followed the Wish-Guided handbook to record down their data. The subjects may have trouble at some part of the process. For example, the subjects may forget that they should be in the customers' shoe at this point. If the subjects are not in the customers' shoe while gathering complains, questions, and motivation, new possibilities may be annulated. The reason to this may be due to the subjects' background, experience, and domain knowledge on the design problem.

However, the domain knowledge will be a key asset when integrating the support technology to the service. If the subjects do not have a lot of knowledge on the current technology, the overall result may be affected as the solution may be out dated.

This study gathered the subjects' opinion and experience after the Wish-Guided design method workshop. Overall, the subjects agreed upon that a transition from a problem-driven solution to a wish-driven solution will have greater chances of producing innovation results. The amount of time required to discover the value proposition is shorten as well. However, subjects had difficulties on identifying what are the customers' intention and purpose in the journey mapping, as well as supporting technology. The reason may due to the subjects' original background, knowledge, and domain etc, which may restrict the subjects' to view the problem from a customer perspective.

4   Conclusion and Suggestion

This research aims to develop a design method that is suitable for NSD by approaching the design problem from customers' wish perspective. The Wish-Guided design method is capable of discover innovation results, which leads to the following three conclusions:

1. Wish-Guided design method is capable of transforming customers' complains into wishes, which can be a short route to identifying the core value of the design problem. However, the detail of the information may be decided upon the team members within the team, as this can impact the overall process and result of Wish-Guided method.

2. The value proposition will be approach from the customers' perspective, while strategic intent is from the service providers' perspective. It is a matter of "What" and "How", this area may require some skills and experience to integrating the information into a quote.

3. There are areas that still can be improved, such as team formation. Team members may not have the correct information on what the customers' actually wish for; they may rely on their own personal experience and interaction with the customer. Therefore, having what kind of person in the team will help benefiting on customer understanding.

4. The Wish-Guided design model is straight forward and easy to understand. The participants will not only look at "outer" part of the problem, but also the "inner" part of it such as "why" and what is the motivation behind it. This can be beneficial, as these "whys" can dig out a possibility that the customer themselves do not even know.

Acknowledgement. This research project would not have been possible without the support of many people. First and foremost, we would like to thank to our advisor of this project, Professor Luh for the valuable guidance and advice. He inspired us greatly to work in this project. Deepest gratitude are also due to the member of Sayling Wen Cultural & Educational Foundation, Phil, Steven and others without whose cooperation and assistance for the workshop, this project would never have been successful. Special thanks must also go to members of ASUS, especially Daniel, Grace and Rebecca for sharing invaluable knowledge and comments during our research. Last but not least we wish to express a sense of gratitude and love to our friends in NCKU for their manual support, strength, and help and for everything.

References

1. Cooper, R.G., Easingwood, C.J., Edgett, S., Kleinschmidt, E.J., Storey, C.: What distinguishes the top performing new products in financial services. Journal of Product Innovation Management 11(4), 281–299 (1994)
2. Edvardsson, B., Gustavsson, B.O.: Problem Detection in Service Management Systems - A Consistency Approach in Quality Improvement. Working paper 90: 13, CTF, University of Karlstad (1990)
3. Edvardsson, B., Olsson, J.: Key Concepts for New Service Development. The Service Industries Journal 16(2), 140–164 (1996)
4. Johnson, S.P., Menor, L.J., Roth, V.A., Chase, R.B.: A critical evaluation of the new service development process. In: Fitzsimmons, J.A., Fitzsimmons, M.J. (eds.) New Service Development: Creating Memorable Experiences, pp. 1–32. Sage Publications, Thousand Oaks (2000)

5. Kim, K., Meiren, T.: New Service Development. In: Introduction to Service Engineering, ch. 12. John Wiley & Sons, Inc. (2012)

6. Lovelock, C., Yip, G.: Developing global strategies for service businesses. California Management Review 38(2) (Winter, 1996)

7. Matthing, J., Sandén, B., Edvardsson, B.: New service development: learning from and with customers. International Journal of Service Industry Management 15(5), 479–498 (2004)

8. Moritz, S.: Service Design Practical Access to an Evolving Field. Stefan Moritz (2005)

9. Ostrom, L.A., Bitner, J.M., Brown, W.S., Burkhard, A.K., Goul, M., Daniels, S.V., et al.: Moving Forward and Making a Difference: Research Priorities for the Science of Service. Journal of Service Research 13(1), 4–36 (2010)

10. Woodruff, R.: Journal of the Academy of Marketing Science 25(2), 139–153 (1997)

11. Zeithaml, A.: Consumer Perceptions of Price, Quality, and Value: A Means-End Model and Synthesis of Evidence. Journal of Marketing 52, 2–22 (1988)

How to Create a User Experience Story

Ioanna Michailidou, Constantin von Saucken, and Udo Lindemann

Technical University of Munich, Institute of Product Development
{michailidou,saucken,lindemann}@pe.mw.tum.de

Abstract. Narratives are a tool used in many disciplines. In the area of User Experience Design (UXD), in particular, a storytelling approach can be applied during the whole design process to improve the quality of developed concepts regarding user experience (UX). Furthermore stories support designers in exploring and communicating their new concept ideas. However, the guidelines on how to create a story are either too abstract or do not focus on the experience elements of the interaction. This paper aims at systemizing the storytelling approach in the context of UXD in a ten-step-methodology for story creation. The proposed approach emphasizes on experience-related elements of interaction. The UX story is written by and aims at designers with the scope to communicate UX and reinforce it in product implementation. Further, the approach is systemized in a ten-steps-description with additional form sheets in order to support the application by designers from various backgrounds. In future projects a systematic evaluation of the tools introduced would validate the observed positive outcomes of applying storytelling in UX projects.

Keywords: storytelling, narrative methods, DUXU processes, emotional design.

1 Introduction

Designing attractive products that evoke positive emotions requires knowledge about the feelings products arouse as well as knowledge about users and their needs. In recent years, research directions such as 'Emotional Design' [7] have appeared, with the common scope to make possible integrating affective, non-technical values in product design. The research fields of User Experience (UX) and User Experience Design (UXD) also focus on analyzing users' personal impression and making the emotional impact of product solutions describable, even measurable.

Narratives are a tool used in many disciplines, from knowledge management and sociology to software engineering and interaction design, with the goal to support communicating, collecting and compiling qualitative information by giving it a human face. In the area of UXD in particular, as suggested by Quesenbery and Brooks [8] a storytelling approach can be applied during the whole design process to improve the quality of developed concepts regarding UX, as well as to support designers in exploring and communicating their new concept ideas [2]. Although this approach is suggested in literature, concrete guidelines and instructions about how to create stories describing UX, are not to be found. Important thereby is that in this case

A. Marcus (Ed.): DUXU/HCII 2013, Part I, LNCS 8012, pp. 554–563, 2013.
© Springer-Verlag Berlin Heidelberg 2013

using narratives is a tool aiming at developers without expertise in writing, so guidelines used in screenwriting or novel writing are rather inappropriate. Meanwhile, stories describing UX are linked with psychological needs and motives and focus on product and interaction specific aspects, in contrast to organizational or other forms of storytelling, which serve different scopes.

These facts all emphasize the need for a simple and flexible tool which enables capturing of emotions, impressions and needs. With the proposed collection of story elements, designers can focus on experience-relevant aspects even from the early phases of the design process and achieve continuity until the concept implementation, without forgetting important UX aspects through the whole design process. A ten-step-description of the story creation process guides members of a design team applying this approach on their work.

The following section presents related work, while section 3 covers the description of the proposed methodological approach highlighted with an example. The paper ends with a discussion of the approach and an outlook on future research.

2   Background

In the areas of **management science and knowledge management** storytelling is suggested as an appropriate method to communicate activities, to inspire and motivate employees, visualize qualitative evaluations and pass on knowledge in a memorable way. In this context, storytelling is defined by Thier [13] as a method by which experiential knowledge of employees about significant events, collected from different perspectives of the participants, is evaluated and processed in the form of a shared experience story. This kind of stories is per definition different from a story describing interaction and has no UX relevance. Although they are used to support communication aspects, their aim is to document experiences from projects and hints in a transferable and usable for the entire company way. They do not focus on interaction or UX elements and cannot serve as guidelines for concept implementation. However, the generic phases of storytelling process [9]: plan, interview, extract, write, validate, and spread can be adapted with focus on UX. Goal of this work is to support in particular the phases extract and write. Extract is according to Kleiner & Roth [9] the most important phase of storytelling, where interview contents are structured under the analysis categories and a draft script is created. In our approach the analysis categories are adapted in the UXD context, described as "UX elements". For the write phase Thier [13] suggests a plot arrangement scheme: problem/initial situation – incidents/milestones – solutions/experiences. In UX stories the plot should be arranged according to an interaction –instead of topic-specific order and respecting the temporal aspects of UX. Another difference is that UX stories should enable the listener to understand motives and emotions concerning an interaction rather than learning something. Therefore in UX stories the role of the character is emphasized.

In the discipline of **design**, narrative methods can often be found as personas, storyboards and customer journeys, used in different phases of the design process but mostly for user research [12]. In **ethnography**, where human behavior and context play a vital role, stories are used as a user research method and as communication tool

[6]. Gausepohl et al. [4] emphasize that stories help understanding the context of use involving user characteristics, tasks, equipment and physical and social environment and are therefore valuable for the elicitation of requirements. In **interaction design** stories are introduced by Erickson [2] as a communication tool that supports the implementation of user information into prototypes. However, the storytelling tool is not systemized, so designers without similar experience have difficulties in applying it.

In **UX design**, as suggested by Quesenbery and Brooks [8], a storytelling approach can be applied during the whole design process to improve the quality of the developed concepts regarding UX, as well as to support designers in exploring and communicating their new concept ideas. The main concept of their work is that stories evolve through the design process. They introduce different story types according to different possible audiences and design phases. Particularly interesting for this work is the technical specification story type, which summarizes useful information in a structure including: presumptions on which the story experiences base, user experiences described in two sentences, goals of the new experience, references and takeaways as a short summary. Still, those stories do not give concrete information about the interaction or the product itself to support the concept implementation.

Summing up, there is a lot of literature on the reasons why applying storytelling. However, the guidelines on how to create a story are either not aiming at designers or do not focus on reinforcing UX. The proposed approach emphasizes on experience-related elements of interaction. The UX story is written by and aims at designers, with the scope to communicate UX and reinforce it in product implementation. Further, the approach is systemized in a ten-steps-description with additional form sheets to be filled, in order to support the application by UX designers from various backgrounds.

3   Approach: Creating Stories with UX Elements

We introduce a methodology for creating UX stories consisting of experience-related elements defined as setting and arranged into a story plot (overview in Fig.1).

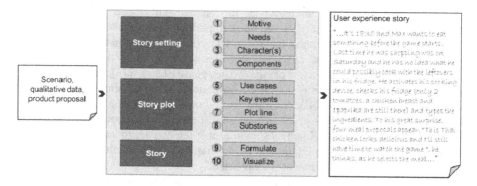

Fig. 1. Overview of the proposed approach with an excerpt of an exemplary UX story as output

3.1   Story Elements

Psychological Needs and Motive

The approach of UX aims at developing experiences via the product usage, which has to meet psychological needs and motives of the user and fulfill or even exceed his expectations [10]. To support this need-oriented approach from the beginning of the design process we suggest that the users´ needs and motives [5] to be fulfilled by the new concept are defined as first story elements. In order to support designers with little background in psychology, we recommend selecting one need from an established set of psychological needs, for instance the set of the 10 psychological needs tested by Sheldon et al. [10]. The concept quality regarding UX could then be assessed according to the degree of need fulfillment. The user motive or motives are, in this approach, expressed as a simple sentence in the form "I want to ..." or "I can ...". This motive-sentence represents the design goal and could serve as title of the story, making the vision for the new product clear to everyone involved in the design process.

Character

One of the main characteristics of stories in comparison to other techniques for modeling applications is that they are personal. To give the story a human face we suggest defining a well-drawn character as main protagonist of the UX story. The study of the story character also emphasizes the user-centered character of the design process. A typical user of the system, defined as persona [1] as result of marketing analysis, can therefore be selected. The authors recommend considering selecting an untypical user as protagonist of the story as well, of course, depending on the development object and goal.

System Components

Subsystems, product components or functions which address the same need as the development object, are proposed to be listed as highly relevant elements to the holistic experience. The integration of more components into a consistent product experience can be a challenging part of designing for UX. This story element is supposed to encourage designers to integrate the new concept into a system of more components that contribute to the fulfillment of the same motive and to reassure the consistency of the experience described in the story.

Use Cases

Roto et al. [10] emphasize the temporal aspect of experiences, highlighting the role of expectation and remembrance. Environment and context factors have an impact on the motives, as well. We suggest that all use cases relevant for the new concept be listed and selected systematically. In this step, designers are supposed to explore how the experience described in their story (and the developed UX) changes over the use in different cases. This step should also serve as basis for the definition of the plot.

Coincidence and/or Disturbing Event (Resulting in Emotions and Activities)
Finally, we recommend the selection of at least one key event for the story, which highlights the need for the new product/concept. This can be a disturbing event -the problem solved by the new solution, or a coincidence -providing the chance for the use of the new concept. Either way, due to this key event, the story character faces critical emotions and the need for activities/actions that are enabled by the new concept. This key event describing the highlight of the experience will also serve as peak point of the story plot. For example, a key point by the end of the story can contribute to creating an exciting story but also to creating of a positive remembrance on the interaction.

Methodology Steps
Our methodological approach consists of 10 steps, described in the following section. Steps 1 to 4 concern the definition of the story setting, which should be filled into *form sheet 1* (Fig. 4), while steps 5 to 8 result in the definition of the story plot. Finally, steps 9 and 10 concern writing and visualizing story in an appropriate format. To further support the designers by the application of the methodology, the description is extended with forms to be filled during the process. The methodology has been applied on the example of a new cooking device, used as short example demonstrating the methodology steps and use of forms in the next section.

1. Determine the main **motive** characterizing the reason for the use of the product. Formulate it in the form of "I want ..." - or "I can ..." - sentence.
2. Choose up to 2 **psychological needs** to be fulfilled by the product. Use the collection of 10 psychological needs.

COMPETENCE
„very capable in what I did"

PLEASURE - STIMULATION
„I was experiencing new sensations and activities"

SECURITY
„my life is structured and predictable"

SELF-ACTUALIZATION-MEANING
„I was becoming who I really am"

RELATEDNESS
„contact with people who care for me and who I care for "

AUTONOMY
„free to do things my own way"

POPULARITY - INFLUENCE
„I was a person whose advice others seek and follow"

SELF ESTEEM
„quite satisfied with who I am"

PHYSICAL THRIVING
„a strong sense of physical well-being"

MONEY - LUXURY
„nice things and possessions"

Fig. 2. Set of psychological needs (based on Sheldon et al., 2011)

3. Choose the **characters** appearing in the story, writing a short description of the character and his usage pattern. *Form sheet 2* (Fig. 3) can be used for support. Note: Does a Marketing Persona already exist? Does it make sense to choose a typical user, or a rather non-typical user? Are one or more characters needed in the story?

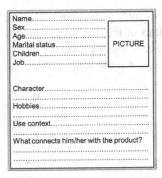

Fig. 3. Form sheet 2 for character description

4. Find other **system components** affecting your product experience. Those can be super-, sub- or other systems, and existing features of the product. Note: Select components that address the same motive and need as your product.

The result of steps 1 to 4 (**story setting**) can be summarized in form sheet 1:

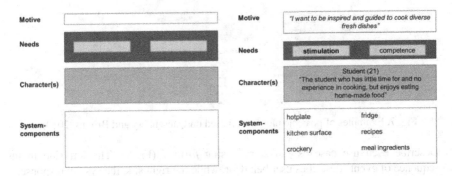

Fig. 4. Form sheet 1 for story setting, as defined in steps 1 to 4, exemplarily filled (right)

5. Collect **use cases** (*form sheet 3,* Fig.5), where your product is used. Choose up to 6 use cases that appear to be particularly interesting / critical in your story. Note: What happens before, during, after use? What role do environment and context factors play?

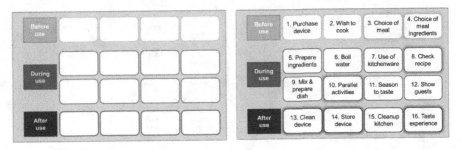

Fig. 5. The form sheet 3 for collecting use cases, exemplarily filled (right)

6. Define at least one "**Key event**", which emphasizes the need for the new product and arouses critical emotions of the character. This may be the problem solved by the new solution, or a chance to use the product.
7. Choose a plot line and arrange the use cases and key events accordingly.

Fig. 6. Example of a plot line with use cases and key events

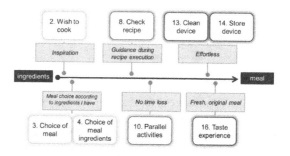

Fig. 7. Examples of possible plot lines (based on Quesenbery and Brooks, 2010)

8. Describe each use case as "substory" using *form 4* (Fig.8). The left side in the sequence of events describes user behavior, while the right side the system response.

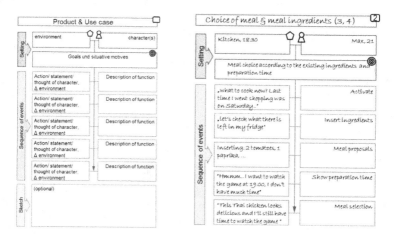

Fig. 8. The form sheet 4 for creating substories, exemplarily filled (right)

9. Formulate each substory as text. The entire text is your story!

Example: *It's 18:30 and Max wants to eat something before the game starts. Last time he was shopping was on Saturday and he has no idea what he could possibly cook with the leftovers in his fridge. He activates his cooking device, checks his fridge (only 2 tomatoes, a chicken breast and 1paprika are still there) and types the ingredients. To his great surprise, four meal proposals appear. "This Thai chicken looks delicious and I'll still have time to watch the game ", he thinks, as he selects the meal.*

10. Visualize your story in a form appropriate for the receiver of your story. Visualization options include: text, illustrated text, storyboard, film.

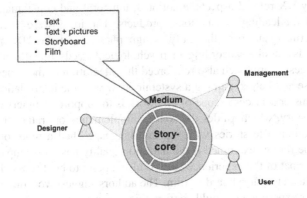

Fig. 9. The choice of visualization form of the story should be made according to the audience

4   Discussion

The proposed methodology for creating UX stories has been applied in student projects. The student teams, consisting of designers without previous experience in UXD or storytelling have been asked to create a UX story using the proposed method description and form sheets. A scenario including information about the development task concerning the market, the environment and the company, as well as a product proposal served as input for their work. Qualitative interview and observation results have been collected to assess the communication of ideas within the teams and the comprehensibility of the process, based on the method description and the use of forms. The UX stories quality has been reviewed in regards to completeness in UX related aspects.

The **communication within the teams** is supported by the use of stories: the common communication platform facilitates cooperation, the discussion about user feelings and motives was encouraged in many stages and the contributions of all team members could be structured as story elements. Moreover, the team shared a common and specific vision about the product to be developed. Still, the need for a moderator should be examined further, since time issues with long discussions and documentation issues (ideas not being documented) have been observed. The method description guided the team in every step of the process. We observed the need for further explanations mostly in steps 2 and 8, so the kitchen device example has been integrated in the method description. The use of forms has clearly supported the process. They have been extended with notes based on the participants' remarks. Another parameter to be further examined is the form of the data given as input: for this work we experimented with scenarios including the product proposal and qualitative data. Another limitation is that since the approach was applied in workshop sessions, it was difficult to evaluate how easy it would be for a team to integrate it into their standard working procedures and furthermore, what consequences it would have regarding time effort.

The main advantage of the **UX stories as result of the process** was that they involved many UX related aspects, emotional, temporal and contextual, and showed high potential for leading to emotional products. The ideas were documented in a presentable form, even from the early design phases, and the UX quality of the concept ideas is possible according to psychological needs fulfillment through the story. The suggested approach also reinforced the integration of the concept ideas into a context of use and helped gaining a systemic view with the interrelations with other relevant systems or services. Scope of this work is to support designers capturing UX elements in a story, which guides the concept implementation, rather than creating a "perfect" narration. The stories with "spoken language" had a more original effect, but it should be further examined if the narration quality has a big impact on the UX quality. The format of the experience story is also a point to be discussed: it can differ from text to illustrated storyboard or film. The authors suggest working primarily with text, but further experiments should confirm this assumption.

5   Conclusion and Outlook

Designing emotional products requires tools which support communication and reinforce integration of UX aspects from the beginning of the design process. In UXD many challenges need to be faced with communication of non-tangible, affective characteristics being essential. UX stories are introduced as a tool to face these challenges and improve the holistic experience. Systemizing the story creation process is very important in this context, since the approach aims at designers with no background in storytelling. Further, UX stories focus on the experience aspects of an interaction and are therefore different from other story types. The advantage of having a simple tool that can be applied from the beginning of the design process is decisive for the use of UX stories, as well as for the improved quality of the stories by the end of the project.

A description of the experience elements composing the UX story, a method description in ten steps as well as form sheets supporting the designer are introduced in this paper. By applying this approach in student projects, we could evaluate, improve and complete the collection of story elements and the methodology steps. The students without background in psychology, UXD and professional writing, were able to create new concepts taking into consideration experience-relevant aspects and stories which helped them structure and communicate their ideas.

In further projects we intend to systematically evaluate the proposed approach and the UX stories themselves, in order to validate the first qualitative data from the application within student projects. We will record the group sessions and analyze the communication [3] to assess comprehensibility of the process and the use of the method description and forms. On the other hand, the quality of the stories as complementary element of the product specification will be assessed. Thereby we also plan to explore different story visualization forms and their impact. The quality of generated concept ideas regarding UX is another parameter we intent to further investigate.

References

1. Cooper, A., Reinmann, R., Cronoin, D.: 'Personas'. In: About Face: The Essentials of Interaction Design, pp. 100–110. Wiley Publishing Inc., Indianapolis (2007)
2. Erickson, T.: Notes on design practice: Stories and prototypes as catalysts for communication. In: Carroll, J.M. (ed.) Scenario-based Design: Envisioning Work and Technology in System Development, pp. 37–58. Elsevier Science B.V., Amsterdam (1995)
3. Hashemi Farzaneh, H., Kaiser, M.K., Lindemann, U.: Creative processes in groups - relating communication, cognitive processes and solution ideas. In: Proceedings of the International Conference on Design Creativity, September 18-22, pp. 13–23. The Design Society, Glasgow (2012)
4. Gausepohl, K., Winchester III, W.W., Arthur, J.D., Smith-Jackson, T.: Using Storytelling to Elicit Design Guidance for Medical Devices (2011), http://erg.sagepub.com/content/19/2/19 (December 13, 2012)
5. Leontjew, A.: Tätigkeit, Bewusstsein, Persönlichkeit. In: Studien zur Kritischen Psychologie. Pahl-Rugenstein, Köln (1982)
6. Lloyd, P.: Storytelling and the development of discourse in the engineering design process. Design Studies 21, 357–373 (2000)
7. Norman, D.: Emotional Design:why we love (or hate) everyday things. Basic Books, New York (2004)
8. Quesenbery, W., Brooks, K.: Storytelling for User Experience. Rosenfeld Media, New York (2010)
9. Roth, G.L., Kleiner, A.: Developing organizational memory through learning histories. Organizational Dynamics 27(2), 43–60 (1998)
10. Roto, V., Law, E., Vermeeren, A., Hoonhout, J. (eds.): User Experience Whitepaper (2011), http://www.allaboutux.org/files/UX-WhitePaper.pdf (December 20, 2012)
11. Sheldon, K., Elliot, A., Kim, Y., Kasser, T.: What is Satisfying about Satisfying Events? Journal of Personality and Social Psychology 80(2), 325–339 (2001)
12. Tassi, R.: Service design tools (2009), http://www.servicedesigntools.org (December 10, 2012)
13. Thier, K.: Storytelling: Eine Narrative Managementmethode. Springer, Heidelberg (2010)

Prototyping with Experience Workshop

Jussi Mikkonen and Yi-Ta Hsieh

Aalto University, Finland
jussi.mikkonen@aalto.fi, ioniqueda@gmail.com

Abstract. In order to investigate deformable user interfaces (DUIs) on mobile devices, an experience workshop was developed to encounter the new interaction style. The design of the workshop strives to bridge form factors and use cases with genuine interaction, which was made possible through prototyping. Prior to the workshop, an explorative experiment was designed to study the role of form in DUI design. Based on the result, several shapes were 3D-printed for further investigation in the workshop. During the workshop, experts in design and engineering experienced a whole design process in which various prototypes were built and the interaction was practiced. The participants were encouraged to practice the imagined scenario with prototypes in real life setting. The result of the workshop became valuable input for building a working prototype.

Keywords: organic user interface, deformable user interface, prototyping, participatory workshop.

1 Introduction

In order to investigate organic user interfaces[1], or more specifically, deformable user interfaces on mobile devices, an experience workshop was designed to encounter the new interaction style. The main idea is to understand how people manipulate a mobile device when its deformation is utilized as an interaction style. Therefore, the workshop involves the identification of three main factors in the new interaction paradigm; the form, the use case and the interaction.

This one-day workshop was designed so that participants could explore the form factors of deformable materials and imagine the use cases. To make real interaction happen, prototyping is utilized as a tangible approach. With the real-life setting, genuine experience was encountered in the workshop. The outcome of the workshop was taken into the next development of a working prototype.

2 Preliminary Preparation

2.1 The Experiment on Form Factors

An experiment was conducted in order to study the form factors of a flexible mobile device. Traditional design methods focus on human's cognitive skills despite the fact

A. Marcus (Ed.): DUXU/HCII 2013, Part I, LNCS 8012, pp. 564–572, 2013.

that other senses are as important as visual skills [2]. Unlike the method in which users invented gestures to associate with given commands[3]–[5], a more explorative manner was adopted in this experiment.

The purpose was to find insights from people's instinct and tactile sense on flexible materials by observing participants' action and response. Shape preference and possible gestures on flexible materials were examined, which became the design hint for the next prototype. In this experiment, four different models were presented to the participants. They were asked to play with and manipulate the models with the presence of stimulus, a video clip.

Four models were built and function as a medium in the experiment (Fig. 1.). In order to achieve flexibility, felt and sponge were chosen as raw material. Starting from the left to the right in the figure, the first model is in cylindrical shape with the intention to manifest one-dimensional characteristics. The second model is in oval shape with plan flat body. The third is basically a rectangular pillow in which sponge is stuffed in the middle. These two models mainly manifest two-dimensional characteristics. The last one is a ball presenting three-dimensional characteristics. Although, in practical, all the models are three-dimensional objects, the intention was to embed different spatial properties into the models so that the interaction in different dimensions can be studied.

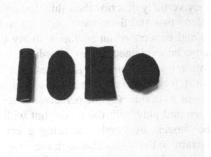

Fig. 1. Four felt prototypes

A video clip was composed for providing content for users to imagine possible interaction while the models are in their hands. That way contextual interaction can be generated accordingly.

There are three parts designed in this video, each with different purposes. The first part consists of geometric objects, which provide a neutral content without specific meaning. This way, users' reaction on stimuli could be observed. The second part is street view enhanced with informative signs. Solid connection between participants' personal experience and this experiment was provided. The last part is simply bubbling water. Similar to the first scene, the setting provides neutral content without specific meaning, while the linearity and predictability were removed.

The procedure can be divided into four steps:

1. Explanation of the experiment

The purpose and the procedure of the experiment were explained to the participants so that they understood the scope and tasks.

2. Participants look at the models and describe their perception without touching

Before touching the models, participants were asked to inspect visually all the four models on the table and describe possible deformation on the models.

3. Participants touch and describe their perception without looking at the models

Participants closed their eyes and played with the models in hand. They were asked to describe their perception.

4. Participants watch, imagine, act and react with the presence of the video

The video was played on a large display in front of the participants. They were asked to watch the video and imagine that there was real interaction created between the content and the model in hand. Their task was to use imagination to interact with the content via the model in hand as a medium. Meanwhile, users were asked to think out loud, which means they verbally describe their thinking and action.

The reason why steps two and three were designed in this manner is to examine how people perceive and understand an artifact's ability through different senses. In Norbert Streitz's study, he explained macro affordance as physical shape and form factor of an object, while micro affordance is addressed as tactile characteristic of the object's surface[6]. In step two, users were able to see the whole model and described their visual perception of it. In this way the perceived macro affordance was revealed. After, they could touch and play with the model but with eyes closed. Users in this stage understood the models by hands exploring every part of the models. The purpose here was to examine the instinct through tactile sense. With a physical object in hands, they were also asked to try to deform the models. At this moment, micro affordance was perceived and action was manifested accordingly.

The findings from the experiment provided insights from three layers: form, gesture, and application of deformable user interface. On the layer of forms, different properties of macro and micro affordance could be revealed. On the layer of gestures, the characteristics that could bridge fundamental functions were identified. As for the layer of applications, physical actions were linked to practical intentions. For example, the application could be starting a car, opening a lock, and similar interactions, whose operation model is based on its mechanical implications. The interactions match those found in prior work[7], but also provide new ones, such as pointing along with twisting.

A set of device shapes was refined for development. After several iteration, a selection of acceptable device shapes were built, and a few chosen for the workshop. The selected shapes were 3D-printed in order to give a proper feel and weight, but to also withstand the rigours of workshop.

2.2   The Material and Locale for the Workshop

One of the tasks designed in the workshop was to build quick mock-ups. Various flexible raw materials were provided, such as rubber, foam cushion, foam board, etc. In the field, a field kit, which included notebook, pen, and camera phone, were given to the teams. Instruction of the tasks in the field was attached to the notebook, and the teams were particularly asked to use camera phones to document their exercise in the field. After the workshop, the kits were collected back for data analysis.

In order to come up with a suitable locale, the metropolis was scouted for different surroundings. We decided to have the workshop along a bustling street with cafes, small specialty shops and groceries, but also with a few larger stores focusing on e.g. second hand shops and antiquities. The core of the workshop was held at a restaurant, which acted as a central location. These were seen as important factors for the exploration and for being able to play in real and authentic user settings. The variety of the shops was seen as support for keeping up the interest, and allowing different situations to be readily available. One could as easily get a feeling from a bridal shop, as from a bookstore. Such approach has been developed during several years[2].

3   Workshop

3.1   The Method and the Context of the Workshop

Three tasks targeting different aspects were designed: prototyping, generating scenarios, and playing in the field. To bridge form factors with applications, the content of each part was constructed first. The form factor of flexibility was explored by quick mock-up building, while application was imagined by understanding the context and discussion in the groups. Practical application cases were then presented as scenarios. Finally, the scenarios were practiced with the prototype in the field, from which, form factors and applications could be bridged by interaction. (See Fig. 2.)

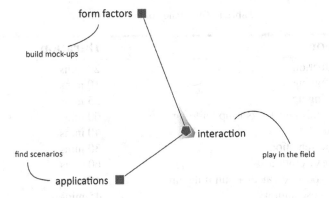

Fig. 2. The form factors and applications are bridged by interaction

The context was derived from the intention of answering the question: how do DUIs enable users to engage with the immediate environment? It is quite common that people immerse themselves in their phones even when walking on the street. A flexible phone might provide interfaces that could avoid the phenomenon of detaching from the immediate environment. The tasks assigned to the participants in the field exploration session especially addressed this issue.

The derived context was then brought into the design of the tasks. In the brainstorming session, groups were told to investigate the detaching issue and imagine solutions based on DUIs. The tasks assigned in the field exploration session were related to the context as well. Since the immediate environment is perceived through our five senses, the groups were asked to imagine and practice how the DUI could mediate the perception of five senses via the prototypes.

3.2   The Procedure and Tasks

The detailed agenda is depicted in Table 1. The workshop started with introduction and ice breaking sessions. Basic information about the workshop and its purpose were presented in the introduction session. The participants did not know each other beforehand. Therefore, the ice breaking session provided an opportunity for each other to get acquainted. Tasks such as naming the team and designing the logo were assigned to inspire the team spirits.

Four teams were formed. Within each team, half of them have technical background and the other have a design-oriented background. The groups were intentionally mixed, so that there would be a clash in the common topics and perceptions. This was deliberate, as our aim was that the other half would understand the technical difficulties, and would perhaps provide technical solutions or see problems, and the other half would see the opportunities and out of the norm solutions. Following the introduction and ice breaking were the sessions illustrated in below.

Table 1. The agenda of the workshop

Session	Duration
Introduction	20 mins
Ice breaking	10 mins
Warming up	25 mins
Brain storming + mock-up building	60 mins
Lunch	40 mins
Mid presentation	30 mins
Field exploration	60 mins
Prototype adjustment + summing up	15 mins
Final presentation	45 mins
Ending	15 mins

Warming Up

The subjects, flexibility and mobile devices, were presented to the teams in this session. Teams were given a short period of time to answer the following questions.

— What are the benefits and limitations of flexible phone?
— What else in your daily life do you want it to be flexible?
— What does your phone mean to you?
— Other than its ordinary functions, i.e. making a call, checking e-mail, navigation, etc., how do you utilize your phone's physicality?

Brainstorming and Mock-Up Building

The context was brought in at this session. The issue of immersing and staring at the phone was brought into discussion. Several questions were designed for this part.

— What are the reasons causing the detaching from the immediate environment?
— How can a flexible phone help with the situation?
— What are the scenarios where flexible interaction can help engaging with the environment?

The participants were asked to reflect on the questions individually before starting group brainstorming. That way, the perspectives could be diversified.

The teams were also asked to build quick mock-ups with the provided raw materials.

Field Exploration

A 3D printed prototype along with a field kit was given to each team. Each kit had one notebook with instruction of the tasks and one camera phone which can be used for documenting the scenarios. Along with the prototype built by them, each team had at least two prototypes. They were asked to practice the following tasks with the prototypes.

— Practice the scenarios presented in previous session in the field. Capture color, sound, texture, smell, and taste of corners in the city.
— Use one prototype to leave your trace (sound, smell, etc.) at some spot, send it to another member who is holding another prototype. Practice sending and receiving.
— Discover your friends' trace.

Prototype Adjustment and Summary

After returning from the field, teams were asked to modify the prototypes and summarize their findings. It was not to compare the two prototypes each team has but to improve the prototypes individually.

4   Interpreting/Adapting the Results of the Workshop

4.1   The Outcome of the Workshop

Away from labs, acting in the field was apparently an involving and encouraging manner for participants to encounter the experience of the interaction scenarios, especially with prototypes in hand. The teams practiced out the scenario in the real-life situation where interpersonal interaction was made possible. It can be seen that the prototypes became tangible medium and involving the surrounding people (See Fig. 3.). The format of the final presentation varied. Some teams performed the scenarios, while others show the video taken in the field.

Fig. 3. Participants acting in the field

In the end of the workshop, six mock-ups were built. Each was associated with scenarios. As for the data collected, there were text and figures drawn on paper, notebooks, post-its and posters. There were also pictures and videos taken by teams via camera phones. The presentation of the teams was video recorded as well. With the help of mock-ups, acting appeared to be an inspiring and involving method in presenting interaction scenarios.

4.2   Findings Considering Flexibility

Shape changing appeared to be one of the major concerns from the participants. The teams explored multiple ways of changing the mock-ups' shape and size to trigger a certain types of event. The gestures were no longer confined in pressing a button but deforming the entire device as action trigger. Furthermore, the possibility of switching operation modes by changing the shape was examined. Different shapes convey different information in terms of affordance. Therefore, different operation modes can be associated with different shapes.

In the tasks of capturing the five senses, the teams performed physical touch on all of the intangible substances. Namely, in the case of capturing the color of a vase, the prototype was bent to align with the curved surface of the vase. In the case of capturing the sound of a surface, the mock-up was placed on it and rubbed against the surface. While the substances to be captured were intangible, the way to capture with the tangible mediator was through physical touch.

Another interesting finding is collective flexibility. In this case, the concept of flexibility was expended from one single physical device to a flexible platform where multiple devices communicate with each other. Flexibility on each device on this platform could form a piece of information. The synergy generated through the platform could result in a greater effect.

4.3   Findings Considering Applications

Environmental awareness is expected so that the devices understand the locale. The point was not only to know the location, but also to be able to provide relevant information associated with the specific locale.

Moreover, a mobile device was also expected to be aware of both the context and the content in the situation. Understanding the intention of the user, a mobile device could provide intimate services. One practical example was to obtain traffic information by the mobile device. The device was expected to know whom the user is, where the user wants to go, and reply with the timetable and number of the bus.

Another interesting finding is the idea of communication between devices. When devices can communicate with each other, the information is able to be shared. That way, social interaction is possible to be extended. Associated with the concept of collective flexibility, communication between devices enables shared information to be delivered in the form of flexibility. Each device manifests different level of flexibility according to the shared information.

Continuing with the social aspect, teams also looked for possibilities in directly involving people to tackle the issue of detaching. A flexible device could be able to foster a situation where all the people can surround and share face to face. Engaging with the environment is not only about the physical objects in the space but also the people in the situation.

4.4   Leading toward the Next Working Prototype

The result from the workshop has provided abundant insights in designing a working prototype. The design of the prototype does not intend to include as much functionality and features as possible; rather, it is to select relevant features so that flexible interaction can be examined on certain applications.

The working prototype consists of a flexible mobile device and an information system that is in charge of processing digital data. A wireless communication channel is built in between so that commends and information can be exchanged between the device and the information system. It is also possible to allow more than one mobile device communicating with each other on this platform. The results from the workshop gave hints on applications that could be implemented on the platform.

5   Conclusion

The design of the workshop enables the encountering of genuine experience of the new interaction style. As a physical representation of hypotheses, prototypes serve also a medium for making real action happen.

Through the workshop, participants developed concepts based on their own experience and discussion within the teams. Starting with understanding the questions, developing concept, building mock-ups and practicing the scenarios, the teams were able to contribute magnificent findings and precious insights on this issue. The findings regarding application provide a basis for associating flexibility with practical application cases. Meanwhile, the findings regarding flexibility give hints on designing flexible interaction.

Acknowledgements. We would like to thank Teemu Ahmaniemi, Merja Haveri, and Johan Kildal, from Nokia Research Center, who actively participate and support in the project.

References

1. Vertegaal, R., Poupyrev, I.: Introduction. Commun. ACM 51(6), 26–30 (2008)
2. Design research through practice: from the lab, field, and showroom. Morgan Kaufmann/Elsevier, Waltham (2011)
3. Herkenrath, G., Karrer, T., Borchers, J.: Twend: twisting and bending as new interaction gesture in mobile devices. In: CHI 2008 Extended Abstracts on Human Factors in Computing Systems, New York, NY, USA, pp. 3819–3824 (2008)
4. Lahey, B., Girouard, A., Burleson, W., Vertegaal, R.: PaperPhone: understanding the use of bend gestures in mobile devices with flexible electronic paper displays. In: Proceedings of the SIGCHI Conference on Human Factors in Computing Systems, New York, NY, USA, pp. 1303–1312 (2011)
5. Schwesig, C., Poupyrev, I., Mori, E.: Gummi: A bendable computer. In: Proceedings of the SIGCHI Conference on Human Factors in Computing Systems, New York, NY, USA, pp. 263–270 (2004)
6. Streitz, N.A.: Augmented Reality and the Disappearing Computer. In: Smith, M.J., Salvendy, G., Harris, D., Koubek, R.J. (eds.) Cognitive Engineering, Intelligent Agents and Virtual Reality, vol. 1, pp. 738–742. Lawrence Erlbaum Associates, Mahwah (2001)
7. Lee, S.-S., Kim, S., Jin, B., Choi, E., Kim, B., Jia, X., Kim, D., Lee, K.: How users manipulate deformable displays as input devices. In: Proceedings of the 28th International Conference on Human Factors in Computing Systems, New York, NY, USA, pp. 1647–1656 (2010)

Keeping User Centred Design (UCD) Alive and Well in Your Organisation: Taking an Agile Approach

Colette Raison and Snezna Schmidt

Adept KM Pty Ltd, 118 Gibraltar Street, Bungendore, NSW 2621, Australia
adeptkm@apex.net.au

Abstract. Using the analogy of user centred design (UCD) as a garden, we explore how to establish, grow and cultivate it to maturity in an organisation. We consider the importance of: having a clear and agreed intent and scope at the start; understanding the environment and culture; planning for success; focusing on the expected outcomes at each iteration; dealing with barriers and risks as they occur; implementing quickly in a scalable manner (according to the Agile methodology); conducting regular 'health checks'; reporting progress; and celebrating achievements along the way.

Keywords: Agile methods, Scrum, Usability, User Centred Design.

1 Introduction

Just as with other organisations around the globe, Agile software development methods are becoming increasingly popular in Australian public sector organisations. Their appeal lies in the fast turn-around from business specifications to developed software and a focus on development rather than documentation. However, given an increasing focus on citizen-centric service delivery, many public sector organisations have discovered that a product developed to suit only business needs may not be usable, useful, or satisfactory from an end user (the voter) perspective. Within the last fifteen years, project managers in Australian public sector agencies have begun to experiment with Agile approaches which included user centred design (UCD) techniques in order to satisfy the political voter pressures and (the user) as well as their agency's business and management stakeholders.

While the intention to include UCD as part of an Agile process to improve quality and performance in systems is to be applauded, it is not an easy task and the outcome is not always achievable. Promoting Agile UCD presumes that there is an existing, and available set of UCD resources from which to draw upon and that the organisational processes, culture and maturity will allow for it to occur. The level of UCD experience and the prominence that the organisation accords to UCD will influence the success of implementing Agile UCD systems design and development.

UCD techniques work best when the practitioners are skilled, supported by management and have the capacity to partner with their Agile cohorts and other teams in the organisation. The 'UCD Garden' in an organisation must be tended, nourished and maintained regularly, like all gardens, in order for it to thrive, become well established and effective.

A. Marcus (Ed.): DUXU/HCII 2013, Part I, LNCS 8012, pp. 573–582, 2013.

1.1   Providing context

Prior to any decision to embark on Agile UCD, organisations need to be clear about what it is they are integrating. To provide some context for this paper, the basic definition for UCD as taken from Webopedia1 is that UCD is a design philosophy where the end-user's needs, wants and limitations are a focus at all stages within the design process and development lifecycle.

UCD is taken to encompass User eXperience (UX), and well as Usability and Interaction Design and to include Usability Evaluations. It is embodied in the ISO-standard 13407 Human-centred design processes for interactive systems. UCD is an interactive, iterative process with key principles [14] such as:

- The active involvement of users and clear understanding of user and task requirements;
- An appropriate allocation of function between user and system;
- Iteration of design solutions; and
- Multi-disciplinary teams.

Disciplined Agile software development is said to be an iterative and incremental approach to software development conducted by self-organising teams within an effective governance framework with stakeholder input and with just enough documentation to meet their needs. [2] Essentially, it includes any iterative design and development process that aligns with the values in the 'Agile Manifesto' [3] where value is assigned more to:

- Individuals and interactions over processes and tools;
- Working software over comprehensive documentation;
- Customer collaborations over contract negotiation; and
- Responding to change over following a plan.

The popularity of the Agile Scrum method is well documented [8] and is the focus of this paper when considering Agile UCD. Scrum methods include an initial meeting to identify a Product Backlog (the entirety of the work to be done), a series of Sprint cycles (2- 3 weeks) to develop software components and daily Scrum 'stand-up' meetings facilitated by a Scrum Master .

This paper explores several projects in a number of Australian public sector organisations that integrated UCD with Agile Scrum processes. It provides practical insights about what worked and what did not and it makes some recommendations about the need to establish, support, grow and maintain UCD capability so that it works effectively in the Agile environment.

---

1 Webopedia at `http://www.webopedia.com/TERM/U/`
`user_centered_design.html` accessed on 28 February 2013

Our research questions were:

1. How is Agile UCD work (or UCD generally) conducted in projects?;
2. Why are some Agile UCD projects less successful (or perceived as less successful) when it comes to the UCD components?; and
3. What (if any) are the common elements shared by projects?;

The next section describes the related literature studies. Section 3 details the research method. Section 4 describes the findings and Section 5 concludes the paper with suggestions for further work.

2   Literature Review

There seems to be an increasing consensus that Agile UCD is a more effective method than either Agile or UCD alone. [8] [16] Early discussions with proponents from both fields (Kent Beck (Agile) and Alan Cooper (Interaction Design)) in 2002 [11] highlighted the process differences in the two approaches, but also seemed to move towards an embryonic consensus on the techniques that could be used as part of an integrated approach.

A systematic review of the existing literature on the integration of Agile software development with UCD approaches conducted in 2010 [14] highlighted how far the integration has progressed from those early days.

The consistent findings from this review and prior research [16] are that:

- The development and the UCD work must be done in two discrete streams with UCD work to always be at least one Sprint ahead;
- Teams must maintain the 'Big Picture' overview of the project throughout the design and development iterations; and
- It is possible to conduct some research and do quick conceptual design work (e.g. Little Design Up Front - LDUF) at Sprint 0 while the developers are also planning and arranging their infrastructure and operating environments.

The interrelationship between the UCD and Agile streams is illustrated by Figure 1.

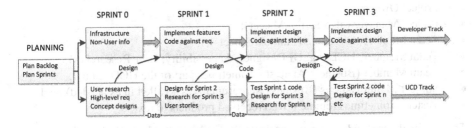

Fig. 1. Agile UCD Process

From a UCD (analysis) perspective, Sprint 0 involves research, a brief requirements-gathering exercise, and clear goals and a clear vision (Intent Statement). The development team prepare the architectural infrastructure and arrange the lightweight agile communication tool (JIRA, TFS, or similar). Developers start coding when the UCD team provides their brief documentation, conceptual design and user stories.

When Agile UCD is done well, it provides demonstrable gains for the organisation [7] [8], but success is not always guaranteed. In some organisations UCD is allocated a less prominent role, is not championed, is under resourced and developing ongoing capability is not seen as an essential organisational priority. This has flow on affects for the individual Agile UCD projects. In other words, the UCD Garden is neglected.

The current research illuminates what is often unseen – the incorrect assumptions about the UCD element of Agile UCD. The exploratory based research using case studies highlights instances of less than optimal projects and provides possible options for rectifying UCD-related issues in future projects. To put it simply, well-tended UCD Gardens provide excellent harvests.

3   Method

This research was very clearly exploratory in nature. We were aware that there were problems with some Agile UCD projects but the extent of the problems and the impact on the organisations (and people) were unknown until subsequent analysis was conducted following the closure of the projects.

We elected to use the case study method [13] because we wanted to find out how Agile UCD was conducted in the projects and why some projects were less successful in their UCD integration efforts. We also wanted to find out if there were any perceived commonalities related to UCD issues shared by those the more successful (and less successful) projects.

During the execution of the projects we were able to speak to some of the team members and we observed interactions between project stakeholders. We also viewed and discussed the tools used to communicate and undertake the work and the project documentation (e.g. UI Specs, one-page Intent Statements and Storyboards).

The roles associated with the projects teams varied, but they usually included:

- Business Stakeholders (Executives and Committee Representatives);
- Project Owner;
- Project Manager (also Scrum Master);
- Team Member (Developer/s and Architects);
- Team Member (UCD e.g. UI Designer, Accessibility, User Researcher);
- Team Member (Business Analyst – sometimes part of the UCD team);
- Subject Matter Experts (Business Representatives – called in as needed); and
- Testers (sometimes remote – who received products to text)

The six focal case studies and the projects are shown in Table 1. Each of the projects related to the design and development of systems (or platforms) within Australian Public Service (APS) agencies. The projects were undertaken from 2010 to 2013 and most had durations of less than 6 months.

Table 1. Six Agile UCD Projects in Australian Public Service agencies

Agency	Project	Type (Agile UCD)	Success
A	Develop a data capture system	Agile UCD	Yes
B	Implement records and sites	Agile UCD	Yes
C	Implement a reporting system	Quasi Agile, min UCD	No
D	Provide a 'single view of client'	UCD, min Agile	Partial
E	Develop an Intranet solution	Agile UCD	No
F	Develop electronic lodgement	Quasi Agile UCD	Partial

4   Findings

4.1   Agency A – Agile UCD - Successful

Agency A is a mid-size and geographically dispersed public sector organisation with a high public profile and international reputation. The project was run largely by the development team who were well versed in Agile Scrum, but unused to UCD. Once the benefits of UCD had been explained and presented to Executives, UCD was endorsed as a core part of the overall analysis process. The team comprised the roles mentioned earlier in this paper and also used the full Scrum method and tools.

Initially, the project commenced with the Development and UCD Analysis being undertaken within the same Sprint because the developers were used to working this way. This meant that there was no time for UCD and analysis personnel to do any background research, to provide the overall intent and vision and to do any analysis on even high level user requirements.

Following a review, it was decided that the first Sprint was a 'practice run' to see how best to incorporate UCD into the mix. The project then adopted the process outlined in previous research where the Development and UCD (and analysis) streams were undertaken in parallel, but with the UCD (analysis) team always one Sprint ahead. The focus was on quick turnaround, minimal documentation and user stories.

What Worked?
- UCD eventually being conducted a Sprint ahead;
- UCD user stories included in the electronic Scrum system;
- UCD *brief* user research and artefacts (Intent Statement) during Sprint 0; and
- UCD and BAs working together and being co-located with developers.

What Didn't Work?
- Initially doing UCD in the same Sprint as development; and
- Reliance on early Scrum tools (JIRA & Grasshopper later used for visibility).

4.2   Agency B Agile, Limited UCD – Unsuccessful

Agency B is a newly created small public sector organisation. It did not have the usual formal structures, governance, policy or procedures in place that would be found in a more mature organisation. Resource limitations meant hiring external consultants and contractors who brought their own models and processes.

The project had experienced several iterations over the life of the agency – all failing to deliver on expectations. Service providers and team members were constantly changed at each review and remediation session. Although purporting to use an Agile Scrum approach, in reality this was only a loose ad-hoc arrangement. UCD had no visible champion and all UCD involvement was disregarded.

What Worked?
- The initial request for UCD services was appreciated; and
- UCD artefacts, design principles, strategies and approach (although not considered useful in this project) were used in all subsequent projects..

What Didn't Work?
- UCD was not co-located with developers and often prevented from access;
- UCD seen as a 'fluffy' add-on or (worse) a project 'blocker';
- UCD usability evaluations on prototypes seen as irrelevant as the prototypes were being shown to business stakeholders for 'feedback'; and
- Usability (and Accessibility) were not as important as getting a product out.

4.3   Agency C - Agile UCD – Successful

Agency B is a small public sector organisation based in one capital city. It was undergoing change to its organisational model and there was a focus on implementing enterprise-wide systems and processes.

The project had experienced several iterations over the life of the agency – all failing to deliver on expectations. There was a churn of project team members until the final project revamp – when a PM with UCD and Agile experience was hired. Once this happened, an effective Agile UCD processes was implemented using Scrum.

What Worked?
- UCD conducted one Sprint ahead;
- Developers using Sprint 0 to plan and setting up infrastructure (non-user related);
- UCD user stories included in the electronic Scrum system;
- UCD *brief* user research and artefacts during Sprint 0; and
- UCD and BAs working together and being co-located with developers.

What Didn't Work?
Earlier project instances with no UCD and no 'real' Agile capability

4.4   Agency D – UCD and Limited Agile – Partially Successful

This high profile public organisation dealt with emotive issues and was receiving negative publicity. Criticisms related to the organisation's ability to respond quickly and to provide a consistent and appropriate client service. UCD was introduced as a panacea to address the client service issues through the inclusion of actual end users, however the introduction of UCD techniques was opportunistic and often personality driven. The iterative nature of UCD led to a recognition that there was a need for more agile processes but the implementation of an actual Agile environment was poor. The focus was on incorporating end users into existing processes rather than on changing the existing processes to make them agile and end user centric.

What Worked?
- Initial 'Sprint' was non-technical and involved data collection and analysis;
- Actual end users were involved;
- Development was iterative and changes from business and users were included;
- Stakeholders were given a voice at planning and update meetings;
- Design artefacts were concise and quick to produce and update; and
- Successes were well publicised.

What Didn't Work?
- Project team members had limited experience with Agile methods;
- Communication between teams was ineffective;
- Stakeholder management was not effective; and
- Changes between each iteration were not prioritised or managed well.

4.5   Agency E – UCD and Quasi Agile - Unsuccessful

This was a high profile intranet redevelopment project in a large, distributed organisation which delivers essential services to clients who are often very critical of service delivery. Agile development was popular for business and executive stakeholders who were keen to see quick and tangible outcomes. UCD was supported by a limited number of sponsors and its implementation did not consider the existing organisational maturity, processes and governance structures. Initial UCD projects used expensive, external staff, promoted UCD as a 'status symbol' (e.g. 'current best practice') which made it inaccessible to internal project staff and caused resentment. Poor implementation did not create a sustainable outcome.

What Worked?
- Actual end users were involved; and
- UCD was integrated into each 'Sprint'.

What Didn't Work?
- UCD was not well integrated in the organisational governance model;
- Focus on documentation was too high;
- Organisational maturity was not considered;
- Internal staff were not included in UCD implementation;
- Communication between teams was ineffective; and
- No process to measure the value of UCD within the Agile process.

4.6   Agency F – Quasi Agile and UCD – Partially Successful

This organisation is compliance focused and encourages applications from its customers – previously mostly in hard copy. Development teams were using an Agile approach but this was inconsistently applied and was not well documented.

The adoption of UCD was considered at a time when external stakeholder support was important. It was hoped that UCD would address the perceived issues with Agile processes. UCD was introduced by a well-respected sponsor who had seen its value demonstrated in other organisations, but support for UCD was inconsistent and it was unfairly 'blamed' when existing issues with Agile did not improve.

What Worked?
- Actual end users were involved;
- Development was iterative;
- Business and executive stakeholders were given a voice at meetings; and
- Design artifacts were concise and quick to produce and update.

What Didn't Work?
- Introducing change on top of existing unstable processes;
- In-effective or not timely communication (e.g. dispersed team); and
- UCD practitioners not familiar with Agile approach and vice versa.

4.7   Summary of Findings

A significant problem was that UCD was seen as an optional 'add-on' or even a blocker to the real development work. The findings for the less successful projects replicated the findings from projects in other organisations [17] where the lack of strategic support for UCD posed problems.

Co-location within an Agile project team and a collaborative team culture was an important finding and is an important Agile UCD principle [5]. When not co-located, UCD was seen as irrelevant or purely a checkbox ticking exercise.

Replicating results from other research [16] Agile UCD conducted in Sprints requires that UCD and analysis is done at least one Sprint ahead.

Perhaps most importantly, analysis of the findings from the projects indicated that success with one particular Agile UCD project does not create or support a sustainable long-term approach for the organisation. Significant cultural change, ongoing sponsorship and an innovative, incremental and holistic approach is needed.

5   Conclusion

Research shows that if Agile methods and UCD are successfully integrated within a project team, Agile UCD is more likely to deliver benefits to the business and to the end user as well. [5]. The research conducted over the past decade shows that as Agile and UCD practitioners we have moved beyond asking why we should integrate UCD and Agile. The benefits in this combined approach clearly demonstrate value to organisations.

We have also moved beyond asking how to integrate them. Agile UCD offers a range of options for how this might occur, from selecting artefacts for small jobs right through to parallel streams for development and for UCD in short Sprints. Research conducted by colleagues has also helped to answer who is involved in Agile UCD and who our customers and users are. Roles are explicitly specified in various Agile approaches and we can identify the differences between customers, stakeholders and users and can recognise the circumstance and need to involve all of them.

We now need to ask what must be in place to achieve success – not only for the project, but for the wider organisation. We need to ask what can be done to ensure UCD is operating well in the projects and within the agency itself. Put simply, we now need to look at the best ways of establishing, growing, and cultivating UCD in our various agencies so that any future Agile UCD project can be assured of success.

This research was exploratory. It provided practical insight into Agile UCD projects and highlighted some outcome project commonalities; however it cannot enable any correlations to be made amongst project elements (variables). Empirical research is now warranted to consider in more detail those common elements contributing to the success or otherwise of an Agile UCD project.

References

1. Agile Defence Adoption Proponents Team, The Business Case for Agile Methods, Association for Enterprise Information (2011), http://www.afei.org/WorkingGroups/ADAPT/Documents/Business%20Case%20for%20Agile.pdf (accessed on February 28, 2013)
2. Ambler, S.: (undated) Disciplined Agile Software Development: Definition, http://www.agilemodeling.com/essays/agileSoftwareDevelopment.htm (accessed on February 28, 2013)
3. Beck, K., et al.: Manifesto for Agile Software Development (2001), agilemanifesto.org (retrieved on February 28, 2013)
4. Blomkvist, S.: Towards a model for Bridging Agile Development and User – Centred Design. In: Seffah, A., Gulliksen, J., Desmarais, M. (eds.) Human-Centred Software Engineering – Integrating Usability in The Development Process, Springer, Dordrecht (2005)
5. Chamberlain, S., Sharp, H., Maiden, N.: Towards a Framework for Integrating Agile Development and User-Centred Design. In: Abrahamsson, P., Marchesi, M., Succi, G. (eds.) XP 2006. LNCS, vol. 4044, pp. 143–153. Springer, Heidelberg (2006)
6. Eklund, J., Levingston, C.: Usability in Agile development, UX Research, pp. 1–7 (2008)
7. Fox, D., Sillito, L., Maurer, F.: Agile Methods and User Centred Design: How These Two Methodologies Are Being Successfully Integrated in Industry. In: Agile 2008 Conference, pp. 63–72. IEEE Computer Society (2008)
8. Hussain, Z., Holzinger, A., Slany, W.: Current State of Agile User-Centred Design: A Survey. Institute for Software Technology, Austria (2009)
9. ISO, 13407: Human-centred design processes for interactive systems, International Standards Organisation, Geneva (1999)
10. McNeil, M.: User Centred Design in Agile Application Development (2006), http://www.thoughtworks.com/pdfs/agile_and_UCD_MM.pdf (accessed on February 28, 2013)

11. Nelson, E.: Extreme programming vs Interaction Design (2002),
    http://web.archive.org/web/20070313205440/,
    http://www.fawcette.com/interviews/beck_cooper/ (accessed)
12. Patton, J.: Hitting the Target: Adding Interaction Design to Agile Software Development.
    In: OOPSLA 2002 Practitioners Reports, pp. 1–7. ACM Press (2002)
13. Rowley, J.: Using Case Studies in research. Management Research News, pp. 16–27
    (2002)
14. da Silva, T., Martin, A., Maurer, F., Silveria, M.: User-Centred Design and Agile Methods:
    A Systematic Review, pp. 77–86. IEEE Computer Society (2011)
15. Sutherland, J.: The Scrum Papers: Nuts, Bolts, and Origins of an Agile Framework. Scrum
    Inc., Cambridge (2012), http://jeffsutherland.com/ScrumPapers.pdf (accessed February 28, 2013)
16. Sy, D.: Adapting Usability investigations for Agile User-Centred Design. Journal of Usability Studies 2(3), 112–132 (2007)
17. Vukelja, L., Opwis, K., Muller, L.: A Case Study of User-Centred Design in Four Swiss
    RUP Projects. Advances in Human-Computer Interaction 2010, 1–10 (2010)
18. Williams, H., Feguson, A.: The User Perspective: Before and after Agile. IEEE, The Computer Society (2007), http://agileproductdesign.com/useful_papers/ucd_perspective.pdf (accessed on February 28, 2013)

Design Thinking Methodology for the Design of Interactive Real-Time Applications

Diego Sandino, Luis M. Matey, and Gorka Vélez

Tecnun School of Engineering. University of Navarra
Paseo de Manuel Lardizábal 13, 20018 San Sebastián
dsandino@tecnun.es, {lmatey,gvelez}@ceit.es

Abstract. In recent years, many interactive real-time applications that simulate real situations have appeared. As with every product, good design is an important aspect in meeting the needs of the majority of users. Interactive real-time applications are no exception; they too must fit users while at the same time simulating reality, creating as perfect a mirror of the real world as possible. Design Thinking establishes a methodology for the development of every project, whether a product or a service, based on the conjunction of user needs, the technologies available and the requirements of the entities that request the project. We in the Design Area at Tecnun, the University of Navarra's School of Engineering, asked ourselves how well Design Thinking would help in the design of interactive real-time applications.

Keywords: design thinking, interactive real-time applications, design process.

1   Introduction

Design Thinking is an approach to problem-solving and projects where we adopt the techniques that designers use, the way designers work and how they approach problem-solving [1-2] in order to re-think different models across a variety of fields (business, health, etc.) and modify them or create new ones that are suitable for users, taking advantage of available technology. In recent years, the number of fields in which Design Thinking is applied has greatly increased [3].

Designers usually develop their work in real environments. The design of different objects, spaces or even entire services almost always refers to everyday situations and spaces.

However, interactive real-time applications have become a tool of particular interest in many contexts. We can find them in recreational environments, work facilities and education centres, among other places. There are several reasons for designing and using interactive real-time applications: avoiding certain dangers, saving money, avoiding the need to transport people and equipment, etc. Regardless of the purpose of the tool, it has to be properly designed and fit the needs of all potential users.

For this reason, at Tecnun School of Engineering we created a methodology based on the Design Thinking process adapted to the design of Interactive Real-Time

A. Marcus (Ed.): DUXU/HCII 2013, Part I, LNCS 8012, pp. 583–592, 2013.

Applications. We supported the methodology by using several tools that designers use to help them obtain all the necessary information while the methodology moves forward. Once we had the methodology, we applied it to a concrete spraying simulator to validate it.

2   Tool Selection

In this section, we describe our process of selecting the tools that define our methodology.

The first step that needed to be taken in order to properly define a Design Thinking methodology for the design of an interactive real-time application was to select the design tools that were most suited to addressing the design requirements for designing these types of applications.

For this purpose, we needed to clearly define what the needs were when designing these kinds of applications. In order to correctly design an interactive real-time application, the most important requirements are that reality is properly mirrored and that the interaction with the application is as pleasant as and similar to the real activity as possible.

With this information in mind, we went through the 51 IDEO Method Cards [4] and selected the ones that provided the most useful information about those requirements.

We chose 11 tools, which shaped the core of the methodology. While choosing those 11 tools, 16 other tools were discarded because of their similarity to the ones selected in terms of the information they provided. Table 1 shows the 11 tools we chose and gives complementary tools, which come from the tools we discarded.

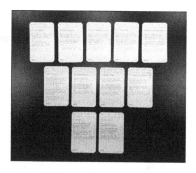

Fig. 1. Tools used in the methodology

Apart from those 11 tools, there were another 9 tools that we left outside the core of the methodology, though we felt they could be applied to any project were they become necessary or of particular interest.

Finally, 15 other tools were left out because they were inappropriate for the design of interactive real-time applications.

Table 1. Tools chosen in the methodology and complementary tools

Tool	Information	Complementary Tools
Error Analysis	This tool helps the team in charge of the design identify every possible error in the activity and in the simulator. When using 'Error Analysis' in the activity to be mirrored, errors that need to be simulated are found because trainees have to learn about them. Other times, errors are detected in order to prevent them from occurring in the application.	Scenario Testing
Activity Analysis	This helps designers identify all the tasks, all the steps to be taken, and all the objects in a process. This tool is very useful when used in conjunction with 'Error Analysis' since once every element of the process is identified and divided into smaller entities using 'Activity Analysis', it becomes much easier to identify every possible error and malfunction during each step.	Cognitive Task Analysis Flow Analysis Draw the Experience
Social Network Mapping	This technique allows designers to identify the different roles in the process; that is, the different jobs and responsibilities of each person involved.	Character Profiles Role-Playing Scenarios
Fly on the Wall	The information provided by this tool is related to how people behave while performing the activity that is being analysed. Designers gather the information through observation, though the people do not know they are being observed, thus avoiding expectancy effects [5].	A Day in the Life Still-Photo Survey
Behavioural Archaeology	Thanks to this tool, the design team gets to know how people organize the space where the activity takes place, what they have to wear, how they use and organize objects, and so on.	Personal Inventory
Rapid Ethnography	Similar to 'Fly on the Wall', with this tool information can be obtained directly from the people involved in the activity. The difference is that with 'Rapid Ethnography' a direct relationship is developed with the people in order to gain their trust, ask them about the activity, and participate in the activity with them.	Cross-Cultural Comparisons Shadowing A Day in the Life Still-Photo Survey Card Sort Foreign Correspondent
Behavioural Mapping	Thanks to this tool designers analyse how people use the space in which the activity takes place (how they position themselves, which areas are most used, and so on).	Guided Tours
Cognitive Maps	Similar to 'Behavioural Mapping', in this case designers ask the people involved in the activity to show them how they think of the space and how they navigate it.	Guided Tours

Table 1. (*Continued.*)

Surveys & Questionnaires	These can be used in different stages of the methodology in order to obtain different kinds of information for designing or testing the activity. It is important to consider that a proper number of interviewees are necessary so that the results are valid [6-8] and that bias can appear while interviewing people. [9-12].	Five Whys?
Narration	Information about the validity of the project can be obtained through users' narrating their experience interacting with the tool in real-time.	-
Try it Yourself	Useful information can be obtained when the design team uses and interacts with the designed application.	-

3   Methodology

The process of Design Thinking is an iterative one with several stages. It starts with a briefing that yields a framework for the future work of the team. After defining the brief, the team starts exploring everything related to what is going to be designed. This provides a good starting point for the next stage, a divergent phase in which the team generates as many ideas as possible, which will be refined in a later selection stage. Prior to the selection stage, Design Thinking encourages a prototyping phase. After choosing the ideas and defining how the product will be, the team must define who is going to do what, in how much time and with what resources. Lastly, the team cannot consider the design as finished when it is developed and in use: they must review the product and check whether it actually fits the needs of the potential users.

In light of this, we can divide the process of Design Thinking into these stages:

Define ▶ Explore ▶ Ideate ▶ Prototype ▶ Select ▶ Implement ▶ Review

Following the above seven stages of Design Thinking, we assigned the selected tools to the stages where their use is necessary and created a proper methodology for the development of interactive real-time applications.

Experience with a simulator for training operators of concrete spraying machinery helped us tune the methodology.

3.1   Define

As explained above, in this stage the designers or the entities requesting the project set a proper framework for the work to be done. This framework can be seen as a series of constraints that guide the subsequent work.

In the case of interactive real-time tools, it is very important to define how faithfully the simulator must reflect reality. At a first glance, it would seem important to reflect reality perfectly, but in many cases only certain aspects need to be simulated rather than the entire activity. Other times, certain effects need to be exaggerated in order to make them noticeable.

3.2 Explore

The purpose of this second stage of the process is to gather information about everything that surrounds the project that is going to be tackled: potential users and their needs, previous solutions to the same issue, etc.

This stage will give the team very important information for the future generation of ideas, as it will help ensure that the ideas will be oriented toward the needs of the project.

The tools that are considered to be most suitable for this purpose are the following:

- Social Network Mapping
- Surveys & Questionnaires
- Rapid Ethnography
- Cognitive Maps & Behavioural Mapping
- Error Analysis

3.3 Ideate

During this stage, it is important to identify the things that are relevant to the people involved in the activity and to generate as many ideas as possible [13] for meeting those needs. Brainstorming is the core of this stage, but it is also important to consider other ways of getting insights for the future design. With that in mind, the appropriate tools for this stage are the following:

- Behavioural Archaeology
- Fly on the Wall
- Try it Yourself

3.4 Prototype

Design Thinking promotes prototyping from the beginning stages of the design process. Furthermore, early prototyping of software design is recommended in order to help users identify their needs in order to make them part of the process, among other reasons [14].

According to the Design Thinking methodology, the prototypes do not usually need to be detailed or working prototypes in the early stages of the process. However, when designing real-time applications, it is helpful to use an evolutionary approach

[15-17] to start developing the simulator so that it becomes the prototype itself. The tool selected for this stage is:

- Error Analysis

3.5   Choose and Implement

These two stages of the design process are merged since the tool that is most suitable for both stages is the same, and its application is based on the analysis of the reality that is being simulated.

- Activity Analysis

When this information becomes available, the development of the simulator can begin, using both the results of the activity analysis and the requirements from the briefing.

3.6   Review

Once the project is finished, the design team will have to keep track of how the product is introduced to the users whether it really fits the purposes it was conceived for, and identify possible areas of improvement and collect information from the people that benefit from the application.

In the case of real-time applications, three tools help the review process, two of which are used in prior stages.

- Fly on the Wall
- Narration
- Surveys & Questionnaires

4   Methodology Applied to a Real-Time Application

Once the methodology was defined, we applied it to a real project in order to validate it. The target was a real-time simulator for training operators in concrete spraying [18]. This application simulates the tasks involved in effectively and safely spraying shotcrete and was developed with the collaboration of the Santa Barbara Foundation (FSB), a training centre located in Spain.

FSB started the first stage, Define, by providing us with a brief with all the requirements of the project.

After that, the rest of the methodology described in the previous section was applied to obtain the necessary information for the development of the application (Table 2).

Table 2. Methodology and tools applied to the concrete-spraying project

Stage	Tool	Information obtained
Explore	Social Network Mapping	Different levels were not identified in the activity. Nonetheless, we found it necessary to set different levels of learning in the application for the operators to gain different skills step by step.
	Surveys & Questionnaires	Several interviews were conducted with different operators to learn about how they use the machine, their work and the environment.
	Rapid Ethnography	Operators in FSB were open to explaining how the machine works and how it is handled. The information was recorded and analysed.
	Cognitive Maps & Behavioural Mapping	Thanks to these two tools, we learned about the possible scenarios in concrete spraying and about how the operators position themselves to perform their activity.
	Error Analysis	This work was facilitated by FSB based on their experience. They gave us a complete dossier with all the possible breakdowns and incidences.
Ideate	Behavioural Archaeology	Thanks to behavioural archaeology we learned that, due to the difficult, dirty and dusty environment while spraying, special protection must be worn and that other objects, apart from the machine controls, are difficult to use.
	Fly on the Wall	Our team took the opportunity to observe the operators in real situation to obtain additional information about the activity.
	Try it Yourself	People on our team were able to test the machines that FSB uses. Thus, we learned first-hand how to operate them and how to use them to obtain perfect results while spraying.
Prototype	Error Analysis	Following the evolutionary approach for prototyping, different betas of the application were shown to FSB and tested to identify all the possible errors within it. In addition, these tests helped FSB find things that were missing in the application.
Choose & Implement	Activity Analysis	With the help of FSB and the observation, our team divided the activity into smaller tasks and steps. We also identified the devices involved in each step and thoroughly analysed their functioning.
Review	Fly on the Wall	After the application was developed, thirty-five people (trainers and trainees from FSB) tested the application. Not everyone did all the exercises but all the exercises were performed at least once.
	Narration	During the tests, people were encouraged to narrate their experience. The information was recorded and subsequently analysed.
	Surveys & Questionnaires	The last tool used in the post-development stage was a questionnaire prepared by our team. The thirty-five people completed the questionnaire and the information was subsequently analysed.

5   Results

After applying the methodology described above, a shotcrete machine simulator [19] was developed that fit the requirements and the results of the entire Design Thinking process.

5.1   Simulator Description

The goal of the simulator was to offer a detailed course for learning to spray concrete. For this purpose, all the possible scenarios where the concrete spraying machine is used and all the possible ways to use it were simulated.

The visual environment of the simulator took into account multiple factors such as shadows, light refraction, water effects, and so on. The sounds that accompany the activity were also simulated to enhance the experience.

To accurately reproduce the interaction with the machine in real life, a device with two joysticks and eight buttons controlled the simulator, thus emulating the real controls of the machine.

Three levels of training were established: basic, intermediate and advanced. This addresses what we observed during the Explore stage using the social network mapping technique.

The computer automatically evaluated the exercise. For those aspects that the computer could not evaluate, an instructor needed to be present to take notes on those aspects.

5.2   Review Stage Questionnaires

As we stated in the Review stage, questionnaires were given out to evaluate:

• Interaction with the simulator
• Realism of the simulator
• Teaching capacities

Table 3. Results of the questionnaire

Question	Median	Mean	SD
To what extent do you feel that the interaction with the virtual environment is natural?	4	3.77	0.57
How similar are both experiences: spraying with the simulator and spraying with real machinery?	3.5	3.55	0.74
How realistic is the way that shotcrete adheres to the surface?	4	3.58	0.82
How realistic is the modelling of the rebound effect?	4	3.69	0.69
How realistic is the modelling of cohesion failures?	4	3.8	0.69
To what extent is training with the simulator more comfortable than training on-the-job?	4	3.95	0.87
How would you rate your motivation while performing the training exercises?	4	3.95	0.84
How would you rate the training capacity of the shotcrete model?	4	3.9	0.74

There were ten questions that respondents rated on a five-point Likert scale. Thirty-five people were given the questionnaire, and the results of the questionnaire were subsequently analysed to obtain the data in Table 3.

6   Conclusions

Design Thinking has shown itself to be an effective methodology for the design of interactive real-time applications.

Following a specific methodology and choosing the correct and most suitable techniques for this kind of project, we balanced the needs of the users, the requirements of the project, the needs of the company developing it (FSB in our particular case) and the technologies available for this tool.

Currently, we are working on applying this methodology to new projects. Many of these projects are related to virtual reality applications.

Furthermore, according to the questionnaire results listed above, we see that the tool has been validated and enjoys wide acceptance among users.

We also validated that the prototyping method we used was correct and suitable for these kinds of projects. The prototype gave us valuable information at every iteration, until the final product was released.

Again, Design Thinking proves that its creativity-based methodology can be of use for any kind of project. Design Thinking also makes it clear that creativity is not only an isolated spark but also a whole system that can bring important results.

References

1. Brown, T.: Change by Design. HarperCollins (2009)
2. Cross, N.: Designerly Ways of Knowing. Springer, London (2006)
3. Stewart, S.C.: Interpreting Design Thinking. Design Studies 32(6), 515–520 (2011)
4. IDEO Method Cards, IDEO (2002)
5. Krejcie, R.V., Morgan, D.W.: Determining Sample Size for Research Activities. Educational and Psychological Measurement 30, 607–610 (2011)
6. Bartlett, J.E., Kotrlik, J.W., Higgins, C.C.: Organizational Research: Determining Appropriate Sample Size in Survey Research. Information Technology, Learning and Performance Journal 19(1) (2011)
7. Creative Research Systems: Sample Size Calculator (2011), http://www.surveysystem.com/sscalc.htm
8. Sax, L.J., Gilmartin, S.K., Bryant, A.N.: Assessing Response Rates and Nonresponse Bias in Web and Paper Surveys. Research in Higher Education 44 (2011)
9. Armstrong, J.S., Overton, T.S.: Estimating Nonresponse Bias in Mail Surveys. Journal of Marketing Research 14, 396–402 (1977)
10. Furnham, A.: Response Bias, Social Desirability and Dissimulation. Personality and Individual Differences 7(3), 385–400 (1977)
11. Paulhus, D.L.: Measurement and Control of Response Bias. In: Measures of Personality and Social Psychological Attitudes, pp. 17–59. Academic Press, Inc., San Diego (1977)
12. Osborn, A.F.: Applied imagination. Charles Scribner's Sons, Oxford (1977)

13. Rosenthal, R., Rubin, D.B.: Interpersonal Expectancy Effects: The First 345 Studies. Behavioral and Brain Sciences 3, 377–415 (1978)

14. Ratcliff, B.: Early and Not-So-Early Prototyping – Rationale and Tool Support. In: Proceedings of Twelfth International Conference on Computer Software and Applications, pp. 127–134 (1988)

15. Gilb, T.: Evolutionary Development. ACM SIGSOFT Software Engineering Notes 6(2), 17 (1981)

16. Hekmatpour, S.: Experience with Evolutionary Prototyping in a Large Software Project. ACM SIGSOFT Software Engineering Notes 12(1), 38–41 (1987)

17. Carter, R.A., Antón, A.I., Dagnino, A., Williams, L.: Evolving Beyond Requirements Creep: A Risk-Based Evolutionary Prototyping Model. In: Proceedings of Fifth IEEE Symposium on Requirements Engineering (2001)

18. Vélez, G., Matey, L., Amundarain, A.: Real-Time Modelling and Rendering of Sprayed Concrete. In: Proceedings of V Ibero-American Symposium in Computer Graphics (SIACG), Faro, Portugal, pp. 141–146 (2001)

19. De Dios, J.C., Ordás, F., Marín, J.A., Matey, L., Suescun, A., Vélez, G., Schelenz, T.: Simulador de Máquina de Proyección de Hormigón. Actualidad Técnica de Ingeniería Civil, Minería, Geología y Medio Ambiente 214, 64–69 (2012)

User Involvement in Idea Brainstorming of Design Process: Finding the Effective Strategy in Social Network Service

Shu-Chuan Chiu[1,*] and Kiyoshi Tomimatsu[2]

[1] Graduate School of Design, Kyushu University, Fukuoka, Japan
mokochiu@gmail.com
[2] Faculty of Design, Kyushu University, Fukuoka, Japan
tomimatu@design.kyushu-u.ac.jp

Abstract. The growth of Social Network Service (SNS) has created a new potential in marketing. The role of SNS has changed the common private and public aspects of life. Many methods have been developed for engaging users in design process. This paper reviews the process of service design development, the area of idea brainstorming innovation though SNS. Specifically, it describes that User Generated Design (UGD) methods for user involvement apply to the development of idea brainstorming and the influence on imagination stimulation. The evolution in design research from a UGD approach to involve users in social innovations is changing the roles of the designer in idea brainstorming process. The results show that the SNS assists the innovation process during the first phases of the new service development process and helps develop innovation ideas. Suggestions for further work are included that include aspects of SNS tangibility, usage areas and UGD innovation.

Keywords: Casual Data, Idea Brainstorming, User Generated Design, Social Network Service, Service Design.

1 Introduction

This study focuses on social network service. In recent years, people are swimming in casual data like never before. The growth of social network service has created a new potential in marketing. Social informatics has taught us that it is important to not only look at technology from the designer's point of view. Technology development is a process in which multiple relevant groups negotiate over its design. Designers have become magicians who grant new life to a product or service.

However, there is a gap between users and designers. Each of these different social groups has a specific interpretation of an artifact and will see and construct quite different objects. Besides appearances and functions of products, user experience has become one of the significant issues that designers and researchers pay attention to. Nowadays, users' demands no longer focus on functional realizations and good usability. A service is always produced in a social and physical setting. More noteworthy is the user experience found in social interaction.

---

* Corresponding author.

A. Marcus (Ed.): DUXU/HCII 2013, Part I, LNCS 8012, pp. 593–598, 2013.

User experience refers to the user's perceptions and responses in regard to their interaction with a product or service [1]. The concept of user experience has evolved to take into account experiential aspects of user-product interaction, such as emotions, feelings and meanings. User experience is intangible and clearly represents something more than the instrumental and utilitarian aspects of the product. From a Human-Computer Interaction perspective, the obvious response to the demand for user involvement is to utilize HCI methods for user and context identification, user requirements elicitation, design, and evaluation.

Due to the importance of user involvement as part of design development process, there is considerable interest regarding how user can innovate within the idea brainstorming. This article also considers existing co-creation research and describes the development and discuss user group develop innovative new idea though social platform. It focuses on how social groups can innovate services through the use of SNS and contributes new informatics to the field of service innovation.

2   Literature Review

Co-creation and User Generated Design are related concepts. This section discusses the concept of co-creation and its relation to idea brainstorming in social platform.

2.1   Co-creation as an Approach to the Development of User Generated Design

The user experience that is created in social interaction is called "co-experience". Co-experience is crucial for citizens to be involved in the design and implementation of new systems. To bring user into the design process, make them become to part of the development team by co-creation techniques. More noteworthy is the user experience found in social interaction [2]. Comparing with a simply attractive product, creating more chances to interact with family members or friends brings much deeper user experience to users. People like to have joyful user experience when communicating with friends through products or devices. With the exception of interacting with friends or family, providing a better user experience in social interaction will lead to a finer and more valuable life.

People do sharing their life experiences with friends, families, or even strangers. For example, people shared their daily life, impression and comments on Twitter, or on Facebook, or on Blogs. And the social information that we call the casual data, companies also utilize these tools to harvest commentary on Twitter, Facebook, and via customer service interactions connecting to the minds of some of their customers' creative commons more than ever. How to effectively participate in service design from the design perspective has become important to companies and designers [3,4].

2.2   Idea Brainstorming in Social Platform: Social Network Service (SNS)

While users communicate and interact via SNS, the context of their conversation which is refer to as casual data can be used to determine their needs or aspirations. User involvement in the development of new products may offer a novel approach to improve methods of meeting customer needs. These users are considered to offer possibilities for generating original, valuable, and realizable ideas leading to successful innovation. The main purpose was to examine the benefit of involving users in suggesting new product ideas in an innovation project.

The trend of product and service design is changing rapidly due to the influence of SNS. SNS has a role to affect the success of a developing products or services. The web users are getting accustomed to interacting with their friends via social media. In addition, SNS has become more diverse; for example, users are able to publish latest news or information about themselves to others in the same network through different social media. As a new product or service starts its development cycle, its popularity and rating can be observed by the quality or quantity of posts within SNS. A good product/service usually received positive feedbacks within the posts. The customer-oriented perspective has facilitated a specific kind of design driven innovation. The main and distinctive focus of service design tools concerns the design, description and visualization of the user experience, including the potentials of different social interaction platforms [5,6,7].

3   Context of This Research

3.1   At the Fuzzy Front End of the Service Design Development Process

The fuzzy front end [8] describes the phase at the start of the New Service Development (NSD) process. The NSD process is related to the New Product Development process (NPD), and refers to the specific differences encountered when innovating in services rather than products. The fuzzy front end is followed by the design development process where the resulting ideas for products are developed into concepts, prototypes, and then refined into resulting products or services.

The fuzzy front end phase of projects has come into focus during recent years, being described as the most important part of service innovation by innovation managers. This is because the earliest phases of the development process offer the greatest opportunity for transformational innovation.

The fuzzy front end is increasingly being focused upon by designers as they are given a more explorative and open brief. This phase is also seen as an opportunity to lift design up to a strategic and tactical level of an organization. Such methods are also important when it comes to building links and supporting innovation in the cross-functional teams that are now used in most development projects during new service development. In the front fuzzy end of the collaborative process there are many divergent activities that take place to identify any fundamental problems, to describe opportunities, and to determine potential designs.

To achieve collective creativity, they emphasize the early phases, user involvement in the very early design process to clear design strategy and define ideas for further development. In this stage, the goal of exploration is to discover design problems, identify opportunities and determine an innovation design approach.

3.2   User Involvement in Idea Brainstorming of Design Process

Users and other figures can become part of the design process as expert of their experience, but in order to take on this role they must be given appropriate tools for expressing themselves.

The designers should provide ways for people to engage with each other as well as instruments to communicate, be creative, share insights and envision their own ideas. The co-design activities can support different levels of participation, from situation in which the external figures are involved just in specific moments to situations in which they take part to the entire process, building up the service together with the designers.

User involvement in the development of new products may offer a novel approach to improve methods of meeting customer needs. These users are considered to offer possibilities for generating original, valuable, and realizable ideas leading to successful innovation. The main purpose was to examine the benefit of involving users in suggesting new product ideas in an innovation project.

We consider the structured symbolism and cultural valence of an activity. In any social interaction and software situation there are multiple perspectives at play that warrant attention at Personal, Collective, Community/Groups/Teams, Collaborations, Newbie, Service Owner, External Developer.

4   Application of the Idea Generation Process

User generated design is a widely used method in designing new products or services. In this method, users and producer are involved in the cycle of product design and development, where inputs and feedbacks are shared together. Although this method is highly efficient and cost-effective, it requires an elaborate system design. A common difficulty that is found during its implementation is the lack of understanding of user's aspiration. Even when the system is successfully implemented, the final product or service design still doesn't meet inherent user needs.

SNS utilization in designing a network service to describe the overview of our proposed concept has been discussed in the previous sections. To be precise, we designed an online service flow that enables two-way communication between product/service developer and user. Product/service developer can use this service for publishing their idea while receiving inputs from its user. On the other hand, user can directly contribute to the cycle of product development by expressing and sharing their idea. We used Facebook to publish user's opinion into Facebook page that redirect to our service, in order to make the system known to general public and broaden its scope in Fig1.

User generated design is a design method where a product is designed as a result of user voice and aspiration. In this research, we propose a system where the producer publishes a question regarding product development and users can openly contribute by suggesting opinions or sketches.

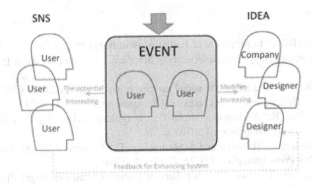

Fig. 1. Feedback Enhancing System Flow

5   Conclusions

There is a gap between users and designers. Each of these different social groups has a specific interpretation of an artifact and will see and construct quite different objects. An experimental user group design was used in order to assess the output in terms of its original, valuable, and realizable merit. The results indicated that ordinary users create significantly more original and valuable ideas. Professional designers created more easily realizable ideas, like product, and ordinary users created the most valuable experiences. The results were discussed from the viewpoint of divergent thinking. It was suggested that divergent thinking was facilitated through the opportunity to combine different information elements that appeared separate at the outset. There is also the social gap between the virtual and reality life. The big problem is that the existing social network groups we're creating online don't match the social networks we already have offline.

While users communicate and interact via social network service, the context of their conversation which is refer to as "Casual Data" can be used to determine their needs or aspirations. Moreover, from a user organization and acquisition perspective, it is contra-productive to single out the software providing a service as the most important entity to design. It is within this context that Service Design operates. Service Design provides an overall design and contextualizes Interaction Design for technology-supported services.

In this paper we have discussed a new method of using Facebook as "Simple Social" in engaging users in design process. In the future works, we will consider how easy these systems can be used as a collaborative platform between product/service developers and consumers. Furthermore, both product/service developers and consumers can receive benefits from SNS service business model. From a Human-Computer Interaction perspective, the obvious response to the demand for user involvement is to utilize HCI methods for user and context identification, user requirements elicitation, design, and evaluation.

References

1. ISO DIS 9241-210. Ergonomics of human system interaction – Part 210: Human-centred design for interactive systems. International Standardization Organization, ISO, Switzerland (2010)
2. Battarbee, K.: Co-experience: the social user experience. In: CHI 2003: CHI 2003 Extended Abstracts on Human Factors in Computing Systems, pp. 730–731 (2003)
3. Lauren, S., Dan, R.: An Introduction to Casual Data, and How It's Changing Everything. Interactions, 43–47 (March-April 2010)
4. John, K.: Abductive Thinking and Sensemaking: The Drivers of Design Synthesis. Design Issues in MIT Press Journals 26(1), 15–28 (2009, 2010)
5. Frances, X.: Frei, The Four Things a Service Business Must Get Right. Harvard Business Review, 1–13 (April 2008)
6. Heskett, J.L., Jones, T.O., Loveman, G.W., Sasser, W.E., Schlesinger, L.A.: Putting the Service-Profit Chain to Work. Harvard Business Review, 118–129 (July-August 2008)
7. Berry, L.L., Shankar, V., Parish, J.T., Cadwallader, S., Dotzel, T.: Creating New Markets Through Service Innovation. MIT Sloan Management Review 47(2), 56–63 (2006)
8. Sanders, E.B.-N., Stappers, P.J.: Co-creation and the new landscapes of design. CoDesign 4(1), 5–18 (2008)

Understanding the UX Designer's
Role within Agile Teams

Tiago Silva da Silva[1], Milene Selbach Silveira[2],
Claudia de O. Melo[3], and Luiz Claudio Parzianello[4]

[1] ICMC/USP - Universidade de São Paulo - Campus de São Carlos
tiago.silva@icmc.usp.br
[2] FACIN/PUCRS - Pontifícia Universidade Católica do Rio Grande do Sul
milene.silveira@pucrs.br
[3] IME/USP - Universidade de São Paulo
claudia@ime.usp.br
[4] Grupo RBS
luiz.parzianello@gruporbs.com.br

Abstract. User-Centered Design spends a considerable effort on research and analysis before development begins. On the other hand, Agile methods strive to deliver small sets of software features to customers as fast as possible in short iterations. Whereas the two methodologies have tensions regarding requirements gathering and upfront design, they also share similarities. For instance, both approaches are iterative and customer focused. However, there is little guidance on how to integrate these two perspectives and a lack of understanding with respect to the User Experience (UX) Designer's role in an agile environment. Based on four ethnographically-informed studies in two large companies, we aim at providing a better understanding of the integration of Agile development and UX Design by describing the different roles that a UX Designer plays within an Agile environment.

Keywords: Agile, User Experience, Designer, Roles, Stages.

1 Introduction

In an increasingly competitive world, where millions of products compete for attracting users' attention, the User Experience (UX) of a product may determine its success or failure. Agile software development methods have also been proposed for the customer's competitive advantage. Despite having different underlying concepts, Agile methods and UX Design aim at producing high quality software. However, it is known that the integration of UX Design into Agile Methods has not been properly addressed [1]. Agile methods have a distinct culture that at first glance seems to conflict with UX Design [2].

Despite their tensions, they also have similarities [3]. The main similarity is that both approaches are iterative and user or customer focused. Notwithstanding, most of the UX Designers have not been concerned about project

A. Marcus (Ed.): DUXU/HCII 2013, Part I, LNCS 8012, pp. 599–609, 2013.

management methods before their first contact with Agile. UX Designers need to be care because, as organizations look for more effective and efficient ways to deliver projects, more and more of them are adopting Agile methods [4].

Frequently, at first glance UX Designers 'notice' that there is no design phase in Agile. From the Designers' standpoint Agile methods strive to deliver small sets of software features to customers as fast as possible in short iterations, implying that design is not a crucial part of the development process. What a UX Designer sees are multiple short deadlines in which working software is delivered and no consideration is given to the many design activities [4].

To the best of our knowledge, there is little guidance on how to successfully incorporate UX Designers into Agile teams. Moreover, there seems to be a lack of understanding regarding the UX Designer's role in an Agile environment [5]. In this regard, the study herein presented aims at discussing the UX Designer's Role in Agile teams based on ethnographically-informed studies in two large companies.

This paper is organized as follows: Section 2 presents the background to the problem. Section 3 describes the studies, data collection and data analysis. Section 4 presents the findings and Section 5 discusses some implications and limitations and presents final remarks of this research.

2   Background

User-Centered Design provides specialized skills in User Interface (UI) Design while Agile approaches prefer generalists and discourage extensive upfront design work [2].

Singh [6] proposes an adaptation of Scrum to promote usability In this adaptation there is the U.P.O (Usability Product Owner) role. The U.P.O. is included in the project effort from the beginning as a peer of a traditional P.O. The two Product Owners work together to first achieve an agreement on the user experience vision for the project. According to the authors [6], the formulation of the vision incorporated the needs of internal customers, developers who have high domain knowledge, and from external customers who would be using the product. Beyer [7] advocates that UX Designers must better understand the Agile principles and presents some practices to the integration of this two fields.

It is not usual to find papers addressing the UX Designer's role in Agile teams despite there are a bunch of studies addressing the integration of UX and Agile in a higher level. Sy [8] describes adjustments on the timing and granularity of usability investigations, and on how the UX Designer reports his usability findings in an Agile environment. Sy [8] states that the Agile communication modes have allowed them to narrow the gap between uncovering usability issues and acting on those issues by incorporating changes into the product. However, she does not address the different roles that a UX Designers play.

Salah [9] provided a software process improvement (SPI) framework for Agile and User-Centered Design integration with generic guidelines and practices for organizations. Despite this study aimed to achieve this integration, it did not mention the UX Designer roles.

A qualitative study presented by Ferreira *et al.* [10] shows that the nature of iterative development facilitates the performance of usability testing, allowing developers to incorporate the results of these tests in subsequent iterations. They say that this can also significantly improve the communication and relationship between UX Designers and developers, showing hope that these practitioners notice that working more closely may assist them in achieving their common goal.

McInerney and Maurer [2] interviewed UX Designers involved in Agile projects and discuss how UX Designers found their role in Agile environments. According to them, the literature does not identify a distinct UX role, so the onus remains on UX to justify and define its role on the team.

Ferreira *et al.* [10] report some implications for the team arrangements. The authors state that the boundaries between the roles of UX Designers and Agile developers are more fluid in the studies where the UX Designer is considered part of the team than in a study where the UX Designers are not part of the team and did not take part in the sprint planning meetings, standups or retrospectives.

As aforementioned, while these studies reported or proposed principles, adjustments or guidelines, and attempted to merge one method to another, none specifically have addressed the UX Designer's role throughout the agile project cycle. However, this role may change significantly throughout the project or product development and it is highly dependent on the context in which it takes place. Agile development and UX Design emerge from the particular problems that practitioners face in the settings in which they work [10].

Our objective is to provide a better understanding of the integration of Agile development and UX Design. We believe it is crucial to understand the UX designer role in an agile environment in terms of the activities and tasks that should be adopted.

3 Cases Description

Four studies in two large companies were carried out to investigate how a UX Designer works in an organizational agile environment. They are ethnographically-informed [10] and, for instance, instead of spending months or years in the field, we spent the amount of time that fit with the development cycles [11]. By adopting the ethnographic approach, we tried to understand practice in its natural setting with minimal researcher intrusion.

We collect our data by observations, interviews and discussions with practitioners, but do not attempt to change or influence practice during the study. We avoid any form of control, intrusion or experiment and so all the data were naturally occurring, as suggested by [11]. Even our interview data may be viewed as naturally occurring, since it was gathered from practitioners reflecting on their practice in their place of work [11]. Finally, the findings and conclusions were confirmed with the teams members involved.

The next sections describe the organizational setting, the projects, who participated in the studies, how data were collected and how analyses were performed.

3.1   Organizational Setting

In Company 1, the team of developers was one of several Scrum teams in the company working on software development[1]. The developers and designers were seated in an open-plan office space located in the same building. However, they were not co-located, *i.e.*, they did not share the same workspace. They were spread in the building, but the UX team members were seated close to each other.

In Company 2 there is no separated UX Team and Developers Team. Each Agile team has its own individuals, *i.e.*, a team does not share developers or UX Designer. These teams were selected because they were the most senior Agile teams in the company. The developers and designers were seated in an open-plan office space located in the same building and in the same floor. Each team is co-located.

3.2   Projects

We followed two projects in Company 1; Project X consists of the development of new features for an existing product of the company. Project Y consists of the development of an existing product of the company for a mobile device.

Company 2 is not structured by projects, but by digital products. It is a digital product-driven business. Two different teams developing two different products were studied. Product X consists of a web portal about agribusiness in the country. Product Y consists of a web portal of services and opportunities in which there are addresses and data from companies and services.

3.3   Participants

In Company 1, our study involved a team of seven individuals and one UX designer. The developers were part of the 'Development Team' and the designers part of the 'UX Team'. The developers had been developing software using Scrum for approximately two years. Although they are called developers, individuals in the team have their own role according to their area and skills. The roles were Project Manager/Scrum Master, Product Owner, Technical Leader, Developer and Tester as presented in Table 1.

Information architects, graphic designers and interaction designers compose the UX team. Each project has one UX designer, but a UX designer usually work with more than one development team. The same goes for Project Managers, and they are also known as Scrum Masters in the teams.

The UX member's role in Project X was to help software engineers to envision new features for this product. In Project Y, the UX member's role was to prototype and design the User Interface and the User Interaction flow for the product. It is noticeable that the UX Designer plays different roles in different projects, even though in the same company.

---

[1] The company also develops hardware.

Table 1. Composition of the Teams

Roles played in Projects	Company 1 - Project X	Company 1 - Project Y	Company 2 - Product X	Company 2 - Product Y
Project Leadership	Project Manager / Scrum Master	Project Manager / Scrum Master	Business Owner / Director	Business Owner / Director
Product Leadership	Product Owner	Product Owner	Product Leader / Product Owner	Product Leader / Product Owner
Technical Leadership	Technical Leader	Technical Leader	Scrum Master	Scrum Master
Development *Team*	Developers – – – –	Developers – – – –	Developers Testers SEO UX Designer –	Developers Testers SEO UX Designer Graphical Designer
Supporting Team	UX (shared)	UX (shared)	–	–

In Company 2, our study involved UX designers and their interactions with an Agile team working on the same product. The teams are composed by Product Leader/Product Owner, UX Designer, Developer, Tester and Search Engine Optimization (SEO), with little differences as can be noticed in Table 1.

One team – Product X – has two individuals focused on UX, a UX Designer and a Graphical Designer, whereas the other team – Product Y – has just a UX Designer who performs the role of a Graphical Designer as well.

The UX designer's role in Product X was to perform user research, benchmarking and interaction design. The Graphic designer's role was to design the User Interface (UI) based on the wireframes provided by the UX designer. Whereas in Product Y, UX designer used to play both roles, performing user research, benchmarking, interaction design and UI design. Again we may notice the diversity of roles that a UX Designer may play in different teams.

3.4 Data Collection

We used two first-degree techniques [12] for data collection: observation and interview.

In Company 1, regarding observations, due to the characteristics of invoking the least amount of interference in the work environment and the least expensive method to implement and still because the company did not allow video or audio recording of the meetings, we choose to manual record the observations of the meetings.

We shadowed a UX person during his activities for 45 days and observed meetings that he was involved, such as meetings of the UX Team of the company and some meetings of two different projects. We also interviewed three members of the UX group that work in different projects and one project manager, as presented in Table 2. The Project Manager was interviewed aiming to define which Agile Method the company uses and how this integration of UX and Agile works from his point of view. The UX Designers were interviewed aiming to understand UX people work on the different projects of the company. In Company 1, our studies were carried out over three months iteratively.

Table 2. Description of the data sources

Data source	Company 1 Project X	Company 1 Project Y	Company 2 Product X	Company 2 Product Y
Observed Meetings	2 Requirements, 1 Planning	3 Planning, 3 Retrospective, 1 Demo, 5 Daily, 2 User Test Sessions	5 Daily	1 Planning, 1 Retrospective, 5 Daily
Interviews	1 Project Manager / Scrum Master, 1 UX Designer	2 UX Designers	1 Scrum Master / Product Leader, 1 UX Designer	1 Scrum Master / Product Leader, 1 UX Designer

In Company 2, as in the first study, we conducted interviews and observations, manually recording our observations. We observed some meetings of two different teams and we interviewed the UX Designer and the Product Leader of the two selected teams, as can also be observed in Table 2. In this company, our studies were carried out over two iterations – 25 working days. The length of the sprints varies from project to project, but for the two teams observed they have three-week sprints.

3.5 Data Analysis

We analyzed data using the open and focused coding techniques. In the open coding, the researcher reads field notes line-by-line to identify and formulate any and all ideas, themes, or issues they suggest, no matter how varied and disparate. In the focused coding, the researcher subjects field notes to fine-grained, line-by-line analysis on the basis of topics that have been identified as of particular interest [13].

Preliminary memos were extracted from the field notes. Having the memos produced, open coding was performed aiming to generate new insights and themes. Focused coding was also performed and this coding consisted of linking the memos generated to key aspects identified in a Systematic Review previously performed [5]. In this process, some new aspects emerged from the analysis of the observations and interviews. Later, some integrative memos were written to relate the field notes, the key aspects and the new codes from the open coding. Our findings with regards to the UX Designer roles are presented as follows.

4   Findings

In this section we present our findings regarding the different roles that the UX Designer may play in Agile teams. In each of the subsections below, we identified their responsibilities and skills, and provided some relevant passages from the observations and interviews.

4.1   User Experience Designer

The User Experience Designer role is **responsible** for the understanding of users.

It is desirable that the User Experience Designer has the following **skills**: User Research, Ethnographic Studies, User Experience Design, User Profiling, Ideation, Competitor Analysis, Design Thinking, Customer Journey Mapping.

It is worth mentioning that we based our skills' classification on the skills listed in [4].

The following quotes represent some of the tasks performed by the User Experience Designer in our studies:

"As we have a set of users (database of volunteers), we can call them and carry out some focus groups. We have 4 different personas with them" [C2 - UXB][2]

"Some User Research is performed by the Marketing Team. In general, the Marketing Team knows what they say they need, not what they really need. It's a not a target effort to gather what the user need' It's a sell visit." [C1 - UX1]

"We perform some speculative research, analysis of competitors" [C2 - UXA]

"We have something that we call Discovering that happens before the planning" [C2 - PLA]

The passages above highlight the activities performed by the UX Designer as User Researcher, or as a User Experience Designer itself as we named this role.

We notice activities like benchmarking, conduction of focus groups and definition of personas, for instance. We may also notice that Company 1 has a Marketing Team that provides some data to the UX Team. However, according to their report, the data gathered by the Marketing Team is more about the users' desires than their needs. This observation highlights the need of having a UX Designer carrying out this kind of research. In general, UX Designers are trained to carry out these activities.

---

[2] The passages are identified by the Company (C#) and the by the team member of each team interviewed (UX#).

It is noteworthy that this role should work alongside the Business Analyst to create a design vision and design direction from the user experience.

4.2 Interaction Designer

The Interaction Designer role is **responsible** for Designing and Evaluating the users' interaction with products or services, both on prototypes as on the developed system.

It is desirable that the Interaction Designer has the following **skills**: Interaction Design, Rapid Prototyping, User Experience Design, Product Design, Guerrilla Testing Sketching, Usability Testing, Ideation, Collaborative Design, Process Flows, Information Architecture, Service Design, Design Thinking.

The following quotes reflects the tasks performed by the Interaction Designer in our studies:

"We don't need to design everything up front" [C1 - UX3]

"We should work at least one sprint ahead the development team" [C1 - UX3]

"Sometimes we add new user stories based on the results of the User Testing. But it depends on the problem. We also can put as a bug" [C1 - UX2]

"We perform some inspection evaluations, peer review with some UX member" [C1 - UX2]

"We put UX criteria as acceptance criteria at the User Stories, or we reference the behavior of the interface in a sequence of wireframes" [C2 - UXA]

"We perform a lot of informal evaluations. Myself and the Graphical Designer" [C2 - UXA]

By researching from the early stages of the project, the UX Designer may build his own 'UX Backlog'. Afterwards, as reported by [C2 - UXB], the Interaction Designer may use these data to design or even prototype one iteration ahead of the development team.

We noticed that whenever the UX Designer works close to the Product Owner, they achieve better results on describing business or users' needs. Developers better understand designs and User Stories when they are built by two members with different backgrounds. Further, User Stories become more clear when enriched by wireframes, for instance.

By having designs, sketches or wireframes, UX Designers may start an evaluation process. We observed UX Designers performing informal evaluations, peer reviewing their designs by pairing with other Designers or Product Owners or even Business Analysts. These early evaluations are very important because they avoid future rework and helps to define what will be built. The Interaction Designer may also works alongside the developers to figure out how it can be built.

4.3 UI Developer

The UI Developer role is **responsible** for the Development of the Graphical User Interface (GUI) and the Design of Graphical Elements.

It is desirable that the UI Developer has the following **skills**: Rapid Prototyping, Collaborative Design, Information Architecture, Visual Design, GUI Design, Service Design, Design Thinking.

UI Developers are often the link between the front end and designers as they can speak both languages. As the Interaction Designer, the UI Developer also works alongside the developers and testers to figure out how it can be built.

In our studies, this is the role least played by UX Designers. Most of the UX Designers observed did not develop the UI. In Company 1, for instance, there are few Visual Designers who answer to the teams just when they are required. However, the following passage reveal that developing may not be trivial to all the UX Designers. This happens due to their heterogeneous backgrounds.

"*It's tricky to UX people to code*" [C1 - UX2]

In Company 2, one of the teams has a UX Designer and a Visual Designer. The other one has a UX Designer has the skill of visual designing and also performs the Visual Design, as follows: "*Once the product is defined, I prototype it in two or three weeks. Paper prototype to communicate between us and some HTML to present to directors.*" [C2 - UXB]

5 Discussion and Final Remarks

We defined three essential roles that a UX Designer may play in Agile teams. Each of these roles encompasses several skills as described in the previous section.

We do not aim to define these roles as an absolute truth. It is just a simple way of defining UX Designers' roles. In contrast, Ratcliffe and McNeill [4] state that UX Designers may be: User Interface, Interaction, and Usability Designer; Experience Designer; UI Developers and Front-End Developers; Information Architects; Visual Designers; and/or Design Researchers. We assume this fine-grained system of seven role may be too detailed to reflect reality in many projects, bearing in mind that based on our experience a UX Designer is usually a single person playing several roles.

Nevertheless, to make these roles happen, it is important that the UX Designer be a full member of the Agile team. One of the reasons is the amount of work accomplished by this role, such as: user research, market research, user-centered design, prototyping, usability inspection, user testing, visual design, coding, providing feedback and so forth.

This workload laid on the UX Designer is highlighted in Figure 1. This figure reveals how the different roles – '*User Experience Designer*', '*UI Developer*' and '*Interaction Designer*' – may be played in the different stages of an Agile cycle.

As we could notice, it is absolutely essential to spend some time before development begins on thinking holistically about the design vision.

Thus, the UX Designer cannot work on too many projects at a time. As a team member said in the study: "*UX Designers must be pigs!*"[3][C1 - PM1],

---

[3] This is a fable told by Scrum practitioners about a pig and a chicken who considered starting a restaurant. "*We could serve ham and eggs*," said the chicken. "*I don't think that would work*," said the pig. "*I'd be committed, but you'd only be involved*".

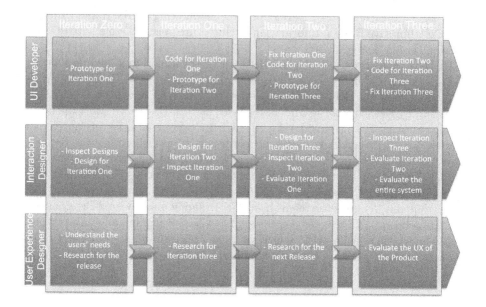

Fig. 1. UX Designer's Roles in the different Stages of an Agile cyel

expressing the importance of role accountability and involvement in projects. However, many organizations still do not consider UX Designers as full-time part of an Agile team. Thus, they keep working on too many projects at a time. This decision does not depend only on the UX Designer, but on the organizational design choices.

Notwithstanding, we should be careful on generalizing from our findings. Although the teams analyzed in these studies are considered to not be atypical, these studies do not cover all the possibilities and the contexts can vary widely.

The major contribution of this paper is to provide a better understanding of the roles played by a UX Designer within an Agile team in the different stages of Agile development.

Finally, we argue that the integration of UX Design and Agile development is a matter of culture. As UX Designers must understand the Agile culture and care because Agile adoption is on the rise and it is a completely different way of working, which requires a new approach and a new attitude toward design [4], Agile developers must understand the importance of having design in the process and how it delivers value to the product.

References

1. Hussain, Z., Slany, W., Holzinger, A.: Current state of agile user-centered design: A survey. In: Holzinger, A., Miesenberger, K. (eds.) USAB 2009. LNCS, vol. 5889, pp. 416–427. Springer, Heidelberg (2009)
2. McInerney, P., Maurer, F.: Ucd in agile projects: dream team or odd couple? Interactions 12, 19–23 (2005)

3. Silva da Silva, T., Silveira, M., Maurer, F., Hellmann, T.: User experience design and agile development: From theory to practice. Journal of Software Engineering and Applications 5(743-751) (2012)

4. Ratcliffe, L., McNeill, M.: Agile Experience Design: A Digital Designer's Guide to Agile, Lean, and Continuous. New Riders (2012)

5. Silva, T.S.d., Martin, A., Maurer, F., Silveira, M.: User-centered design and agile methods: A systematic review. In: Society, I.C. (ed.) Agile Conference (Agile), pp. 77–86 (2011)

6. Singh, M.: U-scrum: An agile methodology for promoting usability. In: Proceedings of the Agile 2008, pp. 555–560. IEEE Computer Society, Washington, DC (2008)

7. Beyer, H.: User-Centered Agile Methods. Morgan & Claypool Publishers (2010)

8. Sy, D.: Adapting usability investigations for agile user-centered design. Journal of Usability Studies 2(3), 112–132 (2007)

9. Salah, D.: A framework for the integration of user centered design and agile software development processes. In: 2011 33rd International Conference on Software Engineering (ICSE), pp. 1132–1133. ACM (2011)

10. Ferreira, J., Sharp, H., Robinson, H.: Agile development and user experience design integration as an ongoing achievement in practice. In: Agile 2012, pp. 11–20 (2012)

11. Robinson, H., Segal, J., Sharp, H.: Ethnographically-informed empirical studies of software practice. Information and Software Technology 49(6), 540–551 (2007)

12. Lethbridge, T.C., Sim, S.E., Singer, J.: Studying software engineers: Data collection techniques for software field studies. Empirical Soft. Eng. (311-341) (2005)

13. Emerson, R.M., Fretz, R.I., Shaw, L.L.: Writing Ethnographic Fieldnotes. The University of Chicago Press (2011)

Designing for Resonance by Evocative Objects: An Experiential Interaction Design Method

Chih-Sheng Su[1,2] and Rung-Huei Liang[1]

[1] National Taiwan University of Science and Technology, Department of Industrial and Commercial Design, No.43, Sec. 4, Keelung Rd., Da'an Dist., Taipei City 106, Taiwan
[2] Shih-Chien University, Department of Communications Design. No.70, Dazhi St., Zhongshan Dist., Taipei City 104, Taiwan
sheng@mac.com, liang@mail.ntust.edu.tw

Abstract. This paper presents a design method that enriches the quality of experiential interaction design. The purpose is to encourage designers to use their own experiences to create. In this paper, we describe how to use an evocative object as a starting point, bringing up a journey of memory, behavior, family relationships, and self-identity, and then translate the inspiration into core elements in an experiential interaction design. This method has six key features: (1) The choice of a designer's own evocative object, (2) The creation of narratives, (3) The creation of visual representations, (4) The search and transformation of the key emotion, (5) The creation of the physical interaction context, and (6) The public exhibition and the final meaning-making process. We claim that this method can establish a dialogue between the designer, the project, and the audiences. It can also enhance the meaning and the quality of the experiential interaction design.

Keywords: Resonance, Evocative Objects, Personal Experience, Dialogical Critique, Interaction Design.

1 Introduction

In discourses of human-computer interaction (HCI), there has been an increasing interest in personal experiences from both users and designers. User-centered design (UCD) has already become a standard in designing interactive technologies and systems in interaction design and Human-Computer Interaction [2]. Regarding the intimacy level with people, designers can create various artifacts with specific functionality, usability, as well as state-of-the-art innovative, superior and insightful, radical products via multiple sources based on designer's personal skills and judgment [1]. To meet user's needs, there are many methods that place users at the center of design process, such as field studies, interviews, and surveys [2], which are research-based ones. There are also storyboard, interactive simulations, user testing, and surveys [3], which are methods relating to prospective and retrospective use analysis.

A. Marcus (Ed.): DUXU/HCII 2013, Part I, LNCS 8012, pp. 610–619, 2013.
© Springer-Verlag Berlin Heidelberg 2013

As instructors in design schools, we deem that meeting user's needs and expectations is one of our educational objectives. To know the users, the attention to psychology and sociology is required. However, due to the lack of knowledge in the two disciplines mentioned above, it is difficult to ask students to understand users from these theoretical perspectives. Hence, we advocate that student designers can use their personal experiences as a design resource, which can facilitate designers' creativity, innovation [2] and ideation. Above all, such a resource could elicit the connection between user's experience and designer's experience, scilicet, the resonance, while enhancing the process of meaning-making and the quality of the experiential interaction design.

2   Background and Motivation

In design school, instructors and students are always looking for a starting point to generate new ideas. As an instructor, one is always looking for a stimulus to inspire students to create. On the other hand, a student is always trying to find a key element to make her work be innovative. To generate new ideas, people used to adopting traditional ideation methods, such as brainstorming, mood boards, card-sorting, and innovation games. These methods provide general association of ideas where the purpose is to meet users' needs and to match their expectations. However, these methods rarely encourage designers to use their personal experience as a resource for design.

For every design major, the process of forming and relating new ideas is the hardest part in the whole design process. At the initial phase of the implementation of a project, students need to find something relevant to rely on and to support them to proceed with their design process with passion. Therefore, it is critical for instructors to help students find the important "keystone". Currently, many designers follow the UCD process to create projects. The purpose of UCD is to discover and to understand users' needs and desires. Through a series of iteration and feedback loops, a thoughtful solution or artifact will be provided to the user by a designer. However, the relation between the user and the solution or artifact might not be strong enough. Once the user does not need the artifact or the solution, the relationship disappears at the same time. To strengthen this relationship and to elicit reflections on the design project, we develop a series of design activity that accomplishes this goal.

This paper presents a design method that centers on personal experience. Using designers' personal experience as a commencement, this design method calls forth one's personal reminiscence and enriches the quality of experiential interaction design process by creating new meanings of it. We argue that designers' personal experience can inform and should be a resource for interaction design, as well as will elicit other people's personal experience.

3   Evocative Objects

There must be some objects accompanying us as we move through different stages of our lives. For example, there might be a security blanket or a baby doll that we used to carry, otherwise we would not be able to fall asleep in our childhood. There might be a pen as a present from a high school teacher for us getting good grades. We get along with these objects during different phases of our lives. In the process of being with and using these objects, we develop affection for them unconsciously.

The existence of these objects is of great significance to us. If we lose them or cause damage to them, we lose some special segment of memory as well. We preserve these objects with care, for they represent some unforgettable memories or experiences. We place all kinds of precious and irreplaceable artifacts above the fireplace in the living room or on the bedside table in the bedroom. Each of the artifacts has a lively anecdote about how it came into our possession. Just as we are collectors of things, things are collectors of meanings [7].

3.1   The Meaning of the Object

According to Borgmann's definitions, there are two terms that objects may refer to: commodities and things. Commodities are objects that have no other significance apart from their main functions. Things, on the other hand, are not just physical objects. They include emotional feelings and meanings that are associated with the objects [8]. In this study, we refer objects to things. Sometimes, the meaning of an object is predetermined by the dominant culture, such as family heirlooms, childhood toys, and travel souvenirs; sometimes, the meaning of an object comes from its aestheticized appearance. Some objects are intended to be interpreted, and some become interpretable accidentally. Once the objects are interpreted, the meaning will be given.

In most of the cases, the meaning of an object is not the value listed from the marketplace or in an auction. Its value is given by its owner. Like a talisman or a mascot, any trivial object can be someone's precious possession. To an owner, the meaning of the object is more significant than the net price of the object. In addition, the object signals a new understanding of who the owner is and what the owner may be interested in. It also emphasizes the inseparability of thought and feeling in our relationship to things [6].

The object itself often represents a certain person: the one who means the most to us, the one who leaves us, or the one who lives faraway from us. The object itself is also a reminiscence of a certain period in the past: a sentimental and ambiguous love affair during the teenage years, or a meaningful and memorable time serving in the military. French philosopher and anthropologist, Bruno Latour, claimed that many participants are gathered in a thing to make it exist and to maintain its existence [9]. When we see an old man kissing a gravestone in a cemetery or a broken doll sitting on someone's bedside table, we know that the objects have particular and unique meanings. They are ordinary things with extraordinary significance [7].

3.2   Personal Experience

Each person's life is a combination of countless wonderful experiences. These experiences are one's most valuable intangible assets. Whether consciously or unconsciously, one experiences something incessantly. There are no two identical experiences in the world because an experience exists in one's inherent unique cognitive system. When a group of people went through a same event, each one generates a unique experience. Even though the same person goes through the same event repeatedly, she will have different experiences because of the different circumstances, or different moods she has at the moment. For example, when reading a novel, different person might have different thoughts and gains, or be touched by different paragraphs from reading the same novel. The same person reading a novel for a second time might have different feelings about it and comprehend differently.

Traditional cognitivist and behaviorist ways of thinking about HCI argue that experience is a sequence of actions that designers predetermined, and they allow users to perform through interfaces [11]. Although this approach to experience does not fully summarize the richness of people's lived experience, UCD has already constructed various theories and methods to assure that designs meet user's needs and requirements. Experience was generated by various events and/or activities that one may gather knowledge, opinions, and skills. Experience is not a rigid and closed thing; it is vital, and hence growing [10], and it can be reflected upon. To understand and to make the best of experience is one of the most important issues to interaction designers. However, we cannot "design" an experience or control an expression that a person will experience via design, since the perception, sensation and the cognition of a stimulation of each person vary. To make the best of experience, we can treat the personal experience as a source for interaction design. In addition, the interaction design artifacts should be personal pathways that allow individuals to find and create their own experiences.

3.3   Resonance

Once the interaction design project is completed, the relationship among the designer, the project, and the participant is formed. The designer delivers messages or provides functions via the project. The participant understands and experiences the project through perceptual system and senses; furthermore, he or she reflects. Being different from senses, human's perceptual system can orient, explore, investigate, adjust, optimize, resonate, extract, and it comes to an equilibrium [12]. The termination of external stimulation does not end the cognitive process. Instead, the process of reflection continues over time.

Typical examples of artifacts made to facilitate reflection are art and music, especially as found in galleries and concert halls [13]. The stimulus of art or music doesn't persist on our way home from an art exhibition or a concert, but our perceptual system keeps working and making us reflect. In slow technology, Johan Redström proposes that we should give people time to think and to reflect in design. Reflection makes the human society various and pluralistic. These unique thoughts in our mind also help the progress of human civilization move forward.

Resonance stems from the theory of ecological or direct perception, and it is a rather unexplored area due to its complexity [14]. Gibson [12] clarified the principle of resonance by using a radio metaphor. When tuning the receiver to change the station frequency on a radio, if the current station frequency matches the frequency sent from a radio station, it resonates to that radio station. In experiential interaction design, the design artifact acts like a radio station that broadcasts information. Our sensory organs act as the receiving antenna on the radio, which must be transparent to the carrier's frequency to let the signal pass through and arrive at our perceptual system. The same process proceeds when a participant experiences an experiential interaction design artifact. When one grabs a puppet dog, touches and feels its fur, this experience and one's childhood memory of keeping a pet may resonate.

Hummels et al. [14] argue that resonance can be a concept that provides respectful and humanistic human computer and product interaction, which allows individuals to find and create their own experiences. They proposed two interactive installations and tried to find the salient aspects of resonance, and they reached some conclusions. First, controlling and experiencing the relation between cause and effect increase resonance. Second, temptation, intimacy, and engagement during interaction are generally considered essential to increase resonance, for they make a user feel in control.

4   Dialogical Meaning-Making

Critique is an important activity in design school. In the critique process, students first take turns to present their work in progress in the class. According to the presentation and the work, the instructors and the students provide the presenter with their opinions and thoughts. Generally speaking, an instructor gets to know a student's design progress through the critique and provides advice to the student to help her work become better. The student then takes the advice and uses it as a reference to improve her design. By implementing this critique process repeatedly, a student can finish her design project gradually with other people's advices and her own reflection. The whole critique process also corresponds to one of the design activities: Iteration. When a student describes her work during the presentation, she can always get a deeper understanding and comprehension via the oral narration.

Bakhtin argues that in this world, any unity is always a matter of work and is always accomplished dialogically. "Dialogically any unity is composed of many voices in unfinalized conversations that cannot be reified monologically [15]." The completion and interpretation of the meaning construction of an experiential interaction design project rely not only on the designer's creative thinking and execution, but also on the dialogue among the designer, the project, and the audience. The whole constructive procedure is an ongoing process that will not be stopped because of the discontinuity of the reaction and behavior of any one of them. People construct the meaning of the project by following through a number of real world contexts, as well as witnessing the responses of others [17].

People make sense of and give value to things based on their own previous experiences and dispositions, their understanding of other people's experiences, and the understanding of the fact that an experience is never terminated [16]. Every time we make a statement, it always remains open for others to discuss. Since the "others" might have different points of view, the true meaning of the statement is multi-dimensional and is open to change ceaselessly. The true meaning thus is always emerging through these dialogical processes. Leung and Wright also articulate that sharing experiences with others as well as telling others about oneself and self-lives is not simply an act of reporting but rather an act of co-construction of meaning.

5   Designing for Resonance by Evocative Objects

Habermas characterizes three primary generic human interests that can determine categories relevant to what we interpret as knowledge: the technical interest in controlling and manipulating our environment, the practical interest in identifying our social interaction and join in communicative activity, and the emancipatory interest in identifying our self-understanding or self-reflection [18]. Habermas argues that Hegel held labor, language and interaction to be constitutive moments of developing Spirit [21]. People use language to communicate and interact with each other and acquire life resources by laboring.

In this design method, we first conducted several repetitionary and continuous dialogues between self and others through the choice of an object, the creation of narratives, and the creation of visual representations. Bakhtin articulates that discourse in life is directly informed by life itself and cannot be separated from life [19]. Gadamer also argues that questioning arises possibilities of meaning, and thus what is meaningful becomes one's own thinking on the subject [20]. We conducted the dialogues in an attempt to give utterance to evocative objects.

Second, we tried to find the key emotion hidden in a context of the language/dialogue built in the first part through the constant labor of one's body and spirit, which was then transformed into a central idea or proposition that a designer intends to deliver. Next, a designer was asked to build up the form of a project by laboring and endowing the behavior pattern, and then invited to present the design artifact in front of the public. Audiences resonated with the design artifact while/after interacting with it, meanwhile, establishing the dialogue with the design artifact and the designer, and then co-constructed the meaning of it.

In this design method we proposed, evocative objects play an important role in externalizing imagination. We emphasize the fact that evocative objects can evoke personal story, memory, emotion, family relationship, and self-identity [6]. We advocate that using an evocative object as a starting point for a design project is an effective design method that elicits rich personal experience. Sherry Turkle points out that most objects exert their holding power because of the particular moment and circumstances in which they come into people's life [6]. Thus, the personal experience elicited by evocative objects, which serve as bearing media of personal meanings, will stimulate focused imagination, and can be a good resource for interaction design.

5.1   Six Key Features

Feature 1: The Choice of a Designer's Own Evocative Object. Everyone must have some objects that accompany her for a long time. When a student chooses a particular evocative object, he or she entails a dialogue with it. The context of the dialogue reinforces the relationship and the emotion the student has with the object. This process mediates the conflicts between one's conscious and subconscious dialogues, and it makes the contradiction in one's mind no longer exist.

At the very beginning of establishing the dialogue between the self and others, a student needs to ask lots of questions for herself: "Where did I get this object?", " What does this object mean to me?", "Who does the object remind me of?" Some of the questions lead to unique answers and help the student to clarify the role of the object, while others lead to deep reflections and help them to establish narratives.

Feature 2: The Creation of Narratives. After students choose their own unique evocative objects, they are asked to write down narratives regarding their personal experience with the chosen objects. Through reflecting on the objects, the students reveal their connections with the evocative objects and other people in the narratives. By constructing the narratives, a student invites audiences to understand the story hidden behind the object.

Gadamer proposes that the art of writing letters consists in not letting what one says become a treatise on the subject but in making it acceptable to the correspondent [20]. By constructing the narratives the designer invites the participants to join the story hidden behind the object.

Feature 3: The Creation of Visual Representations. Based on the appearance of the evocative object and the narratives written in the previous stage, the students create visual representations. This is the last stage of the first part of the method. In order to clarify the utterance of the evocative object, the students make representation of their thoughts and emotions elicited from the evocative objects by all means.

Bakhtin argues that the eventness of an event and the livedness of experience can not be reduced to texts [15]. To have a dialogue with others, it would be easier to refer to an observable material; therefore, a visual representation is necessary.

Feature 4: The Search and Transformation of Key Emotion. In this stage, the students search for the key emotion hidden in the narratives and the visual representations they created in the first part through constant laboring, and they continue to set up internal dialogues to elicit new insights. In the meantime, through several dialogical critiques, an instructor's mission is to guide a student to induce her personal experience, to find a core concept and expression of her emotion, to work out a new interpretation of the evocative object, and to build an empathic relationship with each other.

Hereon, through the internal dialogue with oneself and the dialogical critiques with the instructor and other students, one can extract the key emotion elicited by the evocative object. One is then asked to transform the key emotion into an expression or a statement – something that one wants to deliver to the audiences via the design project or the artifact one creates.

Feature 5: The Creation of Physical Interaction Context. Once the core concept and expression are ensured, a student starts to design the form of a project and endows it with the behavior, that is, the behavioral utterances of the project. Bakhtin argues that behavioral utterances can continuously develop a situation, suggest a plan, and organize for future actions [19]. The form and the behavioral utterances revealed from the project determine how participants will interact with the design artifact.

Kolko articulates that, "Interaction Design is the creation of a dialogue between a person and a product, service, or system." He also argues that the dialogue can be found in the insignificant place of daily life and is nearly invisible [22]. Here, students try to structure this natural dialogue and elaborate it into the form and the behavioral utterances to create the physical interaction contexts for the artifacts of the design projects.

Feature 6: The Public Exhibition and the Final Meaning-Making Process. After the design project is completed, it opens to the public. To finalize the meaning-making process, the audiences meet, feel, interact with, try to understand, and finally resonate with the design artifact of the project. Bakhtin argues that each person occupies a solitary situation. In this situation, there is a unique perception that each of us has seen things that others don't see. Hence, we need others to consummate ourselves [15]. When the participants interact with the design artifact, our conscious minds would meet to co-construct the meaning.

5.2   Two Examples: My Monster Friend and Storyteller

My Monster Friend. Everyone spends her childhood with an invisible friend. It may be a doll or a volleyball. Although it is nothing but an ordinary object, we talk to it and let it be around us. This project combines furniture and puppet. When a participant sits on this project, it will become alive. Depending on the user's different movements, it will have different reactions. When the participant touches the back of the chair, he will smile. When the participant touches his cheek, he will blush. He is just like the monster we imagined when we were young.

The designer of this project uses a chair from IKEA as a basic structure. She first covered the chair with artificial fur and feathers and installed several sensors under them. Then, she connected sensors to a computer and a projector. When the participants interact with the chair, the hidden sensors will detect the motions. Meanwhile, the computer will generate different facial expressions and sounds. Through the projector, they will be projected onto the chair. At the same time, the participants resonated with the reaction of the chair.

Storyteller. This project is inspired by the LEICA of the designer's father. The designer's father is a soldier, who rarely expresses his concern for his son in words. The father's hobby is photography, and he expresses his love through taking pictures of the designer. In this project, there is a gyroscope inside a camera, which is connected to a computer. When a participant picks up the camera and aims at one of the photo frames placed at various heights, a corresponding photo of the designer relating to his height during a period of time in his life will be displayed within the frame. This project reproduces the father's experience of standing behind a camera, documenting and looking after his son's growth. Through the camera, the relationship between father and son is formed. The participants resonate with the behavior of using the camera and the photos that display in the photo frames.

Fig. 1. My Monster Friend. (Left), Storyteller. (Right)

6   Conclusion

We present a design process whereby interaction designers structure a persuasive argument and then invite the participants to join the creation of a dialogue. The work is completed by the presence and synthesis of the audiences [22]. As Bakhtin argues that any unity is always accomplished dialogically [15], in the method we proposed above, the dialogues between the designer, the design artifact, and the audiences accomplish the unity of all meaning-making process.

In this method, we place designers at the center of the interaction design process, and we advocate that designers resonate with an evocative object first. After having a dialogue with oneself, a designer is then able to have a dialogue with others. Ultimately, the dialogue between the design artifact and the audience finalizes the meaning-making process. We found that using an evocative object as a catalyst elevates the resonance of the experience between the user and the designer from both cognitive and emotive aspects. The results of the experiments using this interaction design method show that an evocative object can elicit a hidden story from everyone effectively. This design method allows us to discover a new experience in interaction design.

We discover that this interaction design process evokes the audiences' reminiscences, and it elicits their emotional resonance. We argue that the meaning of an experiential interaction design project does not only rest on the technology applied to the project, but also lies in the reaction and resonance elicited by understanding, experiencing and interacting with the project. It appears that the meaning of the project exists relative to the existence of the audience. To enhance the meaning and the quality of the experiential interaction design, we would suggest that it is a must to obtain and increase resonance among the designer, the design artifact, and the audiences.

References

1. Nieminen, M., Runonen, M., Nieminen, M., Tyllinen, M.: Designer experience: Exploring Ways to Design in Experience. In: CHI 2011 Extended Abstracts on Human Factors in Computing Systems, pp. 2449–2452 (2011)
2. Zhang, X., Wakkary, R., Maestri, L., Desjardins, A.: Memory-storming: Externalizing and Sharing Designers' Personal Experiences. In: Proceedings of the Designing Interactive Systems Conference, pp. 524–533 (2012)
3. Nelson, J., Buisine, S., Aoussat, A.: Design in use: some methodological considerations, http://stephanie.buisine.free.fr/publis/CIRP09.pdf
4. Nam, T.J., Kim, C.: Design by Tangible Stories: Enriching Interactive Everyday Products with Ludic Value. International Journal of Design 5(1), 85–98 (2011)
5. Wright, P., McCarthy, J.: Empathy and Experience in HCI. In: Proceedings of the SIGCHI Conference on Human Factors in Computing Systems, pp. 637–646 (2008)
6. Turkle, S.: Evocative objects - Things we think with. The MIT Press, Cambridge (2007)
7. Gleen, J., Hayes, C.: Taking things seriously. Princeton Architectural Press, New York (2007)
8. Borgmann, A.: Technology and the character of contemporary life: A Philosophical Inquiry. University of Chicago Press, Chicago (1987)
9. Bruno, L.: Why Has Critique Run out of Steam? From Matters of Fact to Matters of Concern. Critical Inquiry 30, 25–248 (2004)
10. Dewey, J.: How we think. FQ Books (2010)
11. Wright, P., McCarthy, J.: The value of the novel in designing for experience. In: Future Interaction Design, pp. 9–30. Springer, London (2005)
12. Gibson, J.J.: The Ecological Approach to Visual Perception. Lawrence Erlbaum Associates, Hillsdale (1979)
13. Hallnäs, L., Redström, J.: Slow Technology: Designing for Reflection. Personal and Ubiquitous Computing 5(3), 201–212 (2001)
14. Hummels, C., Ross, P., Overbeeke, K.: In search for resonant human computer interaction: building and testing aesthetic installations. In: Rauterberg, M., Menozzi, M., Wesson, J. (eds.) Proceedings of the 9th International Conference on Human–Computer Interaction (Interact 2003), pp. 399–406. IOS Press, Amsterdam (2003)
15. McCarthy, J., Wright, P.: Technology as Experience. The MIT Press, Cambridge (2007)
16. Leong, T.W., Wright, P., Vetere, F., Howard, S.: Understanding experience using dialogical methods: The case of serendipity. In: Proceedings of the 22nd Conference of the Computer-Human Interaction Special Interest Group of Australia on Computer-Human Interaction, pp. 256–263 (2010)
17. Forlizzi, J., Battarbee, K.: Understanding Experience in Interactive Systems. In: Proceedings of the 5th Conference on Designing Interactive Systems: Processes, Practices, Methods, and Techniques, pp. 261–268 (2004)
18. Habermas, J.: Knowledge and human interests. Beacon Press, Boston (1971)
19. Bakhtin, M.: Discourse in Life and Discourse in Art. In: Elbow, P. (ed.) Landmark Essays on Voice and Writing, pp. 3–10. Hermagoras Press, Mahwah (1994)
20. Gadamar, H.G.: Truth and Method. Sheed & Ward Ltd and the Continuum Publishing Group, New York (2004)
21. Habermas, J.: Theory and Practice. Beacon Press, Boston (1988)
22. Kolko, J.: Thoughts on interaction design. Morgan Kaufmann, Burlington (2011)

Usagame – A New Methodology to Support User Centered Design of Touchscreen Applications

Pedro Vinagre[1] and Isabel L. Nunes[1,2]

[1] Faculdade de Ciências e Tecnologia - UNL, 2829-516 Caparica, Portugal
[2] UNIDEMI, Faculdade de Ciências e Tecnologia - UNL, 2829-516 Caparica, Portugal
pedrodiogovinagre@gmail.com, imn@fct.unl.pt

Abstract. Touchscreen mobile devices growth resulted in an explosion of the mobile applications. Focusing on touch mobile game applications this study aims to fulfill a research gap, creating appropriate usability guidelines for these applications. Concerns about usability, touch technologies, mobile devices and game testing, provided the background needs for this study. Initial game application tests allowed for the creation and implementation of such proposed usability guidelines into a support checklist (UsaGame), designed to help applications developers. An evaluation test was performed with 20 users in order to assess the validity of the proposed guidelines. Results from the test of the two builds from the same game application allowed comparisons that led to the assessment of the importance of some of the guidelines implemented into the application. Results suggested a usability improvement on the game application implemented with the guidelines. Furthermore results allowed commenting on all proposed usability guidelines.

Keywords: Usability Touch guidelines, Mobile Applications, Usability Checklist, Touch Mobile Devices.

1 Introduction

This study addresses touchscreen mobile game applications. It regards usability and ergonomics concerns about their use and aims to present a usability checklist to support the user centered design of touchscreen game applications.

Mobile technology advances and unique features, such as, slow or unreliable connectivity, small screen size, processing speed, limited power or sometimes inappropriate data entry methods, impose certain difficulties upon usability evaluation [1]. Traditional guidelines and usability test methods used in desktop applications might not be always directly applicable. Consequently it is essential to create or adapt existing usability guidelines and usability evaluation methods, to appropriately evaluate the usability of mobile applications [1].

The purpose of the study presented here results from a research gap in touchscreen mobile device applications, more specifically regarding usability in touch mobile game applications. Therefore the objective of this study is to create a checklist, the UsaGame guidelines, to support the usability evaluation process of such type of

A. Marcus (Ed.): DUXU/HCII 2013, Part I, LNCS 8012, pp. 620–629, 2013.
© Springer-Verlag Berlin Heidelberg 2013

applications, which would help designers and developers throughout the application's development process.

To validate the UsaGame guidelines the initial version of the touch mobile game application (Megaramp) was compared with a new version where the UsaGame guidelines were adopted. The Megaramp game application is a sports' application which allows the users to perform Skate and BMX maneuvers throughout touch inputs. The user can choose its player, customize his own options and execute different maneuvers with its player, besides that users can explore the many options available in the main menu area.

The paper presents the UsaGame guidelines and the findings of the tests performed for assessing this new support tool.

2   Methodology

The methodology used to create the UsaGame (Figure 1) was based on: a literature review which contributed for gathering usability guidelines' knowledge; game tests' performed to a touch game application; and knowledge elicited through the joint-venture with a game development company (Biodroid).

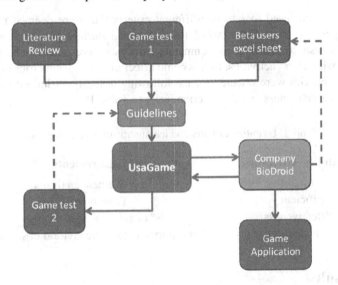

Fig. 1. UsaGame Development Methodology

Therefore the UsaGame guidelines (included as Annex) resulted from the adaptation of existing usability guidelines [2,3] to the context of touch game mobile applications, as well as the creation of new ones. The existing guidelines were mainly heuristic based.

In order to validate the guidelines a usability test comparing two different versions of the Megaramp application was performed. One of the versions of the game was developed with the support of the proposed method. The usability test was performed using a cognitive walkthrough protocol, specifically created for this study.

The usability test involved 20 users, with an average age of 24.5 years (SD = 3.10). All users were made familiar with the cognitive walkthrough protocol in order to properly execute all the required tasks. The usability test that comprehended the execution of four tasks was applied to the two versions (Test A and Test B) of the game.

Test A tested an initial version (version1.0#30) of the application, with no usability guidelines implemented. Test B was applied to a final version of the Megaramp application, which was developed considering the proposed usability guidelines.

The tasks performed in the usability test were:

- Task 1 – Choosing the skate mode, customizing the player and the skate, and checking if they match the ones that appear in play mode.
- Task 2 – Performing the "180 ollie" maneuver in skate mode.
- Task 3 – Playing in BMX mode, going to the pause menu, and learning how to perform the "tailwhip" trick.
- Task 4 – Eliminating a saved game, starting a new one and choosing a character with a different sex from the previous one.

Likert scales were used to rate the different criteria that were deemed relevant for tests' comparison. Users were asked to think aloud during the test sessions, thus allowing analysts to record their comments. Analysts were asked to do so without interfering with users' activities, as this could affect time-on-task metrics [4].

Usability metrics were selected for the following usability attributes: Learnability, Efficiency, Effectiveness and Satisfaction (refer to Table 1).

Table 1. Usability atributes and measurements used in the study

Usability Attributes	Measurements
Learnability	Improvement analyzes
Efficiency	Time-on-task
Effectiveness	N° of errors + Task success
Satisfaction	User reported data + Behavioral observations

3   Results

During the usability test it was recorded data used to compute several usability metrics which were later analyzed to assess the improvements resulting from using the guidelines. Figure 2 shows the average time-on-task values (green and purple markers) and the dispersion intervals (black dots) for completion of each task in both tests.

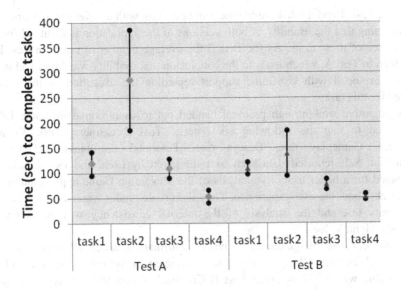

Fig. 2. Average time-on-task and dispersion intervals

From the analysis of Figure 2 one can see that Task 2 presents the highest variation of results, corresponding to the largest standard deviation (228.2 sec in Test A). This can be explained because in this task users were asked to play the game application, which is a task more difficult and more depending on the individual skills to play. Nevertheless, Figure 2 demonstrates that the game version tested in Test B consistently presents better time-on-task indicators which allows us to infer the existence of usability improvements, corroborating the initial hypotheses that UsaGame guidelines can have a positive effect on the application design. This is also confirmed by the lower dispersion of the users' performance observed in Test B when compared to Test A.

When the average number of errors per task of Test A and Test B are compared (see Table 2) the difference in the usability of both versions also becomes evident.

Table 2. Average number of errors per task

	Task 1	Task 2	Task 3	Task 4
Test A	1	12	2	1
Test B	1	3	0	1

Task 2 emerges again as the most difficult task for participants, where the highest number of errors was recorded. This was mainly due to lack of explanatory tutorials.

Results of Task 1 and Task 4 are identical in both tests with an average of 1 error per user; meaning that the usability of both versions of the application is identical for the performance of these tasks. As for Task 3 the average number of errors in Test B is lower than in Test A, which leads to the conclusion that usability was improved in the version developed with UsaGame support regarding the execution of the actions required for this task.

The cognitive walkthrough protocol handed out to users contained some Likert scales used to rate the following six criteria: Task 2 easiness, Task 3's help usefulness, Gameplay rate, Design rate, Tutorials' usefulness and Overall Satisfaction. Self reported data such as rates given by users and user comments, contributed for a better usability analysis of the Megaramp Game application and to gain insight about the user experience. The Likert scale grades were also submitted to a reliability test and the analysis of the internal consistency was based on the Cronbach Alpha Value.

Internal consistency generally provides information about all items and the extent to which they all measure the same concept in the test. Test A Cronbach Alpha Value was 0.737 whereas Test B Cronbach Alpha Value was 0.786. Both values were within the interval of $0.7 < \alpha < 0.95$ which suggests that both tests have an appropriate reliability [5]. The results can suggest an improvement of the game application usability from one test to another. Time-on-task metrics demonstrate the improvements that the game suffered in the versions tested by Test A and Test B. Task 1 achieved 8% time reduction, Task 3 achieved 29% time reduction, Task 4 achieved the lowest time reduction with 3% and Task 2 presented the highest improvement rate with 51% time reduction. These time-on-task reductions provide a positive feedback for the proposed guidelines that were adopted for the second version of the Megaramp game, tested in Test B. Regarding the improvement in the number of errors, Task 2 presented the highest reduction ratio reaching the value of 75% less errors. Task 1 and Task 4 registered the same number of errors per user in both tests. Task 3 presented no errors in Test B compared to 2 errors in Test A.

To better illustrate the improvements of the Megaramp application Figure 3 shows some differences in the two versions tested. It is desirable that users are informed about the status of their performance, whether or not they are succeeding in performing the maneuvers. For instance, in Test A version no information was given to users about the solution to the problems they were having (e.g. not performing the right steps to execute a maneuver) whereas Test B version shows a clear message about the problem the user is having. In the latter version an example of an error message (You didn't release in time) is shown when the user fails to execute the jump command in time. Furthermore Figure 3 shows the differences in the tutorials design. Test A version shows only a background tutorials (red circle), which came as insufficient, whereas Test B version offers new and improved step by step tutorials that clearly inform users on how to use the application.

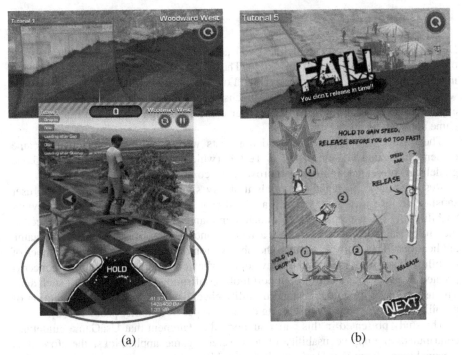

Fig. 3. Examples of differences between Megaramp versions from Test A (a) and Test B (b)

Task assessment clearly demonstrates the improvements from Test A to Test B versions. Test A reached an average 76% task success that was directly related with the low success rate on Task 2. Test B registered a 98% task success which can suggest an improvement of the game usability that led to an increased user performance.

Comparison charts shown in Figure 4 demonstrate the differences in the scores given to each of the Megaramp versions tested.

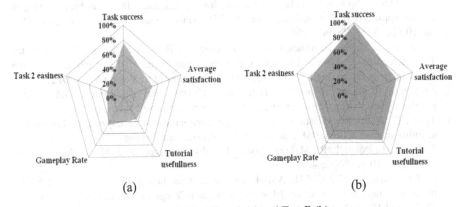

Fig. 4. Comparison of Test A (a) and Test B (b) scores

4   Conclusions

Developing new usability guidelines well adapted for touchscreen applications was one of the main challenges of this study. The goal of this study was to bridge the gap in game applications usability research. For this purpose the UsaGame guidelines were compiled, adapting or creating touchscreen heuristics to the domain of game applications, with the aim of offering user centered design support to touch mobile game application developers.

The results observed in the validation tests were promising. In fact, it became evident that game version tested in Test B (which was developed using UsaGame guidelines) presented significant improvements compared with the other version.

Results suggest that game tutorials usability significantly contributes to the user satisfaction. Results also suggest a significant impact of touch mobile devices usability in the gameplay rate. Touch commands can become hard to execute, therefore usability concerns can be a major contributor to the success of the game applications. This study confirmed the observation done in [6] that a large number of usability issues were identified by developers when considering the usability concerns pointed by user centered design support tools, confirming the importance of such aids. The use of usability guidelines and usability checklists complement the execution of usability testing, eventually disclosing different types of usability problems [6].

The study presented in this paper supports the statement that UsaGame guidelines contributed to improve usability of touchscreen game applications, therefore it is reasonable to affirm that UsaGame is a valuable tool to support user centered design in the fast growing field of game development.

Acknowledgements. This work was funded by National Funds through FCT - Fundação para a Ciência e a Tecnologia under the scope of project PEst-OE/EEI/UI0066.

References

1. Zhang, D.S., Adipat, B.: Challenges, methodologies, and issues in the usability testing of mobile applications. International Journal of Human-Computer Interaction 18(3) (2005), doi:10.1207/s15327590ijhc1803_3
2. Inostroza, R., Rusu, C., Roncagliolo, S., Jimenez, C., Rusu, V.: Usability Heuristics for Touchscreen-based Mobile Devices. Paper Presented at the 2012 Ninth International Conference on Information Technology- New Generations, Las Vegas (April 2012)
3. Nielsen, J.:   Ten   Usability   Heuristics   (2005),   http://www.useit.com/papers/heuristic/heuristic_list.html (retrieved November 14, 2012)
4. Tullis, T., Albert, B.: Measuring the user experience: collecting, analyzing, and presenting usability metrics. Elsevier/Morgan Kaufmann, Amsterdam; Boston (2008)
5. Tavakol, M., Dennick, R.: Making sense of Cronbach's alpha. Int. J. Med. Educ. 2, 53–55 (2011), doi:10.5116/ijme.4dfb.8dfd
6. Ji, Y.G., Park, J.H., Yun, M.H.: A usability checklist for the usability evaluation of mobile phone user interface. nternational Journal of Human-Computer Interaction 20(3), 207–231 (2006), doi:10.1207/s15327590ijhc2003_3

7. Park, Y.S., Han, S.H.: Touch key design for one-handed thumb interaction with a mobile phone: Effects of touch key size and touch key location. International Journal of Industrial Ergonomics 40(1), 68–76 (2010)
8. Sun, X., Plocher, T., Qu, W.: An empirical study on the smallest comfortable button/Icon size on touch screen. In: Aykin, N. (ed.) HCII 2007. LNCS, vol. 4559, pp. 615–621. Springer, Heidelberg (2007)
9. Seward, D.: Designing Usable Mobile Websites: a practical guide, p. 24. Peak Usability, Brisbane (2011)
10. Tiresias, Checklist For Touchscreens (2009), http://www.tiresias.org/research/guidelines/checklists/touch_checklist.htm (retrieved October 17, 2012)
11. Sjöberg, S.: A Touch Screen Interface for Point-Of-Sale Applications in Retail Stores (Master's Degree) (2005), http://www8.cs.umu.se/education/examina/Rapporter/SamuelSjoberg.pdf (retrieved)
12. Simunovic, M.P.: Colour vision deficiency. Eye 24(5) (2010), doi:10.1038/eye.2009.251
13. Neiva, M.: Code ColorADD (2010), http://www.coloradd.net/code.asp#top (retrieved August 22, 2012)
14. Scribd, Game Testing Methodology (2008), http://www.scribd.com/doc/6555758/Game-Testing-Methodology (retrieved October 17, 2012)

Annex – UsaGame Guidelines

	Requirements	Brief explanation
1	Input Target area	Ensure that the selected area is larger than the icon itself
2	Controls size	Controls should be touchable, at least 23x23 pixels or 6mm x 6mm. Most used icons should be 40x40 pixels or 10.6mm x 10.6 mm [7,8].
3	Easy navigation	Allow clear and direct navigation to return to the main menu or exit [2,3].
4	Navigation Features	Support Redo and Undo [2,3].
6	Navigation Features	Do not display too much information; use skipped tutorial and various pages.
7	Navigation Features	Implement a side bar when row or column information is used, for a better knowledge of information location and to skip to end and top in a faster way.
8	Icon Design	Good delineation of the icon gives the users a more precise location of the button, use concave surfaces or movement.
9	Icon shapes	Take advantage of user known shapes and implement consistency throughout the application [2,3].
10	Icon label	Use simple labels along with the icon or create a hover effect to show the label once the button is selected.
11	High contrast visual elements	Text must be readable and links easy to target, use white or yellow text over dark color backgrounds [9,10].
12	Pratical Tutorial	When possible implement tutorials while loadings occur or implement a background tutorial whilst the user is playing the game.
13	Use appropriate touch actions	Implement release response actions [11].

	Requirements	Brief explanation
14	Use appropriate touch actions	Implement the appropriate response time upon clicking [2,3]
15	Use appropriate touch actions	Minimize touch inputs, such as, click to select and click to ok.
16	Support touch gestures	Take advantage of touch gestures, such as, zooming, panning, scroll, rotate and make them intuitive to users.
17	Design for multiple users	Implement a feature that allows the application to be used by left and right-handed, or allow the opportunity to configure icons and implied actions [2,3].
18	Design for multiple users	Avoid the use of red and green in critical decision tasks without symbols, to adapt the application to color-blind users [12].
19	Design for multiple users	Implement a customize feature for color-blinds, that implements symbols (ColorADD®) into icons so users can acknowledge colours [13].
20	Button location	Avoid right screen areas when dealing with one-handed thumb interaction [7].
21	Button location in Landscape mode	Main buttons should be held near the lower corners within thumbs reach and there is the possibility to place icons in between
22	Button location in Portrait mode	Main buttons should be held near the lower corners within thumbs reach and is not advised to place buttons in between.
23	Button consistency	Locate buttons wisely and with consistency to increase learnability.
24	Provide propper feedback	Use 3D-effects in buttons to appear clickable, also implement hover effects, such as color gradients to change button color when selected.
25	Intuitive colors	Use appropriate color conventions for specific actions (e.g., exit buttons in red and undo buttons in green) [2,3].
26	Characters need to be viewed	Show characters in a viewable area whilst users are typing to promote a better understanding.
27	Appropriate loadings	Ensure an expectable loading time (not more than 20 seconds), and implement a loading meter [14].
29	Correct messages	Ensure simple and correct messages are shown whenever errors or savings occur [2,3].
30	Use different feedback means	Implement tactile and sound feedback so users can have knowledge of what happens without obstructing visual attention [2,3].
31	Audio Messages	Ensure that audio messages are kept short and simple, abbreviation use is not advised [10].
32	Exterior feedback	Provide exterior feedback for new messages and device battery status. Generally placed in the right upper corner [2,3].
33	Menu based features	Smartly hierarch features to appear in menus. Most important features must have a highlighted position and be placed directly on the background instead of in drop-down menus.
34	Skip function	Skip buttons should be available in some tutorials and its location should be far from the main buttons, so users do not accidentally activate them.

	Requirements	Brief explanation
35	Memorize players options	Customization of either players or cars should be memorized even if the player quits the game, this way the user does not have to choose it all over again.
36	Wireless connection	Wireless network connection should not be demanding enough that the device cannot support the wireless network connection needed by the game application.
37	Graphical support adaptation	Some devices may not support a large amount of memory dedicated for graphics and fast processing speed, therefore resolution and graphical definitions should be configurable when needed.
38	Language	For the application to be used by multiple users main languages, such as, English, Spanish, French, Chinese, must be available, depending on the public market [2,3].
39	Correct Gameplay	Assure the correct gameplay, depending on the game application being evaluated [2,3,14].
40	Portrayal of real life	Make sure objects collide properly and with the appropriate consequences [2,3,14].
41	Help and documentation	Implement help features [2,3].

A Method for Teaching Affordance for User Experience Design in Interactive Media Design Education

Asım Evren Yantaç

Yildiz Technical University, Interactive Media Design Program, Istanbul, Turkey
evren.yantac@gmail.com

Abstract. Today we are living in a world where boundaries among spatial design, object design and interactive media design (IMD) or human-computer interaction field are disappearing. Technological advances widen the abilities of interactive technologies day by day. We are on the verge of leaving the desktop metaphor behind while more natural and real life like interaction with interactive technologies is already on its way. As mentioned above, this is more about spatially interacting with new interaction modes such as gestures/touch/bio-feedback and new modes of showing content such as seamless/screen-free interfaces projected onto the eye or on different types of surfaces. These facts are highly related with the "user experience" subject. As put forth by Norman (1995), user experience paradigm aims to shift the focus from a more engineering approach to the emotions, behaviors of the human within his surrounding while interacting with the information. Today's designers are to design the user's whole experience, which means that traditional interaction design education concentrating on the media and computer is not enough. With this point of view, one of the aspects that is getting even more important now is ergonomics, thus affordance. This paper is about a method we are using in our interactive media design curriculum to study affordance and trigger the creativity of interaction design students.

Keywords: Interactive Media, Education, Affordance, User Experience, Curriculum, Natural User Interfaces.

1 Introduction

With the advent of interactive technologies, today we make continuous and location-independent interaction with digital information. Regardless of a specific location, we interact with HCI devices while walking, running, focusing on other things, carrying objects or interacting with other devices or people. Human factors research has been dealing with accessibility of interactive devices that are used under disabling conditions. Disabling environment term is used to explain situations that limit users' cognitive and behavioral abilities (Newell and Gregor, 1999). Newell and Cairns (1993) also claim that the design criteria for disabled users are mostly valid for normal functioning users' behaviors under disabling conditions. With another perspective, ARCHIE, an EU project, proved that an office worker nearly has similar

A. Marcus (Ed.): DUXU/HCII 2013, Part I, LNCS 8012, pp. 630–638, 2013.
© Springer-Verlag Berlin Heidelberg 2013

accesibility level as an airplane pilot in the cockpit (Devnani et al. 1995). Both of these examples support the fact that disabling conditions provide valuable information for universally accessible interactive solutions. With this mindset, researchers like Hancock (Hancock and Miller, 1982), Newell (Newell and Gregor, 2002), Landau (Landau, 2002) have long been busy with the subject while it hadn't attracted much attention in design curriculum. However today we are living in a world where we nearly use interactive technologies only under disabling conditions. Here comes user experience design subject telling us that we need to change our design education perspective.

Within this world of continuously evolving technologies, it is getting harder for designers to develop rich, yet efficient, effective and satisfactory user experience solutions. We, in our IMD program in Yildiz Technical University, have been discussing interactive solutions used under disabling conditions as design case studies in IMD curriculum since 15 years. By then, it was an unfamiliar case study to encounter environmentally challenged computer use cases which we used as unfamiliar situations and obstructions for the design students to solve limiting problems like getting into interaction while standing up, moving or partial use of haptic abilities (Ozcan and Yantac, 2009). As a part of our breaking the rules education concept, it was a challenging design problem for the students for triggering their creativity.

But today, as mentioned above environmentally challenged interaction is almost a part of our everyday life. It is not uncommon for most of us, especially the young generation. Every interface has to be designed in a way that they can function effectively in many different environmental conditions. Thus, the careful planning of interaction between the interactive object, the user and the surrounding environment is significant. That is why we believe that affordance of interactive objects is one of the most important subject within the IMD curriculum while we see from the literature that there are not many examples of this. As one of the few examples, Faiola (2007) questions the lack of problem solving courses compared to the high number of usability, interface design and computing skills, and they (Faiola and Matei, 2010) propose the idea of having affordance at the center of HCID education, based on the arguments by Hollan et al (2000) claiming that the field should focus on "complex, networked world of information".

We hereby, in this paper, share our experiences with basic interaction design exercises focusing on affordance of natural objects, with which the students can explore user experience design solutions, pretentious space of interface ergonomics, alternative interaction possibilities, un-cliché design questions while having physical constraints caused by disabling environmental factors. We respectively discuss (i) problem space; (ii) explanation of exercises; (iii) insights from the study and (iv) further studies.

2   Problem Space: Teaching the Fundamentals of "Creative" User Experience Design

As mentioned above, it is clear that a new era of NUIs lies in the future of ubiquitous computing. The technology enables us to interact with computers by means of our everyday gestures and use them anywhere, anytime. But today's systems merely act as an orientation for the up-coming future. We are in the verge of a big change. This brings many new challenges for both today's designers and design education institutions. However the dynamic ground of HCI has always been here. So it is not new that IMD education has to focus on universal design problems and build up a strong design-thinking basis that is not bound up with technologies and trends. For the clarification of the "design-thinking" term, we refer to the definition by Zimmerman et. al. (2007); a whole design process that involves grounding, ideation and iteration. Norman (1999) supports this idea by claiming that the most important components of a successful design are conceptual model and overall consistency.

On the other hand, another critical concern for IMD education is creativity. "Why?" Relying on the fact that creative skills can be learned, we believe that a design curriculum should always have the notion of triggering the "lateral thinking skills" (De Bono, 1990) and give the vision to push the traditional boundaries and be creative. Creativity, in this sense, is "bringing something into being that is original (new, unusual, novel, and unexpected) and also valuable (useful, good, adaptive, and appropriate)" as explained by Osche (1990).

Design research literature has been focusing on these two big concerns of design education; giving design thinking basis and triggering creativity. With regards to research through design approach (Frayling, 1993), which uses education results as research artifacts to create knowledge instead of products (Zimmerman, et. al., 2007), many design curricula takes advantage of studio-based learning to overcome above problems. With the aforementioned perspective for grounding their studio-based design education to creativity and design thinking, Faiola and Matei (2007), consider "affordance" as a key conceptual concern in HCI education. They task their students to start the design process not from abstract functionality but from defining the way the device presents itself physically. With an activity-oriented approach, we believe that affordance seems to be a very good challenge for IMD students in this sense.

With a similar perspective, we have been focusing on natural interaction exercises in our curriculum. This has been a part of our educational approach of "Breaking the Rules" (Ozcan and Yantac, 2009) inspired by Lars von Trier's film Five Obstructions (Leth 2003) for which Von Trier claims that creativity thrives on limitations (Tabak 2004). We want the students to explore non-predictable ideas when they confront unfamiliar or extra-ordinary design problems and obstructions. Regarding the problems of giving a design-thinking basis and triggering creativity in IMD education, we've been employing different "rule breaking" exercises for 15 years such as;

1. Disabling environment (auditory/haptic/visually limited environmental conditions) (Ozcan and Yantac, 2009),
2. Re-reading old cultural traditions for interaction (Ozcan, 2005)

However, due to above-mentioned changes in the field, disabling environment case studies started to be inadequate for triggering the students' creativity when compared to 10 years ago. Instead, we have been employing 2 different exercises for exploring natural user interfaces (NUI);

3. Learning NUI through creative drama (Unluer and Ozcan, 2012)
4. From natural objects to interactive artifacts,

The idea beneath the second of above exercises is to task the students to explore affordance of natural objects, the way we interact with them in real life and imagine how they would turn it into interactive artifacts in unfamiliar situations. We, hereby, share our insights from our studies on this "unfamiliar actions with natural objects" exercise. We will first briefly explain the procedures, pedagogical approaches and a few results of this exercise.

3   From Natural Objects to Interactive Artifacts

Main idea of this exercise is to make IMD students explore natural interaction using ontological metaphors, mediating artifacts, personification with natural objects. These widely used methods for practicing ideation process in architecture, industrial or graphic design schools, is here employed to explore fundamentals of affordance besides triggering creativity and productivity by means of NUI, and forming the basis of design-thinking. Instead of dealing with technological limitations or traditional design boundaries or trends, students focus solely on a natural object and its physical, chemical, material substances in interaction with a user and surrounding.

3.1   Pedagogical Approach

For provoking the productivity of students, the exercise (Figure 1) takes advantage of well-known methods such as personification, mediated artifacts and ontological metaphors (Lakoff & Johnson, 1980) that are used popularly in design education. A natural object is imagined in many different random situations where an action is applied on to it and it replies this action. For the beginning stage, there is no need for detailing but students practice the productive ideation process by exploring many possibilities of interaction sets. Sometimes the object is personified; sometimes the idea comes from ontological metaphors. That is why we want the students to start exploring with action based verbal ideas and play with sentences, words and then continue the exploration process with hand-drawn sketches where they can investigate visual clues of physical attributes and actions. Following this preliminary ideation process, students start to detail the concept in order to turn the object into an intelligent interactive artifact where they confront limitations as a part of our breaking the rules method. They analyze the object the object with its physical, functional, conceptual, lexical attributes. For the interaction design solutions (input, feedback, predictability...), they are forced to stick to some attributes of the original object as well as being limited to one main function for practicing consistency. The process ends by shaping all the interaction map of a re-constructed interactive artifact for which they are free to en-richen the artifact with graphical, auditory, luminous, action related abilities. The artifact is in continuous communication with the user and their surrounding. However, as our education curriculum focuses on IMD and doesn't teach industrial product design or 3D ergonomics in detail, we don't want the students to work on the physical shape of the object but re-think all possible human-object-environment interactions regarding this artifact.

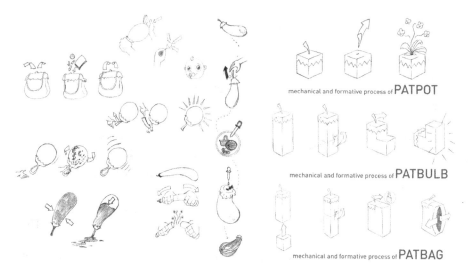

Fig. 1. Sketches on an interactive eggplant artifact (left). Final ideas on the artifact (right) (Mustafa Ahmet Kara, 2008)

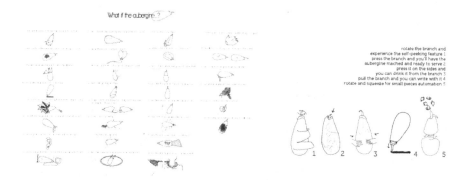

Fig. 2. 4th procedure of the process; defining 40 ideas (left) and 5th procedure; 5 of the eliminated ideas for in interactive eggplant artifact (Bruno Santos, 2008)

3.2   Procedure

From 2008 to 2013, the exercise has been implied to 2 different student groups; 2nd semester (1st year) and 5th semester (3rd year) of an 8 semester, bachelor level IMD program. Each group involved 40 students and 80 students in total did the study. We first tried the study with 3rd year students with a more detailed process running as 12 studio sessions. This was deeply exploring the latter parts of the process by details on efficiency and consistency of the artifact. Later on we started running the study with a more basic format with the 1st year students as a 3-session process. This time we focus more on the ideation process instead of detailed design solutions. Briefly, both studies included following procedures:

1. Define a natural object (We suggest them to work with unusual, provocative, interesting objects that have different parts)

   e.g: A mushroom, pineapple, pomegranate, pine cone, starfish...

2. Explore its substance; Physical attributes, Form, Color, Material, Stiffness... (Here they explore physical attributes of the original object on its affordance)

   e.g: Mushroom's body has a cap on top, pores at the bottom of the cap, elastic stipe carries the cap, yellowish grey, soft, spongy...

3. Investigate all other attributes such as feeling (taste, smell...), function (edible, medicinal, protective...).

   e.g: Strong taste, odor, edible, poisonous, fertile...

4. Write down 40 fictive sentences (Figure 2) explaining how it would react when confronting an unfamiliar action from the user or the surrounding.

   e.g: What would the mushroom do if it was thrown into the air by being turned 360° around itself?

5. Eliminate these interaction stories into 10 consistent functions that would turn the object into an interactive artifact used for a specific need.

   e.g: The mushrooms can be used as small containers used for mixing, storing, duplicating mixtures of sauces or drinks.

6. Reconstruct the natural object in a way that the user can predict how to use its functions and what would the results be; carryout the actions easily; watch results of the interactions (While re-structuring the object, students need to keep some of the attributes such as the main form, but can play with others).

   e.g: The mushrooms cap and stipe can be separated and brought together again when needed. The cap can be screwed on the stipe...

For all of these steps, the student draws sketches (Figure 3) and detailed illustrations explaining interaction steps such as; the first state of the object (predictability); user's first action (input); object's external reaction (feedback, WYSIWYG, mental model); object's internal reaction (functionality, navigation). The process, which is presented as (1) sequential images showing the actions, (2) a still image showing the whole (3) and an animation in the end, is evaluated with jury critics. The jury considers the level of exploring the affordance of the object, creativity in the ideation process, productivity and presentation.

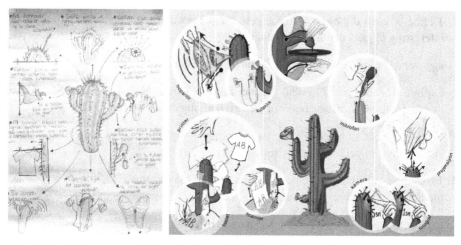

Fig. 3. Two different cactus ideas; An interactive cactus for general home use (Başak Gence, 2013) (left); A second interactive cactus for home entertainment (Özge Kantaroglu, 2008) (right)

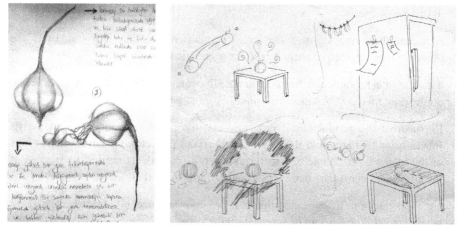

Fig. 4. Preliminary ideas on a garlic artifact used for camping (Birnur Yıldırım, 2013) (left); An orange artifact used for hygienic functions (İmge Akbulut, 2013)

4   Discussion

As detailed above, we started implying the exercise as a more detailed study to the experienced students before they start working on spatial interaction design case studies. But this exercise lacks focus on detailed problem solving. It is more about creativity and productivity in the ideation process and doing this by means of affordance of a natural object. Thus we continued by implying the study to the less experienced 1st year students as a part of the basic interaction design education. In the basic interaction design education, we feature exercises that focus on ideation and presentation skills of students. What we experienced by this change is that this exercise fits better to the early stages of interaction design curriculum to help forming the design thinking skills for user experience design and fundamental interaction design principals.

The effectiveness of these exercises was evaluated through the analysis of 7th semester design studio works, which focus on the design of spatial interaction in a physical space. Generally speaking, these exercises about affordance of natural objects guided the students to have a better understanding of the physical tools and ergonomics of the objects, so they had reached a new level of awareness in choosing/shaping the mediated artifacts in relation with its surrounding and user's experience. Besides, they created inspiring solutions for the use of wearable, mobile and surface technologies.

In this paper, we share our insights from experiences with an exercise we implied for teaching fundamentals of user experience design by means of affordance in interactive media design education curriculum. For the exercise, students choose a natural object, explore its attributes and re-construct it in a way that it is a responsive, interactive artifact which functions efficiently and consistently. This gives a student the opportunity to brainstorm about the interaction of the artifact with the user and their surrounding. We learned from our experiences that these exercises help building the design-thinking basis for user experience design however it functions better when used in the preliminary stages of the curriculum.

References

1. De Bono, E.: Lateral thinking: Creativity step by step. Harper & Row, New York (1990)
2. Devnani, N., Cairns, A.Y., Cobley, A.E., Glynn, H., Ricketts, I., Scott, D.: Inside ARCHIE - A Description of the ARCHIE System Architecture and Functionality. In: Adjunct Proceedings of HCI 1995, Huddersfield, pp. 182–184 (1995)
3. Faiola, A.: The design enterprise: Rethinking the HCI education paradigm. Design Issues 23(3), 30–45 (2007)
4. Faiola, A., Matei, S.A.: Enhancing human–computer interaction design education: teaching affordance design for emerging mobile devices. International Journal Technology Design Education 20, 239–254 (2010)
5. Frayling, C.: Research in Art and Design. Royal College of Art Research Papers 1(1), 1–5 (1993)
6. Hancock, P.A., Milner, E.K.: Mental and psychomotor task performance in an open ocean underwater environment. Research Quarterly, 247–251 (1982)
7. Hollan, J., Hutchins, E., Kirsh, D.: Distributed cognition: Toward a new foundation for human computer interaction research. ACM Transactions on Computer-Human Interaction 7(2), 174–196 (2000)
8. Lakoff, G., Johnson, M.: Metaphors we live by. University of Chicago (1980)
9. Landau, K.: Usability criteria for intelligent driver assistance systems. Theor. Issues in Ergon. Sci. 3(4), 330–345 (2002)
10. Leth, J.: Five Obstructions. Directed by Jørgen Leth. Produced by Lars von Trier. Trust Film Sales (2003)

11. Newell, A.F., Cairns, A.Y.: Designing for extra-ordinary users. Ergonomics in Design, 10–16 (1993)
12. Newell, A.F., Gregor., P.: Extra-ordinary human-machine interaction: what can be learned from people with disabilities? Cognition, Technology & Work, 78–85 (1999)
13. Norman, D.A.: Affordance, conventions, and design. Interactions 6, 38 (1999)
14. Norman, D., Miller, J., Henderson, A.: What You See, Some of What's in the Future, And How We Go About Doing It: HI at Apple Computer. In: Proceedings of CHI 1995, Denver, Colorado, USA (1995)
15. Osche, R.: Before the Gates of Excellence: The Determinants of Creative Genius. Cambridge University Press, Cambridge (1990)
16. Ozcan, O.: Turkish-Ottoman miniature art within the context of electronic information design education. Journal of Technology and Design Education 15(3), 237–252 (2005)
17. Ozcan, O., Yantac, E.: Breaking the Rules in Interactive Media Design Education, Digital Creativity, Routledge, UK, vol. 17(2), pp. 115–124 (2009)
18. Unluer, A., Ozcan, O.: Current Problems in Design Education on Natural User Interface Using Creative Drama Technique. In: Design Thinking Research Symposium (DTRS 2012), the School of Design, April 18-19. Northumbria University (2012)
19. Zimmerman, J., Forlizzi, J., Evenson, S.: Research through design as a method for interaction design research in HCI. In: Proceedings of the SIGCHI Conference on Human Factors in Computing Systems (CHI 2007), pp. 493–502. ACM, New York (2007)

Author Index

Abascal-Mena, Rocío   IV-231
Abdelnour-Nocera, José   II-161
Abromowitz, Scott   III-130, III-140
Abu-Hnaidi, Malak   II-342
Abujarad, Fuad   III-3
Abulkhair, Maysoon F.   II-3, III-130
Aderhold, Andreas   II-321
Adikari, Sisira   I-3
Adukaite, Asta   IV-163
Ahn, DaeSung   III-316
Ahram, Tareq   IV-325
Alacam, Ozge   IV-334
Al-Arifi, Bayan   II-333
Albatati, Reem   III-85
Alelis, Genevieve   III-429
Al-Ghamdi, Amal   II-296
Alhafzy, Maram S.   II-3
Al-Harbi, Shatha   II-342
Abo Al Laban, Tsneem   III-85
Almeida, Ana   III-169
Almirall, Magí   II-180
Al-Ofisan, Ghadah   II-333
Alomari, Ebtesam A.   II-3
Alpkaya, Seda   IV-84
Al-Romi, Norah   II-333
Al-Rubaian, Arwa   II-333
Al-Saggaf, Reem   II-296
Al-Sahafi, Sultana   II-296
Al-Semairi, Ghadeer   II-342
Altakrouri, Bashar   III-327
Al-Tayari, Hadeel   II-342
Al-Wabil, Areej   II-333
Al-Zebaidi, Maha   II-296
Andersen, Kristina   III-548
Andrade, Ana   IV-121
Ang, Chee Siang   III-429
Ang, Kevin Z.Y.   III-120
Aoyama, Hisae   IV-506
Arning, Katrin   I-439, III-10
Asano, Kaho   II-11
Asthana, Siddhartha   I-183
Atkinson, Robert K.   II-276
Attisano, Roby   III-20
Aurelio, David   IV-469

Austin, Ann   II-161
Avery, Josh   IV-601
Ayanoğlu, Hande   III-30

Bakeer, Mai   III-85
Bamasak, Omaima   II-342
Banic, Amy Ulinski   II-209
Baranauskas, Maria Cecília C.   I-459,
   II-518
Barattin, Daniela   I-242
Barnes, Tiffany   II-189
Baroni, Ilaria   III-558
Barros, Helda O.   III-337
Barros, Marina   I-379, II-491
Bas-sam, Malak   II-462
Batehup, Lynn   II-417
Batawil, Samah   III-85
Baurley, Sharon   IV-424
Bavelier, Daphne   II-352
Bayliss, Jessica D.   II-352
Bazo, Alexander   IV-248
Belden, Jeffery L.   II-381
Bellini, Sara   III-558, III-594
Bellows, Brooke G.   I-13, I-144
Bengler, Klaus-Josef   II-89, IV-359
Berlin, Dan   II-407
Biersack, Peter   II-20
Bilgin, Gökhan   IV-651
Blankl, Martin   II-20
Blondon, Katherine S.   II-361
Blustein, Jamie   I-162
Bobrowicz, Ania   III-429
Böhm, Stephan   IV-631
Bordegoni, Monica   I-242
Bouwmeester, Ruben   IV-575
Braik, Roa'a   II-342
Brandenburg, Stefan   I-449
Brangier, Eric   II-558
Brazinskas, Mantas   III-179
Breiner, Kai   I-193
Breuer, Henning   IV-3
Breyer, Felipe   II-266, III-227
Brockmann, Tobias   I-340
Buchdid, Samuel B.   I-459

Burghardt, Manuel   IV-248, IV-432
Byrne, Daragh   II-276
Bystřický, Jiří   I-22

Çağıltay, Kürşat   IV-334
Cai, Guowei   III-120
Çakır, Tuğba   IV-173
Calado, Alexana Vilar Soares   III-345
Campbell, John   I-3
Camplone, Stefania   IV-23
Campos, Fábio   I-203, I-379, II-491,
    III-337, III-345, IV-113, IV-257
Cantoni, Lorenzo   IV-163, IV-696
Cappiello, Cinzia   IV-641
Carignan, Joëlle   II-501
Carlson, Darren   III-327
Carmo, Maria Beatriz   II-442
Cavalcanti, Aline   II-266, III-227
Cavalcanti, Virginia   IV-121
Champagnat, Ronan   I-74
Chang, Chia-Ling   I-469
Chang, Chih-Kai   II-28
Chang, Teng-Wen   IV-402
Chelnokova, Polina   IV-221
Chen, Ben M.   III-120
Chen, Bo-Sheng   II-304
Chen, Chaomei   IV-601
Chen, Frank (Ming-Hung)   I-545
Chen, Kuo-Pin   III-446
Chen, Ting-Han   III-246
Chen, Yuanyuan   I-479
Chiou, Megan   IV-67
Chisnell, Dana   IV-193
Chiu, Shu-Chuan   I-593
Cho, Yen-Ting   IV-478
Choensawat, Worawat   II-171
Choi, Jung-Min   III-40
Choi, Young Mi   III-75
Chou, Hsin-Yin   II-304
Chou, Wen-Huei   III-446
Chu, Sauman   II-371
Chuang, Miao-Hsien   III-455
Chung, Wei-Ming   III-306
Chung, WonJoon   I-29, I-125
Chynał, Piotr   I-212
Clarke, Martina A.   II-381
Clarkson, P. John   IV-457
Cláudio, Ana Paula   II-442
Combe, Nicola   III-49
Conn Welch, Karla   III-105

Conti, Antonia S.   IV-359
Cordeiro, Erimar   IV-121
Correia, Walter   I-203, I-379, II-491,
    III-337, III-345, IV-113, IV-257
Corte, Joao   IV-113
Coursaris, Constantinos K.   IV-274
Coutinho, Solange   II-219
Cugini, Umberto   I-242
Cui, Jinqiang   III-120

Damásio, Manuel José   IV-13
Danylak, Roman   III-465
da Silva, Daliton   II-266
da Silva, Fernando Moreira   III-419
da Silva, José Carlos P.   IV-265
Da Silva, Régio Pierre   I-330
da Silva, Tiago Silva   I-599
da Silva Augusto, Lia Giraldo   III-150
da Silveira, Dierci Marcio Cunha   I-409
das Neves, Andre Menezes Marques
    II-508
de Carvalho, Breno José Andrade   II-508
de França, Ana Carol Pontes   I-68
de Lemos Meira, Luciano Rogério   I-68
de Lera, Eva   II-180
Demetrescu, Emanuel   IV-238
de Miranda, Leonardo Cunha   II-518
Dennis, Toni A.   III-3
de Oliveira Passos, Marcel   II-286
de Souza, Clarisse Sieckenius   I-115
D´Garcia, Germannya   IV-121
Dias, Patrícia   IV-13
Di Bucchianico, Giuseppe   IV-23
Dinis, Susana   III-475
Dong, Hua   I-171, III-49
Dong, Miaobo   III-120
Dong, Xiangxu   III-120
Donovan, Jared   III-352
Dorey, Jonathan   II-79
Drewitz, Uwe   I-449
Drexler, David   IV-533
Du, Shiau-Yuan   III-246
Duarte, Emília   III-30, III-189, III-205,
    III-362, III-419, III-475
Duckworth, Jonathan   II-391
Dumas, Joseph   I-349

Eibl, Maximilian   III-411
Ekşioğlu, Mahmut   IV-173
El Said, Ghada R.   II-38

Erbil, Mehmet Ali   III-179
Erdal, Feride   IV-334
Eriksson, Joakim   I-262, IV-238
Esteves, Francisco   II-442
Eugene, Wanda   II-189
Evans, Andrea L.   I-222

Fabri, Marc   III-484, III-585
Falcão, Christianne Soares   IV-342
Faroughi, Arash   I-38
Faroughi, Roozbeh   I-38
Febretti, Alessandro   I-232
Fei, Qian   II-44
Feijs, Loe   III-494
Fernandes, Fabiane R.   IV-265
Ferrise, Francesco   I-242
Fesenmaier, Daniel R.   IV-212
Filgueiras, Ernesto   III-205
Filho, Epitácio L. Rolim   III-337
Filippi, Stefano   I-242
Fineman, Andrea   IV-193
Fischer, Holger   I-252
Flanagan, Patricia J.   I-48, I-58, III-439
Følstad, Asbjørn   I-506
Ford, Rebecca   I-312, IV-486
Ford, Treschiel   II-209
Ford, Yelena   IV-424
Fortier, Sara   I-29
Francis, Jon   III-372
Fukatsu, Yoshitomo   III-255
Fuks, Hugo   III-237, III-439
Fukuda, Yutaka   IV-506
Fukuhara, T.   II-435
Fukumoto, Makoto   III-264
Furbach, Ulrich   III-270

Gabriele, Felipe   II-257
Gandhi, Rajeev   III-372
Gao, Jie   IV-183, IV-352
Gao, Yi   III-504
Garduno, Elmer   III-372
Gasser, Jochen   III-513
Gençer, Merve   IV-651
Ghinea, Gheorghita   II-401
Gisbert, Mercè   II-180
Gockel, Bianca   I-262
Godara, Jaideep   II-548
Göktürk, Mehmet   III-57
Goldwasser, Eliad   II-548
Gong, Yida   III-75

Gotsis, Marientina   II-470
Götze, Martin   IV-359
Gouda, Sara   II-105
Gould, Emilie W.   IV-496
Gower, Andy   IV-140, IV-150
Graf, Holger   I-262, II-321, IV-238
Greenspan, Steven   IV-581
Greenwood, Kristyn   I-273
Grønli, Tor-Morten   II-401
Guo, Xiaopeng   IV-183, IV-352
Gurgel, Andrei   II-286
Güvendik, Merve   IV-173
Guy, Olivier   I-74
Gyoda, Koichi   III-65

Hachimura, Kozaburo   II-171
Hama, Daiki   I-283
Hamasaki, M.   II-435
Han, Junghyun   III-316
Hansen, Jarle   II-401
Hao, Yu   III-75
Hardt, Wolfram   III-411
Hardy, Delquawn   II-424
Harrell, Cyd   IV-193
Harrison, David   III-49
Hass, Chris   II-407
Hattori, Kanetoshi   IV-560
Hayashida, Kousuke   III-280
Heemann, Adriano   IV-414
Heidt, Michael   II-54
Heikkilä, Päivi   IV-660
Heimgärtner, Rüdiger   II-20, II-62, II-95, II-139
Hekler, Eric   II-424
Henriques, Sara   IV-13
Higgins, Jordan F.   I-13
Hirako, Hajime   IV-506
Hirao, Akemi   IV-560
Holme, Thomas   I-389
Hooker, Louise   II-417
Hornung, Heiko   II-518
Hsieh, Ming-Hsuan   I-488
Hsieh, Yi-Ta   I-564
Hsu, Hung-Pin   IV-666
Huang, Cheng-Yong   I-488
Huang, Chiwu   III-455
Huang, Scottie Chih-Chieh   IV-367

Ibrahim, Lamiaa F.   III-85
Ienaga, Takafumi   III-264

Igler, Bodo   IV-673
Iitaka, Toshikazu   IV-682
Imamura, Ken   I-283
Inoue, Satoru   IV-506
Inoue, Sozo   III-280
Inversini, Alessandro   IV-163
Ishibashi, Takuya   II-538
Ishii, Hirotake   III-530
Islam, Muhammad Nazrul   I-84

Jaimes, Luis G.   III-520
Jakobs, Eva-Maria   I-439
Jang, Yung Joo   IV-30
Jansen-Troy, Arne   II-452
Janß, Armin   II-452
Järventie-Ahonen, Heli   IV-660
Jeong, Eunseong   IV-274
Jiang, Nan   I-294
Jimenez, Yerika   IV-376
Johnson, Andrew E.   I-232
Johnson, Ian   I-417
Johnson, Steven L.   IV-212
Johnston, Angela   I-273
Joyce, Mary   I-303
Ju, Da Young   IV-103
Jung, Eui-Chul   II-199, IV-30, IV-385,
     IV-515
Jung, Yvonne   II-321

Kakara, Hiroyuki   III-95
Kang, Namgyu   I-498
Kang, Shin Jin   I-322
Kao, Chih-Tung   II-129
Kao, Hsin-Liu   III-306
Karahasanović, Amela   I-506
Karlin, Beth   I-312, IV-486
Karwowski, Waldemar   IV-325
Kato, Mariko   I-283
Keenan, Gail M.   I-232
Keinath, Andreas   IV-359
Kelner, Judith   II-266, III-227
Khashman, Nouf   II-79
Kierkels, Jeanine   III-494
Kijkhun, Chommanad   II-171
Kim, Chang Hun   I-322
Kim, Jeongmi (Jamie)   IV-212
Kim, Kyong-ho   III-393
Kim, Min Soon   II-381
Kim, Si-Jung   IV-740
Kim, Sunyoung   II-199

Kim, Yeolib   IV-203
Kim, Young Bin   I-322
Kim, Youngtae   IV-515
Kirakowski, Jurek   I-303
Kırış, Esin   IV-173, IV-581
Kistmann, Virgínia   IV-414
Kitamura, Koji   I-516, II-568
Kitamura, Satoru   I-516
Kitamura, Takayoshi   III-530
Kitamura, Yoshinobu   IV-560
Klasnja, Predrag   II-361
Knolmayer, Gerhard F.   IV-221
Kobayakawa, M.   II-435
Kohno, Izumi   I-525
Komischke, Tobias   IV-691
Kondo, Akira   IV-525
Kondo, Naoko   IV-525
Koopman, Richelle J.   II-381
Kosmala-Anderson, Joanna   II-417
Kouroupetroglou, Georgios   IV-575
Koyutürk, Efsane D.   IV-173
Ku, Vincent (I-Hsun)   I-545
Kulkarni, Anand S.   III-105
Kulpa, Cínthia Costa   I-330
Kumar, Janaki   II-528
Kuno, Yuki   III-255
Kuramoto, Itaru   II-538
Kurani, Kenneth S.   III-578
Kurioka, Mai   I-283
Kurosu, Masaaki   I-94

Lai, Ih-Cheng   IV-402
Lam, Miu-Ling   III-290
Lamontagne, Valérie   III-296
Langdon, Patrick   IV-457
Langhorne, Anna L.   III-112
Lawler Kennedy, Sally   II-501
Lawrence, Kira   II-209
Le, Hang   II-548
Le, Nguyen-Thinh   IV-533
Leão, Crystian   II-266
Lecca, Nicola   II-247
Lee, Douglas   IV-37
Lee, Lin-Chien   IV-392
Lee, Tong H.   III-120
Leitão, Carla Faria   I-115
Levi, Dennis   II-352
Li, Kun   III-120
Liang, Rung-Huei   I-610, III-306
Liang, Zhi-Hong   IV-450

Lin, Feng   III-120
Lin, Ming-Huang   IV-392
Lin, Tsen-Ying   III-306
Lin, Tz-Ying   IV-47
Lincoln, Dino   I-203
Lindemann, Udo   I-554, IV-130
Liu, Haibin   I-294
Liu, Qing   IV-543
Liu, Zhengjie   I-479
Lo, Chia-Hui Nico   IV-402
Loi, Daria   IV-57
Lopes, Eder   II-442
Lopez, Karen Dunn   I-232
López-Ornelas, Erick   IV-231
Lourenço, Daniel   II-219
Lu, Chia-Chen   I-535
Lu, Haind   I-340
Lucci Baldassari, Guido   IV-238
Luh, Ding-Bang   I-469, I-488, I-535,
    I-545, IV-47, IV-450
Luo, Delin   III-120

Ma, Chia-Hsiang   I-488
Maas, Alisa   II-209
Maciak, Adam   II-480
Maciel, Francimar Rodrigues   II-229
Madhavan, Krishna P.C.   IV-543
Mahdy, Hind H.   II-3
Maier, Florian   IV-94
Makanawala, Prerna   II-548
Mankodiya, Kunal   III-372
Mankovskii, Serge   IV-581
Marache-Francisco, Cathie   II-558
Marchetti, Emanuela   II-238, II-311
Marcus, Aaron   II-72, II-247, III-130,
    III-140, IV-67, IV-696
Maron, Markus   III-270
Martins, Edgard Thomas   III-150,
    III-160
Martins, Isnard Thomas   III-150, III-160
Martins, Laura B.   II-257
Martins, Rolando   III-372
Marx, Thomas   II-480
Matera, Maristella   IV-641
Matey, Luis M.   I-583
Matthiessen, Neil   I-100
McDonald, Craig   I-3
McGee, Mick   I-349
McKenna, Ann F.   IV-543

Medeiros, Rodrigo Pessoa   II-508
Meenowa, Joshan   IV-140, IV-150
Meier, Florian   IV-248
Mejia, G. Mauricio   II-371
Melo, André R.   IV-257
Melo, Claudia de O.   I-599
Melo, Miguel   III-169
Memon, Mohsin Ali   IV-706
Ménard, Elaine   II-79
Mendonca, Saul   IV-113
Michaelides, Mario   II-161
Michailidou, Ioanna   I-554, IV-130
Mielniczek, Witold   III-179
Mikkonen, Jussi   I-564
Milewski, Allen E.   IV-37
Min, Kyung-Bo   IV-385
Miwa, H.   II-435
Mizoguchi, Hiroshi   I-516, III-95
Mizoguchi, Riichiro   IV-560
Moallem, Abbas   I-107
Modi, Sunila   II-161
Mont'Alvão, Claudia Renata   IV-714
Monteiro, Ingrid Teixeira   I-115
Moody, Louise   II-417
Moore, Joi L.   II-381
Morreale, Patricia   IV-376
Motomura, Yoichi   II-435, II-568
Moura, Guilherme   II-266
Muehlhans, Heike   III-10
Murray, Tylar   II-424, III-520

Nahum, Mor   II-352
Nakajima, M.   II-435
Nakajima, Tatsuo   II-587
Nakamura, Akemi   IV-560
Nakamura, Masato   III-280
Nakanishi, Miwa   I-283
Nakashima, Naoki   III-280
Narasimhan, Priya   III-372
Narula, Chirag   IV-67
Nebe, Karsten   I-252
Neves, André   II-491, IV-113
Neves, Maria   I-203
Newby, Ethan   IV-193
Niebuhr, Sabine   IV-533
Nishida, Yoshifumi   I-516, II-568, III-95
Nishikawa, Masahiro   I-525
Nishimura, Satoshi   IV-560
Nishimura, Takuichi   II-435

Nohara, Yasunobu   III-280
Noriega, Paulo   III-30, III-205, III-362, III-419, III-475
Nunes, Isabel L.   I-359, I-620

Obermeier, Martin   IV-568
Ocak, Nihan   IV-334
Oe, Tatsuhito   III-255
Oettli, Michael   IV-77
Ogaick, Tara   I-125
Okazawa, Naoya   IV-408
Okimoto, Maria Lúcia L.R.   II-89, IV-414
Olaverri Monreal, Cristina   II-89
Oliveira, Sabrina   IV-414
Oono, Mikiko   II-568
Orehovački, Tihomir   I-369
Osen, Martin   III-383
Osmond, Jane   II-417
Öztürk, Özgürol   IV-284, IV-623

Pagano, Alfonsina   I-262
Pakkan, Ali   III-57
Panagis, Tasos   IV-77
Park, Hyesun   III-393
Parzianello, Luiz Claudio   I-599
Paschoarelli, Luis Carlos   IV-265
Peng, Kemao   III-120
Peng, Yuan   II-247
Penha, Marcelo   I-379
Pereira, Roberto   I-459, II-518
Pescarin, Sofia   I-262, IV-238
Petersson Brooks, Eva   II-238, III-504
Peterson, Matthew S.   I-144
Phang, Swee King   III-120
Phillips, Robert   IV-424
Picciani, Stefano   IV-23
Picozzi, Matteo   IV-641
Pierce, Graham L.   IV-274
Pinheiro, Tânia   II-442
Pinkwart, Niels   IV-533
Plogmann, Simon   II-452
Pohlmeyer, Anna Elisabeth   III-540
Post, Lori A.   III-3
Pradhan, Neera   II-209
Prata, Wilson   IV-714
Prior, Stephen D.   III-179, IV-304
Prisacari, Anna   I-389
Propst, Dennis B.   IV-274
Provost, Gabrielle   I-399

Quaresma, Manuela   IV-714
Quesenbery, Whitney   IV-193

Radermacher, Klaus   II-452
Rafelsberger, Walter M.   IV-553
Raij, Andrew   II-424, III-520
Raison, Colette   I-573
Rebelo, Francisco   III-30, III-169, III-189, III-205, III-362, III-419, III-475
Redish, Janice (Ginny)   IV-294
Reis, Bernardo   III-227
Reis, Lara   III-189
Riihiaho, Sirpa   IV-660
Rızvanoğlu, Kerem   IV-284, IV-623
Robert, Jean-Marc   I-399
Roberts, Michael   IV-581
Rosca, Daniela   IV-37
Rosi, Alice   III-558, III-594
Rughiniş, Răzvan   II-577

Sadauskas, John   II-276
Sade, Gavin   III-352
Sadler, Karl   IV-424
Said, Tarek   IV-359
Sakae, Ken-Ichiro   I-516
Sakamoto, Mizuki   II-587
Sakamoto, Y.   II-435
Sakarya, Cem   IV-84
Salazar, Jorge H.   III-215
Samson, Audrey   III-548
Sandino, Diego   I-583
Sanna, Alberto   III-558, III-594
Santa Rosa, José Guilherme   II-286
Sapkota, Nabin   IV-325
Sasajima, Munehiko   IV-560
Sasaki, Toshiya   IV-506
Schaffzin, Gabriel Y.   I-134
Schieder, Alex   III-199
Schieder, Theresa Karolina   IV-696
Schmidt, Snezna   I-573
Schneidermeier, Tim   IV-94, IV-432
Schoper, Yvonne   II-95
Schrader, Andreas   III-327
Schricker, Johannes   IV-94
Schulz, Christian   III-401
Schütz, Daniel   IV-568
Seevinck, Jennifer   III-352
Shalash, Wafaa M.   II-462
Shawly, Ghada   II-462

Shen, Siu-Tsen   III-179, IV-304
Shieh, Meng-Dar   III-568
Shilli, Rudainah   III-85
Shimoda, Hiroshi   III-530
Shin, Hyunju   III-316
Shin, Min   IV-103
Shinker, Jacqueline   II-209
Shizuki, Buntarou   III-255
Shum, David   II-391
Silva, Luiz Bueno   III-169
Silve, Sarah   IV-424
Silveira, Milene Selbach   I-599
Simões-Marques, Mário   I-359
Singh, Amarjeet   I-183
Singh, Pushpendra   I-183
Sini, Viola   IV-221
Smith, Melissa A.B.   I-144
Smythe, Kelli C.A.S.   IV-441
Soares, Marcelo Márcio   I-68, I-203,
    I-379, II-491, II-508, III-150, III-160,
    III-337, III-345, IV-113, IV-257,
    IV-342
Sobecki, Janusz   I-212
Sonntag, Daniel   III-401
Sookhanaphibarn, Kingkarn   II-171
Spiliotopoulos, Dimitris   IV-575
Spinillo, Carla Galvão   IV-441
Spruijt-Metz, Donna   II-424
Spyridonis, Fotios   II-401
Stavropoulou, Pepi   IV-575
Steege, Linsey M.   II-381
Stevens, Susan Hunt   II-597
Stieglitz, Stefan   I-340
Stifter, Janet   I-232
Stillwater, Tai   III-578
Strenge, Benjamin   I-252
Strube, Gerhard   II-105
Sturm, Christian   II-105
Su, Chih-Sheng   I-610
Sugawara, Satoshi   I-525
Sun, Huatong   II-115
Sun, Vincent C.   II-129
Sunaga, T.   II-435
Suto, Hidetsugu   I-498
Swierenga, Sarah J.   III-3, IV-274
Szwec, Lee   IV-631
Szymański, Jerzy M.   I-212

Tabosa, Tibério   IV-121
Taileb, Mounira   II-296

Takahashi, Hiroe   IV-560
Takamatsu, Asao   III-530
Takaoka, Yoshiyuki   IV-560
Tallig, Anke   III-411
Tanaka, Jiro   III-255, IV-706
Tanaka-Ishii, Kumiko   I-152
Tang, Da-Lung   II-129
Teixeira, Fábio Gonçalves   I-330
Teixeira, João Marcelo   II-266, III-227
Teixeira, Luís   III-30, III-205, III-362,
    III-419, III-475
Teixeira-Botelho, Inês   IV-13
Teles, Júlia   III-362
Thianthai, Tim   II-602
Thin, Alasdair G.   II-470
Thomas, Patrick R.   II-391
Thomas, Robert L.   I-417
Tomimatsu, Kiyoshi   I-593
Toyama, Takumi   III-401
Trapp, Marcus   IV-723
Trevisan, Bianka   I-439
Trevorrow, Pip   III-484, III-585
Tseng, Jin-Han   IV-450
Tsonos, Dimitrios   IV-575
Tsuei, Mengping   II-304
Tsujino, Yoshihiro   II-538
Turner, Andy   II-417
Tussyadiah, Iis P.   IV-733

Umbach, Elisabeth   IV-3

Vainio, Juhani   I-479
Valente, Andrea   II-311
Valverde, Llorenç   II-180
van Lieshout, Marjolein   III-494
van Schijndel, Nicolle H.   III-494
Vasconcelos, Luis Arthur   II-266, III-227
Vaughan, Misha   I-349
Vedamurthy, Indu   II-352
Vega, Katia Fabiola Canepa   I-48,
    III-237, III-439
Vélez, Gorka   I-583
Velez-Rojas, Maria C.   IV-581
Vicini, Sauro   III-558, III-594
Vilar, Elisângela   III-205, III-362,
    III-419, III-475
Vinagre, Pedro   I-620
Vogel, Marlene   I-449
Vogel-Heuser, Birgit   IV-568

von Saucken, Constantin   I-554, IV-130
Vorvoreanu, Mihaela   IV-543
Voyvodaoğlu, Tansel   IV-651

Wakeling, Jon   IV-140, IV-150
Waldron, Julie A.   III-215
Wall, Andrew   III-484
Walser, Kate   I-427
Wang, Biao   III-120
Wang, Fei   III-120
Wang, Man-Ying   II-129
Wang, Pi-Fen   II-121
Watanabe, Kentaro   II-435
Webb, Erika Noll   II-608
Weber, Markus   III-401
Welch, Shelly   IV-740
Wilkie, Diana J.   I-232
Wilkinson, Christopher R.   IV-457
Wilkosinska, Katarzyna   II-321
Wille, Cornelius   II-480
Williams, Doug   IV-140, IV-150
Wilson, Jennifer   II-189
Wilson, Peter H.   II-391
Windl, Helmut   II-139
Wolff, Christian   IV-248, IV-432
Wolze, Zeno   IV-3

Xu, Tao   IV-601
Xu, Yu-Jie   II-149

Yamada, K.C.   II-435
Yamamoto, Keiko   II-538
Yamaoka, Toshiki   IV-408
Yamazaki, Kazuhiko   II-11, IV-506
Yang, Beiqing   III-120
Yantaç, Asım Evren   I-630
Yasmin, René   IV-723
Yasu, Hiroko   I-525
Yasuda, Junko   I-516
Yılmaz, Merve   IV-173
Yin, Mingfeng   III-120
You, Manlai   II-149
Youmans, Robert J.   I-13, I-144
Yu, Allan   IV-67
Yuan, Xiaojun   IV-591, IV-601
Yule, Daniel   I-162

Zahabi, Liese   IV-611
Žajdela Hrustek, Nikolina   I-369
Zan, Özgür   IV-651
Zeng, Yujing   IV-183, IV-352
Zepeda-Hernández, J. Sergio   IV-231
Zhang, Bin   I-171
Zhang, Tao   IV-313
Zhang, Xiangmin   IV-601
Zhang, Zhenghua   IV-183, IV-352
Zhao, Shiyu   III-120
Zhou, Bingjun   II-602
Ziefle, Martina   I-439, III-10
Zillner, Sonja   III-401